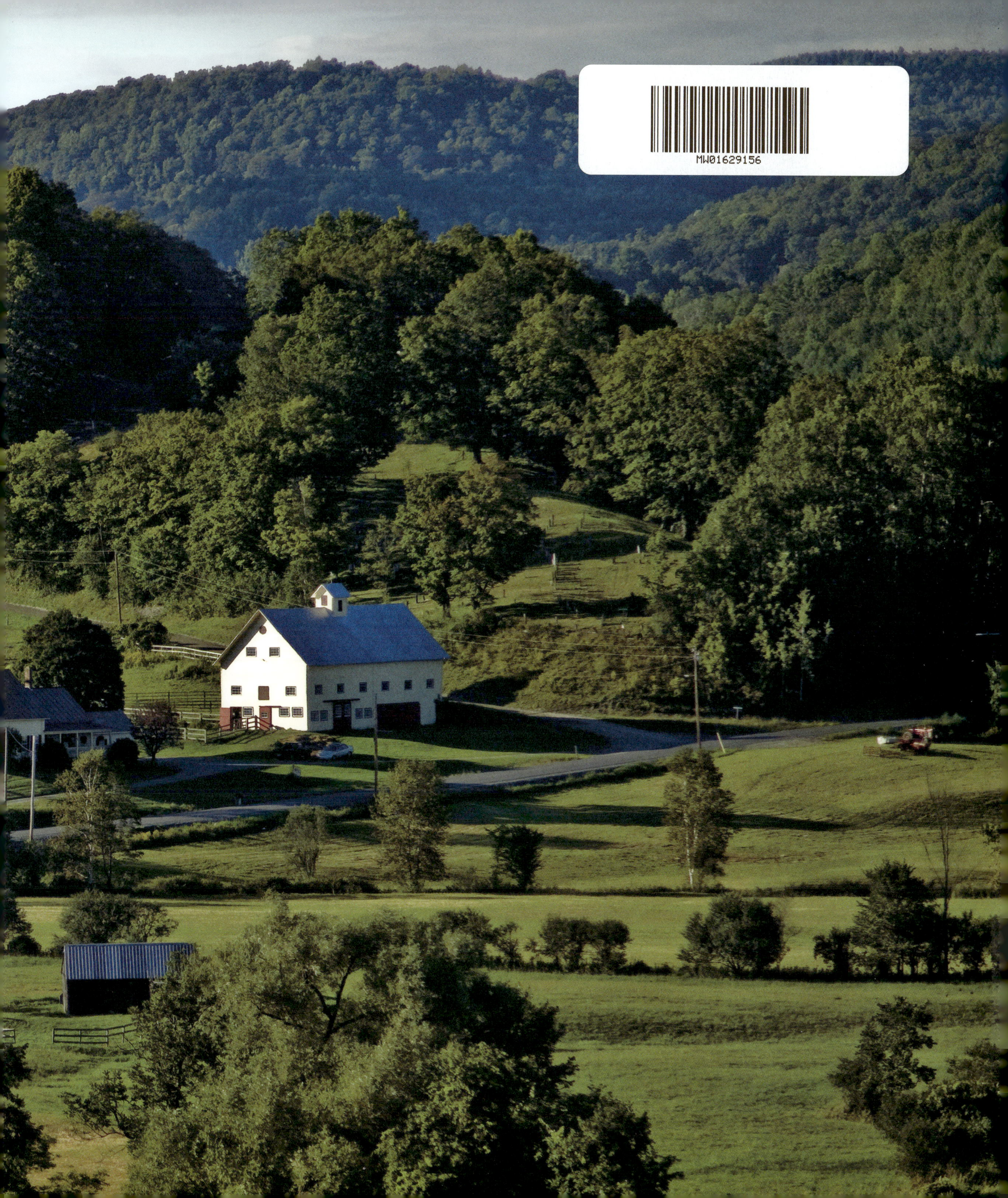

Old Homes of New England

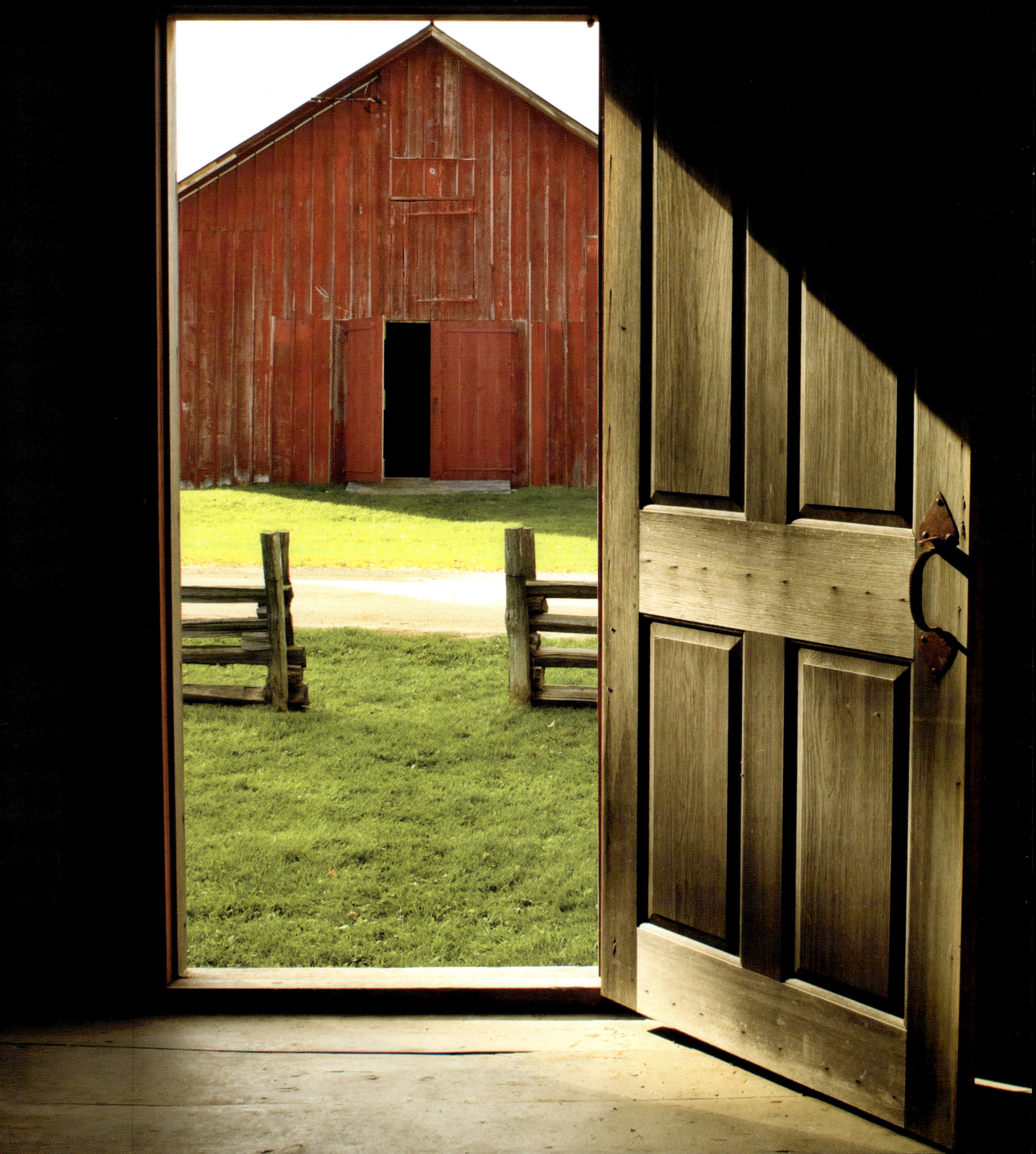

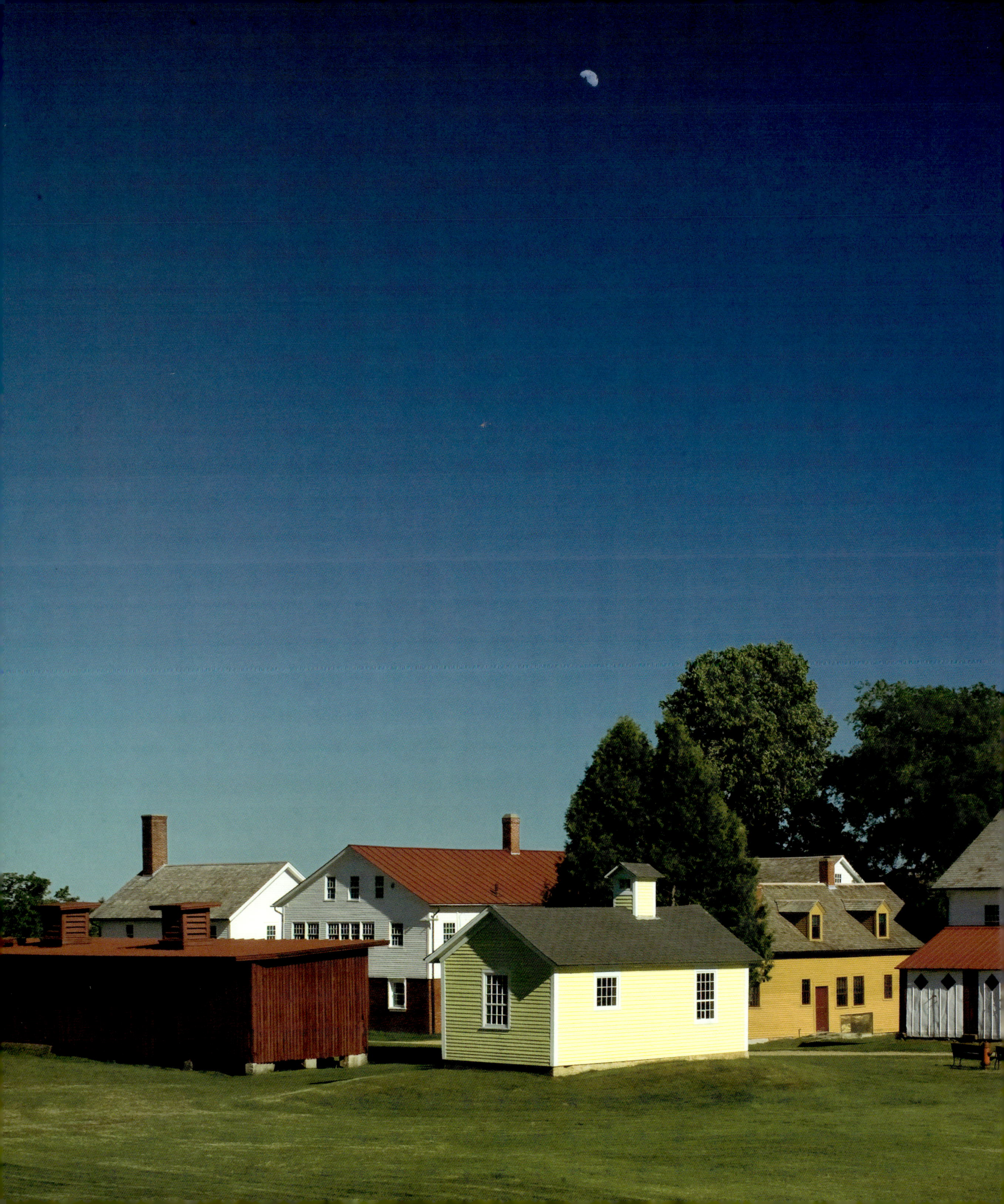

Old Homes of New England

Historic Houses in Clapboard, Shingle, and Stone

Text by Roderic H. Blackburn   Photography by Geoffrey Gross

Foreword by Richard Guy Wilson

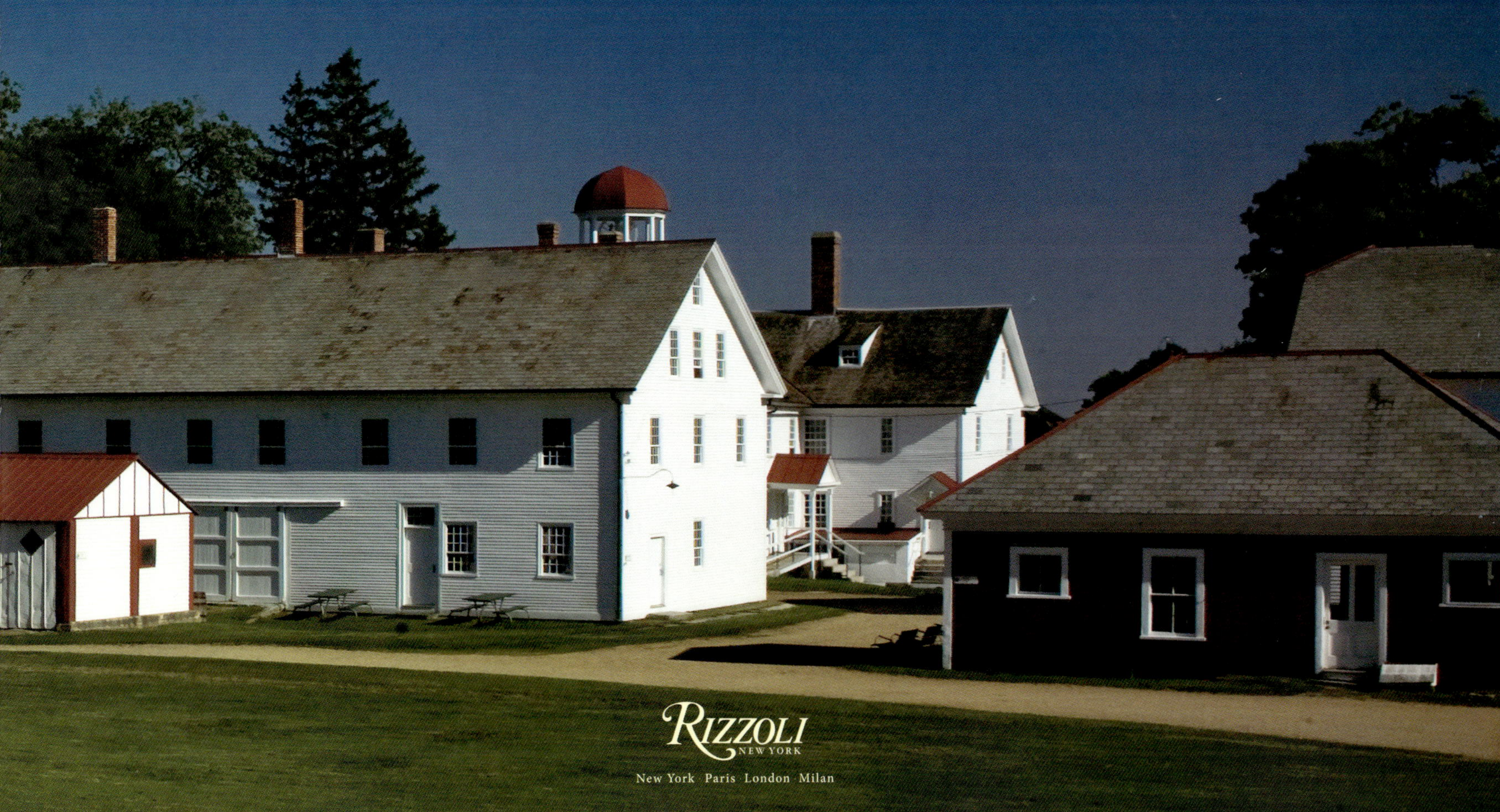

RIZZOLI
NEW YORK
New York Paris London Milan

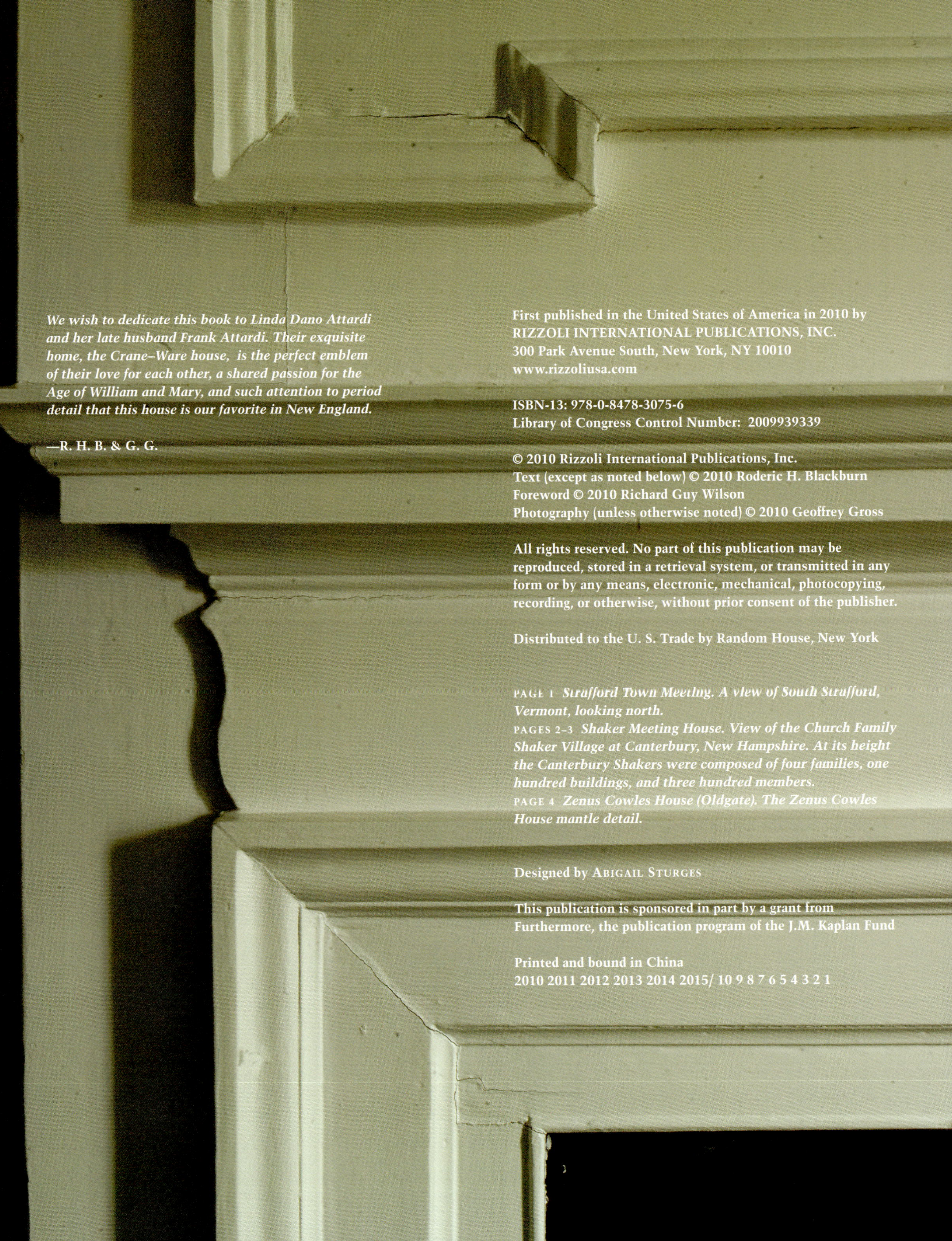

We wish to dedicate this book to Linda Dano Attardi and her late husband Frank Attardi. Their exquisite home, the Crane–Ware house, is the perfect emblem of their love for each other, a shared passion for the Age of William and Mary, and such attention to period detail that this house is our favorite in New England.

—R. H. B. & G. G.

First published in the United States of America in 2010 by
RIZZOLI INTERNATIONAL PUBLICATIONS, INC.
300 Park Avenue South, New York, NY 10010
www.rizzoliusa.com

ISBN-13: 978-0-8478-3075-6
Library of Congress Control Number: 2009939339

Distributed to the U. S. Trade by Random House, New York

PAGE 1 *Strafford Town Meeting. A view of South Strafford, Vermont, looking north.*
PAGES 2–3 *Shaker Meeting House. View of the Church Family Shaker Village at Canterbury, New Hampshire. At its height the Canterbury Shakers were composed of four families, one hundred buildings, and three hundred members.*
PAGE 4 *Zenus Cowles House (Oldgate). The Zenus Cowles House mantle detail.*

Designed by Abigail Sturges

This publication is sponsored in part by a grant from Furthermore, the publication program of the J.M. Kaplan Fund

Printed and bound in China
2010 2011 2012 2013 2014 2015/ 10 9 8 7 6 5 4 3 2 1

CONTENTS

FOREWORD

RICHARD GUY WILSON

The George Ingraham House (Emerson–Wilcox House), York, Maine. The crewel-embroidered set of bed hangings are the work of Mary Swett of York, Maine, from around the time of her marriage to Dr. Alexander Bulman in 1730. This is the only complete American set surviving from the eighteenth century.

With the words "New England," a host of images comes to mind for many Americans. They can include colorful fall foliage, maple syrup tapping, Pilgrims marching off to church, a valley of greenery with a white steeple rising up, a common surrounded by upright houses clad in weatherboard or shingles, or perhaps a farmhouse with an extended el and a barn stretching out in a bucolic pasture. New England, of course, contains much more than such romantic images: the textile and manufacturing industries were born there and flourished for many years, its major cities all contain tall glassy skyscrapers and the debris of our automobile culture clutters the roads. Still, though, the popular image and one that remains historically very important lies with the houses, farms, meeting houses, and churches as shown in this book.

The buildings treated here, from the earliest, the Whitfield (1639) and Fairbanks (1641),to the latest, the Fisher and Fessenden (both c.1801), represent a cross section of some of New England's finest historic architecture. The inclusion of meeting houses and/or churches is of critical importance in understanding the houses, since religion in its varied practices was central to daily life and the structures served as community landmarks. Yes, there are a few non-religious public buildings in early New England, but essentially government took place in the meeting houses in the form of the town meeting. Some of the buildings shown in this book, such as the Parson Capen House and the Old Ship Meeting House, are icons of American architecture; they appear in most books on the history of American architecture. Others are not as well known though they should be and illuminate the incredible richness of the subject.

What to call these buildings, or the stylistic terms to be applied to them, has been an ongoing problem since Americans began to appreciate them in the mid-nineteenth century. Sometimes the term "period" is invoked, such as "first period": 1620–1710, meaning houses with overhangs and more medieval in character, and "second period": 1710–1810 for buildings with more classical details. Another alternative is "Colonial" for the buildings dating from the first period, and "Georgian" referring to the English kings, for those from c.1710 to c.1780, and that show pedimented doorways, shell-like built-in cabinets, and paneled interior shutters. The classical detailing, of course, did not stop with the Revolution, but since we had gained independence other terms appear, such as "Federal" or "Early Republic" for buildings dating from c.1780 to 1810. But not every house conforms to these stylistic dictates and alternatives exist such as the Dunnell House (which is called "Cape Cod" in form, even though it resides in Berwick, Maine). No matter the stylistic terms employed, these buildings show an evolution both in form and also details, from medieval to classical, and from pegged joints to finely turned balusters. Buildings are more than form and the real artisanship is in the wrought iron hinges and latches, the newel posts, the chamfered summer beams, the Delft tiles around the fireplace, and the furnishings.

Behind all the buildings lie many stories about those who commissioned, built, and lived or worshiped in them, and then the many generations who came later. But also important are those who saved and restored them. Why have these houses survived while so many disappeared? Who is responsible for the loving care and preservation? Most of the houses went through tremendous evolutions as different facades were applied, wings added, interiors partitioned or gutted, and in some cases moved. Names do appear of the organizations and societies involved, such as Historic New England (or Society for the Preservation of New England Antiquities), Topsfield Historical Society, Canterbury Shaker Village Inc., and others, along with the restoration architects Norman Isham, Fred Kelly, Joseph Everett Chandler, Morgan Phillips, and John Milner, among many. They made choices; Isham discovered upstairs in Newport's Mumford–Wanton–Lyman–Hazard House some odd wall painting and decided to preserve it rather than paint the room white, which was the standard practice of the 1910s. The saved painted marbleizing is probably the earliest surviving interior decoration in the United States and indicates the aspirations of the early owners. Others added and embellished such as Nina Fletcher and Bertram Kimball Little at Cogswell's Grant. The Littles were leading scholars and collectors of early American and folk art; they furnished the house with their treasures and lived there, as the television set on p. 152 indicates. What this book and the wonderful photographs show is a tremendous commitment to preserving vital portions of New England and ultimately American history as shown in the these buildings.

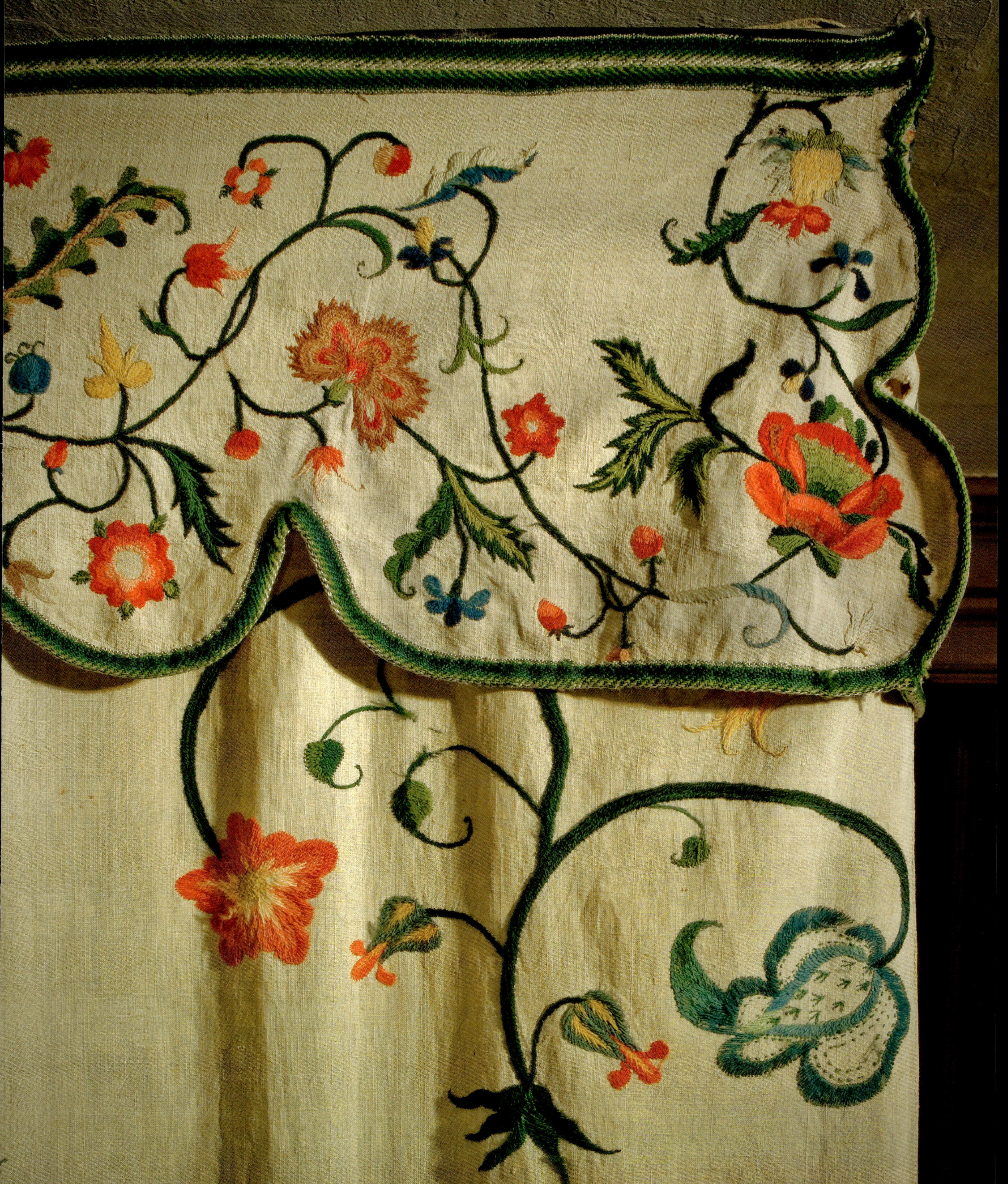

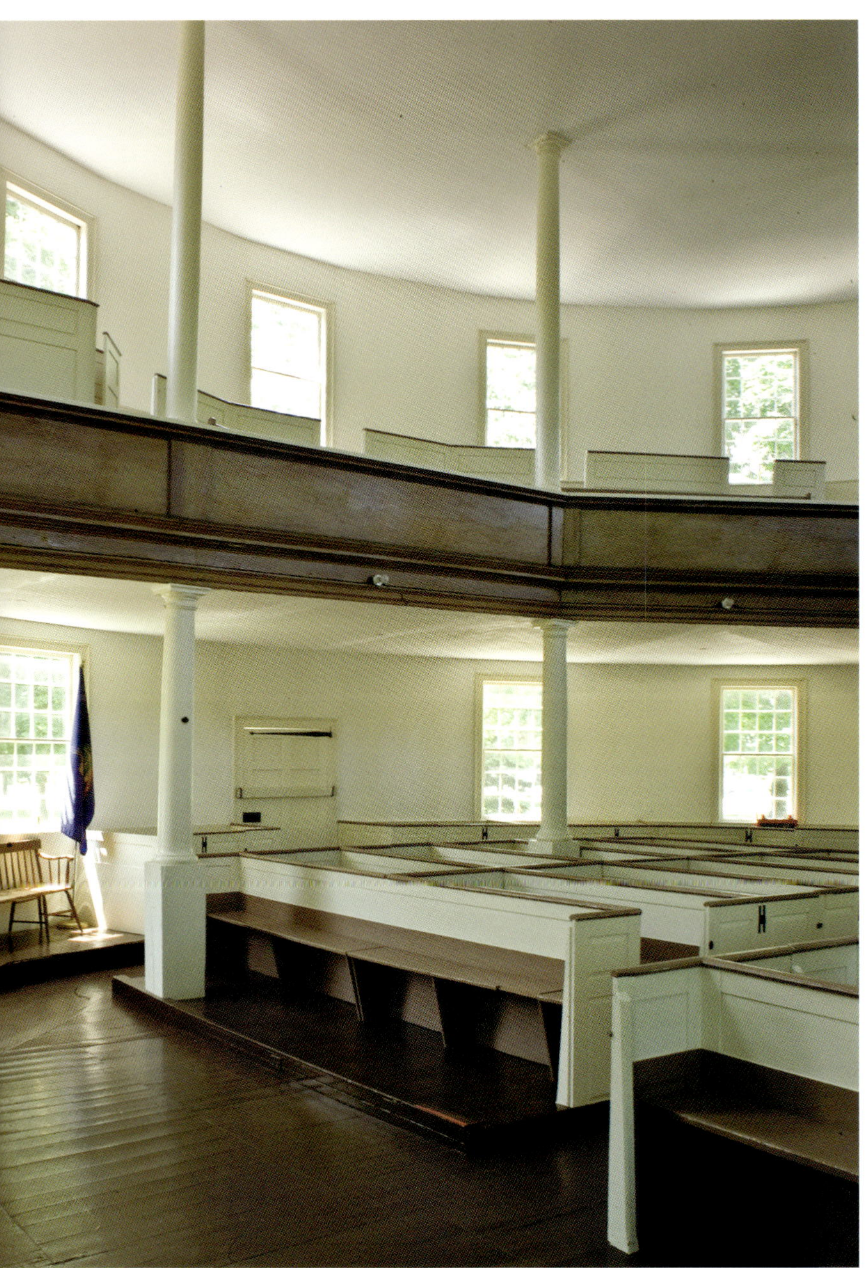

The Old Round Church

ABOVE *Despite the apparent complexity of joinery, a multisided building has the advantage of being concentric for greater strength and visibility within.*

FACING PAGE *This structure is the only sixteen-sided meeting house in New England. Some early Dutch Reformed churches in New York were six- or eight-sided.*

INTRODUCTION

THE GENESIS

New England's origins are found not in its political freedom, economic opportunity, refugee retreat, heathen conversion, or empirical expansion, but in dissension from the Church of England. King Henry VIII dissolved England's ties to the Catholic Church in 1534, creating the Protestant Church of England with himself as its head. For generations both the church and sovereigns were beset by Catholics attempting to reinstall Catholicism as the state religion and by reformers from within advocating a purer church, decentralized and based closely on scripture. Subsequent sovereigns, as heads of the church, viewed both tendencies as nearly treasonous.

Among the reformers were the Puritans who advocated, unsuccessfully, for Parliament to make changes in the Church of England. They were more successful among the populace as advocates for greater individual commitment to Jesus Christ and thus greater personal holiness. Though most remained within the church, some, known as the Separatists, left the church. Some migrated to the more liberal Netherlands, and one group of Pilgrims pioneered immigration to New England in 1620. King Charles I took a dim view of these attempted reforms, rigorously enforcing laws against ministers who dissented from church practices.

"Puritan" was originally a pejorative term directed at those who referred to themselves as "the godly." As such they were not a religious group or sect but those who ascribed to a purity of worship, doctrine, and personal morality. Their faith challenged each to resolve inherent contradiction in their lives: how to find wisdom and understanding, and to live virtuously, in a world beset with evil, and how to reconcile Christian liberty with the absolute authority of the Word and God's omnipotence. The supreme authority of God over human affairs, as expressed in the Bible, was their central tenet. From this principle they sought individual and corporate conformance to the teachings of the Bible and thus to moral and ecclesiastical purity.

THE PURITANS OF EAST ANGLIA

East Anglia, an eastern region of England, is today rural and retired, but in the Puritan era it was the most densely settled part of England, replete with skilled craftsmen, artisans, and merchants. It had the highest literacy rates in the country and a high

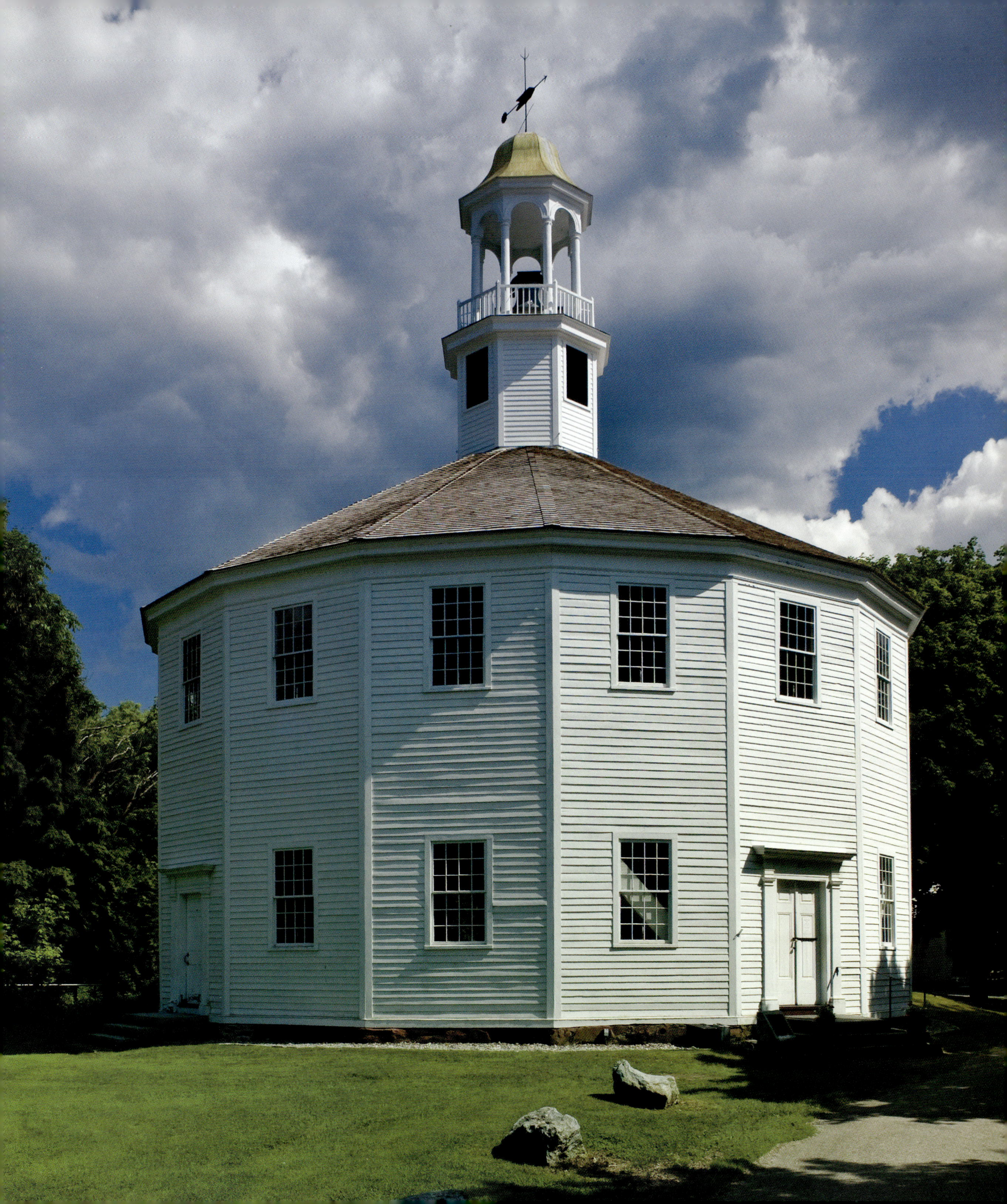

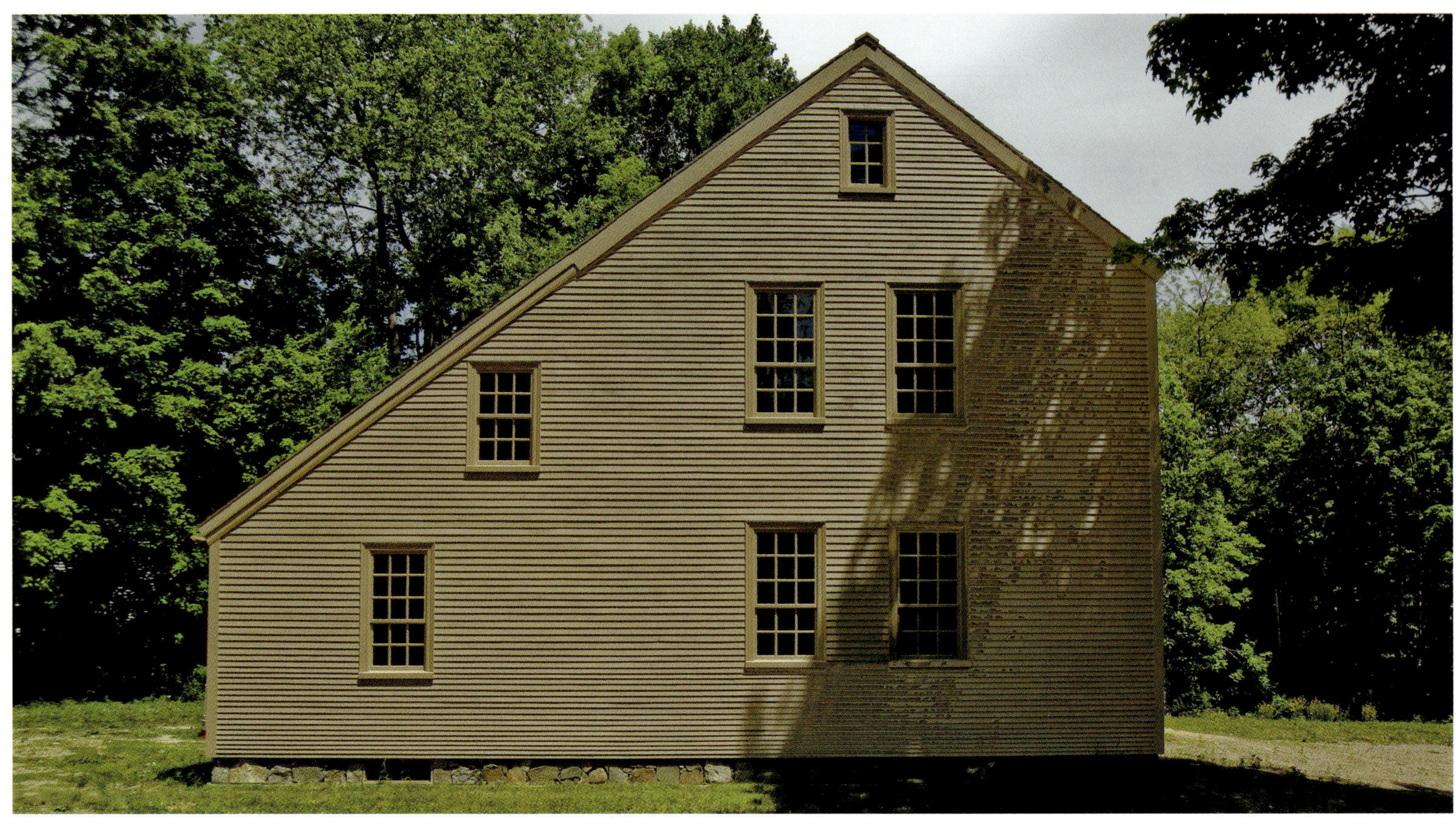

Col. Paul Wentworth House

ABOVE *Colonel Paul Wentworth built this house around 1701 in what is now Rollinsford, New Hampshire, then a frontier town on the Salmon Falls River, which appealed to a saw miller and lumber merchant if not to others who feared French and Indian raids. It is a characteristic center-chimney salt box structure, long the pride of its small town as the oldest surviving house in the village. In 1936, a Wentworth descendant, apparently unable to part with his past, hauled it off to Danver, Massachusetts, where it was rebuilt. After he died, it was slated for demolition until the people of Rollinsford reclaimed it and raised the funds for its restoration within sight of its original place.*

FACING PAGE *Stairway of the Wentworth House.*

percentage of scientists and scholars. Furthermore, as the base of Cambridge University, many Puritan ministers were educated here. The Protestant Reformation had already spread through this region in the sixteenth century, and out of this movement Puritans gained their largest number of converts. Their great enemy was Archbishop William Laud of the Church of England, who purged them from the church, branding Puritans—some literally—as heretics for their dissent from certain principles and practices of the Anglican Church.

It was out of this cauldron of conspiracy that many Puritans left England to found their own Bible Commonwealth in America. Although a few had come before, 1628 marked the beginning of the Great Migration. More people—almost all Puritans—arrived on Massachusetts shores over the next fifteen years than came for decades thereafter. This concentration of common belief, will, and organization was unique in American colonial history and had a profound influence upon New England culture for centuries thereafter.

NEW ENGLAND BEGINS

Though the Puritans came to Massachusetts by design, the Pilgrims arrived there by accident. The vitality of a rigorous, invigorating climate and fertile, if scattered, valleys and marshes contributed to a rapidly expanding population. Like many later Puritans (Separatists), Pilgrims saw salvation in emigration, in their case

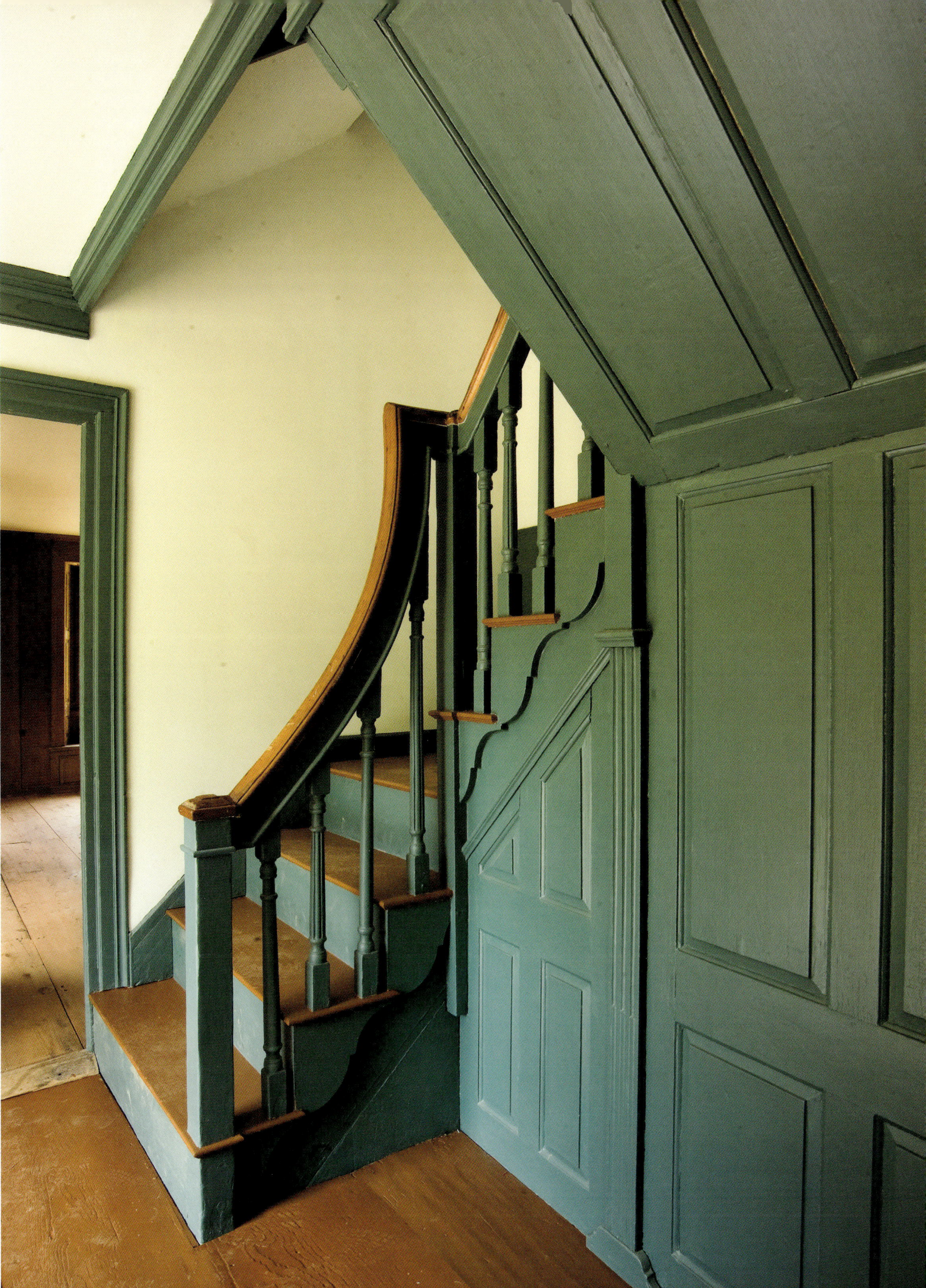

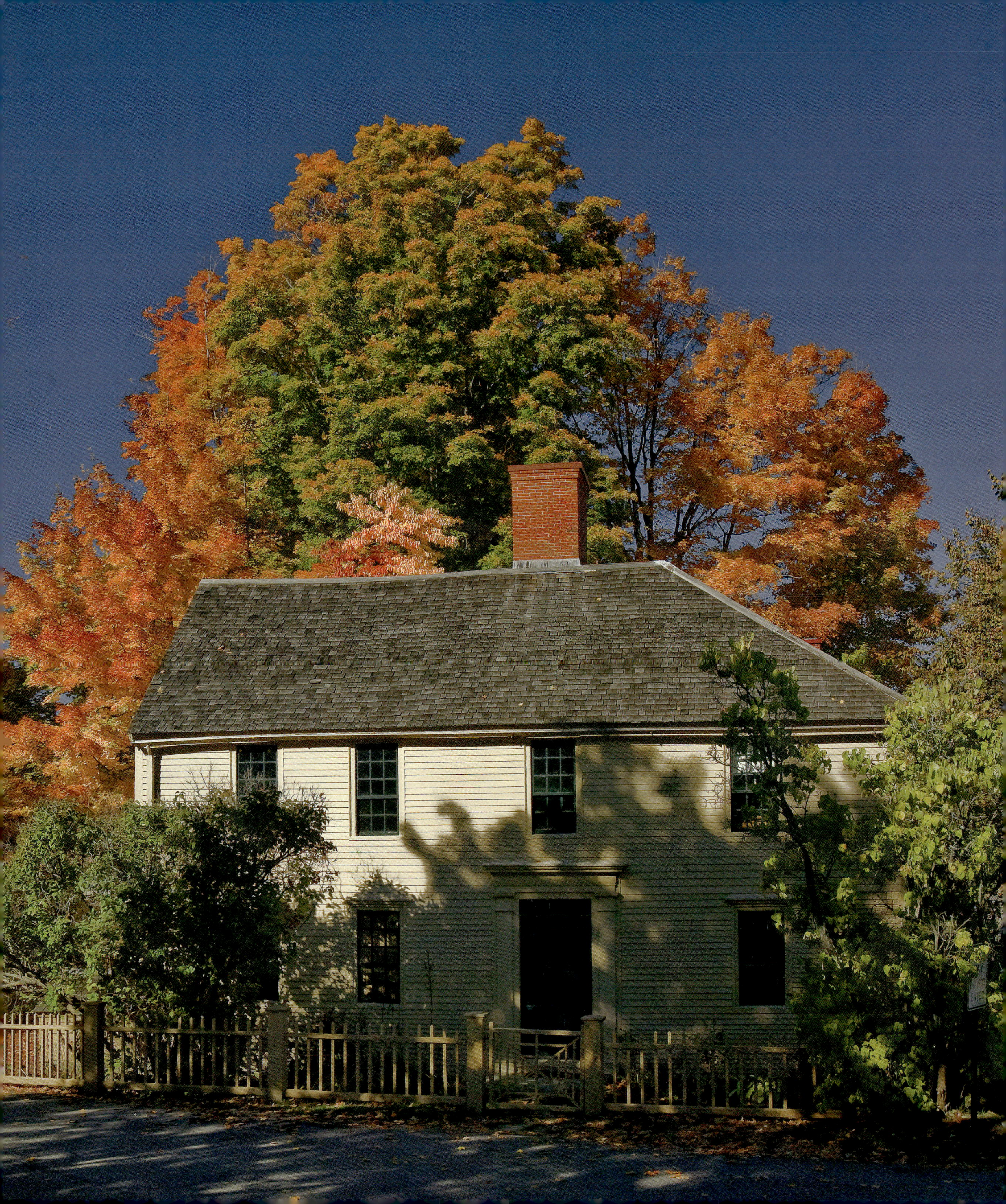

The George Ingraham House (Emerson-Wilcox House)

FACING PAGE *Built by George Ingraham in 1742 in York, Maine, as a one-room-deep center chimney home, it originally had a parlor and hall with two bed chambers above. Edward Emerson acquired the house in 1760 and attached a c.1710 house to form the "L" addition behind. A second addition was added in 1817, yet the whole retains much of its Georgian period character despite use as a general store, tavern, tailor shop, post office, home, and now a museum featuring York antiquities.*

RIGHT *Stairway.*

BELOW RIGHT *The parlor features early furnishings from the town.*

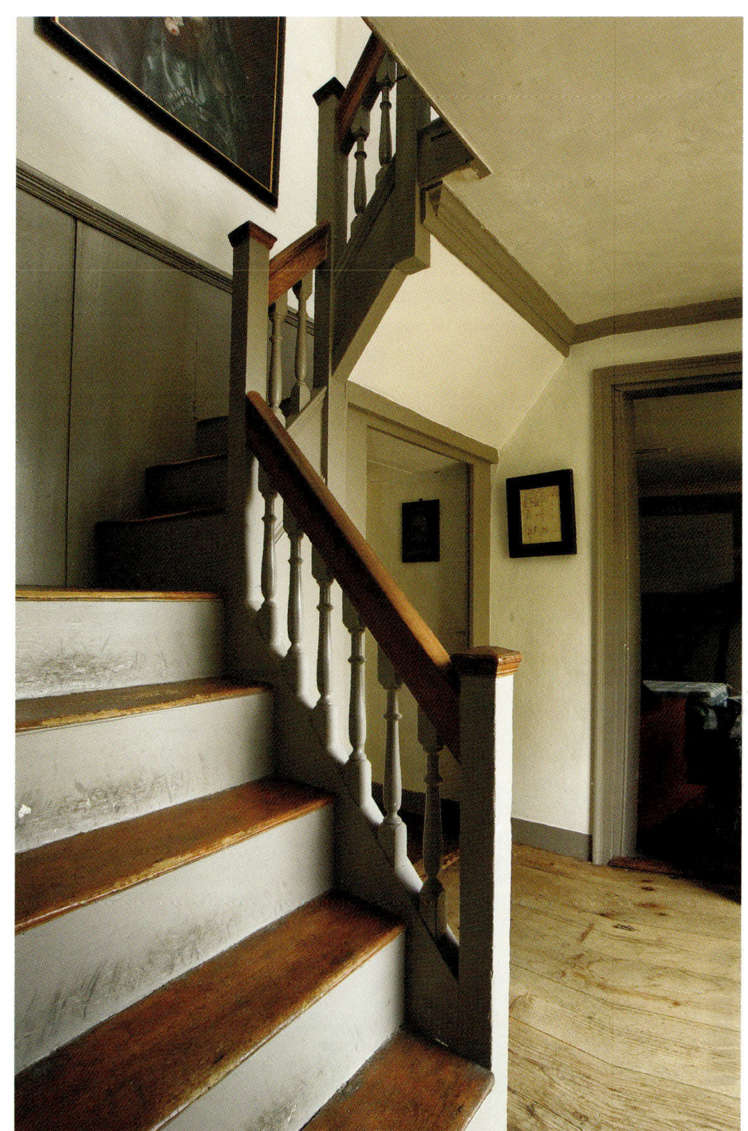

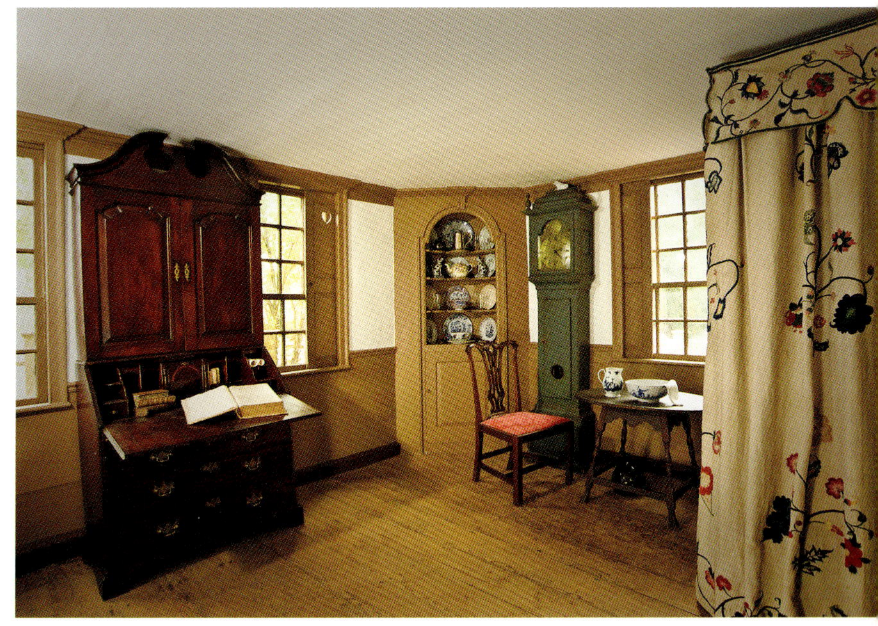

leaving England for tolerant Netherlands in 1608. Concerned that they would lose their identity among the Dutch, they set off for the New World in 1620, picking up far more non-Pilgrims in England on the way. They intended to settle at Virginia where other English settlers had gone before. Landfall, however, came at Cape Cod just as winter was upon them. With no grant for land and fearful of the intentions of the majority of strangers among them, they drew up the Mayflower Compact to establish a new home, Plymouth Colony, under democratic principles of self-government. The first winter was a near disaster: half the 102-person group died of malnutrition, disease, or lack of adequate shelter.

Undaunted by such adversity and driven by similar Separatist convictions, other English émigrés followed in 1623 to Gloucester on Cape May and in 1626 to Naumkeag (Salem). Two years later, Puritans led by John Endecott came to Salem under the auspices of the New England Company, which, a year later, received a Royal Charter for the Massachusetts Bay Company, its successor. This was the foundation of government for Massachusetts with a governor and general court as the legislative body. The next group, lead by John Winthrop, established the Bay Colony capital at Boston. Subsequent groups of the Great Migration established towns along the coast and inland. Each town was chartered with its own representative government, which restricted membership to accepted members of the town congregation. These freemen gained the right to directly elect governors of the Colony in 1632 and deputies to the general court two years later.

THE GREAT MIGRATION

The Great Migration of Puritans continued until 1643, involving over eighteen thousand immigrants. After Massachusetts, Connecticut next attracted settlers. Some from Plymouth Colony took up lands far up the Connecticut River at Windsor (1633), Wethersfield (1634), and Hartford (1636). Groups from England founded Saybrook (1635) and New Haven Colony (1638)

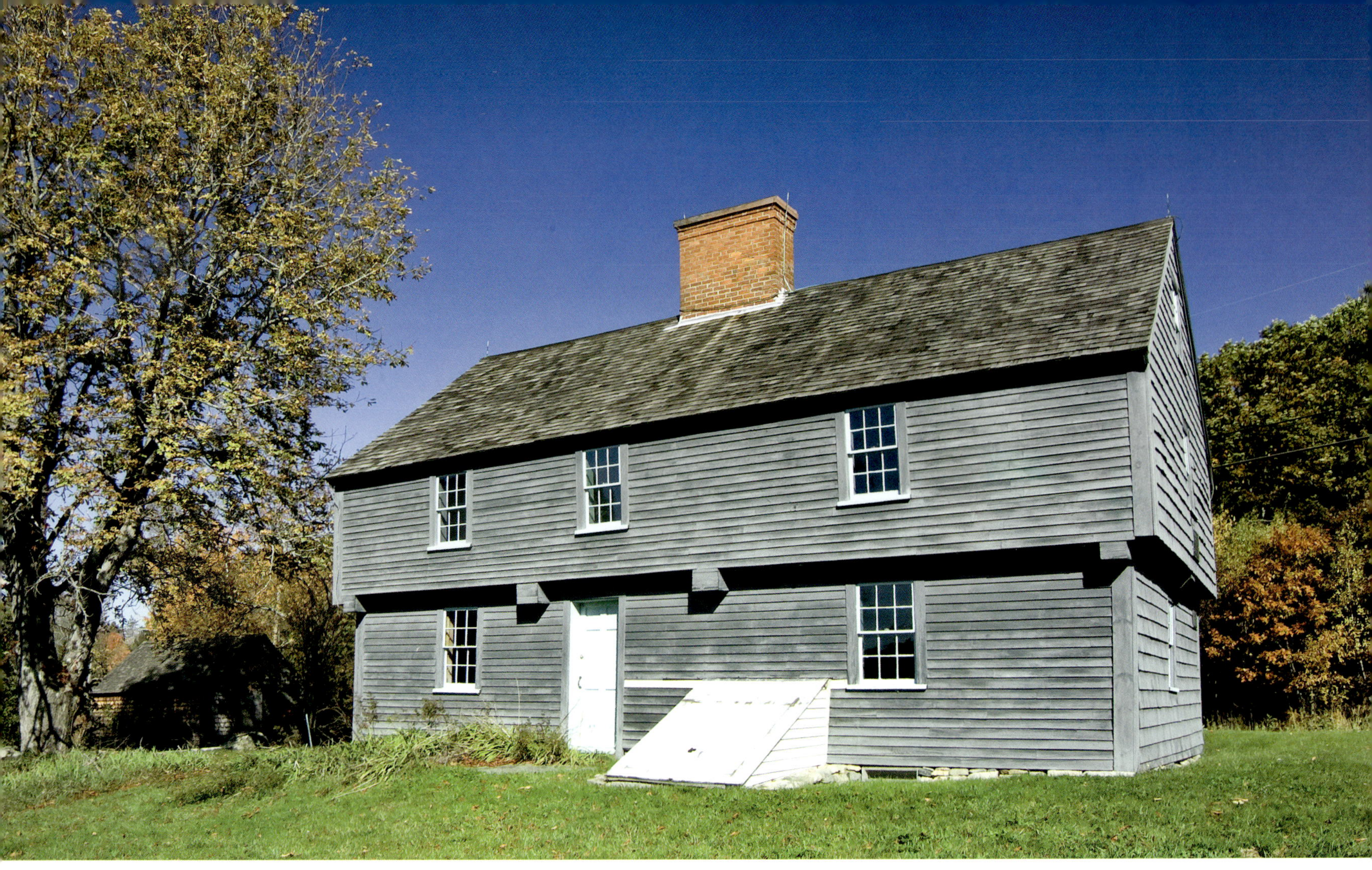

Micum McIntyre House

ABOVE *The Micam McIntire House was restored with sash windows and clapboard siding of later additions.*

FACING PAGE *In this view one can see the Micam McIntire House gable end and rear. While many First Period houses had overhanging second (even third) floors, the garrison houses are the only ones to overhang on all four sides. In that way they do relate to defensive block houses of the period and later western forts.*

on the coast. However, the move inland brought the Connecticut colonists into conflict with regional American Indian tribes. War with the Pequot Indians (1637) encouraged alliance and defense measures amongst these more distant settlements. The Bay Colony formed the New England Confederation, which included Plymouth, Connecticut, and New Haven Colonies.

American Indians had lived in New England for more than 10,000 years, since the retreat of the last Ice Age. By 1600 several tribes of Algonquian-speaking peoples had invested themselves throughout New England, mostly along river valleys and on the coast, and numbered perhaps 25,000. Prominent among these were the Massachusetts, Wampanoag, Narragansett, Pennacook, and Abnaki. When Europeans first began to settle coastal regions, they met some of these peoples, but in diminished numbers. European diseases had already killed many in at least one epidemic (1616–17), giving the settlers the impression that much of the land was empty and ripe for their own acquisition.

ENGLISH SOCIETY IN NEW ENGLAND

English society had always been structured on what was seen as the divine plan for human destiny wherein each person

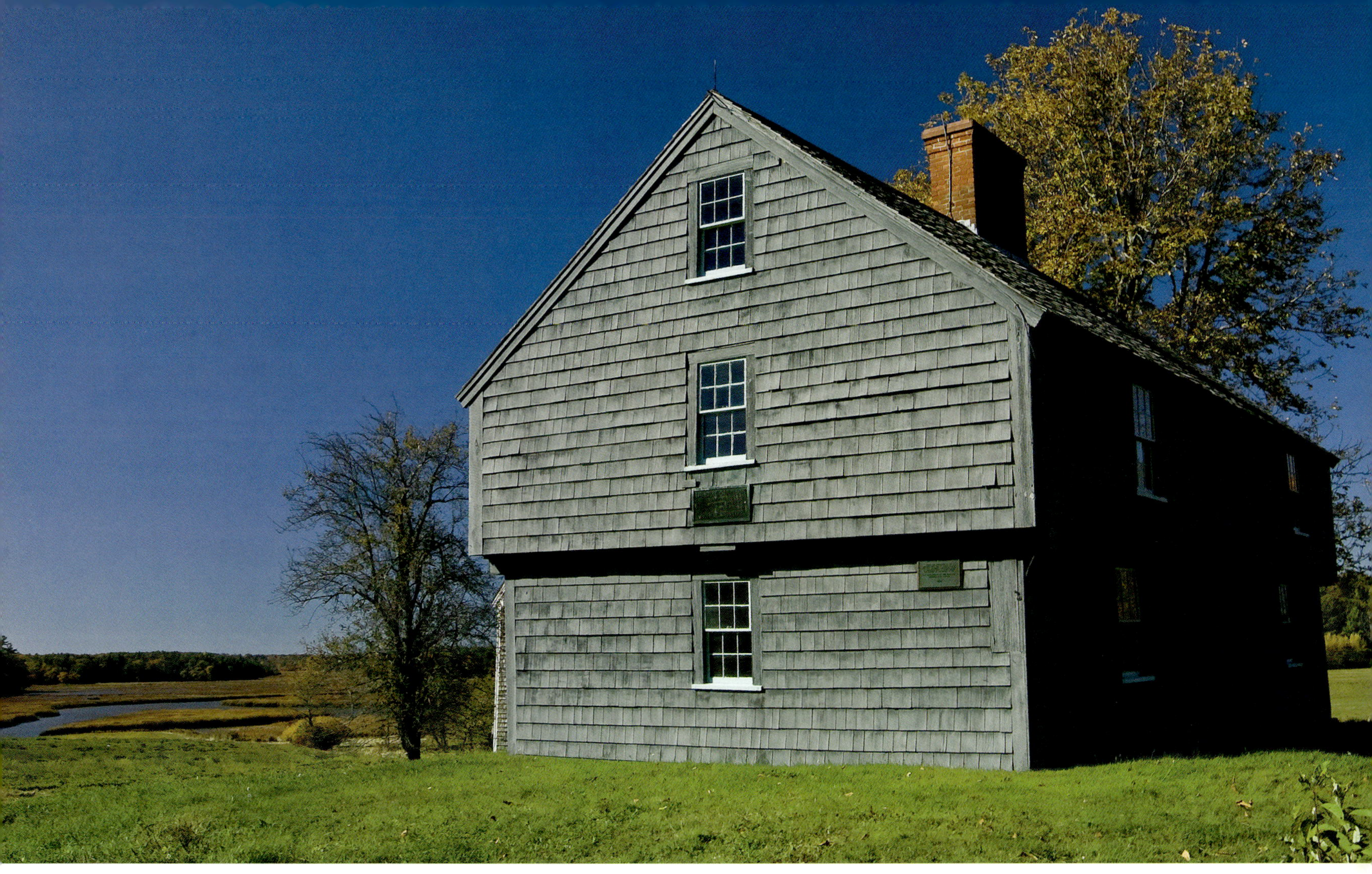

was born to a social rank and served there through life. As trade and crafts developed, especially in East Anglia, yeomen, who had the right to own property and to vote, began to accumulate modest wealth and aspirations to join the gentle ranks. Property possessions now began to convey rank, not just inherited position. Yeomen who had been farmers began to invest in the trades, spurring the beginnings of a middle class based on individualism and a consumer culture. This was happening just as the Great Migration was taking place, bringing to New England a material basis for establishing one's rank in an otherwise generally homogeneous Puritan society. In later periods and in other colonies subsequent immigrant groups became the lower rung on the ladder of rank and labor, but in early New England, every man, excepting the educated ministerial elite, achieved his rank through his own labor and accumulated wealth.

RAISING PURITANS

Congregations were autonomous—each led by a knowledgeable pastor. Worship emphasized preaching and was devoid of any superfluity not justified in the Bible. Modesty and simplicity extended from church to everyday life.

The family was the fundamental unit of society wherein roles of authority and obedience—what to know and what to do—were first learned as preparation for entering the wider society and the church. While a husband's authority over his wife was a given, mothers had religious and moral authority over the children, duties not open to them in public. To prepare children for the discipline of adulthood, education was deemed important, especially for the religious purpose of reading the scriptures. As the Reverend John Cotton wrote in *Christ, the Fountaine of Life*, "Zeale is but a wilde-fire without knowledge." By the 1670s New England colonies (except Rhode Island) mandated literacy for children. Boys could go on to "Latin" schools to learn grammar through Latin, Hebrew, and Greek studies in preparation for college. In their requirement for universal education New England Puritans were singular.

Their conviction that they were creating a new type of society grounded in the truth of the scriptures made it intolerable to accept the liberties taken by other faiths who did not share all their truths. Those, like Roger Williams and Anne Hutchinson, who openly preached their own tenets of faith, were admonished and sometimes driven out of Massachusetts, and Rhode Island became a sanctuary for Baptists, Quakers, and Jews.

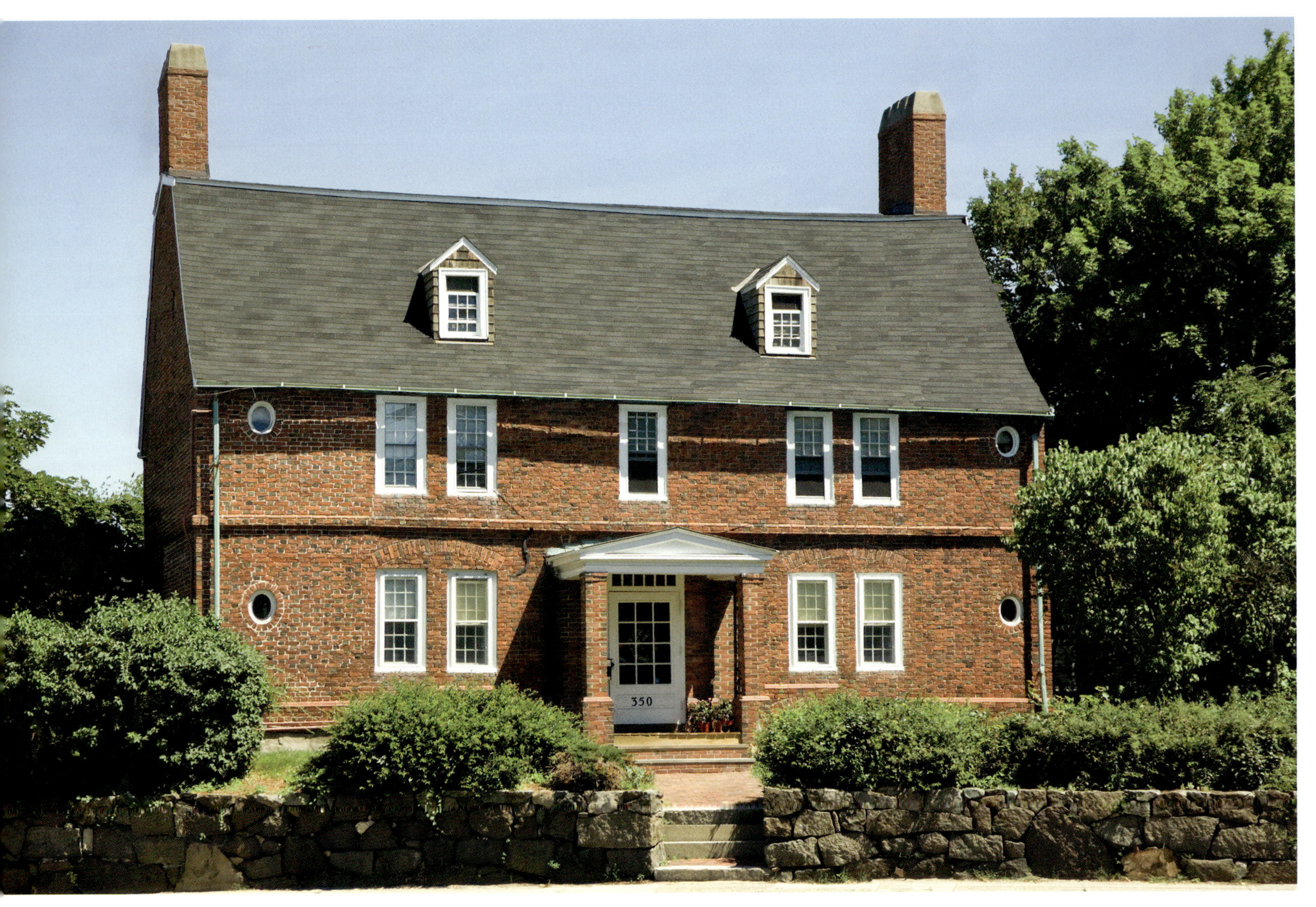

GOVERNANCE BY GOD AND MAN

To organize and govern a community the Puritans began with a covenant, a contract between God and his elected people, charging them with a mission from God. One type of covenant acknowledged that each congregation had the authority to be self-regulating, hence the term Congregationalist. Members covenanted themselves to each other, pledging to obey the word of God, and every member testified to their experience of grace to insure the purity of the church and its members. Church organization and authority was separate and independent from town government, though their organizations mirrored each other. Congregational male members elected selectmen to run the town's day-to-day affairs. Acceptance of the covenant and election to the church was a prerequisite to being able to live in a community, own property, and elect officials. A member wishing to leave a community required permission or suffered forfeiture of property. Thus church, government, membership, and citizenship were closely intertwined in a web of rights and responsibilities. The ultimate authority in both spheres was the word of God, but commitments made to the community and to the congregation via obedience to covenants ensured separation and order. This came to be known as the Congregational, or New England, Way.

COMMUNITIES

United by a common faith and arriving primarily from the same region of England, it is not surprising to find that Puritans formed a more homogeneous social group than other colonies, which drew immigrants for economic or social opportunities. Most were yeomen (landowning farmers) and husbandmen (tenant farmers); few were from the bottom layer of society.

The names of the earliest settlements are a reflection of where each community originated in England. Regionalism was

Peter Tufts House

FACING PAGE *The gambrel roof, Flemish brick bond, a brick water table course, central hallways, and end chimneys of the Peter Tufts House (1675) are all features of later Georgian houses.*

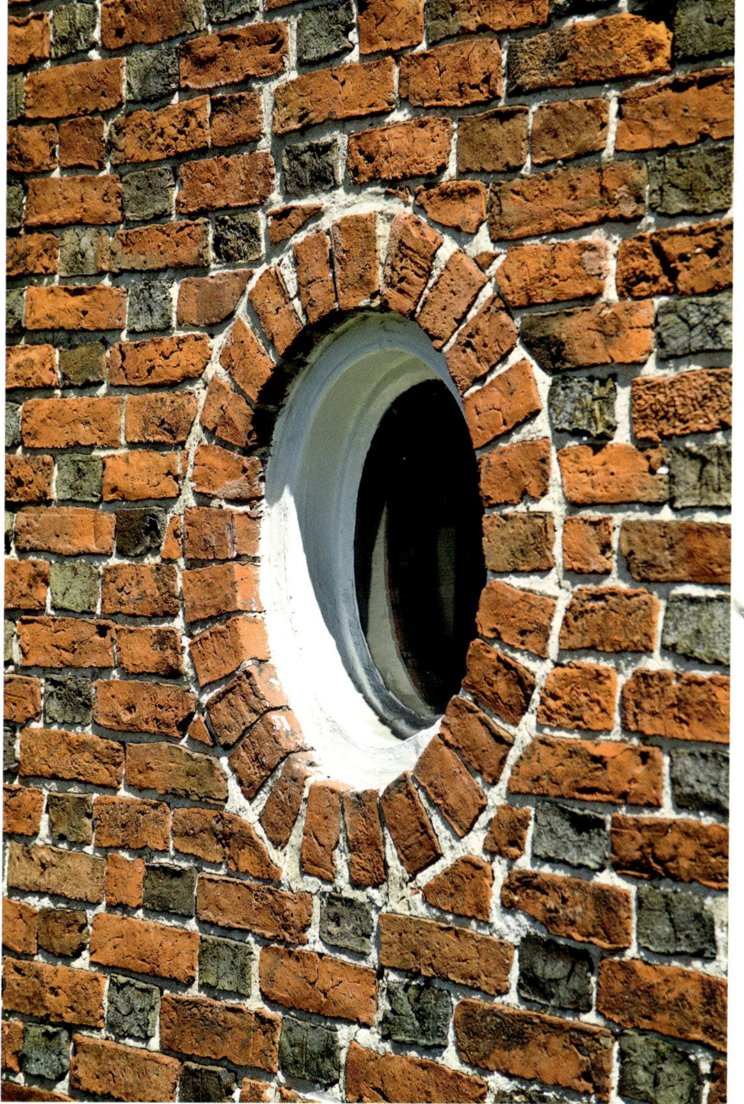

RIGHT *The Peter Tufts House brick porthole window is one of four on the front and two on one gable. They were never on the rear of the house. Brick bonding patterns vary with the facades: front is Flemish bond, left gable is English bond, right gable in American bond (likely rebuilt in the nineteenth century), and the rear is all three.*

especially evident amongst the leadership of Puritans. Magistrates and ministers were overwhelmingly from the eastern counties: they were well educated, had gone to the same schools, knew each other long before emigrating, and continued to intermarry. These experiences were especially common among the clergy who, though they were forbidden to hold political office, formed an influential elite.

As communities founded by and for believers, those admitted to membership were obliged to lead godly lives, have a clear understanding of their faith, and be able to demonstrate they had experienced the working of God's grace in their souls. Each person should be continually reformed by the grace of God to fight against sin. As believers in original sin, they interpreted Eve's sin as extending to all women, thus marginalizing them in the church hierarchy, excluding them from speaking in church and from participating in government. Collectively they sought to establish a Bible commonwealth as a model for mankind.

Each New England settlement remained a tight-knit group of families for as long as four generations until, at the end of the seventeenth century, out-migration to other towns or places of work became widespread. The population expanded rapidly compared to Europe. An earlier age of marriage and better infant health resulted in average family sizes of seven to eight children. Economic expansion followed population expansion. Family farms on fertile soil, without the need for high capital investment (such as slaves), soon produced exportable surpluses of grain and cattle, which led to the rise of the shipping industry as well as expanded imports.

An informative if anonymous and brief manuscript dating from the 1630s tells us what Puritan New Englanders thought a town should be. It was to be laid out in concentric circles within a six-mile square. At the center was the meeting house surrounded by homes. Just beyond was a ring of common fields farmed by the town's residents. Later it would be sold off as freehold land. The outer edge of this ring was to be no more than one and a half miles from the meeting house. The land in the next ring was reserved for "men of great estate" to accommodate their greater number of stock in as much as 400 acres each lot. No farmhouses were to be built at a greater distance than two miles from the meeting house, not so much for safety but for convenience of attending town or religious meetings. Beyond was the fifth circle, which was comprised of common lands such as swamps and unusable land. And still further, the wilderness, abutting the same such land belonging to the next town. As such the town was seen as a self-contained, largely self-governing community. Particular circumstances of topography and settler experience soon clashed with this ideal as each community sought to apportion lots on equitable grounds and individuals sought exception for their circumstances.

CHURCH AND MEETING HOUSES

The center of community life was the meeting house, sharing both sacred and secular functions on different days. This dual purpose accounts for the persistent use of the term "meeting house" rather than "church," which was reserved for the body of

Peter Tufts House

BELOW *The Peter Tufts House parlor fireplace and summer beam follow the more traditional Massachusetts practice from this period.*

FACING PAGE *The open hallway configuration of the stairway of the Peter Tufts House, although altered, is far in advance of other houses of this era.*

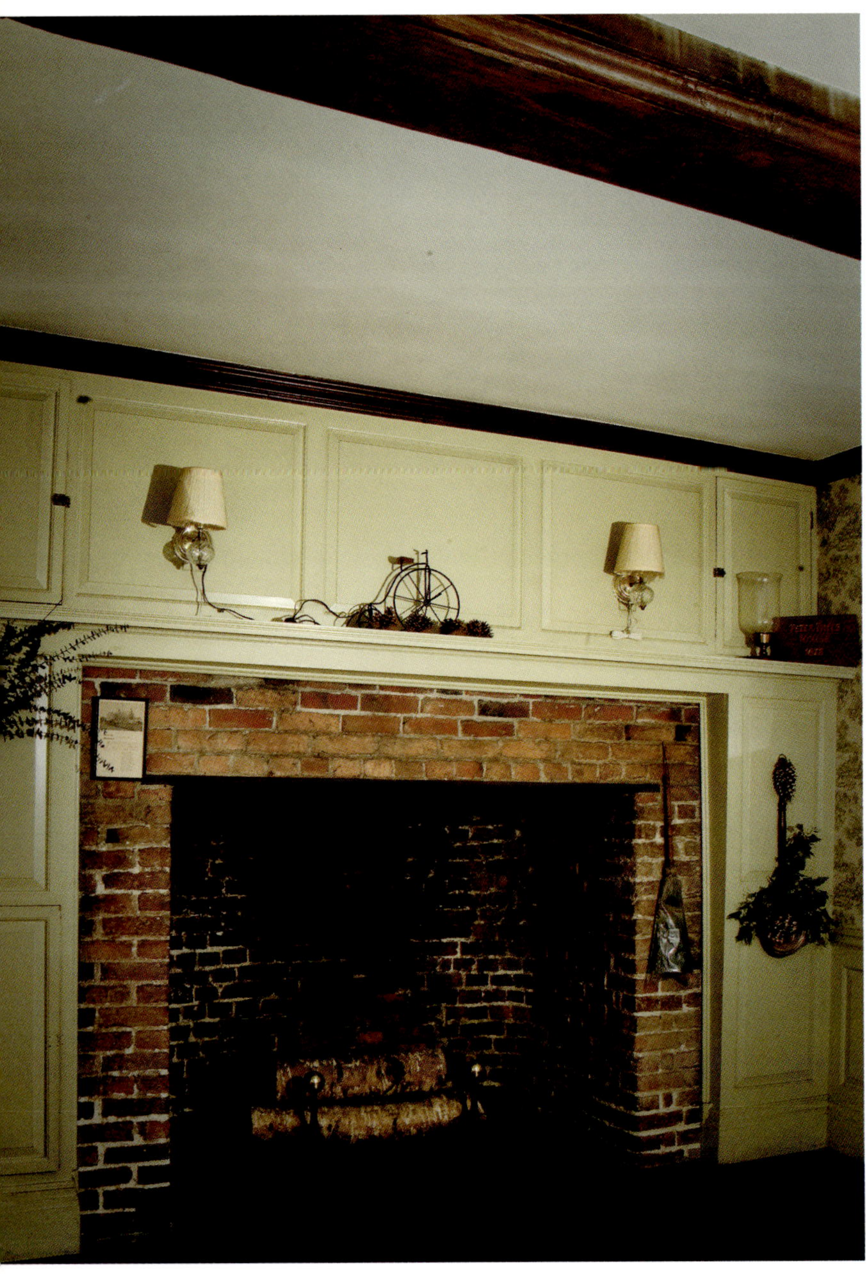

members in faith, not a building. Each meeting house was to be large enough to contain the community, functionally sufficient for protection from the elements, but plain and unadorned. The Puritans sought to sharply distinguish their practices from Anglican Church high ritual and elaborate appearances. Before the seventeenth century had ended, two hundred meeting houses had been built of which that at Hingham (see the Old Ship Meeting House, p. 80) is the oldest and best-surviving example from the early period. A meeting house tended to be a two-story-high square with a four-sided hipped roof and a modest steeple with bell and weathervane at the central apex.

They had a similar appearance to English secular buildings like courthouses and market buildings but were most closely modeled on Calvinist meeting houses throughout Western Europe. Often set on a rise or hill, they were left unpainted inside and out. Inside they were more like a lecture hall than a church. There was no altar; opposite the entry door (on a long side) was a high pulpit with sounding board above. Below the pulpit the elders sat, facing the congregation. Men sat on one side, women on the other, each section arranged in order of wealth and status. There was no ornament—no curtains, lights, or heating—nothing to distract from the spoken word except the all-seeing eye painted on the face of the pulpit. Sunday services were the only time the community met together each week, and each week was a recounting of the purpose of their founding, holding community and its culture together in the face of an ever-changing sectarian outside world.

Included in this book are five meeting houses from the Puritan to the Federalist era. Though they differ in physical configuration, they retain the austere plainness the Puritans deemed necessary to hear the spoken word and avoid the visual temptations of secular desires. Today the spoken word comes not from the pulpit but from the town's citizen, who, within a plain building, can all feel equal in their opinion.

ON THE LAND

One requisite of obedience to God was self-control, which found its outward expression in personal behavior and by bringing order to all within one's responsibility—namely, farm and family. Two types of farms were brought to New England. From the southeast and the midlands came a farm with a barn for grain processing and storage and another barn for sheltering cattle in winter and for milking. The second farm type, a "longhouse," was associated with northern and western English counties where the barn and house were conjoined, but fewer of these were established as there were fewer immigrants from these areas. A longhouse had the risk of burning both home and barn if either caught fire. Rather than adopt these types of farms, New Englanders opted for a variation. By joining the shelter of stock and grain under one roof they settled on a large single barn separate from the house. This configuration persisted for two centuries and is still seen through much of New England, though now rarely used in the original manner. The importance of the barn in the yeoman's view was such that it was often placed closer to the road than the house, never behind the latter. More practically, the house most often faced south to absorb the sun's warmth in winter and had its back to the winter winds. The barn was placed to help break that wind. The average farm was just ten acres, but within it were sufficient space for hay and crop fields, a kitchen garden, and lesser structures, such as a sheepfold, horse stable, corncrib, milk house, shop, and sheds.

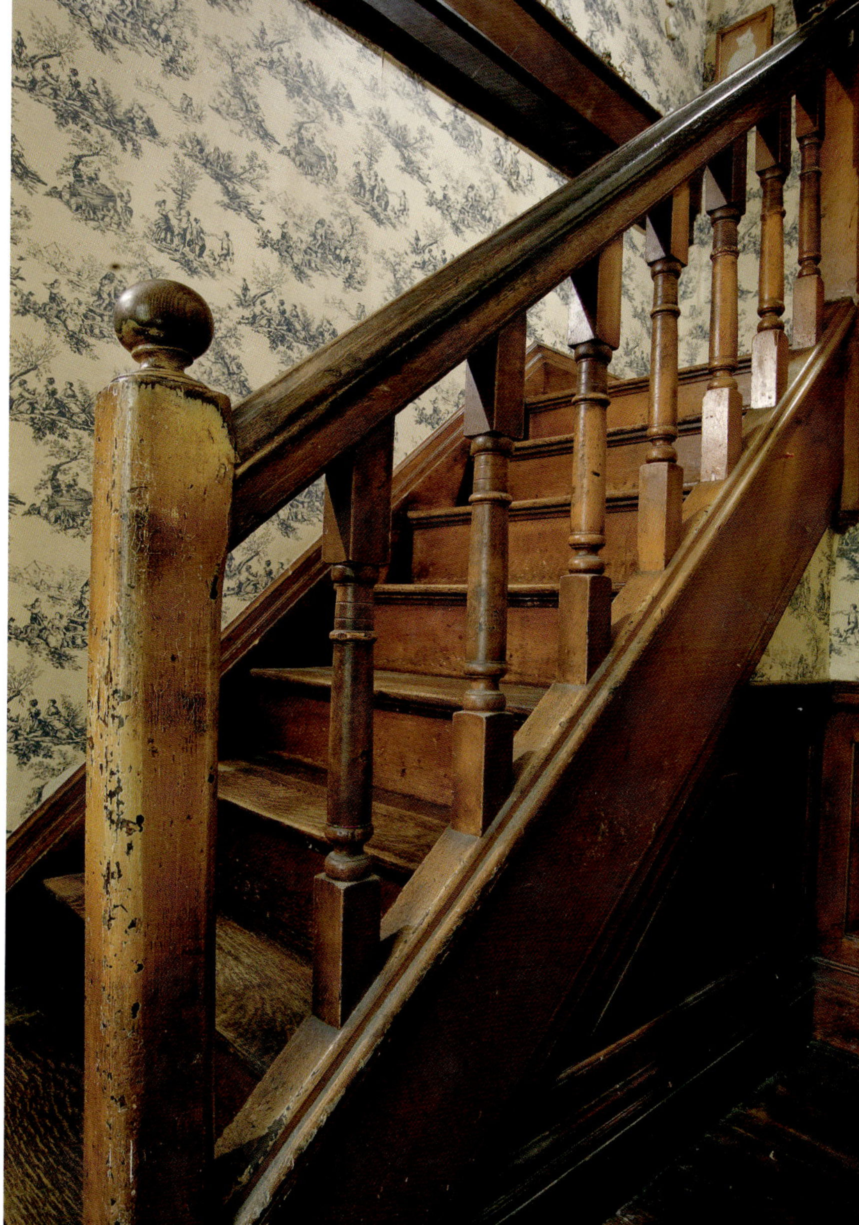

THE HOME

From the beginning, as soon as substantial houses were built, they took the East Anglican form. First and foremost, all were wood houses. The New England house shared with East Anglia's wood house a similar post-and-beam structure, pegging, wind brace, shaping, mortise, and tenon joinery, and shape of crown posts, rafters, purlins, and scantling.

The ubiquitous saltbox form of house (see the Jethro Coffin House, p. 94) in New England had precedent in East Anglia and Kent. Likewise, the Cape Cod–style one-and-a-half-story house (see the John Dunnell House–Tare Shirt Farm, p. 186) also had precursors in the same region as did the more elaborate multi-gabled house (see the Judge Jonathan Corwin House, p. 52). In both East Anglia and Kent, a projecting second floor, called a "jetty," became widespread in the seventeenth century (see the Parson Joseph Capen House, p. 88). These house types were built in different sizes and elaborations. Some were simple one-room structures, more an accommodation to modest budget than familial need, which could be easily added to.

By the end of the Great Migration Captain Edward Johnson, shipwright and historian, could honestly boast that "the Lord hath been pleased to turn all the wigwams . . . built at their first coming into orderly, fair, and well-built houses, well-furnished many of them, together with orchards filled with goodly fruit trees and gardens with a variety of flowers."

INTERIOR

Interior arrangements around the central chimney stack followed an English pattern as well: a small central entryway (in larger houses often enclosed in a projecting porch as on the Judge Jonathan Corwin House, p. 52) with a three-run "dog leg" stairway before the chimney stack leading to chambers above. To the left and right of the entry were two large rooms. One was a hall, a holdover from the medieval hall, which was the center of all public life in a manor house. It served as kitchen and great room. The other was the parlor, a room of formality, which was reserved as the owner's bedchamber but also reception room on high occasions. From this plan the New England house expanded, usually first with a one-story extension across the entire back for a kitchen (the hall retaining its dining function), pantry, and dairy. Other extensions could be off the gable end(s) or to the rear (forming an "L" shape), all to accommodate more residents.

The frame was composed of heavy oak posts and beams interlocked and pegged at each joint. Each room's floor and ceiling were supported by a massive summer beam running from chimney stack to outer wall, which in turn supported a closer-spaced set of smaller joists running from summer beam to the other two walls. This was repeated on each story.

First Period structures were usually clad with narrow clapboards of riven (split) oak, but coastal houses were more often sheathed in shingles to withstand the ocean weather. Exterior walls were filled with wattle (sticks) and daub (mud and

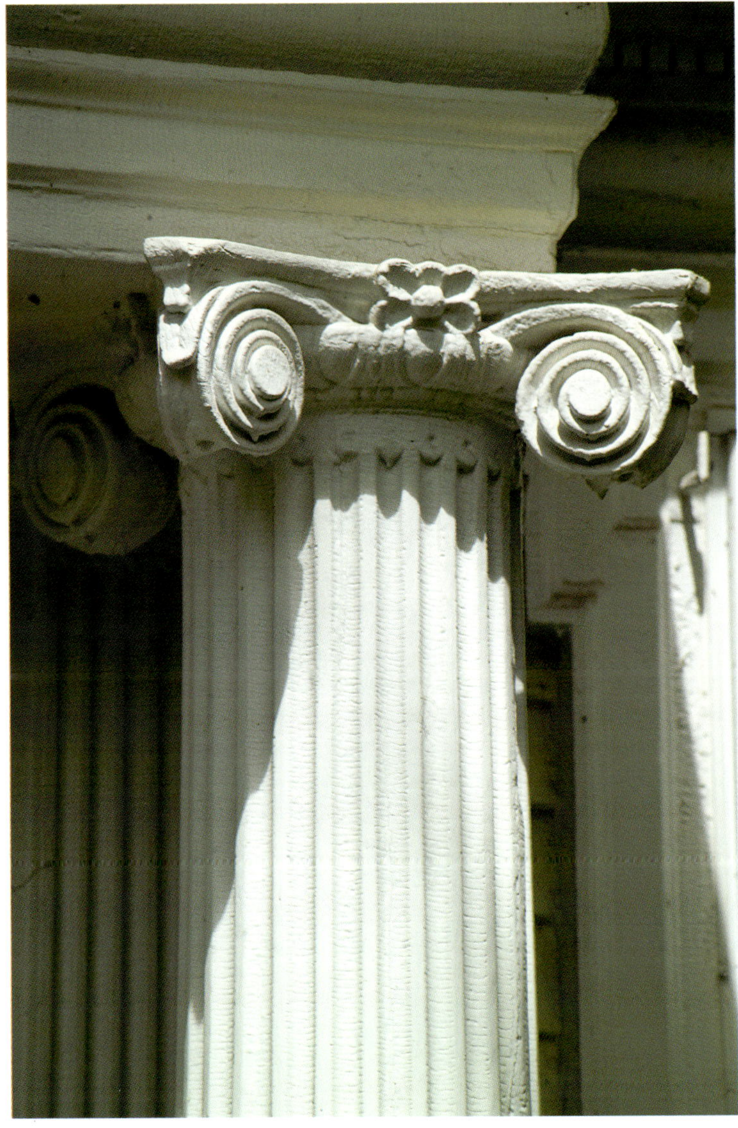

Zenus Cowles House (Oldgate)

ABOVE *The Zenus Cowles House front column is fluted with an Ionic capital.*

FACING PAGE *The Zenus Cowles House front exterior with a projecting pedimented pavilion with large Palladian window.*

clay) to form a windproof seal. The interior side of this infill was smoothed and plastered, with the large posts projecting into the room slightly. Flooring was composed of wide planks. The interior weight of the structure rested half on outer walls, half on the centrally located massive chimney stack. Placement of doors and windows owed more to function than symmetry, although most second-story windows aligned with those on the story below.

Stepping up to the second floor, two rooms were usually enclosed by walls and ceilings forming the hall chamber and the parlor chamber, each with a fireplace for the comfort of winter sleeping. If there was a lean-to kitchen, the area above was for storage. These chambers had multiple functions: sleeping rooms, storage spaces, and spinning and weaving textiles. On the ground level, the kitchen lean-to was for more than just cooking on the hearth. One end held the dairy. Here, earthenware basins and wood containers held milk and cream, and butter and cheese were processed and stored. At the other end was the pantry for food and utensil storage. Garret (attic) and cellar were primarily for storage of supplies and food. A cellar fireplace was useful as a cooler summer kitchen.

In these characteristics the early New England house followed southeastern English styles quite closely. Where exceptions to the early center-chimney house form are found—for instance the "stone-ender" houses of Rhode Island (see the Eleazer Arnold House, p. 104), their origin can be found in the western counties from which some Puritans emigrated. By the late seventeenth century, expansion turned inward. Instead of adding additions, the main block of the house became larger, two rooms deep on either side of the chimney on both floors. This required shifting the centerline of the roof backward to the centerline of the gables. As a result the saltbox profile changed to a symmetrical shape, which has been the dominant form ever since.

Symmetry also extended to room and window sizes and placement as New Englanders became acquainted with a new set of architectural principles derived from the Classical (see *Great Houses of New England*). Those principles were increasingly accepted as New Englanders became more affluent and could afford to separate front spaces from rear work spaces. As the house became two rooms deep it allowed for more chambers, reflecting the desire for greater privacy within the family. These trends were behind a major shift in house design when the central chimney was removed to permit a front-to-rear central hallway, an elegant and spacious public entryway into the house, and, just as important, separate and private doorways to all rooms. Fireplaces, formerly and conveniently radiating out from one chimney stack, now were shifted to either the gable walls as separate chimneys or to the central wall between front and back rooms forming back-to-back fireplaces. This was the Georgian central hall plan—the medieval had succumbed to the Classical. The elaborate and sophisticated Georgian style is what New Englanders finally aspired to by the time America won its independence.

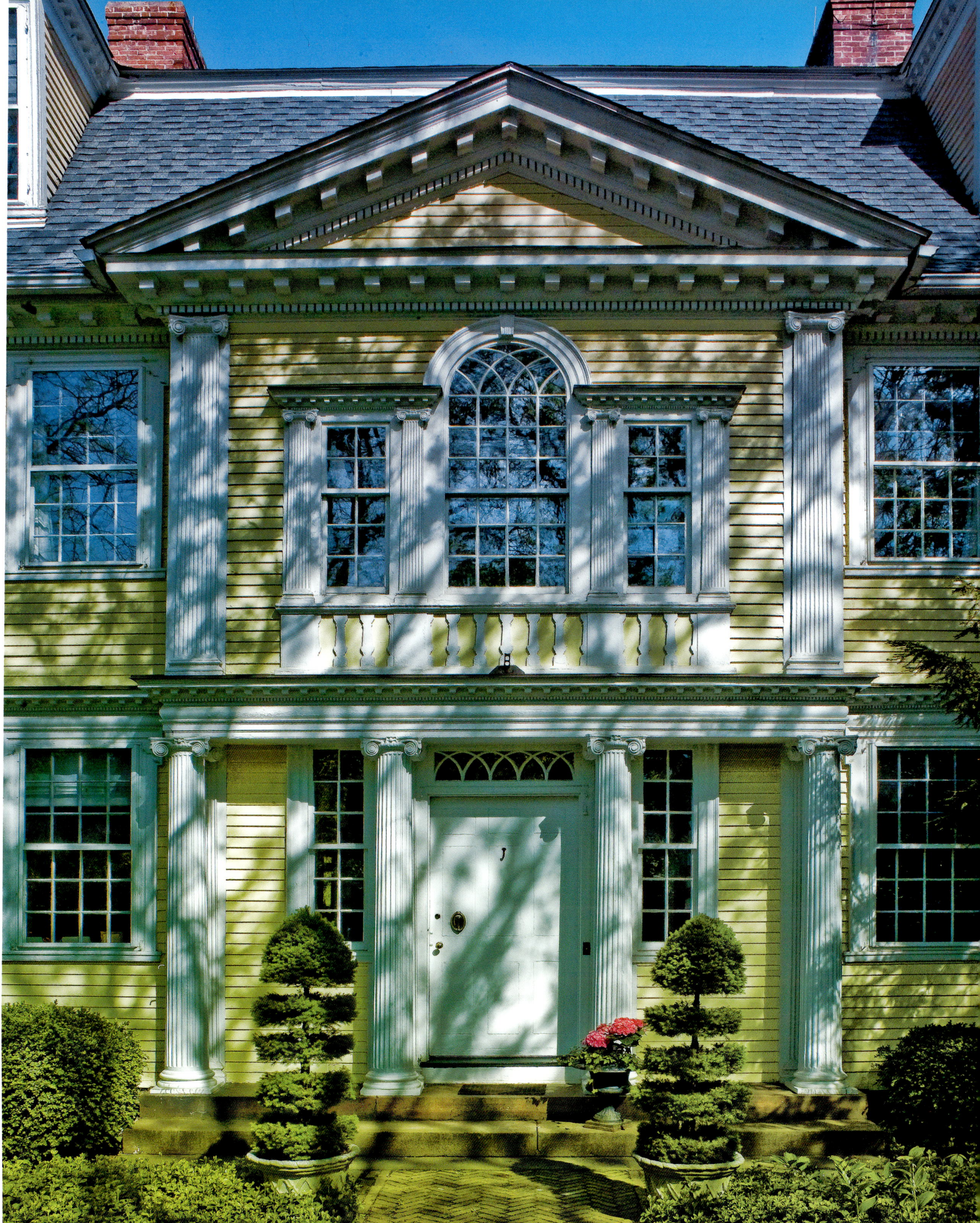

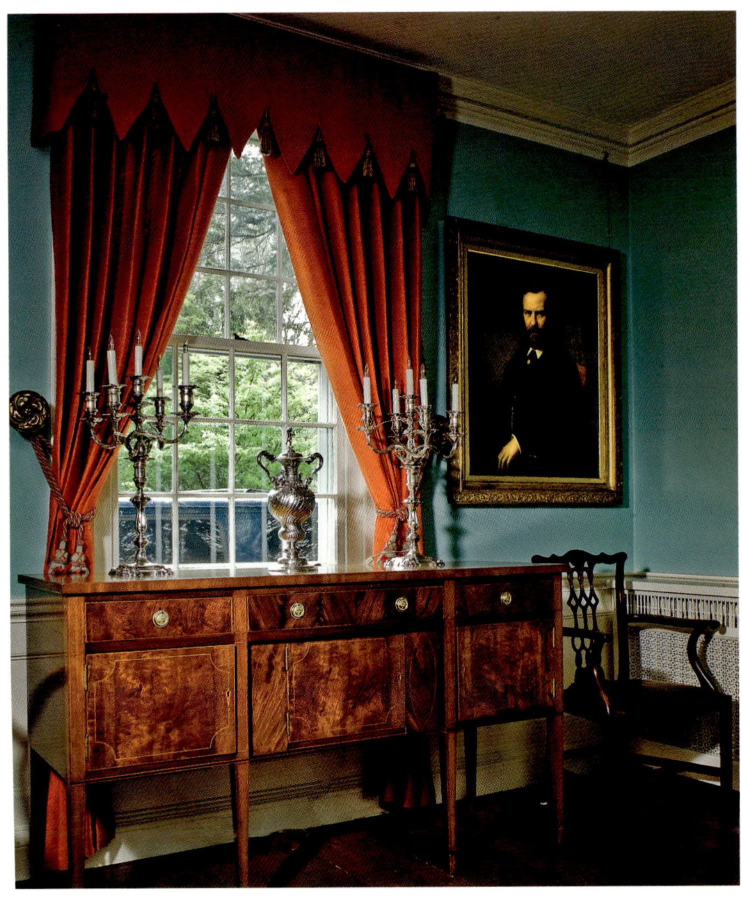

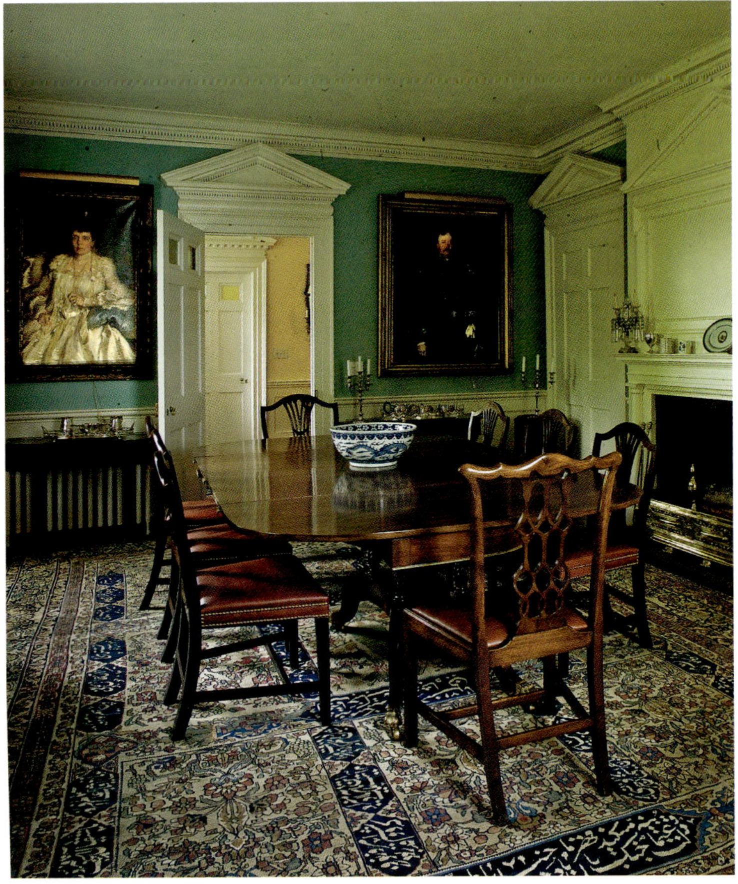

Zenus Cowles House (Oldgate)

LEFT *In the Zenus Cowles House dining room, to the right of the sideboard is the portrait of Anna's father Theodore Roosevelt Sr., painted by Daniel Huntington (1816–1906). Roosevelt Senior was a New York merchant, and a founder of the New York Orthopedic Hospital (which later merged with the New York Presbyterian Hospital), The American Museum of Natural History, and The Metropolitan Museum of Art. He was father of Anna, Theodore (later president), Elliot, and Corinne Roosevelt.*

BELOW LEFT *In the Zenus Cowles House dining room, the pedimented doors and chimneybreast are indicative of an architect versed in English design concepts. The portrait to left is of Anna Roosevelt Cowles by Ellen Emmett Rand (1876–1941); to the right is a portrait of her husband Admiral William Sheffield Cowles by the same artist. William served in the Navy during the Civil War on blockade duty, then attended Annapolis, and returned to the Navy for his career. In 1893 he was naval attaché in London where he met Anna. They were married two years later. On his retirement they made Oldgate, the family home, their residence. A son, William Sheffield Cowles Jr., resided in the house, as does his son's family today.*

FACING PAGE *Zenus Cowles House (Oldgate)*
Long before the modern era the swastika appeared in many cultures. The word is from Sanskrit svastika, which means good luck and thus is an appropriate welcoming emblem on an entry gate.

AN ABBREVIATED LIST OF SOURCES ON NEW ENGLAND HISTORY AND ARCHITECTURE

Cummings, Abbott Lowell. *The Framed Houses of Massachusetts Bay, 1625–1725*. Cambridge, 1979.

St. George, Robert Blair. "'Set Thine House in order': The Domestication of the Yeomanry of Seventeenth-Century New England." In Jonathan L. Fairbanks and Robert F. Trent, *New England Begins: The Seventeenth Century*, Vols. I and II. Boston: Museum of Fine Arts, 1982.

Fischer, David Hackett. *Albion's Seed: Four British Folkways in America*. New York: Oxford University Press, 1989.

Garvin, James L. *A Building History of Northern New England*. Hanover and London: University Press of New England, 2001.

Kimball, S. Fiske. *Domestic Architecture of the American Colonies and the Early Republic*. 1922. Reprint, New York: Dover Publications, 1966.

Morgan, Edmund Sears. *The Puritan Family: Essays on Religion & Domestic Relations in Seventeenth-Century New England*. Boston: Trustees of the Public Library, 1944.

Morrison, Hugh. *Early American Architecture from the First Colonial Settlements to the National Period*. 1952. Reprint, New York: Dover Publications, 1987.

Nylander, Jane C. and Diane L. Viera. *Windows on the Past: Four Centuries of New England Homes*. Boston: Society for the Preservation of New England Antiquities and Bulfinch Press/Little Brown and Company, 2000.

Smith, Gwenda. *The Town House*. Strafford, VT: Strafford Historical Society, 1992.

Waterman, Thomas Tileston. *The Dwellings of Colonial America*. Chapel Hill: University of North Carolina Press, 1950.

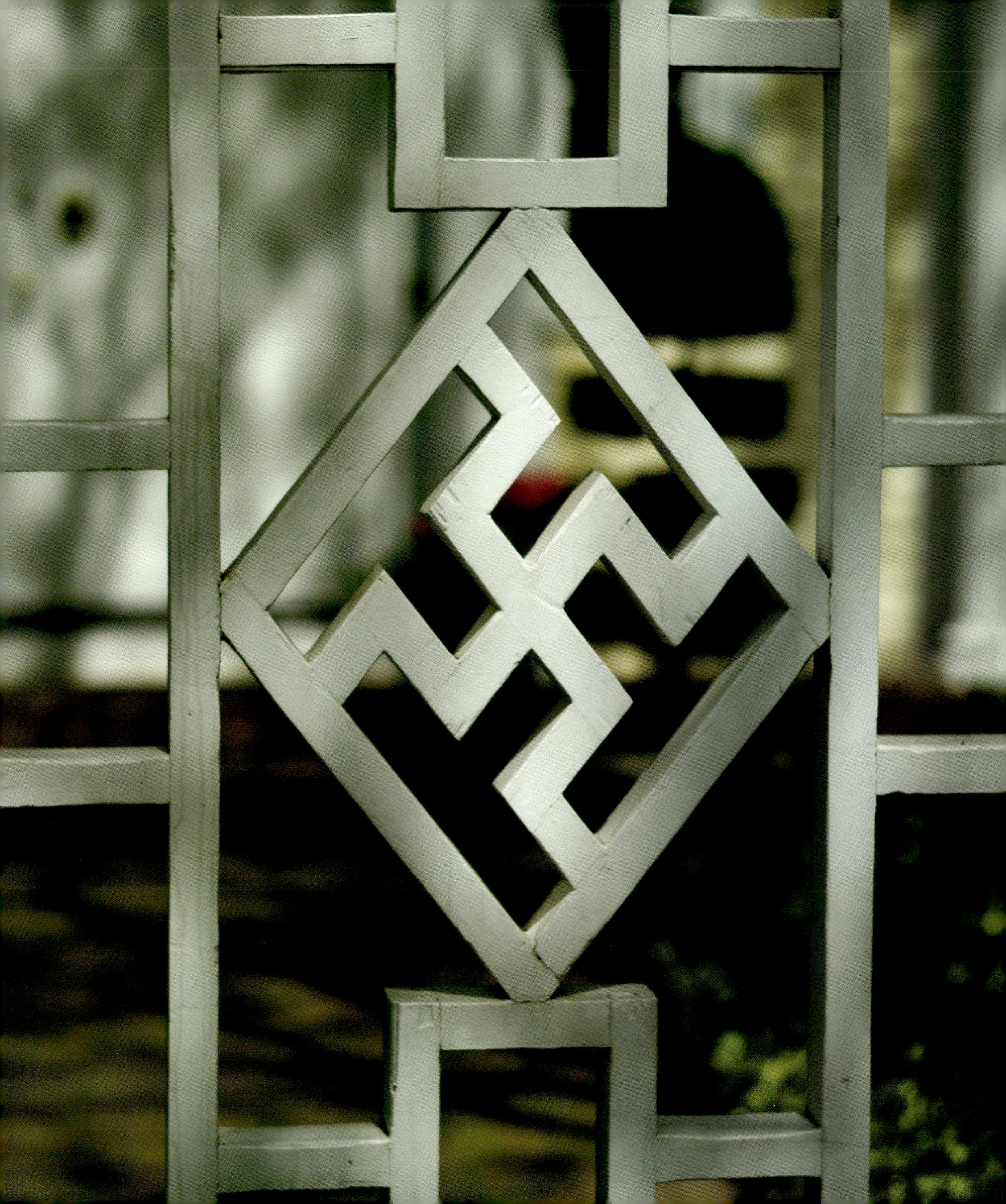

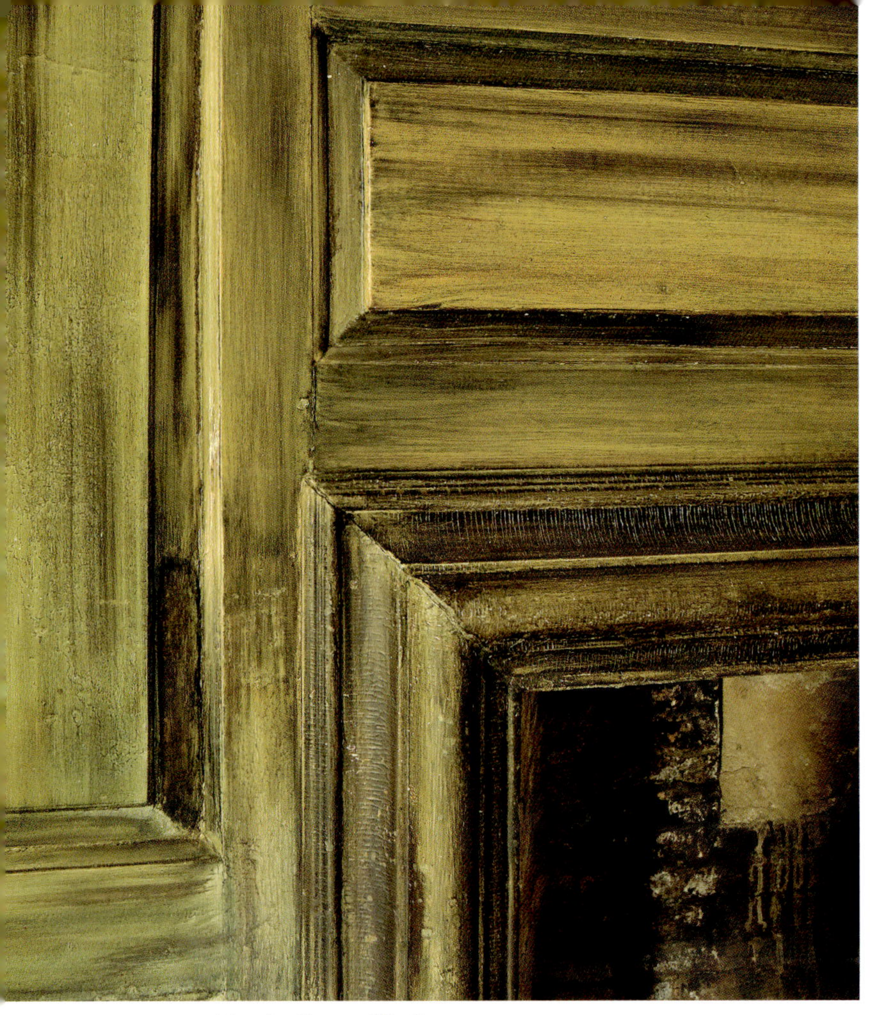

ABOVE *Mantle, Cogswell's Grant.*
BELOW *Door handle, Canterbury Shaker Village.*

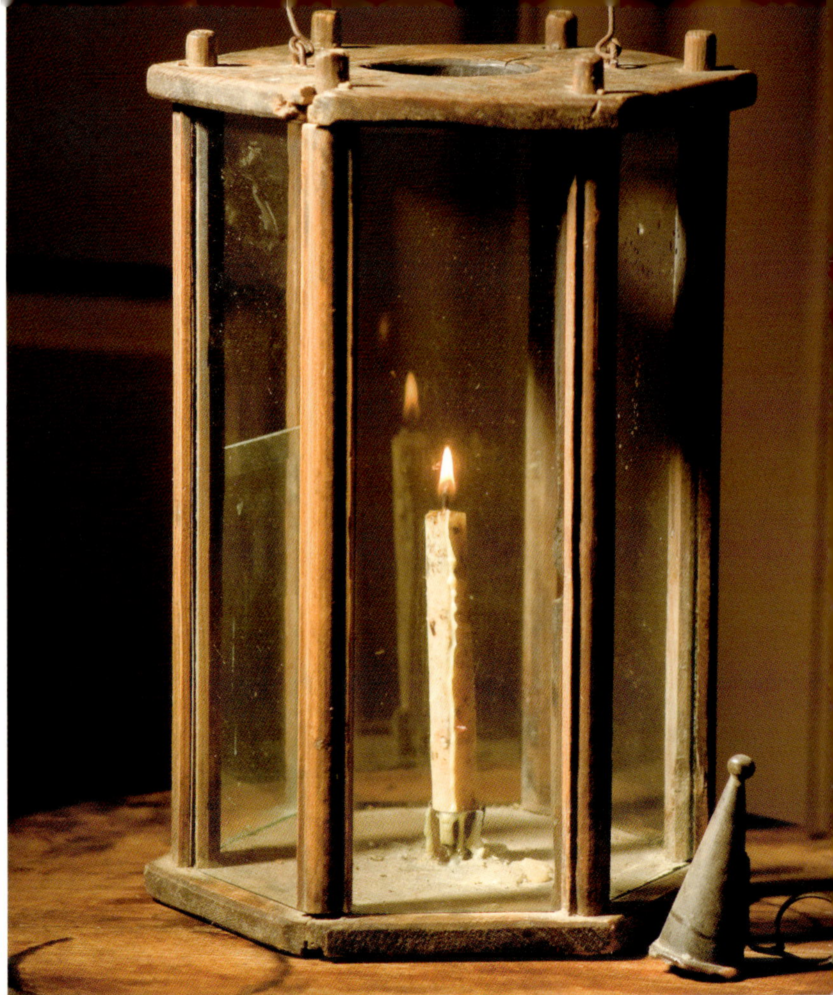

ABOVE *Lantern, Major John Giles House.*
BELOW *Top of newel post, Joseph Fessenden House.*

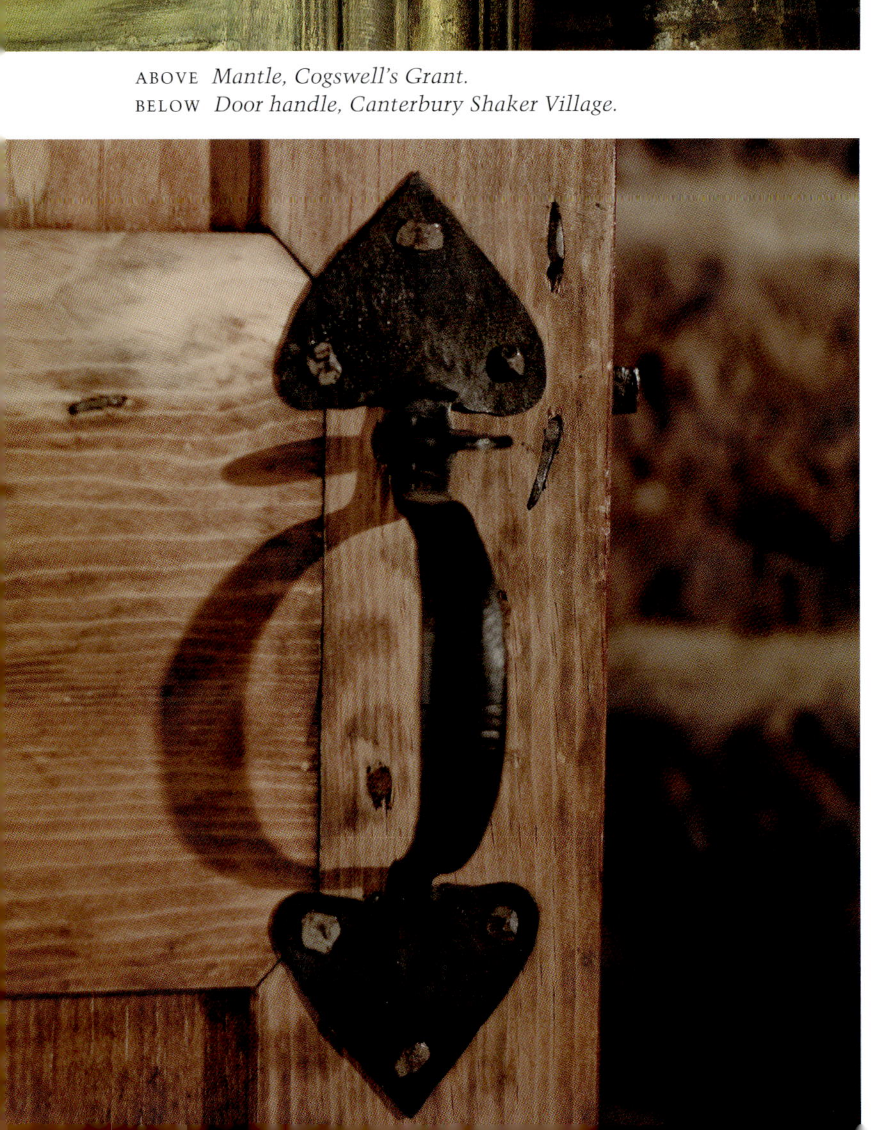

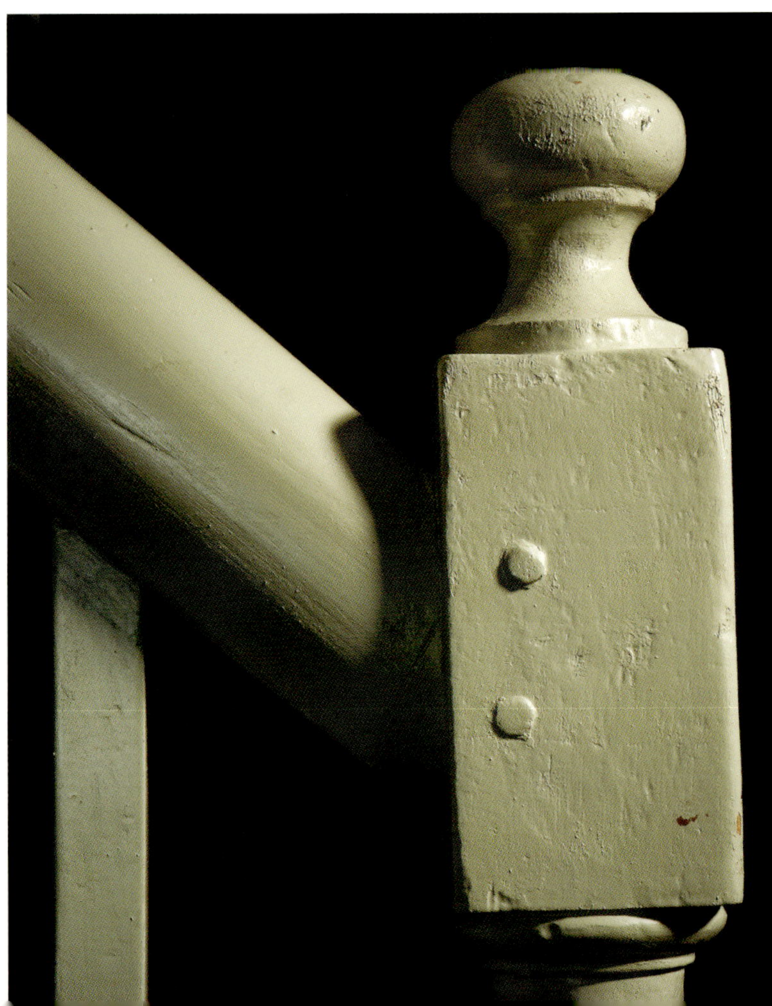

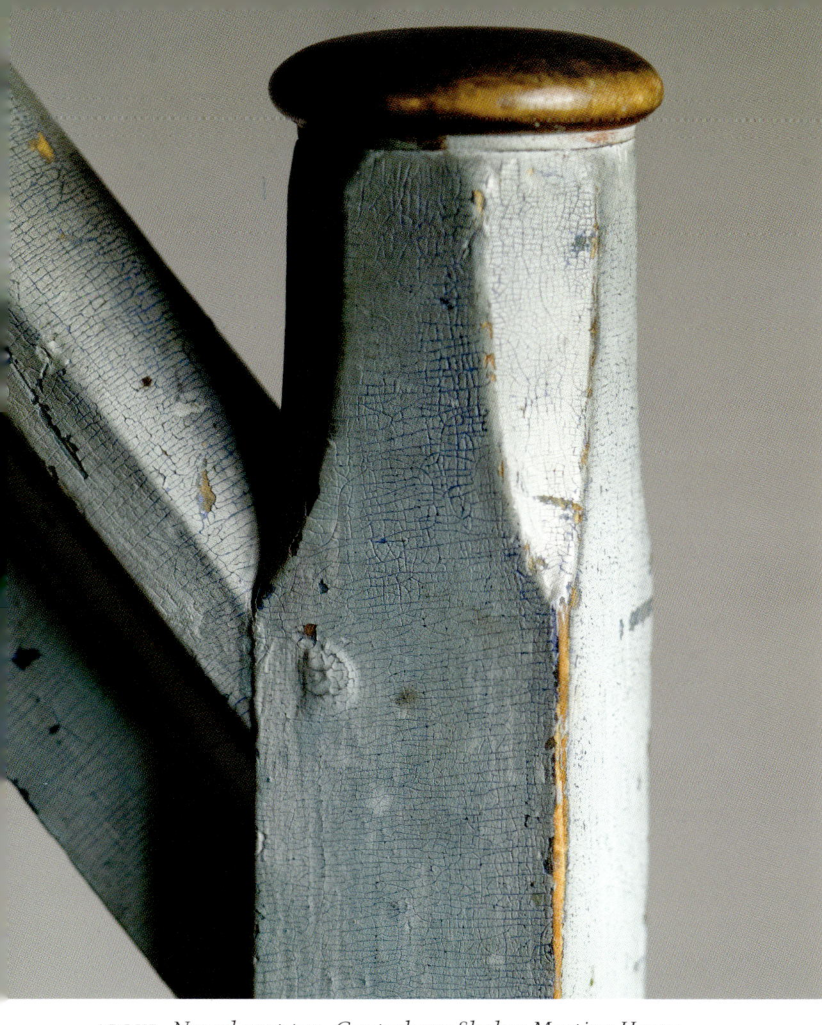

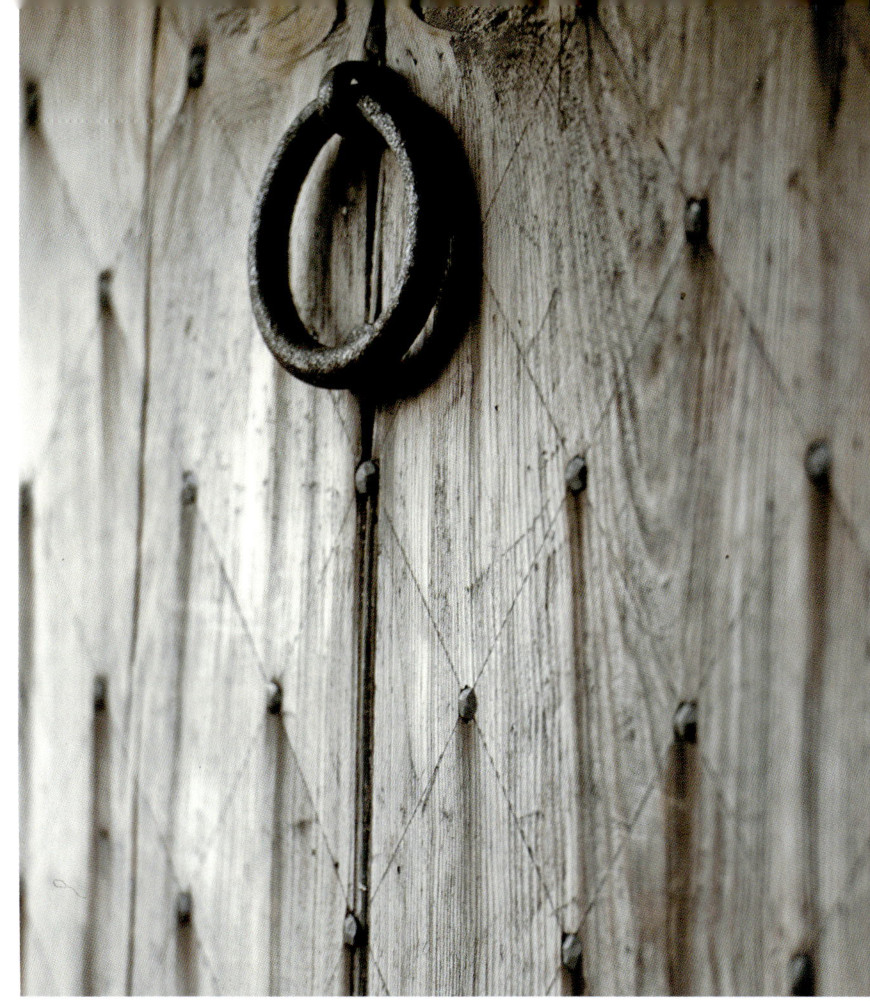

ABOVE *Newel post top, Canterbury Shaker Meeting House.*
BELOW *Box lock and latch, Joseph Fessenden House.*

ABOVE *Knocker door, the Henry Crane–Samuel Ware House.*
BELOW *H hinge, Canterbury Shaker Meeting House.*

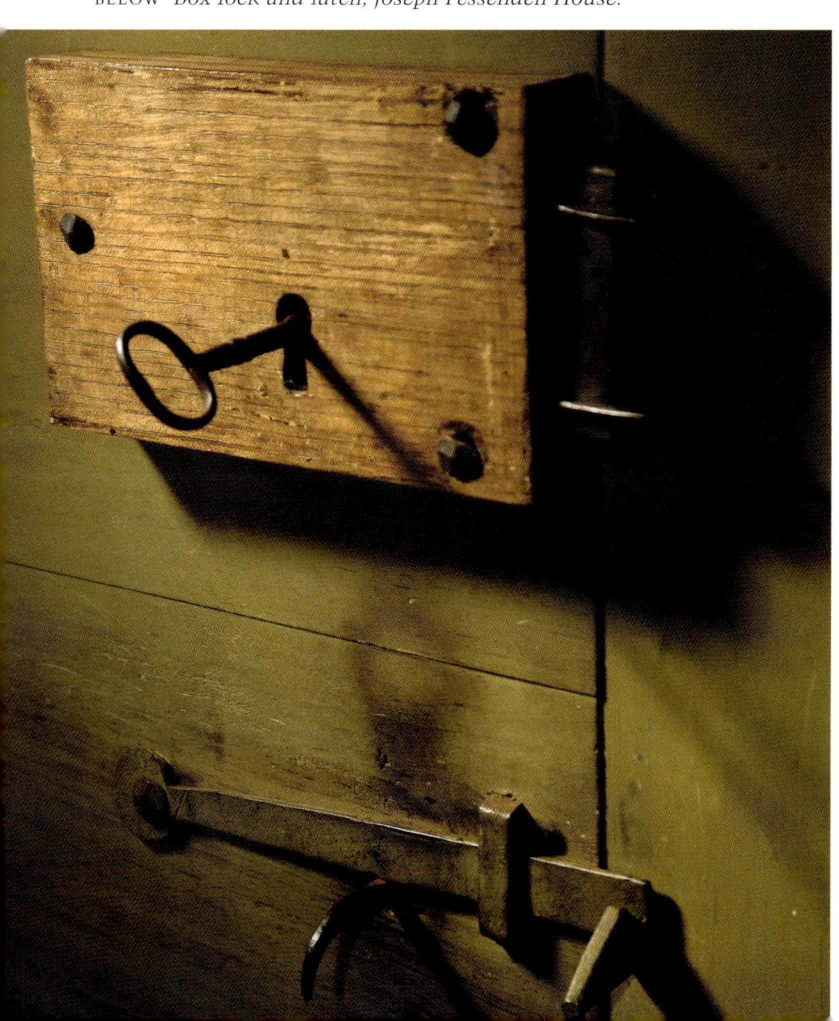

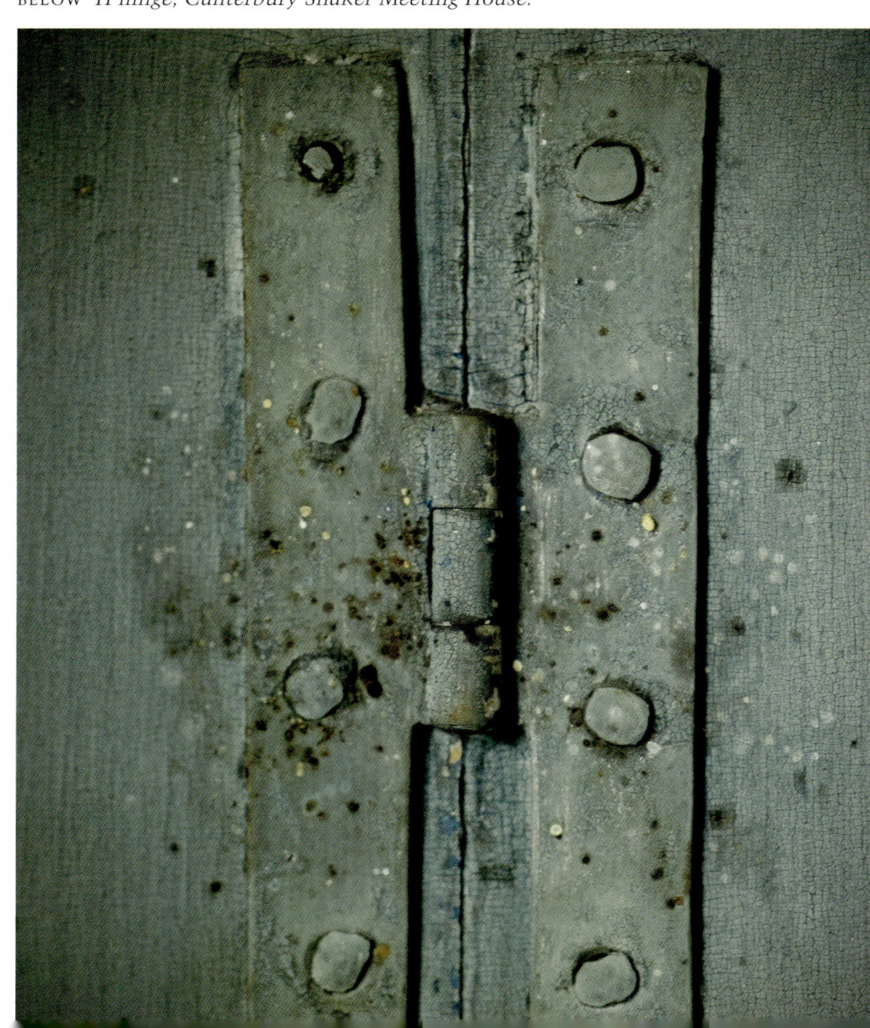

HENRY WHITFIELD HOUSE

Guilford, Connecticut, 1639 (with later modifications)

The European settlement of what is now Connecticut began when the Dutch of New Netherland (later New York Province) laid claim to the region in 1633 by establishing a trading post at the present location of the city of Hartford on the Connecticut River. Both Dutch and New Englanders were aware of the fertile bottom land of this river valley. In 1632 a ship from the Plymouth Colony had explored the Connecticut River and in 1633 (just three years after Winthrop's fleet had arrived on the Massachusetts coast), a group from the colony formed an English trading post on the Connecticut River in competition with the Dutch. Sailing north they found the Dutch fort, defied its injunction, sailed on, and established a trading post at what is now Windsor. This was the beginning of the end of Dutch claim to the area. Without sufficient arms or settlements the Dutch relinquished claim by 1654.

Two years later the first English settlement began at what is now Wethersfield, ten miles south of the English trading post, followed closely by people from Dorchester, Massachusetts, who came to Windsor in 1635. The next year the Reverend Thomas Hooker brought his congregation from Newtown (later renamed Cambridge, Massachusetts) and created the town of Hartford. The three towns joined together to provide a framework of civil government and chose deputies to represent each town at a general court (legislative body), and they selected a governor and magistrates to regulate their lives.

Meanwhile, in 1635 John Winthrop, the younger, established a fort on the Connecticut coast of Long Island Sound, close to the mouth of the Connecticut River, now known as Saybrook. These settlements had hardly been built when war with the Pequot Indians broke out in 1637, culminating in decimation of

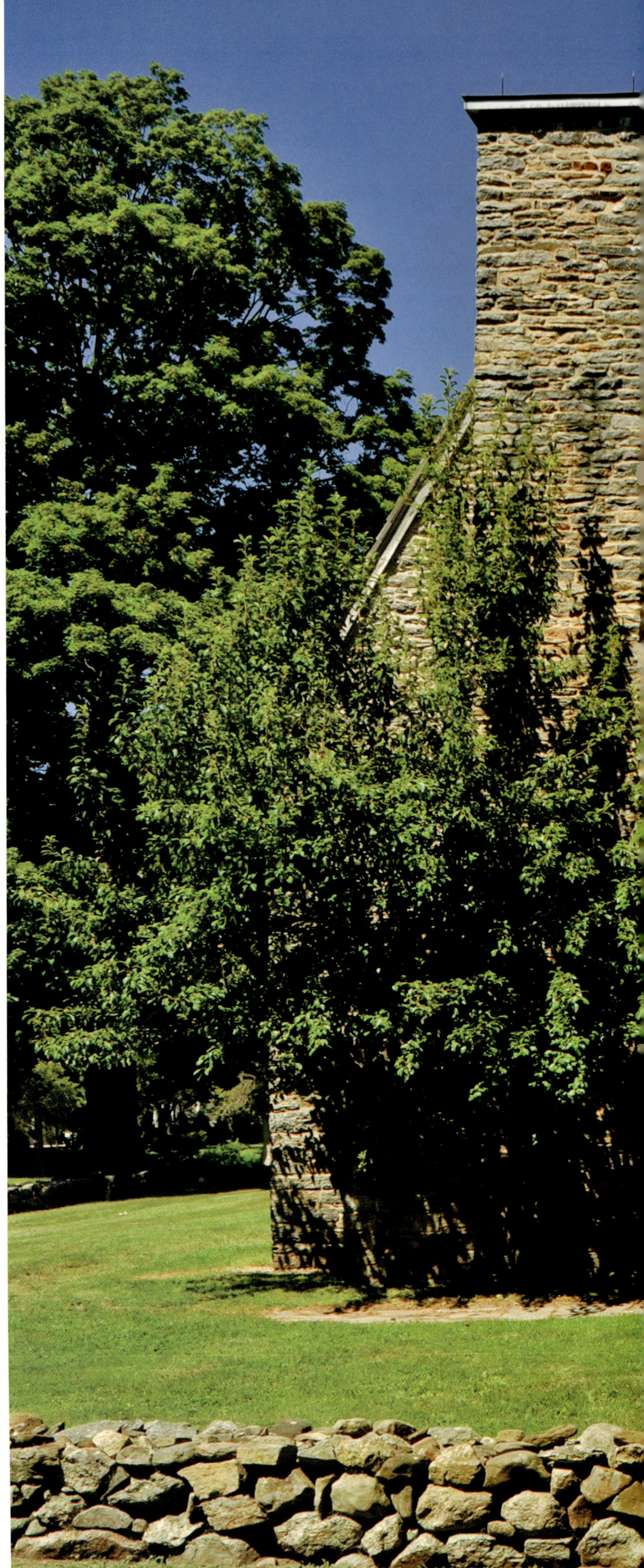

Although related in form to English houses of the time, the Whitfield House is unique in New England for its rare use of stone, no doubt inspired by a recent American Indian war, since four similar houses were built at that time. This is the last surviving and the oldest house in New England—at least its walls—dating from 1639. The massive chimney stacks have more to do with accommodating the irregular sizes of rubble stone than volume of smoke.

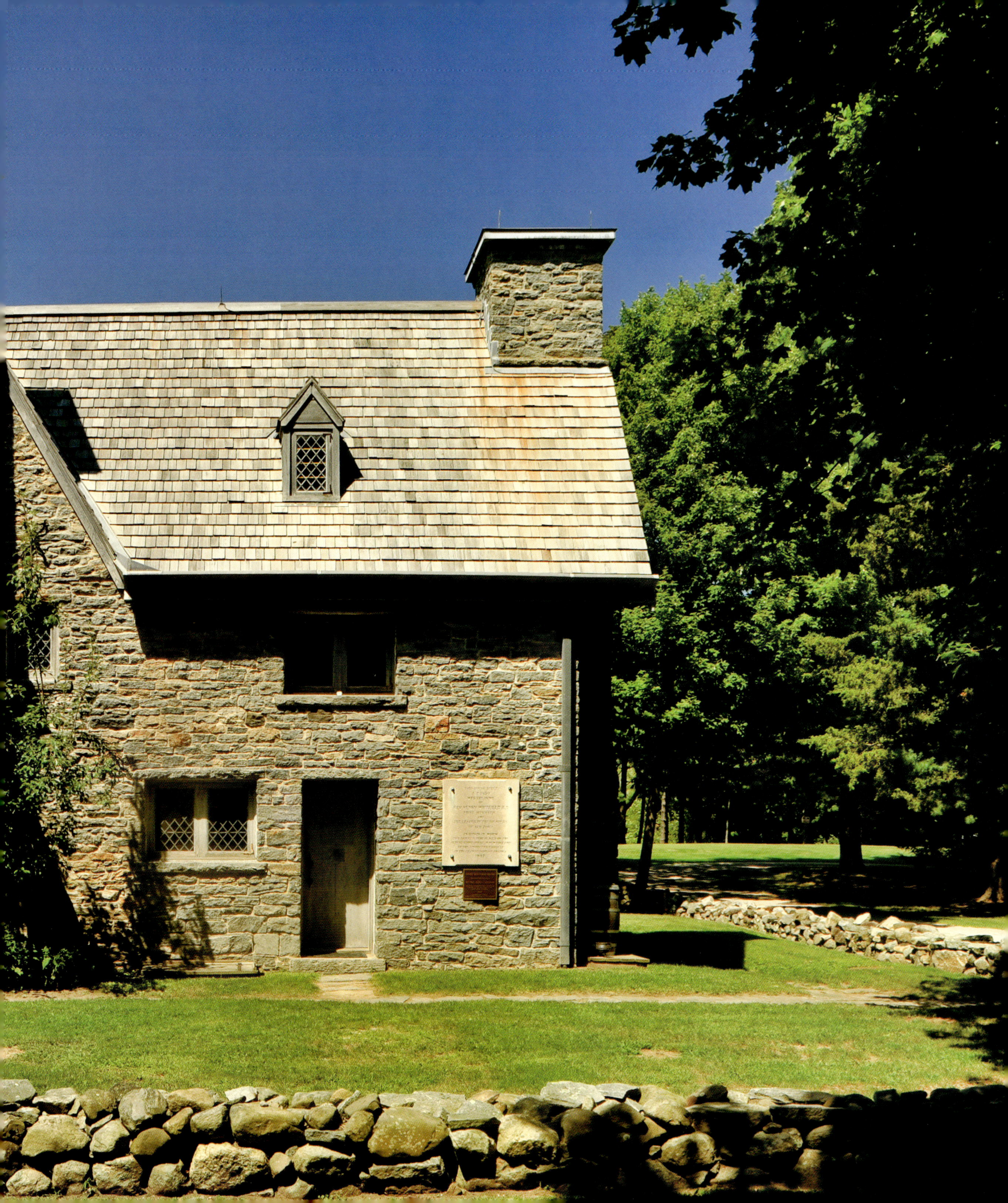

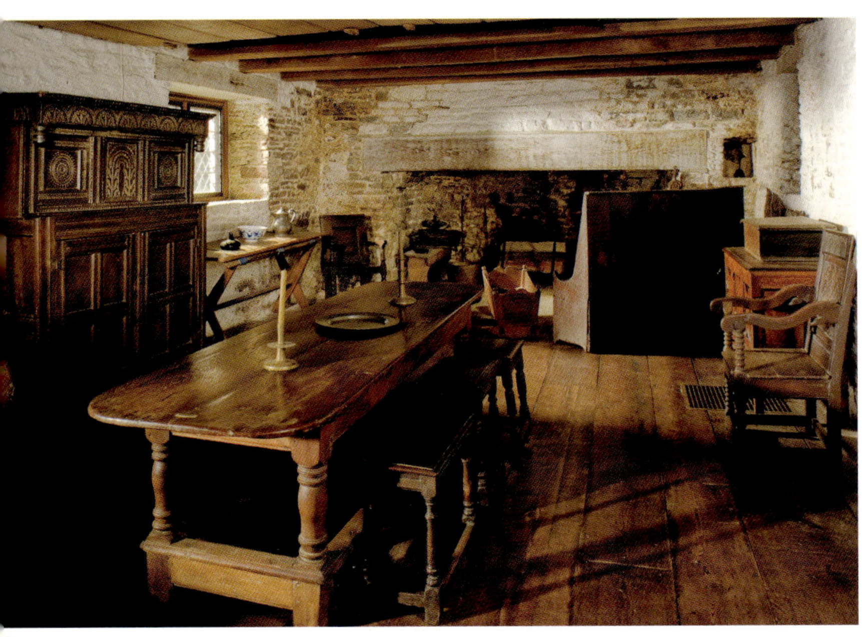

ABOVE AND RIGHT
In the great hall, the width of the fireplace was characteristic of early hall/kitchen hearths. Seventeenth-century furnishings include English pieces and a Guilford, Connecticut, communion board (left) and chest from the Scranton family (right).

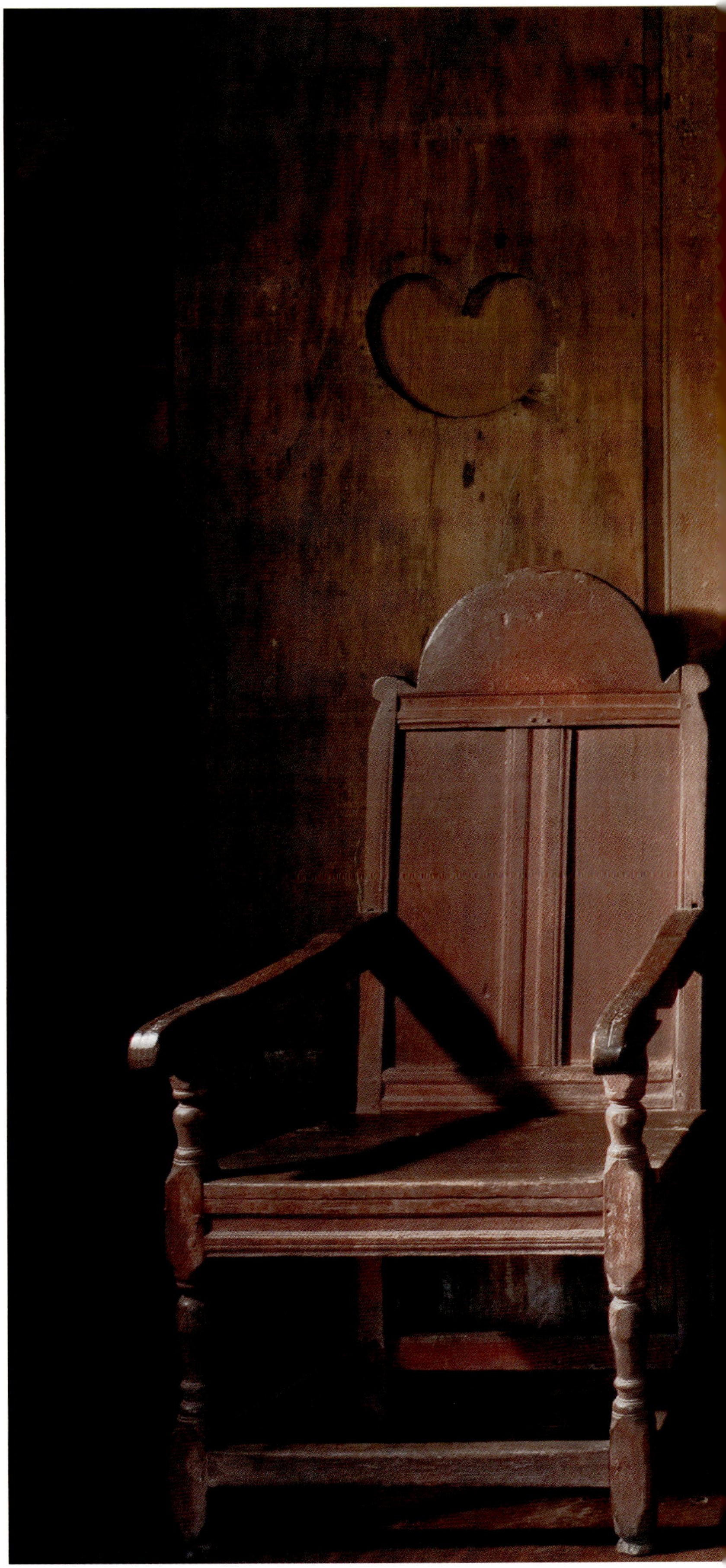

the tribe and ending any major threat to the expansion of European settlement. Within a year settlement resumed and Reverend John Davenport and Theopolis Eaton brought settlers to found what became known as New Haven Colony in 1638. The following year his friend, the Reverend Henry Whitfield, brought forty families from London to New Haven, the first group to come to Connecticut directly from England. Intent on their own settlement, they purchased land on the coast from the Menuncatuck Indians halfway between Saybrook and New Haven. Erecting rudimentary houses around a village green, this community did not follow the common practice of encircling the settlement with a palisaded wall; rather, they built four large stone houses to act as residences for the leaders of the community and as defensive refuges in case of attack. Henry Whitfield's house is one of these and is the only one to survive.

Guilford later became a part of New Haven Colony, which itself was merged with other Connecticut settlements to form

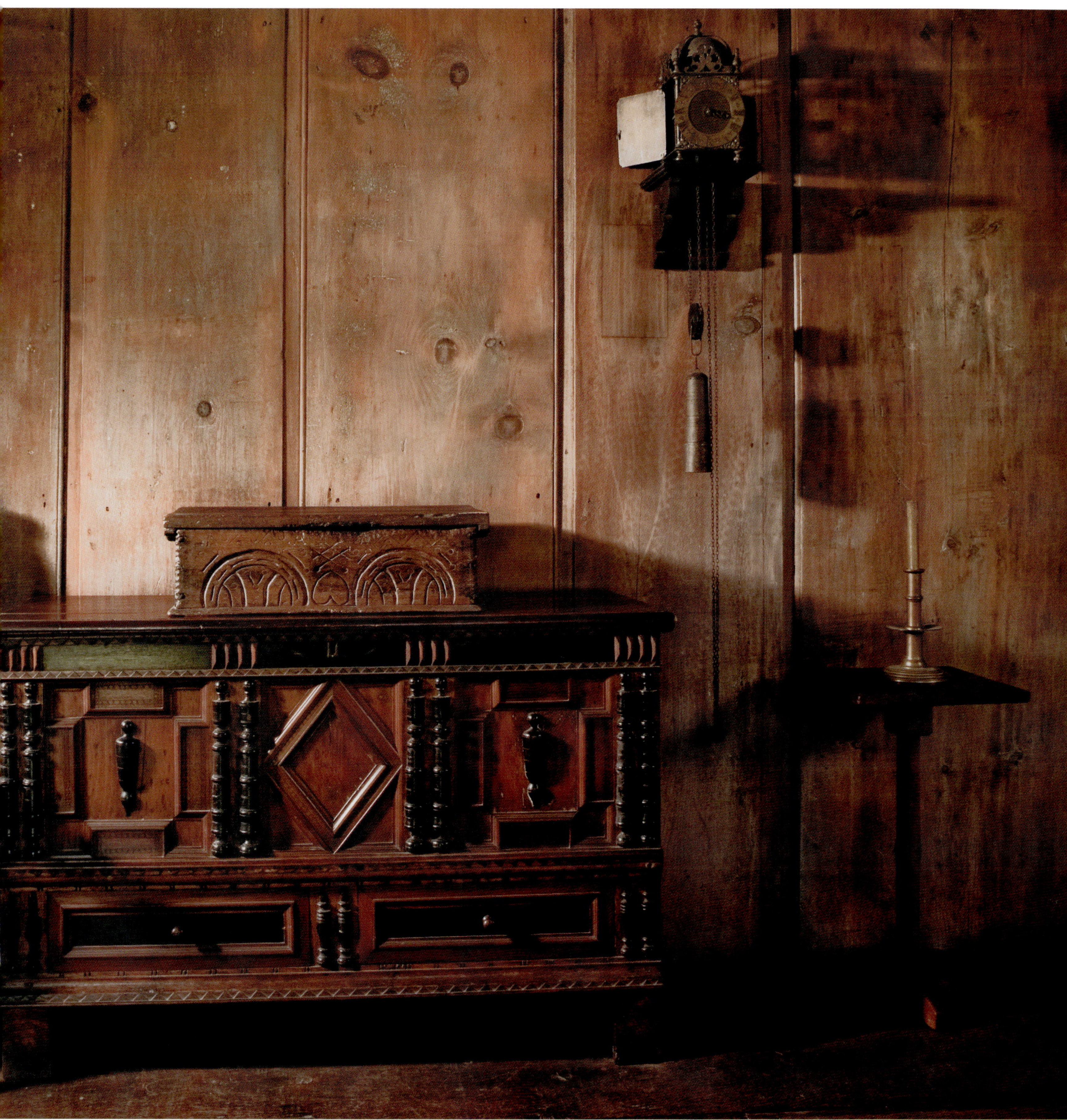

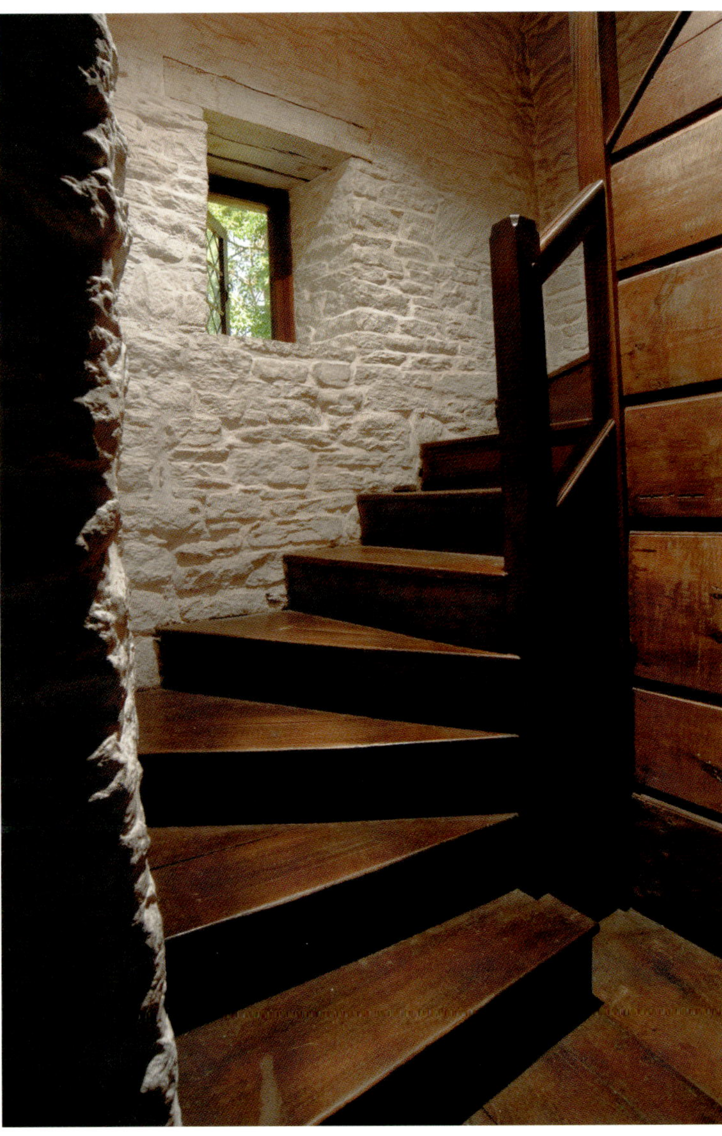

LEFT *The stairway's corner position is unlike other New England houses, which typically located the stair against the chimney in front of the entrance door. This particular stair is a re-creation.*

FACING PAGE *Furnished as a sleeping chamber, the large fireplace and small window in this room reflect economy—plenty of firewood and little expensive imported glass.*

Connecticut Colony with essentially the same bounds as today. Guilford's economy derived from agriculture and maritime trade. Its prosperity is evidenced by the many surviving colonial period homes. Like so many New England communities, its expansion over three centuries was driven by a succession of businesses, in this case shipbuilding, sea trade, manufacturing, quarrying (including granite for the Statue of Liberty), and in the last century tourism based on its appealing coastal resorts, followed by year-round expansion brought by the interstate highway.

Henry Whitfield's house was likely built in 1639 and as such could lay claim to being the oldest surviving house in Connecticut and oldest stone house in New England. While age alone may earn reverence, its size and stone construction are so singular that it has attracted community pride and owner investment over a long period. Indeed, it could be considered the poster child of historic preservation in New England. When the state bought the property in 1900, it hired noted restoration architect Norman M. Isham to prepare it for museum use. He found much of the interior walls and first-floor ceilings to be of a later date than 1639 and removed them, creating a two-story open exhibition hall in the front part of the house. We now know the interior had been destroyed by fire in 1860 and thus was extensively remodeled in the 1870s. In the 1930s, architect J. Frederick Kelly undertook a restoration of the house. By picking through the remaining evidence, it was determined that only the granite walls were original. Beam pockets, old window openings, and other scraps of evidence, combined with educated conjecture, suggested what the original interior may have looked like and was the guide for completing the restoration, which is essentially what is seen today. A later rear section was removed, stucco removed and stone repointed. From 1999 to 2000 the exterior was renovated following the 1930s plan; this fixed the effects of weathering. Extensive archeological excavations over the past thirty years have added many new insights for interpretation.

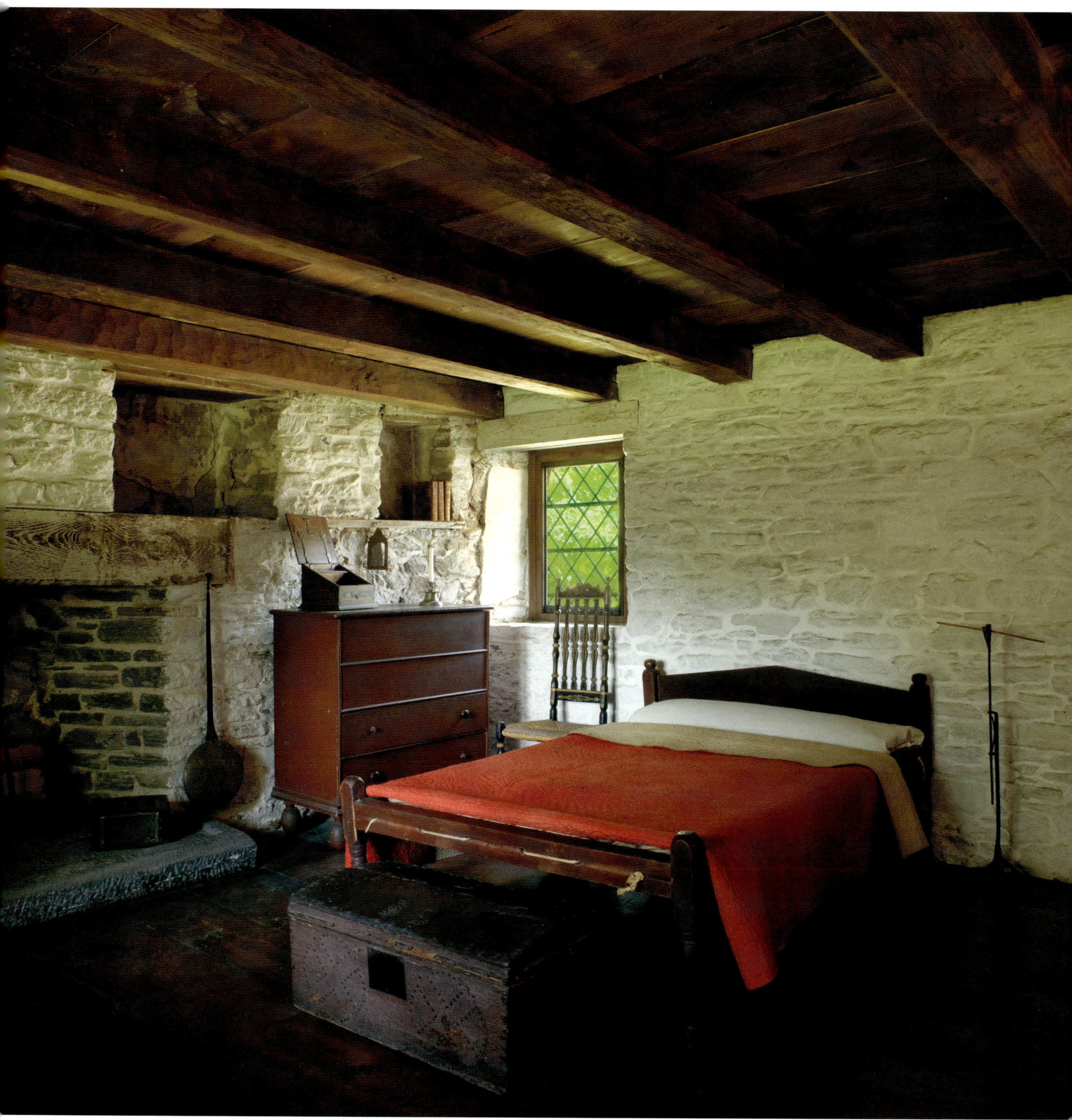

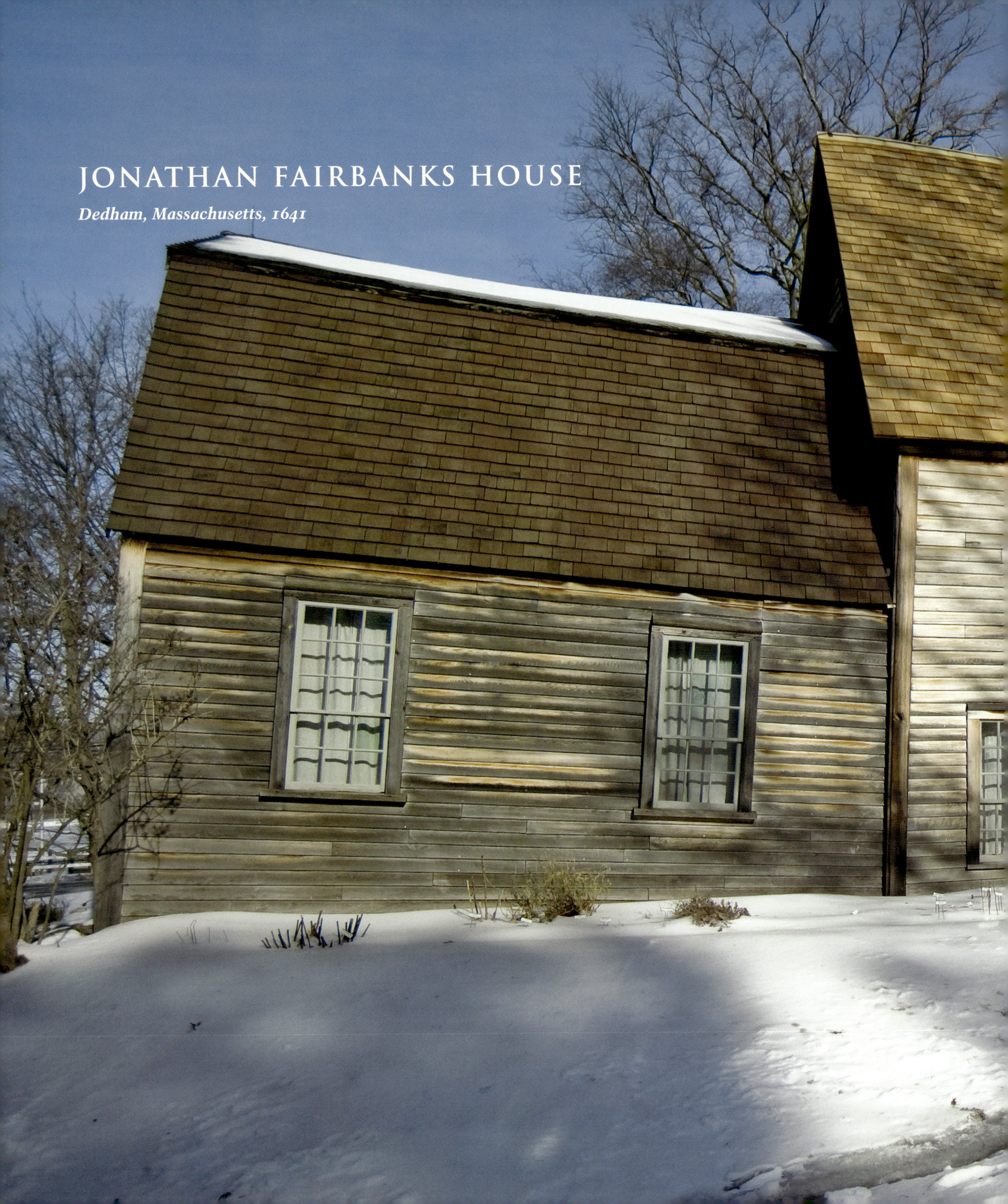

JONATHAN FAIRBANKS HOUSE

Dedham, Massachusetts, 1641

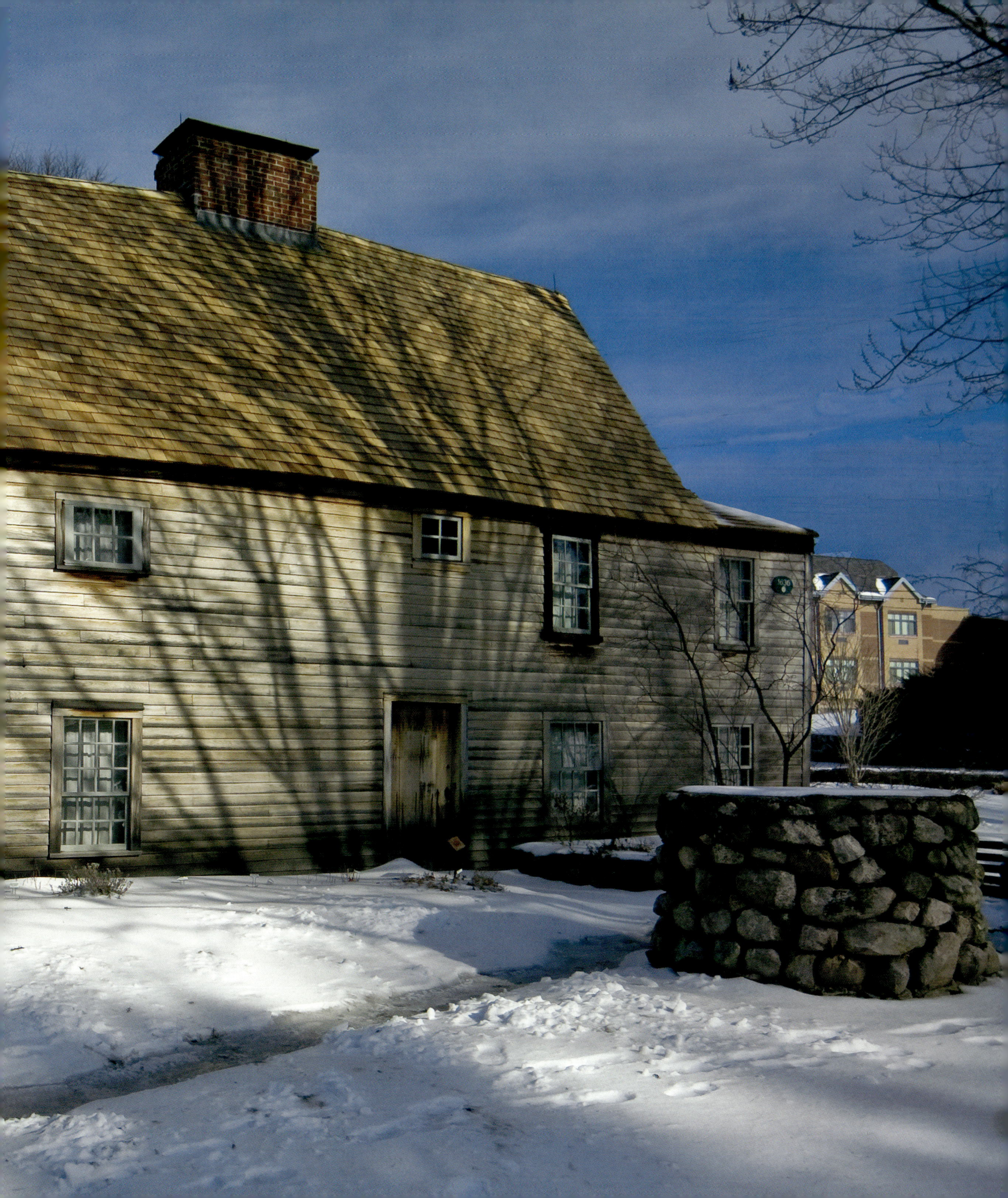

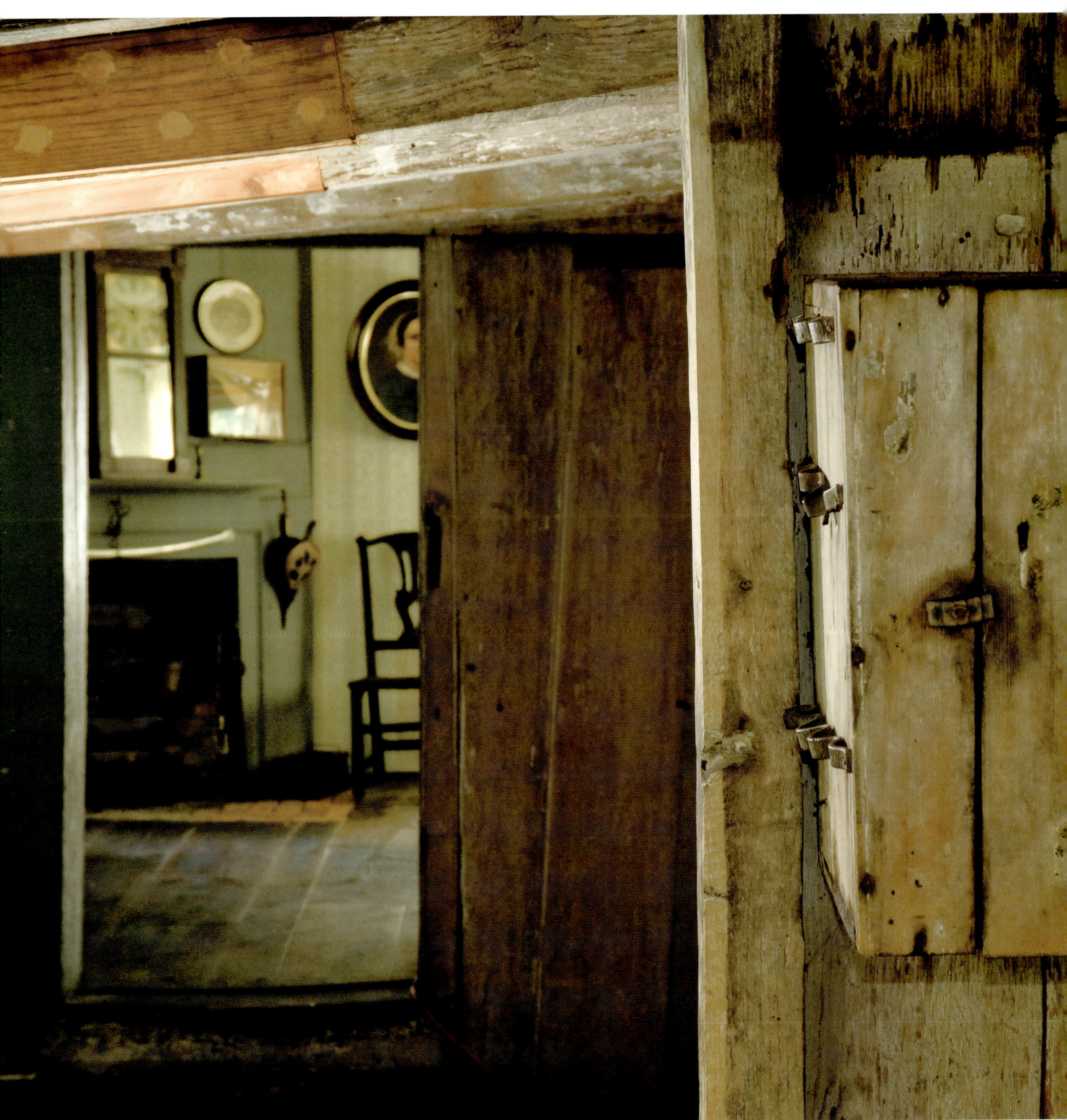

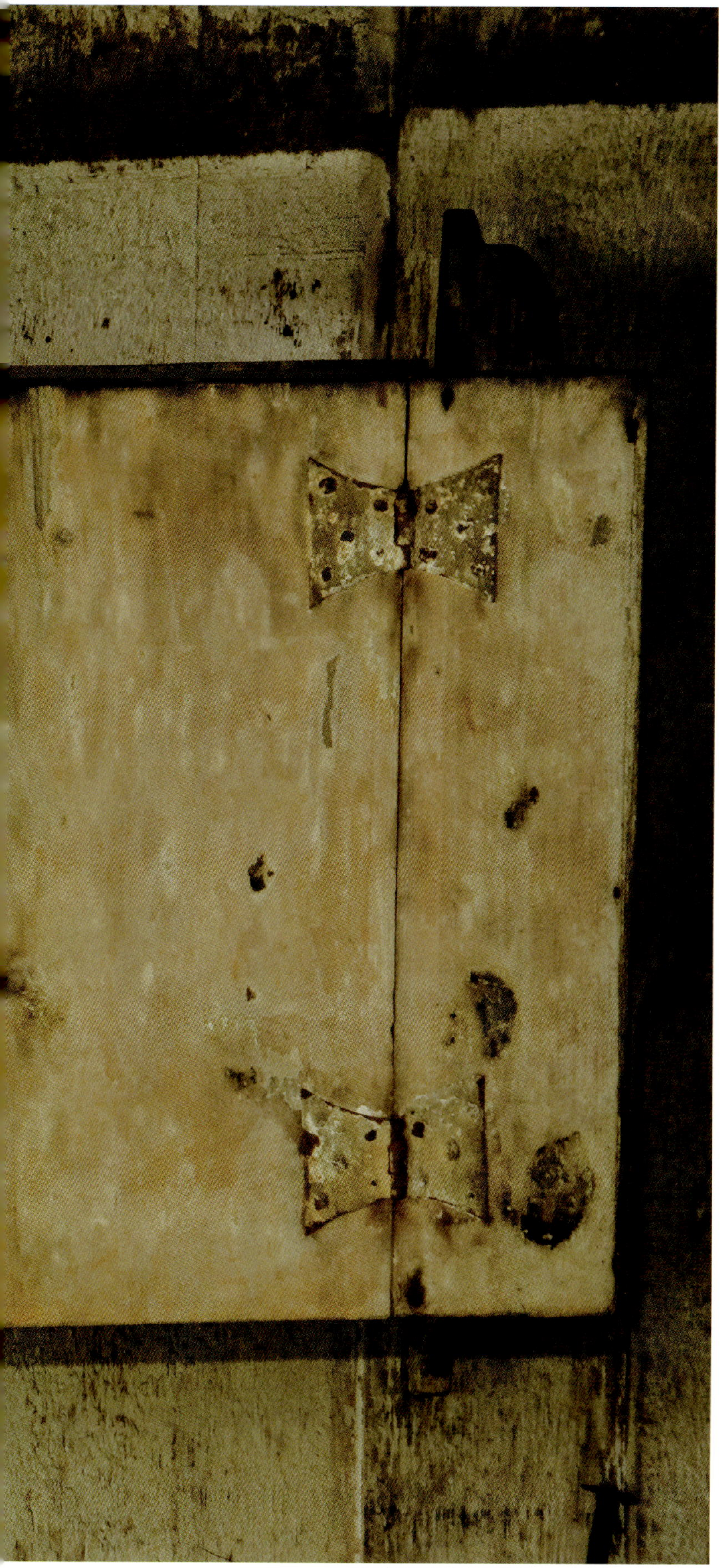

PREVIOUS PAGES *The large central section is the earliest part of the Fairbanks House, and the wings date from the late eighteenth century. There are two rooms for each floor, a hall (early parlance for what became the kitchen), and a parlor. From Fairbank's inventory the parlor was a formal sitting room and also bedroom for the couple. Above were two chambers, one of which was used for storage.*

LEFT *From the old section of the house one can see into the later right wing. Rather than update the old house, the family added wings as function required in the prevailing style.*

BELOW *A pewter dresser (open cupboard), bake oven, and large fireplace speak of the hall's purpose. Other houses moved the kitchen functions to a rear lean-to, but in this case it remained as originally positioned in the left front of the house.*

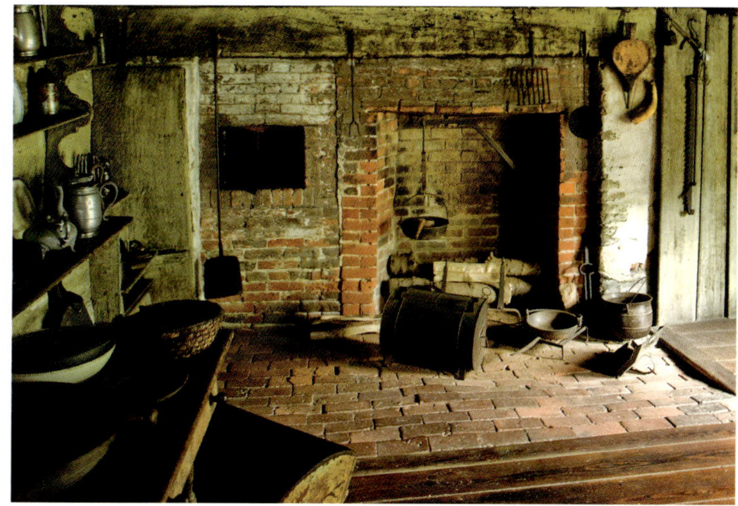

With the Great Migration influx of Puritans to Massachusetts beginning in 1630, coastal communities were densely settled. When rumors started of raids by American Indians, the Massachusetts General Court (the legislative body of the Massachusetts Bay Colony) established two large inland townships in 1635, Dedham and Concord, as buffer communities that would also relieve population pressure near the coast. Dedham was an attractive virgin wilderness stretching from Boston to Rhode Island and drew thirty Puritan families from Roxbury and Watertown. Paddling up the Charles River they established a town they called Contentment—the general court preferred Dedham—and formed a town meeting government (shortly delegating regular administration to a group of selectmen) and their own church.

The location meant nearly all made their living by farming. Though two rivers transect the town, neither had a sufficient drop for waterpower. However, a 40-foot difference between the rivers resulted in an ingenious device: a canal was dug in 1639 between the rivers, creating the power for mills.

Among the early settlers in the town was Jonathan Fairbanks (c.1595–1668), his wife Grace and six children, originally

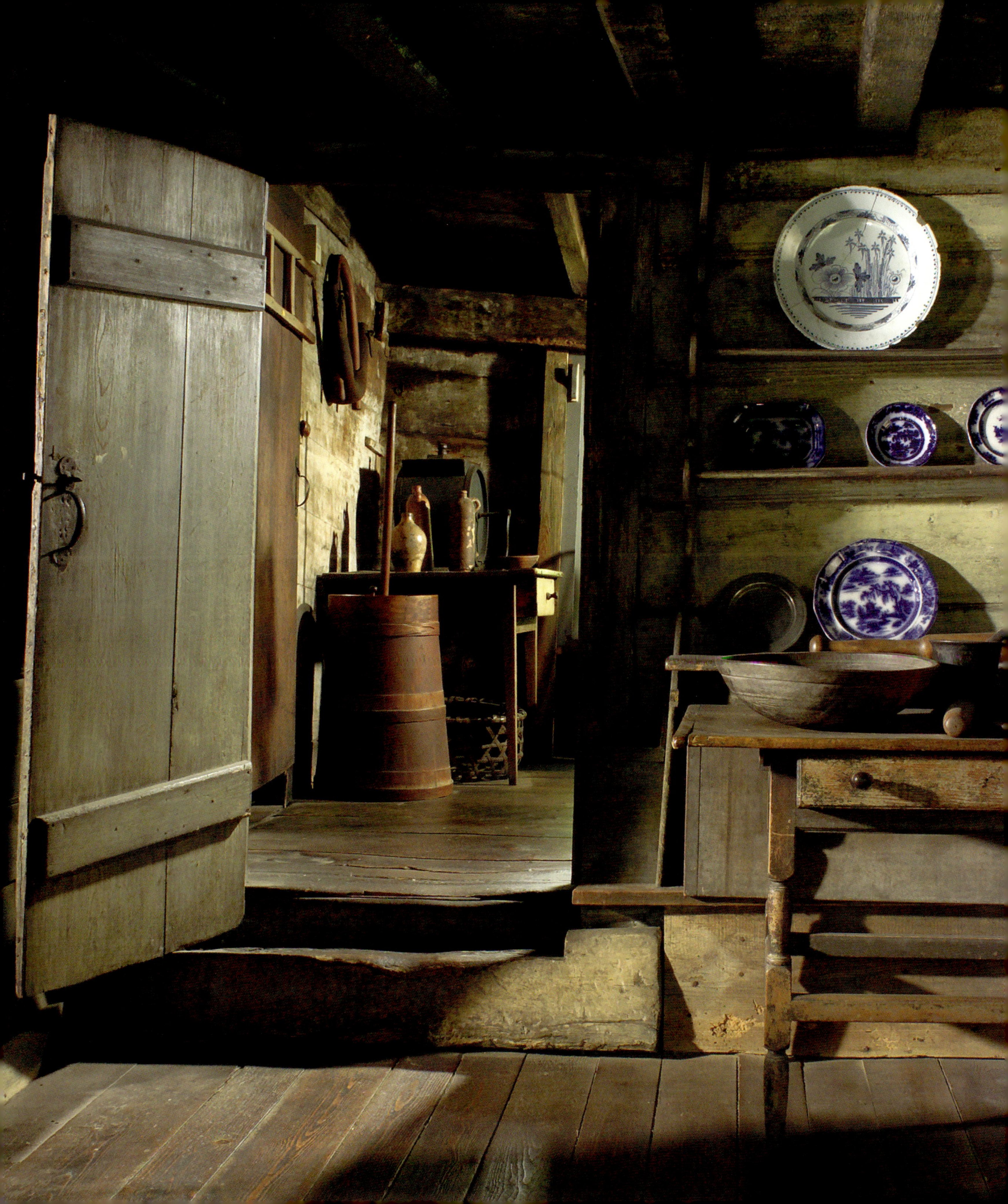

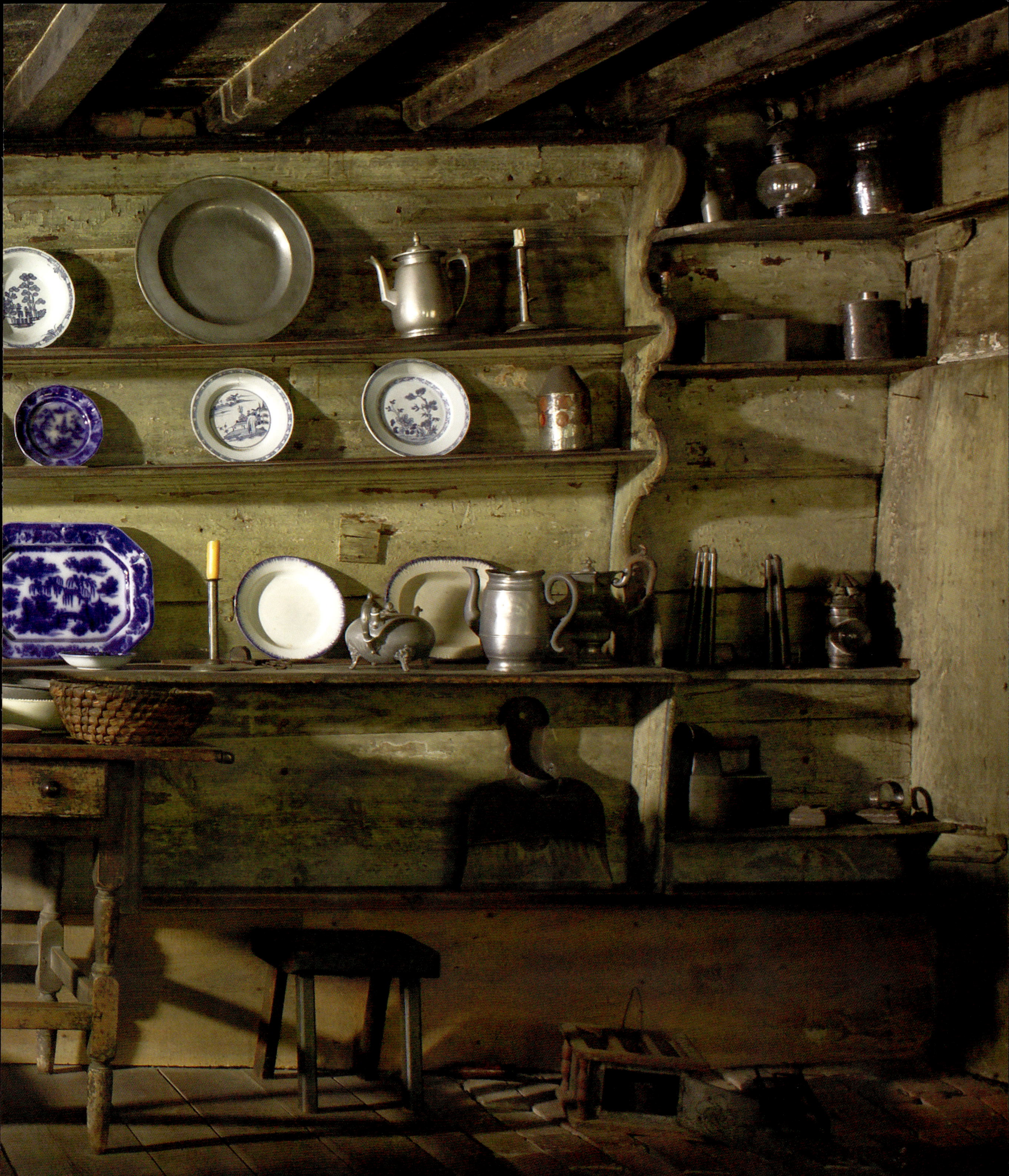

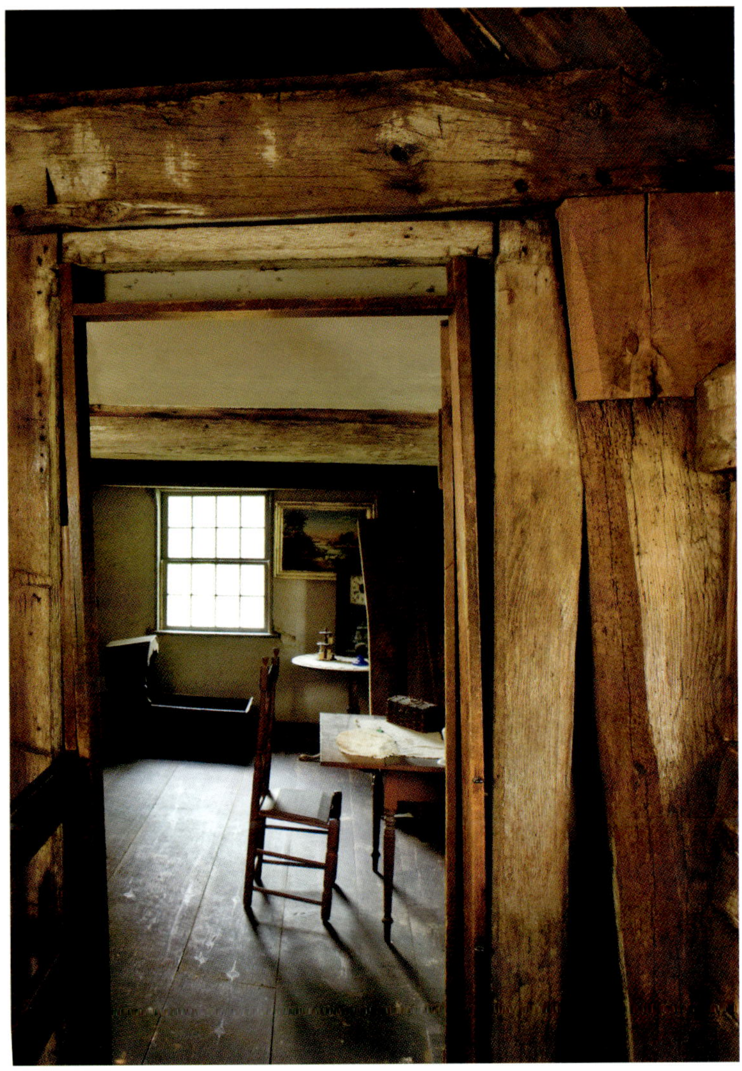

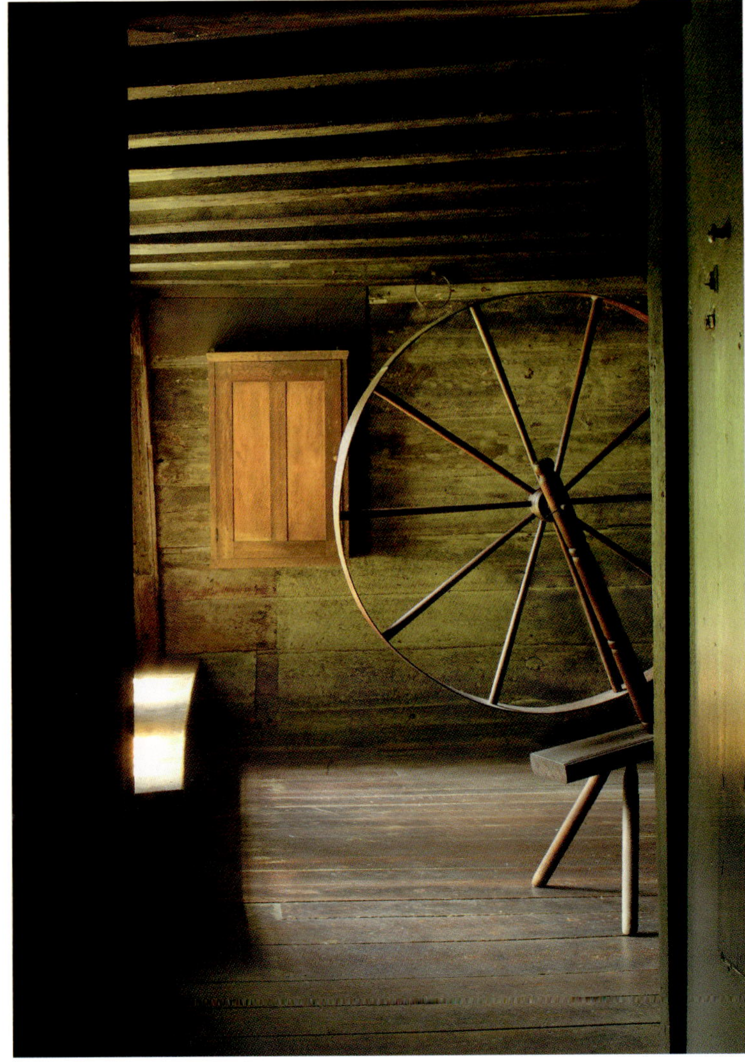

PREVIOUS PAGES *From the hall (kitchen) one can see into the rear lean-to.*

ABOVE *Looking into the right chamber of the old house, the consequences of great age—settlement, warping, looseness, and water—are evident. These factors led to the demolition of so many First Period houses, but family sentiment has preserved the Fairbanks House almost unaltered.*

ABOVE RIGHT
In the old hall (kitchen), centuries of cooking and eating sustained the family as if in a time capsule.

FACING PAGE LEFT *In the lean-to, as elsewhere, the aged early surfaces are evocative of a family's life, with no hint of the self-conscious lifestyle yearnings that altered other early houses.*

FACING PAGE RIGHT *From the lean-to one can see the east wing.*

FOLLOWING PAGES
The front faces the street and south, with later additions on the east (right) end. This family favored functional space over modernization, preserving a rare sense of how it felt to live in an early house.

from Yorkshire, England. In 1637 he was accepted under the covenant as a member of the town and received that day his allotment of 12 acres on which he would shortly begin to build his house. The next year he was appointed with another to survey the Charles River, the artery of connection to other towns. Joining the church took longer—until 1646. He had "long stood off from the church upon some scruples about public profession of faith and the covenant, yet after divers [sic] loving conferences . . . he made such a declaration of his faith and conversion to God and profession of subjection to the ordinances of Christ in the church that he was readily and gladly received by the whole church."

According to recent tree-ring dating (the science of dendrochronology) the original section of the house was constructed by 1641—historical tradition had indicated 1636—which makes it the oldest surviving timber-frame house in America. It is remarkable not just for its age but for its retention of so many original features; it is the most authentic structure from this early period for understanding how Massachusetts Puritans lived at home. The survival of these early features owes much to the fact that it

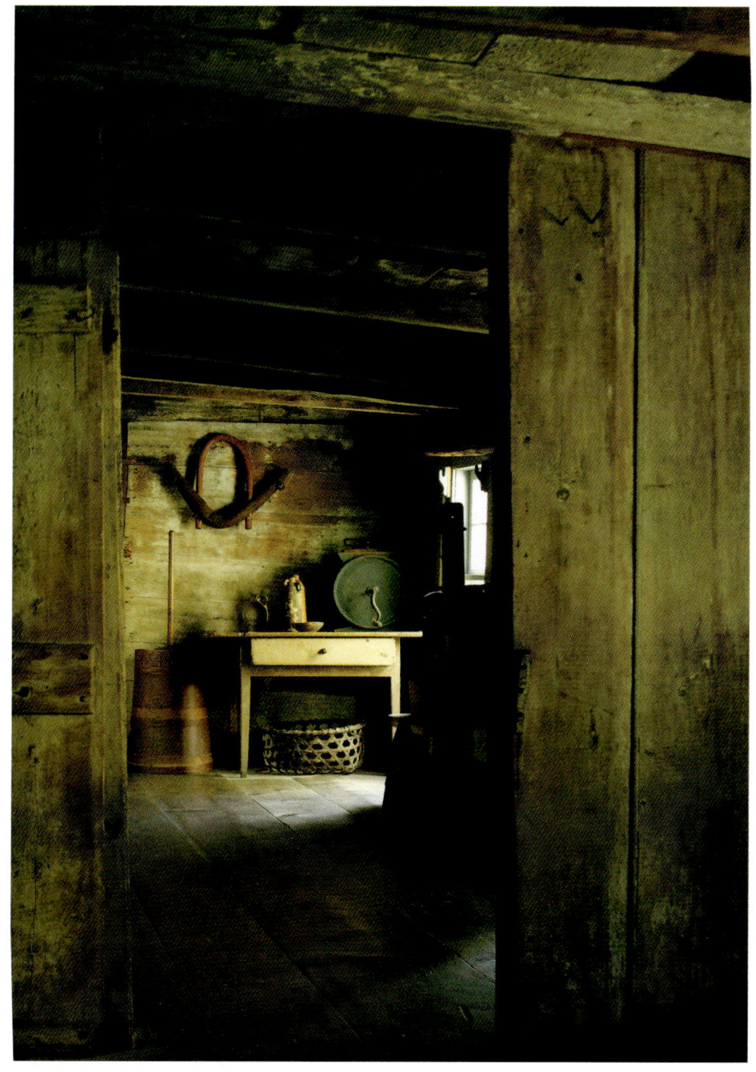

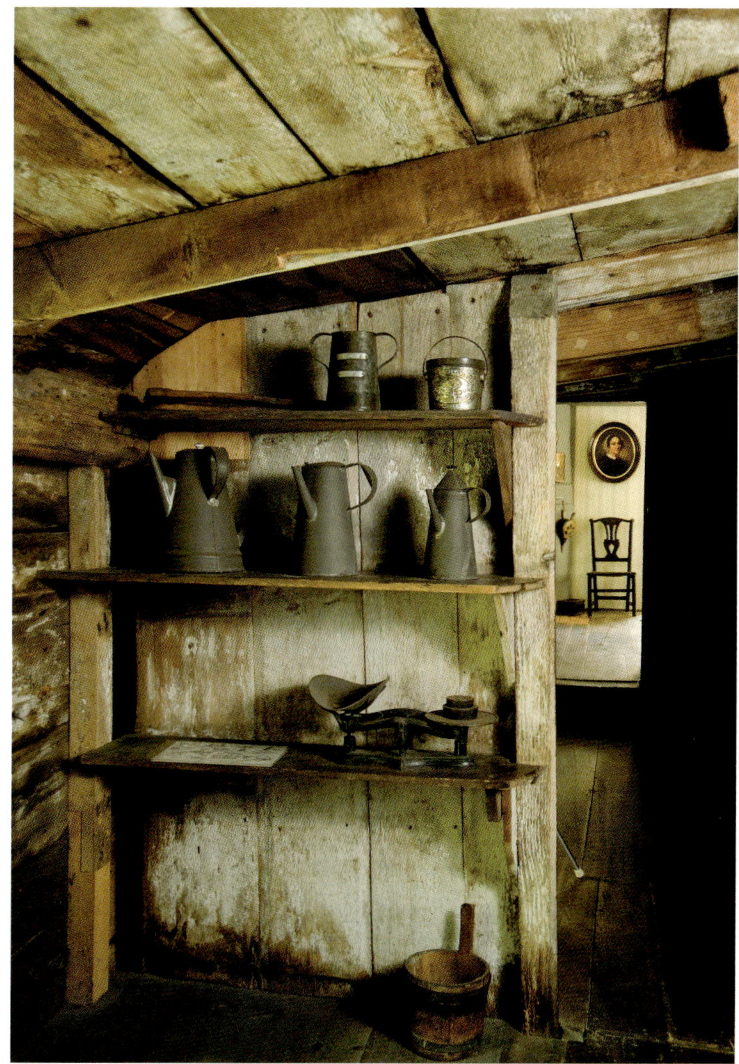

remained the home of Fairbanks family descendants for eight generations. When Rebecca Fairbanks moved out in 1904, the house was acquired by the newly organized Fairbanks Family Association, which has preserved it ever since as a museum, a time capsule of family domestic history unaltered for this last century.

The original house, the center section of the present house, was built two and a half stories high on a central chimney plan, facing south with a "hall" (kitchen) to the left or west side, and a parlor on the east side. In subsequent years additions were made and are still preserved. From Jonathan's 1668 estate inventory we learn of an addition called the "new house," which, in fact, held farm and woodworking tools and cheese-making equipment. It is not clear if this addition was the lean-to across the back (north) or a west end addition later replaced by the present addition from c.1780–1800. In the inventory the hall was furnished for cooking and eating while the parlor was a sitting room, a public area for entertaining guests, which also contained the principal bedstead (with linen and wool bedding, the most valuable things in the house). Upstairs the hall chamber was used as a storeroom for tools, hops, flax, and wool. We also learn that by this time Jonathan had acquired a good deal of land and had swine, cows, and a barn full of hay. The presence of woodworking tools and the mention of his building a bridge for the town indicates that he was more than a farmer.

Another century went by before more additions were added. In the last quarter of the eighteenth century a west addition with a bedroom and a stairway to a chamber above was added, an east wing was created out of two earlier buildings moved to the main house, and within the east wing a new chimney was built. Later its roof rafters were raised and converted into a gambrel roof. Around 1800 a small room was added on the west side (by 1881 it was used as a privy) and the parlor expanded to the east. This is a complicated set of alterations characterized by expansion rather than modernization. The family valued the functional advantages of space over style upgrades seen in many other dwellings. The Fairbanks Family Association has followed this tradition of preservation rather than restoration; the house today illustrates evolving construction styles across two centuries.

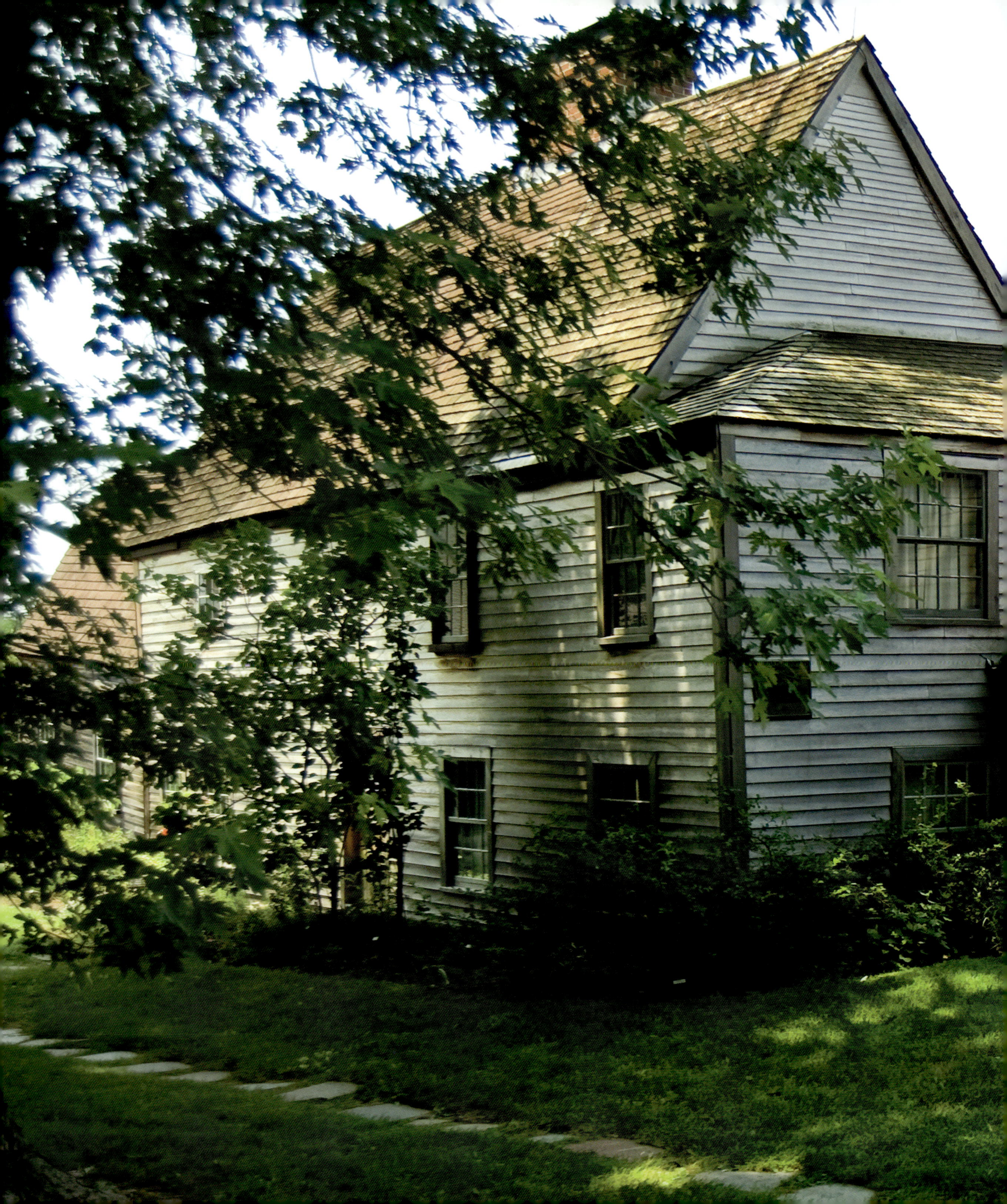

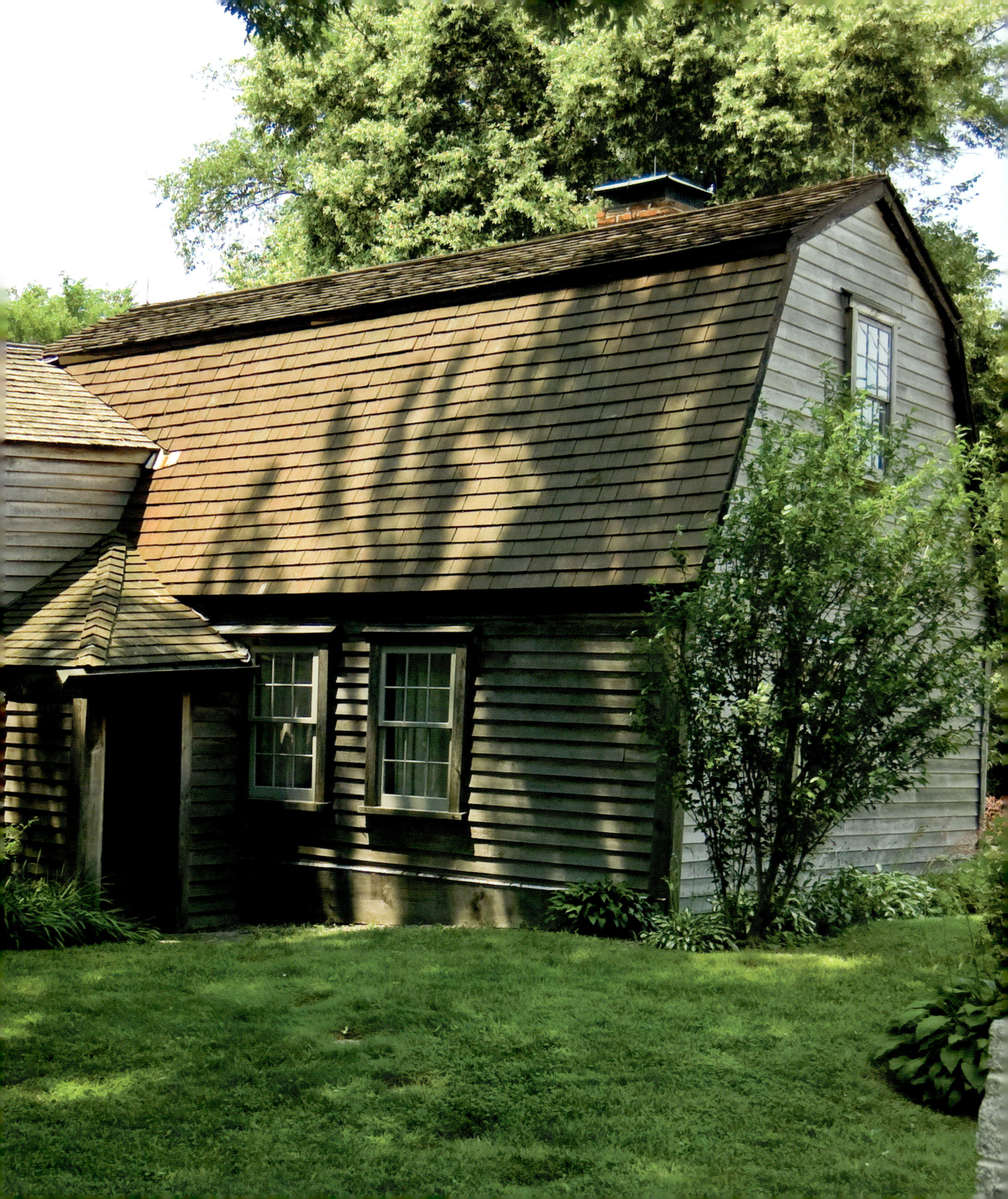

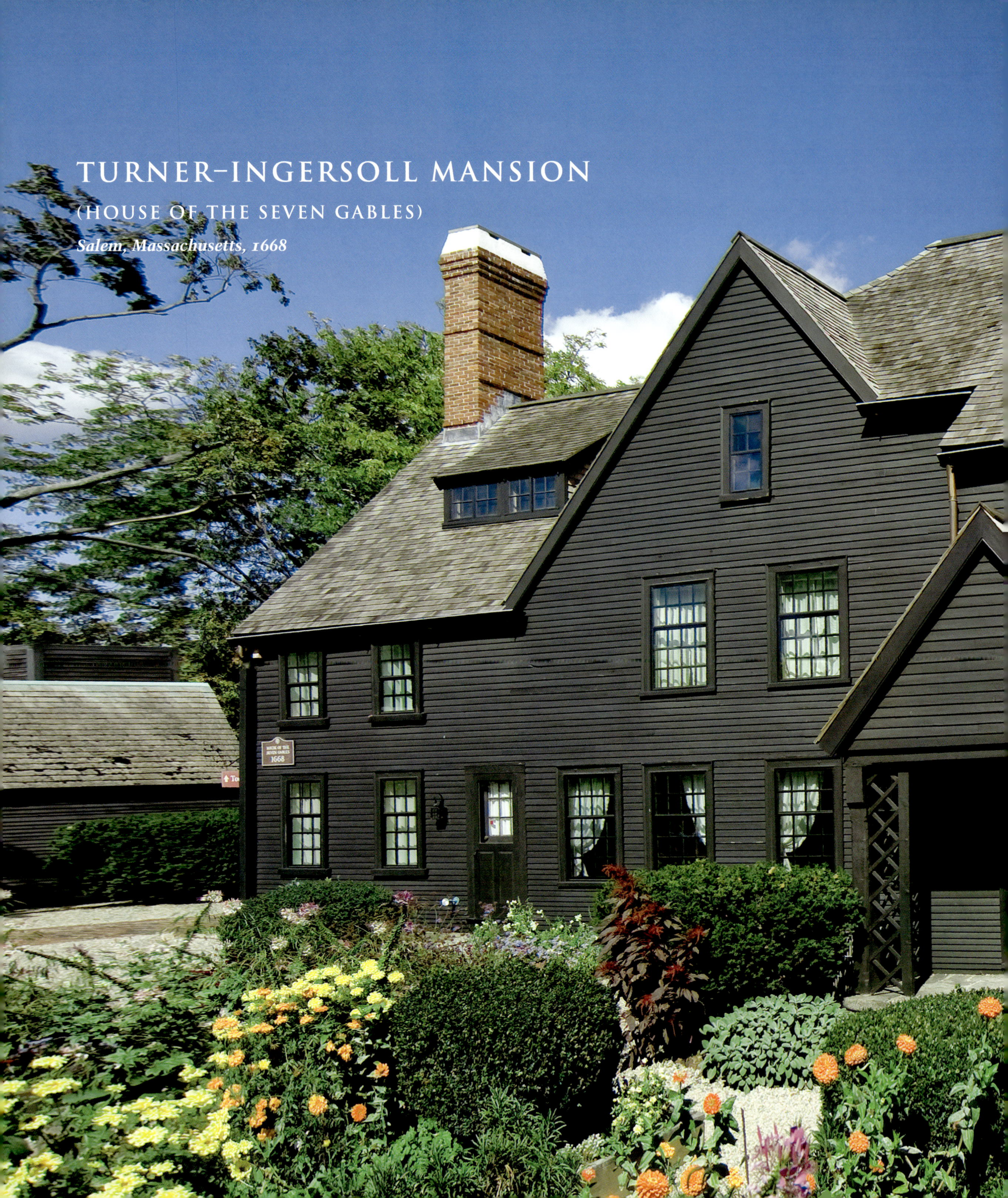

TURNER–INGERSOLL MANSION

(HOUSE OF THE SEVEN GABLES)

Salem, Massachusetts, 1668

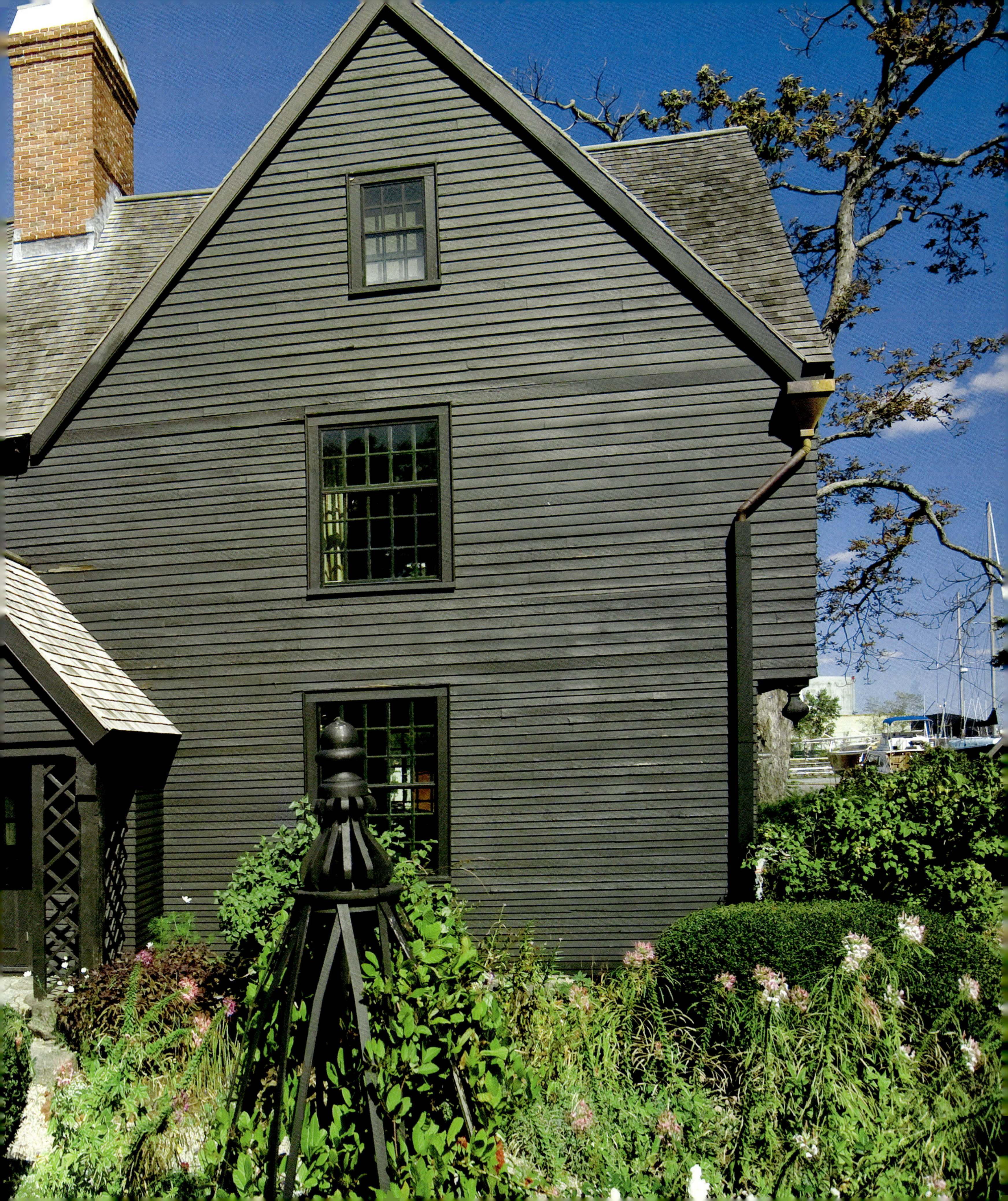

PREVIOUS PAGES *What is now the largest early house in New England began with the center section in 1668. Within eight years a kitchen wing was added (left)—later demolished and then rebuilt in the last century—and a larger section (right).*

ABOVE *Like so many other houses, the Turner-Ingersoll Mansion evolved in size and style throughout its long history. The dining room dates from 1676 but its features reflect the next two centuries.*

RIGHT *The 1676 addition included this large parlor with paneling from the eighteenth century.*

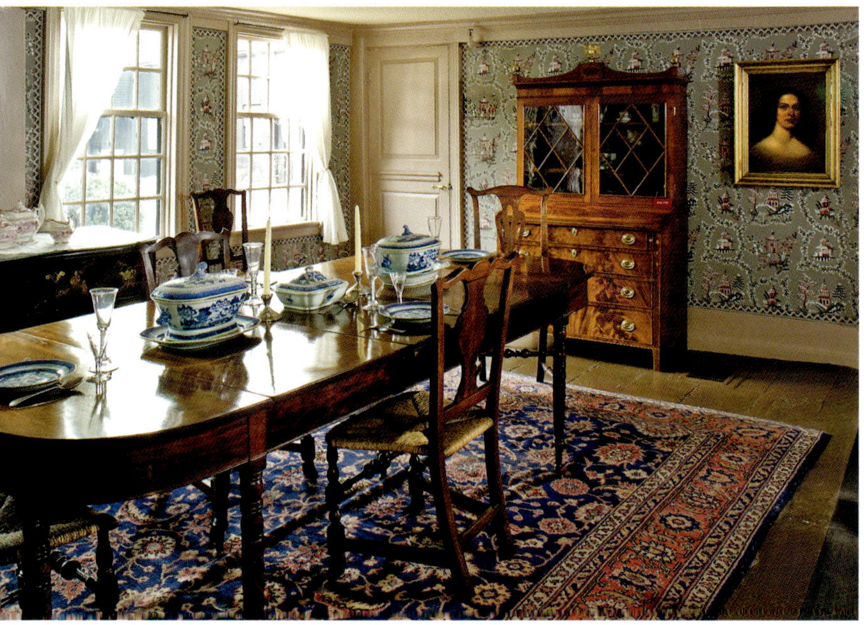

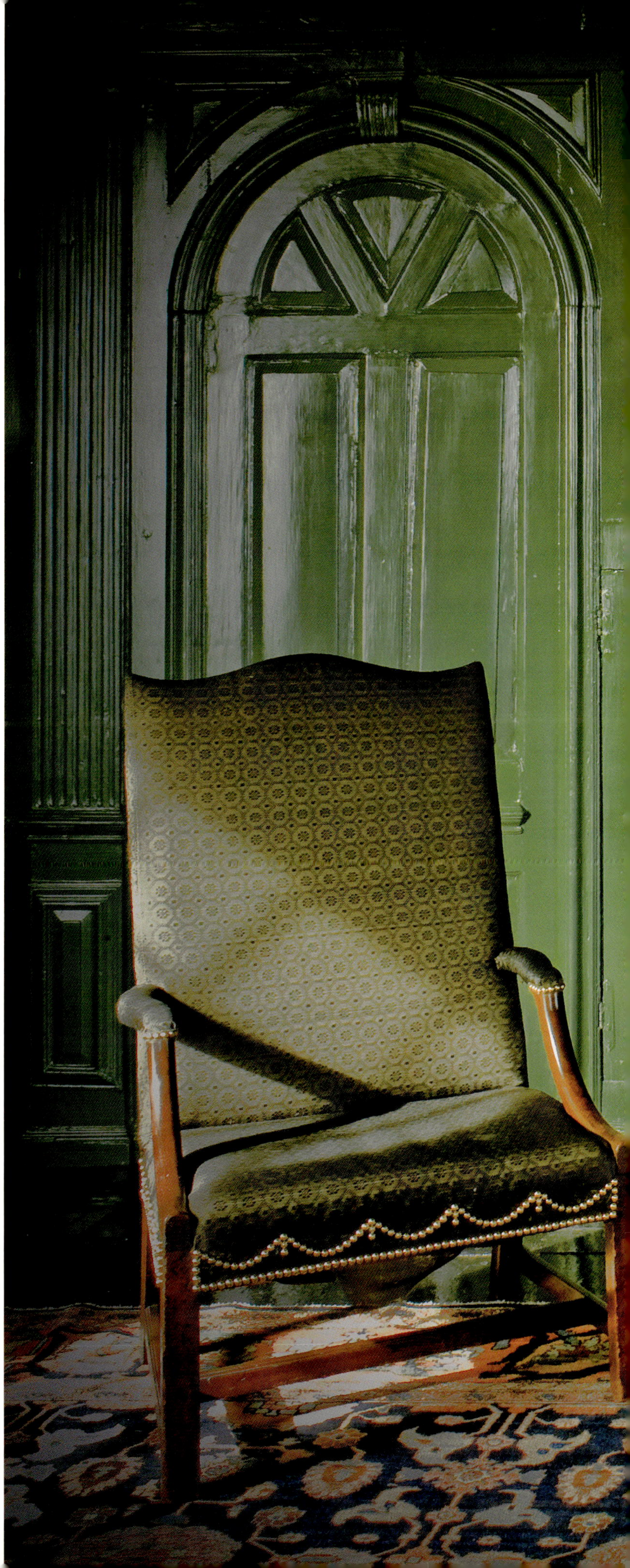

Before the Great Migration of 1630–39, Salem (from the Hebrew *shalom* and Arabic *salaam,* which mean "peace") was established by fishermen from Cape Ann in 1626. Incorporated as a town in 1629, it was geographically larger and included many other places soon populated by the Puritan influx, which would become separate towns. Fishing was its early destiny; shipping and shipbuilding later gave it great wealth and population.

Overlooking the harbor from the north side, the House of the Seven Gables is a large multi-gabled structure built for Captain John Turner (1644–80) in 1668. The original house was three floors including the garret with cross-gables and a large central chimney. This portion is now encompassed within the middle of the present house. A few years later a kitchen lean-to was added; then, in 1676, Turner added a large extension to the harbor front of the house. This became the parlor with bedchamber above, with an additional chimney servicing both. The ceilings are higher

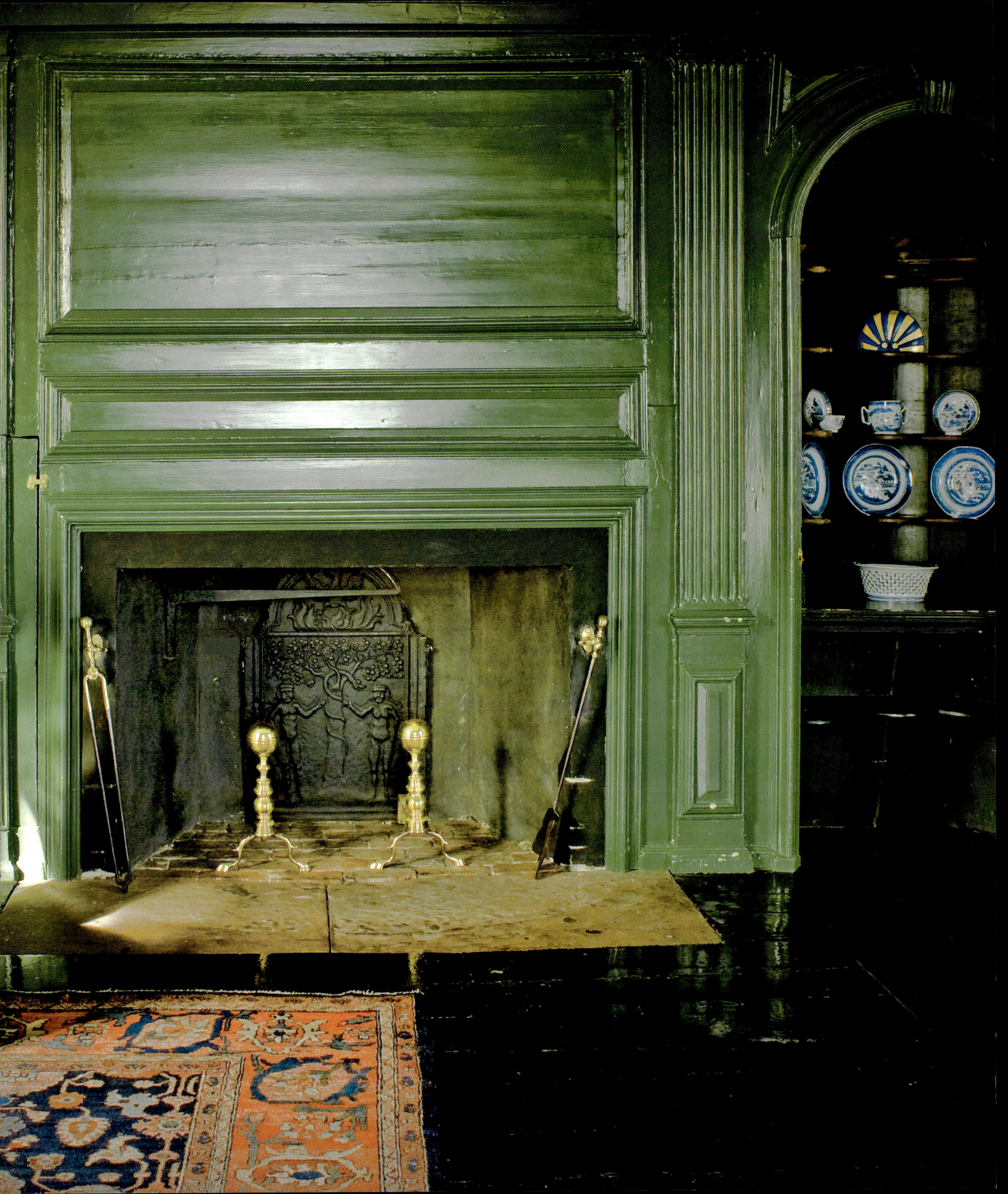

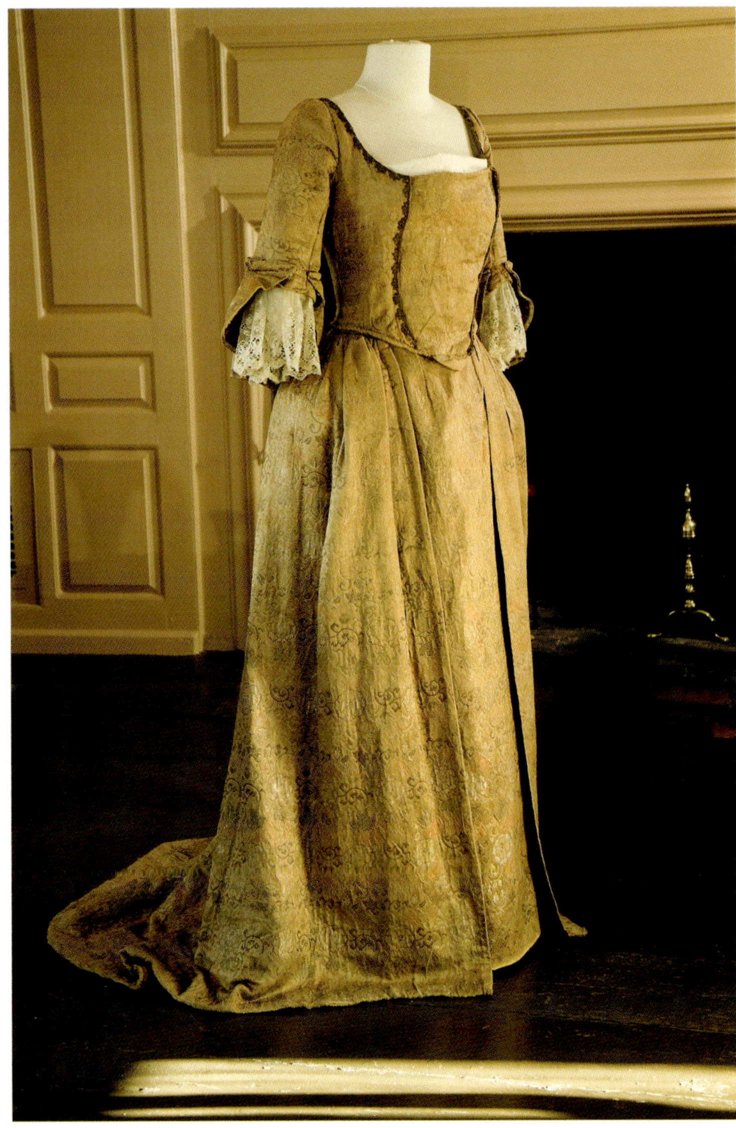

ABOVE *The most ephemeral of early objects are clothes, which wore out, were recycled, or were given away. This is a rare survivor: an eighteenth-century dress that reflects the prosperity of the families of this house.*

FACING PAGE *The south bed chamber is unusually large. It is supported below and above with a double set of summer beams. Tester beds with many yards of hand-loomed textile offered privacy and winter warmth when fires died down in the night. Tester bedsteads and bedding were frequently the highest valued inventory items.*

than the original section, windows are double casements, the second-floor overhang has carved pendants, and the whole addition was capped with a triple-gabled garret.

John Turner II was in possession of the house by 1692 when he added a small brewing room adjacent to the kitchen. About 1710 he remodeled the house in the new Georgian style with room paneling and sash windows, which remain today. John Turner II was the wealthiest of the Turners; upon his death in 1743 his probate inventory spanned over fourteen pages and contained valuable silver and textiles, including imported silks acquired through his lucrative overseas trade.

The house passed to John III but, alas, he lost the family fortune, and the Ingersoll family acquired the house in 1782. Captain Samuel Ingersoll updated the house significantly, removing four of seven gables, the 1670s kitchen wing, and a stairway. He and his son perished at sea, leaving the entire estate to daughter Susanna. It was during this period that Susanna's cousin Nathaniel Hawthorne (who also shared the loss of a father at sea) came to know the house. He wrote, "Halfway down a by-street of one of our New England towns, stands a rusty wooden house, with seven acutely peaked gables, facing toward various points of the compass, and a huge, clustered chimney in the midst." That opening sentence of his novel *The House of the Seven Gables* has since done much to popularize and preserve this largest (seventeen rooms) of First Period houses. Susanna pointed out evidence of the missing gables and inspired Hawthorne with family stories. Her adopted son told the young author a story about lovers, which later become the basis of Longfellow's poem "Evangeline."

In 1908 Caroline Emmerton, a Salem philanthropist, purchased the house and, with the help of noted preservation architect Josesph Everett Chandler, restored the property as a museum to benefit a settlement house for children. The four gables and kitchen el returned. Taking advantage of the house's renown—largely thanks to Hawthorne's novel—it was opened to the public, its promotion and interpretation heavily influenced by the content of the novel such as the newly installed Cent Shop and "secret" stairway. Today, the House of the Seven Gables continues to be associated with family and children's programs in Salem.

Salem's continued popularity rests as much on historical fiction (literature) and fictional history (belief in witches) as on the distinguished architecture that those fictions helped preserve—the whole, creating a tourism bonanza.

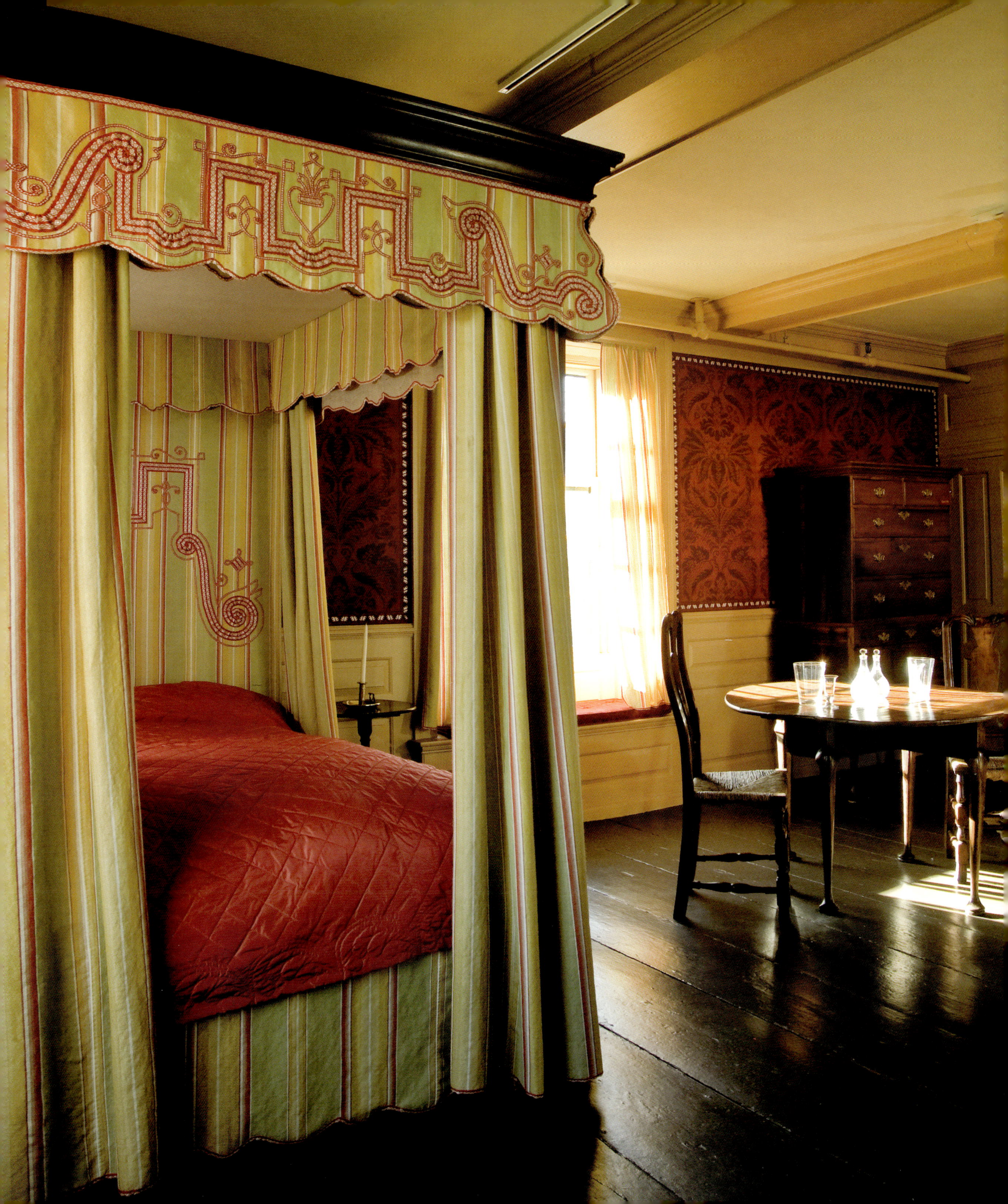

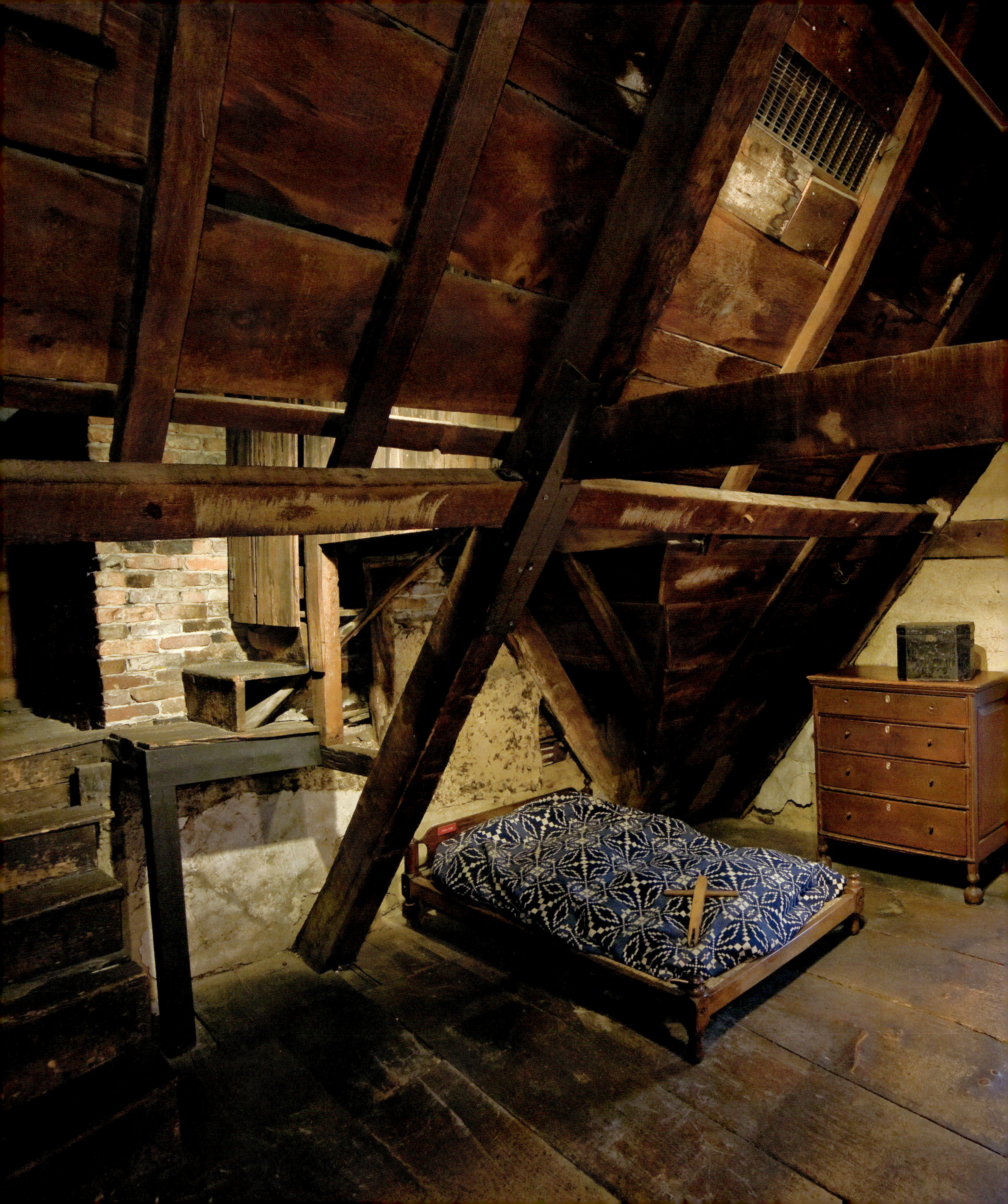

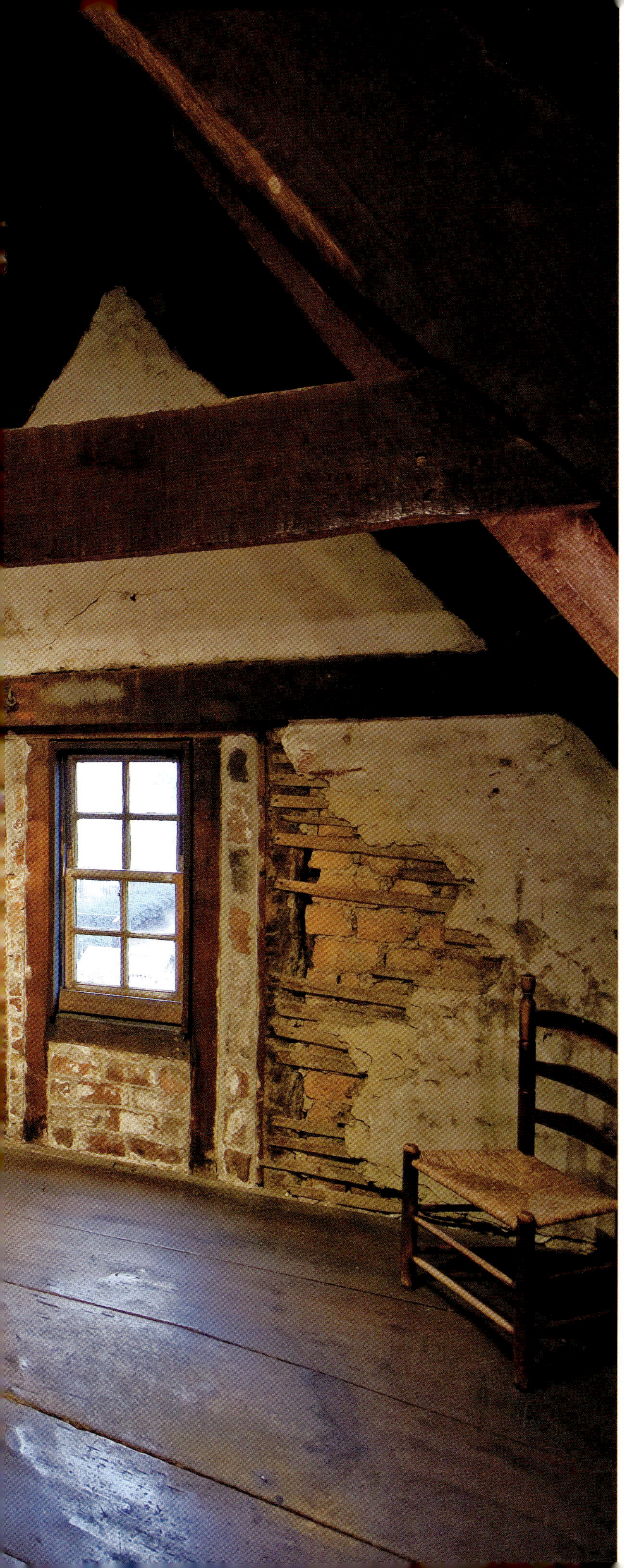

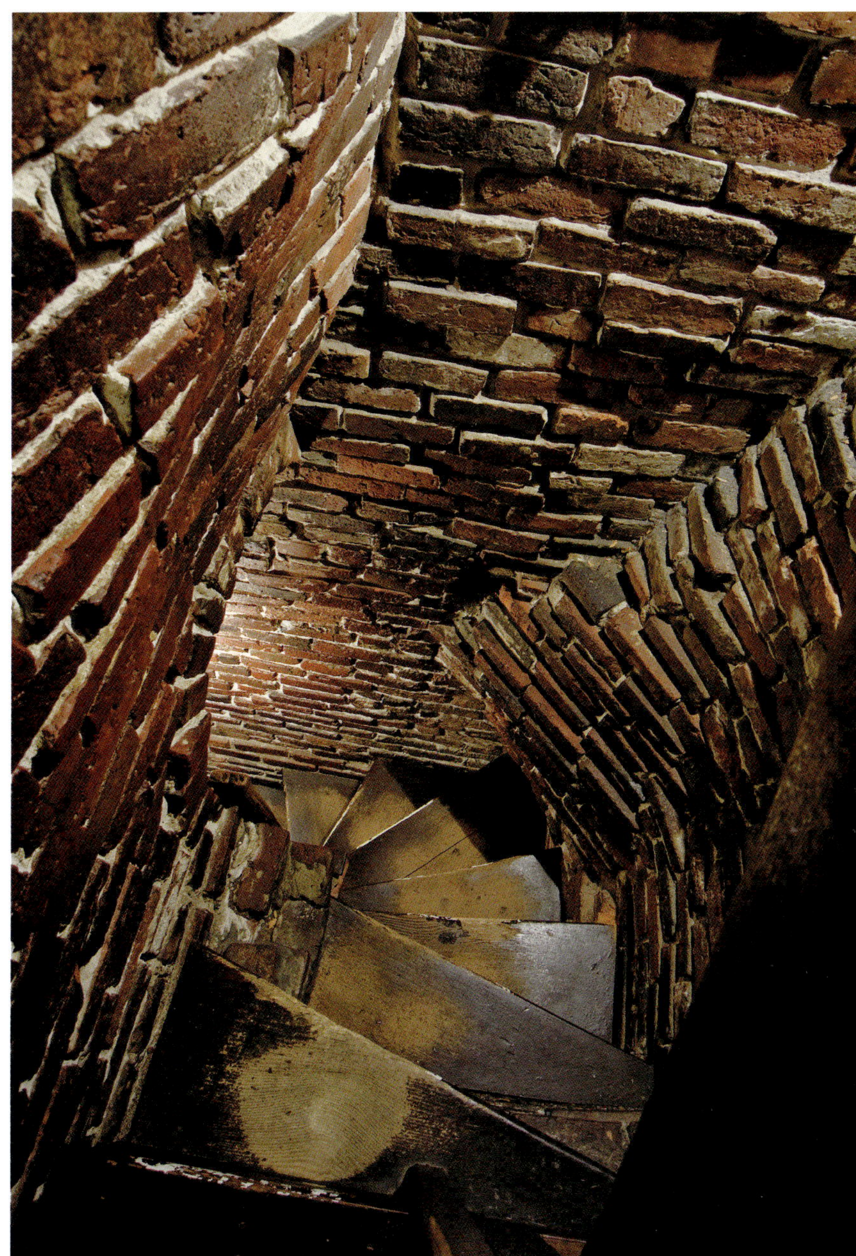

LEFT *Away from public view, this garret (see p. 42, on the left) is essentially unchanged since 1668. The brick nogging for insulation in the wall, sheathed over with split lathe and plastered, is associated with rooms for living, not a storage garret.*

ABOVE *The secret stairway winds by the kitchen fireplace. Long rumored as a hiding place from the American Indians, in fact it is a twentieth-century addition to heighten the mystery and appeal of an already legendary house.*

FOLLOWING PAGES *Captain Turner found the ideal location to keep eye on his shipping business, facing the busy harbor of Salem. The view from the garden includes the adjacent seventeenth-century-style house, a re-creation of an original house in Maine.*

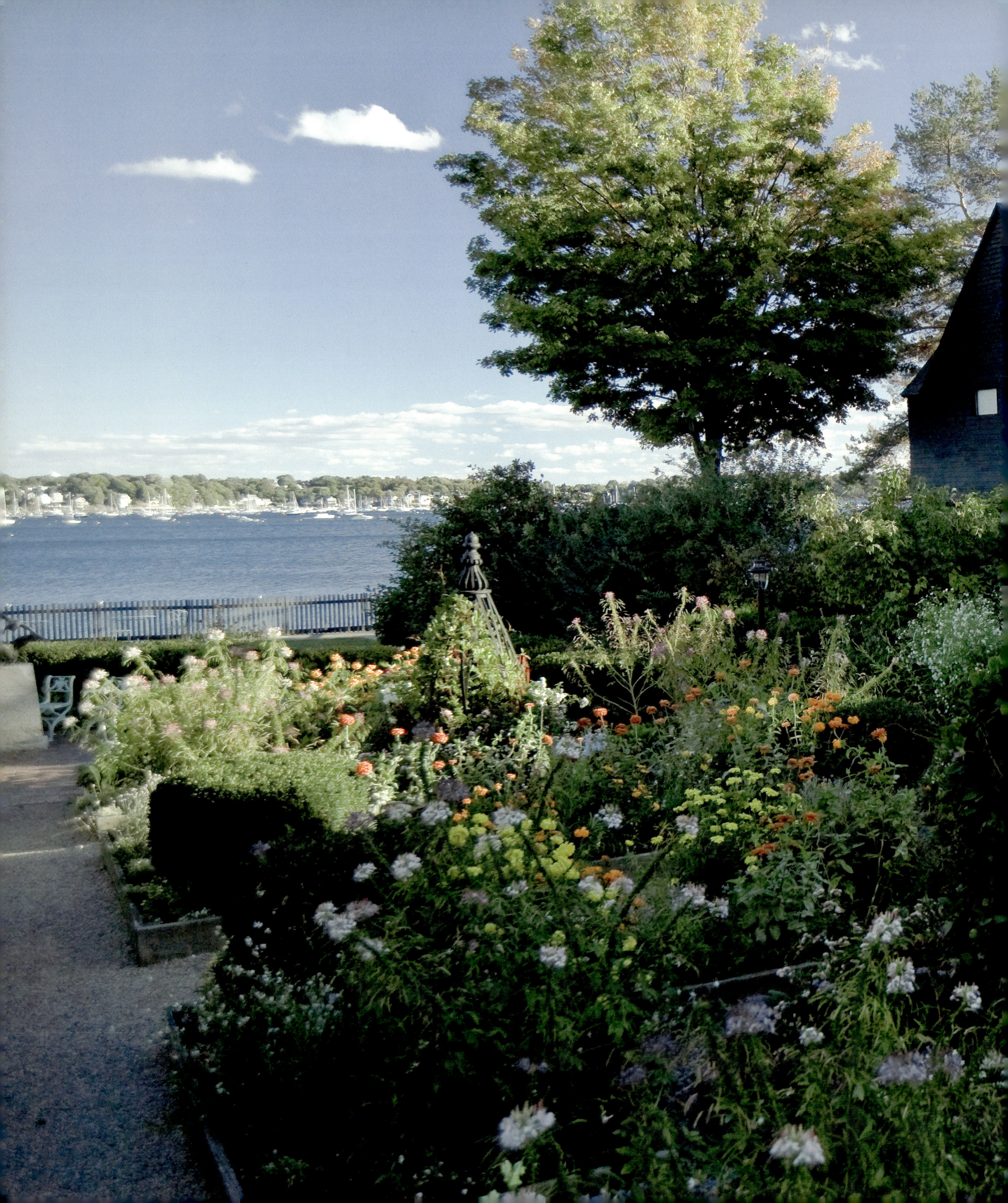

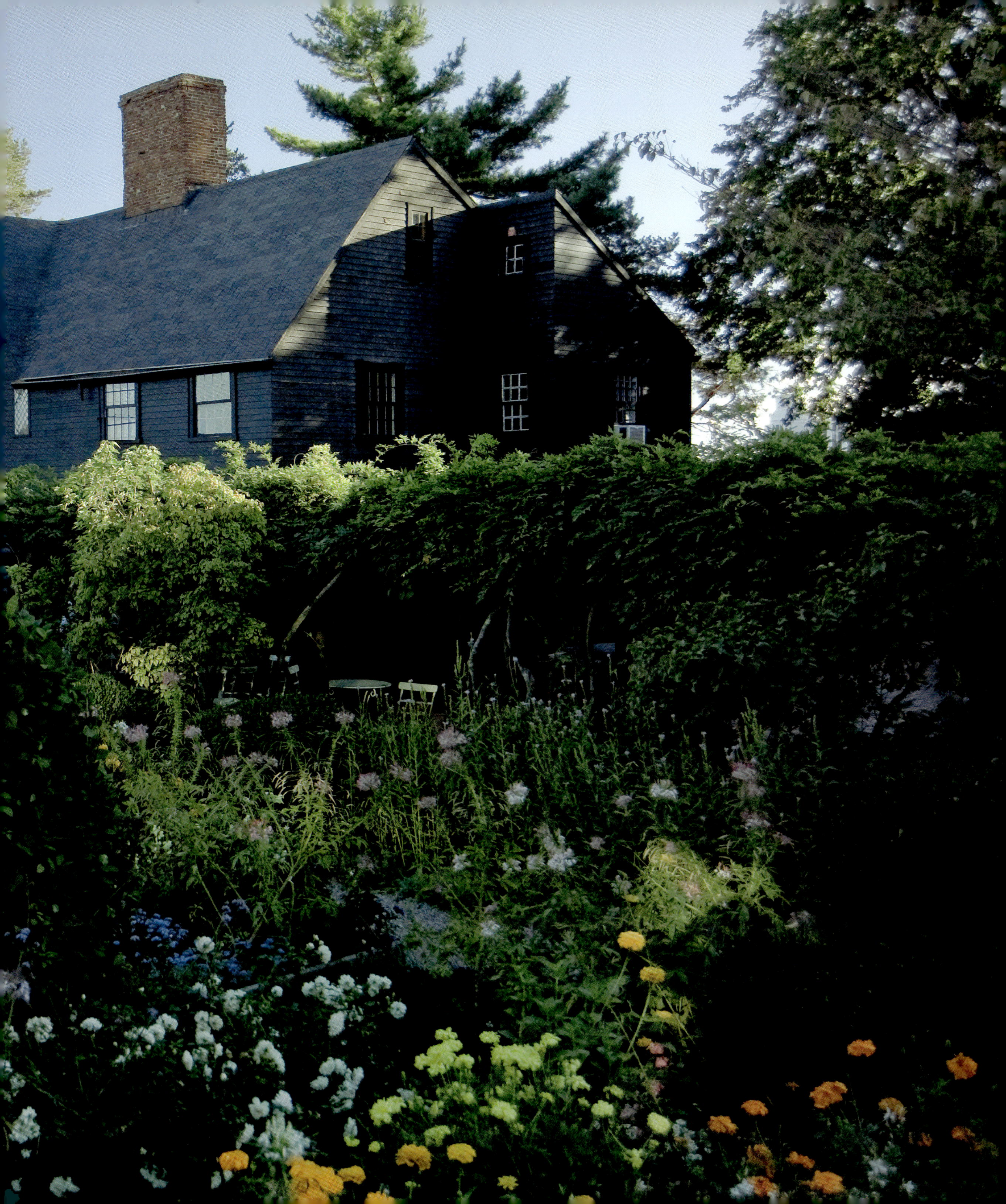

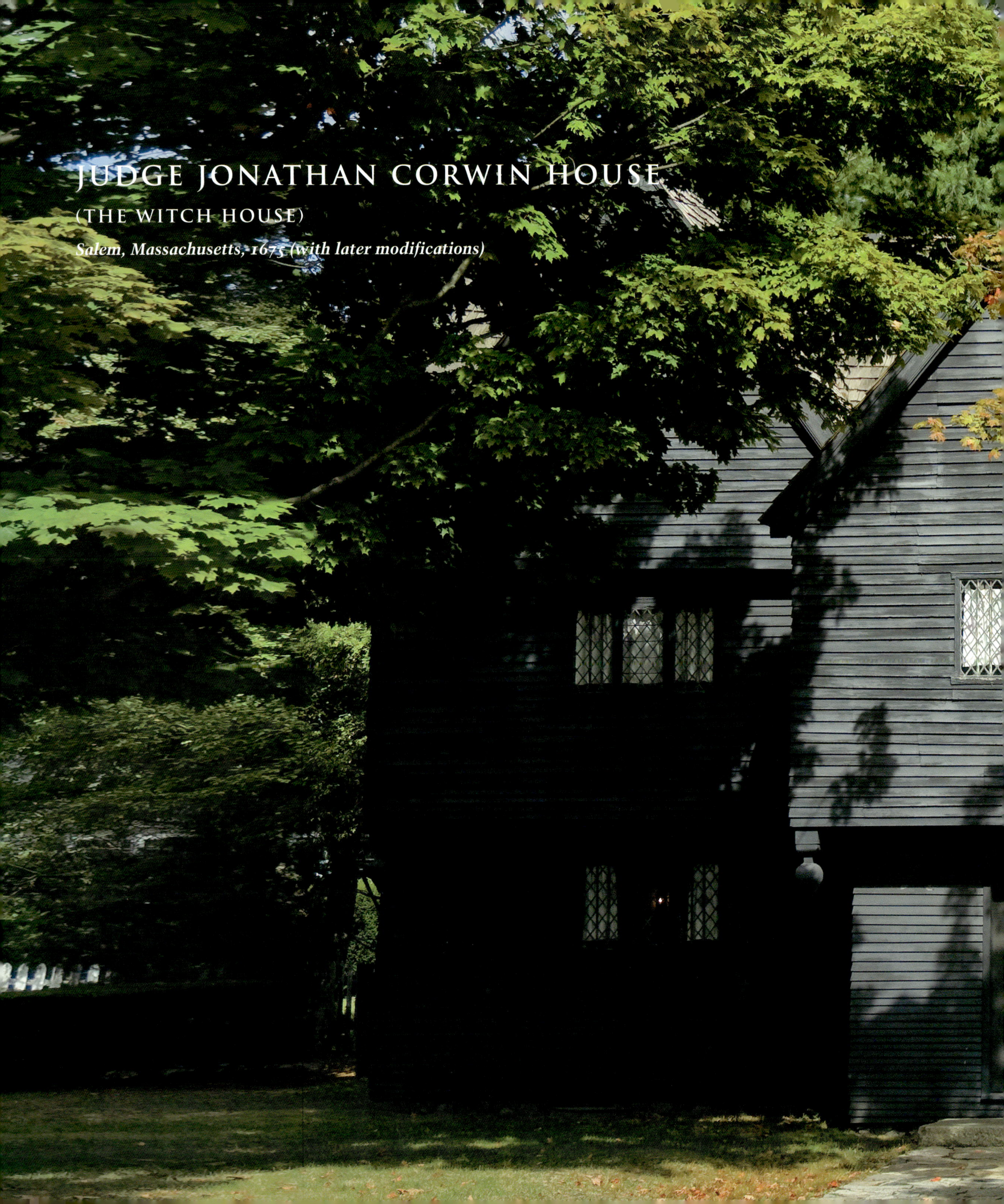

JUDGE JONATHAN CORWIN HOUSE

(THE WITCH HOUSE)

Salem, Massachusetts, 1675 (with later modifications)

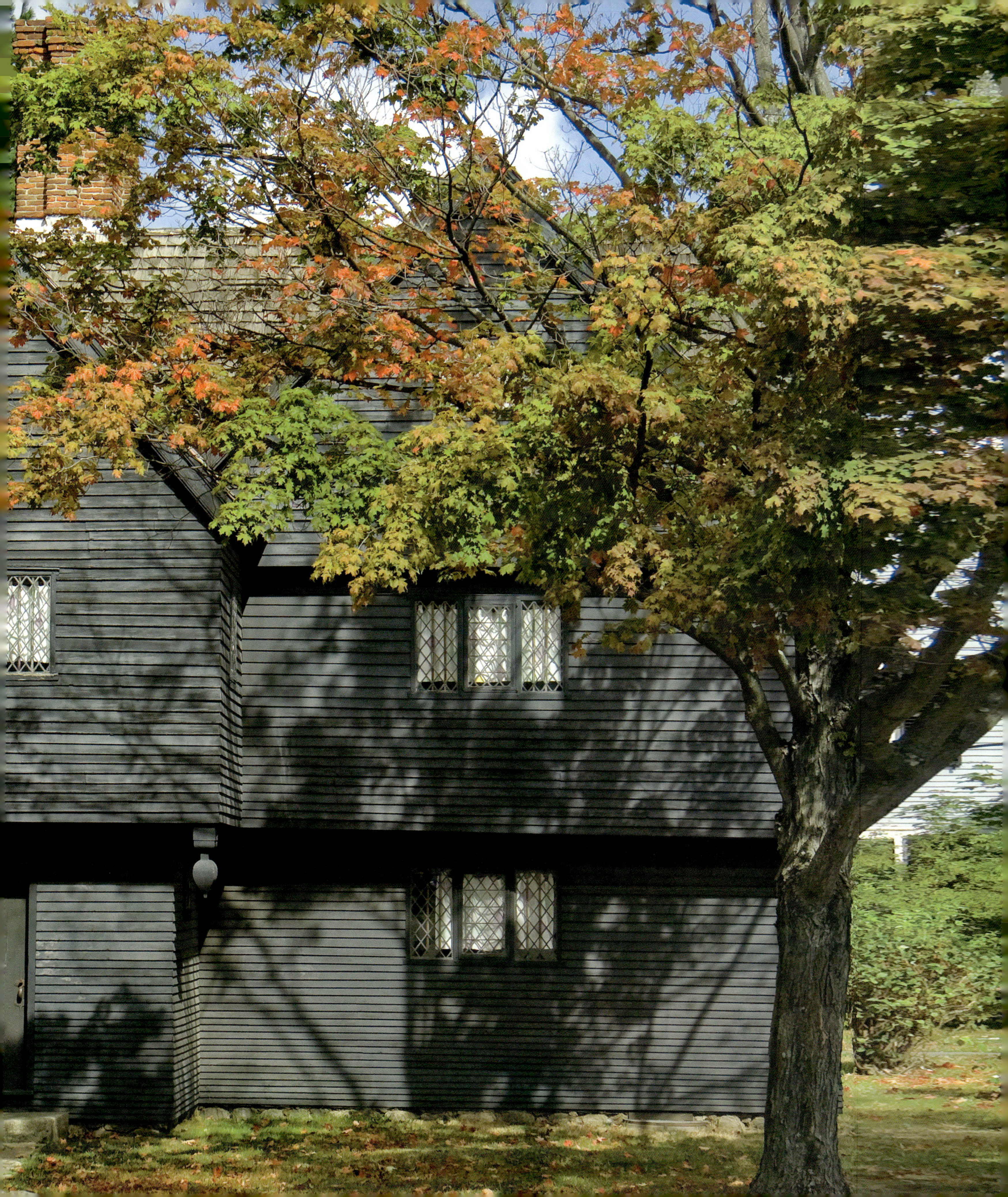

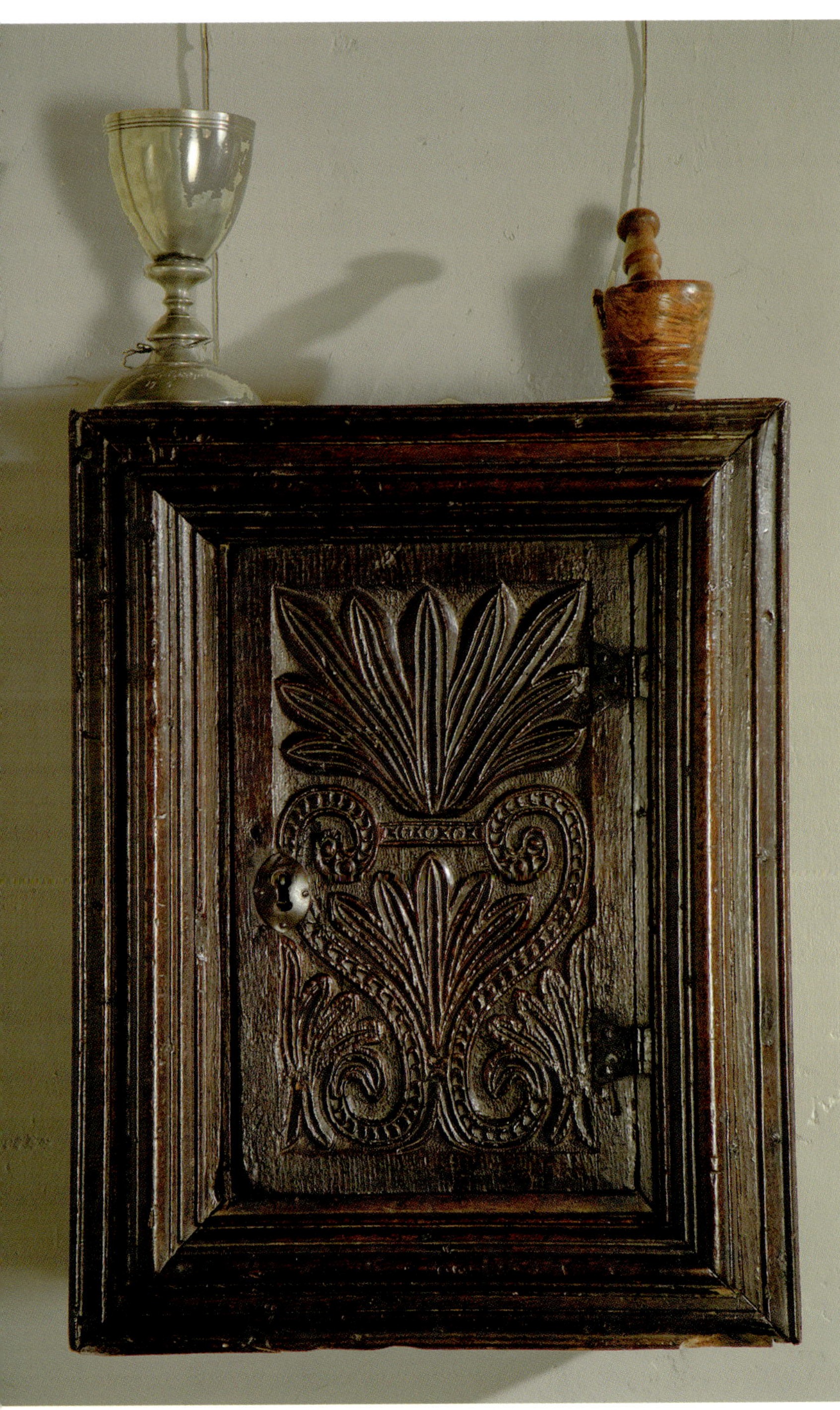

PREVIOUS PAGES *The Corwin House, as restored in the 1940s, has the features of a fully developed medieval New England house: a projecting gabled porch, two addition front gables (not evident behind the trees), and overhangs (jetties) on both floors from which ornament hangs like architectural earrings.*

LEFT *In early homes, which were largely devoid of elaborate furnishings, small objects like this wall cupboard could be decorative at little cost.*

FACING PAGE *The medieval character of these houses is evident in the dining room (to the left of the entry): exposed structural members in natural color and small lead-camed glass windows whose modest light is reflected by whitewashed walls.*

FOLLOWING PAGES *A small door hinge provides functional yet inspiring modest decoration with its shaping and the inscribed lines joining nails. Puritan culture frowned on superfluous decoration, but aesthetic tweaking of structural and functional features, like the overhang drops outside, did not violate their strict interpretation of the Bible.*

Despite the meaning of its name—peace—Salem's history has been overshadowed by the opposite, a series of witchcraft accusations and trials in 1692 that tore the social fabric to the breaking point. Present-day fascination with this phenomenon, so alien to our own beliefs, supports Salem's economy—a testament to Yankee ingenuity as old industries have faded away. Many of the popular historic sites of Salem are interpreted through the lens of this social aberration, including two sites discussed here.

Witchcraft beliefs are remarkable in America for their rarity; they were far more widespread in other nations of the world, and still are today in the developing world. In times and places where seemingly inexplicable events (death by lightning, for instance) and abnormal behavior (some forms of mental illness) were not understood logically, psychological explanations gain currency, especially when tolerated or sanctioned by authority. This is what happened in greater Salem—several communities were involved—in 1692–93, when young girls professed to have been bewitched (possessed by the malevolent powers of witches) by mostly older women. Fits of hysteria, accusations, interrogations, imprisonments, and trials took place, most of the latter in Salem where twenty-nine were tried, all convicted, and nineteen condemned to death. Fourteen women and five men were hung, one who refused to enter a plea was crushed under stones in an attempt to extract a plea, and five died in prison. When accusations, reaching into the hundreds, began to spread to leading citizens—the wife of the governor in one case—the authorities who had been conducting the trials called a halt to the tumult. The beliefs in, and fears of, the wickedness of humanity were submerged, only to reappear sporadically in latter-day guilt, culture,

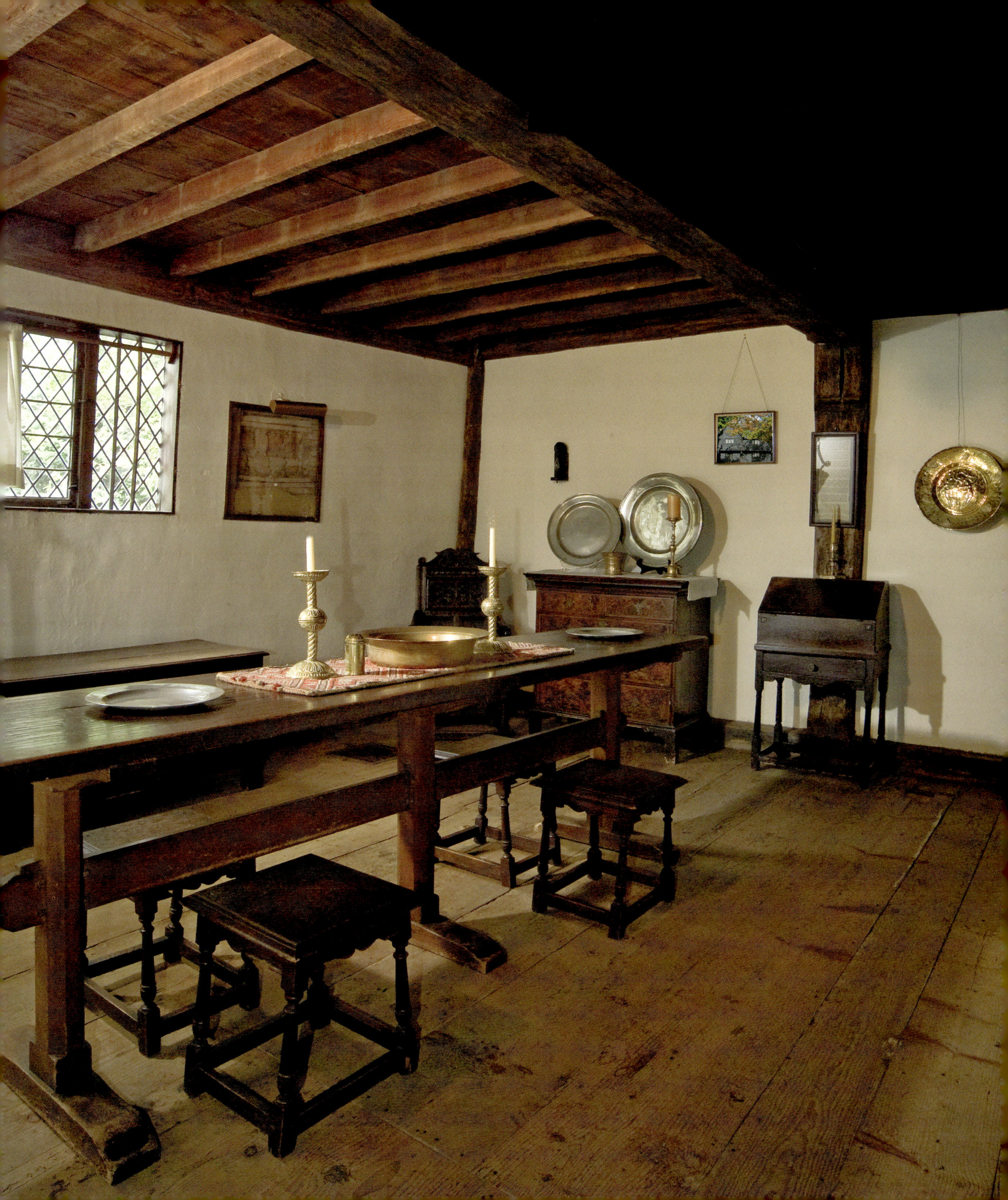

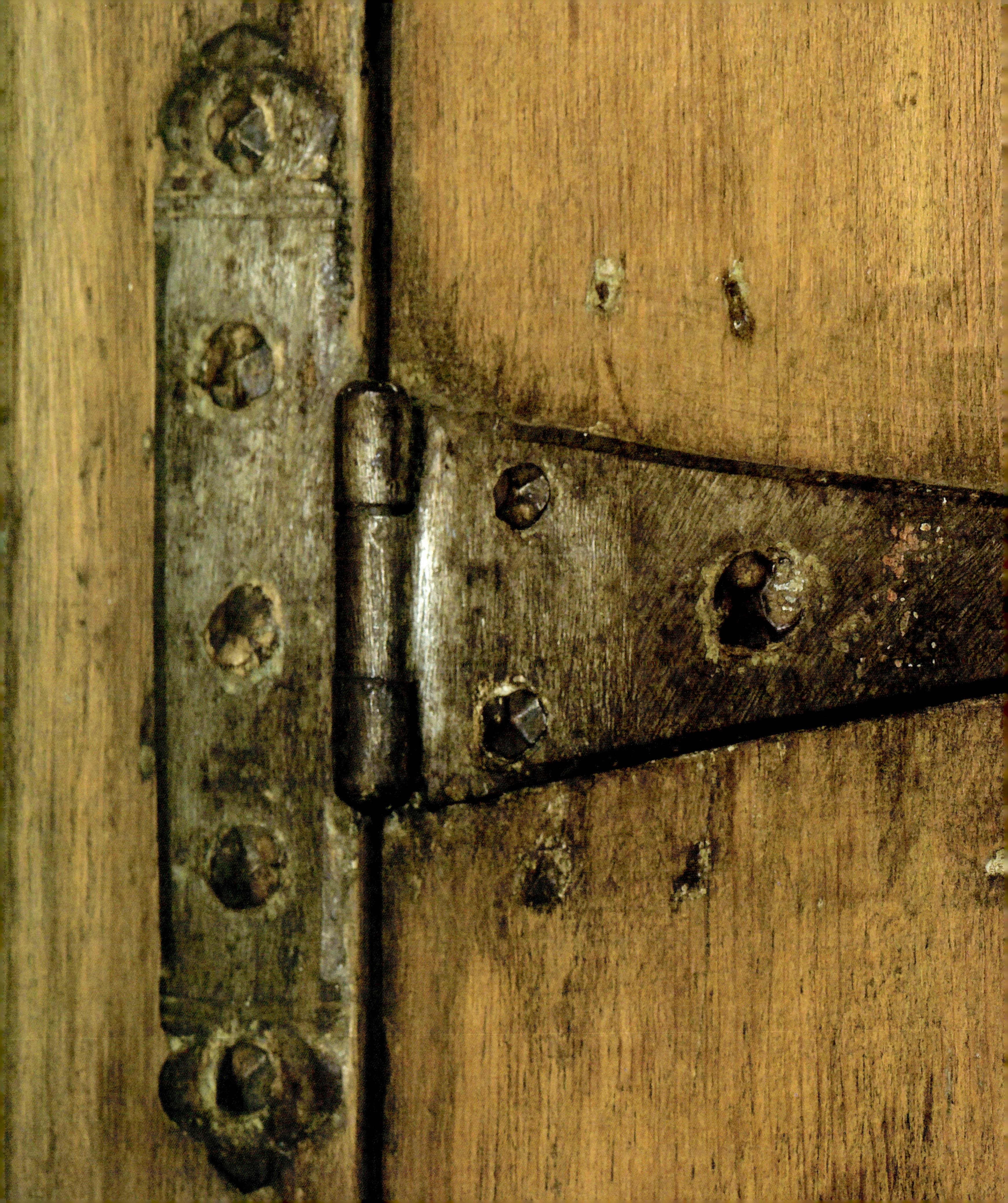

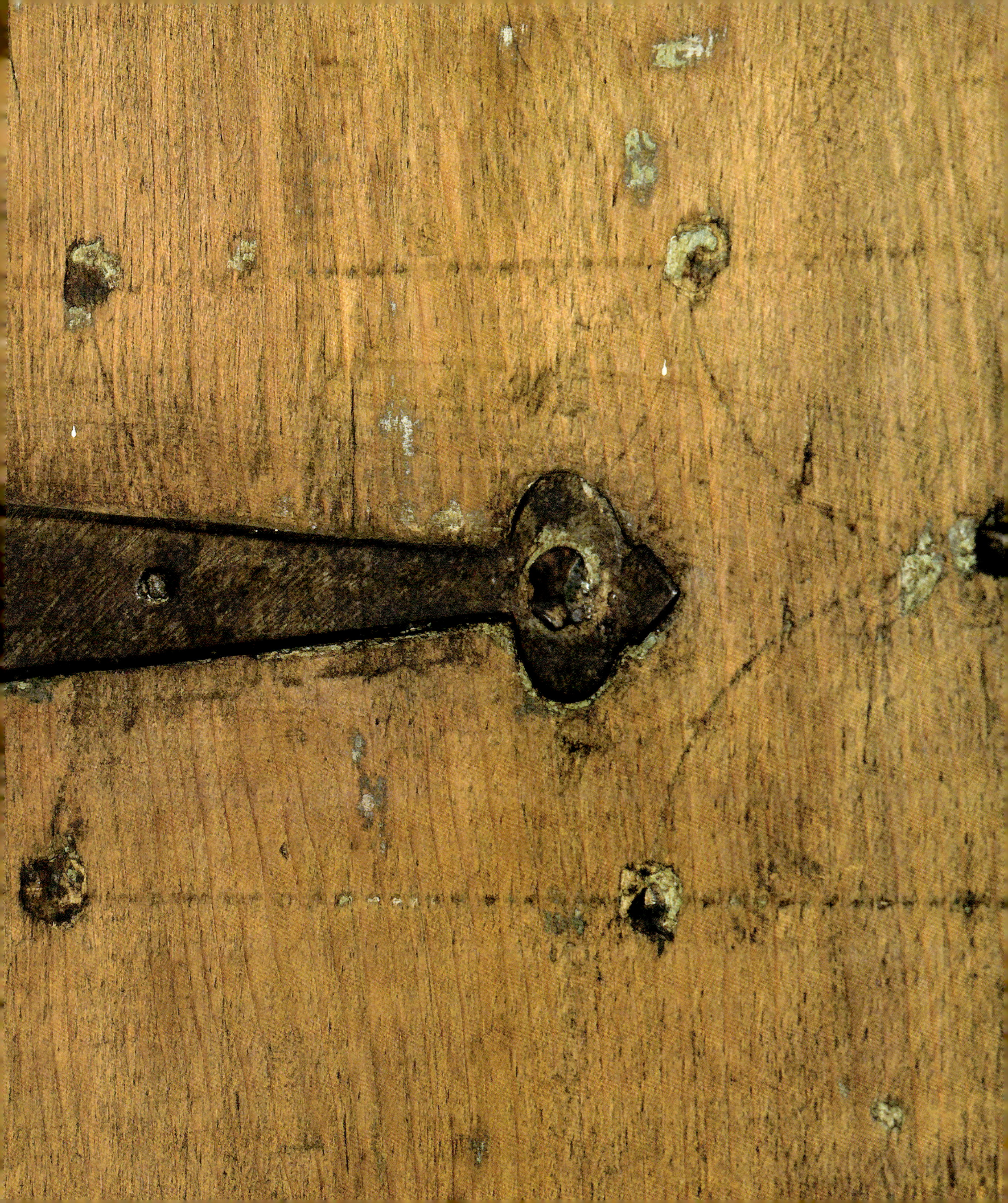

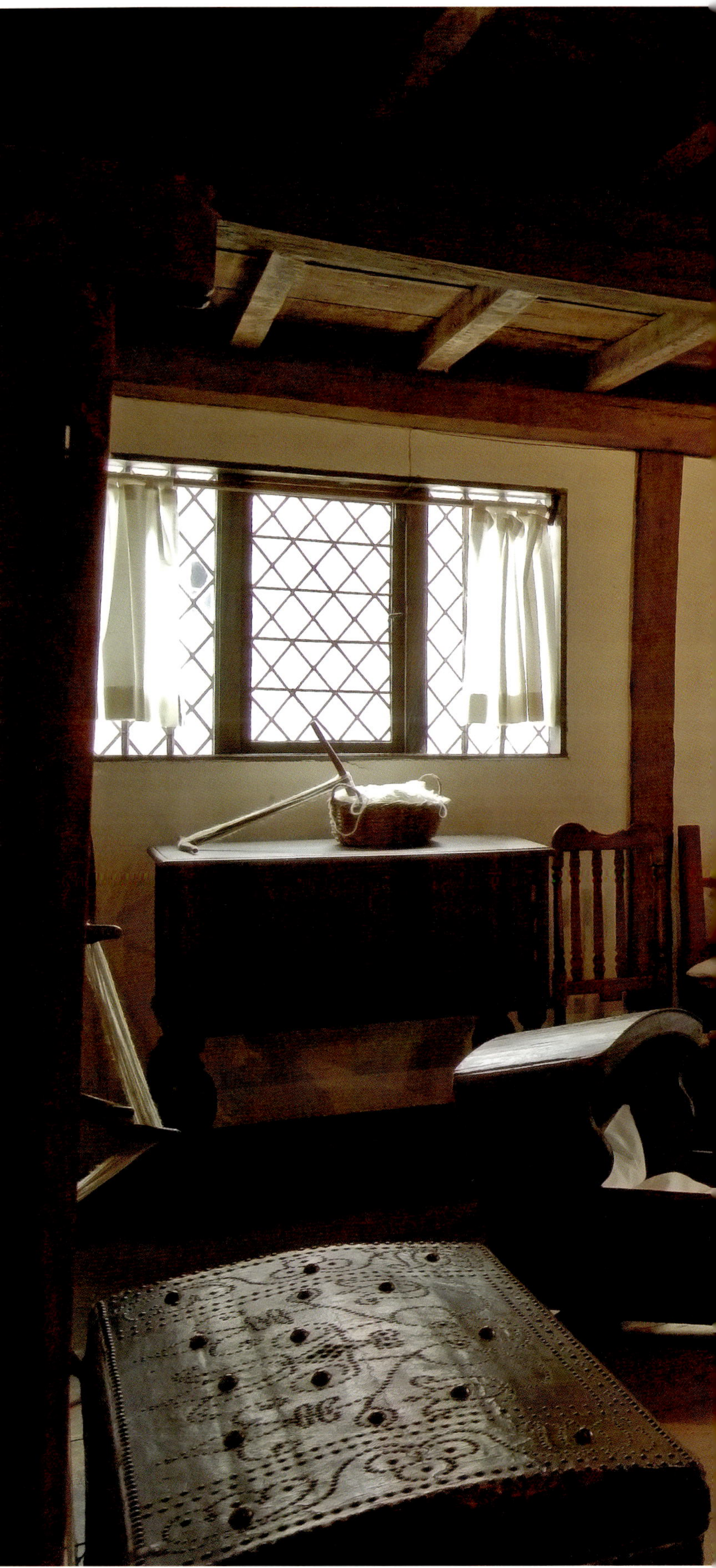

RIGHT *Unlike in most of their other colonies, the English imported house design here that was of especially complex joinery, usually a full two stories high, indicating separate bedrooms for some family members (this is the upstairs right chamber). This reflected an interest in privacy, which would grow in generations to come as houses evolved and became larger in the Classical mold.*

literature, and economy. The Jonathan Corwin House owes its survival to this witchcraft legacy.

In 1944 the Corwin House was in the way of modern traffic, which required the widening of the street. Fearing the loss of the last remaining house in Salem with some association to the witchcraft phenomenon, citizens rallied to form Historic Salem, Inc., to move the house out of harm's way and undertook restoration. It was the beginning of the historic preservation movement in Salem, which has saved many structures.

Jonathan Corwin (1640–1718) was a young man when he bought in c.1674 a house already built, if not finished, by Captain Nathaniel Davenport. His contract for renovation mentioned "filling, plastering, and finishing," which implies the structure was up but the wall in-fill and perhaps other features were not yet installed. A lean-to is mentioned in the contract. Corwin was of a merchant family, exporting timber and fish to England and the West Indies, which likely accounts for his precocious purchase of a large house as a young newlywed. He and his wife Elizabeth lived here the rest of their lives.

His grandson George inherited the house in 1718, and when he died in 1746, the inventory showed the house unchanged in plan from when it was bought long before. In that year, however, his widow Sarah removed a projecting enclosed porch forming a small entry hall and its stairway, and rebuilt the pitch roof into a more fashionably Georgian gambrel roof. These changes were reversed in the 1940s restoration when architectural consultant Frank Chouteau Bron inserted the gables (there is evidence of original projecting gables in somewhat different positions), substantially rebuilt the front porch, and restored the pendants and casement windows—perhaps inspired by an 1819 sketch of the house by a Mr. Bartol. The fireplaces and chimneys appear to be original throughout the house, though the chimney tops have been rebuilt.

The notoriety of the house rests on Jonathan Corwin's role in the witch hunts. He was a civic leader and magistrate in Salem, serving on the Court of Oyer and Terminer. It was his role (and that of fellow magistrate John Hathorne, ancestor of the novelist Nathaniel Hawthorne) to investigate witchcraft allegations by interrogating some of the accused; these interrogations have long been thought to have taken place in dining room of his house. No documentation supports this, but accounts do mention the pub or "ordinary" of Nathaniel Ingersoll as the place of the first stages of the proceedings. Later Corwin assisted in judging and condemning nineteen people to death.

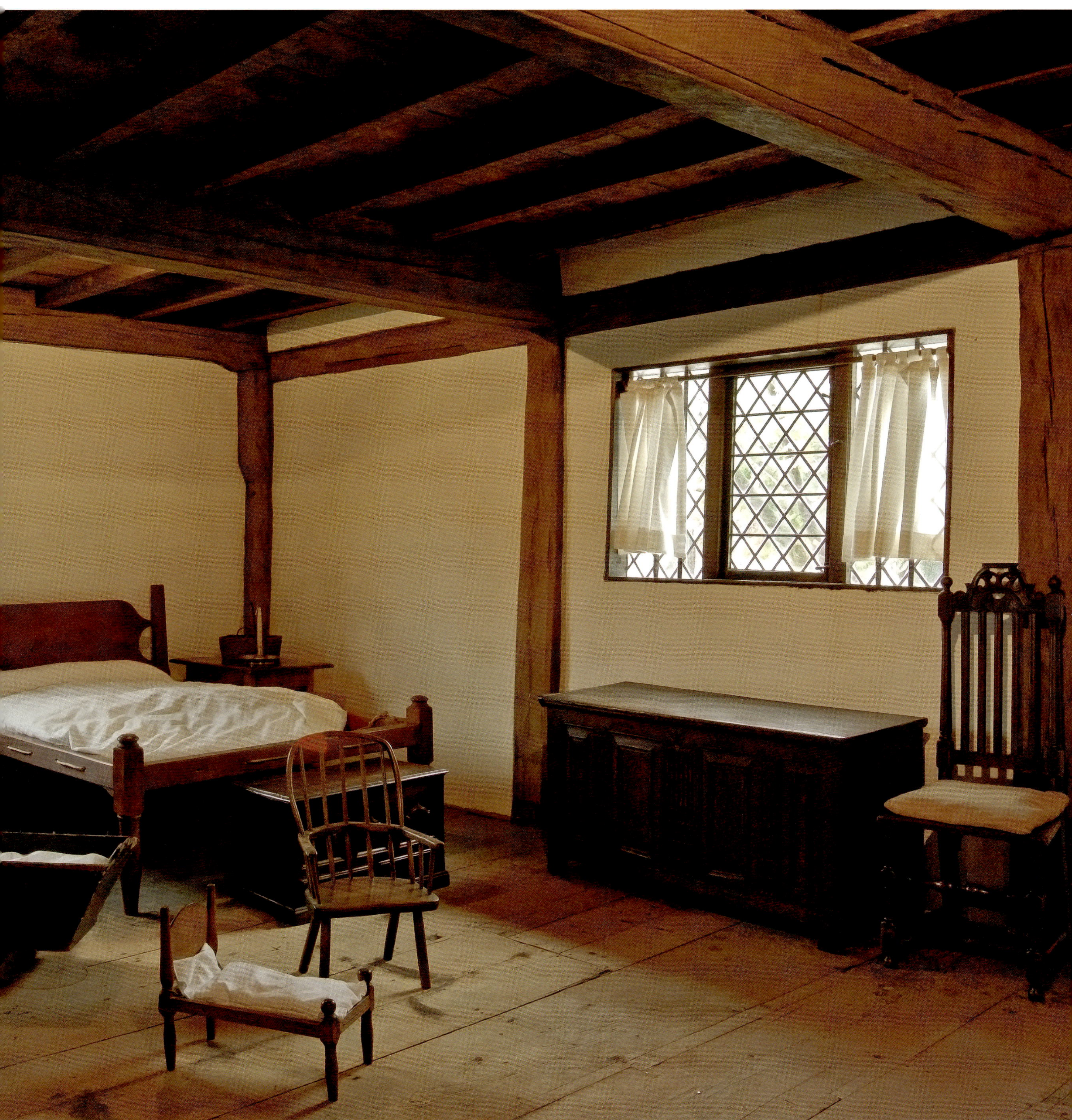

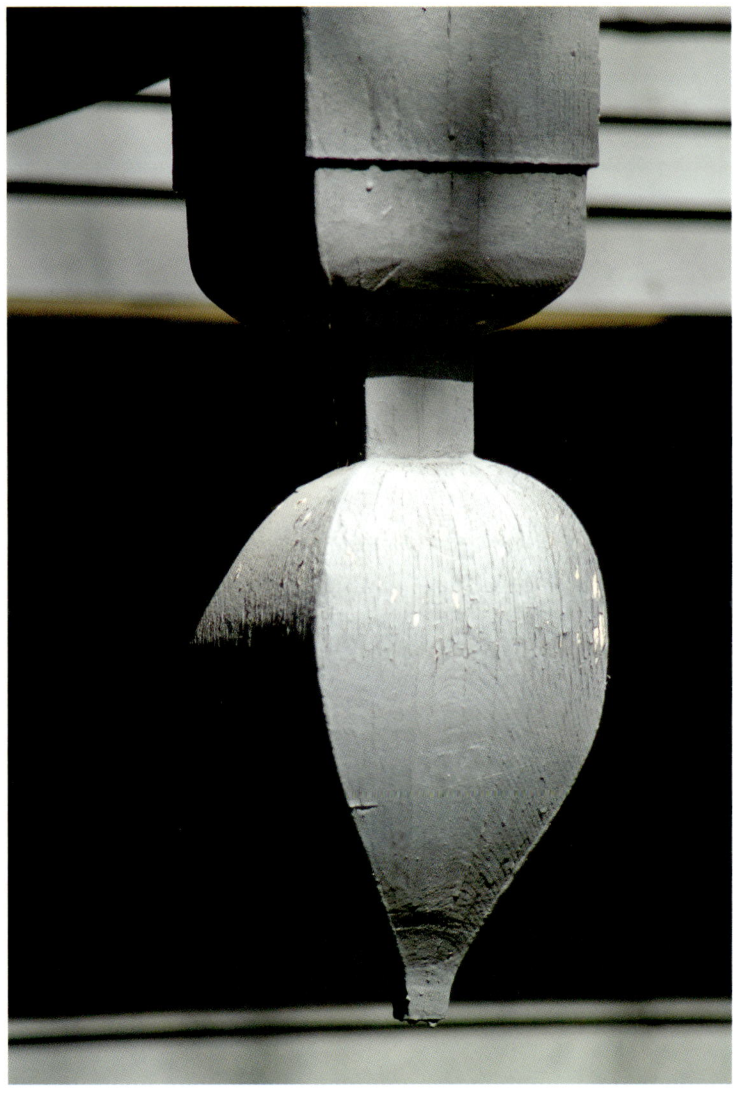

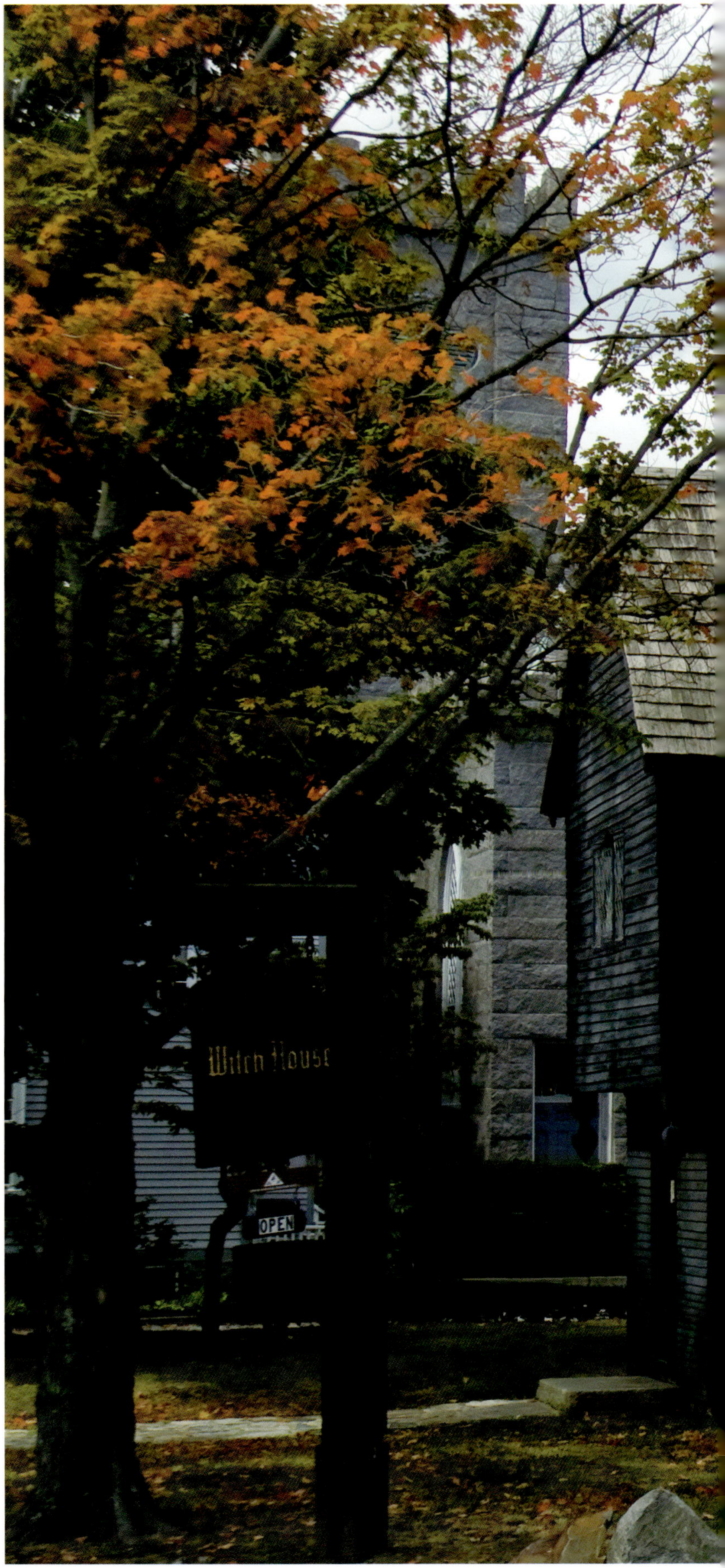

ABOVE *Unlike so many medieval house features, the drop had no practical function other than visual appeal.*

RIGHT *The add-on lean-to, moving the cooking function from the hall to a rear kitchen, is evident here. Symmetry and balance were not cardinal rules of early New England houses, or of their English medieval ancestors, as the shift in roof pitch indicates.*

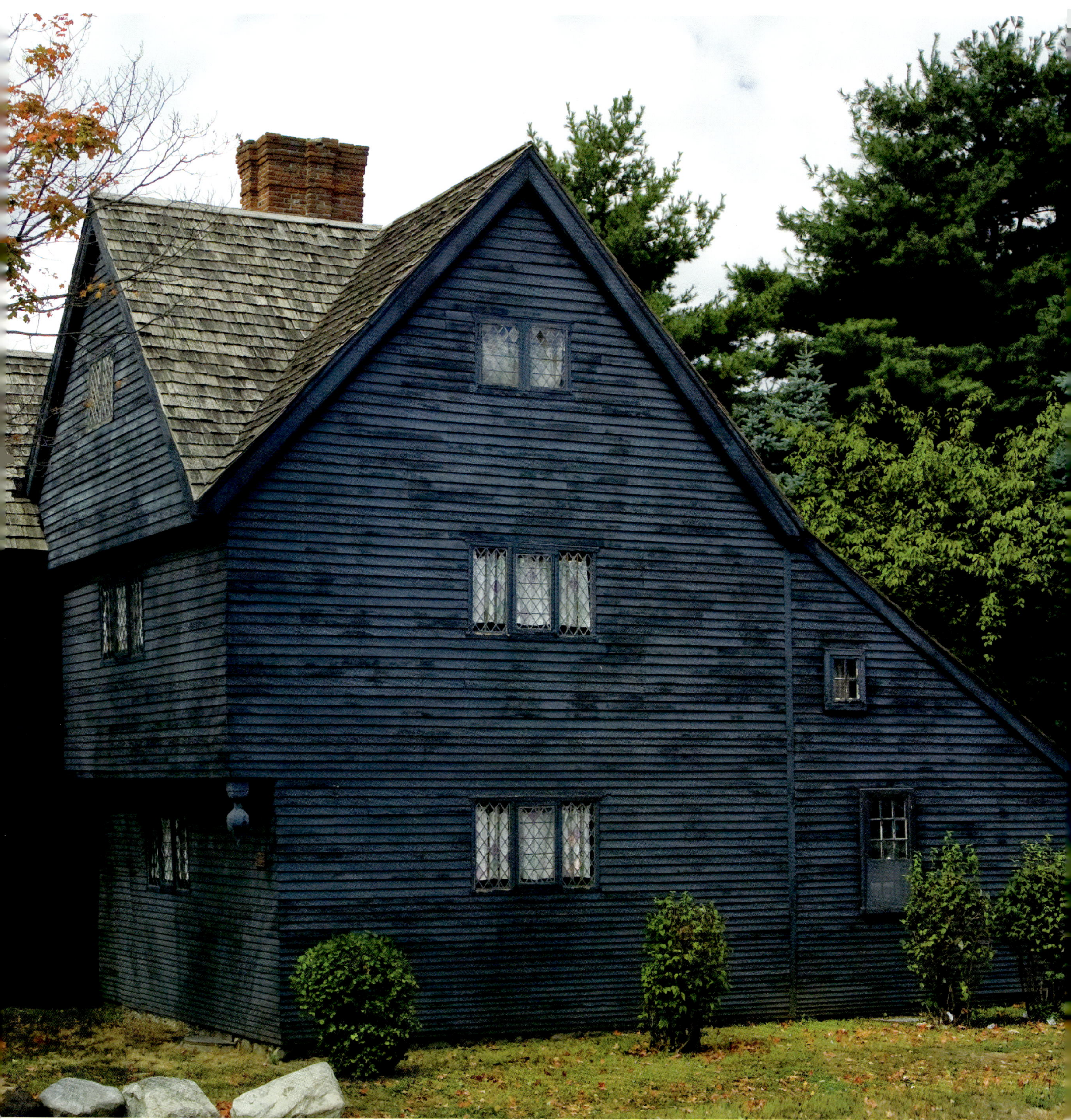

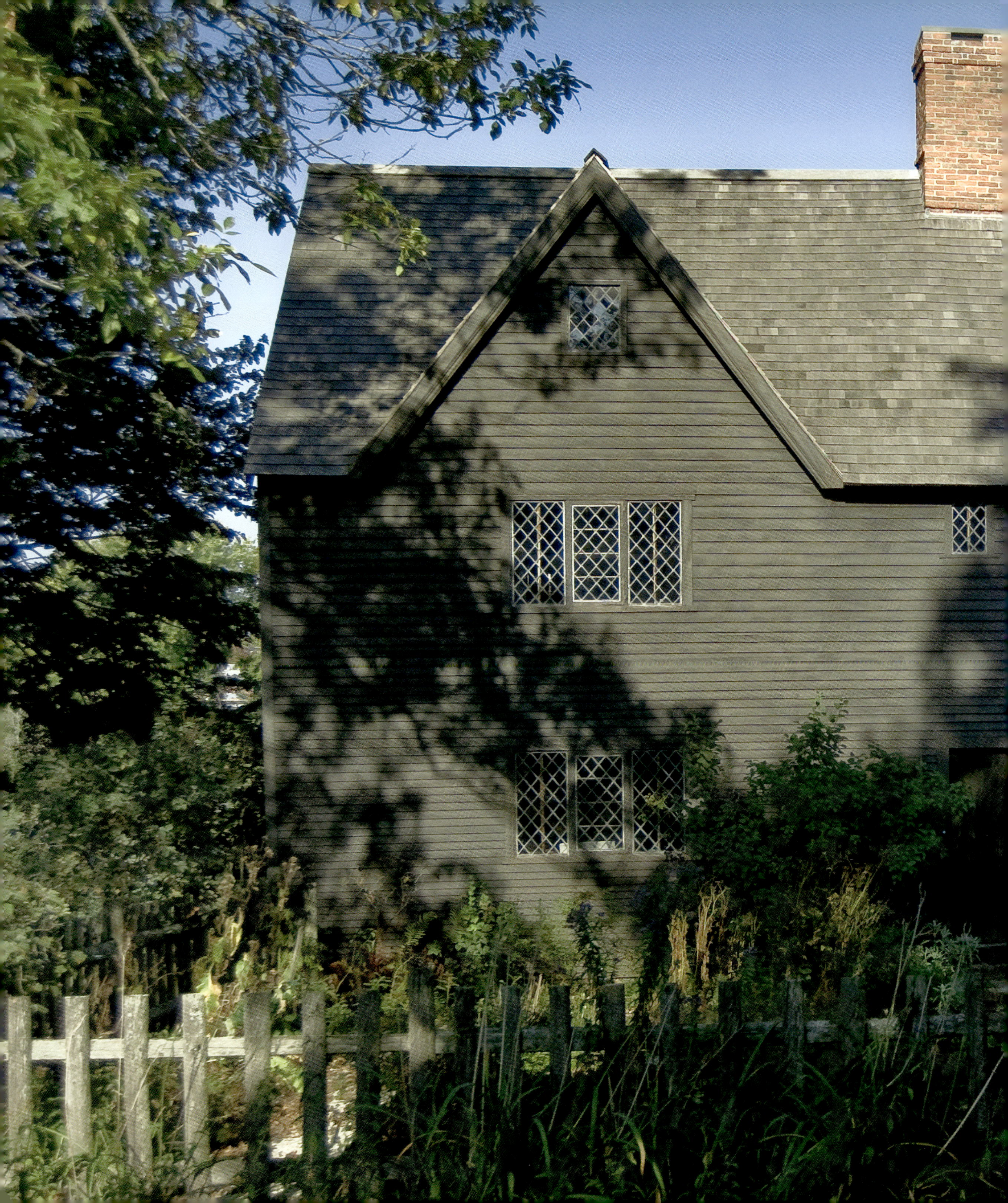

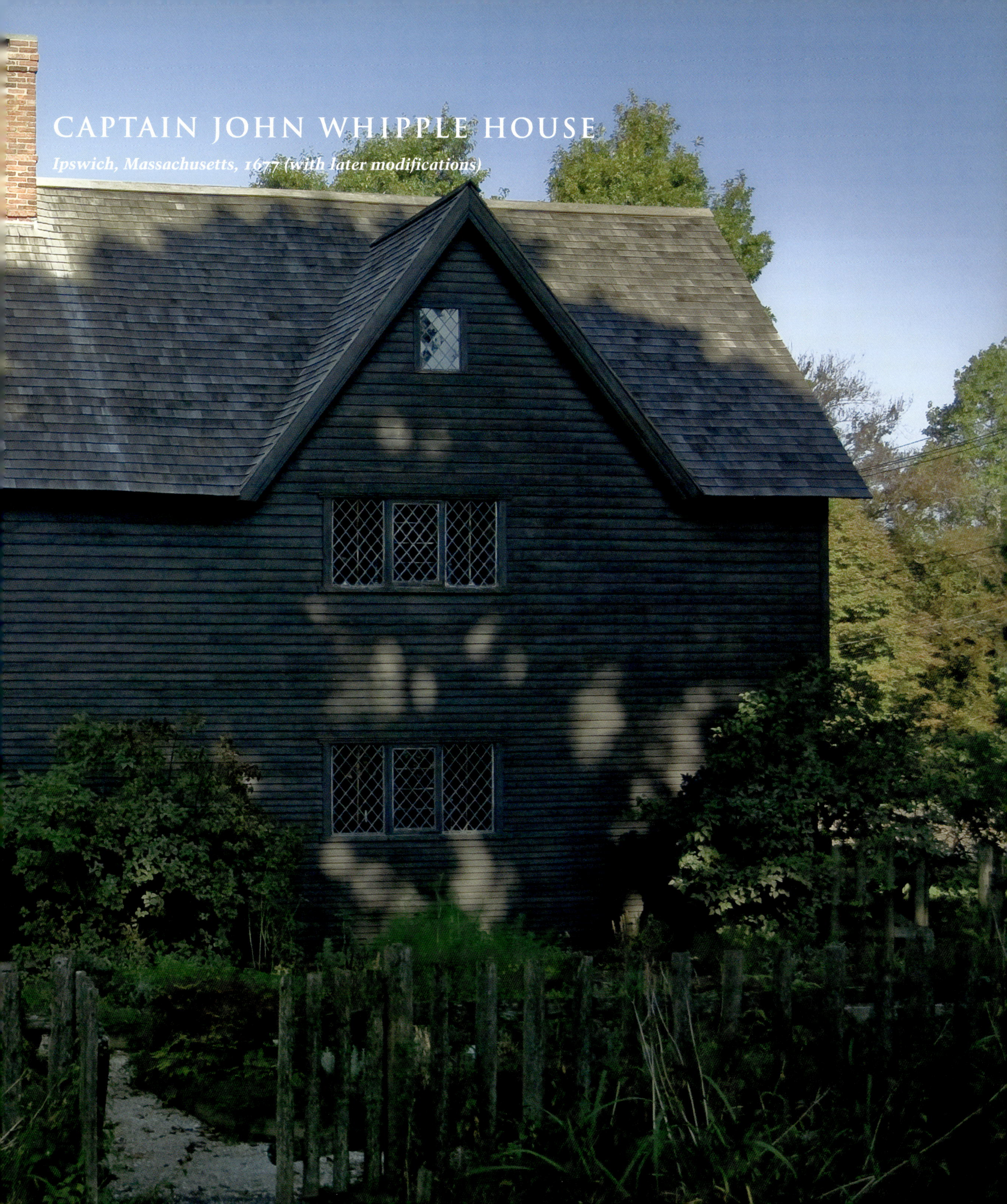

CAPTAIN JOHN WHIPPLE HOUSE

Ipswich, Massachusetts, 1677 (with later modifications)

PREVIOUS PAGES *John Whipple's house started as a modest one-room structure with no front gable (the left side of the present house). Around 1690 he doubled its size by adding the parlor section and two front gables, and he later constructed a lean-to across the back.*

BELOW AND RIGHT *Though furnished with objects of the next century, they are faithful descendants of earlier forms, just less bold, a reflection of English Puritan culture disbursed to the countryside where old ways died slowly. Mostly made of pine and maple, which when new have a flat white appearance, they were almost always originally painted to give them character.*

FOLLOWING PAGES *The English (and New England) court cupboard was an impressive piece to behold. The Reverend Wallace Nutting, a great romancer of colonial antiquities, had this one made. The quillwork sconces are rare survivors of the early period.*

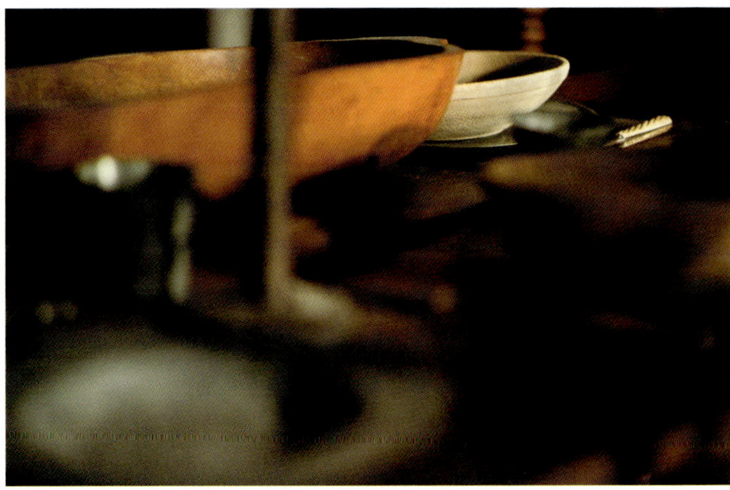

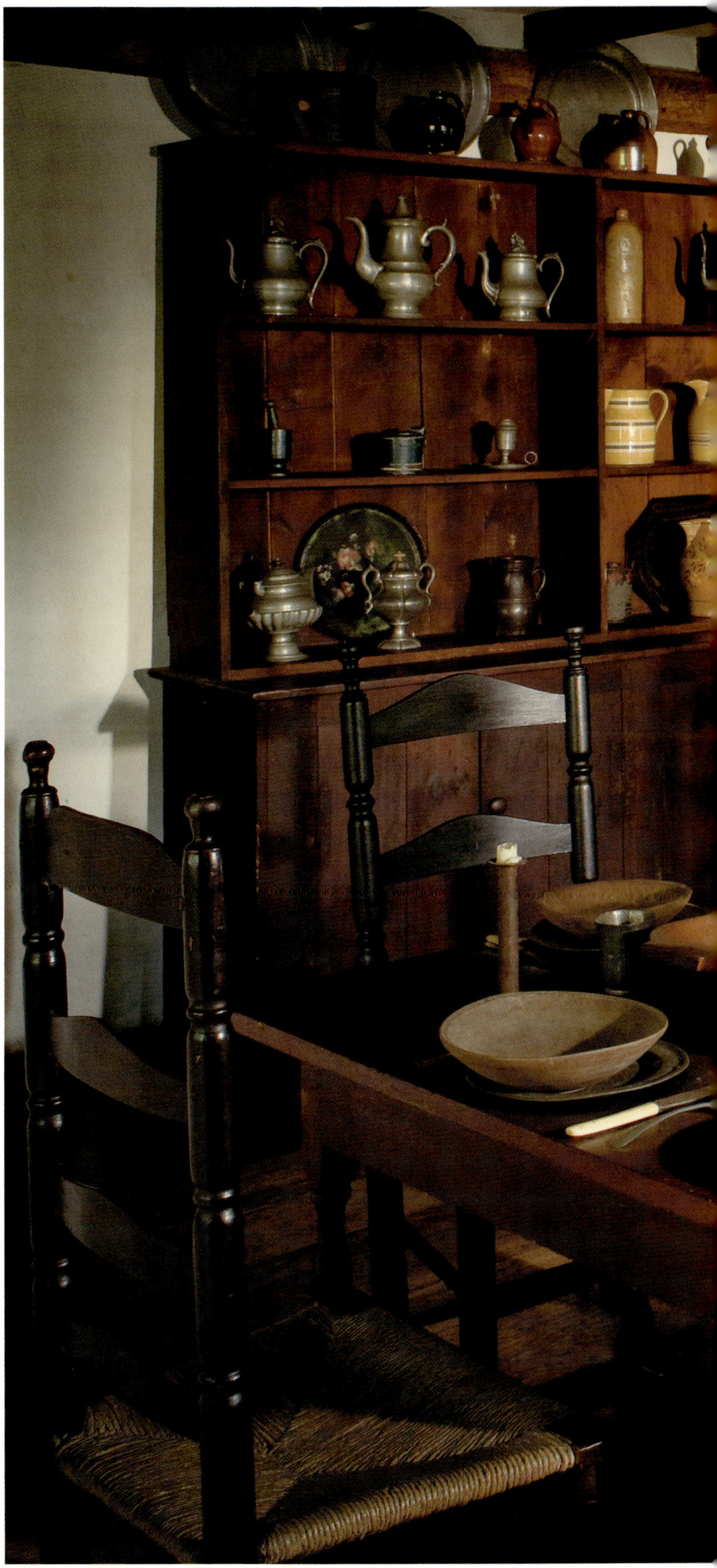

What the natives had called Agawam became Ipswich when John Winthrop Jr., son of the founding governor of Massachusetts Bay Colony, brought a group of settlers to the shores of a river north of Boston. There, in 1633, they found freshwater, potential for waterpower, fine fishing, and easy access to the ocean, yet shelter from it. By 1646 nearly eight hundred had followed, making their living at fishing primarily, but also farming, shipbuilding, and trading. A certain independent spirit was evident from the start. Nathaniel Ward, an assistant pastor, wrote the first code of laws for Massachusetts. In 1687 many residents, led by pastor John Wise, protested a tax imposed by Royal Governor Andros, arguing that taxation without representation was unacceptable. Some went to jail, and Andros was recalled to England. For this rebellion, Ipswich later referred to itself as the "Birthplace of American Independence."

When larger ships required deeper harbors, upriver Ipswich lost out to other ports, but more modest growth helped preserve a number of its earliest houses. Prominent among these is the Whipple House (1677, confirmed by dendrochronology),

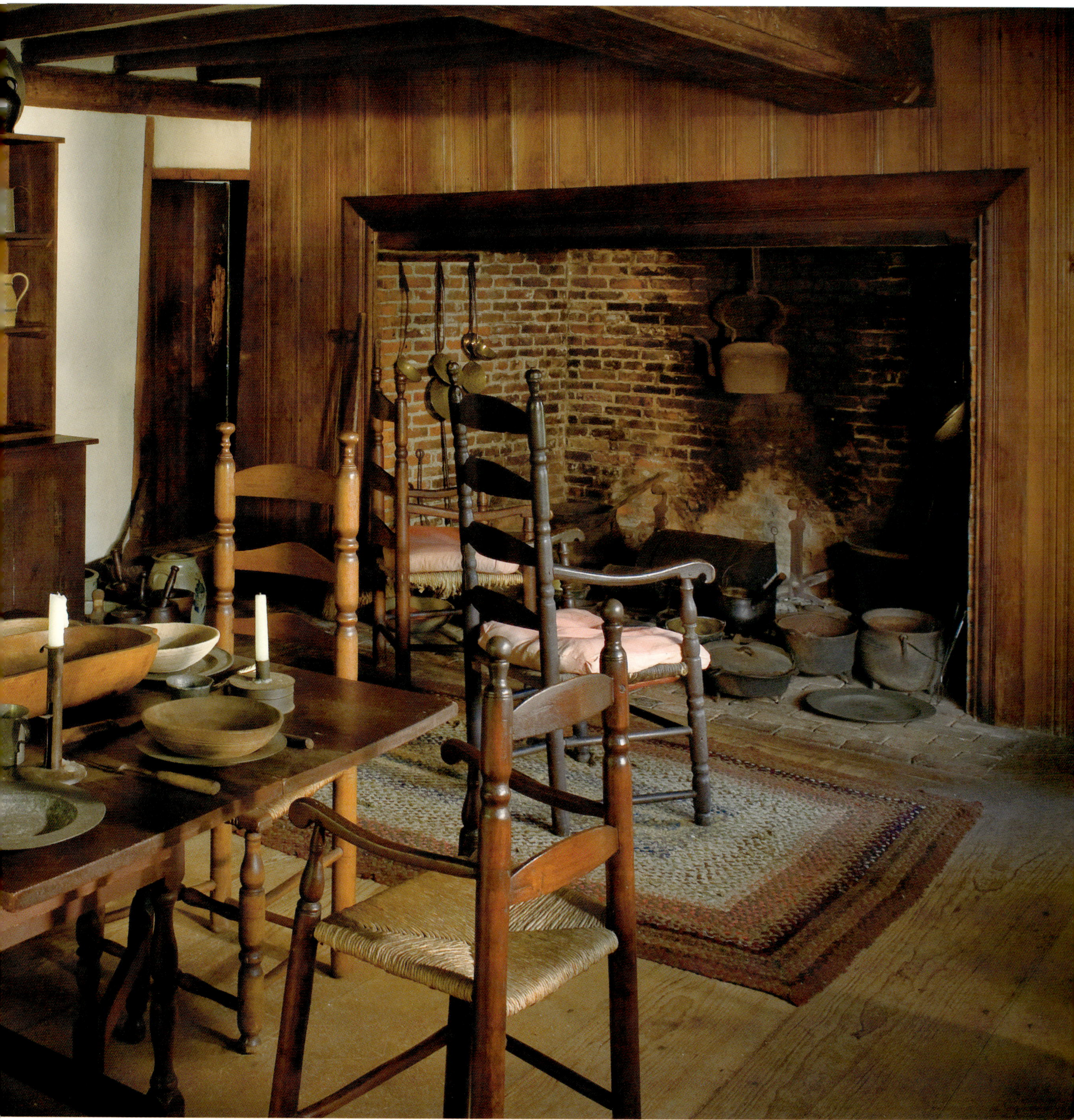

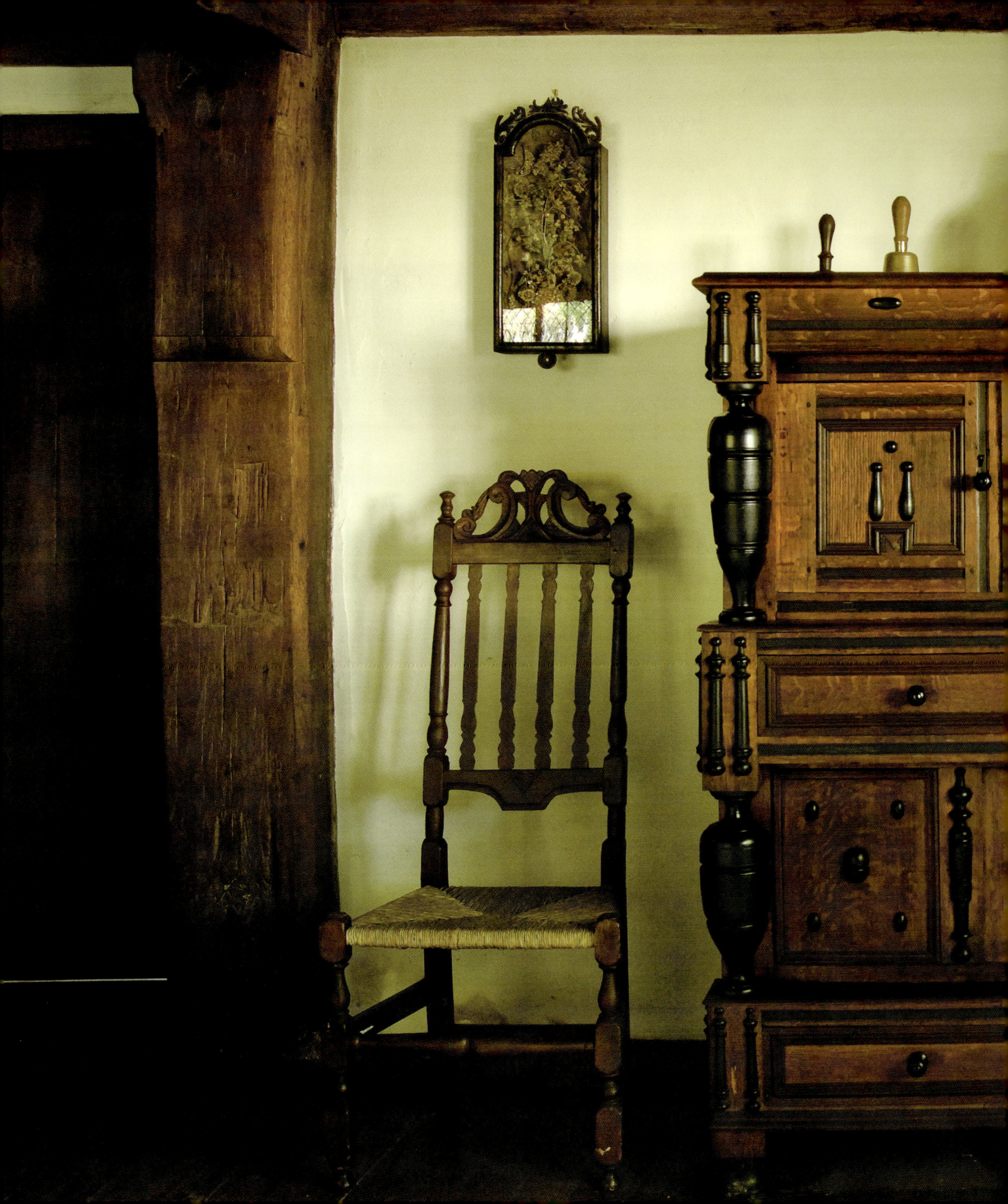

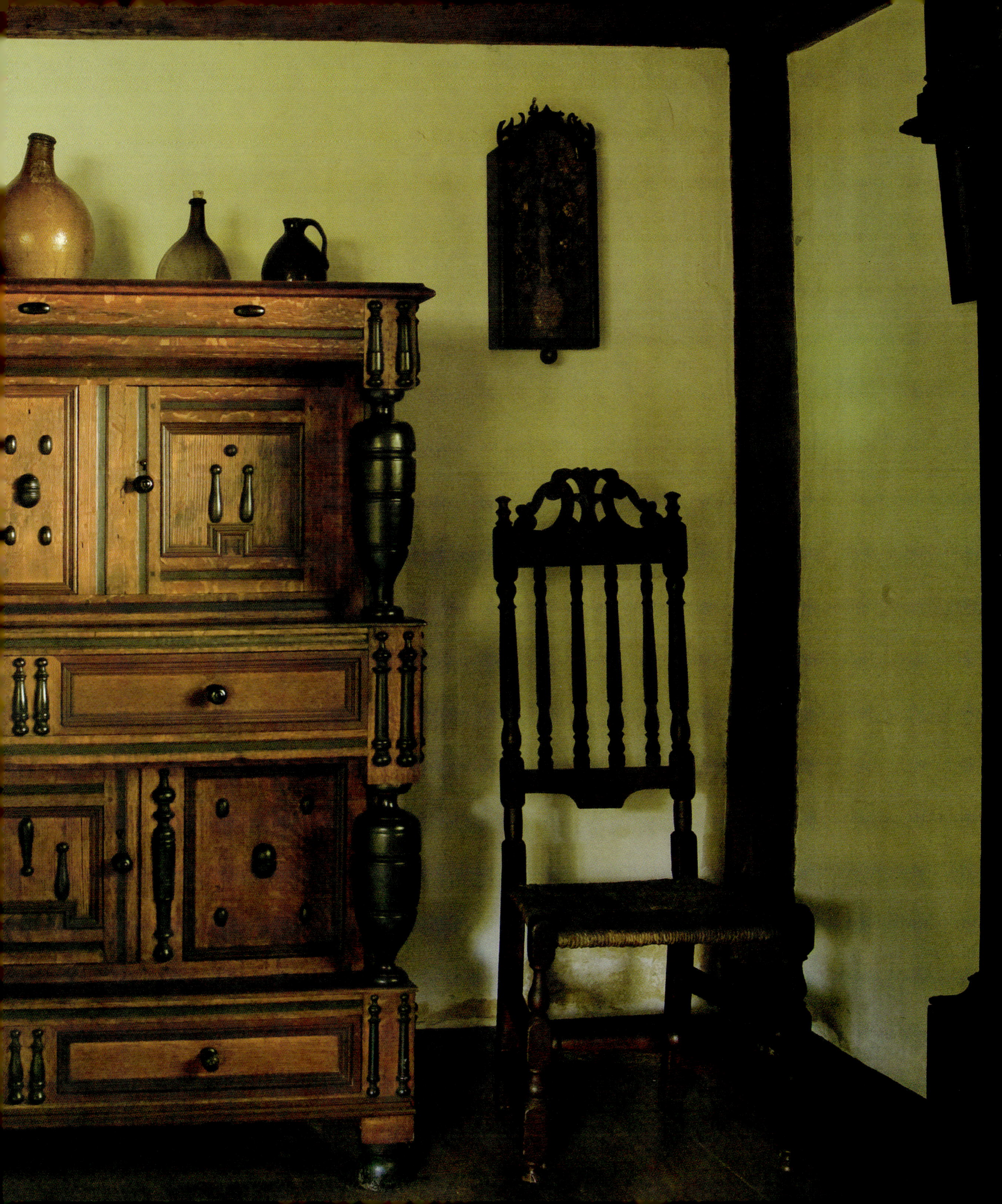

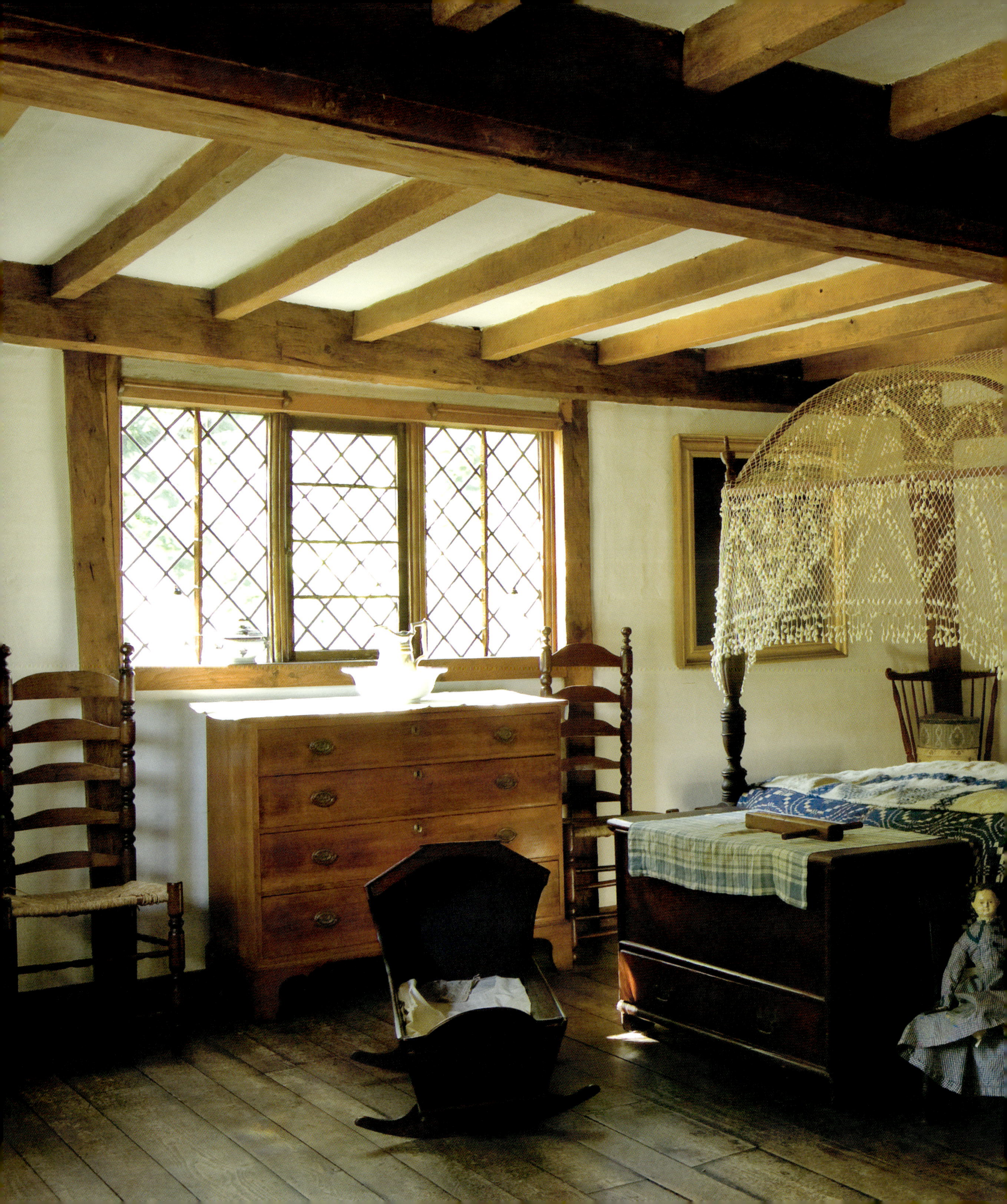

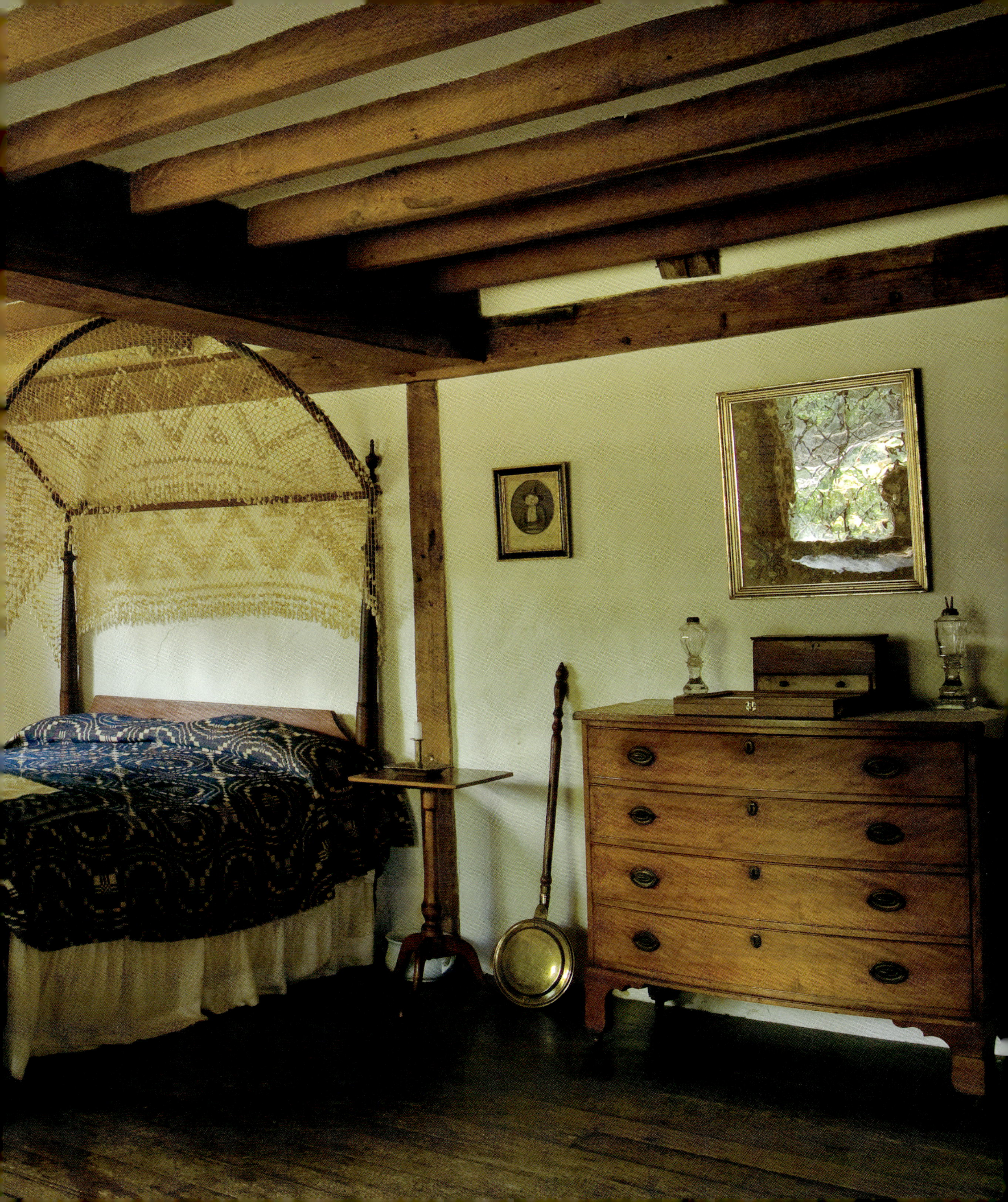

PREVIOUS PAGES *Above the kitchen, the chamber is furnished with a variety of New England furnishings of the post-Revolutionary period. Its structure and restored windows reflect the house's early period.*

RIGHT *As originally built, siding was of narrow riven (split) oak pieces, each overlapping the next. Left unstained and unpainted, it weathered to a dark brown. Modern restorations have used long milled clapboards protected by stain or paint.*

built by Captain John Whipple (1625–83) on a single-room plan in the center of the village (at the corner of Saltonstall and Market Streets). In addition to being a militia officer, Whipple was a successful businessman with interests in a malthouse, fulling mill, and a sawmill. His son Major John Whipple (1657–1722) inherited the house and around 1690 expanded it with a large parlor to the right, creating a conventional center-chimney home with more chambers above. By the time of his death in 1722 he had added a lean-to at the rear, bringing the house to essentially its present form of fifteen rooms: six for the family in front and nine in the lean-to for servants.

On his death Whipple's house passed to daughter Mary and her husband Benjamin Crocker. He was a well-regarded legislator and chaplain. They had two children, but Mary would die only a year after having inherited the house. Her husband married Experience Coolidge in 1736, and, when she died in 1759, he married Elizabeth Williams. This apparently called for a redecoration of the house in the Georgian style by removing the ancient front gables, replacing leaded casement windows with larger sash ones, adding a new ceiling to hide the beams and joists, and removing wooden walls from around the central chimney. Crocker's son, Deacon John (1723–1806), was the fourth generation to own the house and thereafter it passed to yet another son John—who inherited most of the house—and their daughter Elizabeth, who received and would hold the "great west chamber"—as long as she remained unmarried. John sold his share to his brother Joseph who sold it to a married sister, again reserving the room for Elizabeth. Finally, in 1833 the house was sold out of the family to a peddler for $501. By 1897 it was tenement housing for a local mill, in poor condition when the Reverend Thomas Franklin Waters organized a group to purchase the house. The following year the Ipswich Historical Society undertook its restoration to its pre-Georgian appearance to convert it to a house museum, as it remains today. In 1927, wealthy Richard Crane of Ipswich gave the Society land where the house was moved intact. From 1953 to 1954 the Society began another restoration, replacing facade gables and casement windows and adding a caretaker's apartment in the rear. A seventeenth-century-style "housewife's garden" was also created based on extensive research by Isadore Smith, who, under the pen name Ann Leighton, later published three noteworthy books on early American gardens.

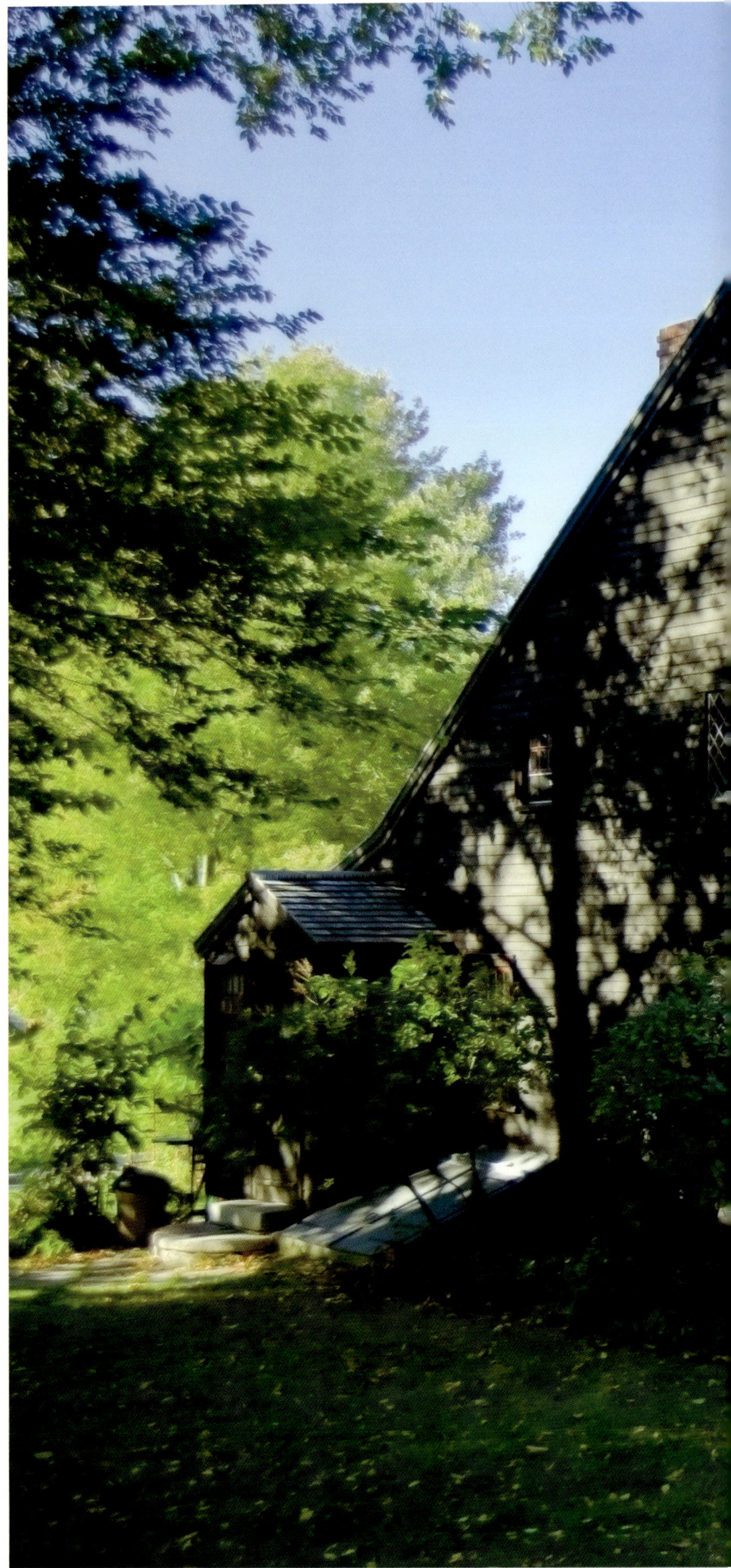

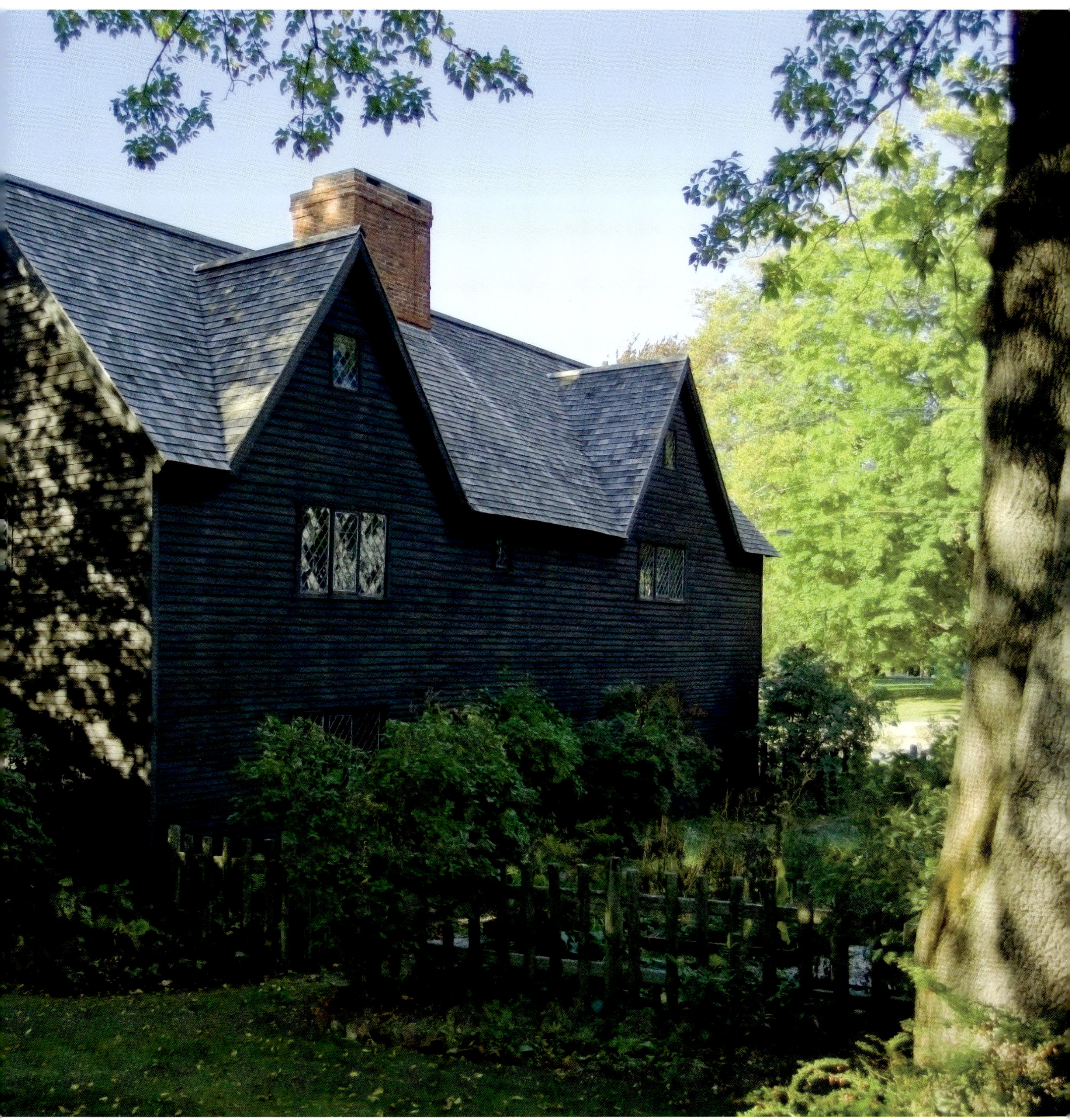

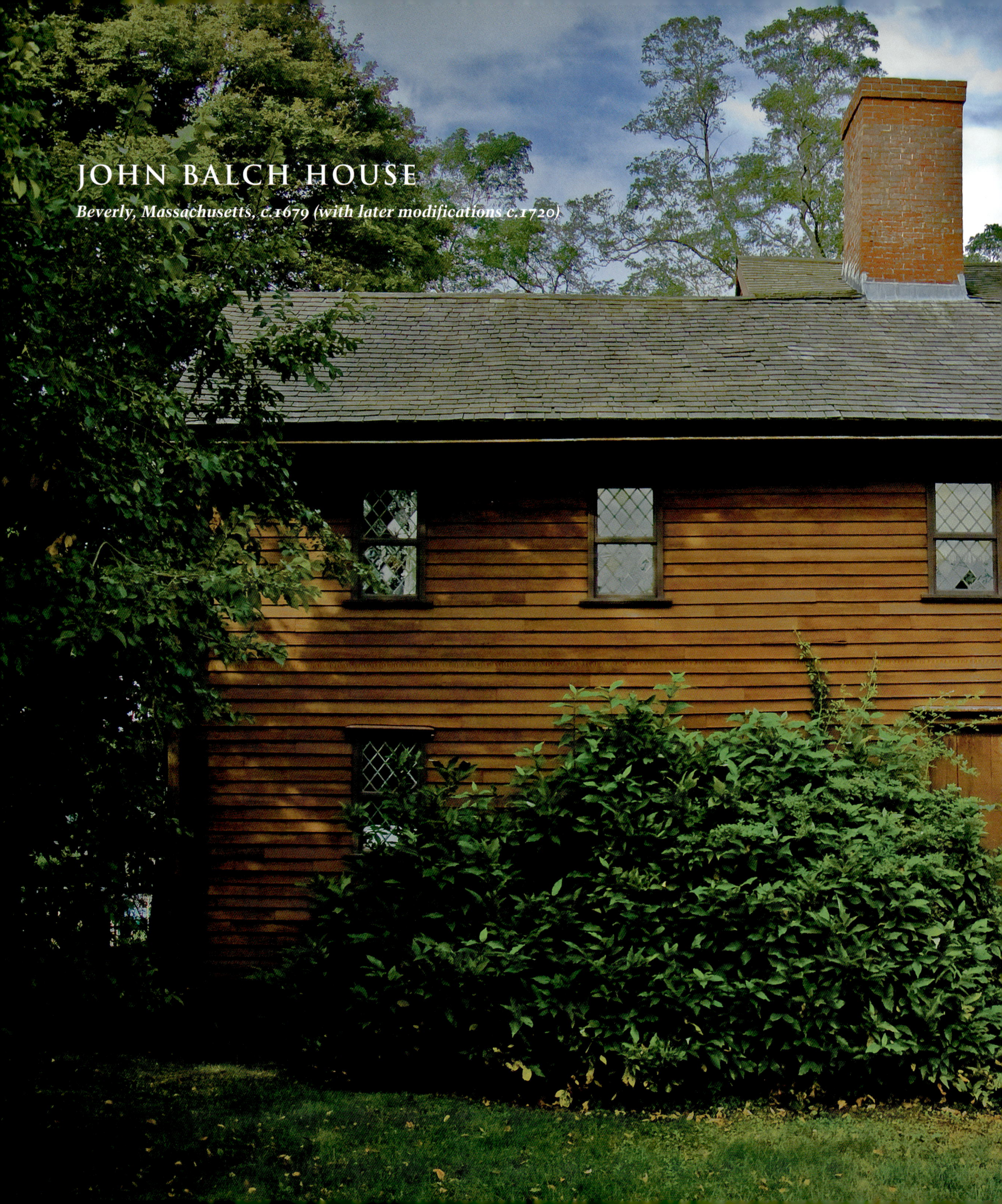

JOHN BALCH HOUSE

Beverly, Massachusetts, c.1679 (with later modifications c.1720)

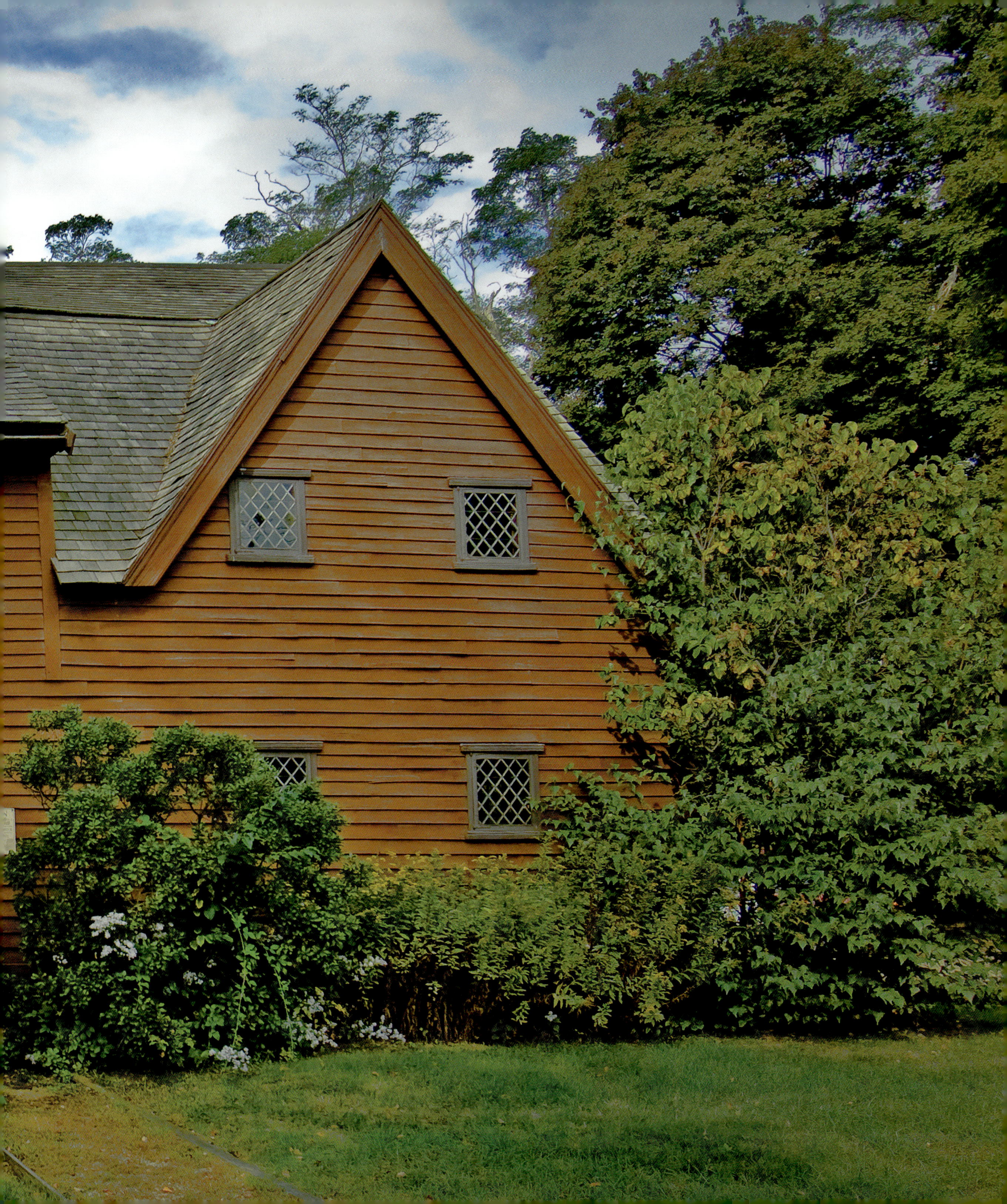

PREVIOUS PAGES *John Balch built the old section of the house (right) in 1670 as a modest one-room, one-and-a-half-story home, which served his family's needs for two generations. His grandson, Benjamin, added the two-story addition (left). A third addition and roof changes resulted in the present structure.*

BELOW AND RIGHT *In the old house the first floor is a one-room hall (kitchen) that served all family's needs except for sleeping, which occurred in the chamber above.*

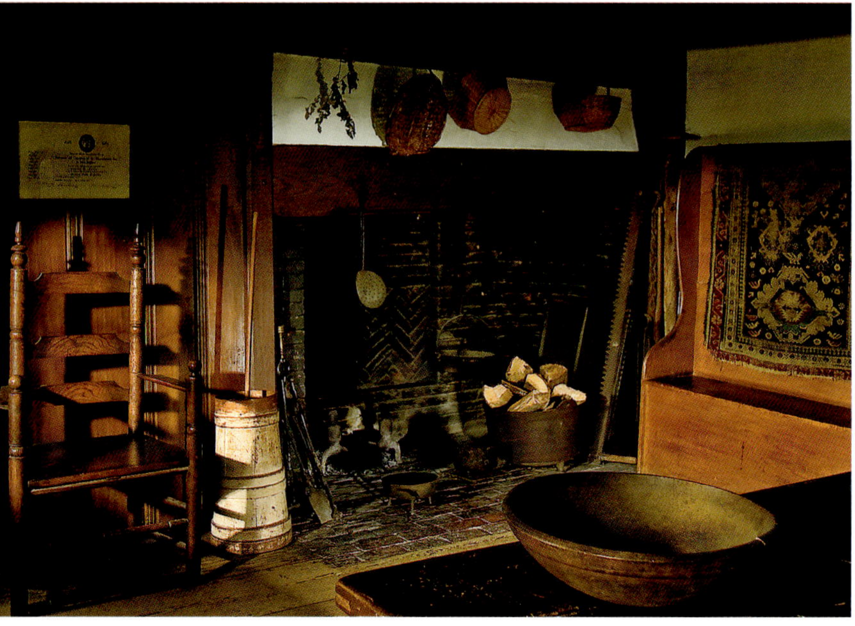

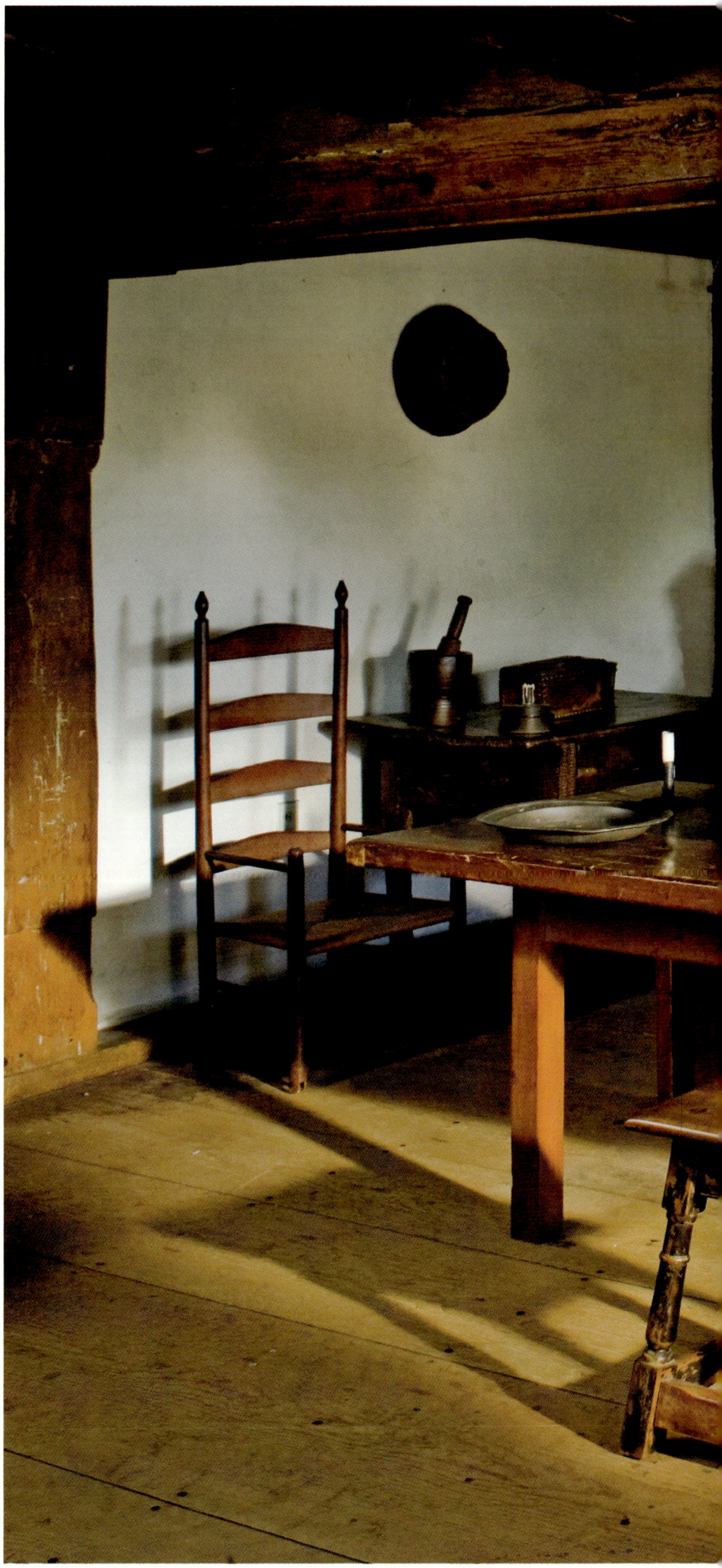

John Balch was born in Somerset, England, in 1579 and arrived with the Dorchester Company at Cape Ann in September 1623. The remnant of this group, including Balch, settled at Naumkeag (now called Salem) in 1626. In 1635 five of them, including Balch, received a 1,000-acre grant at what is now Beverly, Massachusetts, and moved there. Beverly became a "nuclear village," so mandated by a Massachusetts General Court ordinance requiring that no house be constructed more than a half mile from the meeting house, except a mill or farmhouse if the owner already had a village home. This was, in part, a defensive measure, and each proprietor received "outfields" of farmland to be plowed or tilled, or to remain as meadows for hay and pasture for grazing. "Infields," the village common land, usually a wedge-shaped "square," was used by all for grazing stock. At Beverly, as elsewhere, the New England village changed between 1680 and 1760 to a "range town," as people moved to the countryside.

John and Margary Balch were founding members of the First Church in Salem. John was active in the town government and served as one of the "overseers and Layers out of Lotts of ground." On his portion of the grant, Balch built a farmhouse, assumed until recently to be the present house. A recent dendrochronology study, however, dates the present building to the 1670s. The ear-

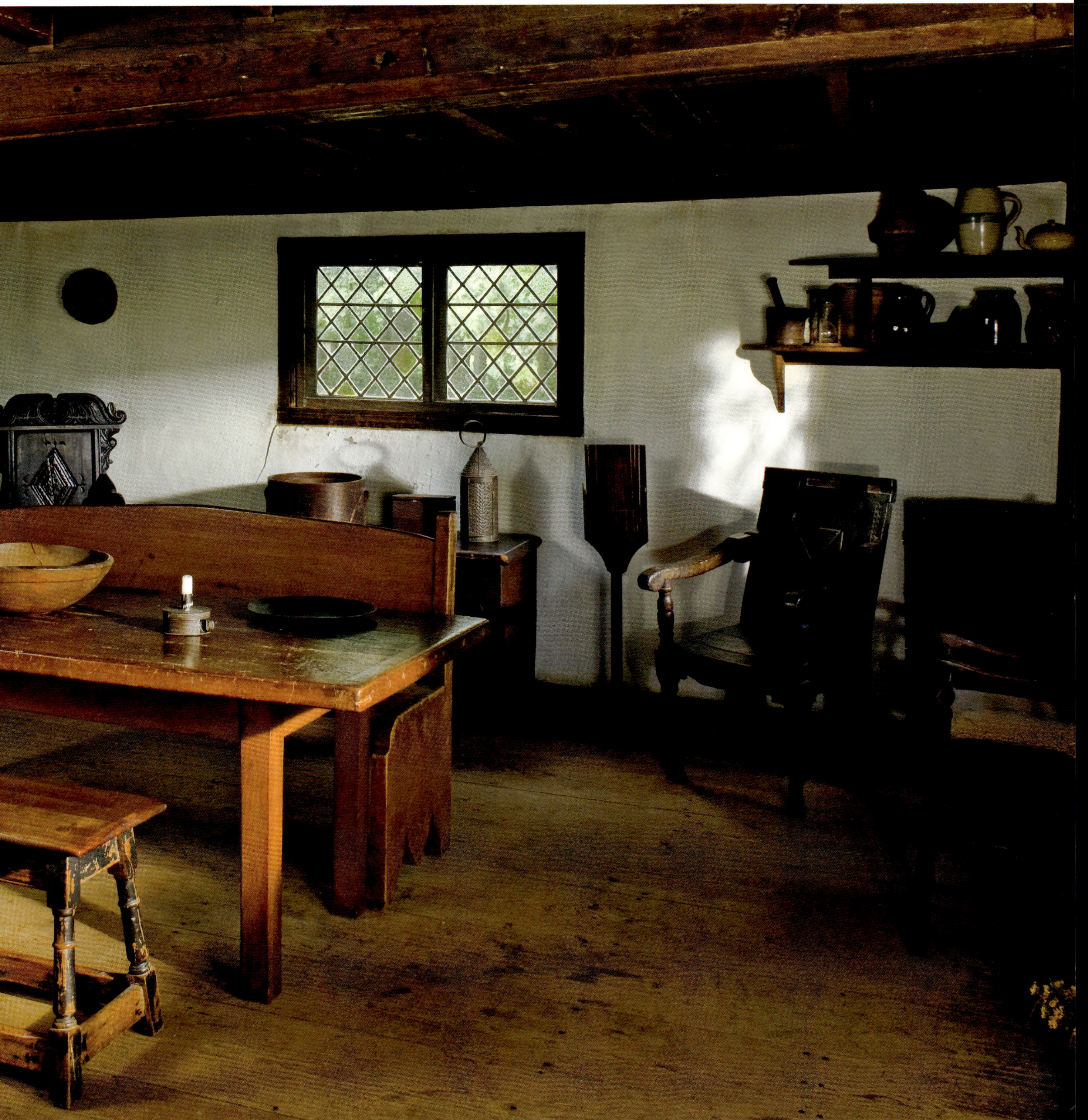

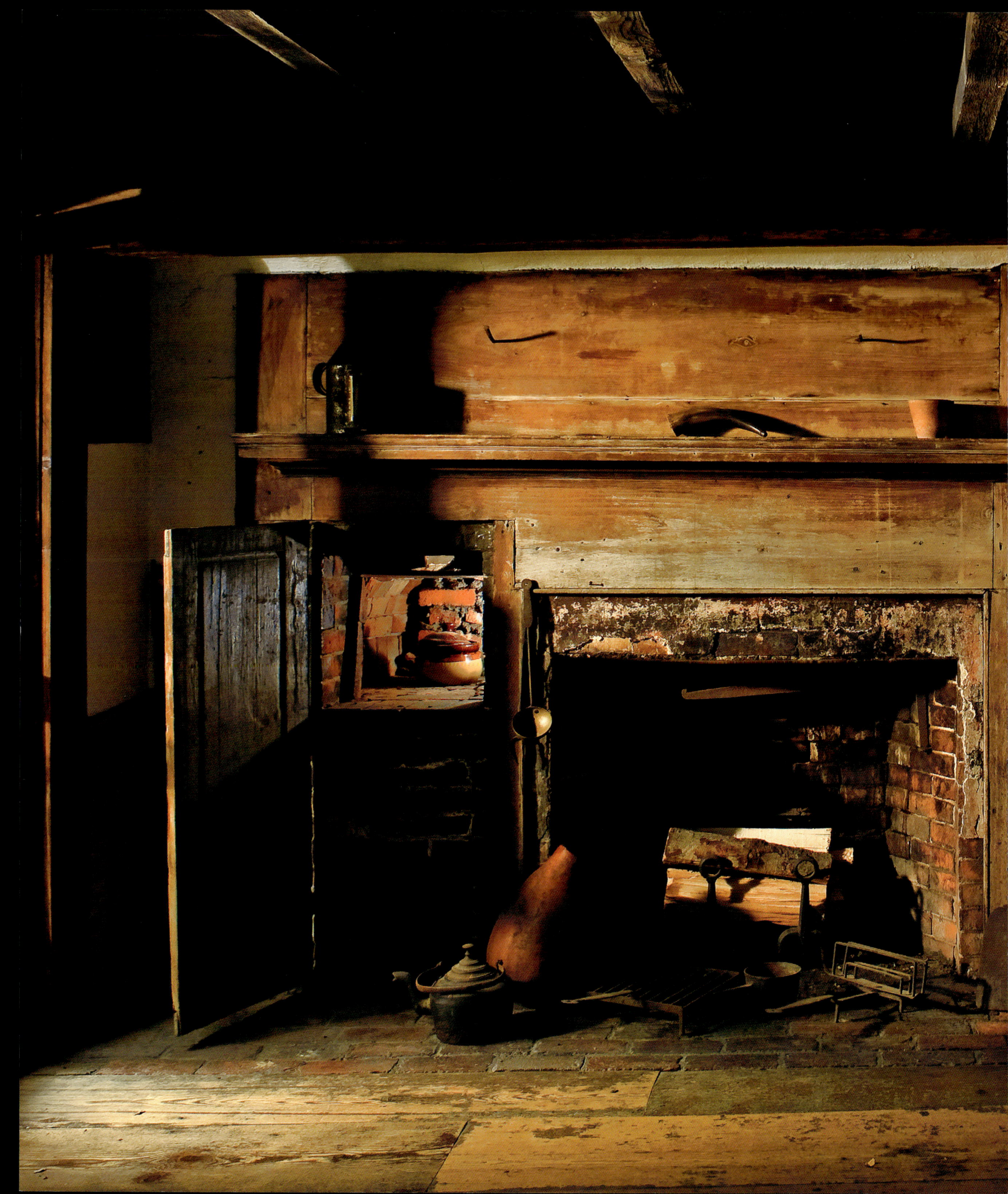

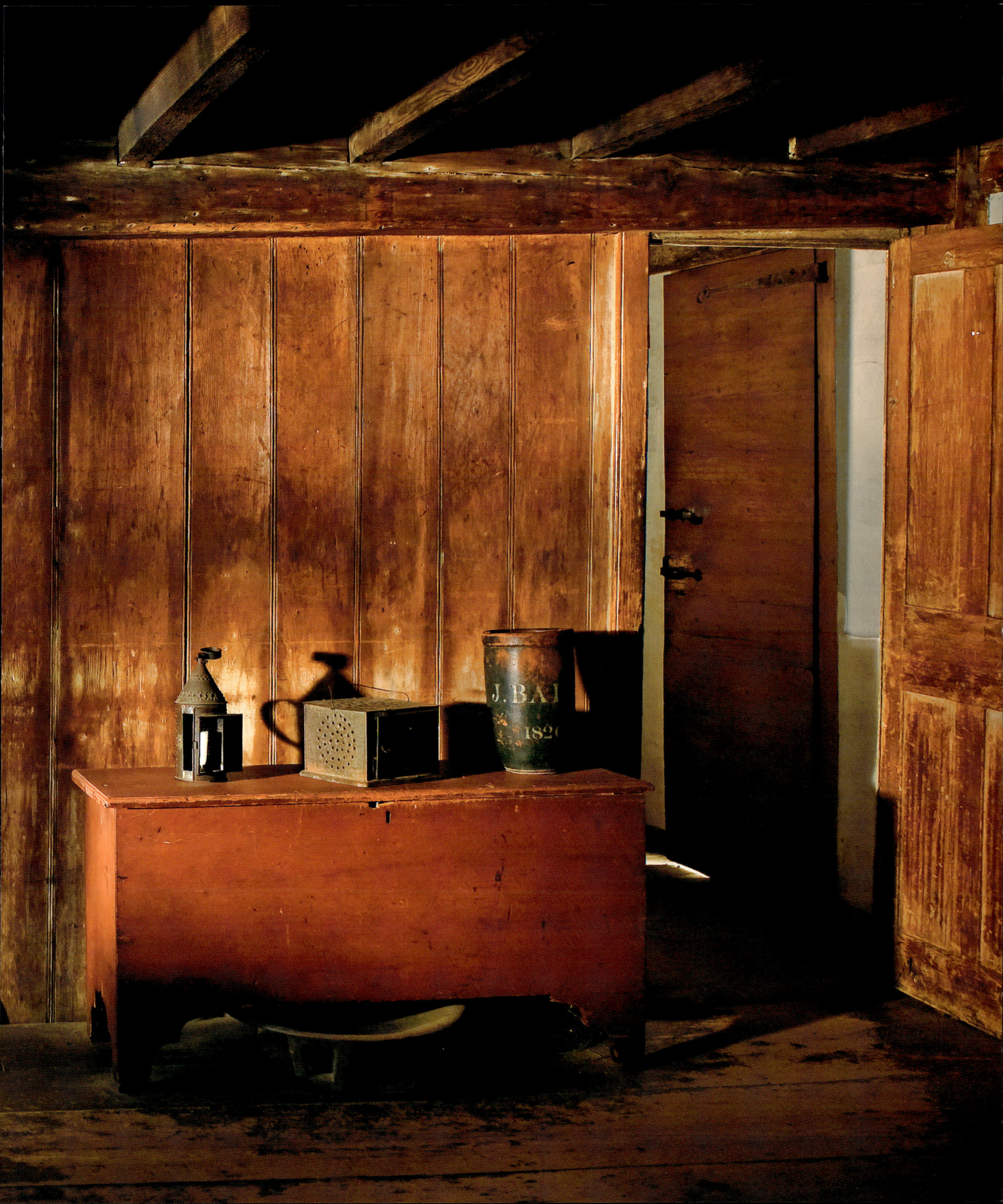
J. BA
182

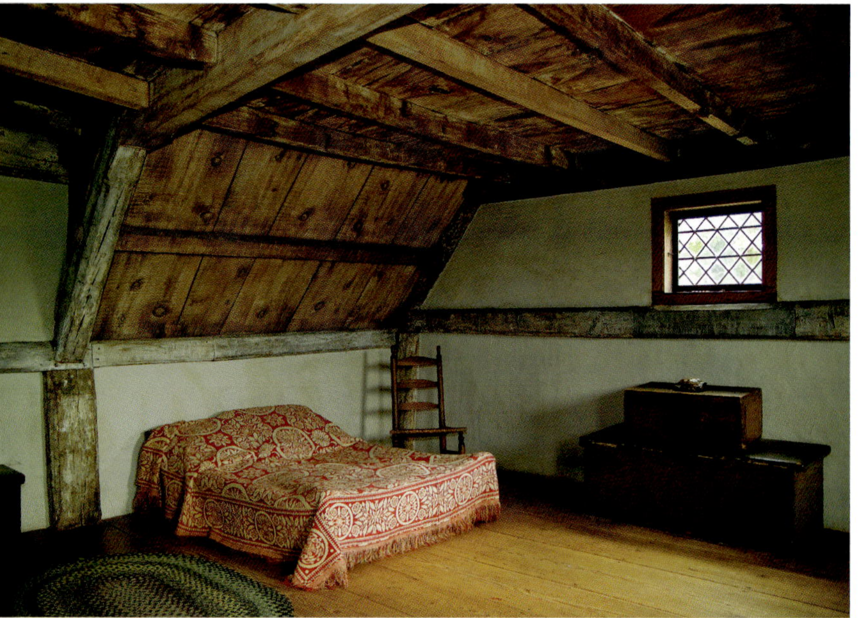

PREVIOUS PAGES *Entering the later section of the house, the kitchen (left) has an eighteenth-century-style bake oven in the left jamb of the fireplace. In this case the oven can be closed off with a wood door when not in use.*

LEFT *The chamber of the old section of the house.*

RIGHT *A window was an expensive affair: blown glass spun into a thin sheet then cut into diamond-shaped pieces in Europe. Imported and fastened with lead cames braced with iron bars and set in a wood casement frame, windows were by economic necessity small and few in number. Glass color varied with the impurity of the sand from which it was made.*

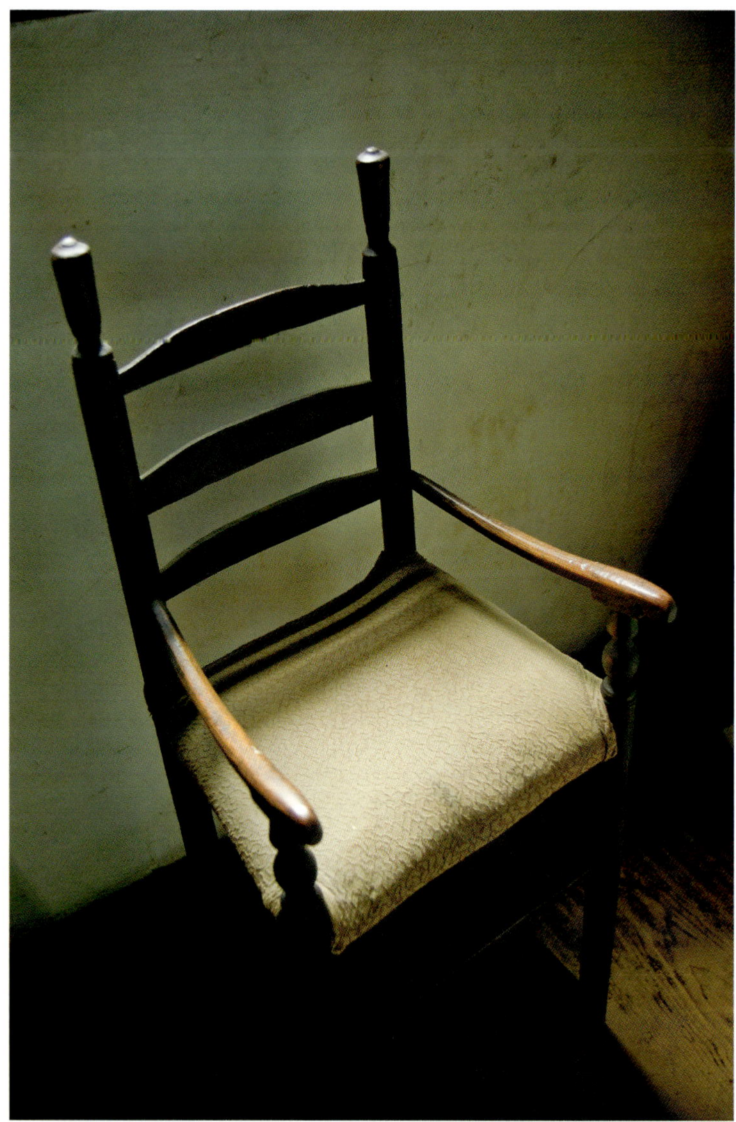

liest built portion was probably a single one-story room and a half house that form the northeast section of the current house. Benjamin Balch, grandson of John, added the southern part of the house, a one-room two-story structure. The two sections were connected by a common roof and a central chimney. Still later, the original north end and chimney bay were enlarged to the west. A symmetrical gable roof, higher than the roof of the southern room, was built over the widened structure.

Beverly, like many other communities throughout Essex County, was affected by the witchcraft hysteria of the 1690s. David Balch, grandson of John, was bedridden with a fatal illness in the early months of 1690 at the Balch House. His name was later entered in the witch trials testimony as one of the earliest victims of spectral visitation by witches. Mary Gage, a Salem resident, testified against the accused Dorcas Hoar, claiming she had tormented David Balch prior to his death on April 17, 1690.

The Balch ancestral home was owned by Balch descendants until 1916, when it was purchased by the Balch Family Association through the efforts of Balch Association member William Sumner Appleton, who was also the founder of the Society for the Preservation of New England Antiquities (now Historic New England). The first restoration of the house, which recreated the original roof slope on the east facade, was done at this time under the supervision of historical architect Norman Isham. The property was turned over to the Beverly Historical Society in 1932. Another restoration was undertaken in 1960–61 by Roy Baker. The Society continues to preserve and interpret the Balch House.

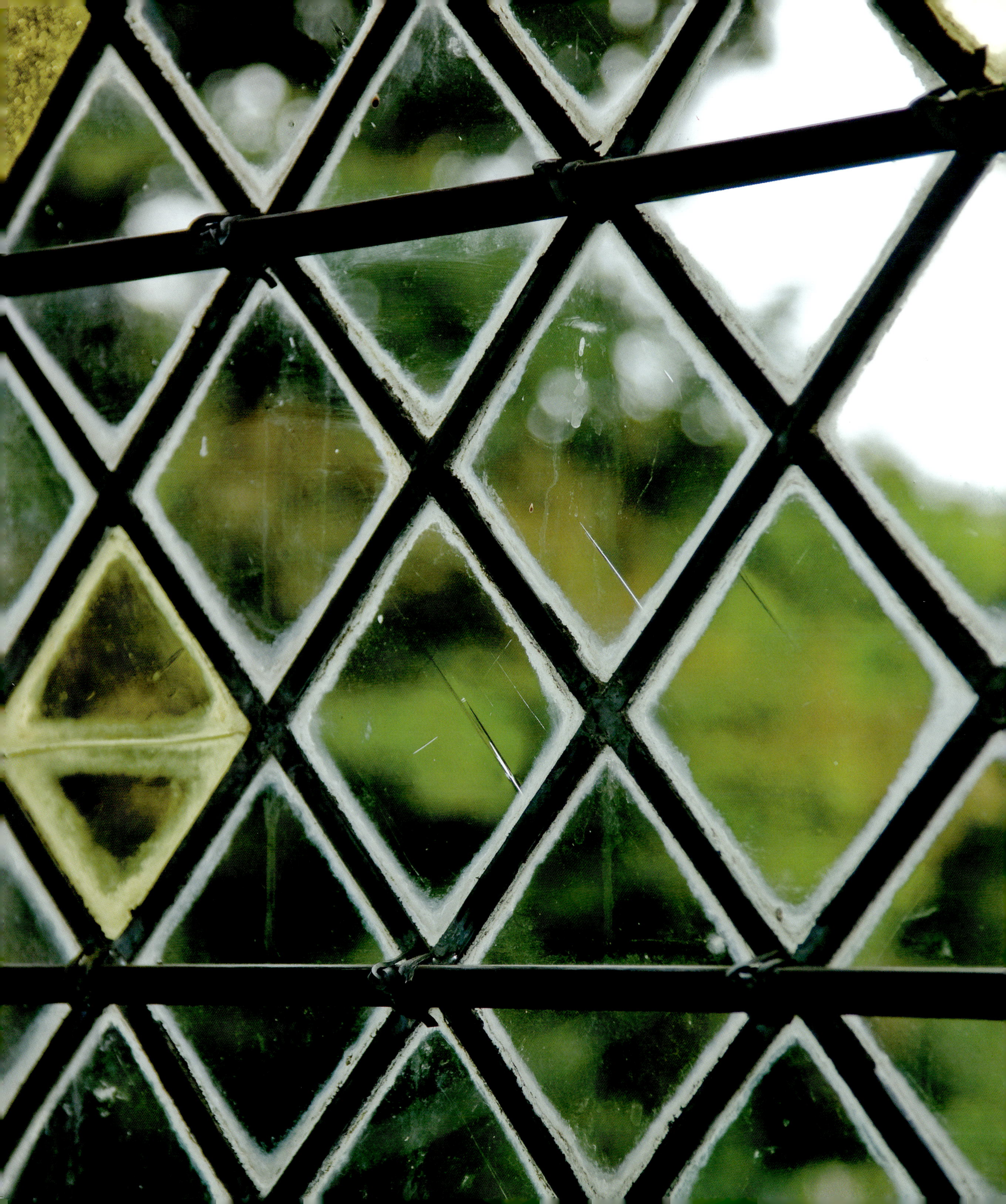

OLD SHIP MEETING HOUSE

Hingham, Massachusetts, 1681 (with later modifications)

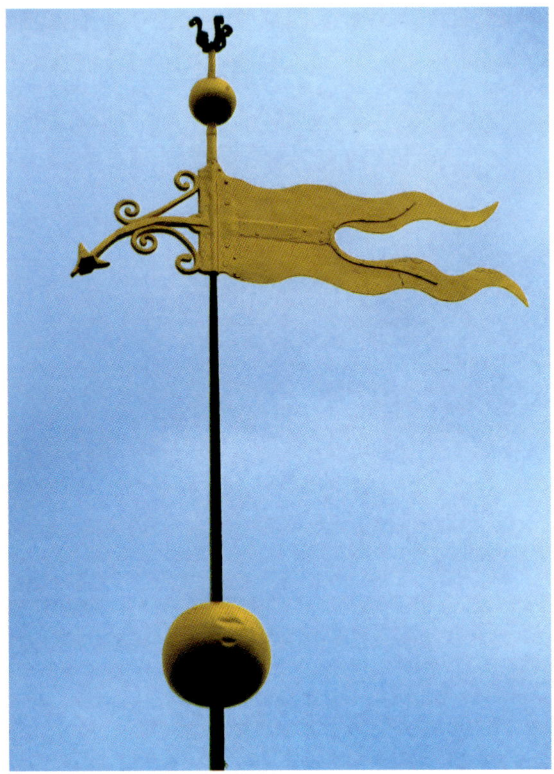

ABOVE *Weathervanes, like the Bible, foretold coming events. Like the steeple bell, its central location on the meeting house was convenient so all residents could be kept informed. This weathervane took a tumble once and still inadvertently points downward.*

RIGHT *This is the oldest surviving meeting house in New England. Despite additions (and some subtractions of Victorian features) it retains much of the character of First Period meeting houses. The enclosed entry porch was also found on some houses (see Judge Jonathan Corwin House, p. 52).*

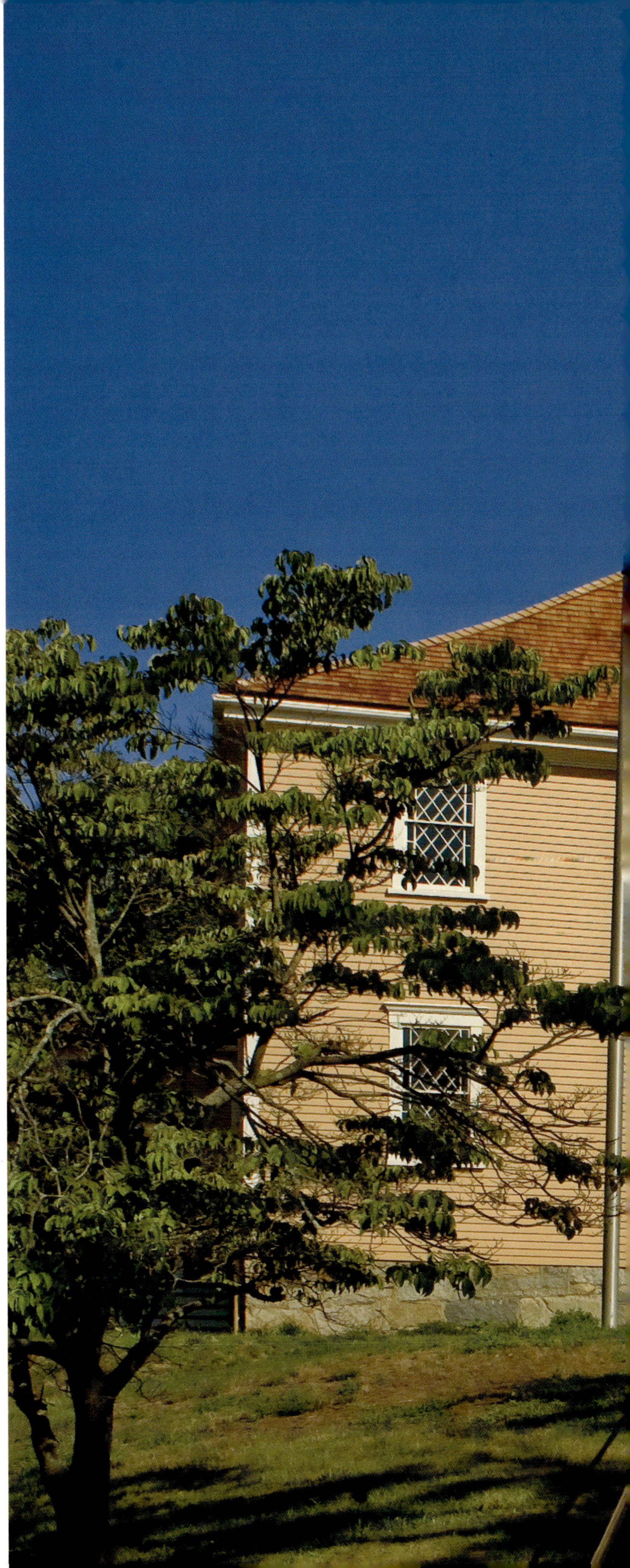

Hingham, 14 miles southeast of Boston, drew many of its first settlers from the town of the same name in Norfolk County, England, beginning in 1633. The Reverend Peter Hobart established the Parish of Hingham in 1635 when the town was organized and lands granted to families. With access to Boston Harbor, Hingham's future was wedded to the sea.

The town's location had an additional implication: it was on the border between Plymouth Colony (noted for relative tolerance), and the stricter Puritan settlements to the north. Reverend

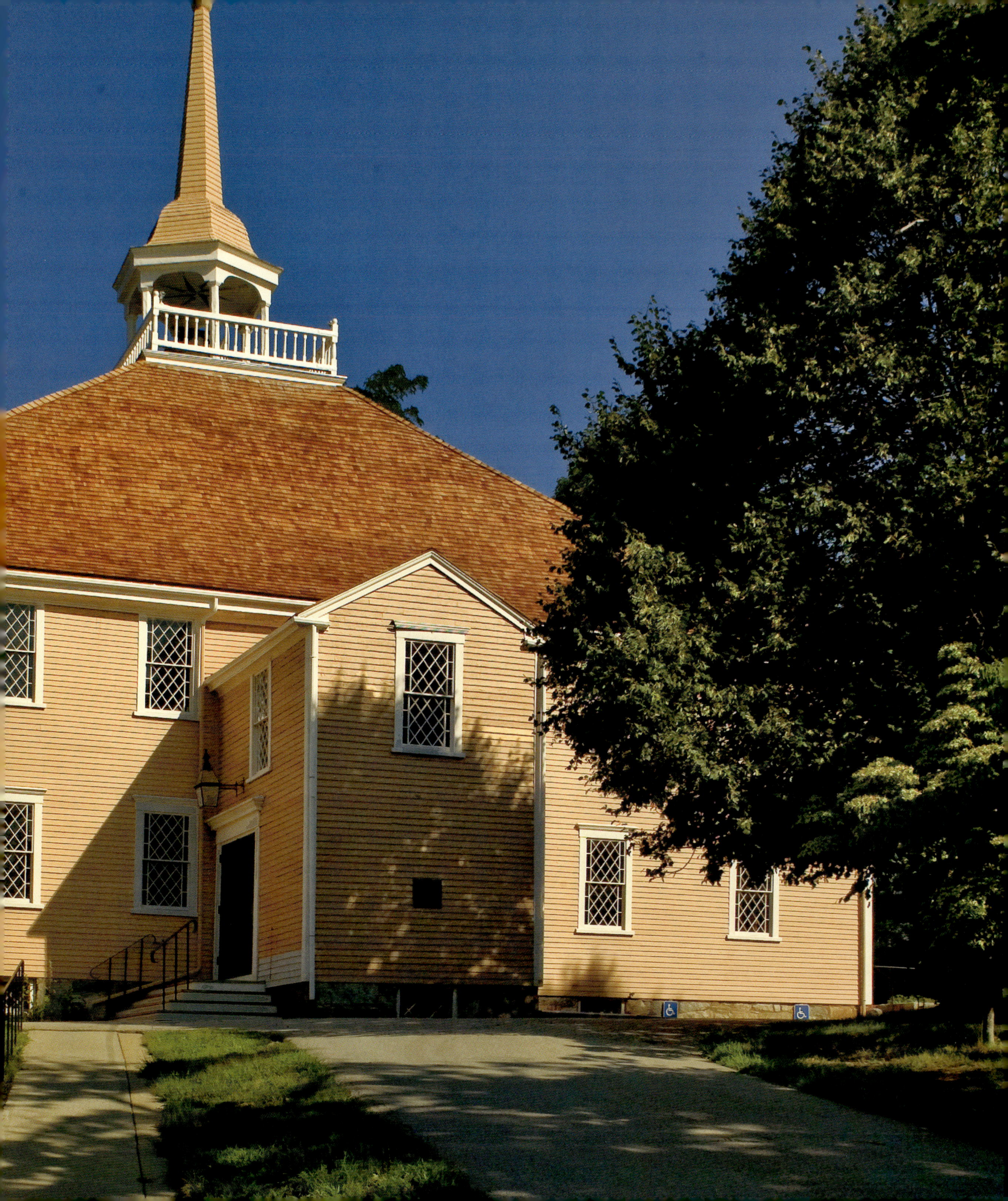

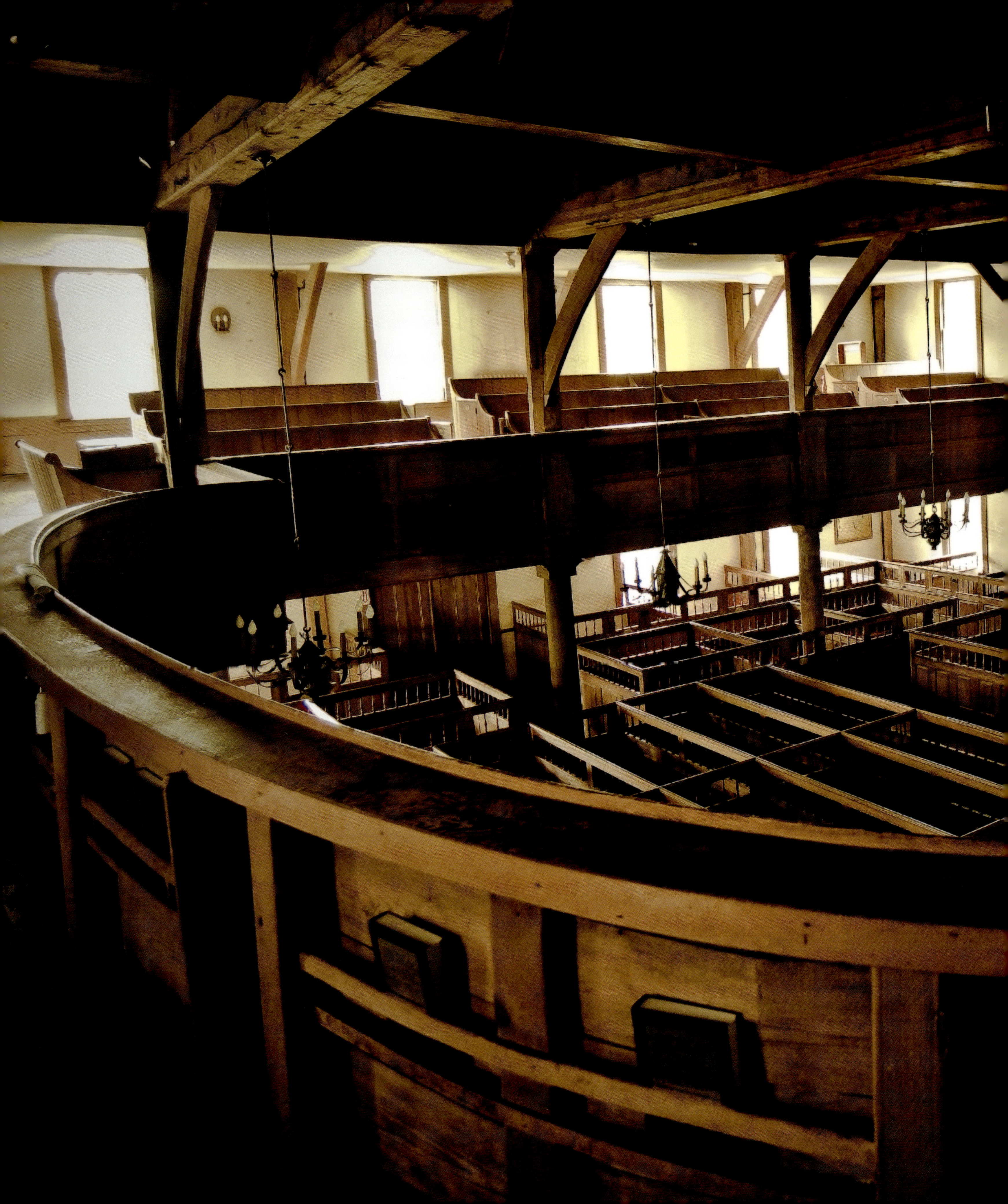

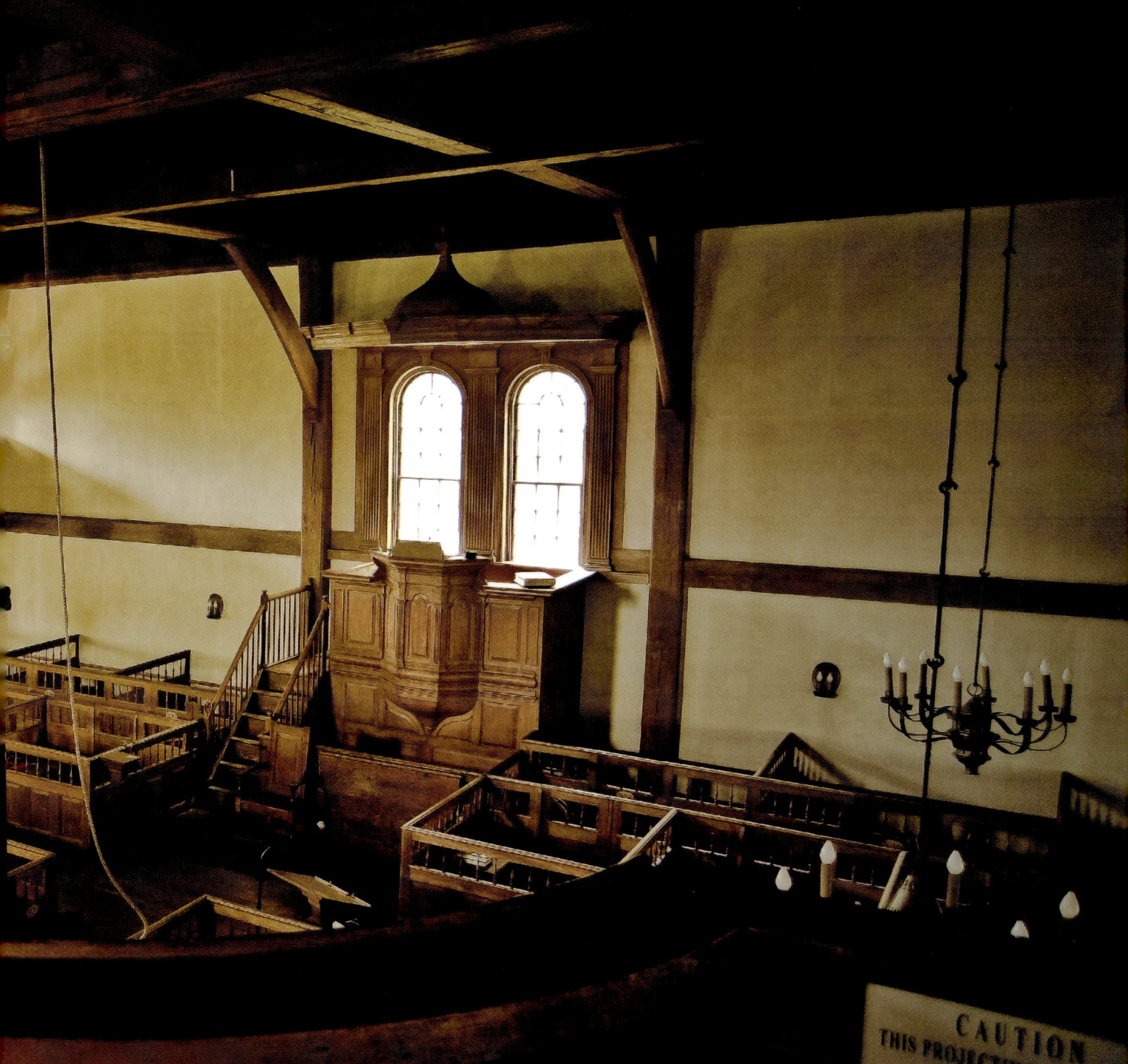
CAUTION
THIS PROJECTING
IS LIMITED TO

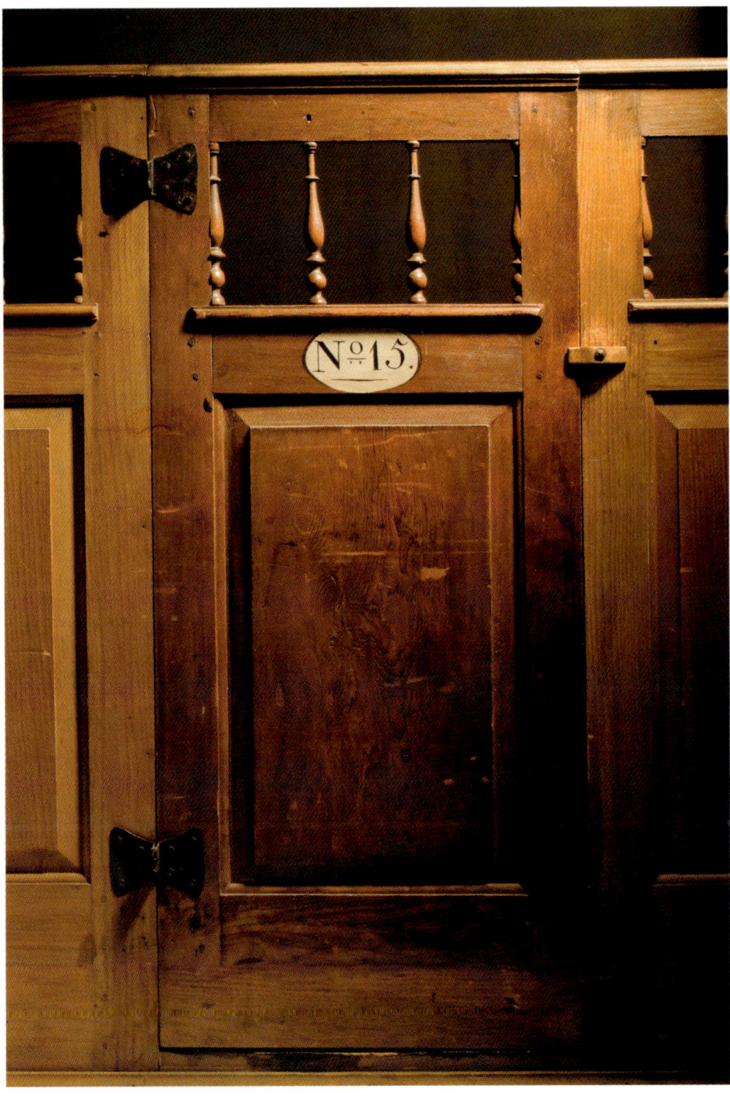

PREVIOUS PAGES *The original 1681 structure was contained within the braced posts. The side galleries were added on in 1731 and 1755. In the later year the second-level gallery was installed on three sides, and pews replaced existing benches. In 1869 the entire interior was Victorianized only to be undone in 1930 to its present appearance.*

LEFT *Pews replaced benches in many meeting houses in the mid-eighteenth century. Selling pews to families for their exclusive use became an efficient fundraiser for building later meeting houses.*

FACING PAGE *Centered on the long wall, across from the entrance, the minister preached for hours Sunday morning and afternoon, with only the pulpit windows to light his manuscript and a sounding board to carry his voice.*

Hobart's attitude of defiance to Governor John Winthrop characterized Hingham's Puritanism. To direct the civil and theological business of the town, a simple public meeting house was soon built that served until 1681 when a larger meeting house was built. This, of all the community houses in New England, is the only one to survive to the present day. For the religious Puritans, building a meeting house rather than a church appears puzzling to modern sensibilities. In fact, its logic conforms to the tenents of their faith—they considered it idolatrous to believe that holiness resided in building materials. No Puritan meeting house was ever consecrated. As such it could serve multiple purposes, including the civic center of the community for town meetings—still the New England form of local government—where decisions, including voting on taxes and electing officials, were made by all.

The singular appearance of this medieval structure derives not just from being the last of its type but from its dissimilarity from any domestic houses of the period and from all later churches whose Classical edifices derived from those built by architect Christopher Wren in post-fire London. As a result of this uniqueness, speculative interpretation led to the meeting house being called "Old Ship" because its roof structure was thought to resemble an inverted hull. In fact, the roof is a conventional hipped roof, rising from all four sides, a design suitable to covering a large structure. The meeting house is 45 feet by 55 feet, large for its time and place.

From town records, raising the meeting house was a community undertaking. After much discussion in the small old structure, each freeman contributed to the cost in accordance with his worth. Its interior arrangement departs emphatically from the Anglican church model—not surprising, since Puritanism was a dissenting faith from the mother church and its head, the king. Instead of a long sanctuary focused on an altar in the nave, the meeting house was nearly an egalitarian square, focused on a pulpit with backless wooden benches running the length of the space. Rigorous self-testing of the faithful extended to no heating or lighting devices nor any ornamentation save some chamfering on the plain-hewn roof beams.

In subsequent years major changes were made. One side was widened by 14 feet in 1731, as was the other side in 1755, creating side galleries. That same year, the benches were replaced by pews, a second-level gallery installed on three sides, leaded-glass windows were replaced by sash windows, and two porches were added with Georgian features. Outside, original small gables centered on each side of the roof were removed, the roof extended over the side additions, and the belfry rebuilt. Inside, walls were plastered and a ceiling installed covering the roof structure. The new upper-level gallery in the rear was for the use of black servants and was known as the "slave galleries." A replacement pulpit of mahogany was installed in 1832.

Then in 1869, shortly after the last of the pews were constructed, all were torn out and replaced with curved and cush-

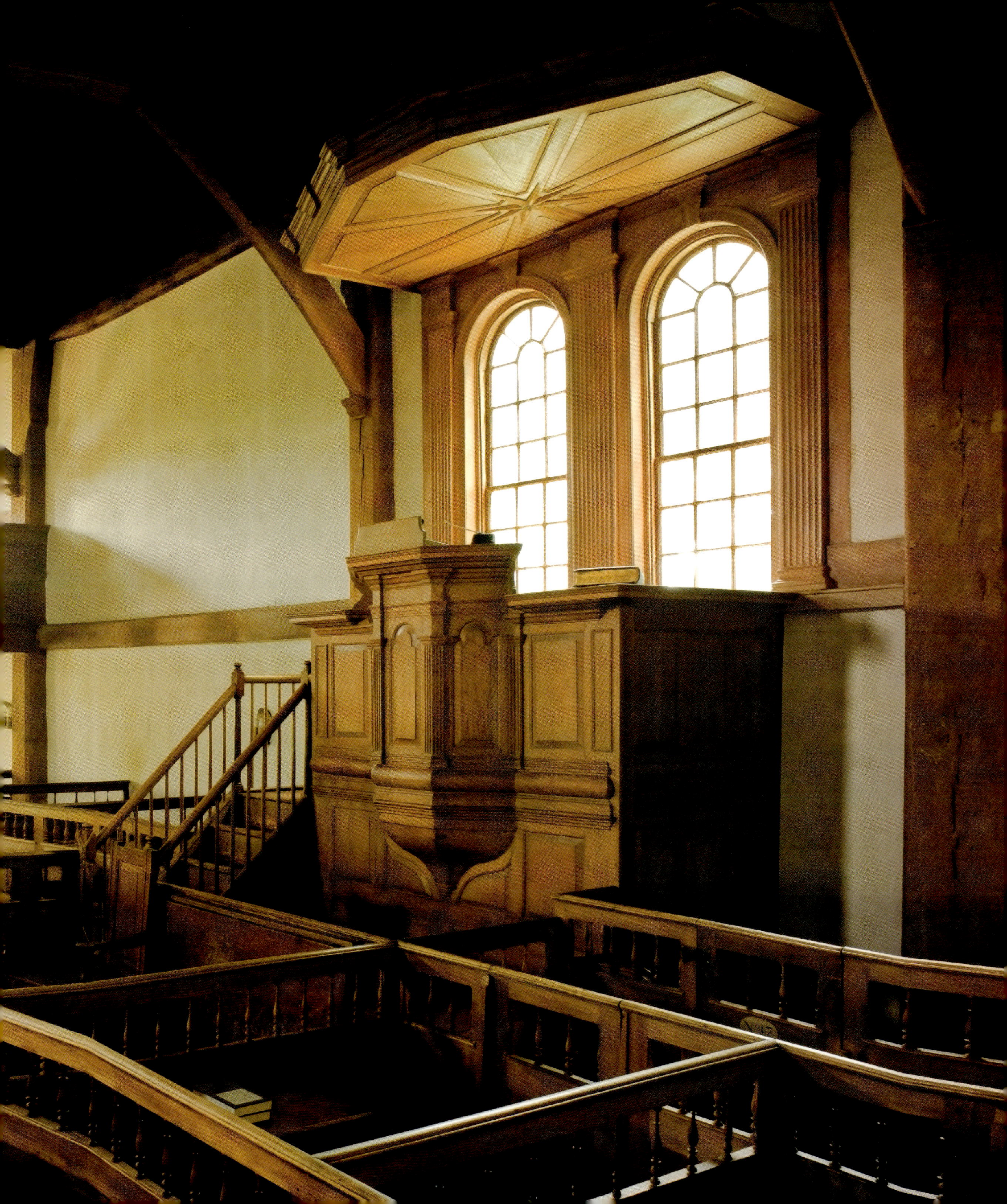

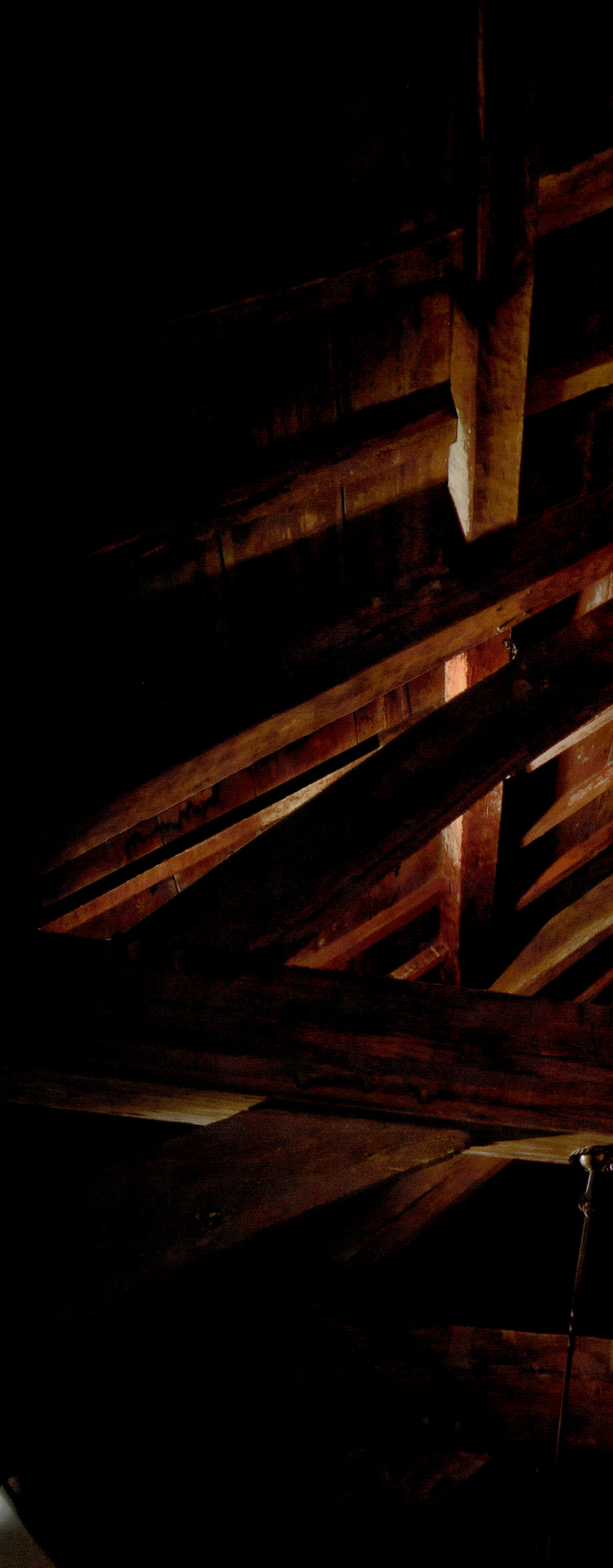

RIGHT *With thoughts drifting during long sermons, puzzling out the complexity of the roof structure must have bemused many. A line of vertical king posts joined curved lower rafters and main horizontal beams to form strong triangles supporting the heavy roof of major and minor rafters, purlins, joists, roof boards, and shingles. The arched lower rafters, like sailing ship ribs, provide extra tension strength to support the main rafters. This was a formidable challenge for housewrights building one- and two-room houses.*

ioned benches and the entire interior decorated in ornate Victorian style. In 1906, a two-story wing was added at the rear of the building, which contains the church parlor with its large working fireplace, a kitchen with good catering facilities, an office, a nursery, and a large ballroom. The second-floor ballroom has over the years been used by various local groups for theatrical performances, as a nursery school classroom, and as a dance school studio. The Victoriana lasted until 1930 when a descendant of a long serving eighteenth-century minister funded the restoration of the meeting house to its early appearance, including returning many of the eighteenth-century pews and uncovering the roof structure.

A parish, of course, is people more than structure. The First Parish of Hingham enjoyed the ministering of exceptional pastors, most serving lengthy periods of time. The Reverend Peter Hobart set the tone of relative liberalism, which persisted with most of his successors. It was during the thirty-five-year tenure of his successor, the Reverend John Norton, that the 1681 meeting house was built, and it is a credit to Norton's persuasiveness. He was followed by Ebenezer Gay, a young Harvard graduate who spent the rest of his ninety-year life as pastor to Hingham, spanning most of the eighteenth century. His distinctively liberal theology laid the foundation for the congregation's future Unitarianism. In 1805 the Reverend Henry Ware, who had followed Reverend Gay as pastor at Hingham, was called from this parish to become professor of divinity at Harvard College. Harvard was founded in 1636 in part to ensure the New World a supply of educated ministers; half of all graduates followed the Calling. His appointment was controversial at Harvard because of his liberal preaching, leading to a split in Puritanism into its Unitarian and Congregational wings (the American Unitarian Association was founded in 1825). His leaving Hingham also precipitated a division in the congregation over the choice of a successor, part of which established their own congregation.

Yet, like this rare surviving structure, the Unitarian Universalist congregation has also persisted. The Old Ship is believed to be in continuous ecclesiastical use longer than any other meeting house (its civil function continued to 1780). Its congregation continues the tradition of welcoming persons of diverse outlook. Today, the meeting house is supported by the Friends of the Old Ship Meeting House, a nonsectarian charitable trust formed in 1971.

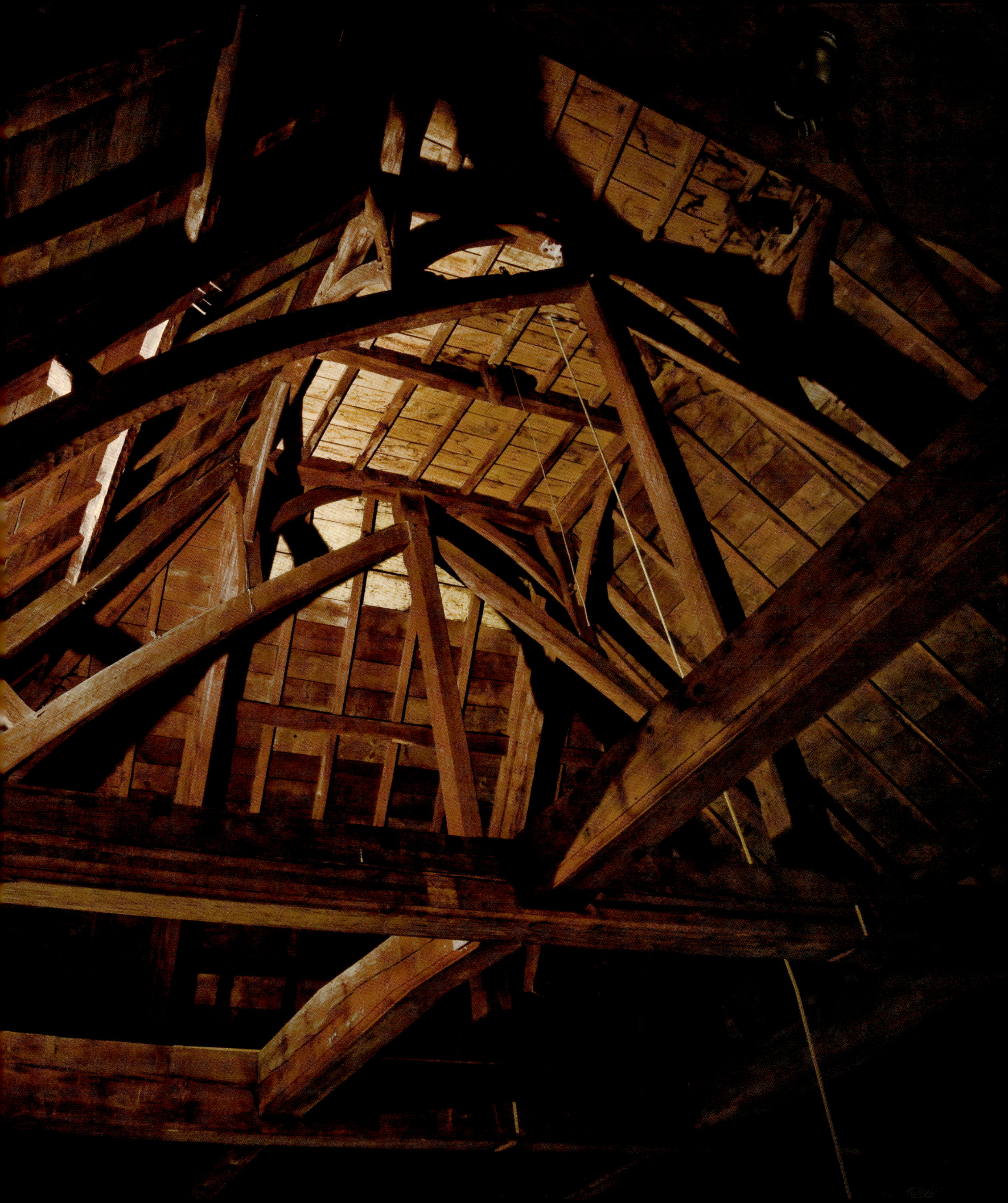

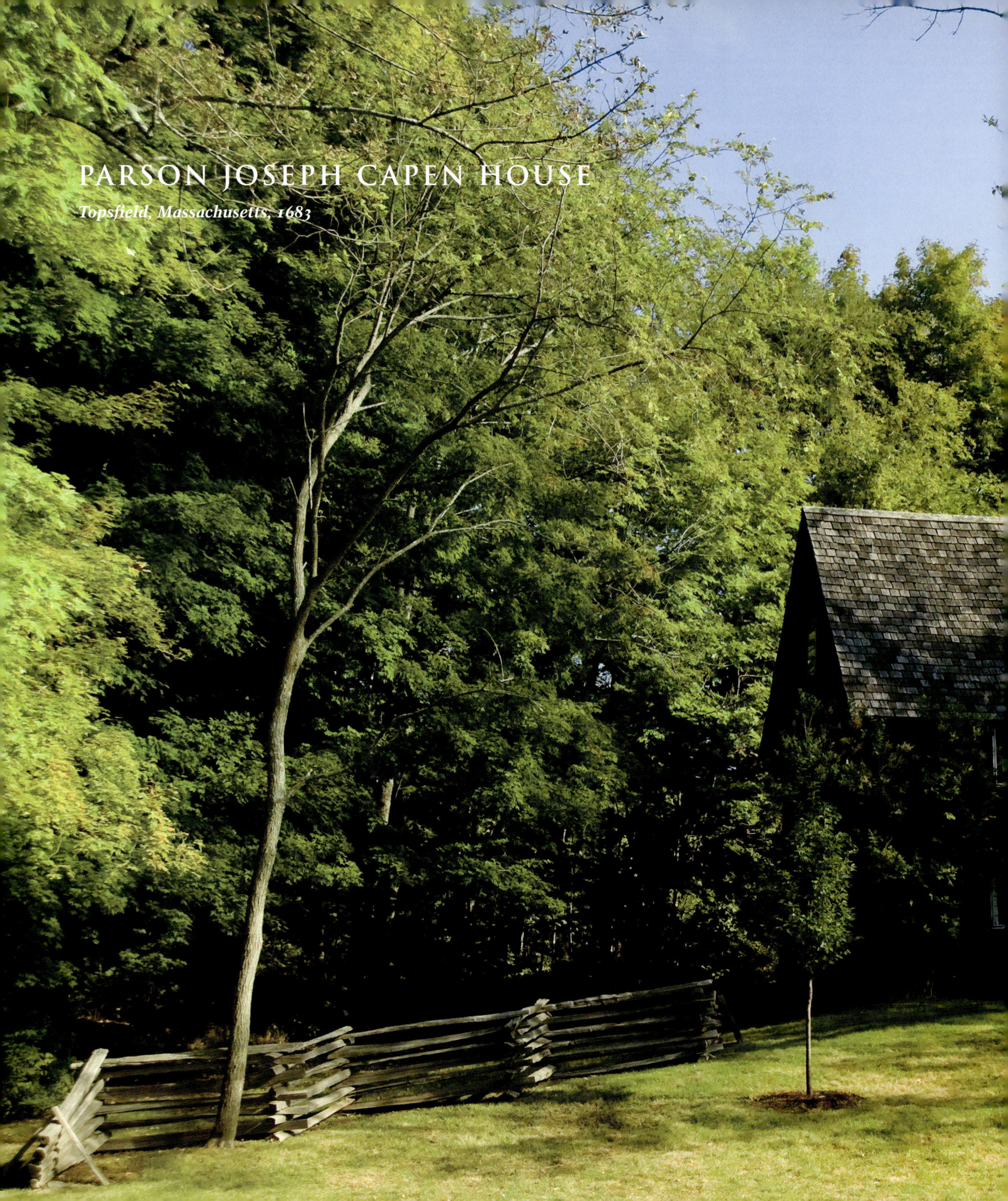

PARSON JOSEPH CAPEN HOUSE

Topsfield, Massachusetts, 1683

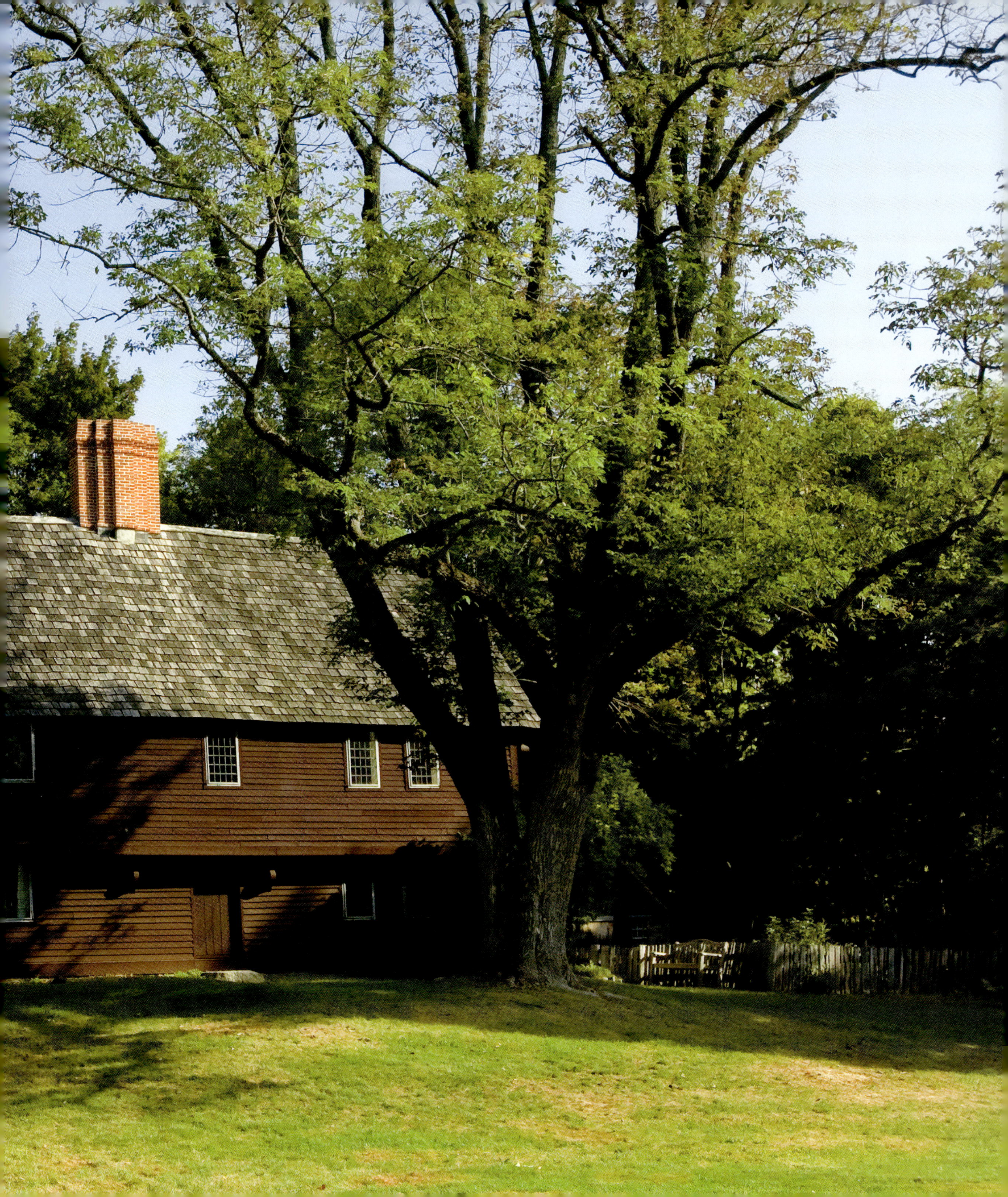

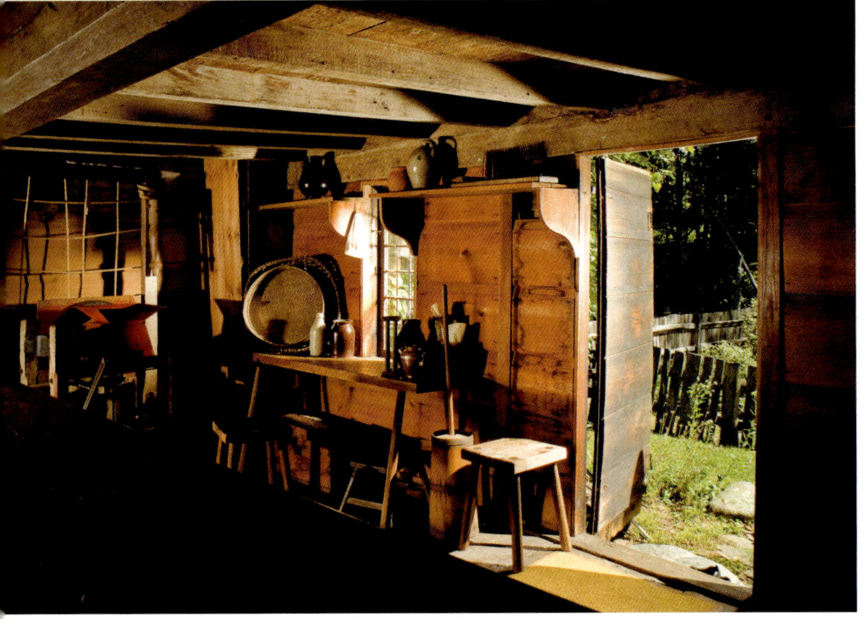

PREVIOUS PAGES *Parson Capen's house has an elegance that has been lost or perhaps never existed in most other early New England houses. Although not large or symmetrical, its pilastered chimney, triple overhang, shaped drops, and brackets are as impressive as its site on a rise overlooking the common.*

LEFT *The clutter of this hall (kitchen)—with a folding bed at the rear—shows the density of family life, which was centered in this one room. The utter lack of privacy—only the husband and wife got the privacy of the parlor (left of front door)—was a prime motivation for the eighteenth-century adoption of the large Classical house with multiple bedrooms.*

FACING PAGE *In the corner of the hall (kitchen) is the pantry.*

FOLLOWING PAGES *The hall (kitchen) fireplace is remarkably wide (8 feet), which required the support of a 16-inches square hearth beam. This is one of the few early houses which did not have a rear lean-to added. Thus the hall continued to serve as the kitchen and dining room throughout its life.*

Essex County, north of Boston, was first settled along its coast, and in the 1630s fertile agricultural lands inland attracted Puritans to New Meadows along the Agawam (now Ipswich) River. This town was incorporated as Topsfield in 1650 with a meeting house built by 1658. Despite the promising land, the Congregational Church itself had got off to an awkward start. Two of the last three ministers had difficulty getting paid, and another was put on trial for intemperance. In 1683 the Reverend Joseph Capen (1650–1725), fresh out of Harvard College, joined the church as minister. Granted 12 acres on a knoll just off the common, he built this handsome house in lieu of taking up the more modest parsonage, which his wife Priscilla objected to. She was from the well-off Appleton family, which may account for this special accommodation. Its heavy oak frame twice bears the inscription "JUL Ye 8. 1683," establishing a firm date, which is a rarity among early houses.

Many have remarked on the Elizabethan-style perfection of the house, pointing out its steep roof, tall pilastered chimney, and overhanging second floor (and on the gable ends, third-story overhangs) decorated with pendants and brackets. Entering the house, to the left is the larger room, the parlor, which required two summer beams to span its ample 17-1/2-by-19-foot space, suitable for ministering to his congregation. To the right, the somewhat shorter hall (kitchen) has an 8-foot-wide fireplace with a massive 16-inch square fireplace beam, rounded back corners, and a bake oven. Before the central chimney, the original stairway winds to sleeping chambers above.

Parson Capen's long tenure in Topsfield (he resided in the house for forty-two years until his death) included the 1690s witchcraft accusations. Some of his parishioners had been accused, and, seeking to resolve differences, he attempted a meeting at his house, to no avail—three women from his congregation were tried and hanged. Later he signed a petition condemning the use of spectral evidence—the main weapon of the accusers—and helping to bring the trials to an end. On another occasion one of his parishioners, John Gould, was charged by neighbors with uttering treasonous words against the king, their accusations leading to Gould's incarceration in Boston. Capen brought the parties together and affected a reconciliation. The growing congregation was reflected in the much larger meeting house built in 1703, which held more pews and galleries—and was closer to Capen's home.

The structure of the community was well represented by how such meeting houses were laid out. Those of status—large land owners, militia officers, constables, court appointees, surveyors, fence viewers, and others responsible for community order—sat with their families in pews, while commoners sat on benches, farther from the pulpit, men on one side, women on the other. By his death Capen could be satisfied to see Topsfield a prosperous and well-regulated community, partially from his contributions.

As the most distinguished of early houses in Topsfield it was logical that residents would seek the preservation of the Capen House. In 1913 the Topsfield Historical Society purchased the property through the efforts of George Francis Dow, founder of the society and noted historian. Dow subsequently undertook its restoration. Observing that much change had taken place on the interior over the years, the restoration was guided by original features found in other early houses.

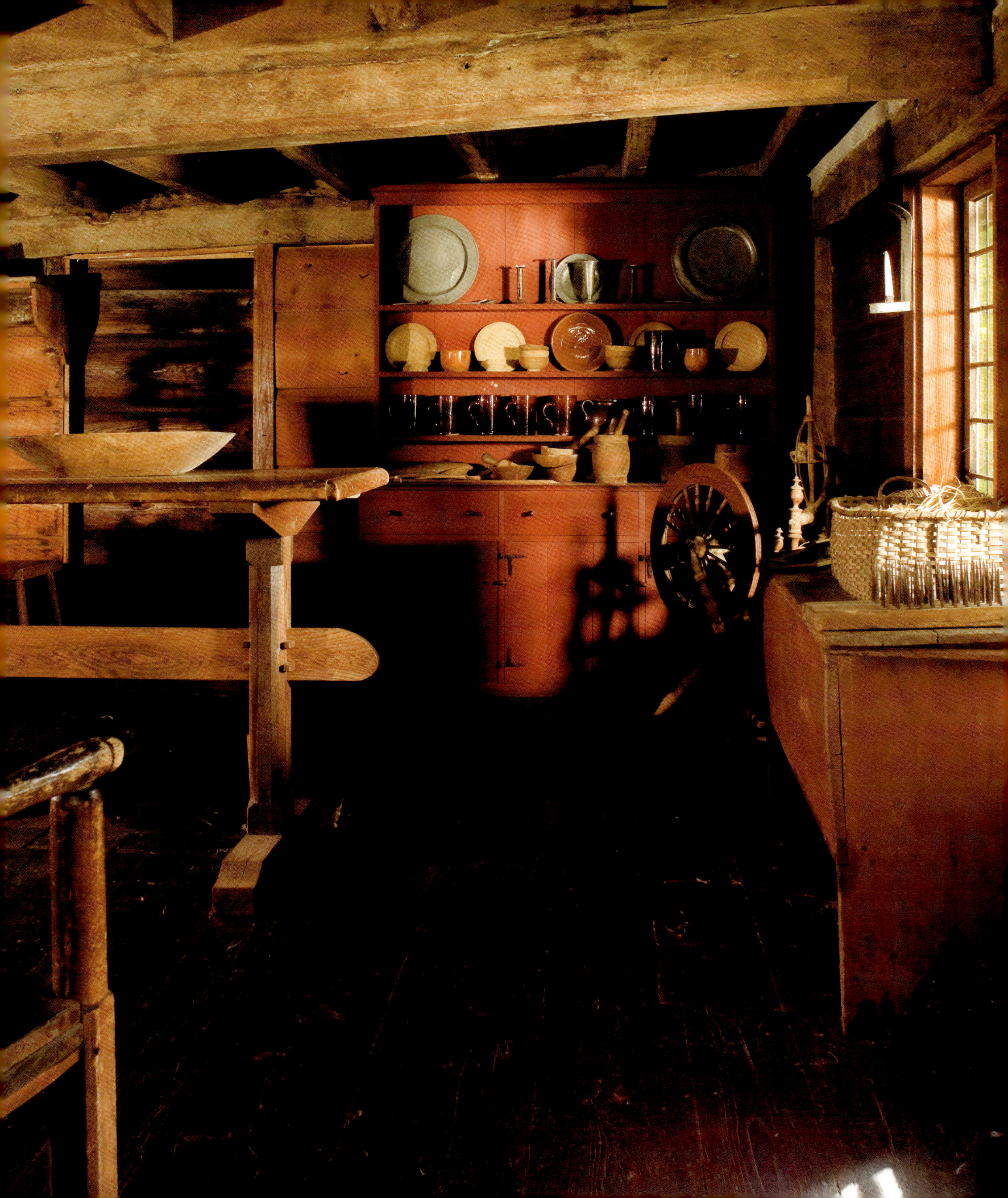

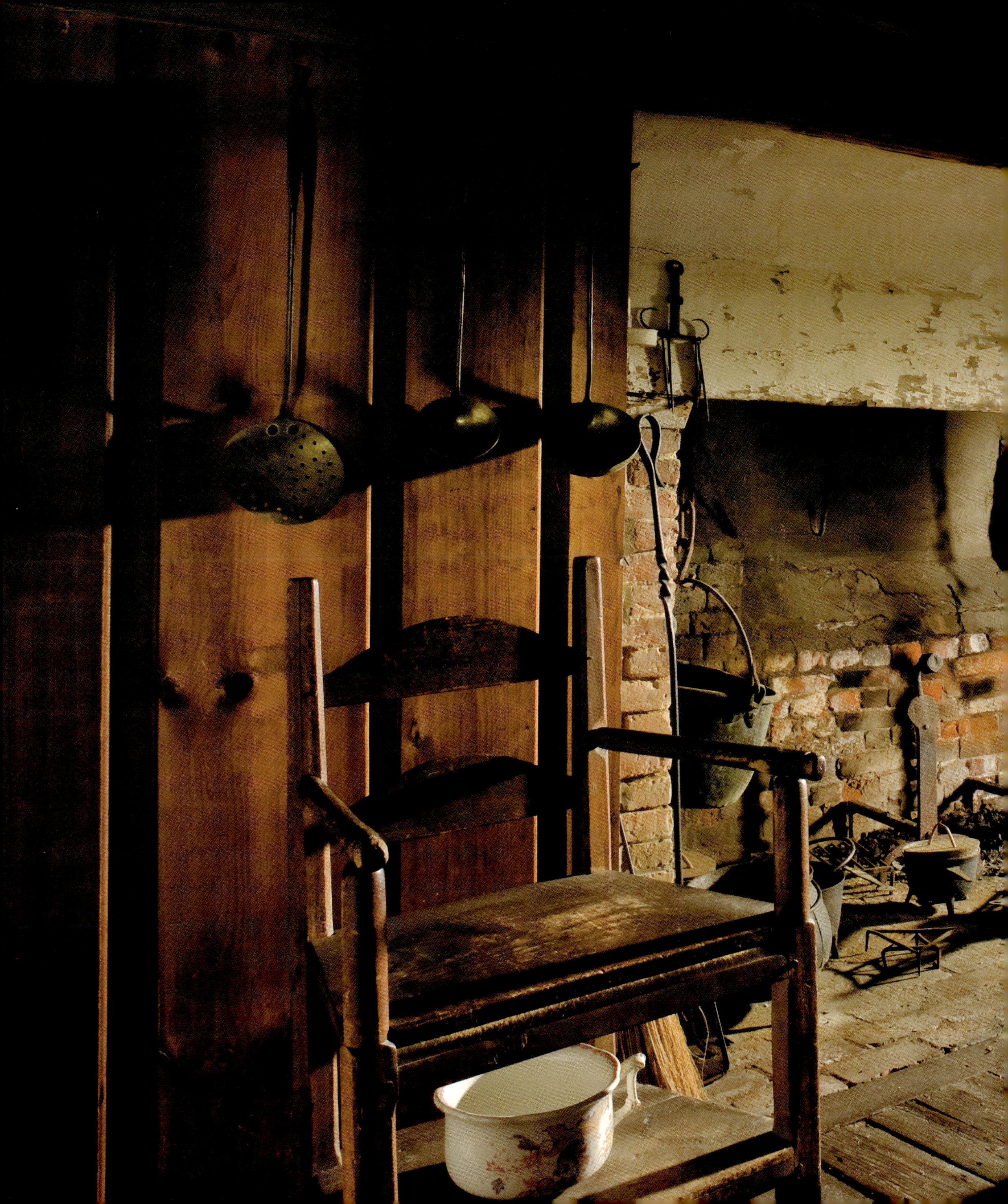

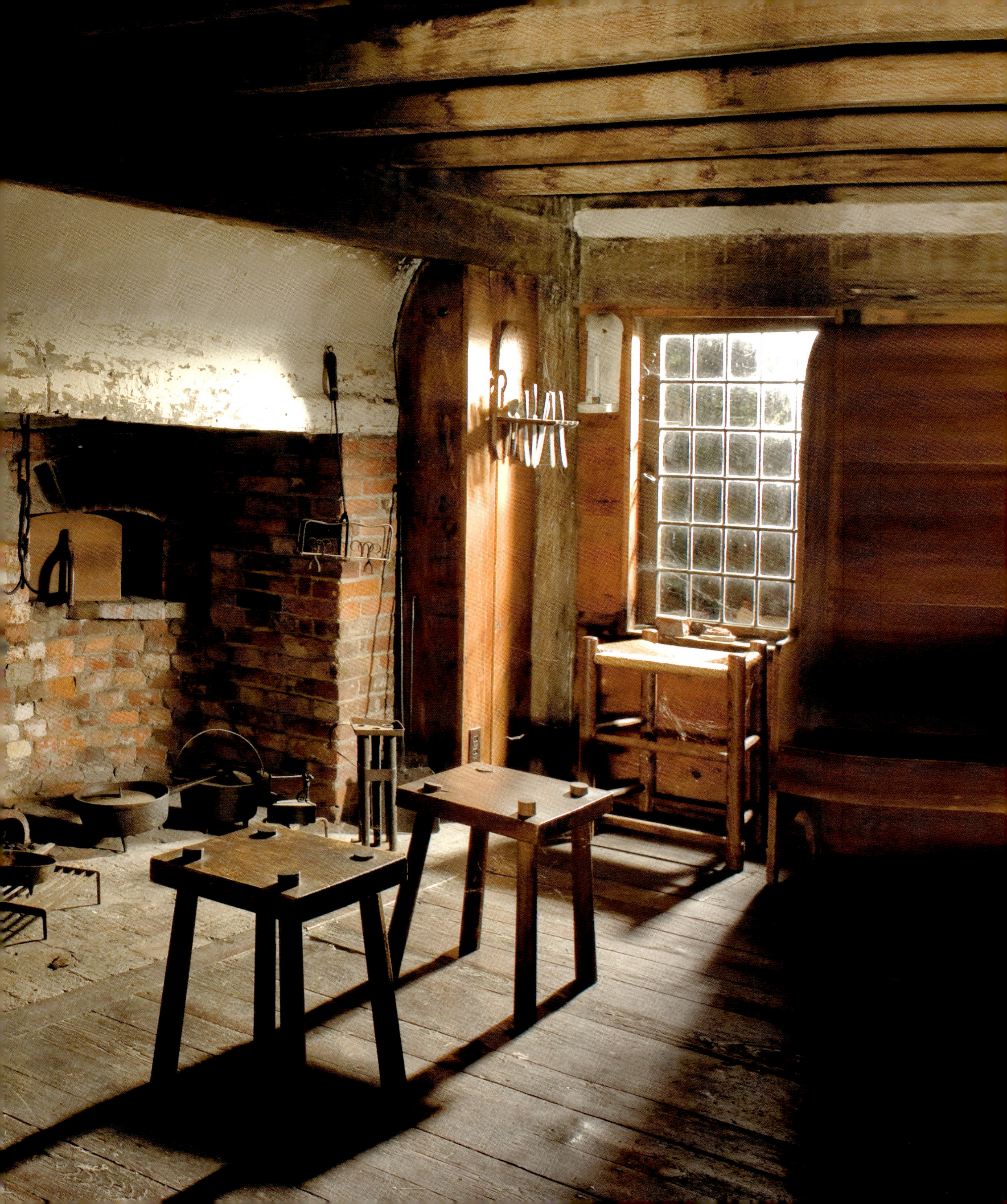

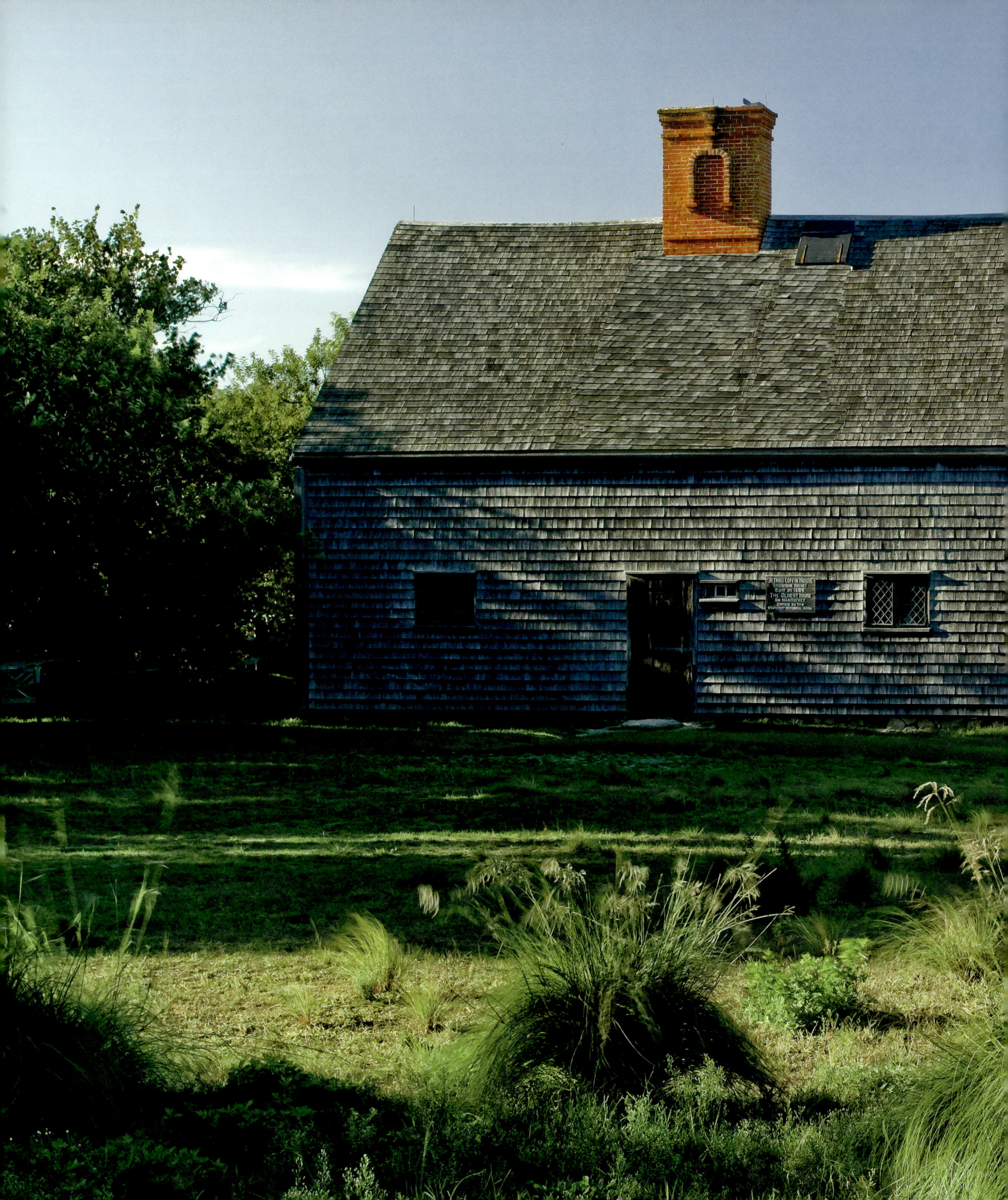
JETHRO COFFIN HOUSE
BUILT IN 1686
THE OLDEST HOUSE
ON NANTUCKET
OWNED BY THE

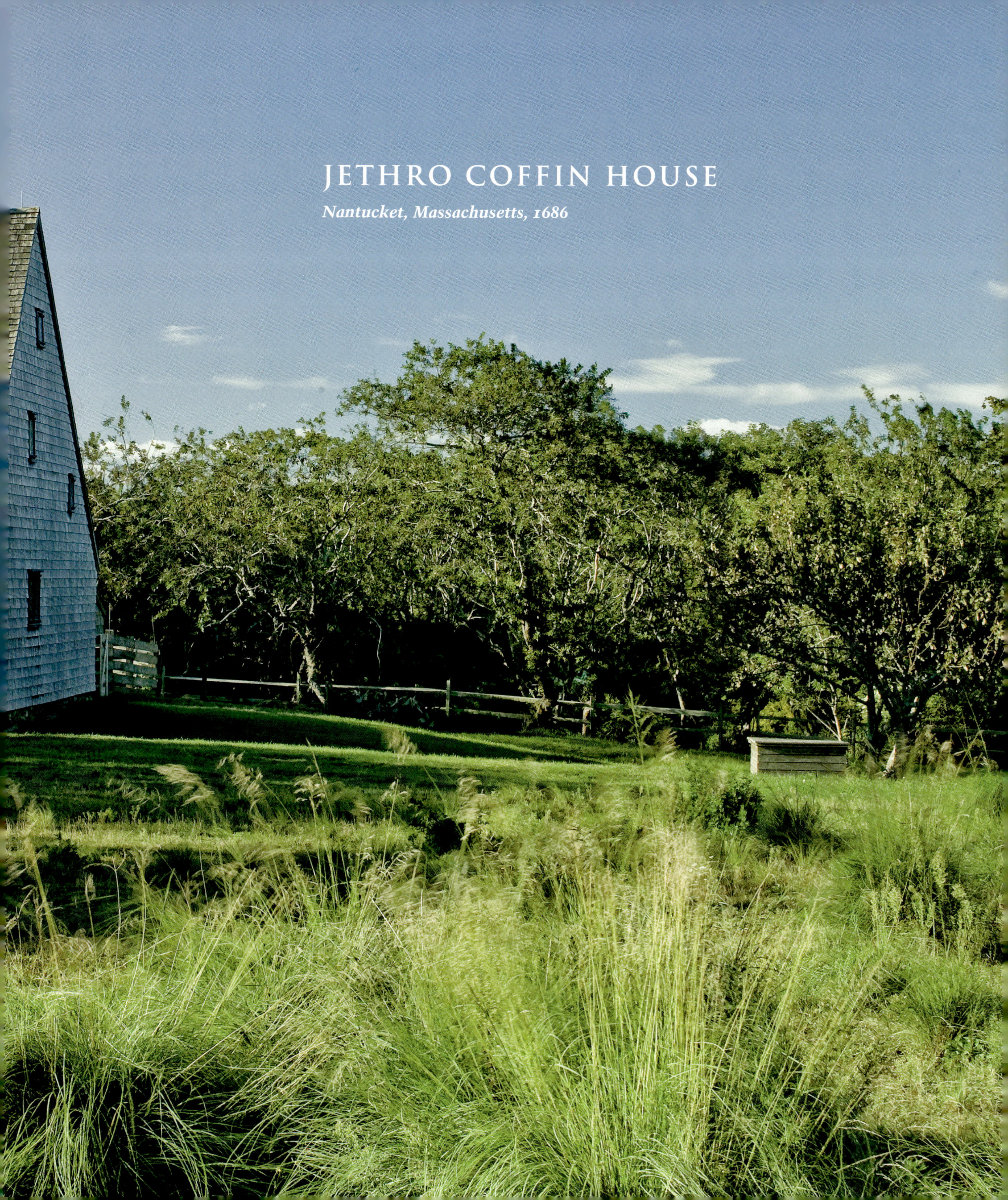

JETHRO COFFIN HOUSE

Nantucket, Massachusetts, 1686

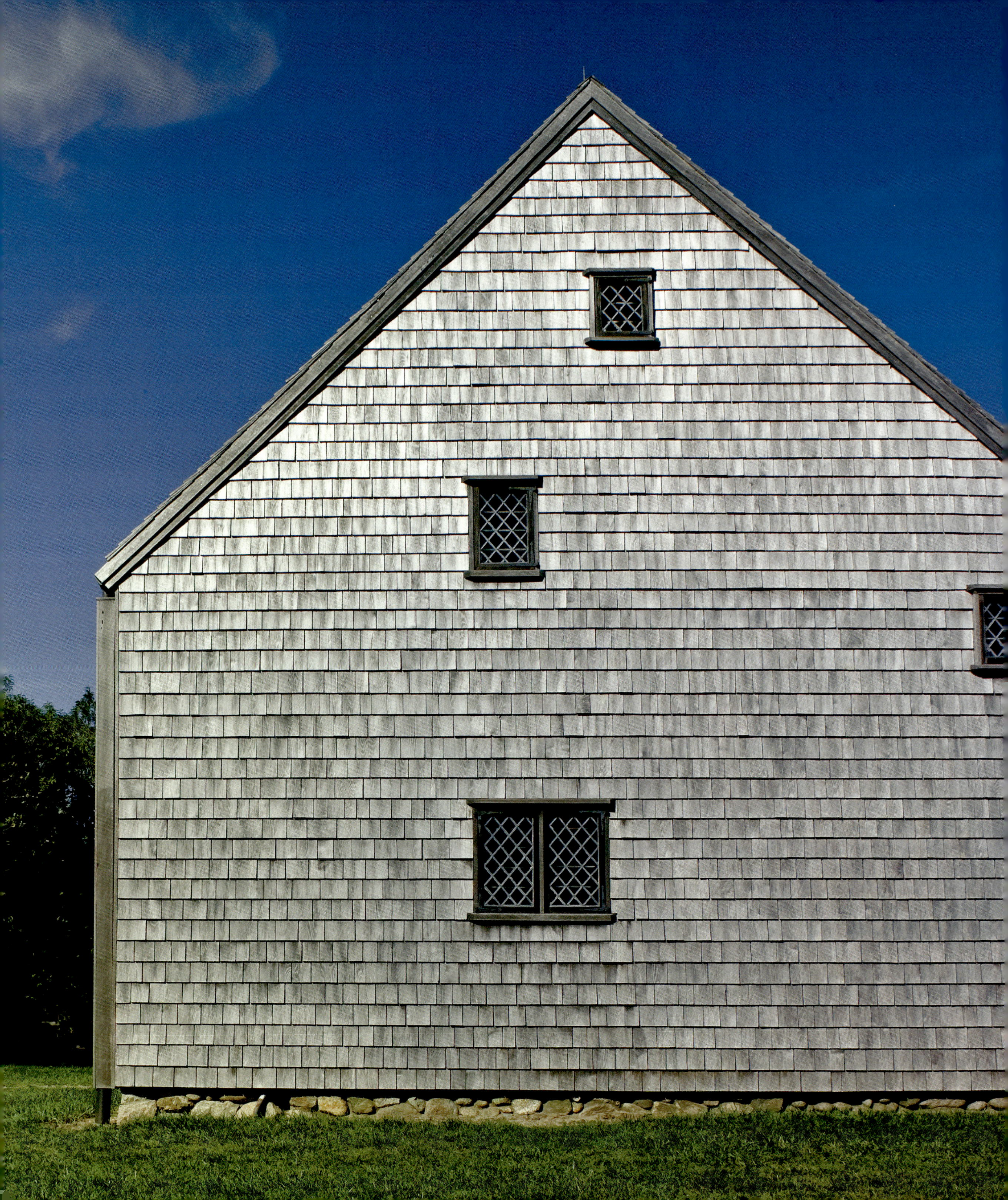

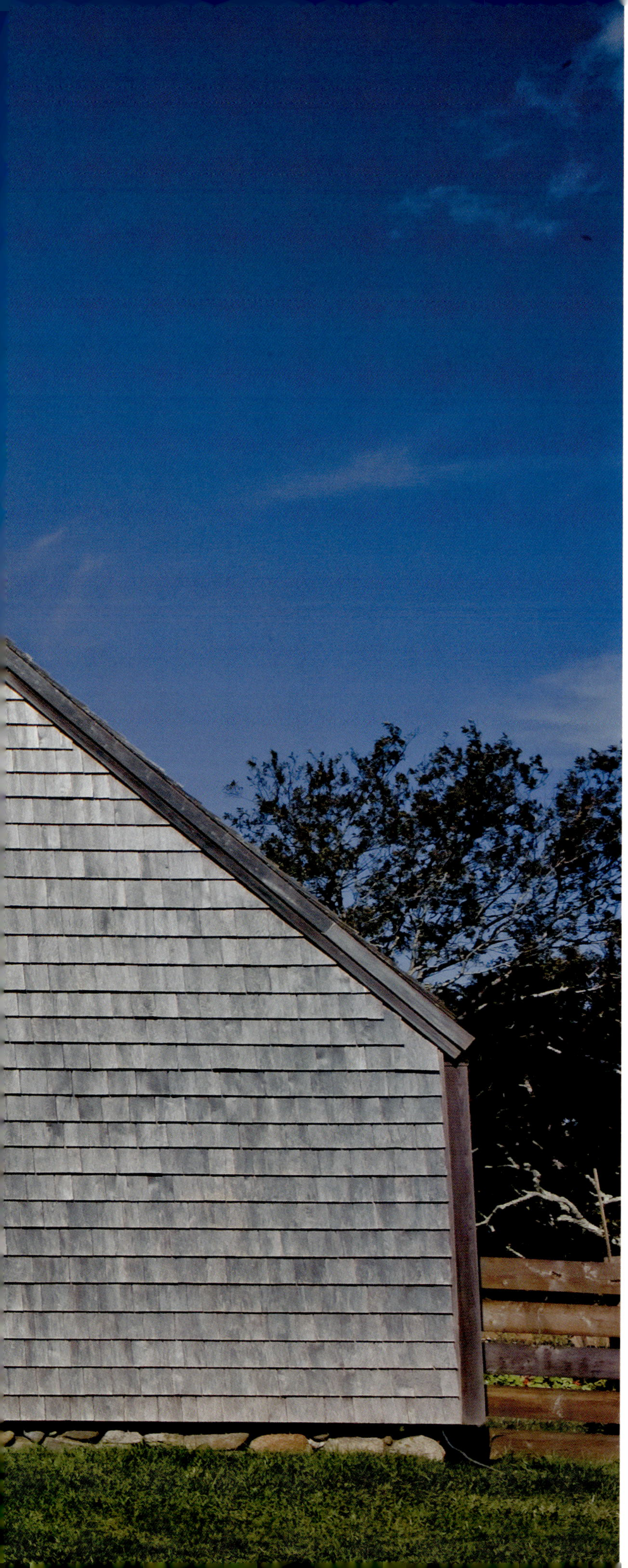

PREVIOUS PAGES *Medieval houses, although not intended to be aesthetic statements, are often arresting to the eye. The Coffin House is just such an expression of Puritan life—stunning in its simplicity. Two centuries later the Shakers, out of a similar dedication to a simple life of faith, left us with an analogous visual statement.*

LEFT *Completely asymmetric—a common characteristic in medieval structures—the windows bestow a sense of balance to the whole.*

BELOW *The kitchen in the lean-to differs from others as the fireplace is built out into the room rather than being enclosed within the massive chimney stack.*

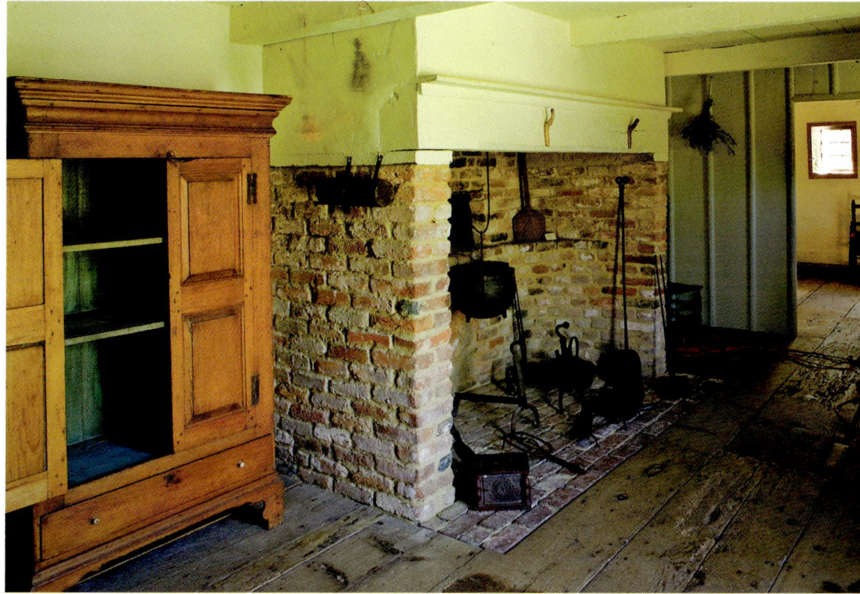

Nantucket has been a special island from its first sighting, perhaps by Norsemen in the eleventh century. Captain Bartholomew Gosnold of Falmouth, England, sailed past in 1602, putting it on the map. The native Wampanoag lived there undisturbed until 1641 when the island was deeded to Thomas Mayhew, merchant of Watertown and nearby Martha's Vineyard, who sold it off to a group of nine in 1659 for thirty pounds and two beaver hats (for the seller and his wife). Until 1691 it was part of New York Province, and then it was transferred to the newly formed Province of Massachusetts.

The oldest and only surviving seventeenth-century residence on Nantucket is the Jethro Coffin House, built in 1686 as a wedding present to blacksmith Jethro Coffin (d. 1727) and his wife Mary Gardner by their parents. He was a grandson of one of the original nine proprietors of Nantucket Island, Tristram Coffin, progenitor of a prolific family in America. Jethro sold the house in 1708 to island weaver Nathaniel Paddack, who in turn sold it to cooper George Turner in the 1840s, who abandoned it in the Civil War depression years. A large portion of the town had been destroyed by fire in 1846, the whaling industry was in decline, and Nantucket suffered a century of neglect and depop-

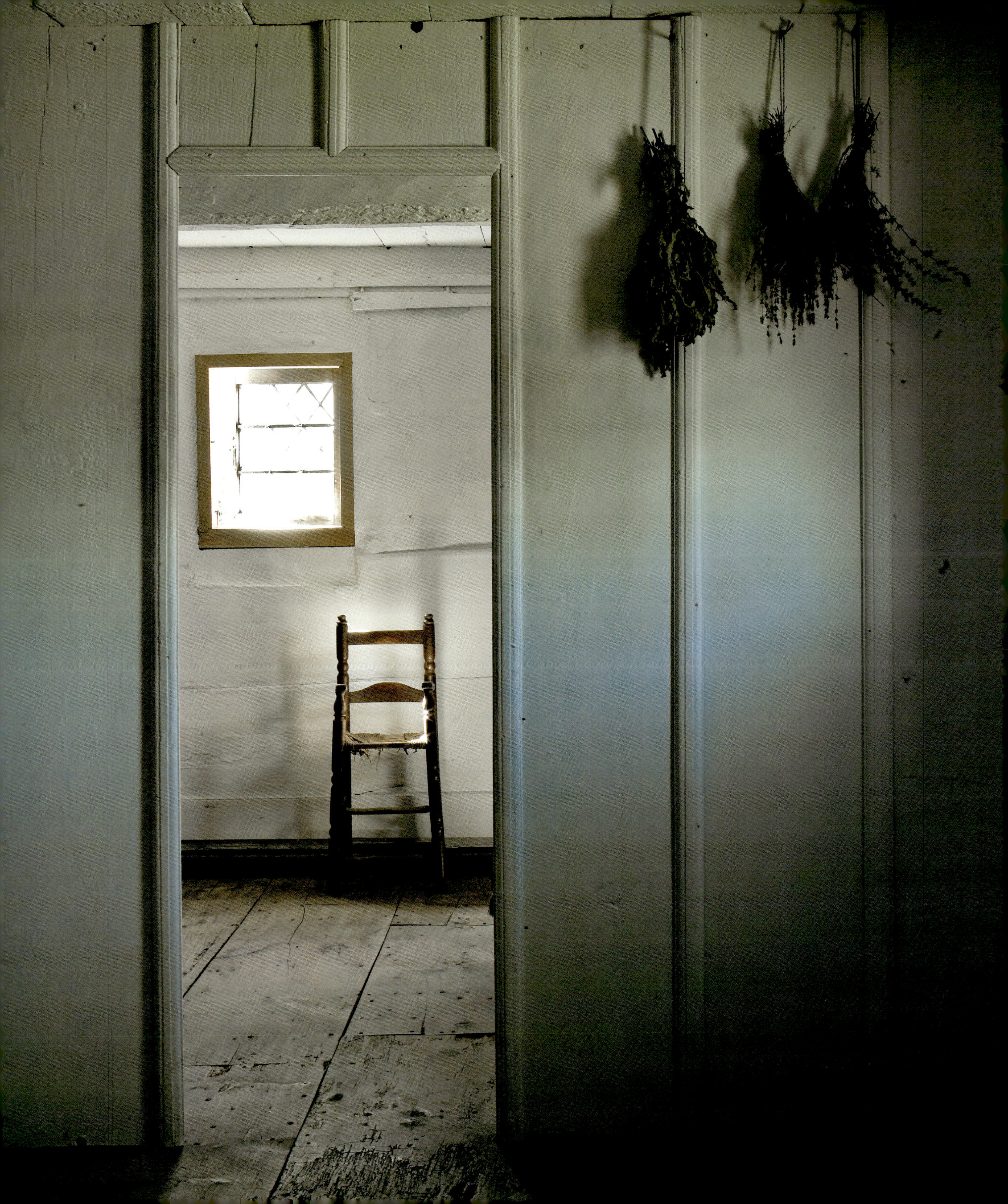

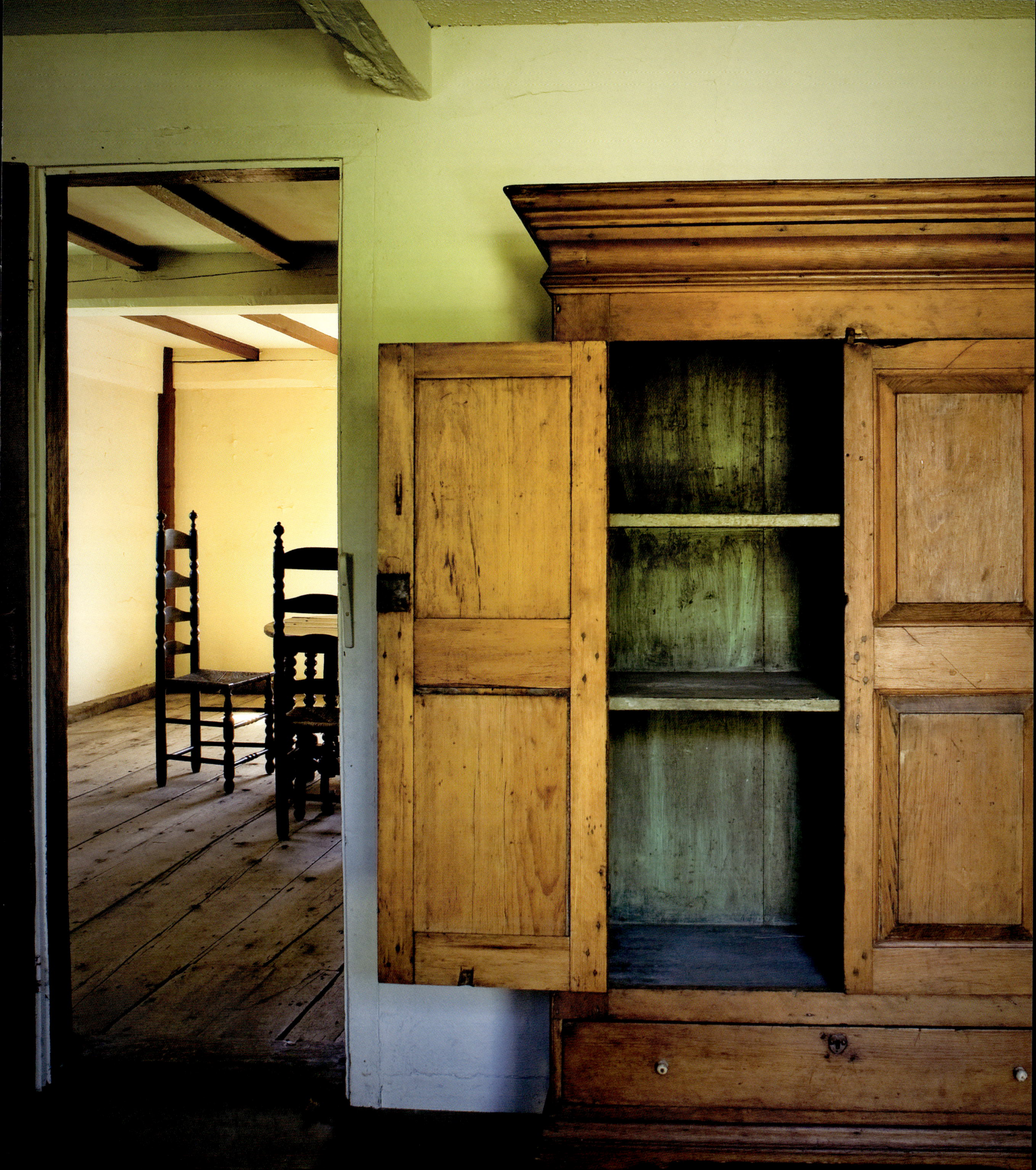

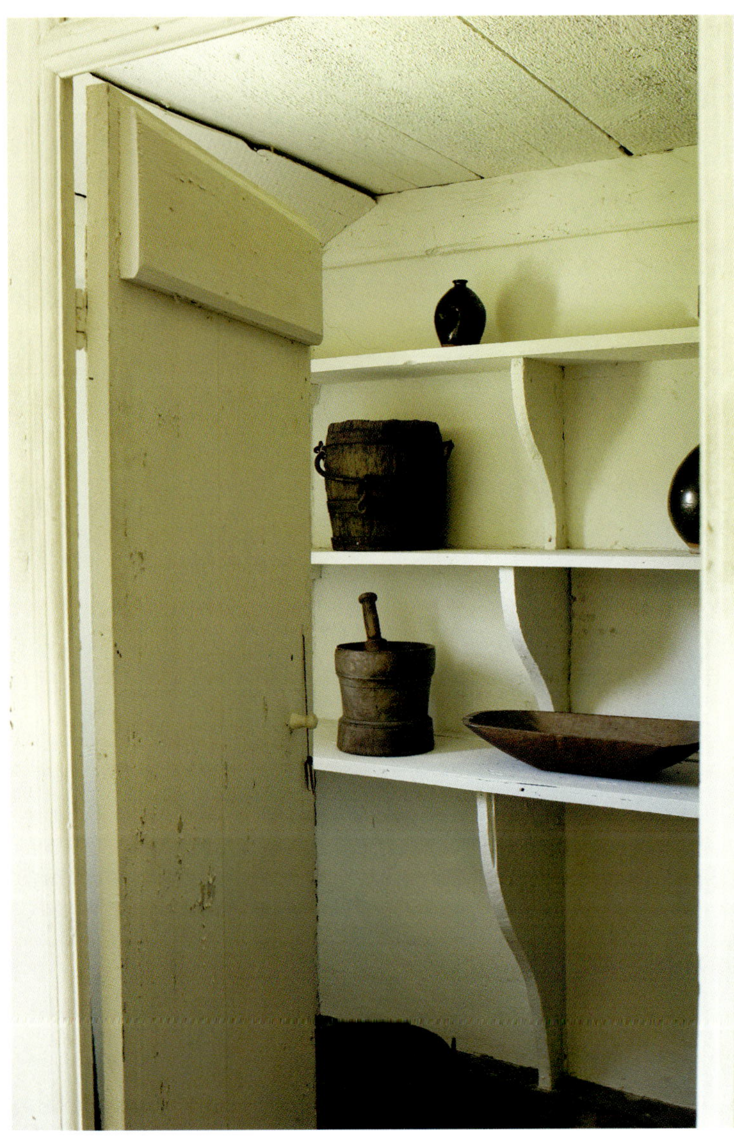

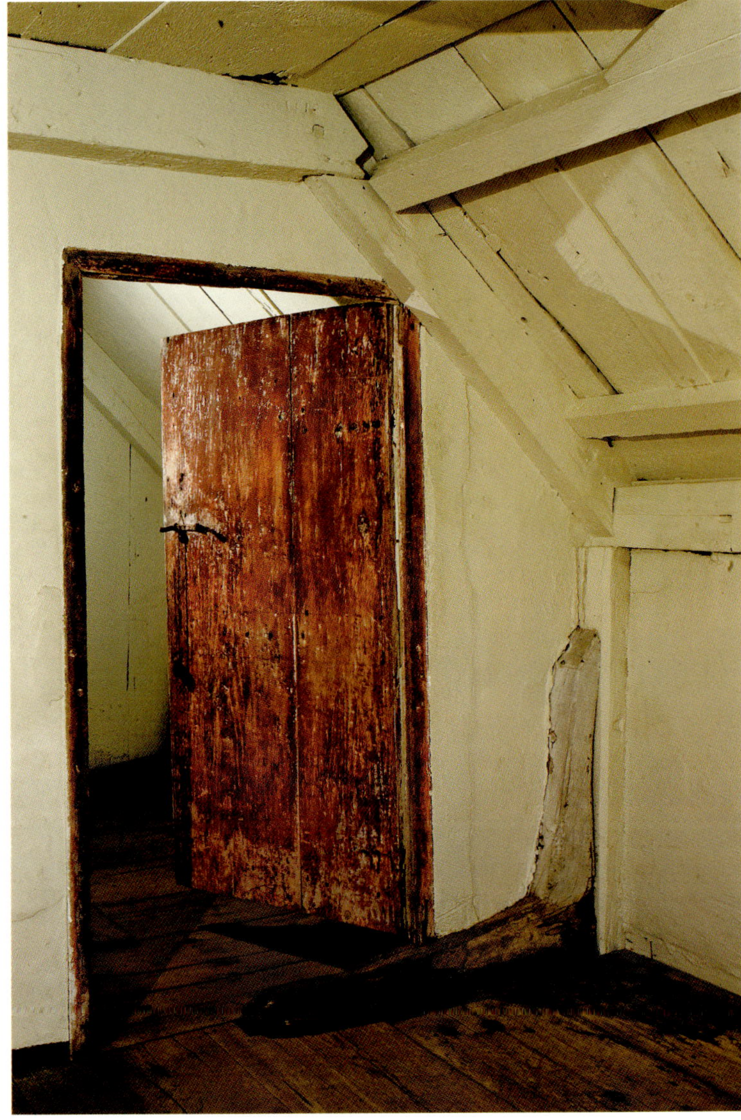

PREVIOUS PAGES LEFT *At the end of the lean-to is a small room, likely the dairy, where basins held milk and cream, some of which would be processed into butter and cheese.*

PREVIOUS PAGES RIGHT *Looking from the kitchen toward the front of the house, one can glimpse a room set for dining.*

ABOVE LEFT *At the other end of the lean-to from the dairy was the pantry for food and utensil storage.*

ABOVE RIGHT *Unsure of the rigidity of the original frame, this knee brace was added. The color red was common to early houses in all colonies, mostly because of its wide availability and low cost*

FACING PAGE LEFT *Detail of the fireplace in the second-floor chamber.*

FACING PAGE RIGHT *Nail holes in old timbers are a testament to the centuries of reworking a house to accommodate different families and their needs.*

ulation until the mid-twentieth century. The Coffin Family Reunion of 1881 rallied interest in the house's preservation, which was taken up when the Nantucket Historical Society purchased it in 1923. Nantucket has a remarkable number of historical houses from later periods, built with the wealth of whaling, surviving thanks to benign neglect—which is a great preserver. With the second-home repopulation of Nantucket in recent decades, active preservation has become a popular preoccupation.

As built, the house is a "saltbox," including an original rear lean-to with common rafters from ridge to eaves. Facing south, the entry has a winding stairway behind which is a large chimney stack with three fireplaces on the first floor in three rooms: the east hall, the west parlor, and the north kitchen. The lean-to section also contains the buttery and a chamber. Over the hall and parlor are two chambers with the parlor chamber having a small fireplace. From this level steep, narrow steps lead to a higher small garret.

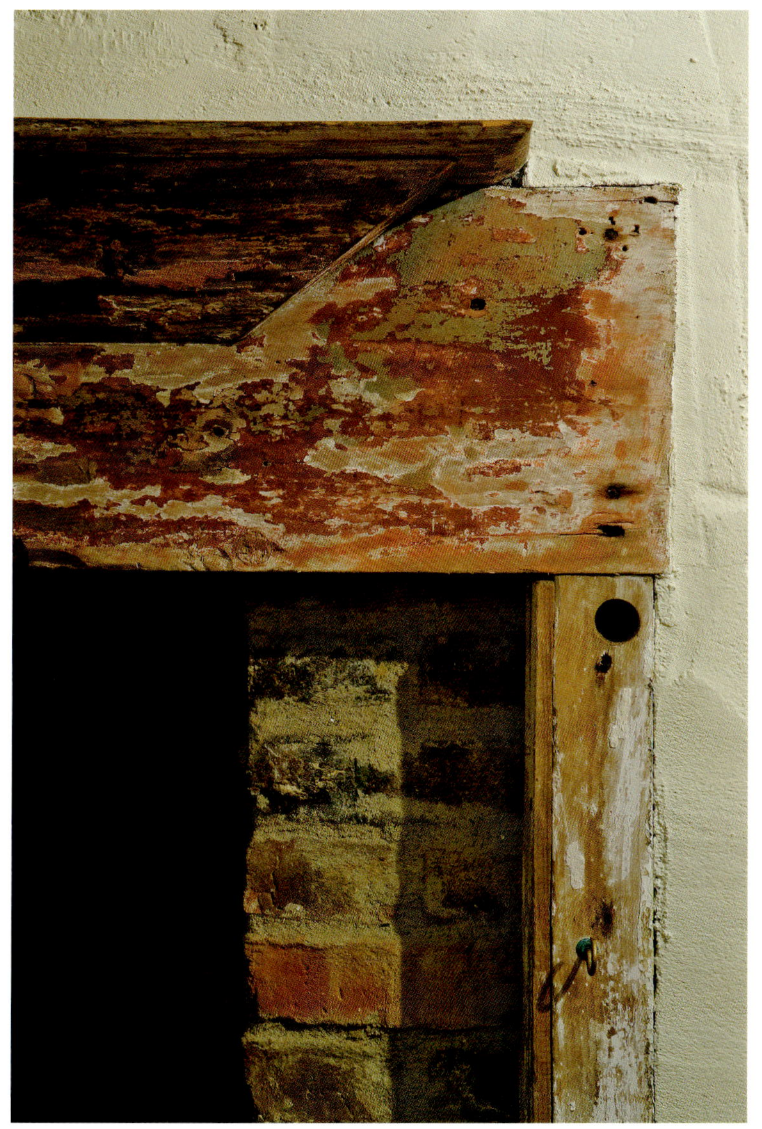

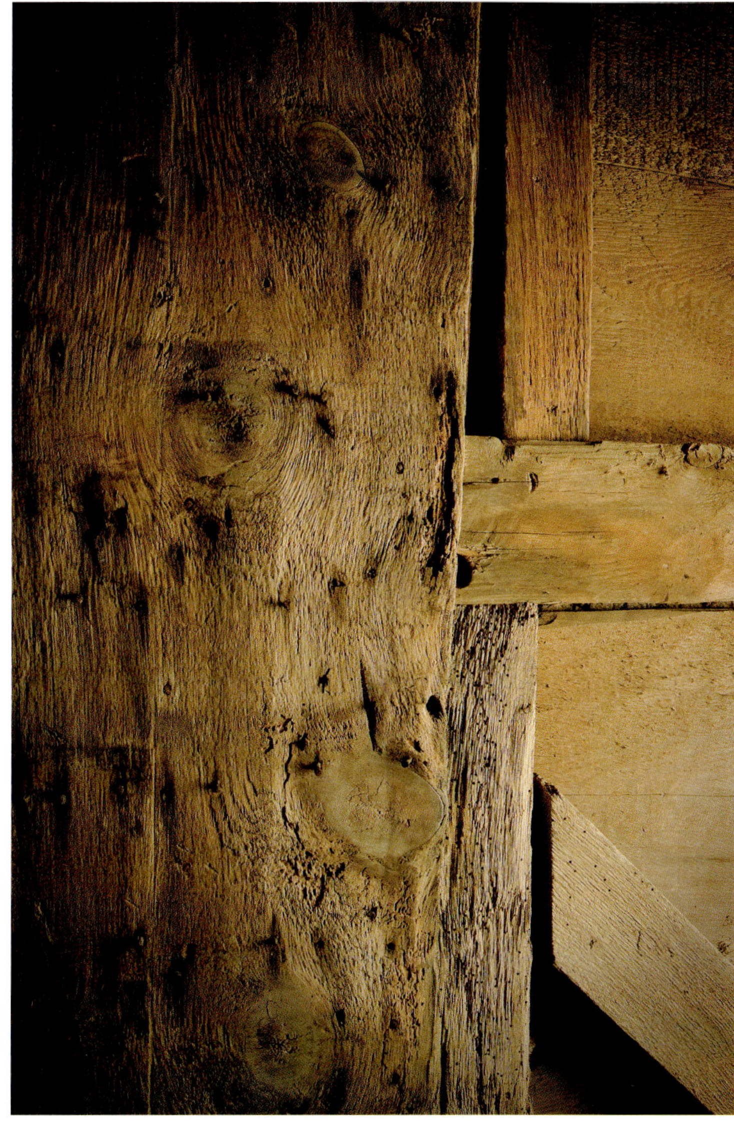

Beside the four fireplaces, the main features of the rooms are the ceiling summer beams and joists. In the hall the large fireplace has a bake oven and a wall consisting of vertical boards. These boards and the ceiling beams and joists were painted red. The parlor's summer beam is chamfered with lamb's tongue stops; the intersecting joists have a distinctive decorative paint design on their sides. The second floor has decorative diamond shapes incised on the doors.

The exterior walls are insulated with mud and straw daubing over which sheathing of wide horizontal boards are fastened to posts with rosehead nails. Since at least the nineteenth century, the house has been shingled; originally, it may have been clapboarded. Evidence from the south, or entry, facade indicates that it had two gable dormers, which, according to folklore, were removed within ten years because they leaked. Physical evidence also indicates there once was an over-door "hut" or pentice.

The house has undergone three known restorations. In the 1880s it was "fixed up" and opened as a museum. A fire had partially destroyed the lean-to and original casement windows had been replaced with sash windows. In 1928 the Society for the Preservation of New England Antiquities restored the house to its seventeenth-century appearance, the lean-to was extended to its original size and leaded-glass casement windows were reconstructed for surviving frame evidence. Careful documentation of the existing structure, of the restoration process, and of replacements (parts were replaced only if the fabric was beyond repair, each member dated) was invaluable for the preparation of the 1987 historic structures report by Morgan Philips and the subsequent restoration by the firm of John Milner Architects in 1989 following a lightning strike that caused the building to nearly explode (most mortise and tenon joints broke but were carefully consolidated). Despite nineteenth-century neglect and devastation by lightning, careful study and restoration has preserved most of the early features of the house.

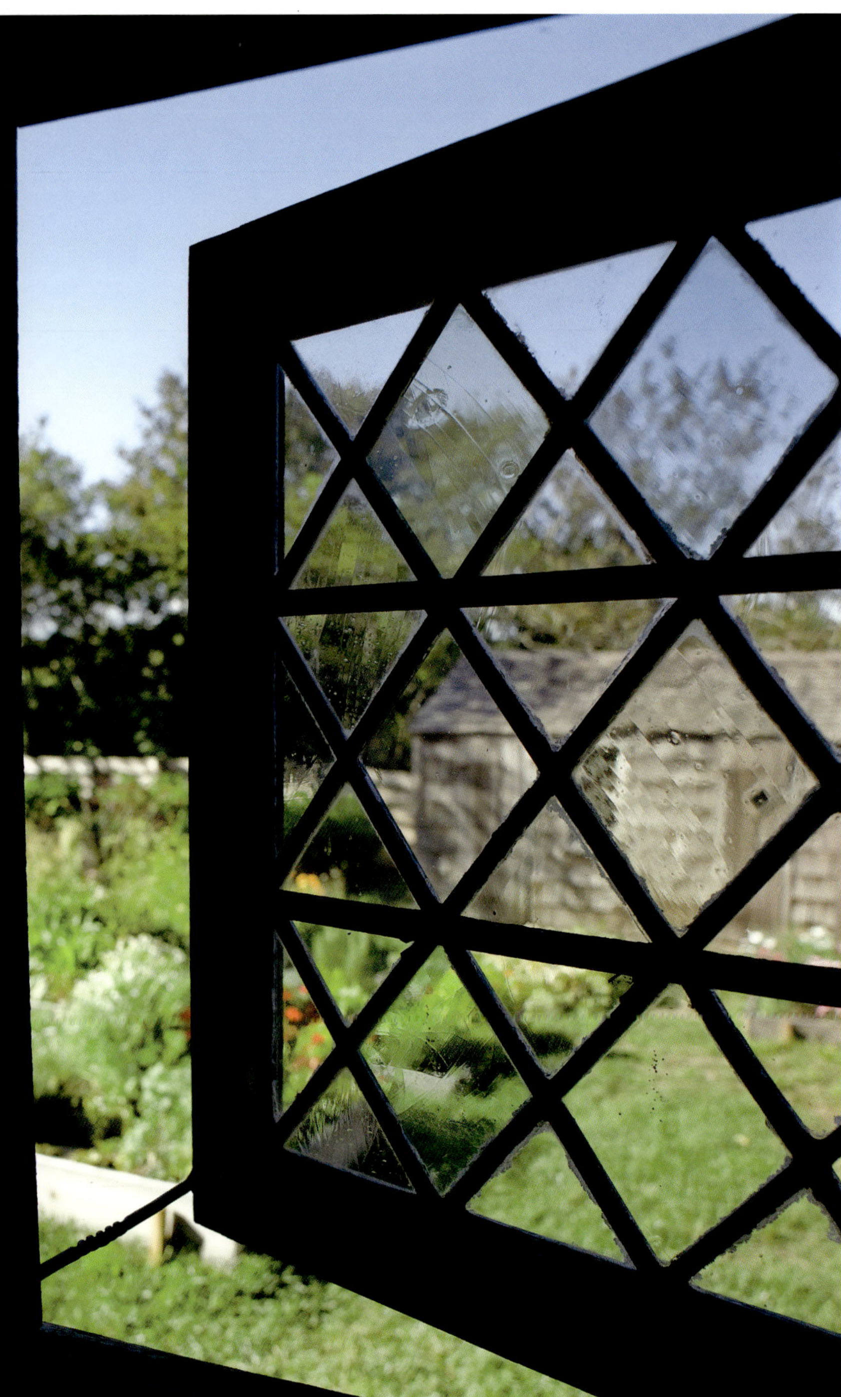

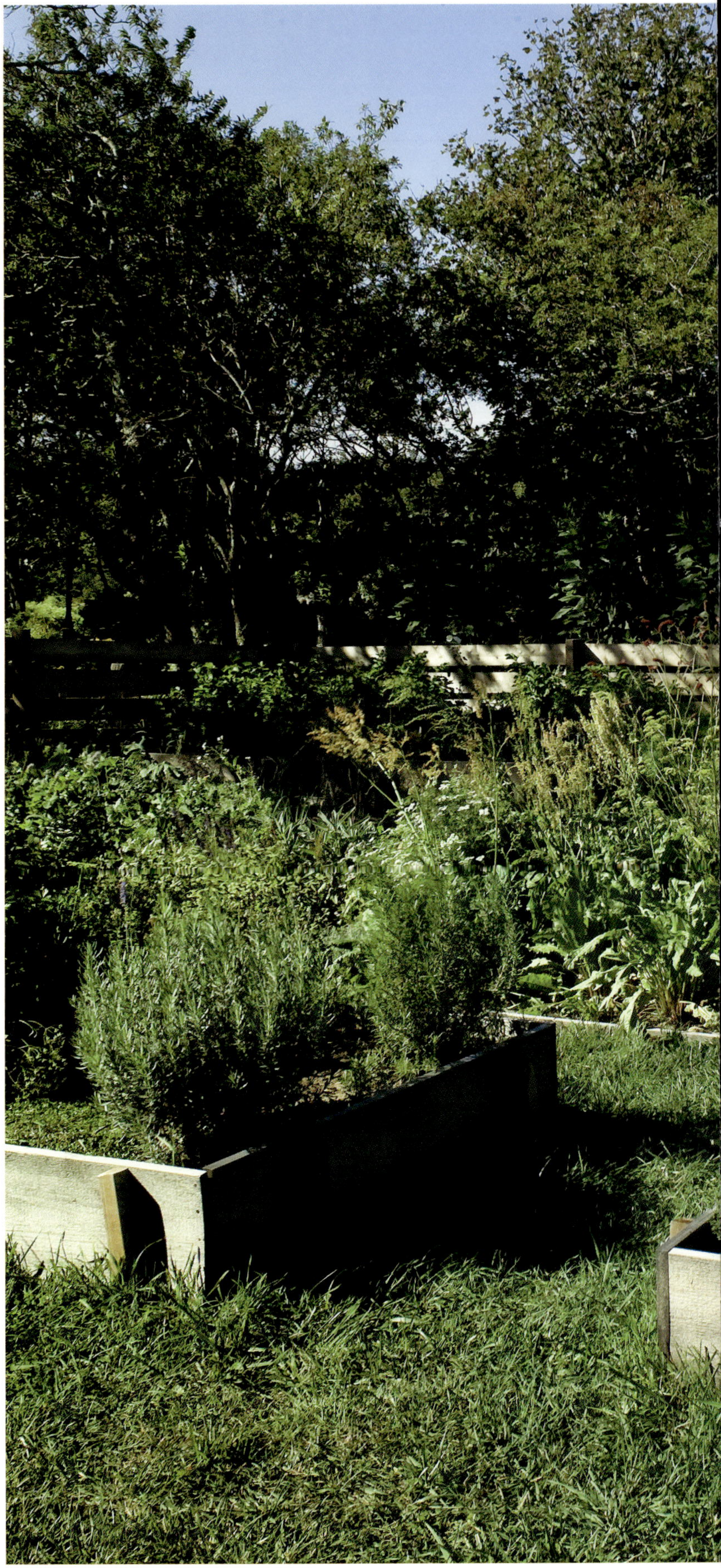

ABOVE *Almost all windows in early houses today are restorations to the common form in the seventeenth century: hinged or sliding casement sashes using small diamond-shaped glass set in lead cames and reinforced with iron bars. These were widely replaced with sliding double-hung sashes in the next century using then-available larger panes of glass set in wooden muntins.*

RIGHT *A kitchen garden is set out with raised boxes and boundary fencing, the better and easier to contain plants and control weeds and animals. This medieval garden tradition is increasingly appreciated by the public for its aesthetics and practicality.*

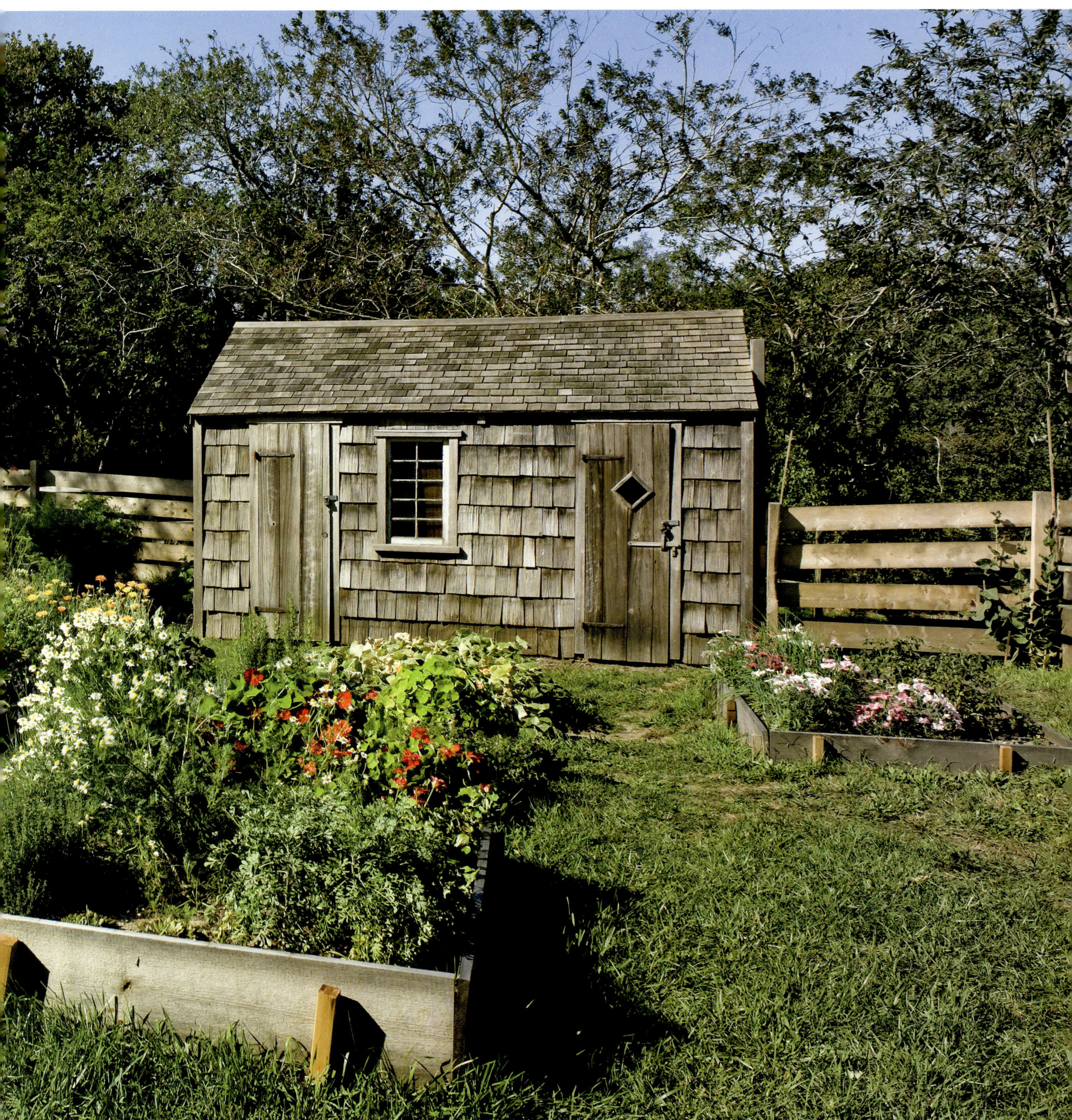

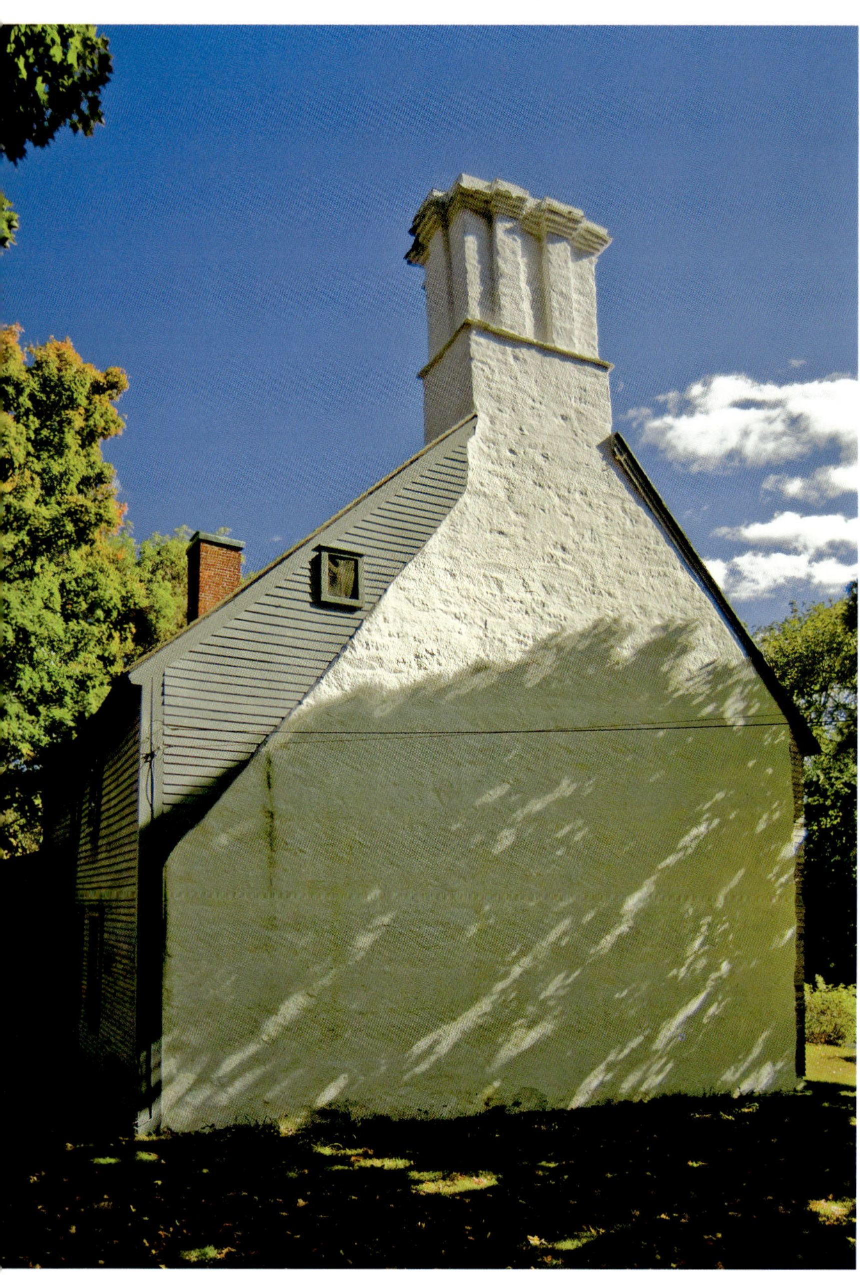

ABOVE *Rhode Island "stone-enders," derived from the west of England, are two rooms deep but only one-room wide and are thus quite different from the houses inspired by east England prototypes elsewhere in New England. With two fireplaces at one gable end, it made sense to build them as one stack with joined flues.*

FACING PAGE *Eleazer Arnold framed his house two stories high and laid a brick chimney with multiple pilastered forms*

ELEAZER ARNOLD HOUSE

Lincoln, Rhode Island, 1687

As Massachusetts became the refuge for Puritans fleeing English persecution, Rhode Island almost as quickly became a refuge from Puritan persecution. In 1636 Roger Williams was exiled from Massachusetts for his dissenting beliefs. Accompanied by others, he bought land from the Narragansett Indians as a safe haven. From its founding Rhode Island earned a reputation for spirited individualism and religious tolerance. Quakers, Jews, and Christian dissenters soon followed. As late as the American Revolution its citizens were quick to challenge outside authority, shedding the first blood of the war in 1772 when John Brown organized the burning of the British revenue cutter the *HMS Gaspee*.

Thomas Arnold emigrated from England to Watertown, Massachusetts, in 1636. Finding the Quaker community at Rhode Island more appealing, he moved there by 1661. A founder of the Quaker community on the Moshassuck River, which became the Saylesville area of modern-day Lincoln, he held local offices and, like most, was a farmer. His son Eleazer (1651–1722) inherited a parcel of land there from his father in 1685 on which he built a house about two years later—which exists today—and raised a family of ten children. Ambitious but well respected, he served on the Providence Town Council in the 1680s, eight times as deputy of the General Assembly from 1686 to 1715, occasionally as justice of the peace, limestone processor, and tavern keeper, and he, reportedly, amassed considerable wealth.

Immigrants to the province came primarily from western England where a tradition of building homes of stone proved suitable to Rhode Island's rocky land, which included a rarity in New England, limestone for making mortar. The characteristic early houses of this region are known as "stone-enders" for the massive gable-end stone chimney, serving both the kitchen and parlor fireplaces. The Arnold House is perhaps the most impressive surviving example: two stories high (most were one-and-a-half stories high) with one of the most impressive chimneys in New England,

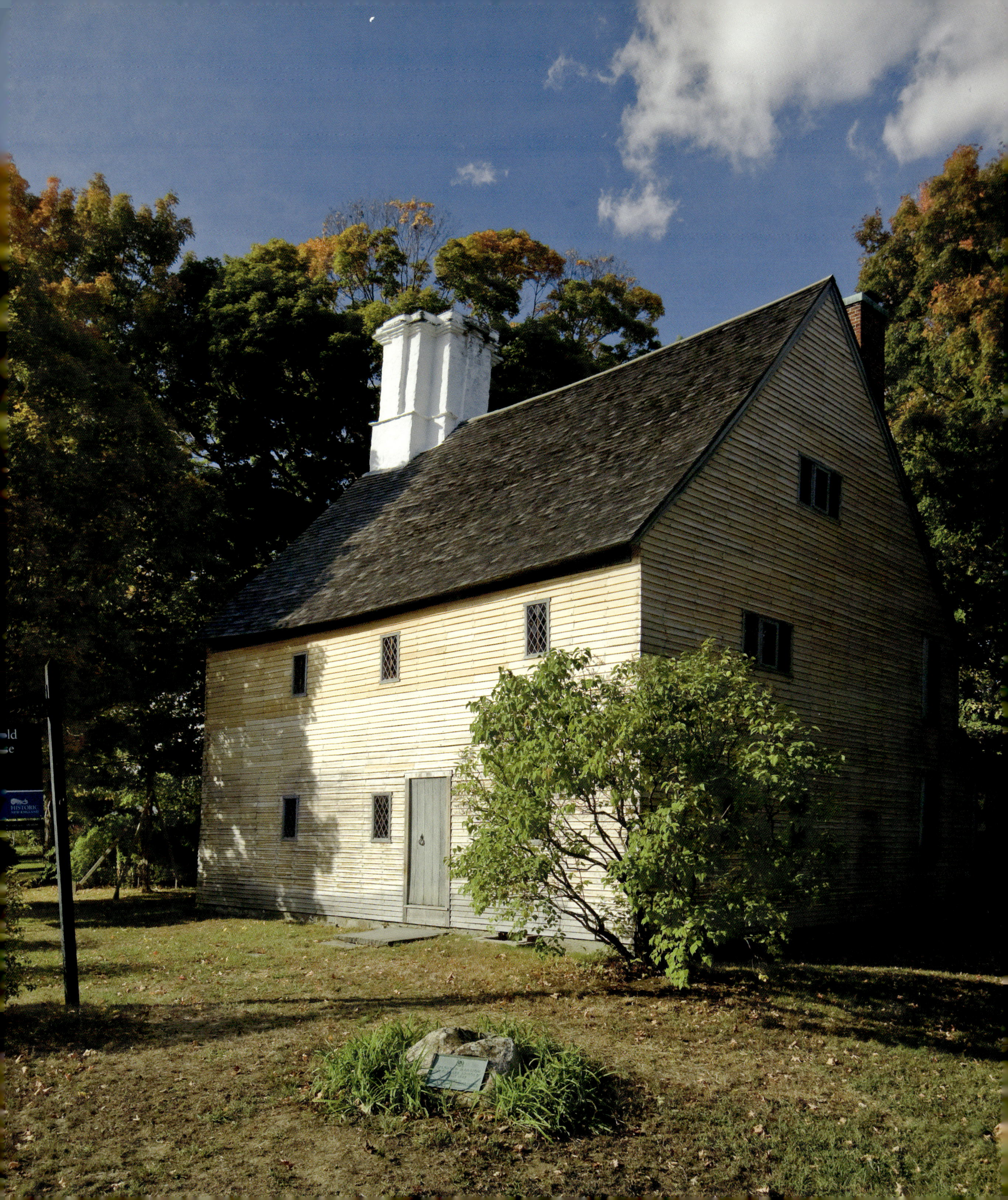
HISTORIC

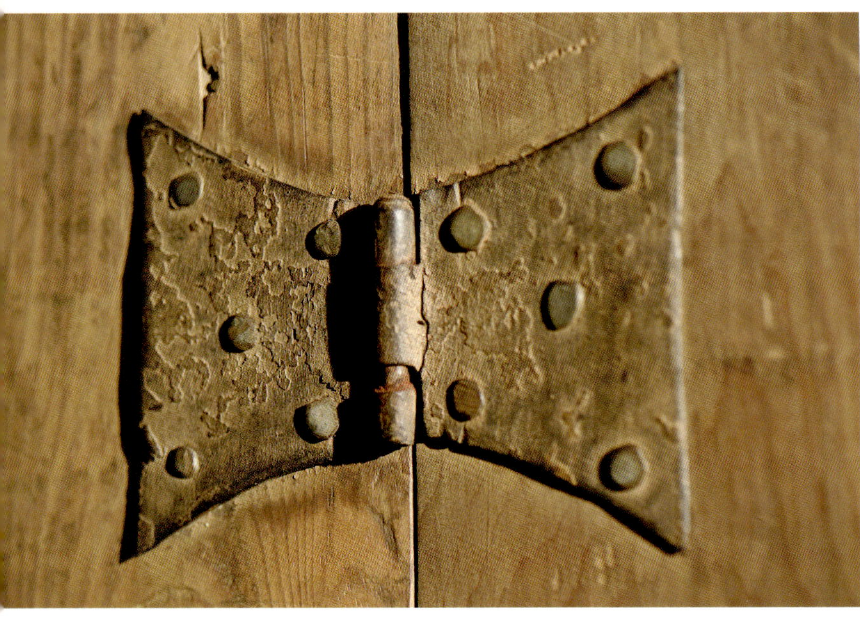

ABOVE *The butterfly hinge was easily surface mounted, and its spread accommodated the security of extra nails.*

RIGHT *The hall, or great room, of the Arnold House is configured differently from others since its chimney stack is in the gable end. The stairway is set in the corner. A smaller kitchen fireplace, also in this gable end, is in the lean-to.*

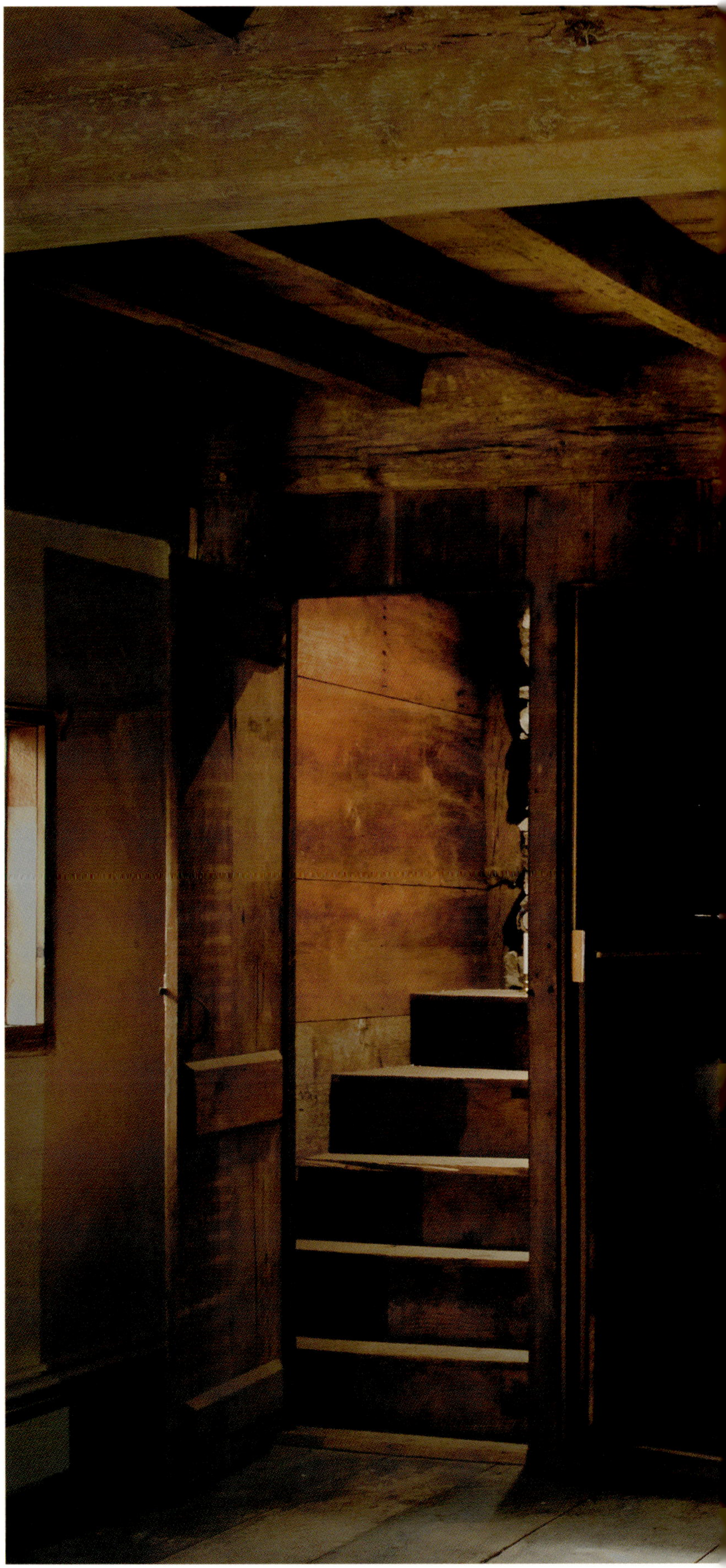

a pilastered brick chimney harkening back to Elizabethan prototypes. In Eleazer's time and after it was referred to as his "Splendid Mansion."

Such stone-enders were built primarily before 1700. Many were burned during King Philip's War (1676), sometimes rebuilt to a full two stories by the addition of a lean-to behind. Like their inspiration—the stone cottages of the highlands of Sussex, Wales, and the West Counties—the entry door opened into the parlor (then known as the Hall or Great Room), not into a small entry hallway, as elsewhere in New England. The Arnold House has four rooms on each floor, the first with the adjacent Great Room and kitchen at the left or west end, and two smaller rooms on the east end, later served by fireplaces. Above the Great Room is the Great Chamber with a fireplace, plus three smaller bedrooms. A garret forms the third floor, once used for storage and sleeping (there were once seven slaves). In the garret framework is evidence of an early but later removed gable.

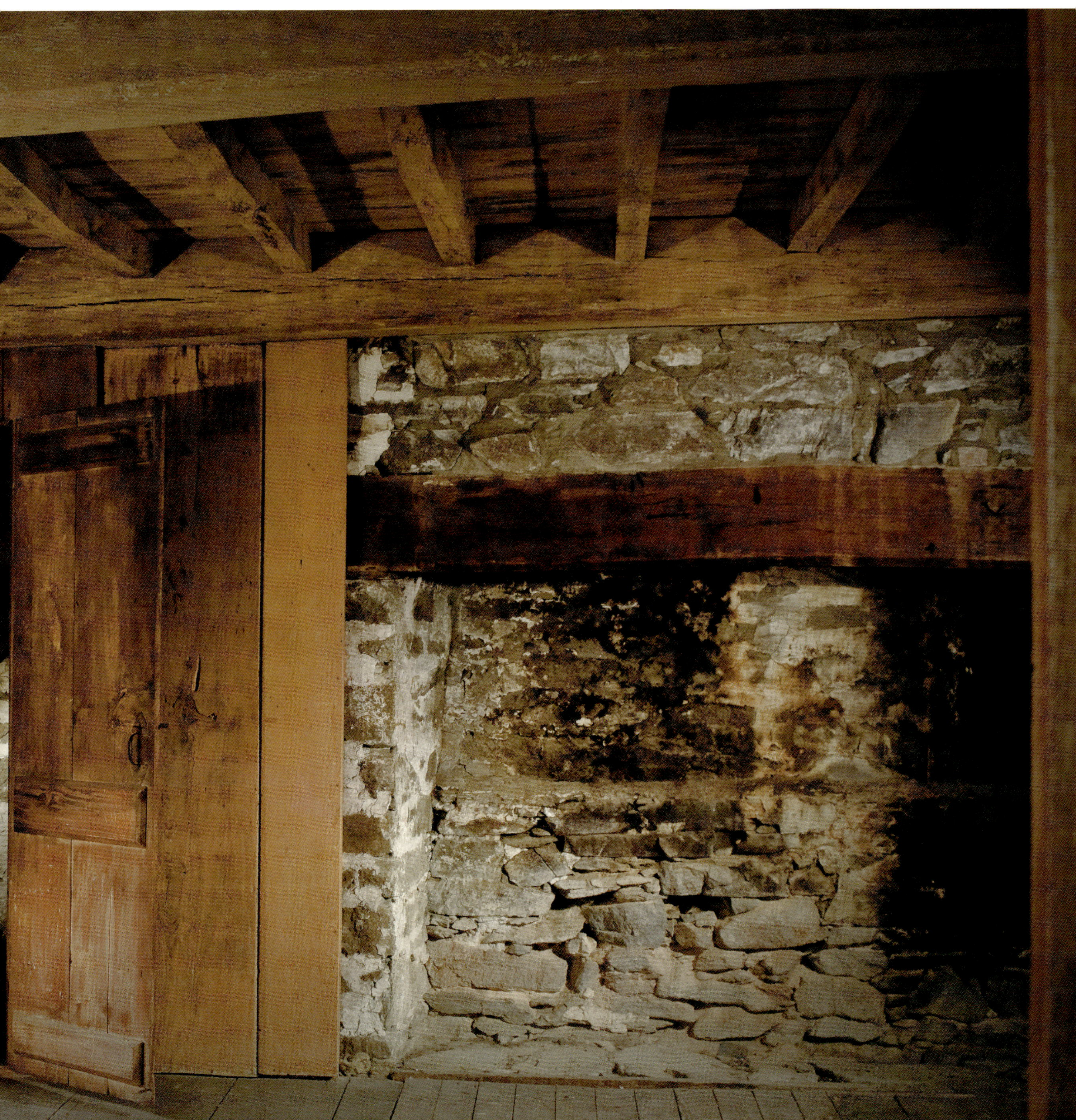

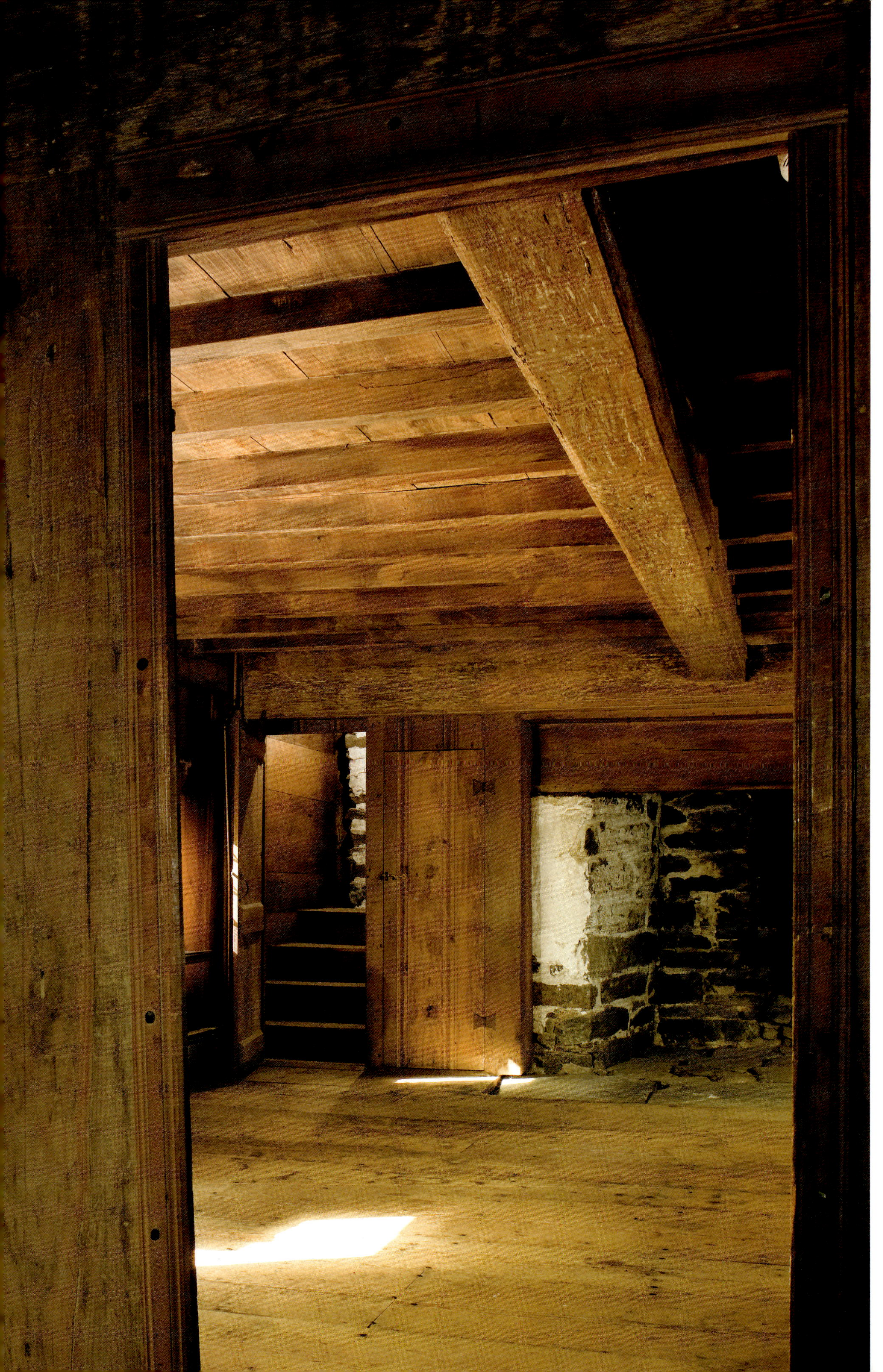

LEFT *From the chamber above the first-floor main room, the corner stairway continues up to the garret. In the ceiling structure of this chamber, the large beams and smaller joists reverse their orientation from the floor below.*

FACING PAGE *With an eye to defense (many stone-enders were burned in King Phillip's War of 1676), small windows had advantages, but the door was most vulnerable. Two boards thick and nailed through, this door was both weather and war tight. The original handle served as both latch bar raiser and door knocker.*

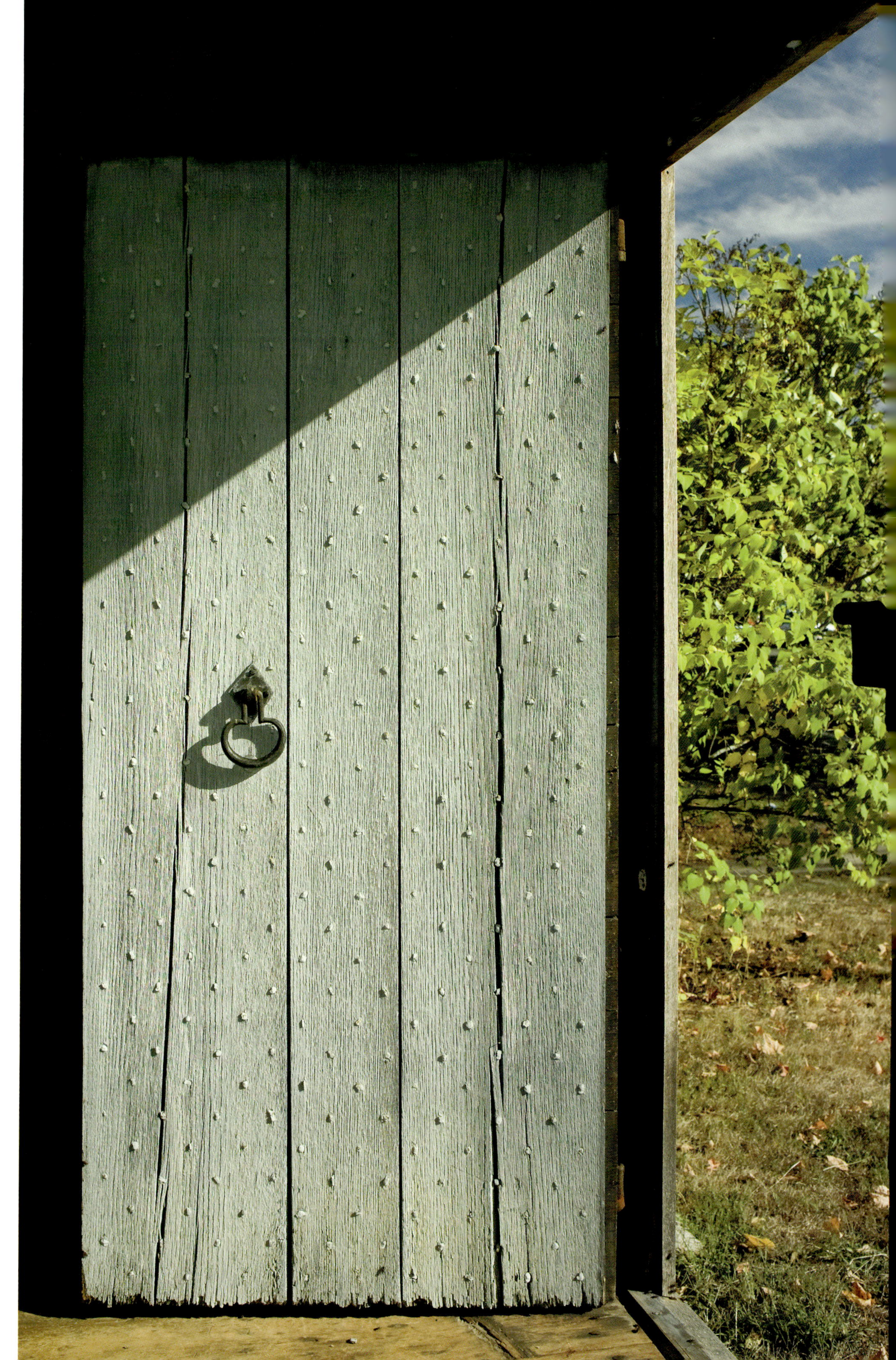

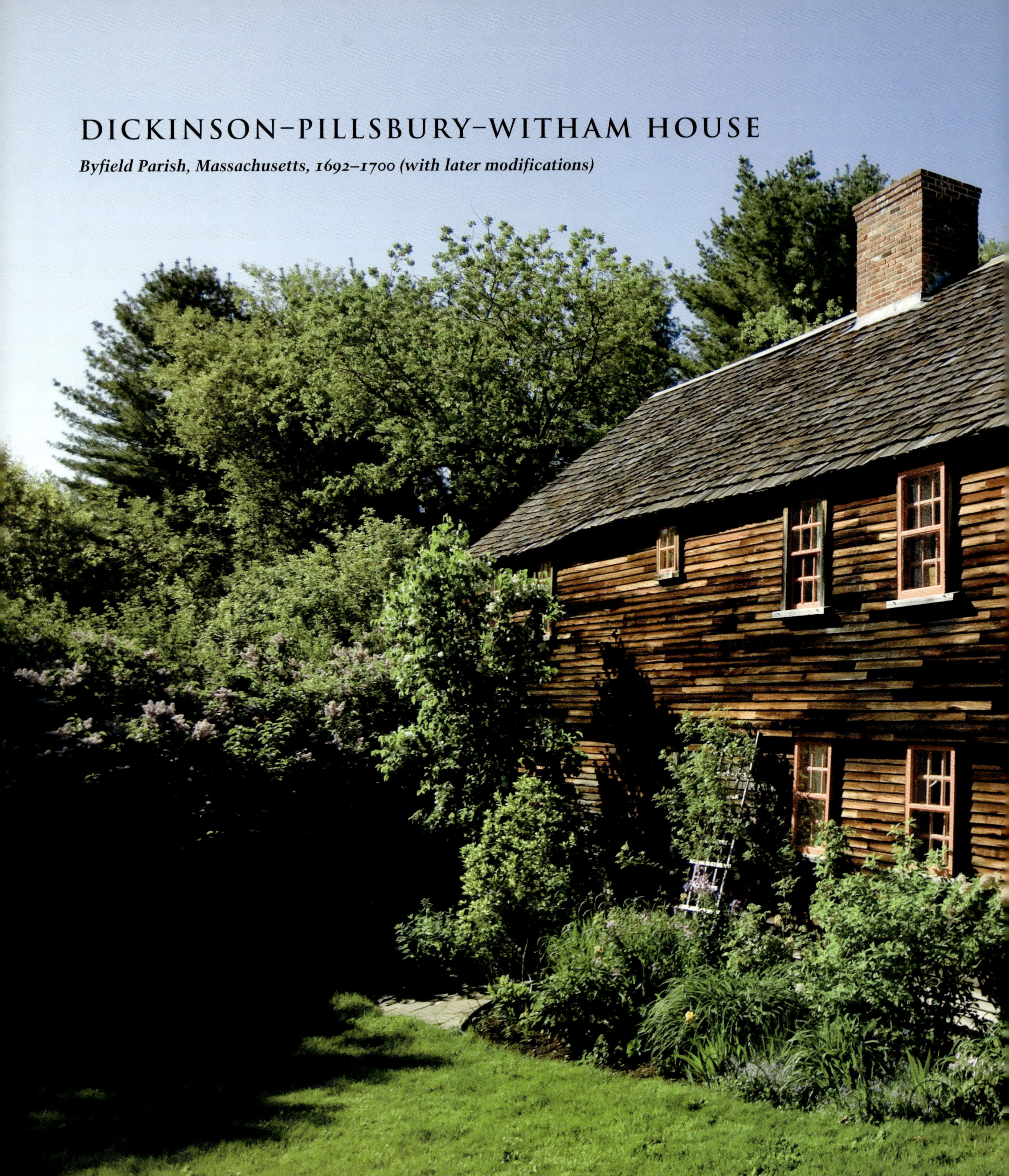

DICKINSON–PILLSBURY–WITHAM HOUSE

Byfield Parish, Massachusetts, 1692–1700 (with later modifications)

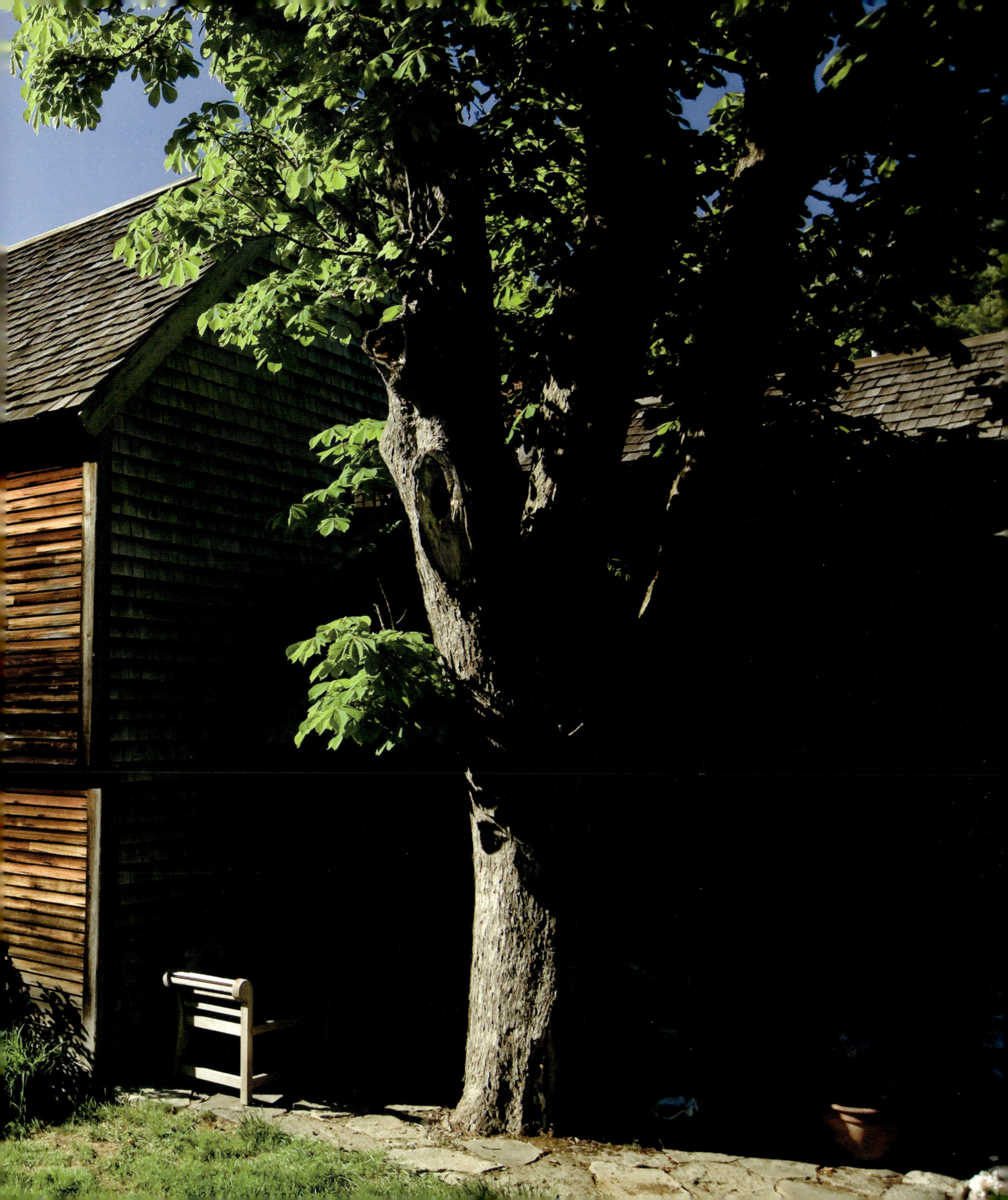

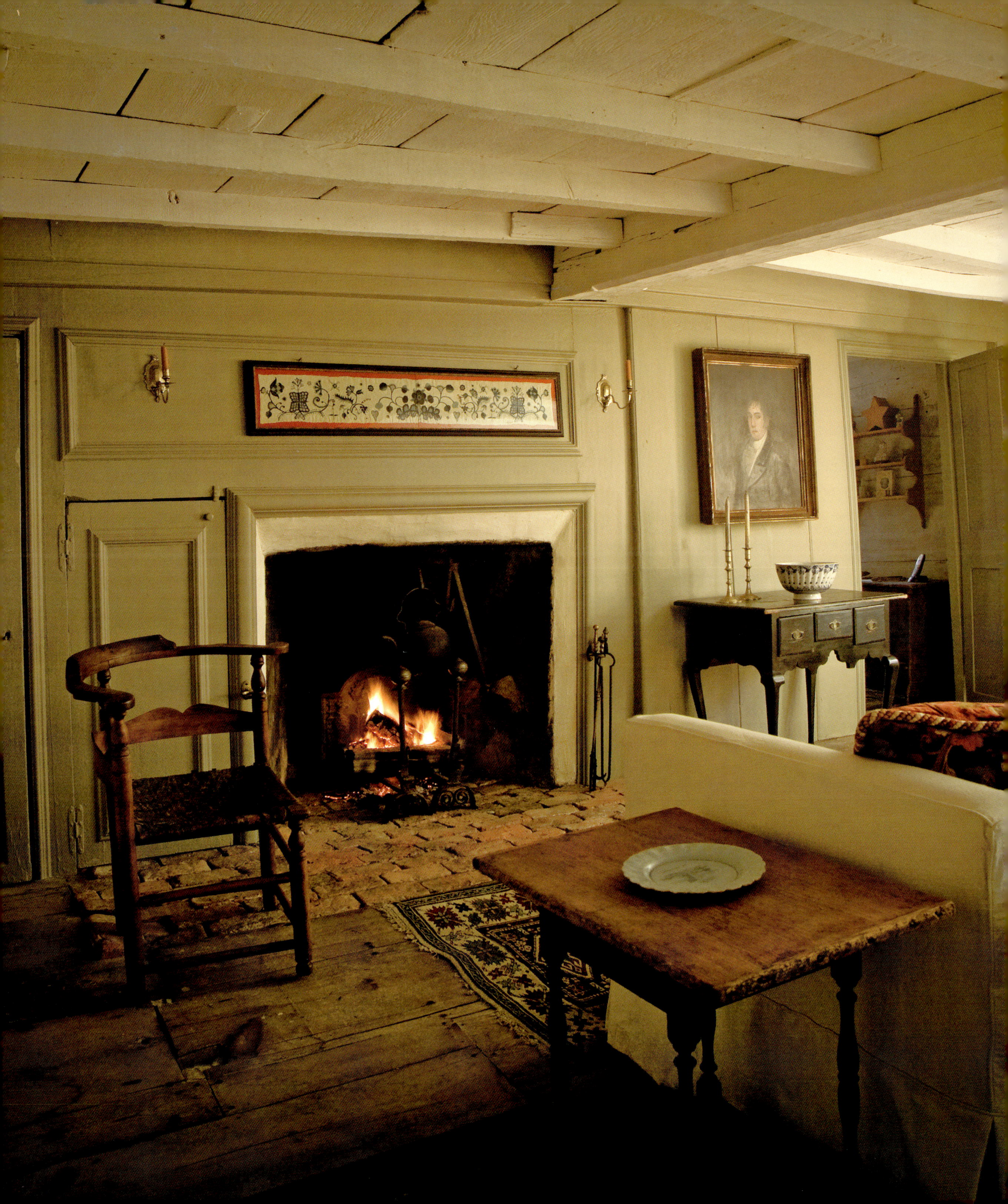

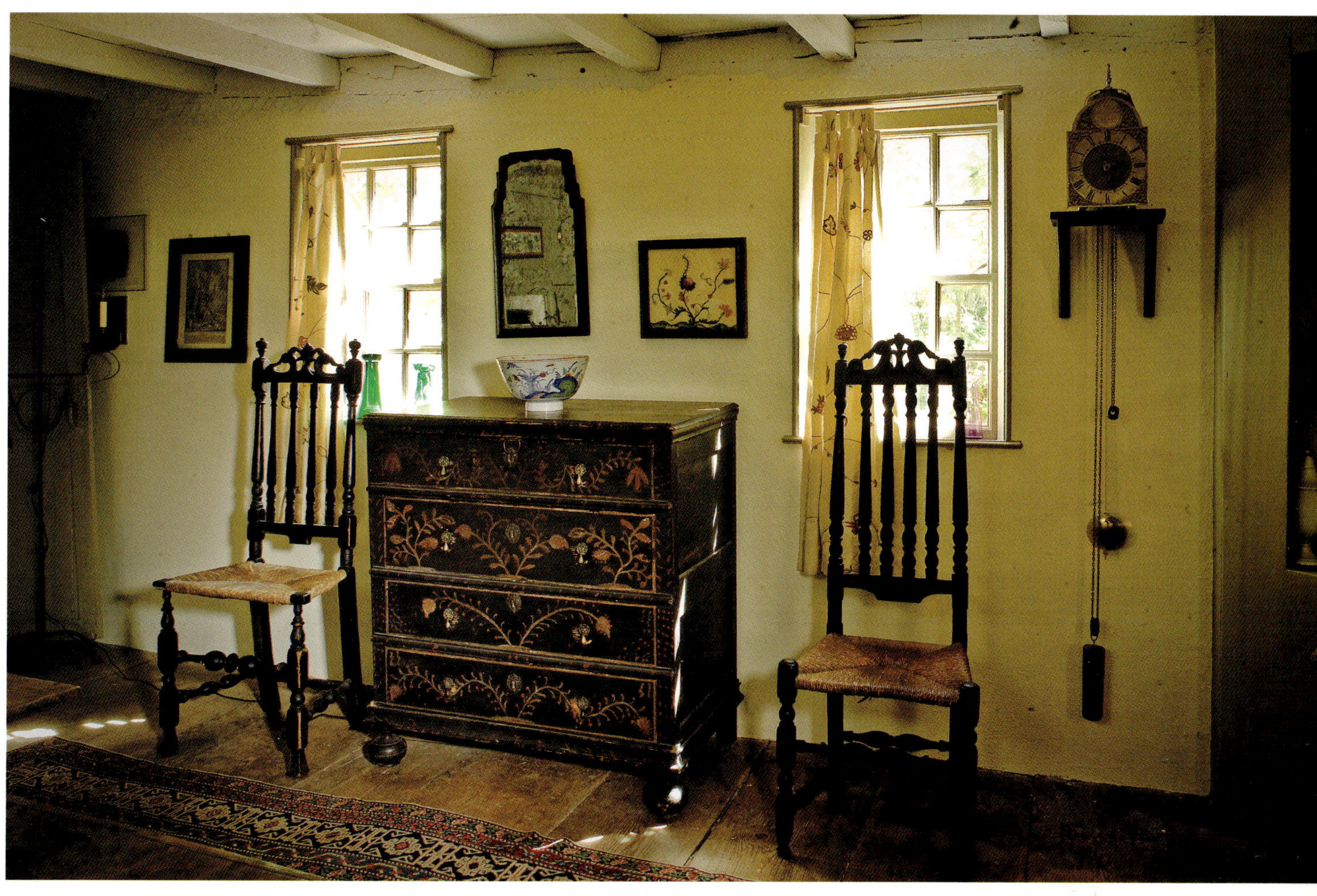

PREVIOUS PAGES *The right half is the original two-story house to which the left half was added a generation later, extending the overhang, or jetty, across the front and on the left gable. The narrow siding has been left to age naturally, giving it the authentic appearance of what early houses looked like in the seventeenth century.*

FACING PAGE AND ABOVE *The parlor was built in the eighteenth century as an addition to the original house. Colors and furnishings from the period capture a sense of its past*

FOLLOWING PAGES *The kitchen is in the original section of the house, opposite the parlor. Many early houses—whether private or public restorations—seek to evoke the feeling of their original era. The continued appeal of these homes lies in their ability to make history a tangible experience to new generations far beyond pupils' often jaded textbook impressions of the past.*

Byfield Parish was incorporated in 1838, but its birth was two hundred years before when a small group of Yorkshire families led by Reverend Ezekiel Rogers set sail in 1638 from Rowley, England, for Salem, Massachusetts, on the ship *John*. Mr. Rogers and his party of about a hundred men, women, and children, having arrived late in the year, remained in Salem for the winter living in common houses. Within a year of arrival the group purchased land between Ipswich and Newbury that they called Rowley and moved there. By 1670 fertile meadows on the west side of their lands, suitable for cultivation and cattle, attracted a small group of families, and a small settlement grew up, later to be called the village of Byfield Parish.

One of those attracted to this area was James Dickinson, who, sometime between 1692 and 1700, built the house shown here. His background and activities are not known, but the house speaks of prosperity, however short-lived, as it and the farmstead

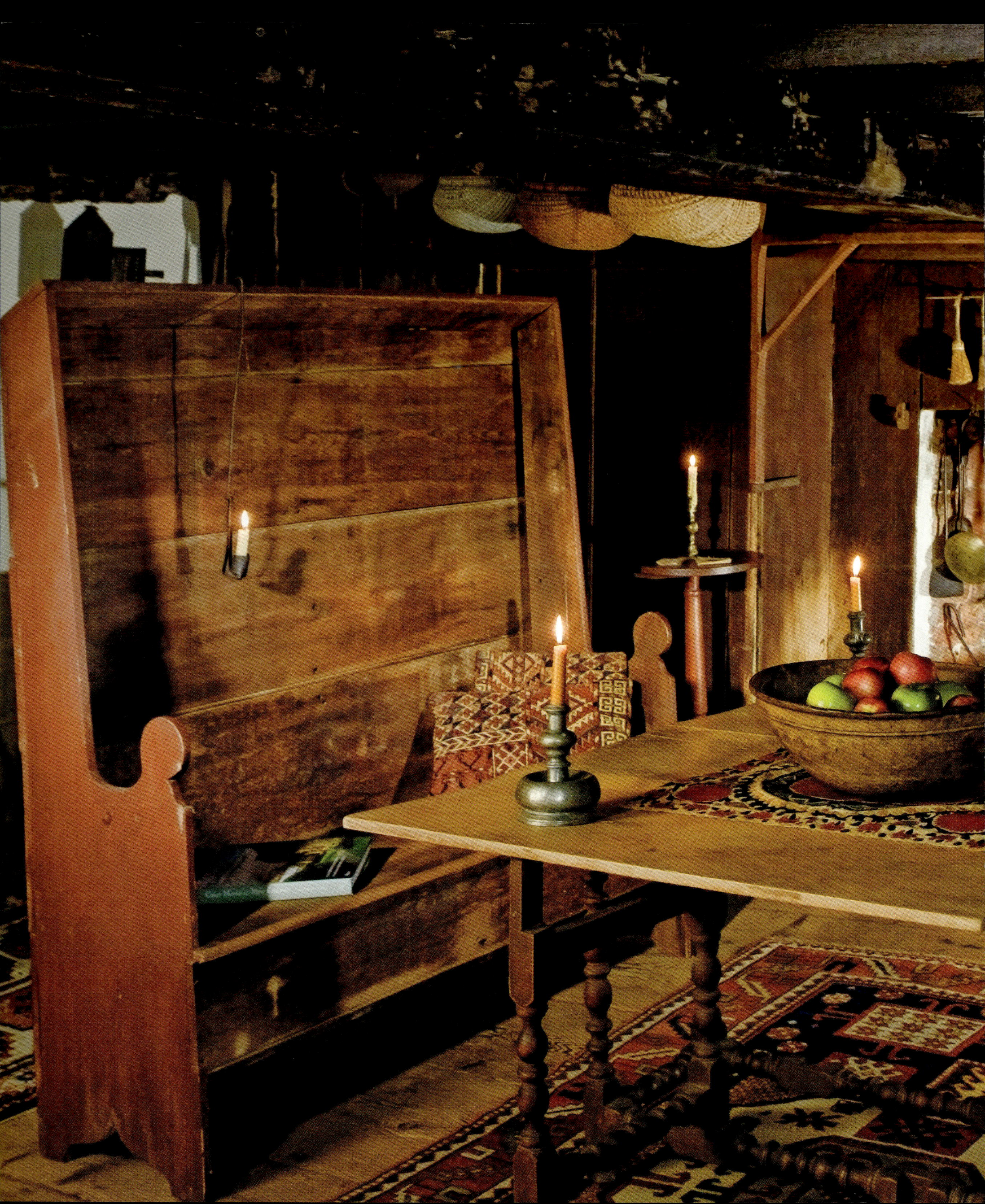

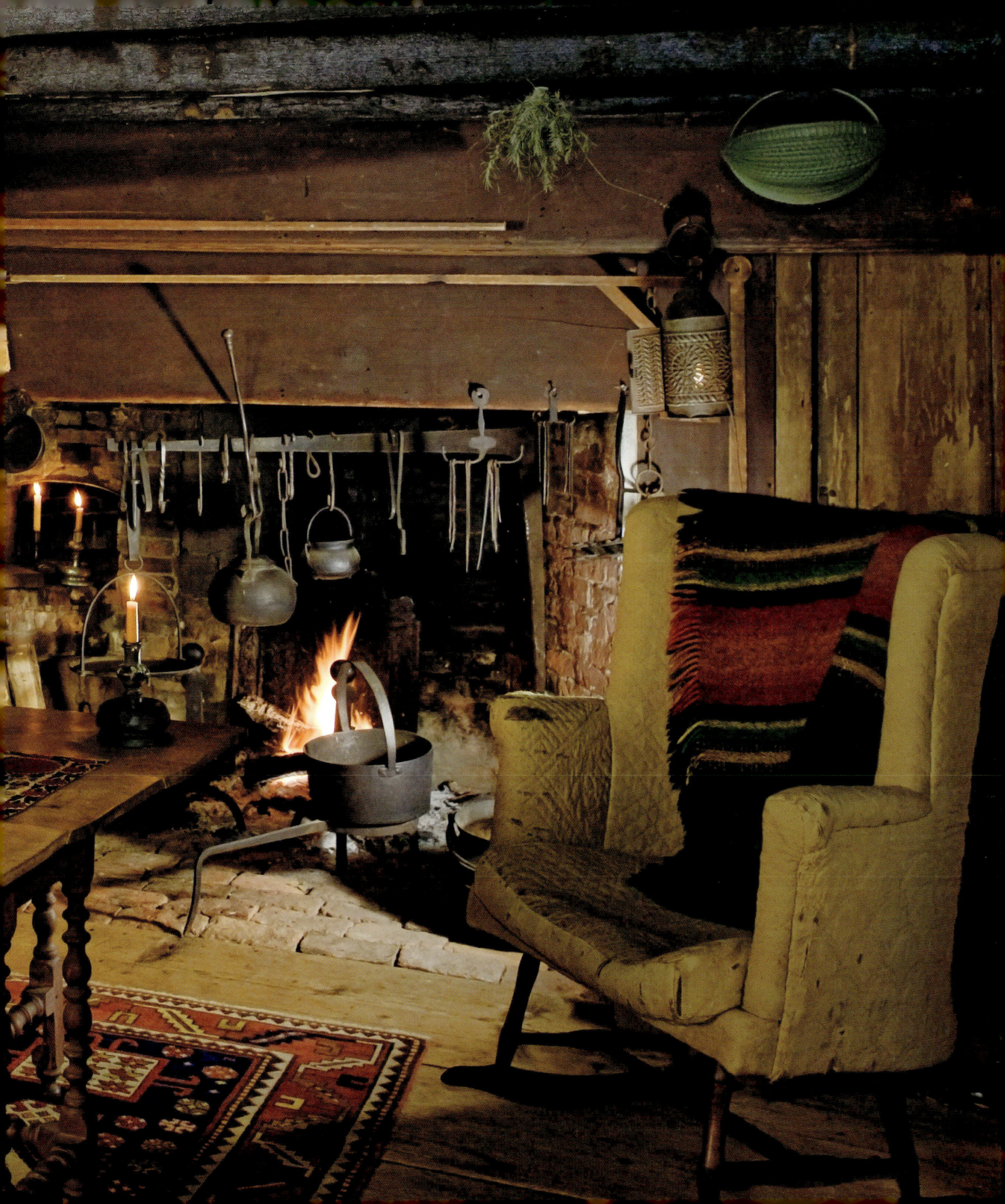

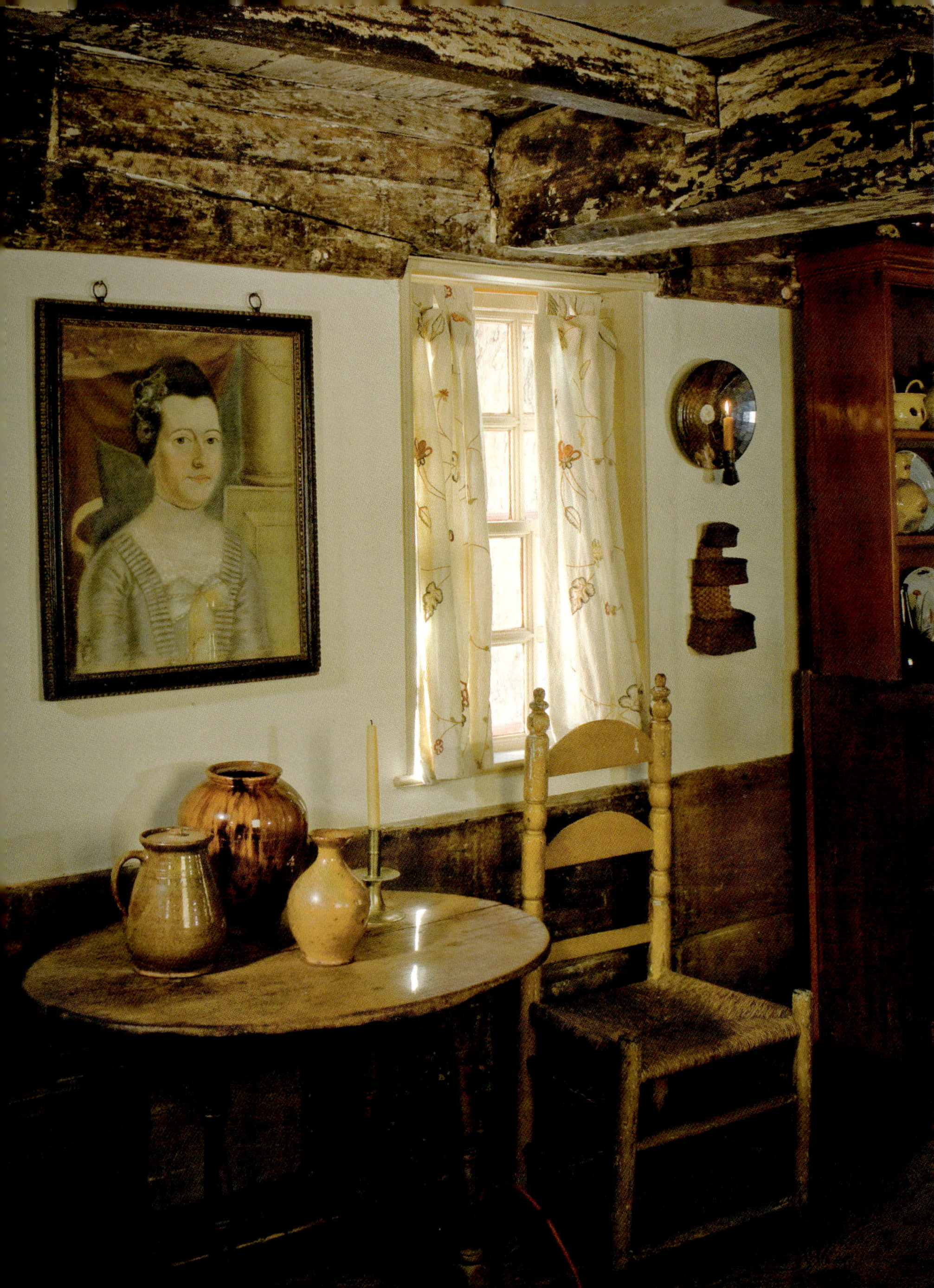

LEFT *While most early homes have been much changed (then later restored), this one, its kitchen shown here, has stayed remarkably the same with its early whitewash and paint.*

FACING PAGE *From the hallway, looking into the kitchen, one can see the open dresser, which contains ceramic pieces that match the ceramic shards found in the ground around early houses.*

FOLLOWING PAGES *This chamber is furnished with early chests, which points to the lack of closets in early houses. Clothing and other textiles were the product of slow handwork and thus expensive and few in number. The bed hangings are crewel embroidery, the epitome of a wife's personal handiwork and a testament to her personal qualities as a woman and her contribution to her home when married.*

came into possession, by inheritance, of his son Samuel Dickinson in 1704, in whose family it descended for nearly a century. About 1801 Paul Pillsbury acquired the home from his uncle Oliver Dickinson. A talented inventor, among Pillsbury's patents was a shoe pegging machine, which presaged one of the principal industries of the town in later years. In recent times the property came into the Witham family before passing to the present owner.

Like some other early houses that remained in the same family for generations, the Dickinson House has survived without the extensive modernization of successive new families imprinting their own identities on their new home. As first built it had a single-room plan, two-stories high, with a front overhang to which, within a generation, the left side of the house was added (with overhang on front and gable sides), creating a center chimney clapboard home characteristic of First Period Puritan homes. An 1865 addition was moved to the rear right-hand end, forming an ell to accommodate the family of the son of Samuel Pillsbury, son of Paul Pillsbury. The main rooms are 19 feet square, framed with massive summers and joists. Much original design is evident: the fireplaces and chimney stack, the stairway, doors, paneling, cupboards, hardware, and early whitewash and paint. Survival of so many early features and surfaces gives us a rare feeling for how other houses of the period once looked.

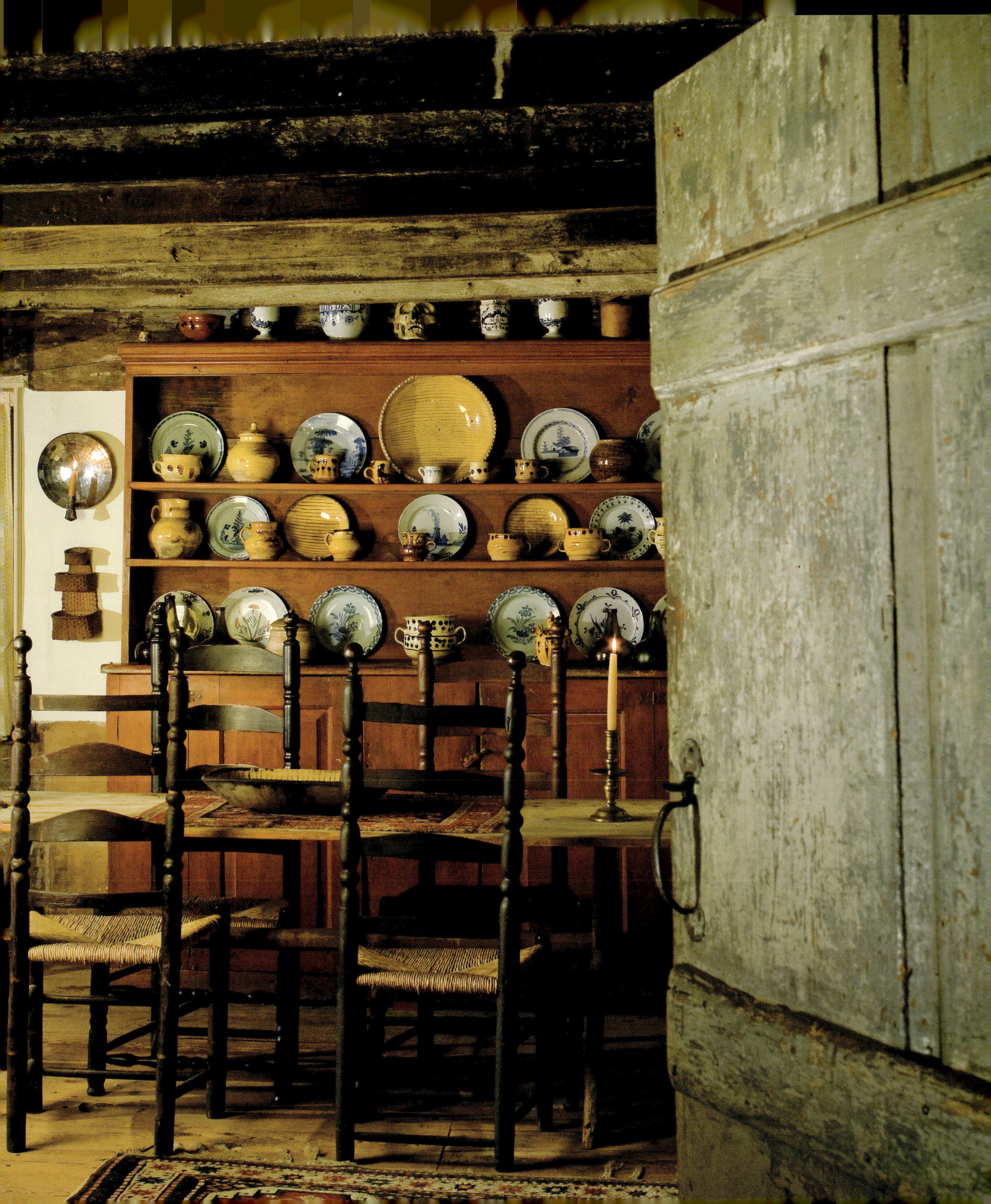

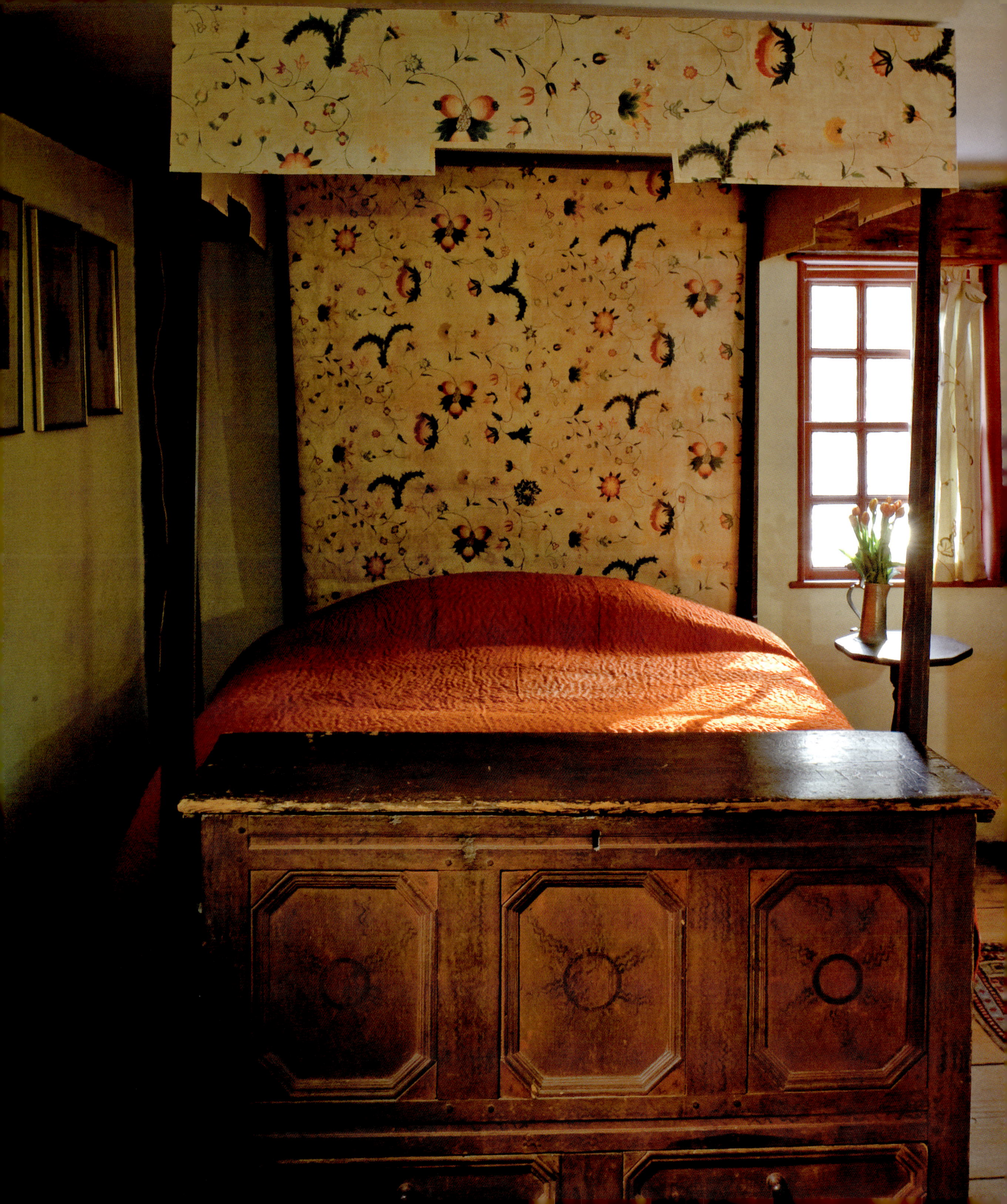

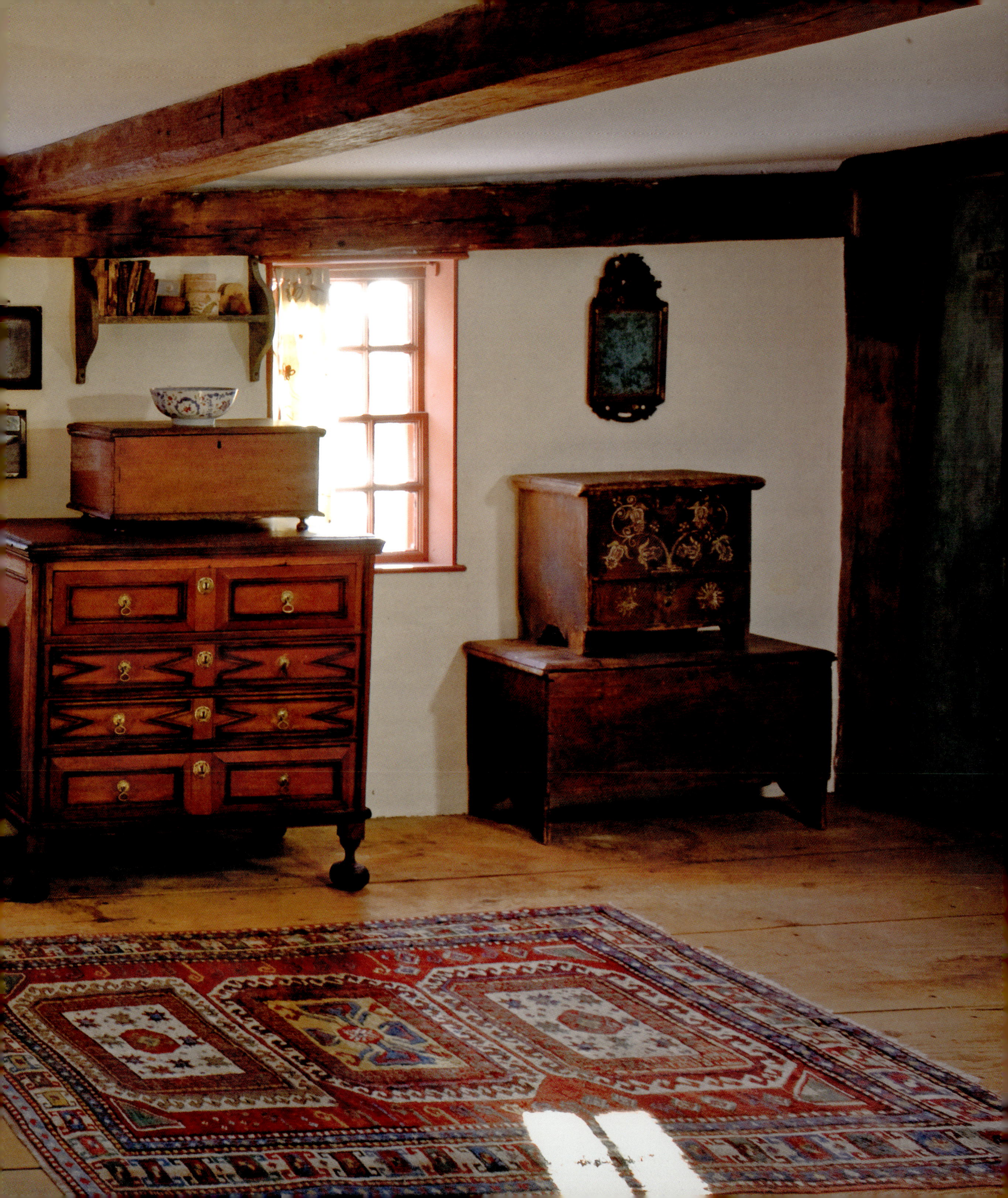

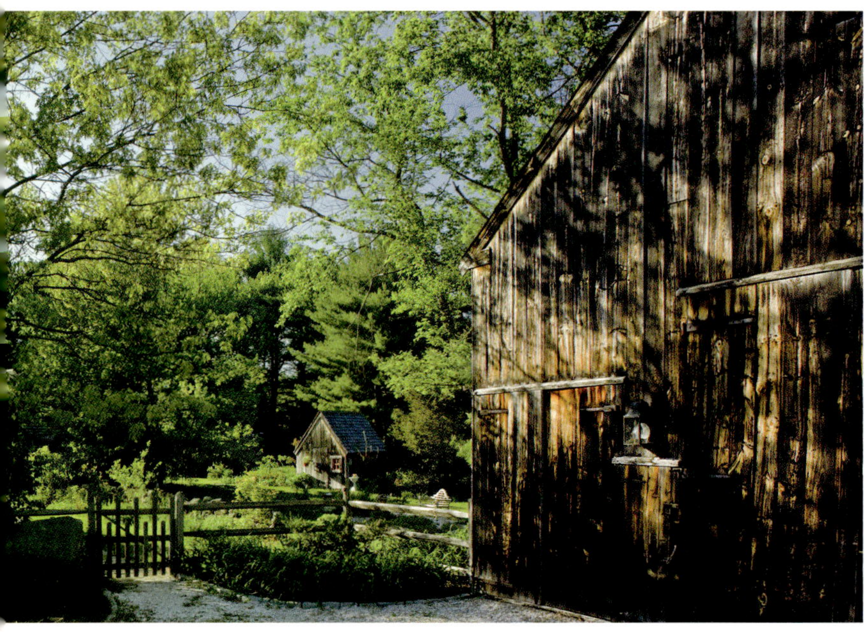

ABOVE AND RIGHT *Among the rarest of early structures to survive are outbuildings, in this case an eighteenth-century barn, adjacent to a period-style garden*

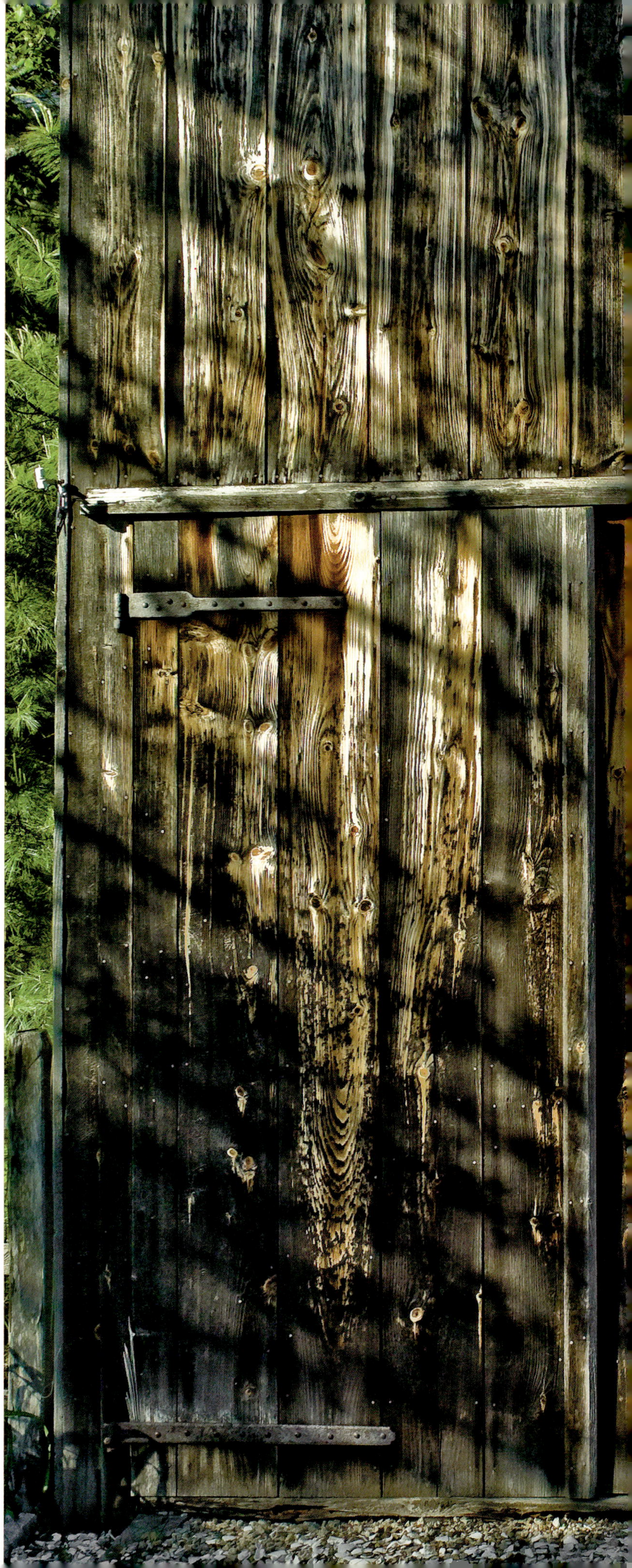

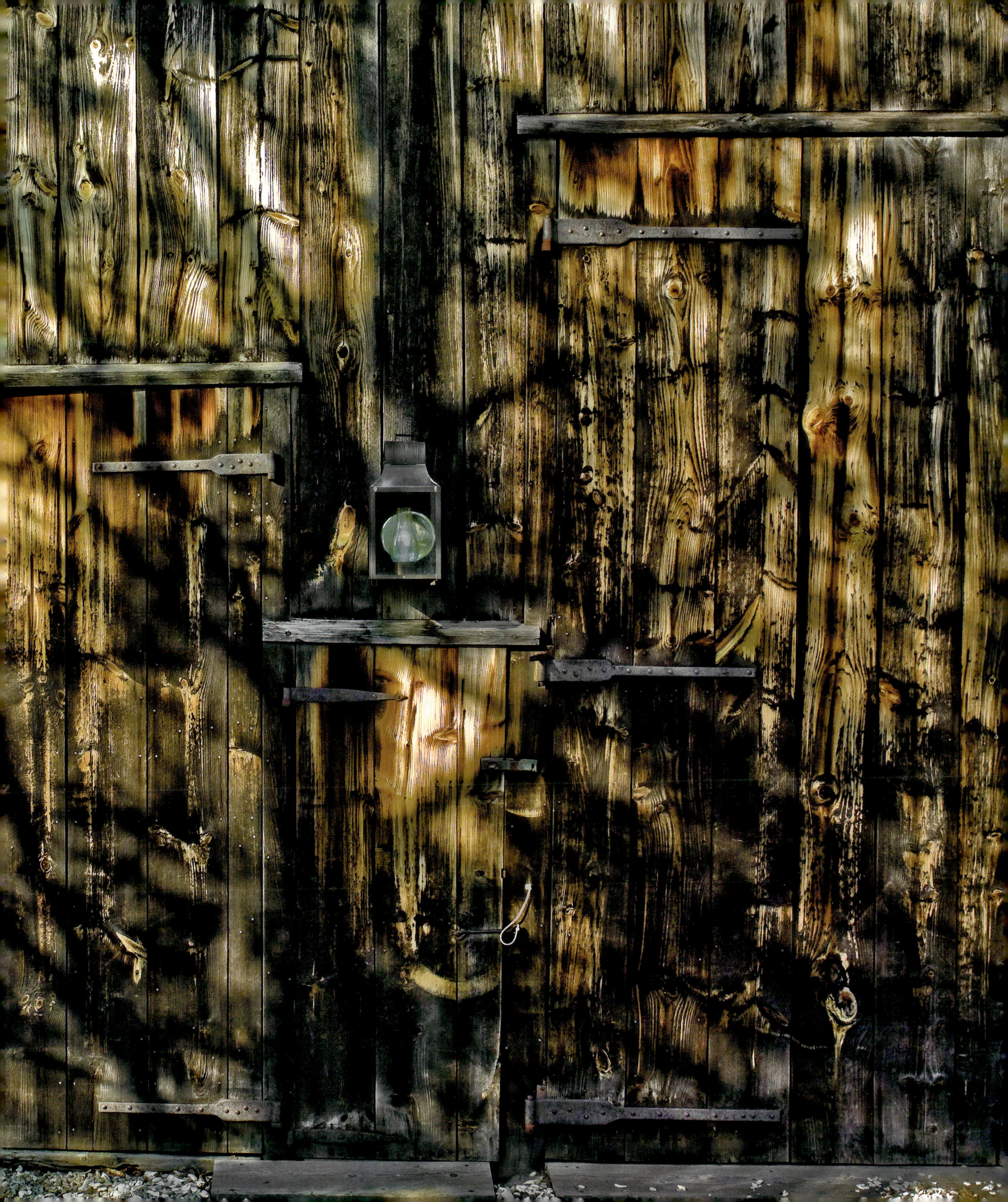

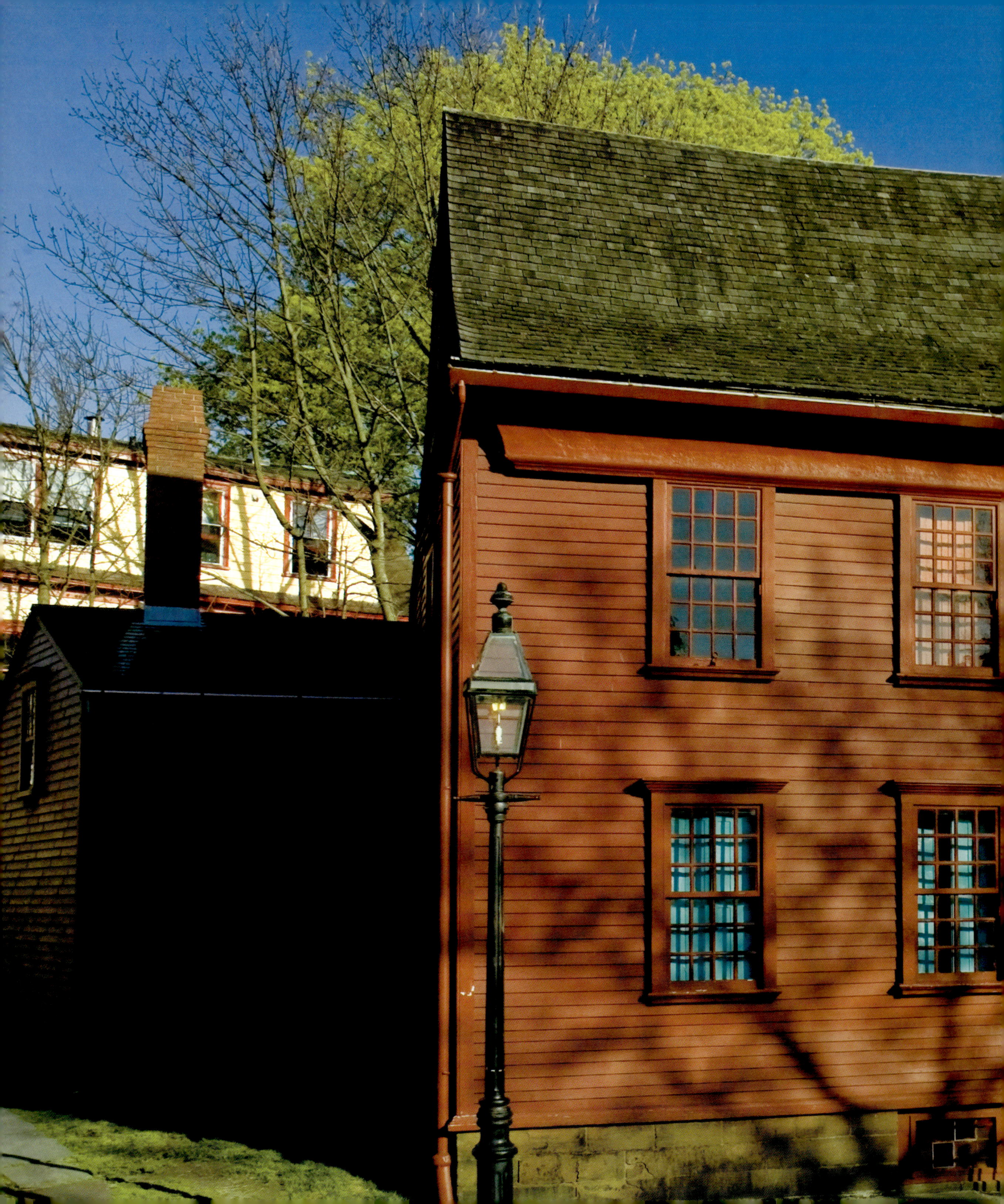

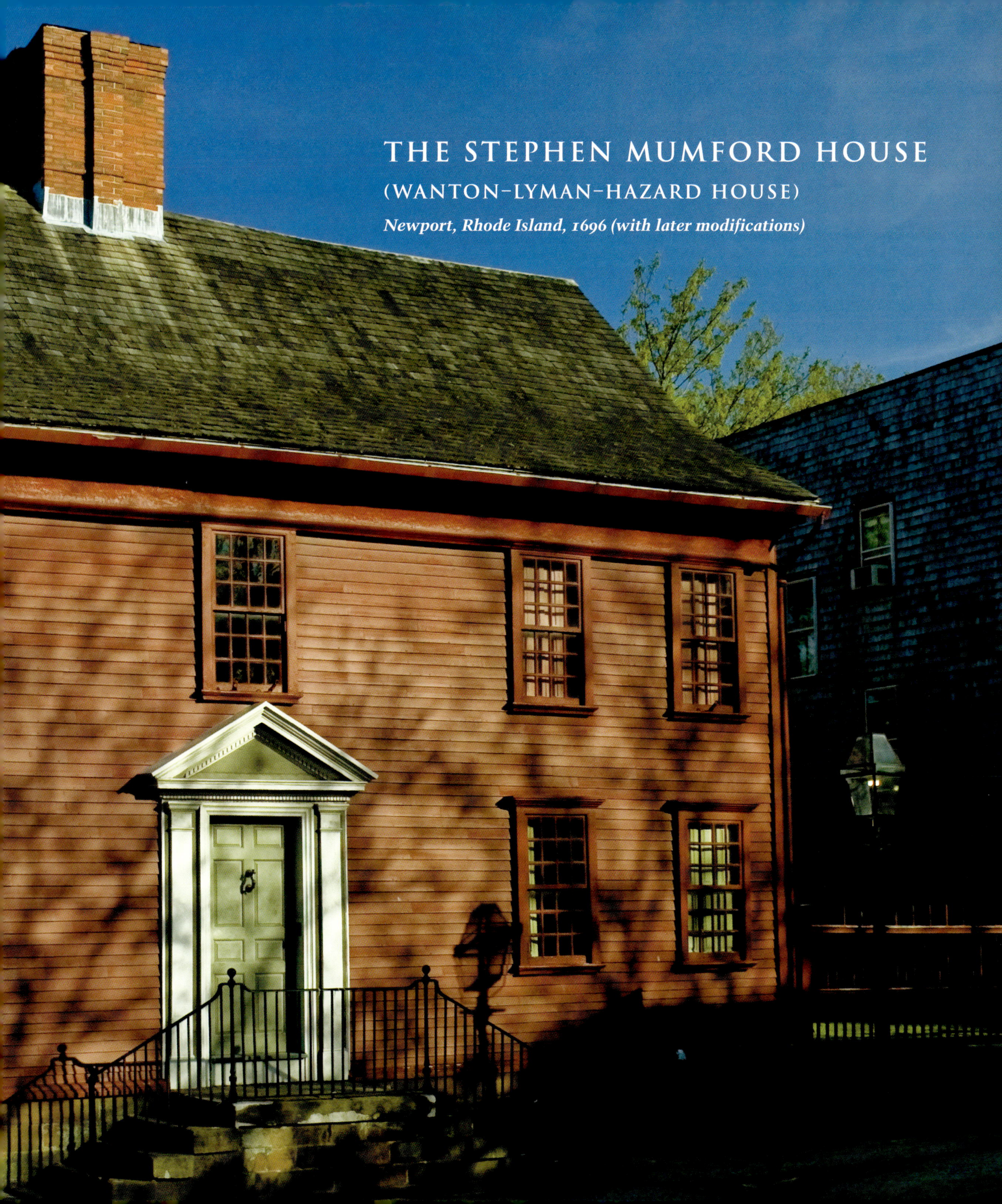

THE STEPHEN MUMFORD HOUSE

(WANTON-LYMAN-HAZARD HOUSE)

Newport, Rhode Island, 1696 (with later modifications)

PREVIOUS PAGES *Stephen Mumford's 1696 house is a study in how multiple owners changed a house over the next century, both inside and out. On the front, a Georgian doorway and sash windows are modest updates.*

BELOW *In more upscale houses, bed chambers rivaled parlors of simpler houses. Paint analysis of early layers informed the colors used in the restoration of the Mumford House.*

RIGHT *The parlor is inside the entry. Georgian paneling in the eighteenth century introduced a new aesthetic, new colors, and the practicality of cupboards.*

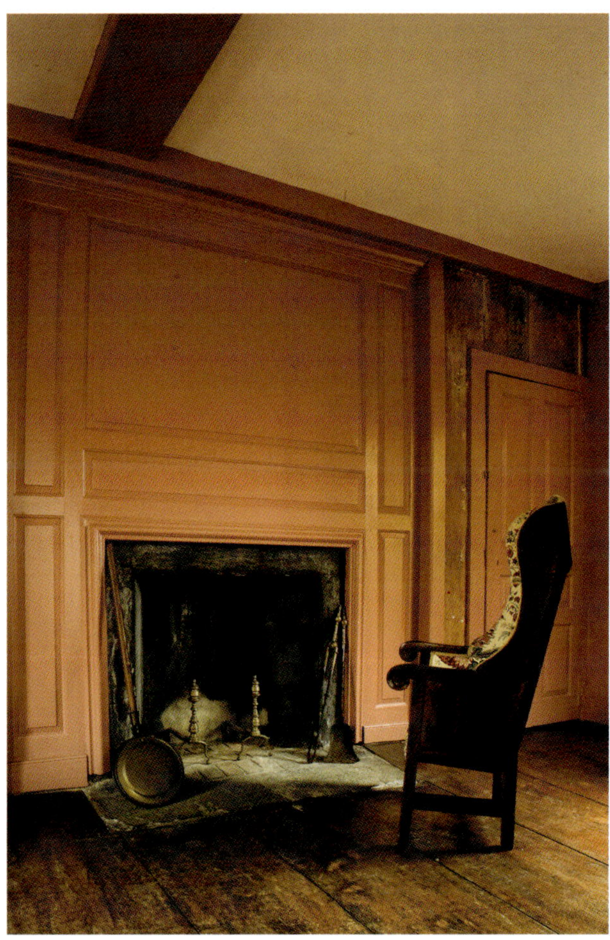

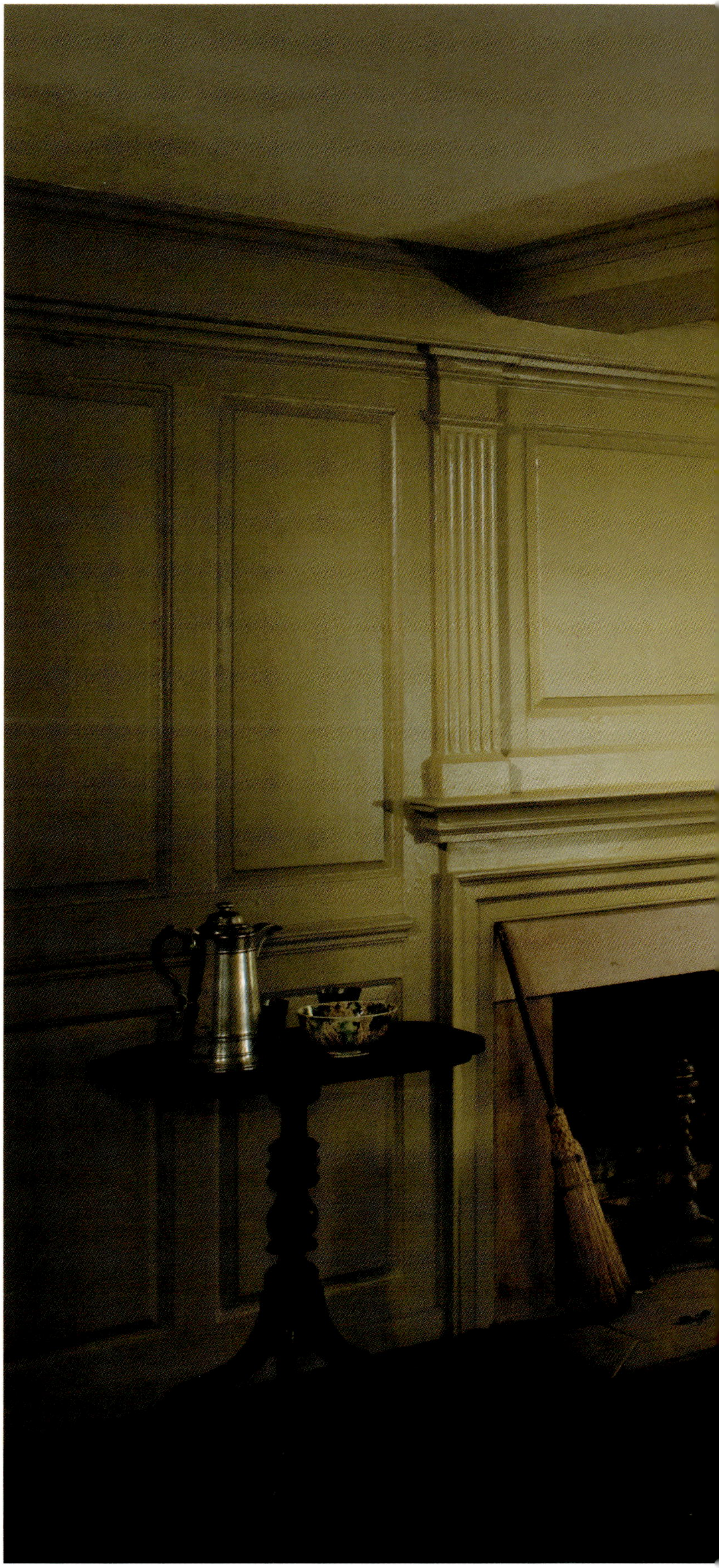

As Massachusetts became a refuge for Puritans, Rhode Island became a sanctuary for those of other faiths who were not well tolerated by Puritans despite a common desire to seek a new life in the wilderness. Among the faithful to head for Rhode Island were members of the Seventh Day Baptists, whose adherence to worshiping on the last day of the week (Saturday), belief in strict adherence to all Ten Commandments, practice of water baptism for adults only, and the "laying on of hands" caused friction with otherwise similar Baptists. The first of these to come to Newport was Stephen Mumford and his wife, Anne, in 1665. He was a successful businessman, sea captain, and founding member of the Seventh Day Baptist Church.

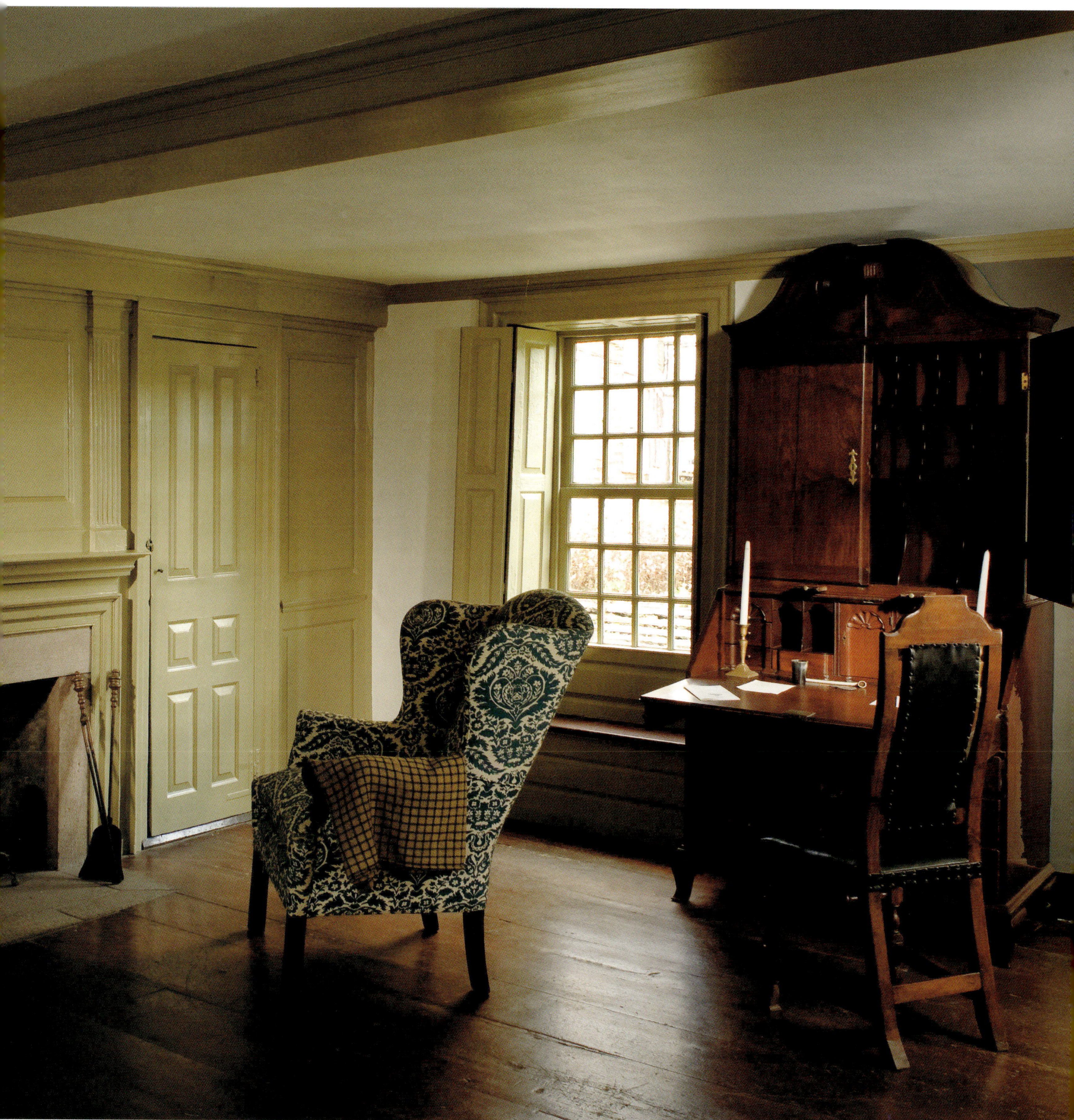

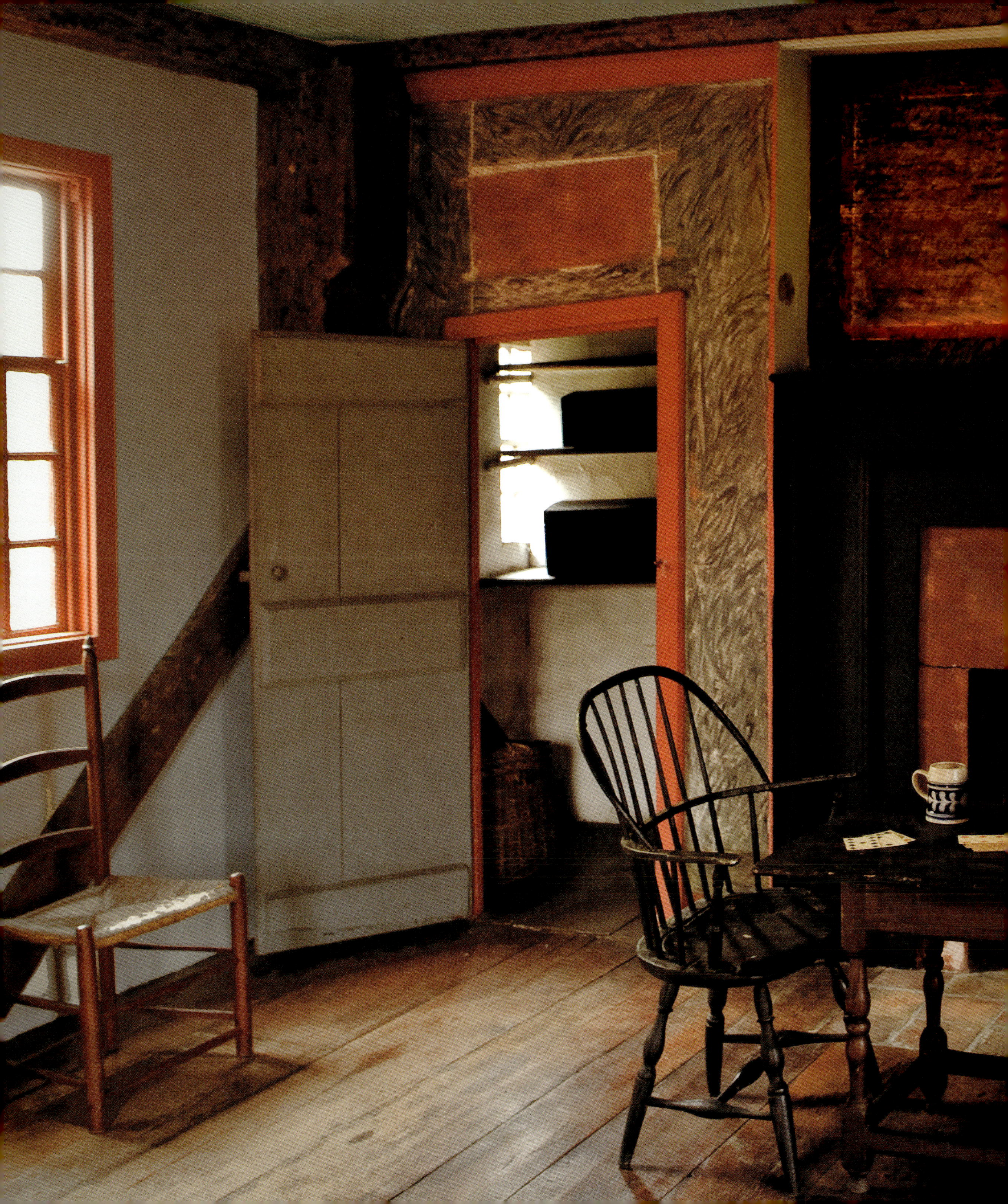

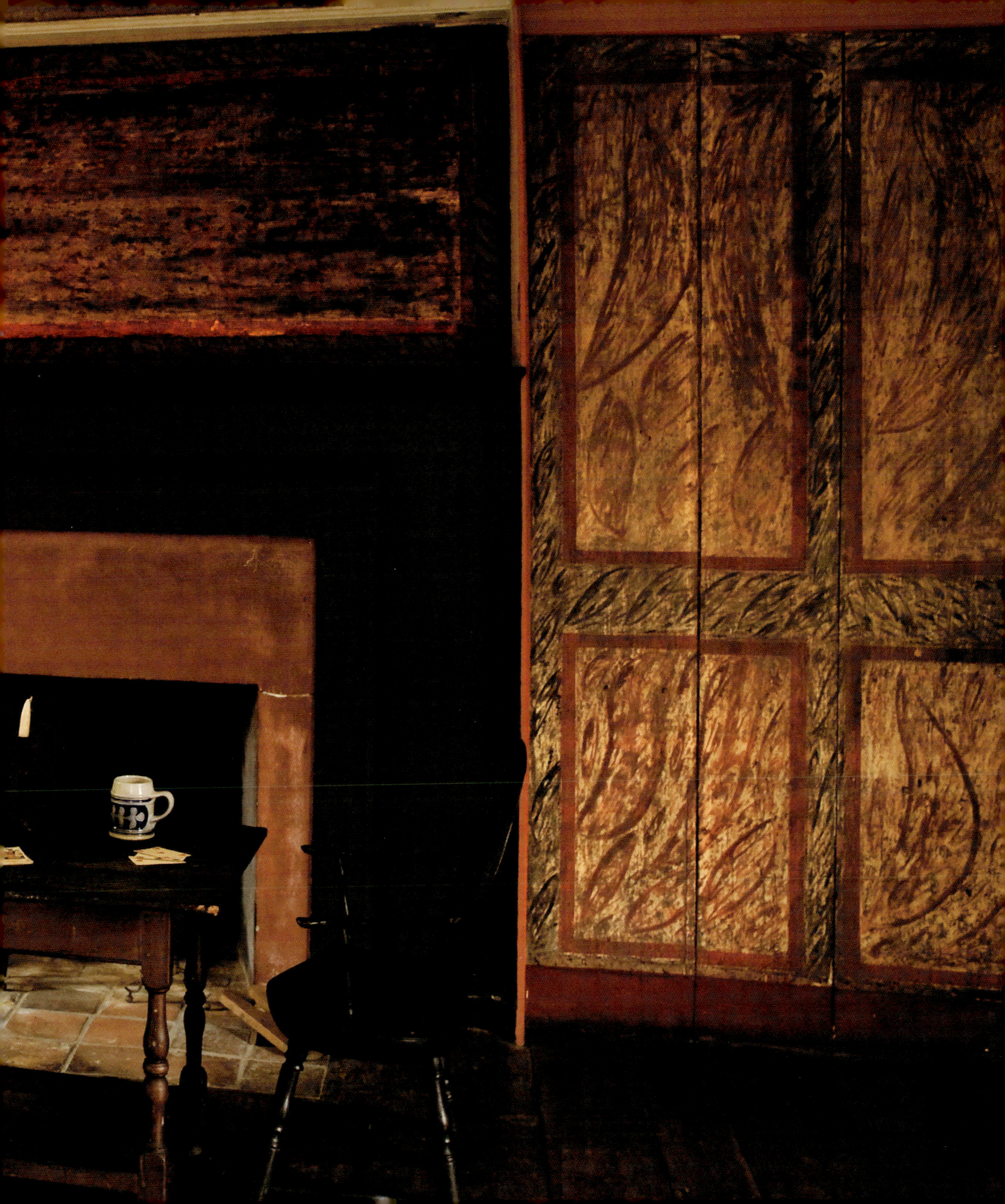

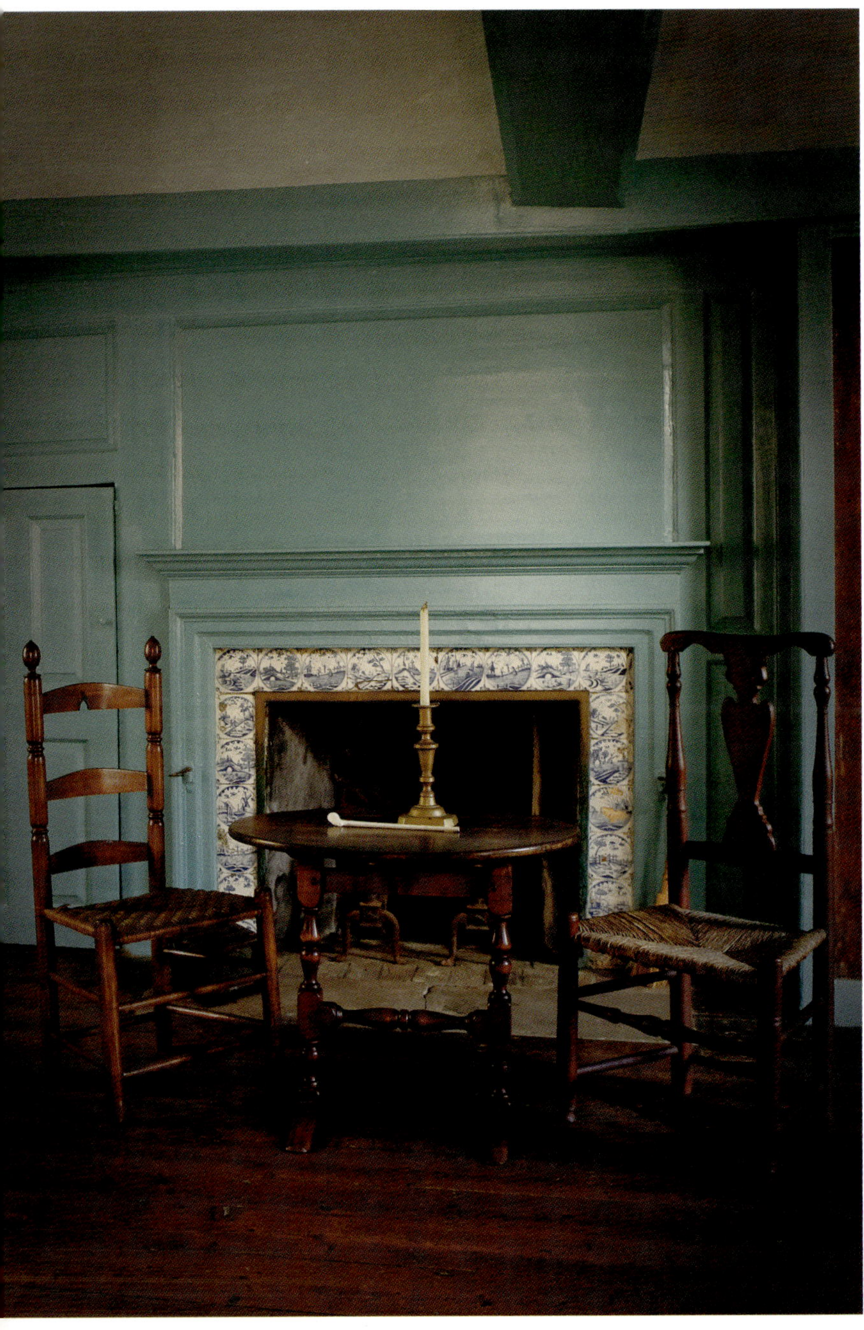

PREVIOUS PAGES *Puritan houses were plain; Georgian style introduced decoration for its own sake. Raised panel walls were preferred but, if too expensive, decorative painters could simulate these in paint, usually with wood graining, sometimes with more imaginative effects, as here in the bed chamber. Few such efforts have escaped the changes of fashion and taste.*

LEFT *This first-floor room was likely once the dining room. By the mid-eighteenth century, imported fireplace tiles (usually Dutch) became affordable to an increasingly affluent society, but they still, however, kept their covenant with God by preferring tiles based on Bible stories.*

FACING PAGES *Despite all upgrades, the house retains its early stairway for at least one practical reason. Restricted to a small space before the chimney stack, and both expansive and expensive, a Georgian redo would make insufficient improvement for the cost.*

Mumford had a house erected in 1696 on the conventional plan: center chimney with a room on either side, two stories in height with a garret. Mumford enjoyed its pleasures for just ten years before his death, at which point his son Stephen Jr. inherited the house, adding a lean-to kitchen at one corner. He later sold it to Richard Ward, a lawyer who became governor in 1741. Martin Howard Jr., a lawyer loyalist, bought the house in 1757, adding updated moldings and paneling. In 1765, as an outspoken member of a Tory group that chastised opponents of the Crown for disregarding Royal and Parliamentary authority, he and others were hanged in effigy during Stamp Act riots, and a crowd attacked and vandalized their houses. Howard fled Newport, and the house was sold at auction in 1772 to John G. Wanton, a prosperous Quaker merchant. It was gifted to Wanton's daughter, Polly, who married Daniel Lyman, a lawyer and Revolutionary War veteran. They added a large two-story addition to the rear in 1785 and then gave it to their daughter, Harriet, who married another lawyer, Benjamin Hazard. The last Hazard family owner died in 1911.

The Newport Historical Society purchased the then-neglected property and had noted restoration architect Norman Isham refurbish the building, preserving many changes owners had made to show the evolution of the house and owners. The early steep pitch roof, plaster cornice, and 1720s kitchen are still evident. The 1785 Lyman addition was removed, and the second-floor bedroom restored to its seventeenth-century appearance. The Newport Historical Society from 1997 to 2001 undertook further stabilization and restoration (paint analysis was used to reinterpret the house's paint scheme), including restoration of the grounds and garden. Today, it is the oldest surviving intact residence in Newport, a town widely recognized for its many well-preserved homes and public buildings.

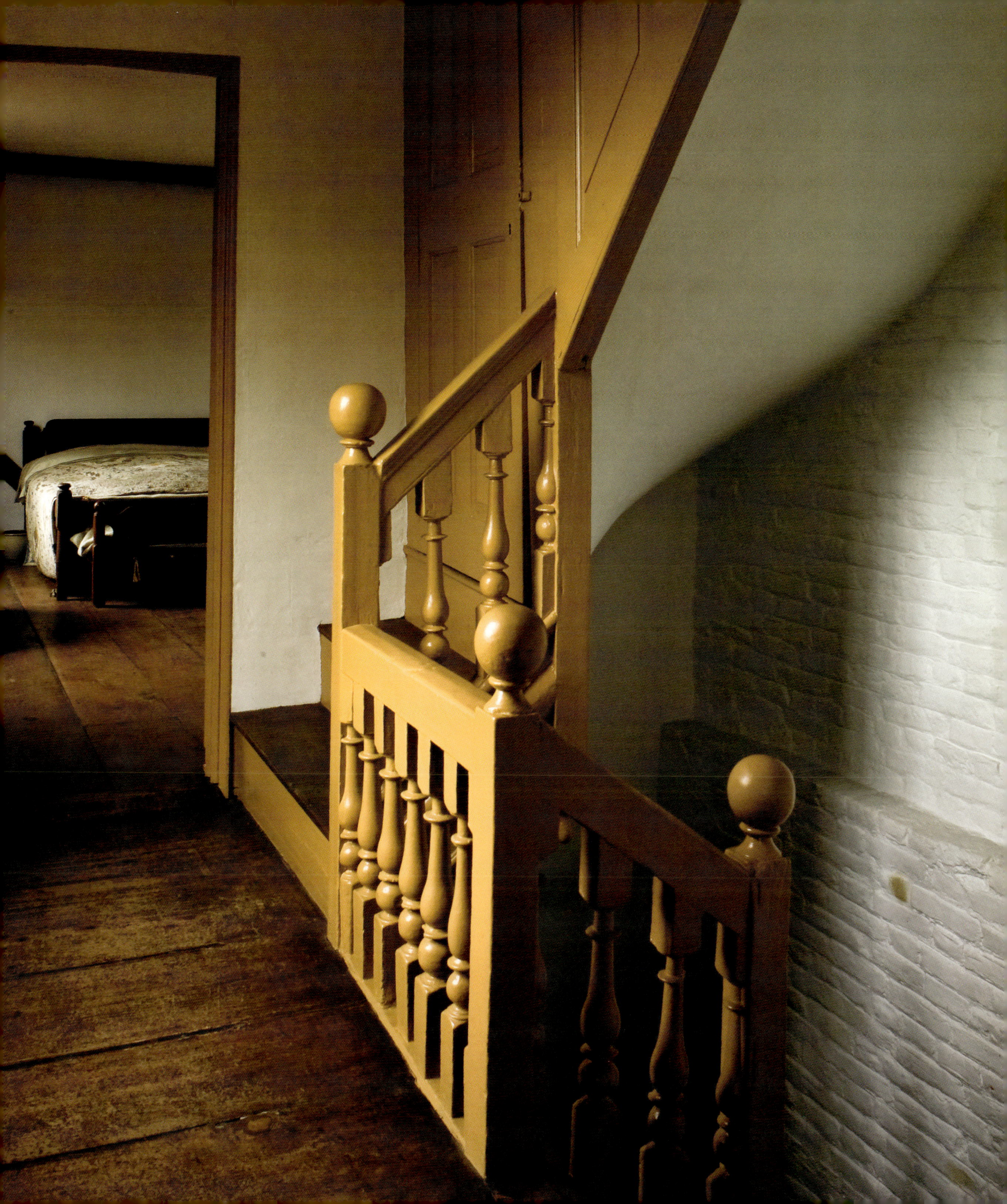

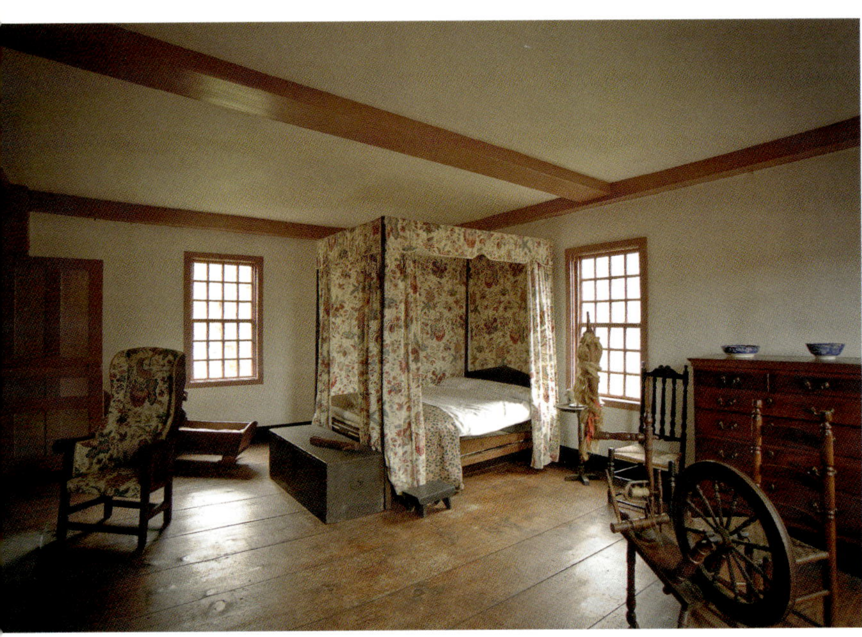

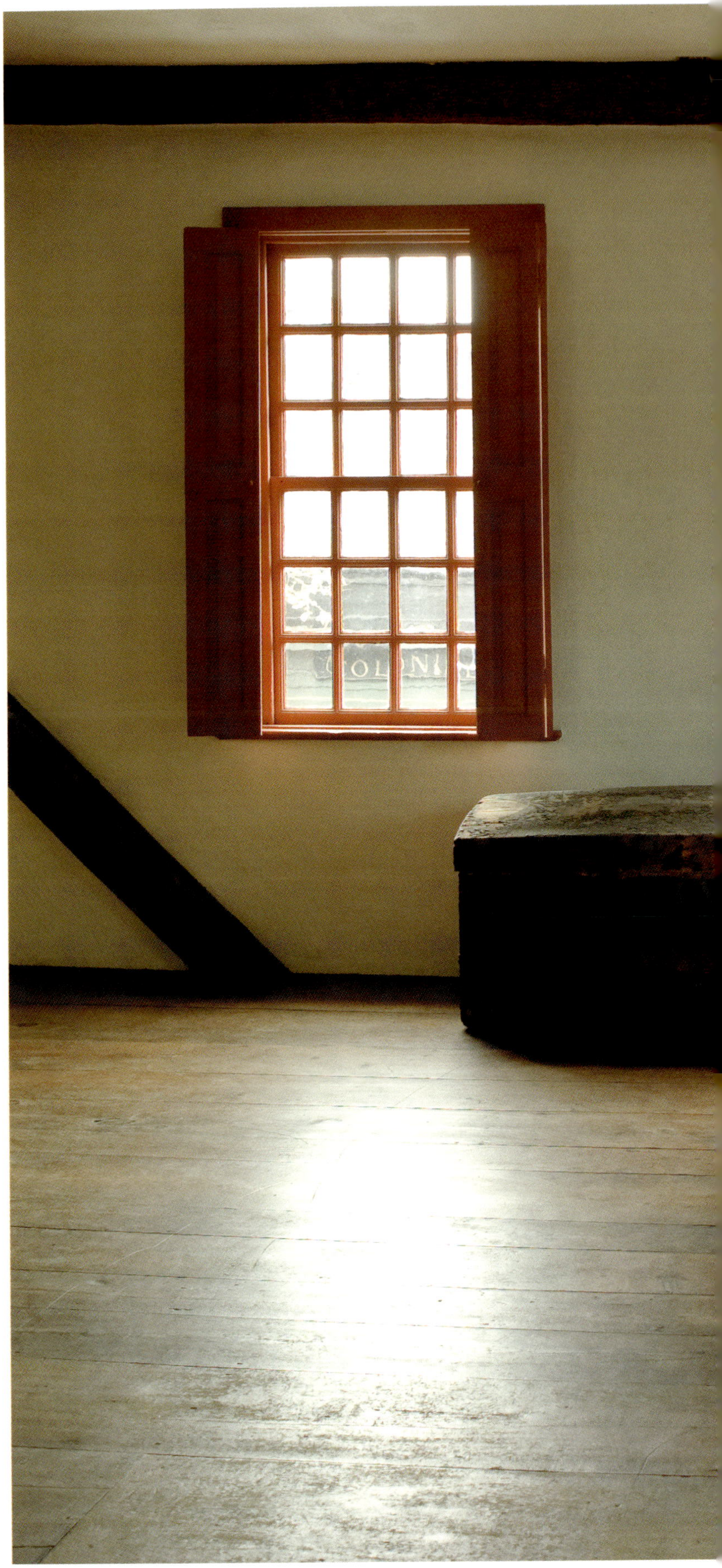

ABOVE *In the right bed chamber only part of the summer beam is shown, giving truth to the house's early origin. All the rest, including furnishings, are in the eighteenth-century mode.*

RIGHT *The left bed chamber escaped modernizing in the eighteenth century, except for the windows. Medieval construction stands out, and was no offense to Puritans who saw the revealed truth of the world as important.*

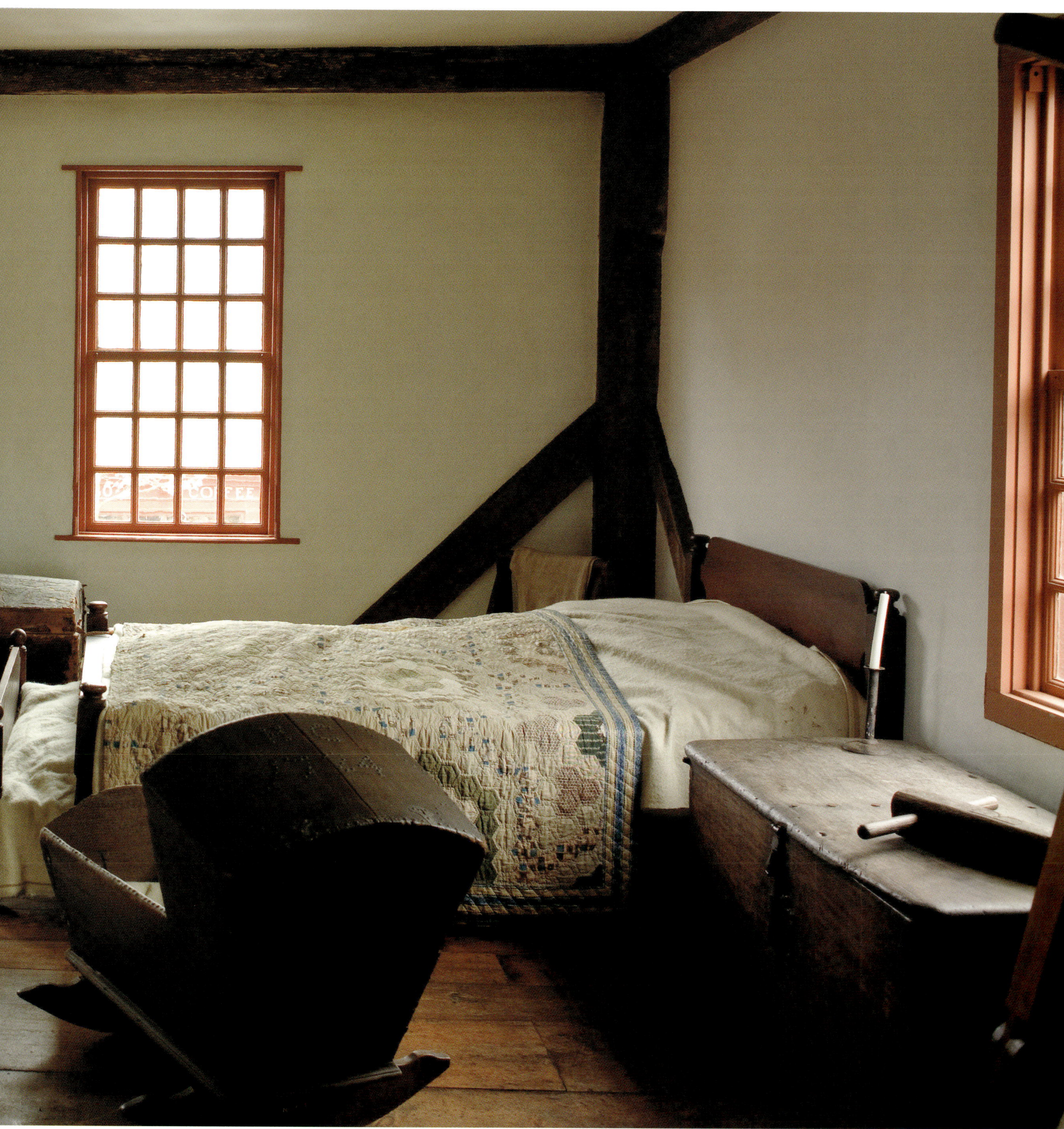
COFFEE

GREAT FRIENDS MEETING HOUSE

Newport, Rhode Island, 1699 (with later modifications)

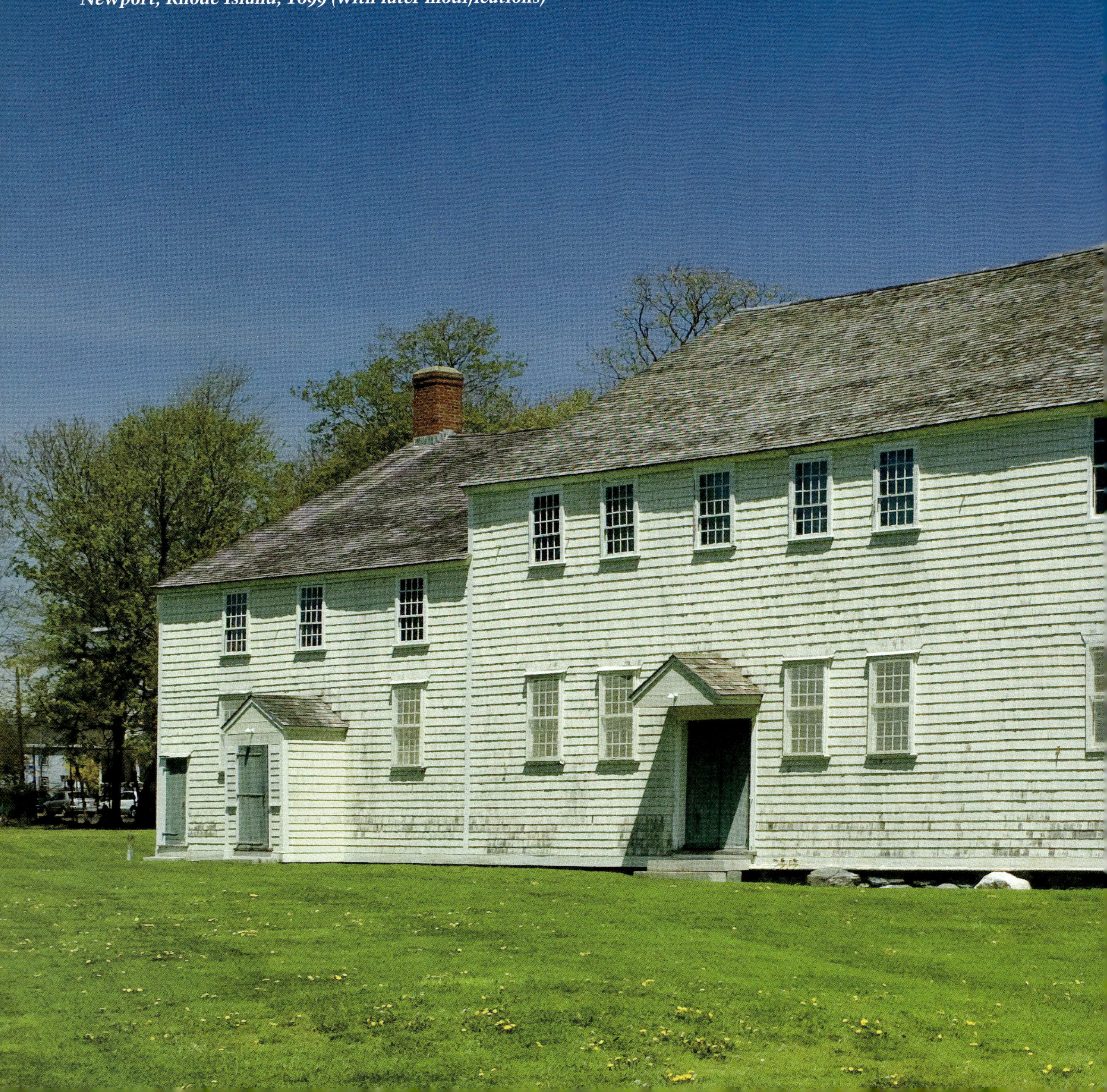

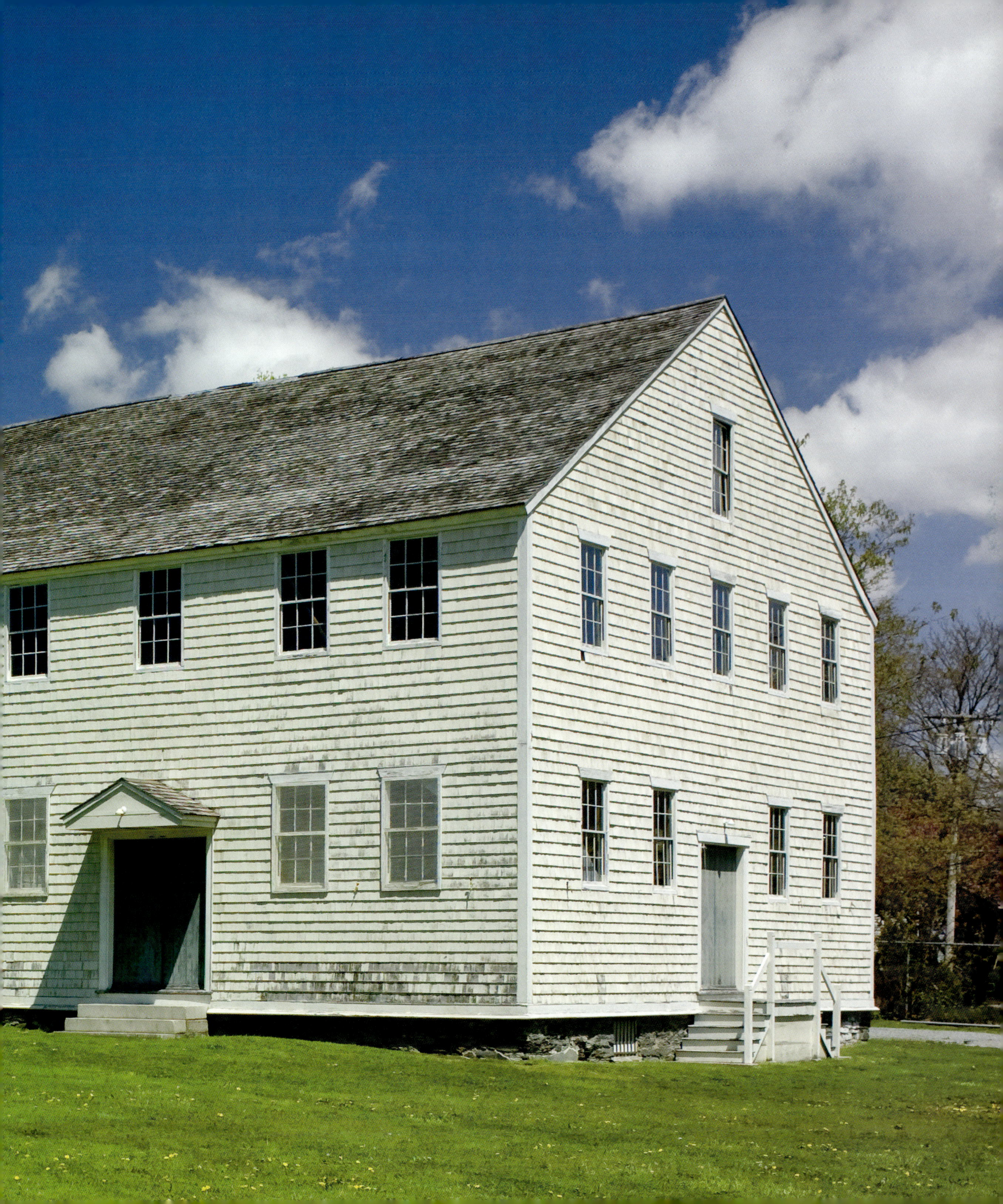

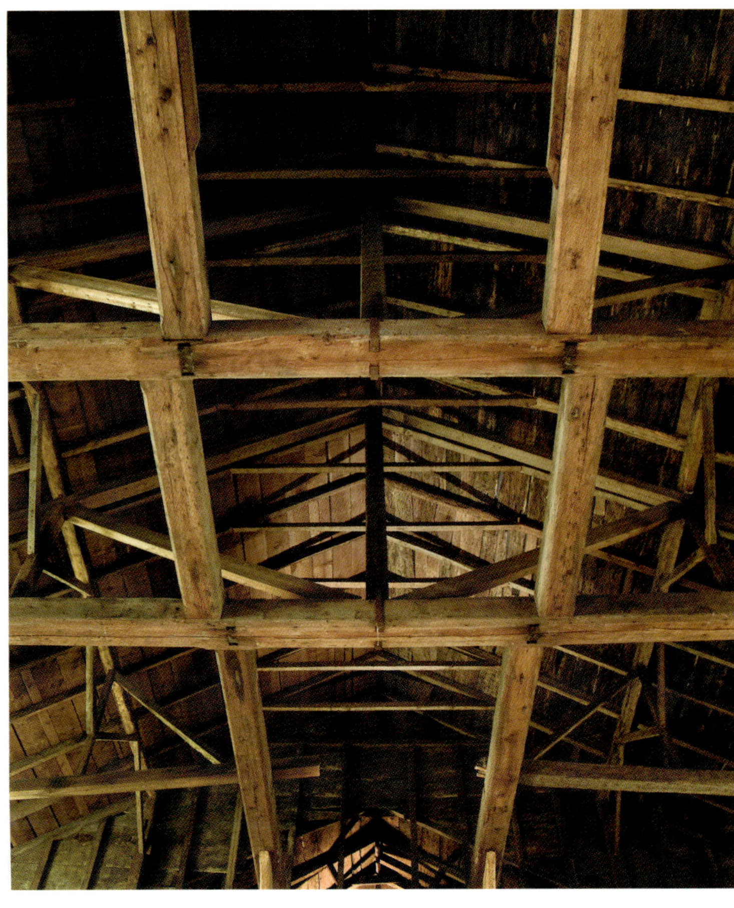

PREVIOUS PAGES *Built in 1699, the center section was the earliest. It had a hipped roof and steeple much like the earlier meeting house at Hingham. Adding extensions to opposite ends during the next two centuries required changing the hipped roof to a pitched roof so all roof ridges aligned.*

LEFT *A pitched roof structure required a quite different system than the Hingham hipped roof. Although the main heavy beams connecting opposite walls are similar to a hipped roof, the structure above is not.*

RIGHT *The original gable wall was partially retained when the large addition was built, but it was opened enough for communication between sections. Quaker worship was centered on the individual's silent communication with God, though each might in turn arise to share his experiences with others. As such the meeting had no need for the accoutrements found in the buildings of other faiths: no pulpit, altar, ornament, or even a steeple.*

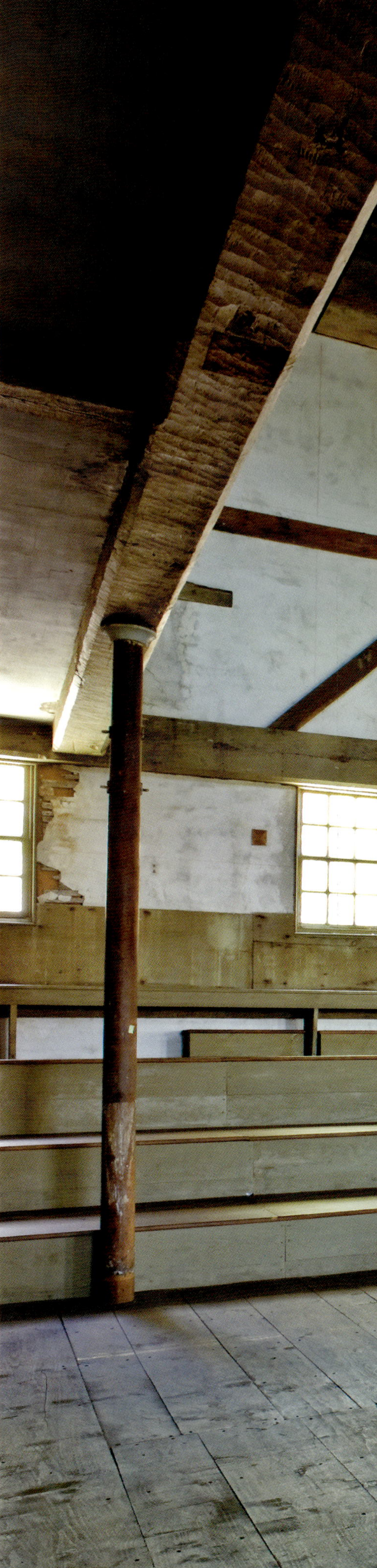

Starting in the 1630s Rhode Island drew settlers seeking a refuge for their differing beliefs. Freethinkers like Anne Hutchinson, Quakers like Mary Dyer, Baptists, and Jews fleeing persecution all arrived here. Tolerance—but also opportunity and ready access to the sea—made Newport the principal port and colonial capital of Rhode Island from the seventeenth century to the Revolution. Tolerance also extended to business, privateering, and smuggling. Newport was a rum manufacturing center and an active port where the slave trade played a role in the activities of many of the prominent merchants, and was the basis of many fortunes. Iconoclastic beliefs also extended to politics; when the Revolution began, Newporters were ready to throw off British authority. Rhode Island's culture of liberty of conscious and religious beliefs, first embodied in Newport's 1641 Town Statutes and codified in the 1663 Royal Charter, became a beacon of beliefs, a prototype of America to come.

In 1640s England, religious dissident George Fox began preaching the concept of "inner light," the basis of what soon became the Quaker faith. Persecuted as a threat to established religious order, many fled to the colonies. In Puritan New England

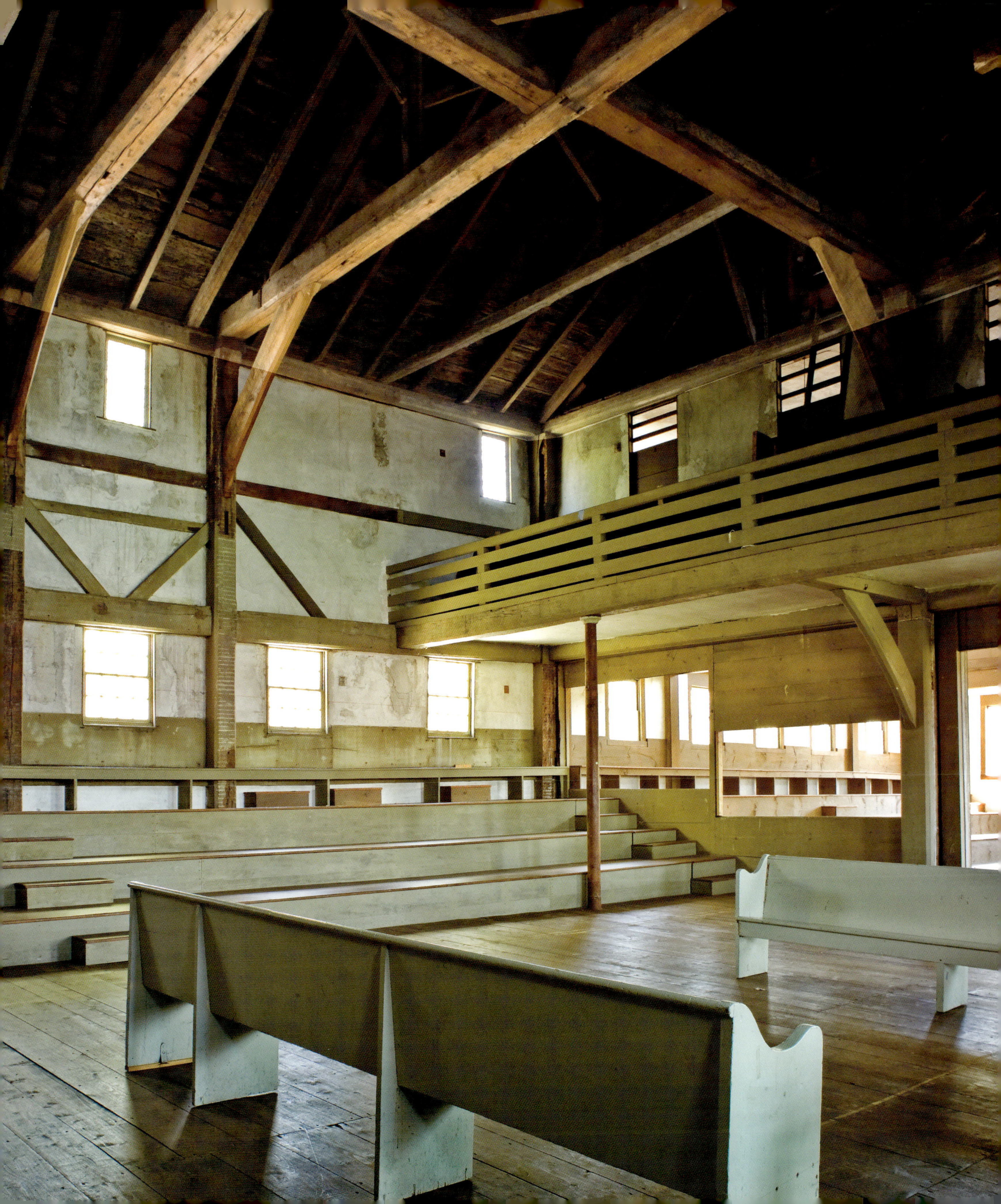

RIGHT *So fitting for a faith of inner contemplation, the Friends Meeting House is as utilitarian as a barn, except for walls broken by windows to allow light inside.*

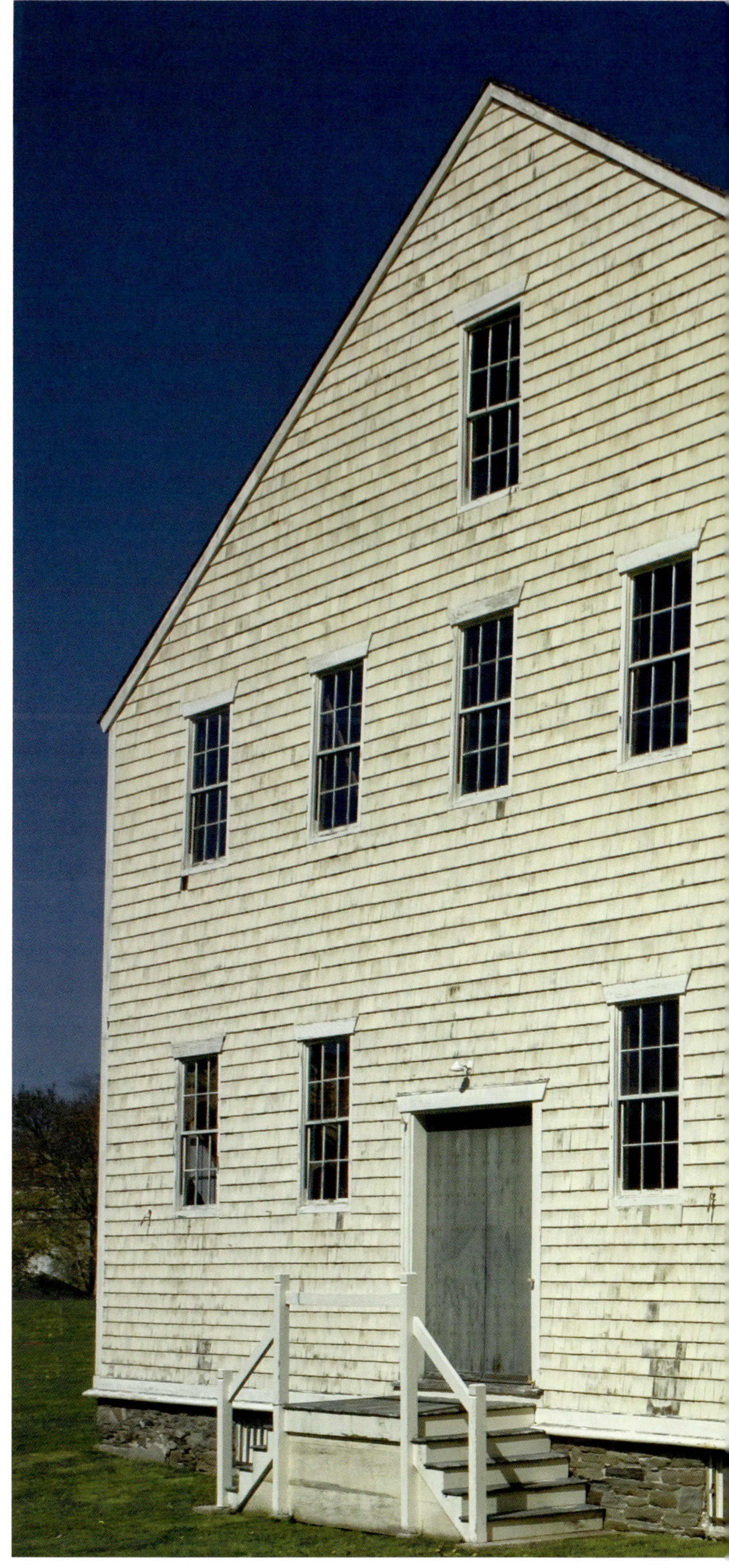

they were outlawed, sometimes accused of witchcraft, their pointed hats becoming associated in our folklore with that spectral role.

The Quakers began arriving in Newport in the 1650s, as did the Jews. Quaker pacifism inspired peaceful relations with American Indians (who limited aggression in Rhode Island during the 1675–76 Indian uprising known as King Philip's War) and passage of the first conscientious objector law in the colonies. By 1700 these members of the Society of Friends were more than half of Newport's population. Many were converted Baptists and followers of Anne Hutchinson. They dominated the town's social and economic life. Their "plain style" of living was reflected in dress and buildings.

An early convert to Quakerism in Newport was Nicholas Easton, who bequeathed his home on Farewell Street to the Quakers in 1676. This may have become the first formal meeting house, which was definitely active by 1677. In 1699, however, the need for a larger house resulted in the presently surviving structure. Built like the meeting house at Hingham, it was square with a hipped roof and cupola. "For the convenience of the women's meeting," it was enlarged in 1705 and again in 1729. It was the largest structure in Newport even at its original size.

Quaker worship meetings were silent and contemplative, each attendee "centering down" within the self to discover the "inner light" before being inspired to commune, silently, with God. In turn, individuals might then rise to share this experience with those assembled. Logically, personal-centered worship dispensed with the accoutrements of other faiths: pulpit, steeple, stained glass, or ornament of any kind would be distractions. The spare, plain-painted structure itself was then, and is today, all that was required.

In 1807, 1857, and 1867 further additions were made to accommodate the thousands who came to the New England Yearly Meeting, which continued here until 1905. Thereafter, the building was used as a recreation center, then a meeting place for the African-American community. In the 1970s it was restored under the guidance of architect Orin M. Bullock and then presented to the Newport Historical Society.

Newport was a cradle of ecclesiastical architecture, much of which has been carefully preserved. It is the site of one of the earliest Quaker meeting houses in the colonies (Flushing, New York, is the earliest), the oldest extant Jewish synagogue (Touro Synagogue, built in 1763 to leading architect Peter Harrison's design), the oldest Baptist congregation, and one of the earliest Episcopal churches (Trinity Church, built by Richard Munday in 1725, the prototype for countless later high-steepled white churches throughout New England).

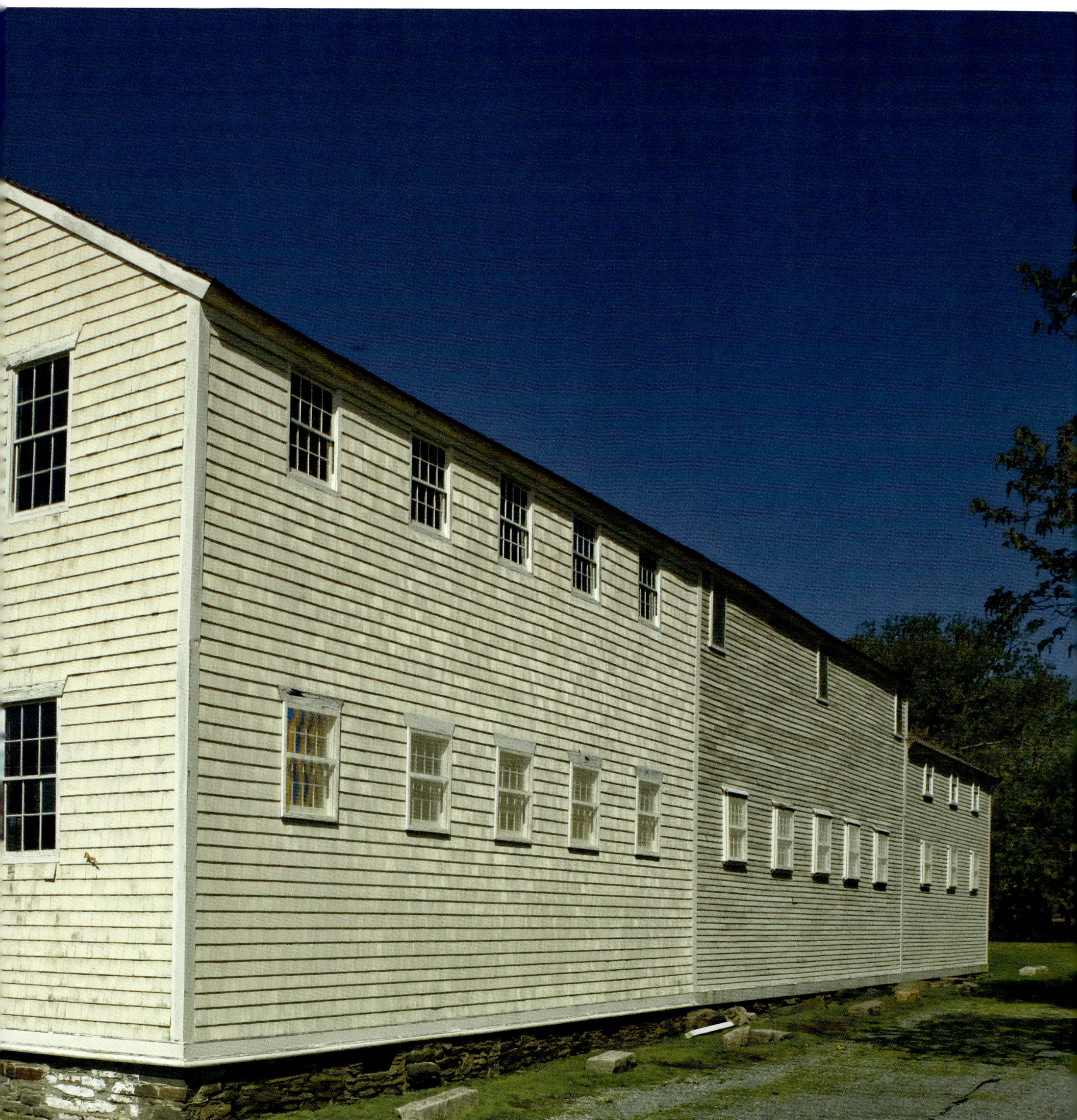

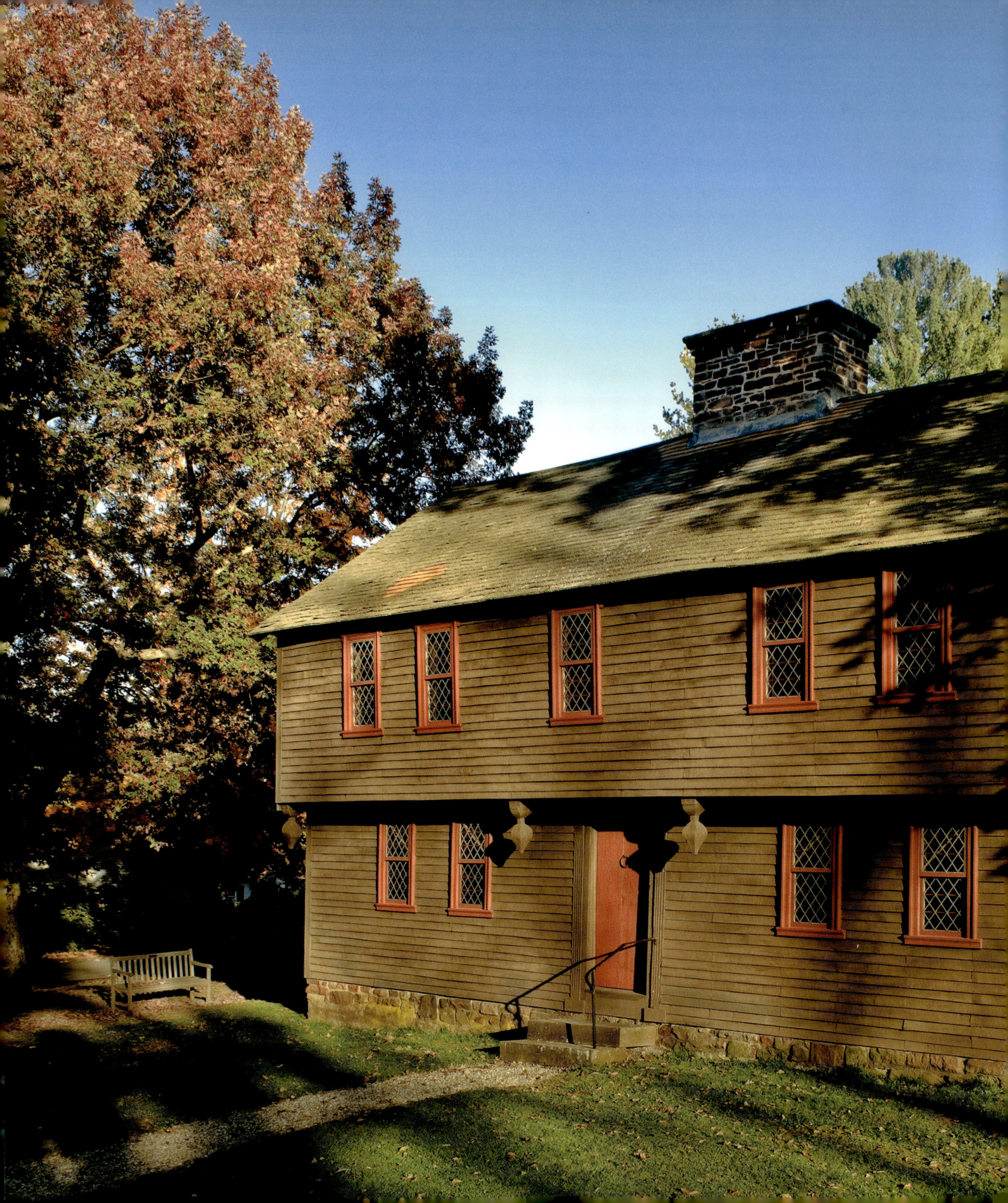

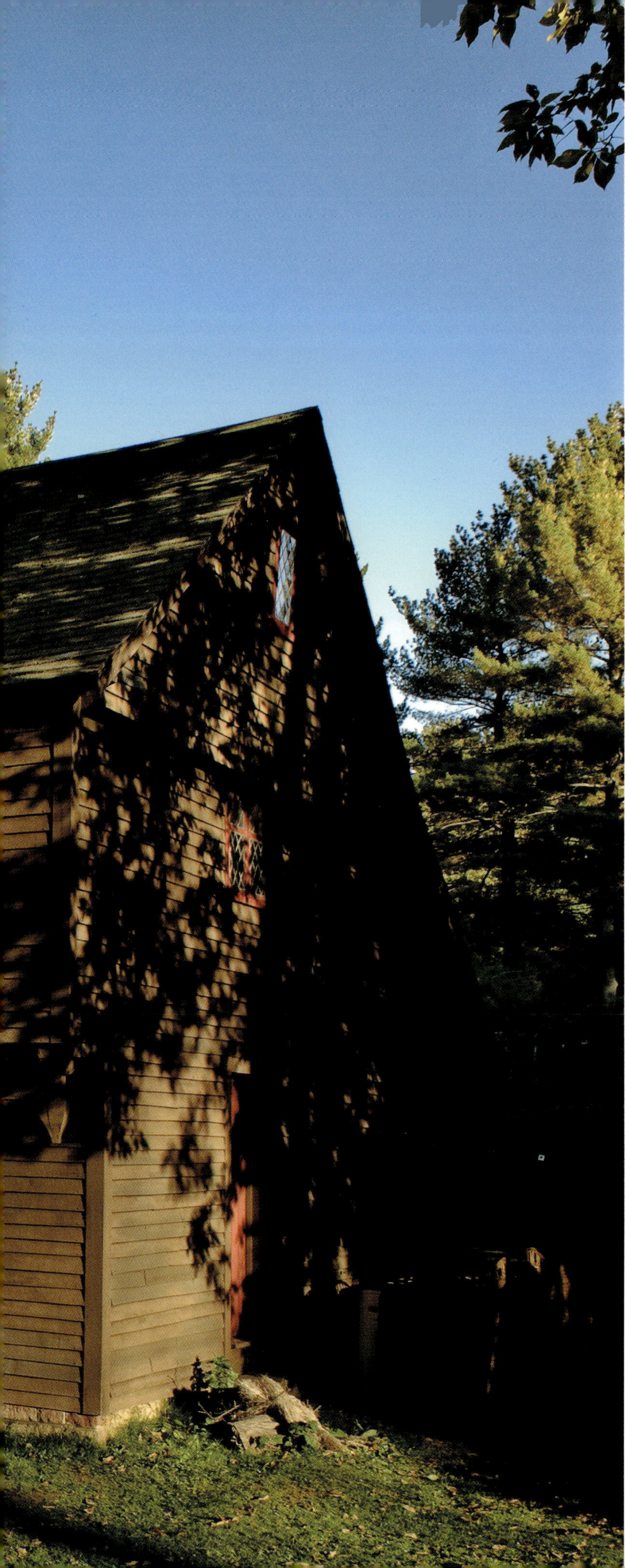

STANLEY-WHITMAN HOUSE

Farmington, Connecticut, 1709–20

The earliest English settlements in Connecticut were not on the coast but near the head of navigation on the "Fresh" River (Connecticut River) at Windsor (founded 1633), Wethersfield (1633–34), and Farmington (1640). They were a checkmate to the New York Dutch Fort Good Hope at what soon become Hartford. Fertile bottom lands just west of Hartford on the Farmington River became the site of the town of Farmington, which for a century prospered on agriculture, then manufacturing. Modest growth but growing wealth has left an unusual legacy of fine early homes, earning the name "Preservation's Valley." Even General George Washington remarked on "the village of pretty houses."

One of the older houses to survive was built before 1720 (possibly as early as 1709) by Deacon John Stanley. He sold it with 6 acres to Ebenezer Steel in that year, and when Steel died in 1722, his daughter Mary inherited it. She married Thomas Smith in 1725, when she was 18. By 1736 Solomon and Susannah Cole Whitman owned the house. Both the Smith and Whitman families were well off, educated, and members of the Congregational Church. Although primarily farmers, they had other income sources. Smith was a weaver, and Whitman a shoemaker (also serving as arbitrator, justice of the peace, probate judge, and town clerk). The Whitman descendants continued to live here until 1922, when D. Newton Barney acquired the house with the intention of creating a museum. After an extensive restoration in 1934, it opened as the Farmington Museum. It was given to the Farmington Village Green and Library Association in 1935 and has continued as a house museum since. It was designated a National Historic Landmark in 1960.

Although a product of the eighteenth century, the house's features are essentially those of a prior generation: a four-drop

LEFT *Remote settlements tend to be more conservative as they are far from the urban coastal centers of imported new ideas. Farmington was far inland and Stanley's new house was already old fashioned by east Massachusetts standards when built in the early eighteenth century. The stubby chimney points to occasional local innovation. It is built of dressed sandstone, locally available material, instead of brick.*

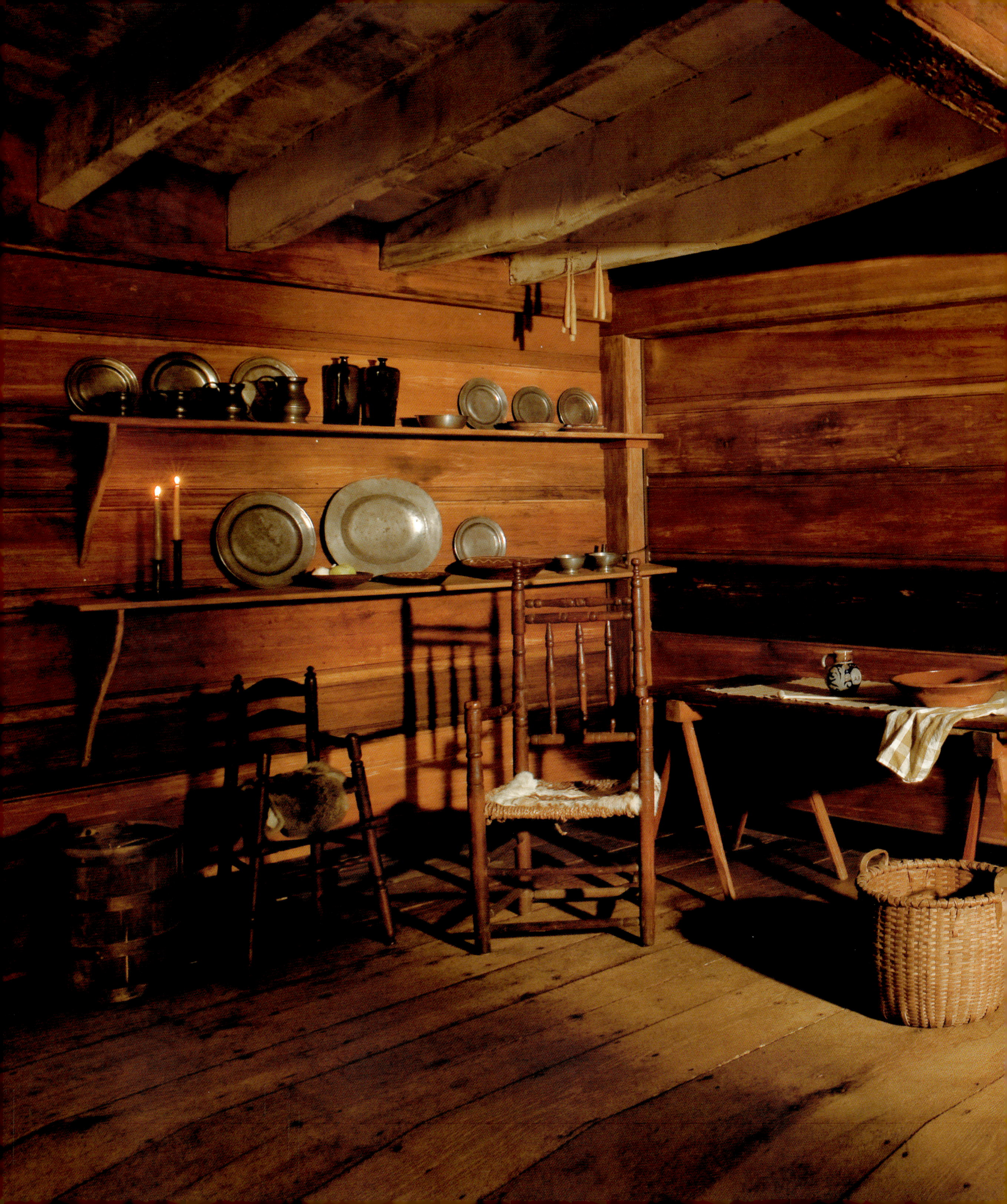

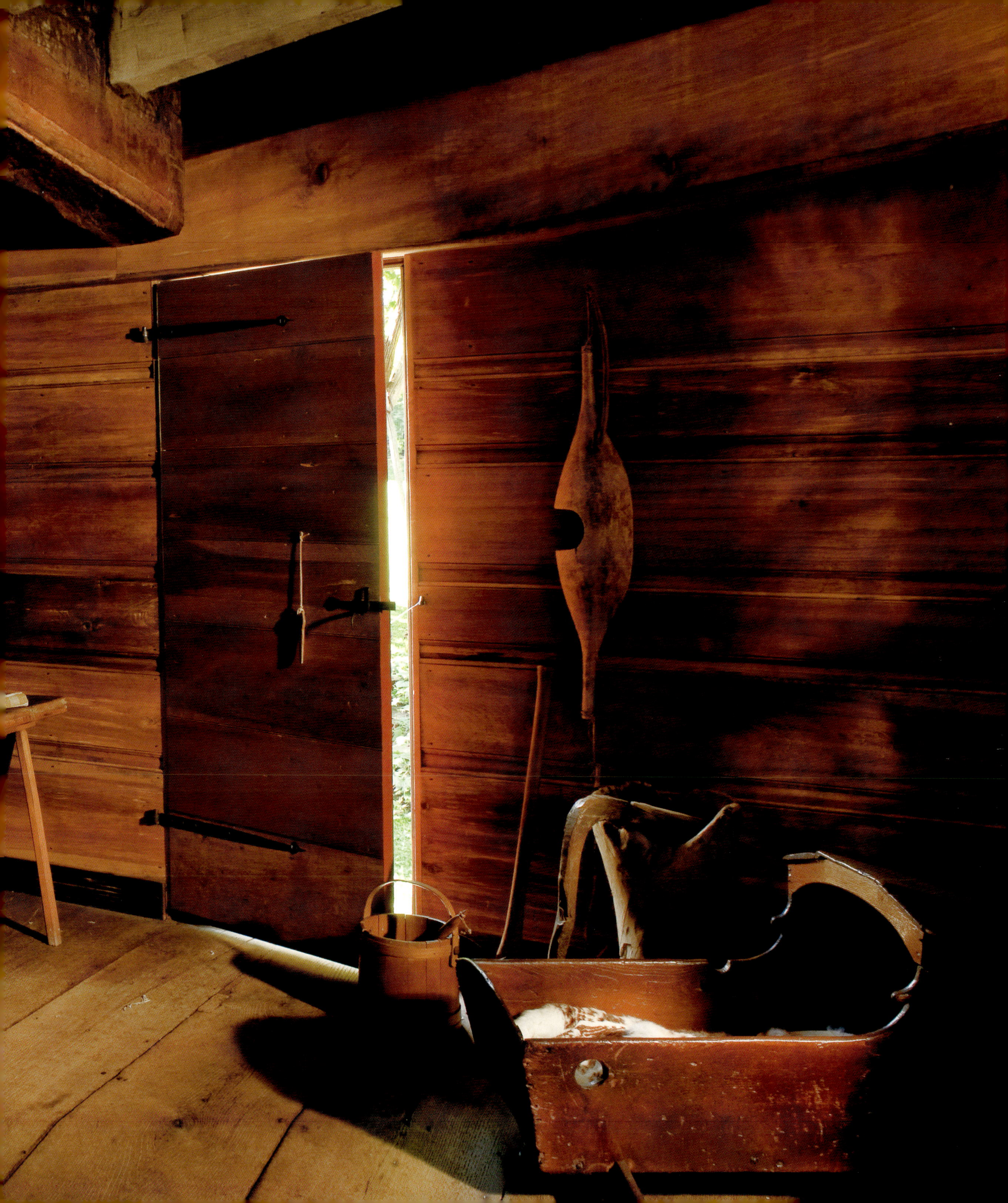

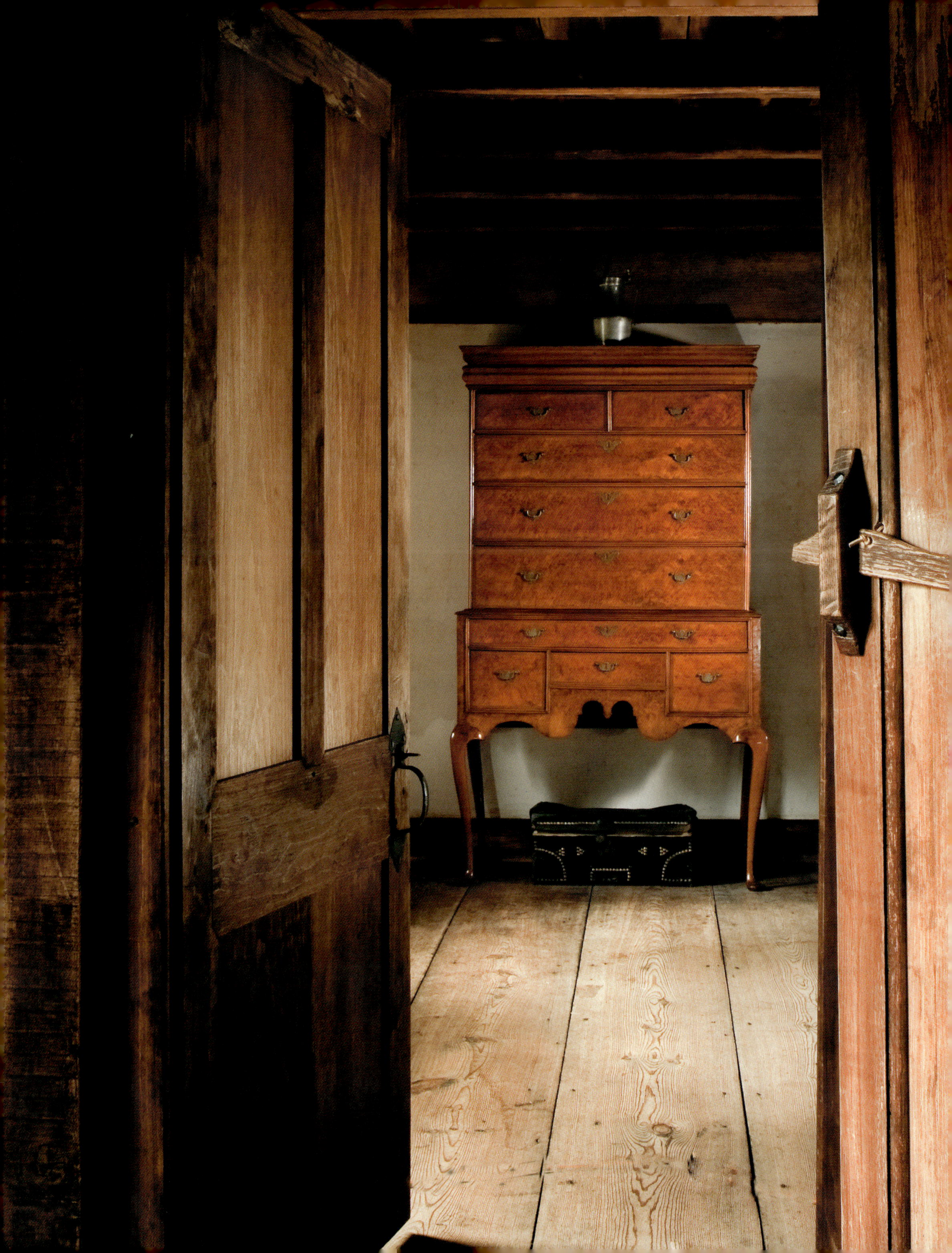

PREVIOUS PAGES *Inside the entryway is the kitchen. This unusual gable-end second entry suggests a special need for this doorway, which is now long forgotten.*

FACING PAGE *The wood-finish plainness of this house is another attribute of early Puritan sensibility, suitable for Deacon John Stanley, a church officer. The elaborate high chest in this chamber is from a later period, a closet for clothes of the newly affluent.*

RIGHT *A painted feather board wall in the parlor is modest pretension to elegance. The greater elegance of the tall clock came in the post-Revolution era. Local sandstone made for substantial fireplaces, and was more durable though less orderly than brick.*

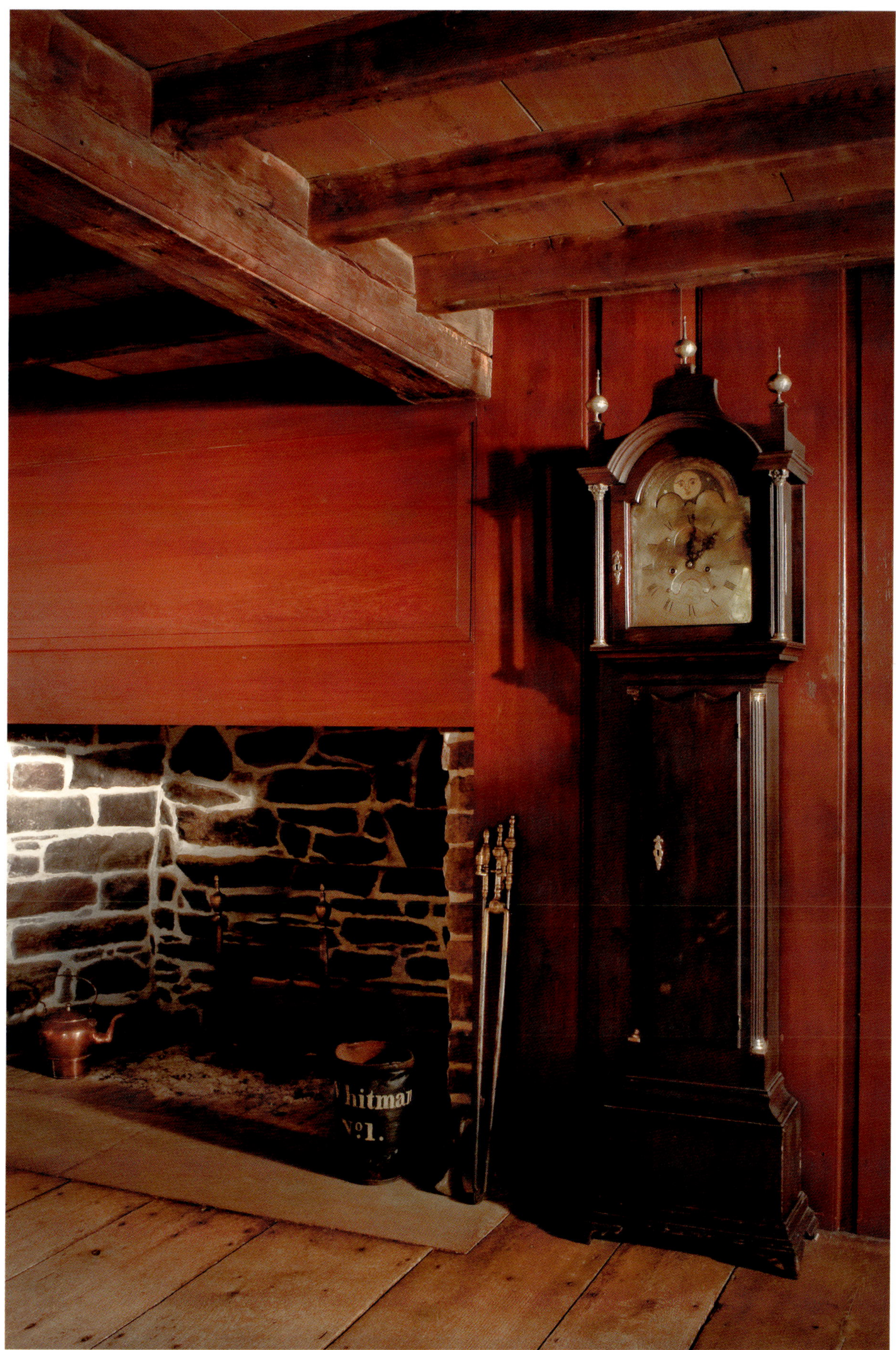

RIGHT *In contrast to the elegant bed hangings of other museums, this sparsely furnished parlor and tester bed likely represent what was common to most early houses.*

FOLLOWING PAGES *While the lean-to dates from the eighteenth century, the two story el is just over a century old and a further extension was more recently built to accommodate museum functions. The raised box garden fits the early period of the house.*

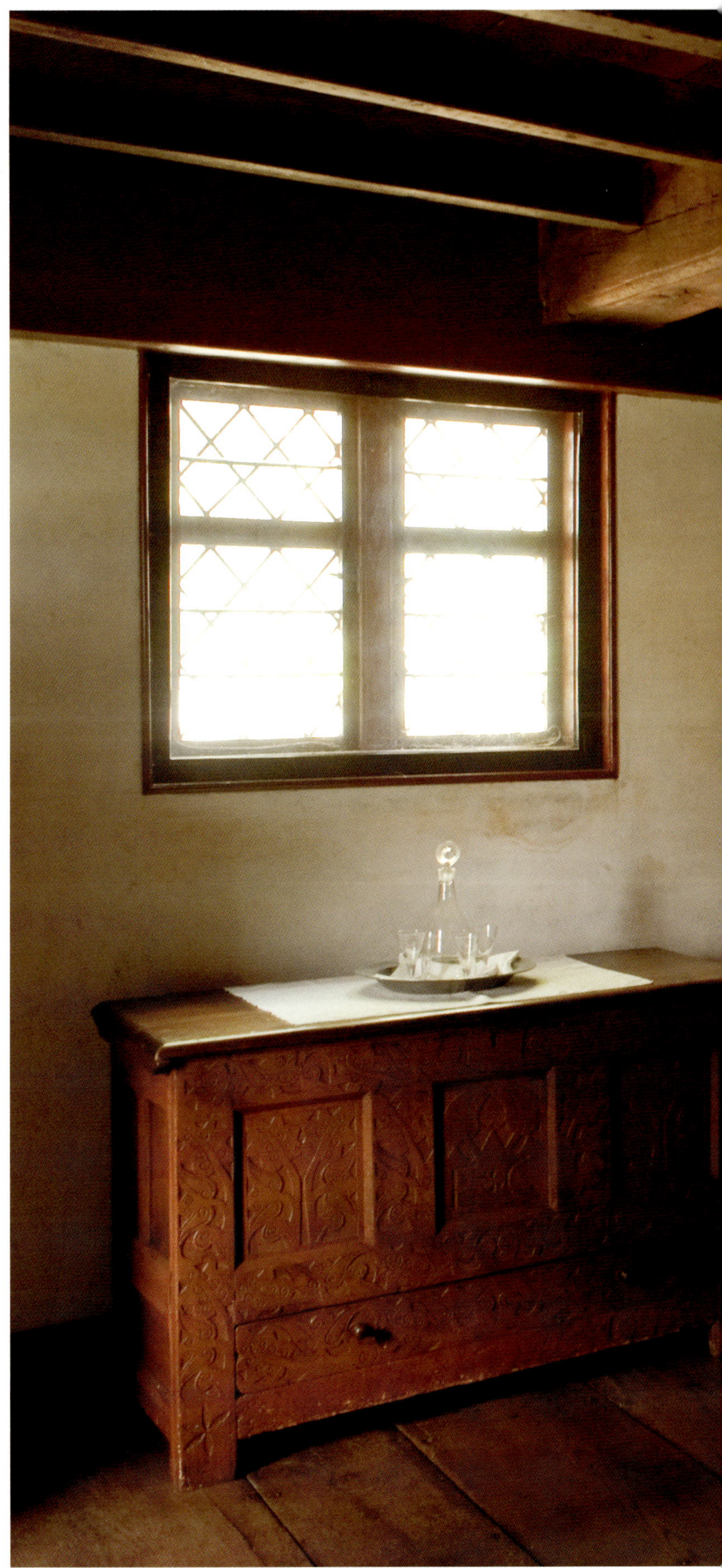

overhanging second floor and large central chimney. Diamond-shaped leaded glass windows were replicated in the 1980s from archeological fragments. The long, spreading lean-to dates from the mid-eighteenth century, entirely consistent with much earlier saltbox houses. The ell, east off the lean-to, dates from c.1890–1900 while the new additions of 2004 branched east of the ell. The house is organized in the traditional plan of central stairway entry and large chimney behind, with hall and parlor to either side.

The mid-eighteenth-century lean-to never had a fireplace and therefore was not used as a kitchen. At either end were rooms used as a buttery and as Solomon Whitman's office. The second-floor front overhangs the wall below—with hanging pendants—in a manner associated with earlier houses.

Despite the long availability of brick, the above-roof chimney, while appearing to be of brick, is of reddish sandstone blocks shaped like bricks and laid up with clay rather than the hard-to-get lime. Farmington and nearby Portland had brownstone quarries affording cheap material for chimneys, foundations, gravestones, and even highway markers.

The house is later than its post-medieval seventeenth-century appearance would suggest, likely attributable to a continuing Puritan conservatism, which one can see in other houses dating to the late eighteenth century.

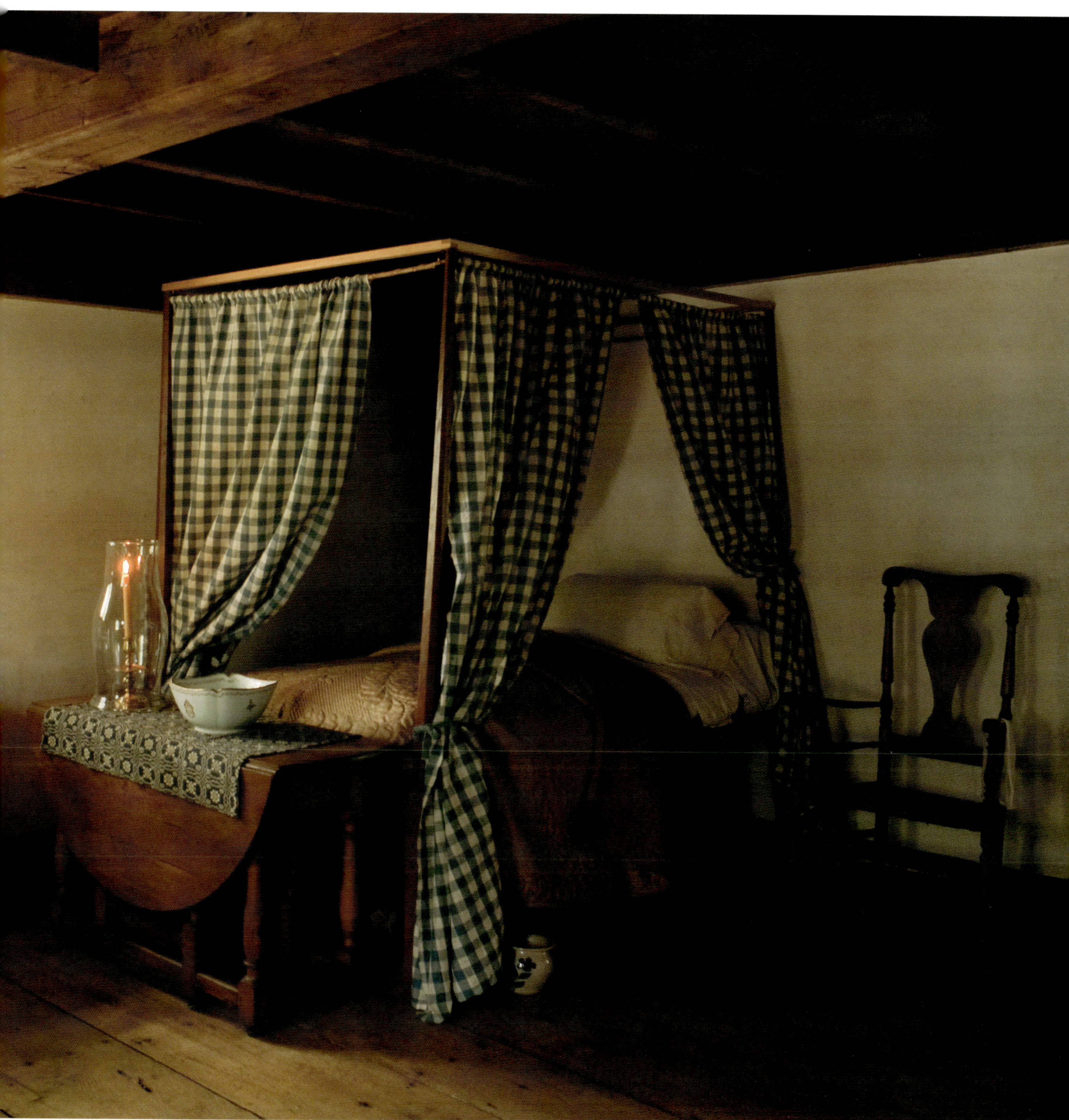

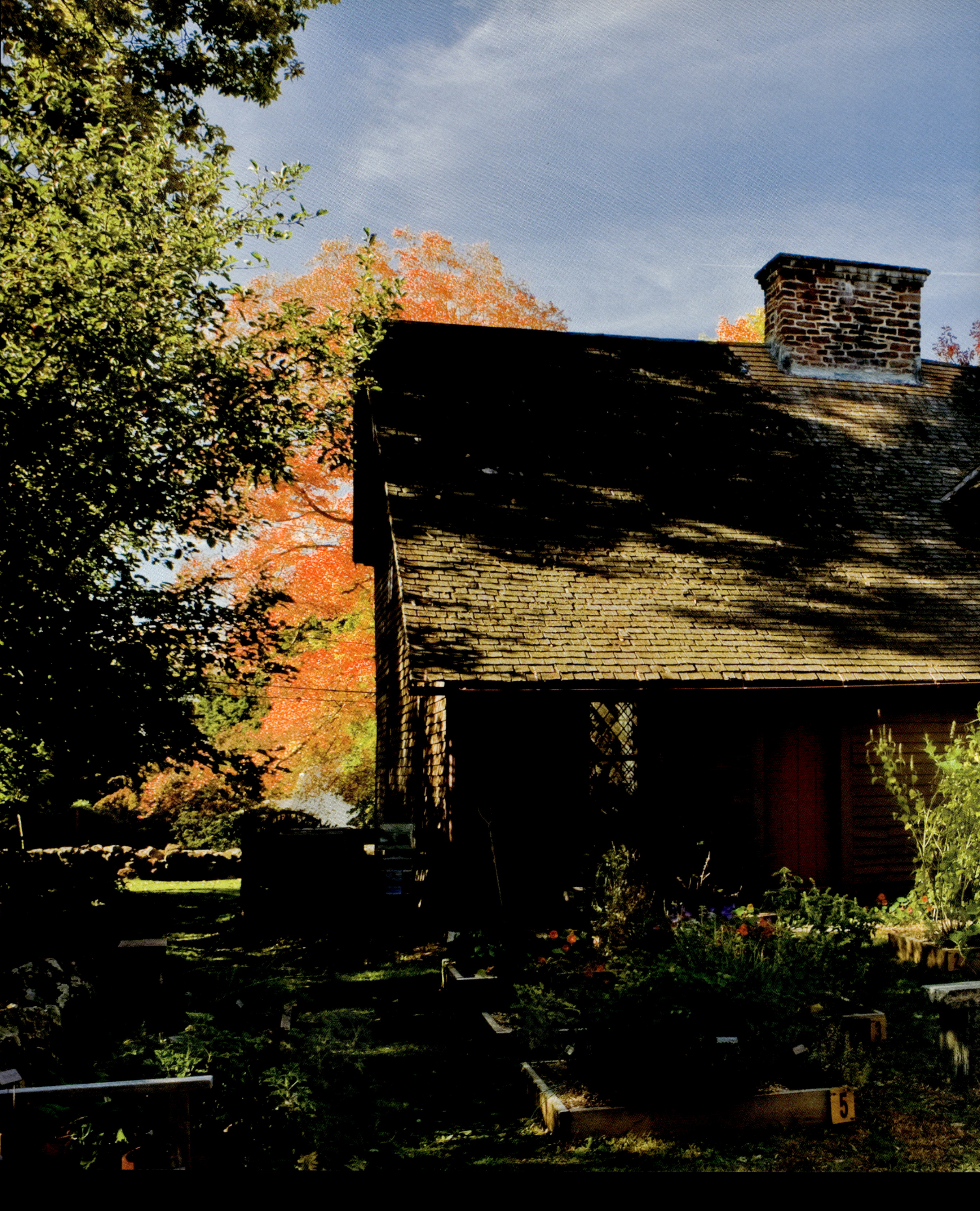

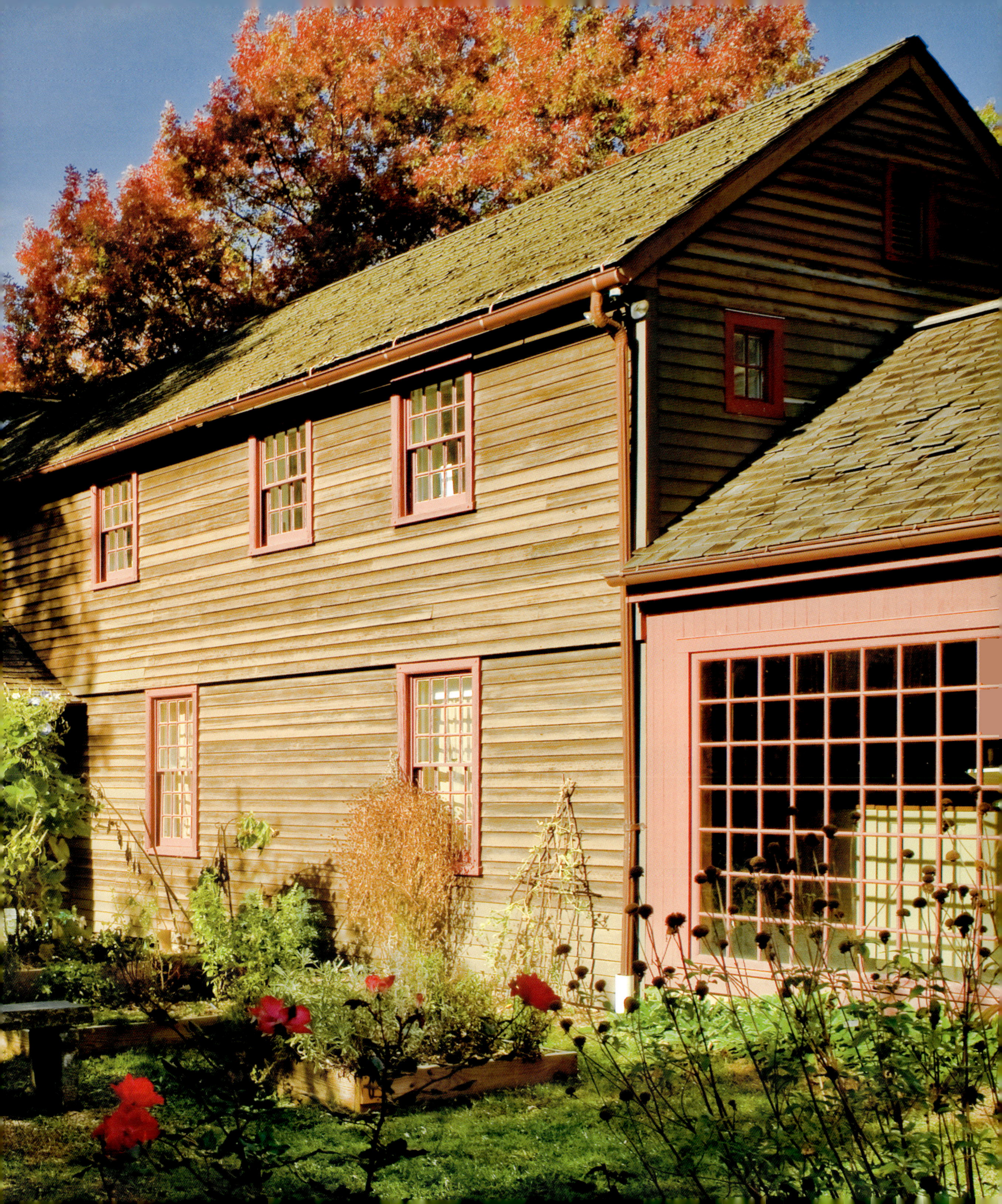

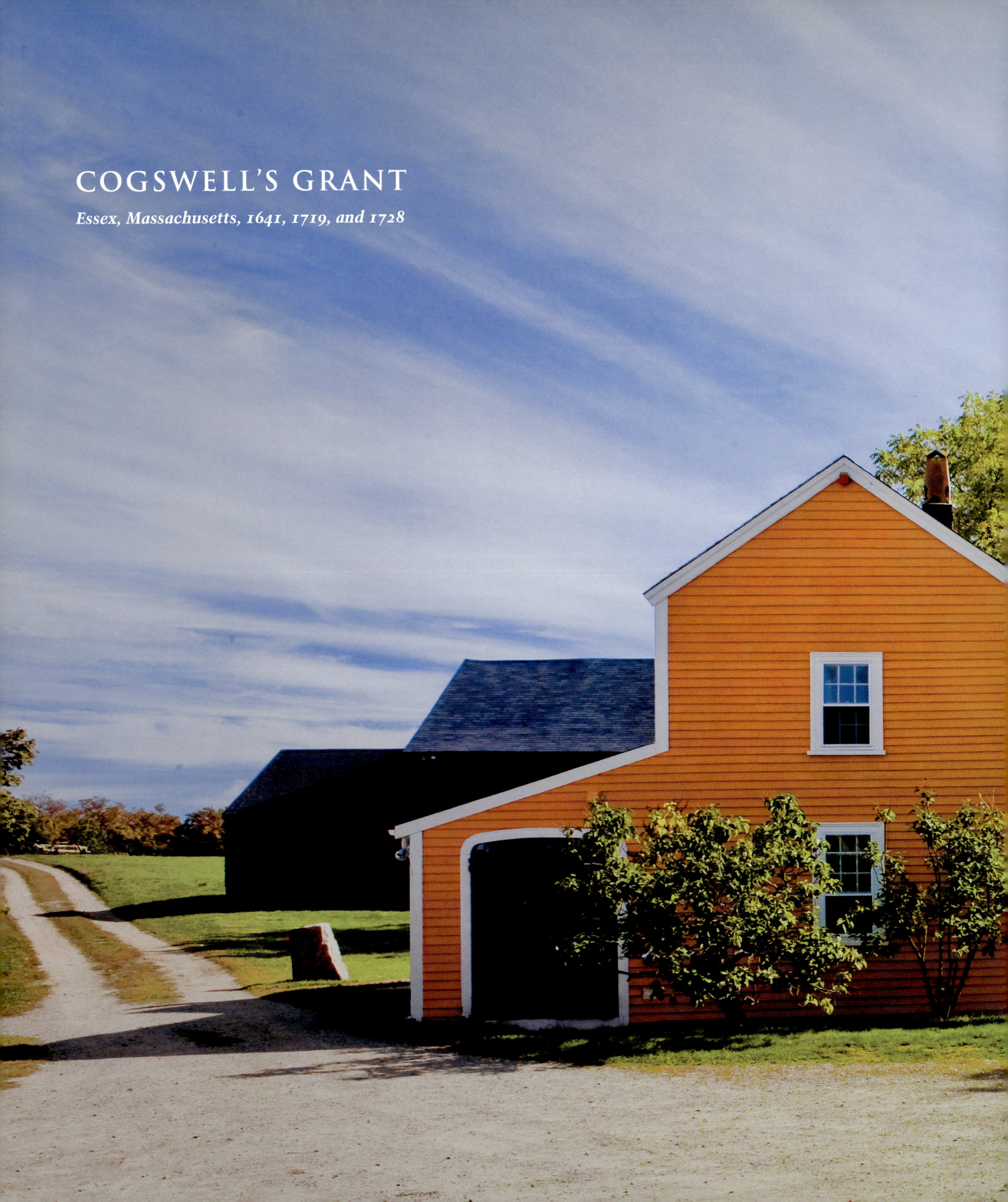

COGSWELL'S GRANT

Essex, Massachusetts, 1641, 1719, and 1728

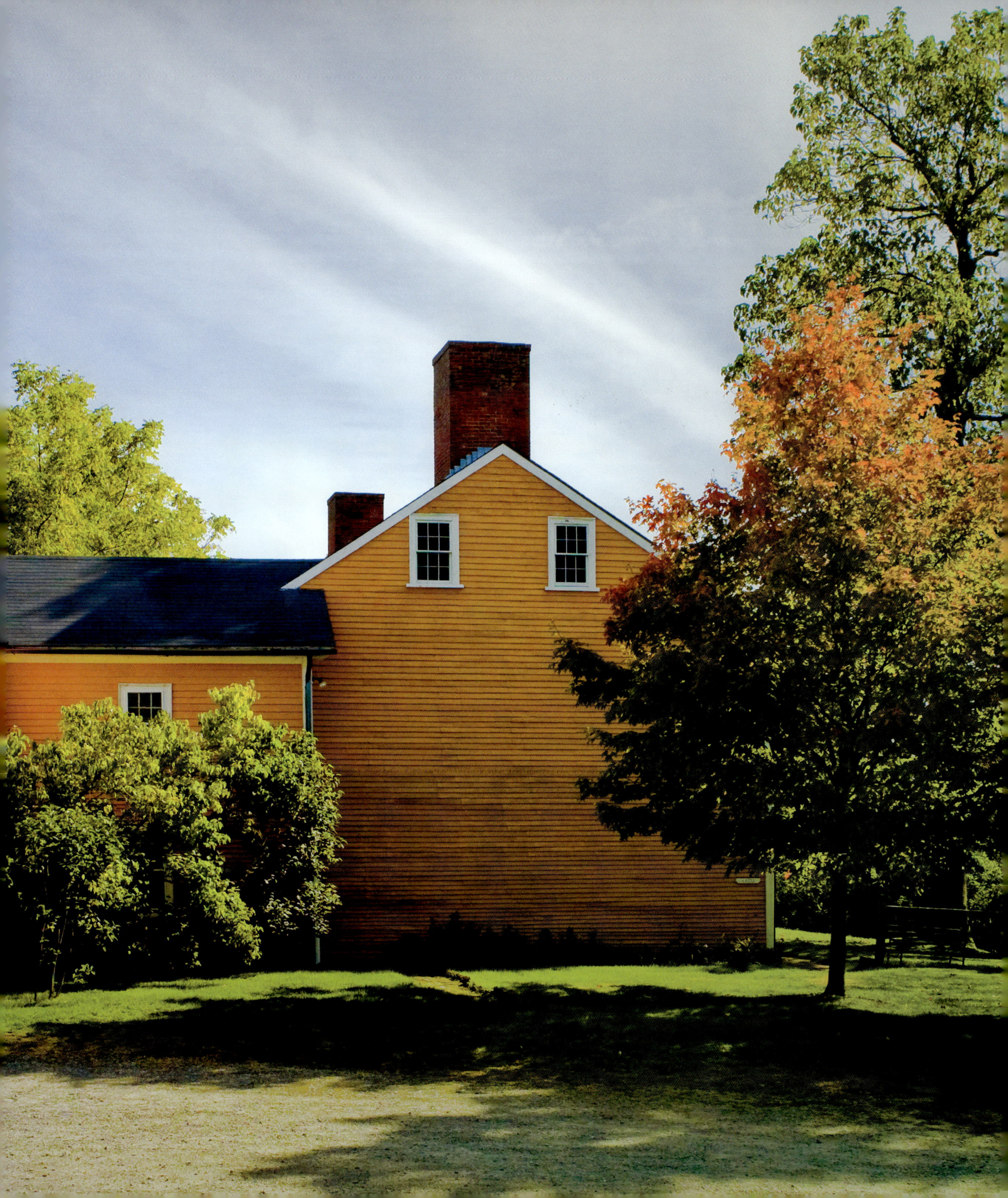

PREVIOUS PAGES *The house is presently in three sections; the section between the chimneys is the oldest. If viewed from the front, the center hall house today started as a smaller seventeenth-century structure onto which Jonathan Cogswell added the stair hall and rooms on two floors (on the left) in 1730, which still exist. In 1770 the old house was torn down and replaced with the right side of the present house with two rooms on each floor. The rear extensions are later additions.*

RIGHT *Almost all period house museums are interpreted around the theme of their architectural style and early history. Cogswell's Grant is different. The richness of its recent owners' collection is such a treasure that the house is background. This parlor is at the rear of the 1770 section.*

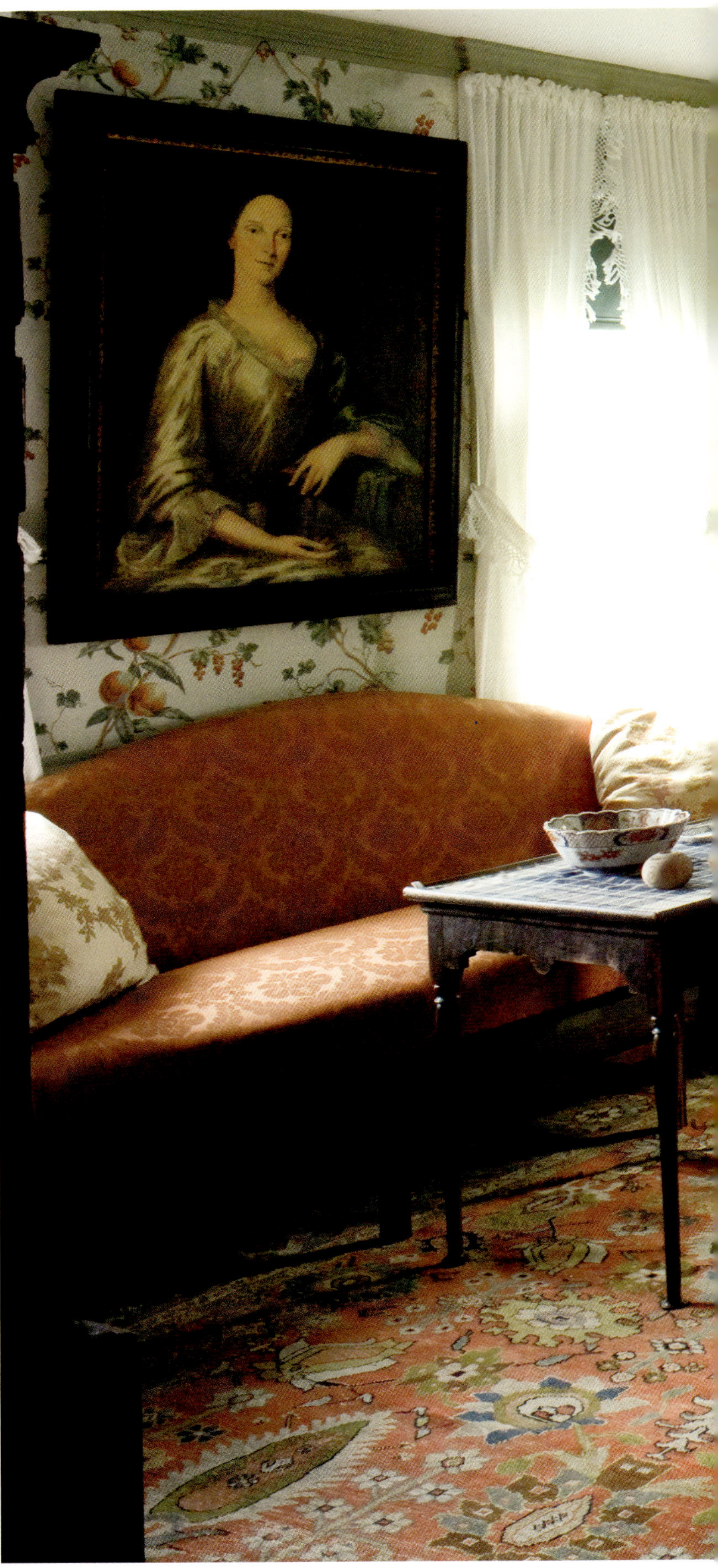

In the town of Essex was a region called Chebacco by the American Indians. The first Anglo-Americans began settlement there in 1634. Two years later John Cogswell (1592–1669), along with his wife Elizabeth (Thompson) and two sons, recently from Westbury Leigh in Wiltshire, England, was granted 300 acres in Chebacco Parish. Records attest to a "house and appurtenances" built by 1641. Through generations, the farm remained in the family until 1839. It still retains most of its early aspect. John's son William (1619–1700) was a successful farmer, serving as selectman and parish meeting moderator. He cleared the land for pasture and arable fields, and built stone walls, hedges, and rail fences. Crops included barley, hay, thatch, and salt marsh hay from the marshes. He operated a ferry ("two pence a person") over the Cebache River, and likely a sawmill, malthouse, and a gristmill—he had a tidal pond dug, which could create power. When he died, his estate inventory also listed pork, butter, cheese, apples, pears, and cider stored in the cellar, and forty sheep, a horse, cow, four yearlings, and two oxen. His four sons inherited portions of the farm.

One son was Captain Jonathan Cogswell (1661–1717), already a merchant, justice of the peace, and militia officer. He inherited the present house (the oldest existing part) and 80 acres in 1700. At his death in 1717 he owned 165 acres, the same as the farm has today. His son Jonathan Cogswell Jr. (1687–1752) built the salt hay barn in 1719 and the western addition to the old house in 1728. By 1749 three generations of improvements resulted in the second highest assessment in Ipswich. When Jonathan Cogswell Jr. died three years later, the farm consisted of upland and salt marsh, orchards, tillage, mowing fields, pasture, house, barns, and outhouses with livestock of three horses, nineteen cows, twelve oxen, fourteen other cattle, one hundred fifteen sheep, and nine pigs.

His second eldest son, Jonathan Cogswell (1740–1819), was colonel of the Second Regiment during the Revolution, a delegate to the U.S. Constitutional Convention of Massachusetts, state representative four times, justice of the Sessions Court, as well as holding other offices. A town tax valuation describes the farm

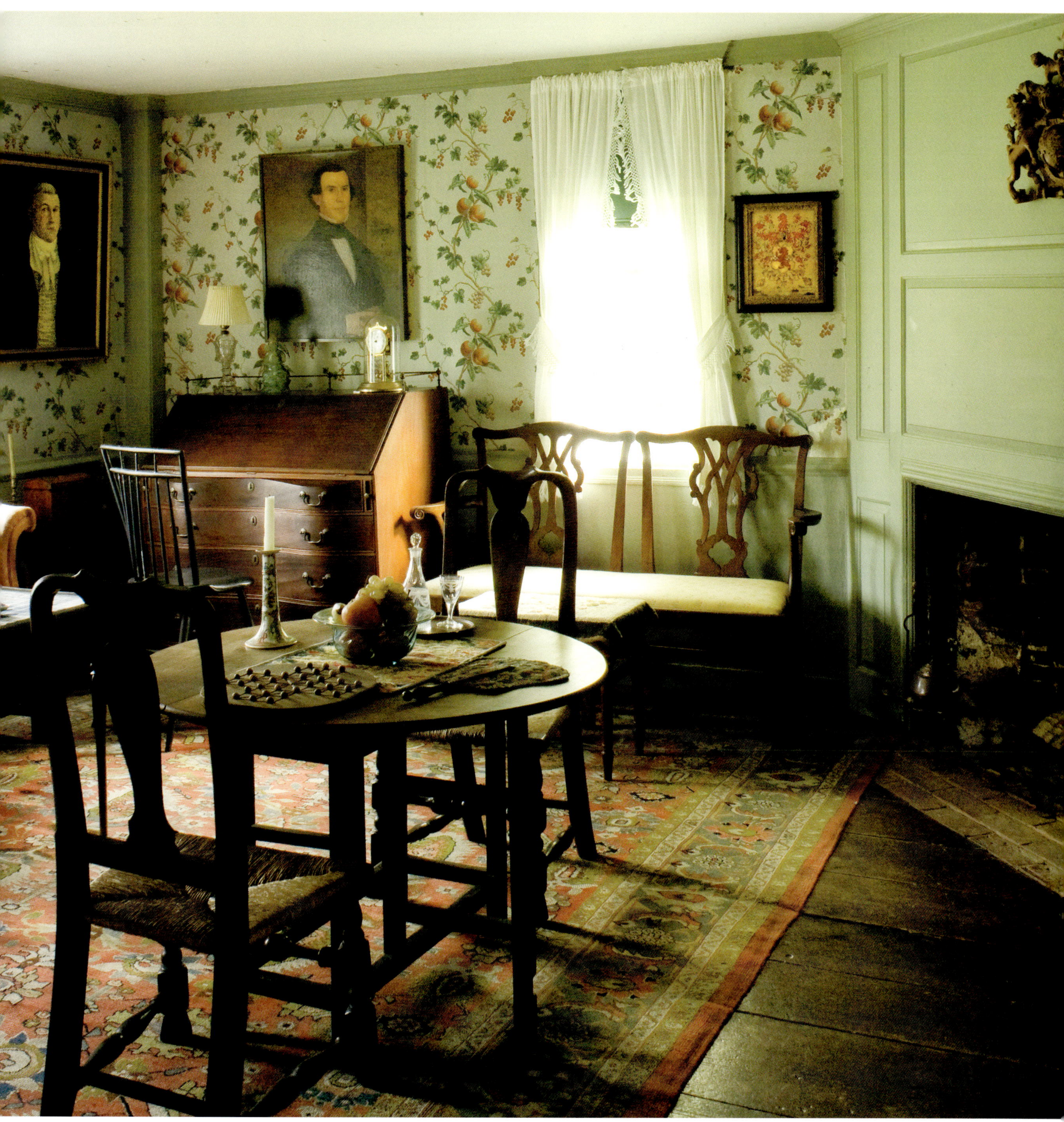

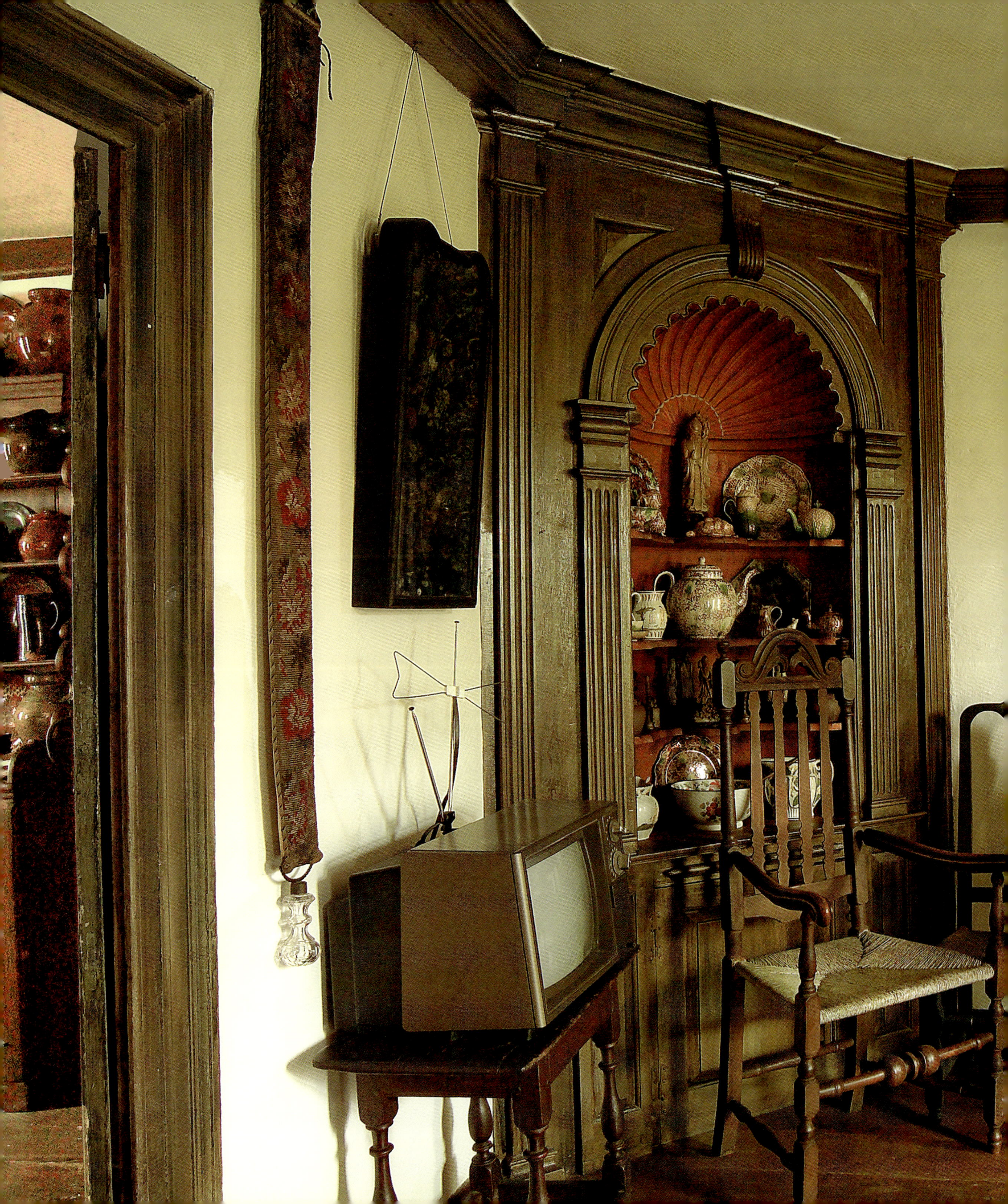

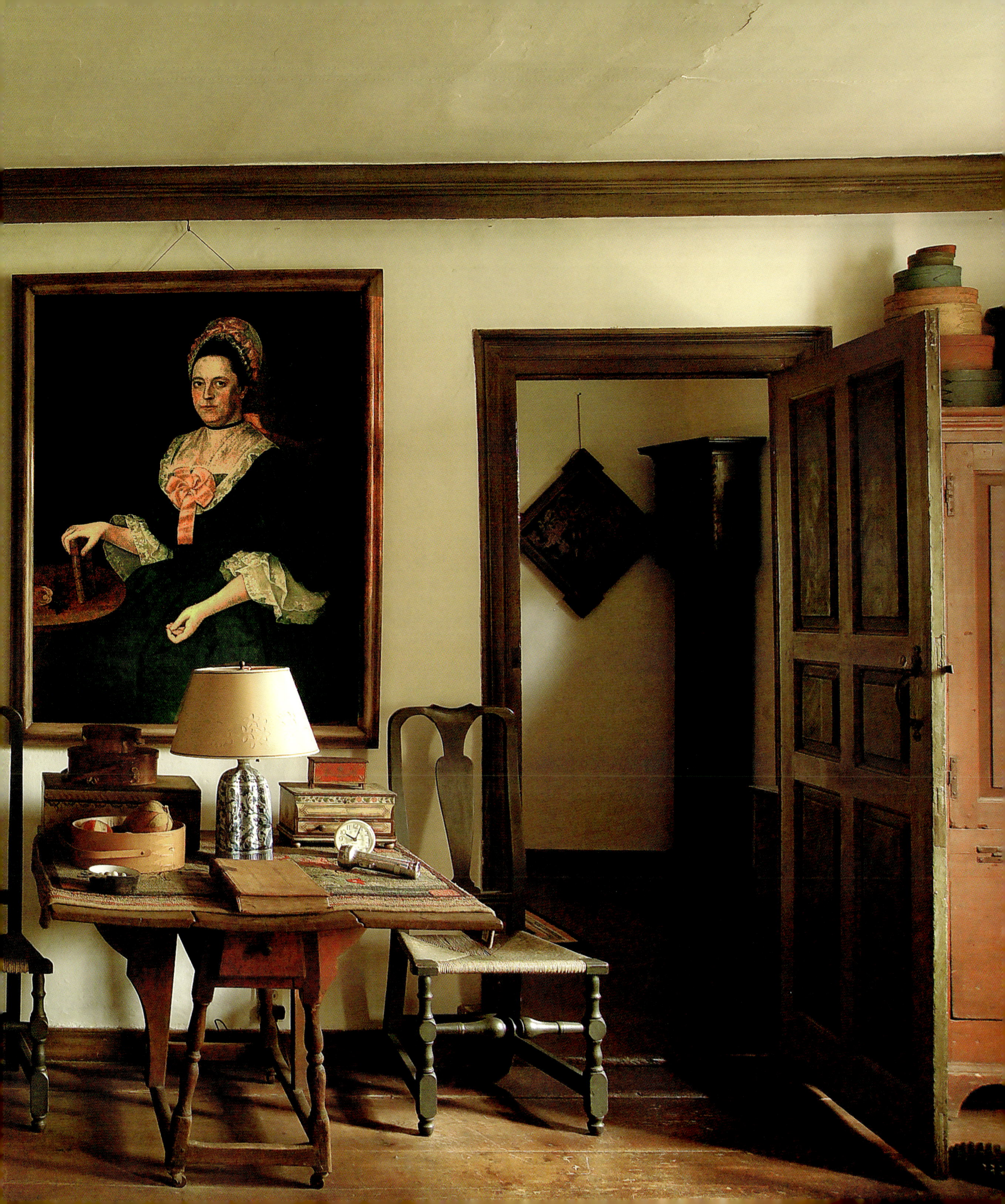

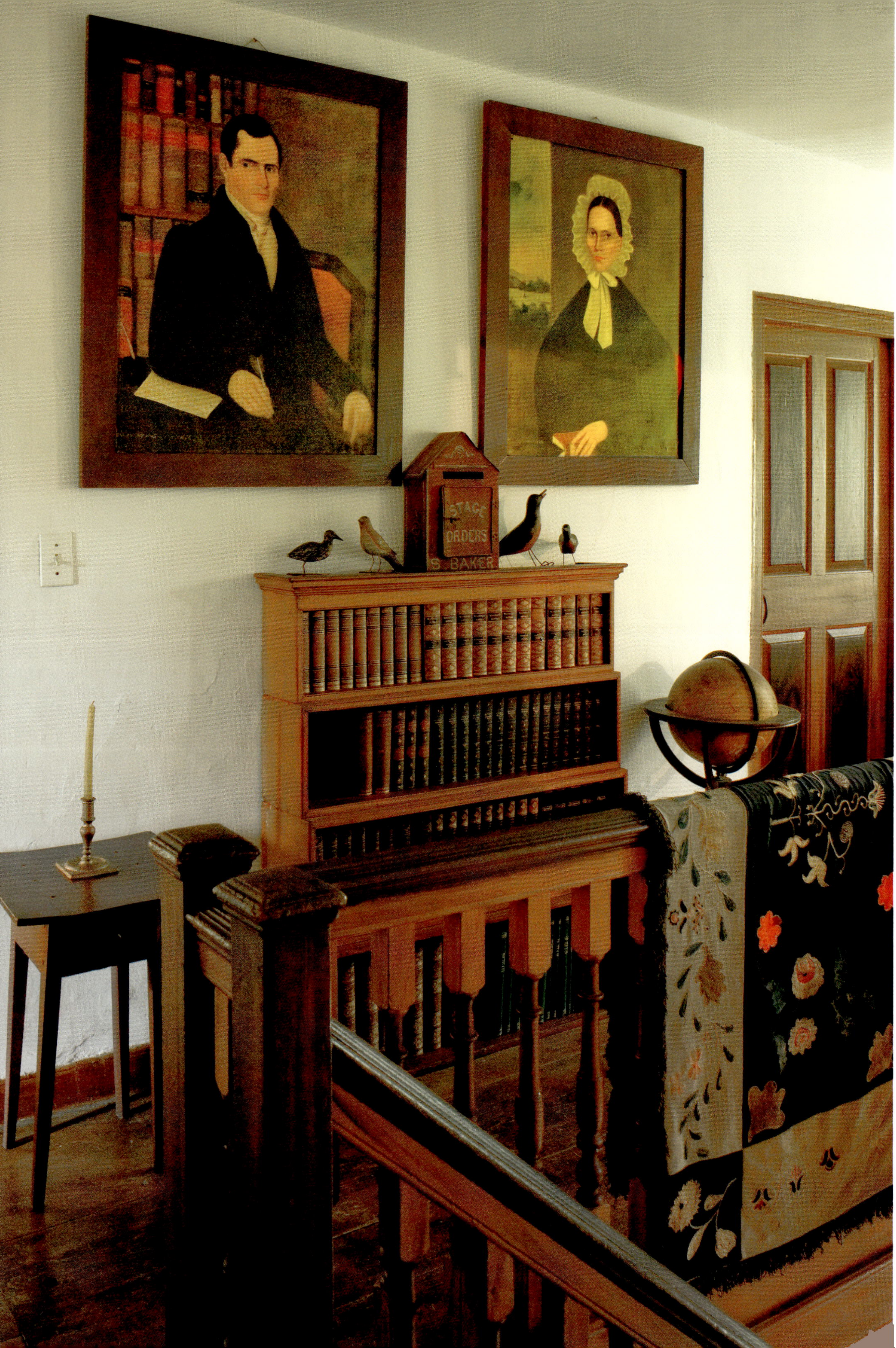

PREVIOUS PAGES *The parlor has made use of a room corner, usually dead space, for a display cupboard.*

LEFT *Ancestral portraits were once the only visible reminder of a family's ancestors who built the house. House, portraits, and descendants were expected to remain inseparable, all having no idea of how mutable their world would become after the unforeseen Industrial Revolution. In our time, all three have been separated almost entirely. Unlike the English system of primogeniture, which ties the family for centuries to the estate, American equal inheritance has disbursed nearly all such estates.*

RIGHT *Heavy summer beams in the rear chamber (1730) testify to the persistence of the medieval framing system in what was becoming a Georgian house. The corner fireplace provided efficient use of a single gable-end chimney. Corner fireplaces, a Swedish influence, are an unusual feature in early New England, although they are found in New Jersey and Pennsylvania.*

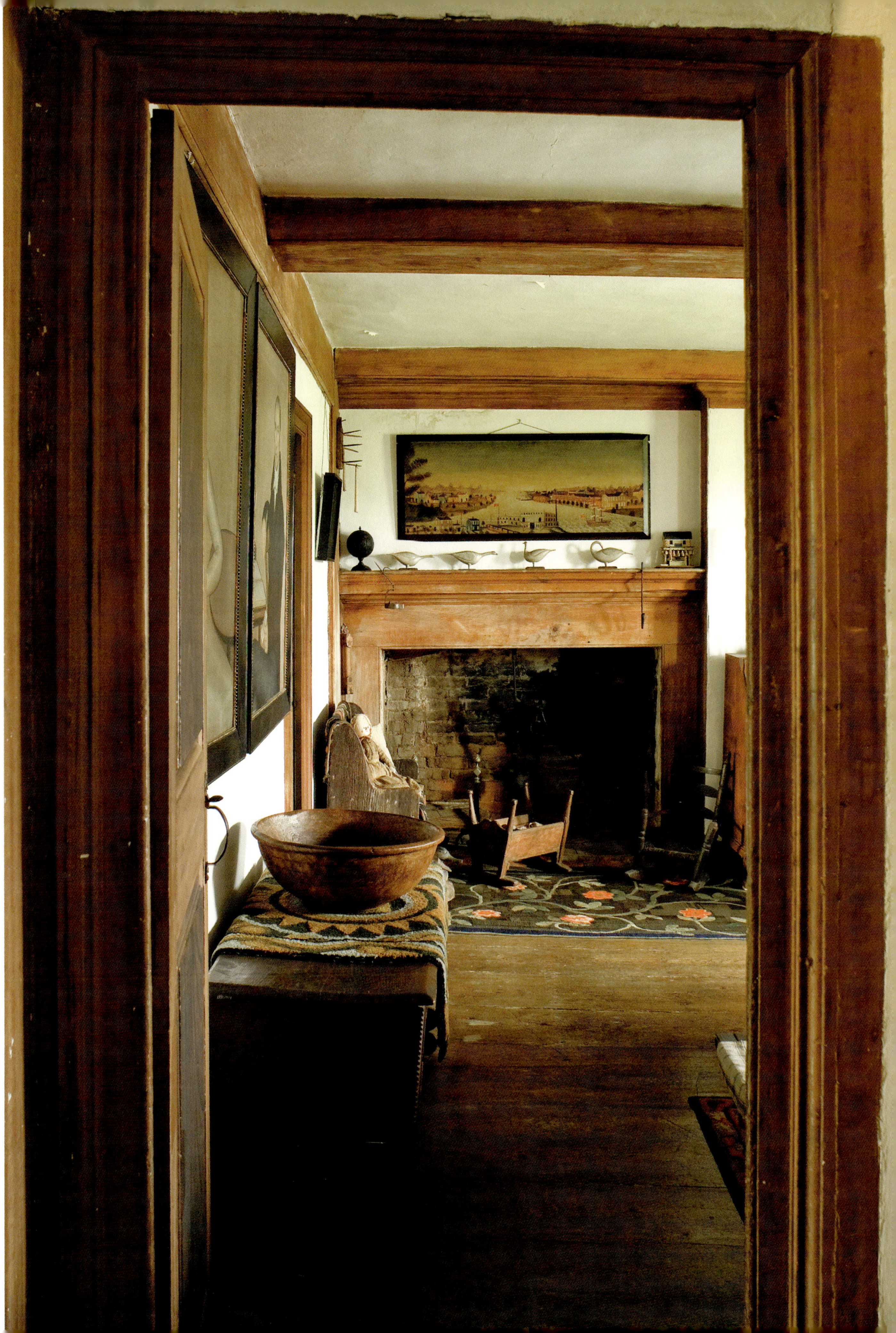

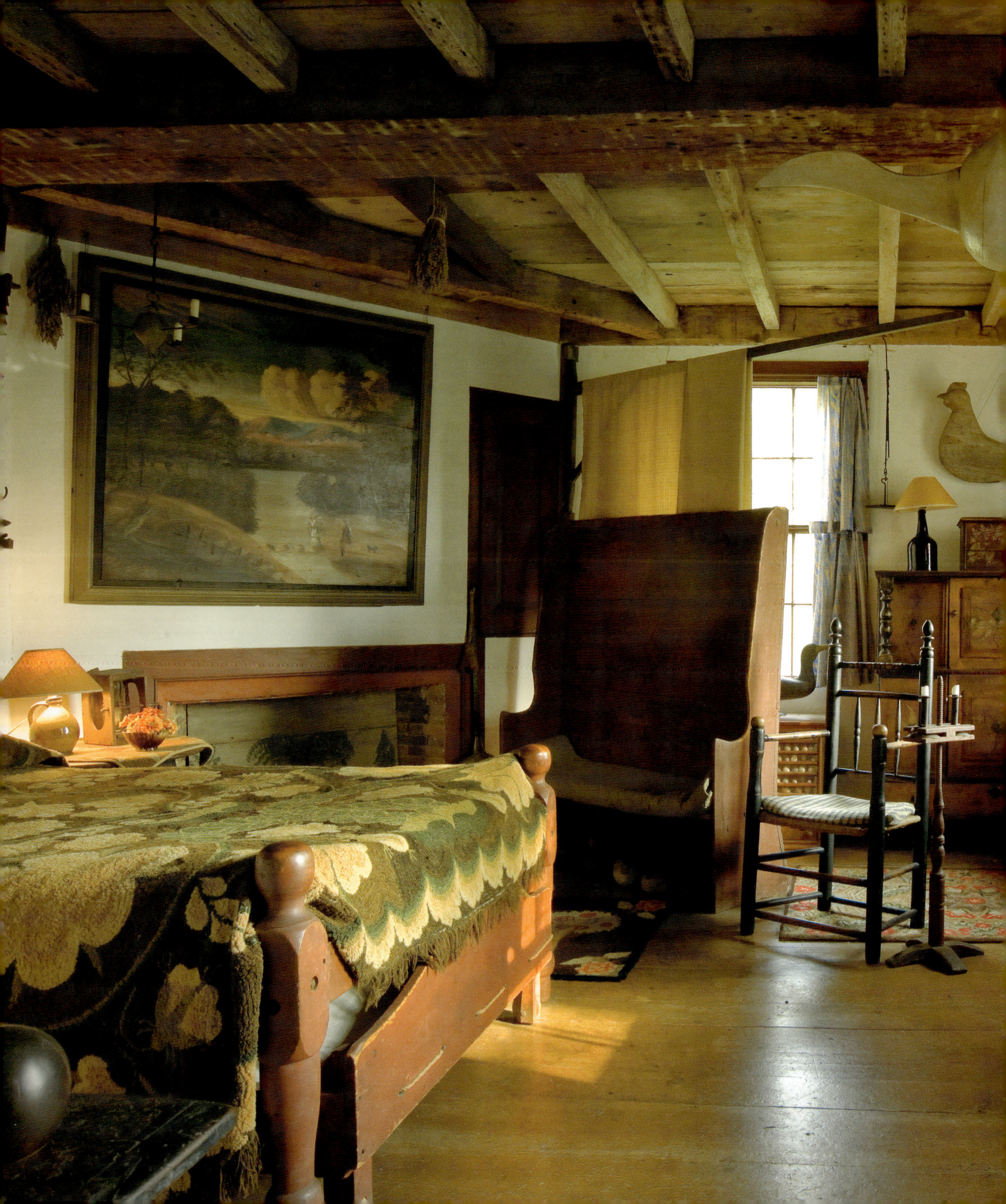

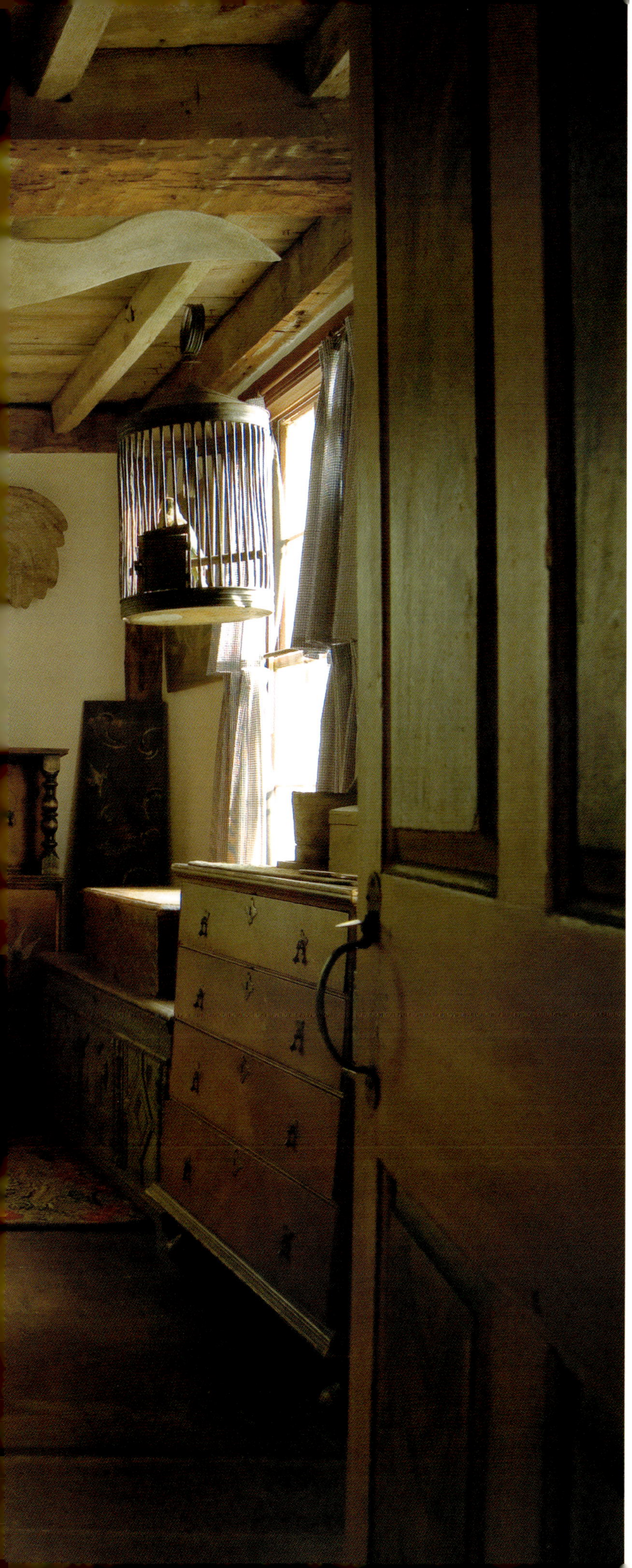

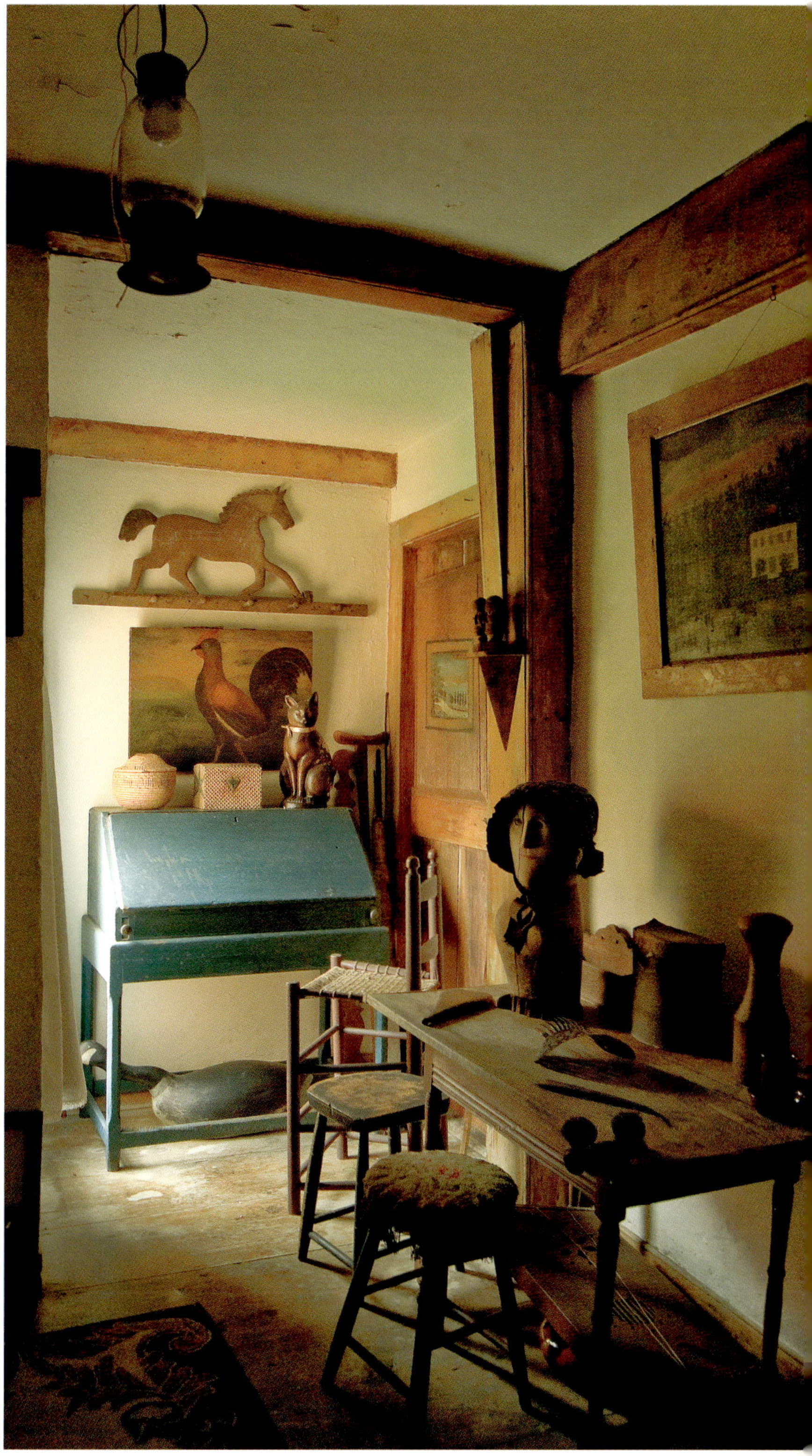

LEFT *The rooms of Cogswell's Grant, like this front chamber, are a cornucopia of objects, a delight to the antiquarian's eye, in far greater profusion than inventories indicate was normal in the early period.*

ABOVE *The furnishings are an artful accumulation of early and late periods, high style and vernacular objects, remarkable for their evocation of the spirit of New England, past and present.*

RIGHT *The grain painted decoration is a restoration of the original 1730 treatment of the woodwork in the front bed chamber. From Puritan plain to Victorian elaboration there was a constantly evolving aesthetic of house decoration through three centuries. We observe ever more color on surfaces, more carving and molding on furnishings and structure, and textiles wherever function or display was permitted. This is a long cycle of fashion, now unwinding to simplicity over the last century and a half.*

FOLLOWING PAGES *A product of consistent family enterprise, the farm today retains most of the structures erected over its long history, including a 1719 salt hay barn, cow barn, horse barn, workshop, sheds, and more.*

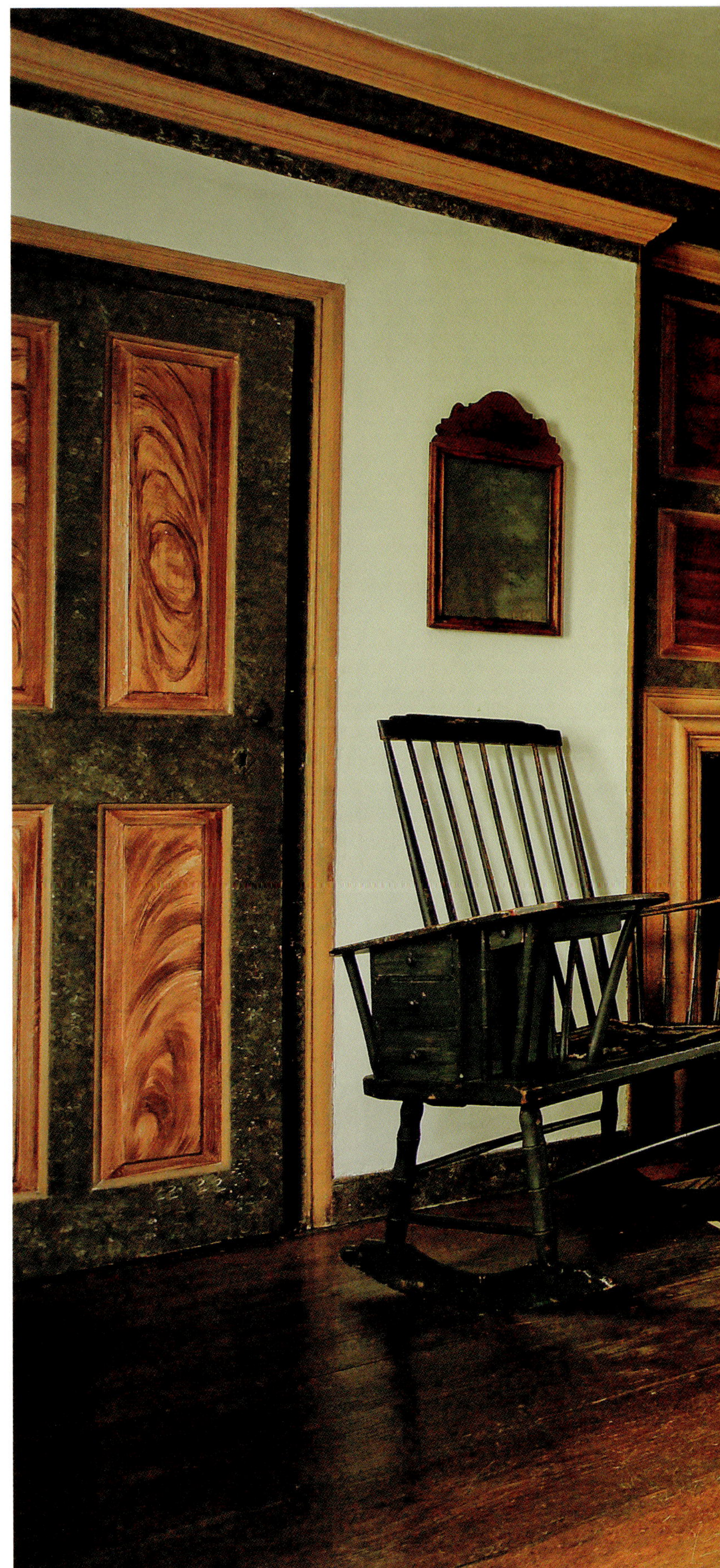

much as it looks today. In 1791, with three daughters, he and his wife moved closer to Cebacco center, the farm was leased and then sold when his widow died in 1839 to Adam Boyd (d. 1865), a prominent shipbuilder. Descendants of Boyd owned the farm through until 1925, running it as a farm, building a horse barn near the cow barn, adding other structures, and maintaining a milk route. By foreclosure it sold in 1925 to Arthur Dana Story (1854–1932), a shipbuilder, who resided elsewhere and let the farm to families until he sold it in 1937 to Nina Fletcher (1903–1993) and Bertram Kimball Little (1899–1993).

The Littles sought a summer home for their family that would accommodate their expanding collection of early American antiques. They preserved the farm much as it was found, restoring buildings after the neglect of the Depression years and built a garage. They added extensive plantings, farm animals, and vegetable gardens suitable to their own (and caretakers') needs. In 1984 they deeded the property to the Society for the Preservation of New England Antiquities (Historic New England) with life tenancy. In 1990 it was placed on the National Register of Historic Places for its significance in agriculture, architecture, archeology, art, and conservation. In 1998 Cogswell's Grant opened to the public as an historic house museum complete with the Littles' extensive collection of period furnishings, a richly visible legacy of a lifetime's passion for American history, art, and antiques, carefully documented by more than a hundred scholarly articles and twenty-five books. They were the leading collector-scholars of their time in New England.

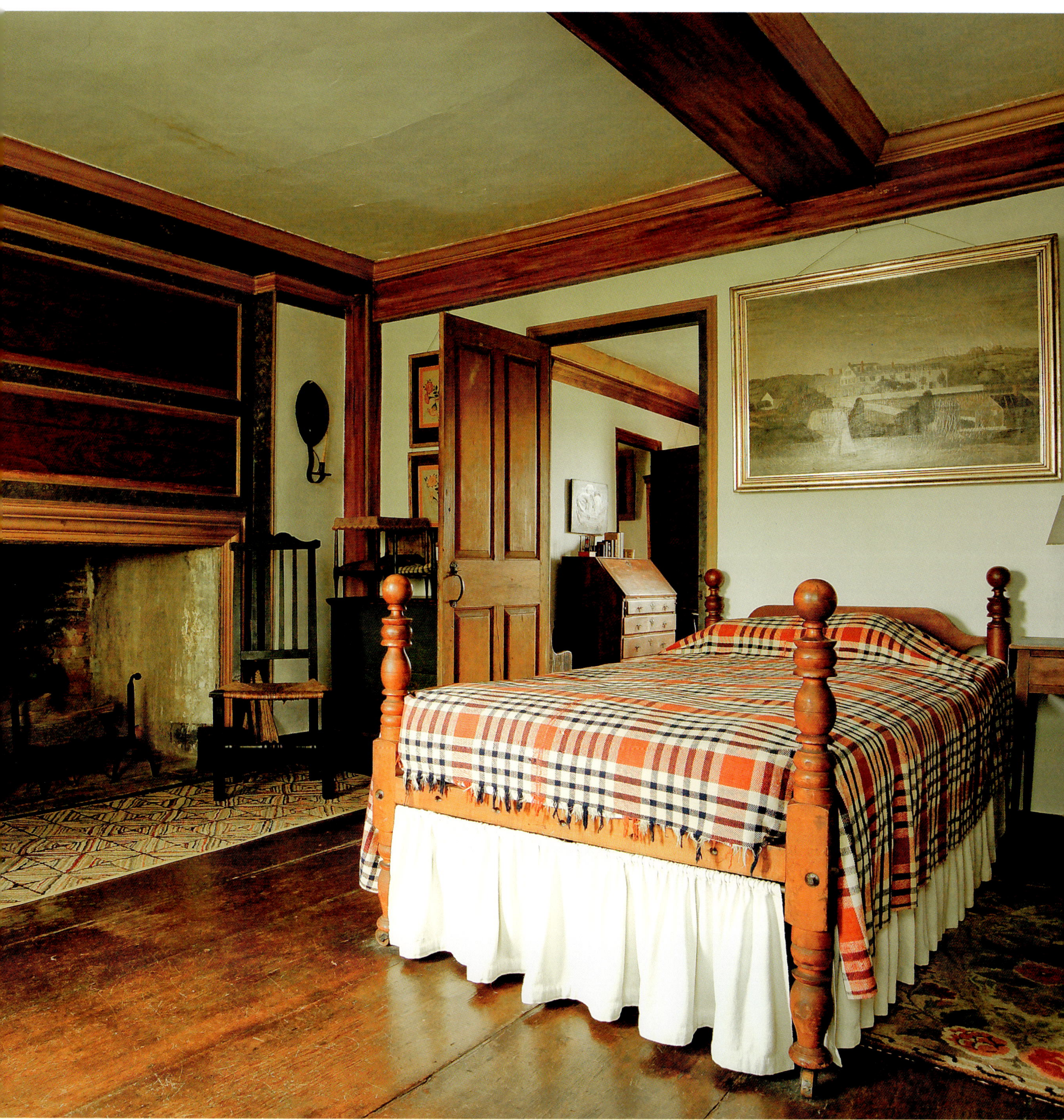

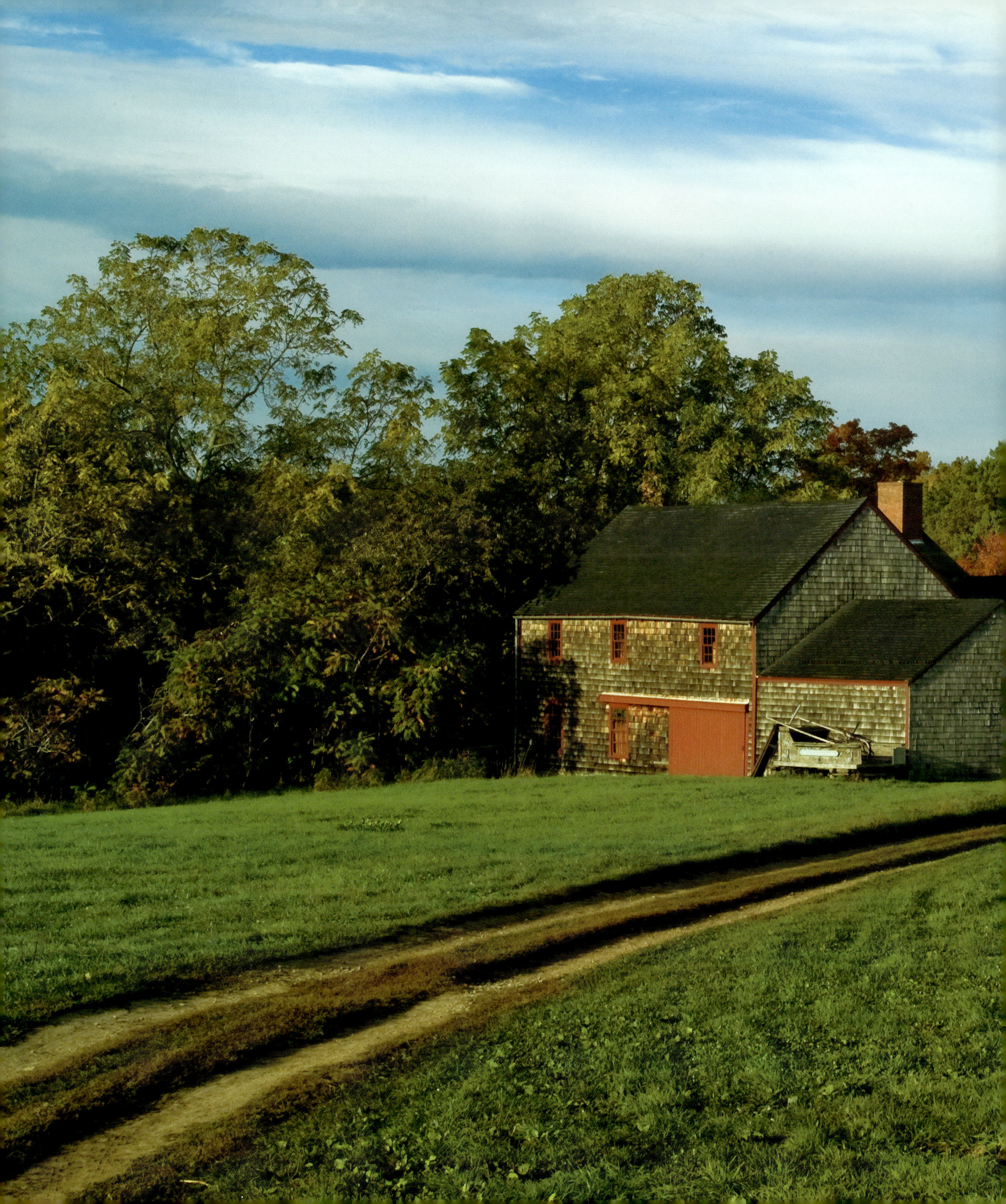

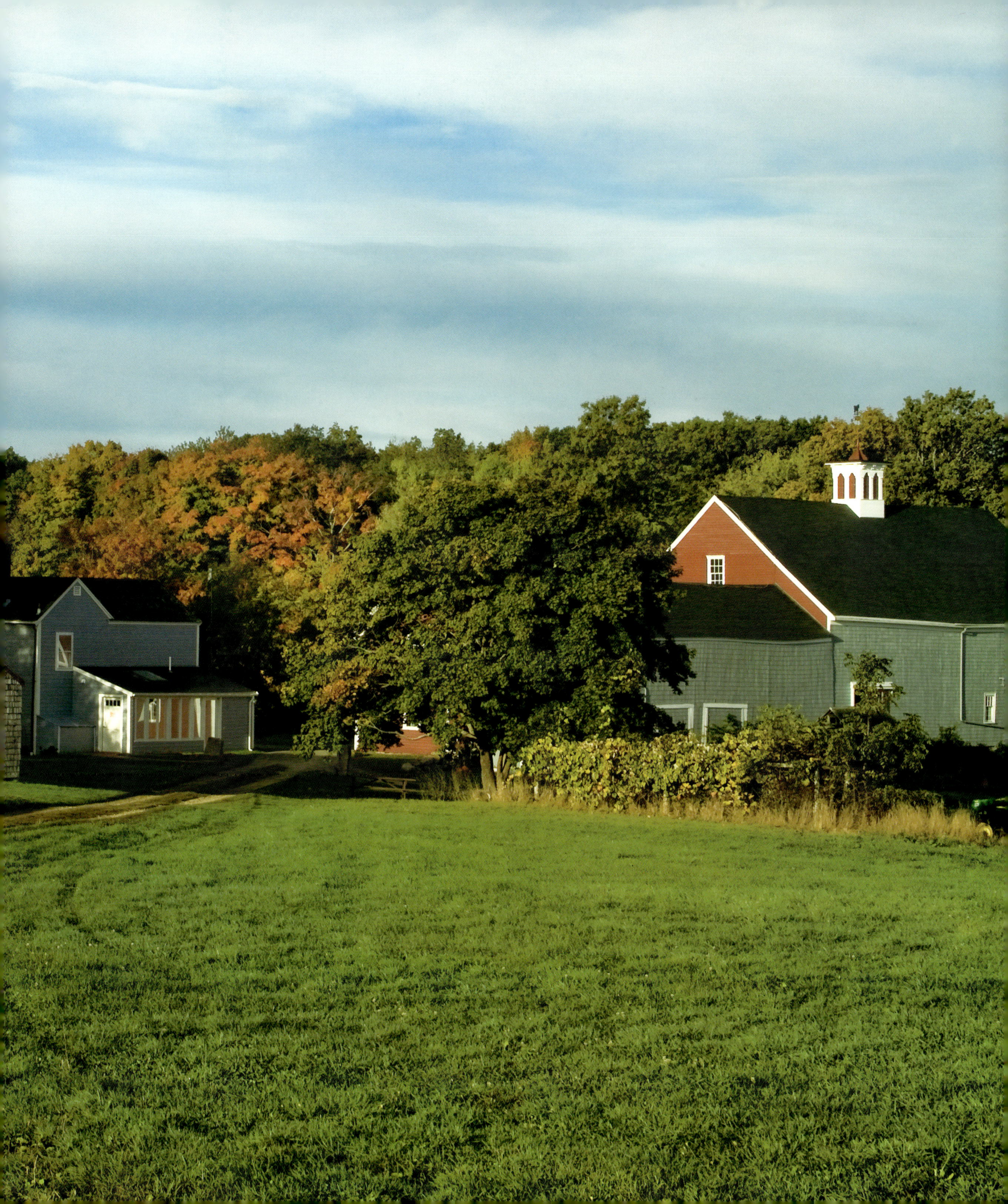

THE HENRY CRANE–SAMUEL WARE HOUSE

Litchfield County, Connecticut
c.1703 (Crane) and 1745 (Ware)

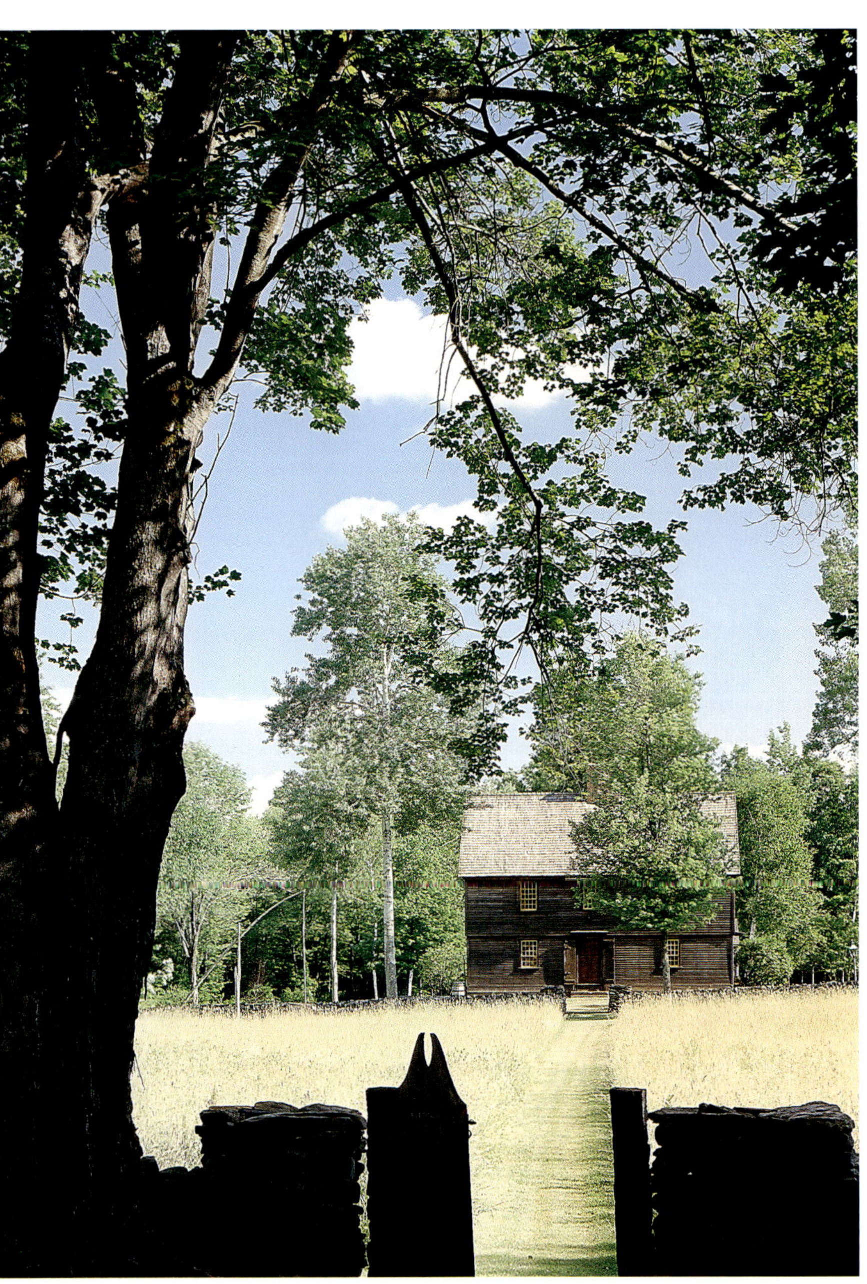

ABOVE AND FACING PAGE *Darkly brooding, this is a house entirely a part of its landscape in any season.*

The Crane–Ware House is actually two houses moved to the present location in western Connecticut in recent years and carefully restored and furnished in the period. The front section was erected in the early eighteenth century by Henry Crane (1675–1741) at the time of his marriage to Abigail Flood of Wethersfield (c.1703) in the newly created town of Durham, partway between Hartford and New Haven. Like his father, Henry was a "planter" and a leading citizen, serving for many years representative of his town to the general court (legislature) of the colony, justice of the peace for the county of New Haven, captain of the local militia, and deacon of his Congregational Church. He amassed more than a square mile of farmland and had many children, of which his eldest son, Silas, inherited his home.

In keeping with his position Henry had a substantial two story-house built with a kitchen lean-to behind, the front consisting of the characteristic center-chimney plan, tight entry stairway, a hall to left, parlor to right, and two bedchambers above. Structurally it continued the post-medieval English house form, with overhanging second floor, already a century old style in New England. The beginning of Georgian innovations is seen in the pedimented front doorway and raised, paneled walls in the two main rooms. For these pious Puritans, modest and belated decoration, with plain exteriors concealing from public eyes a grudging but growing acceptance of once-hated courtly and high church styles hidden within. As some Englishmen said, a proper gentleman should appear plain and pious on the outside while concealing an exciting intellect and imagination within. Even on the frontier yeoman farmers were evolving into county gentry. The more enterprising were turning to water-powered manufacturing, creating a new class of wealth who came to bypass the old agrarian aristocracy in the next century. So it would be for the Cranes and so many other landed families—their many children moving to more fertile lands opened in the west after the Revolution. Henry Crane's grandchildren all moved away from Durham.

The second house, now the "L" to the Crane House, was found in New Braintree, Massachusetts. Built by Samuel Ware

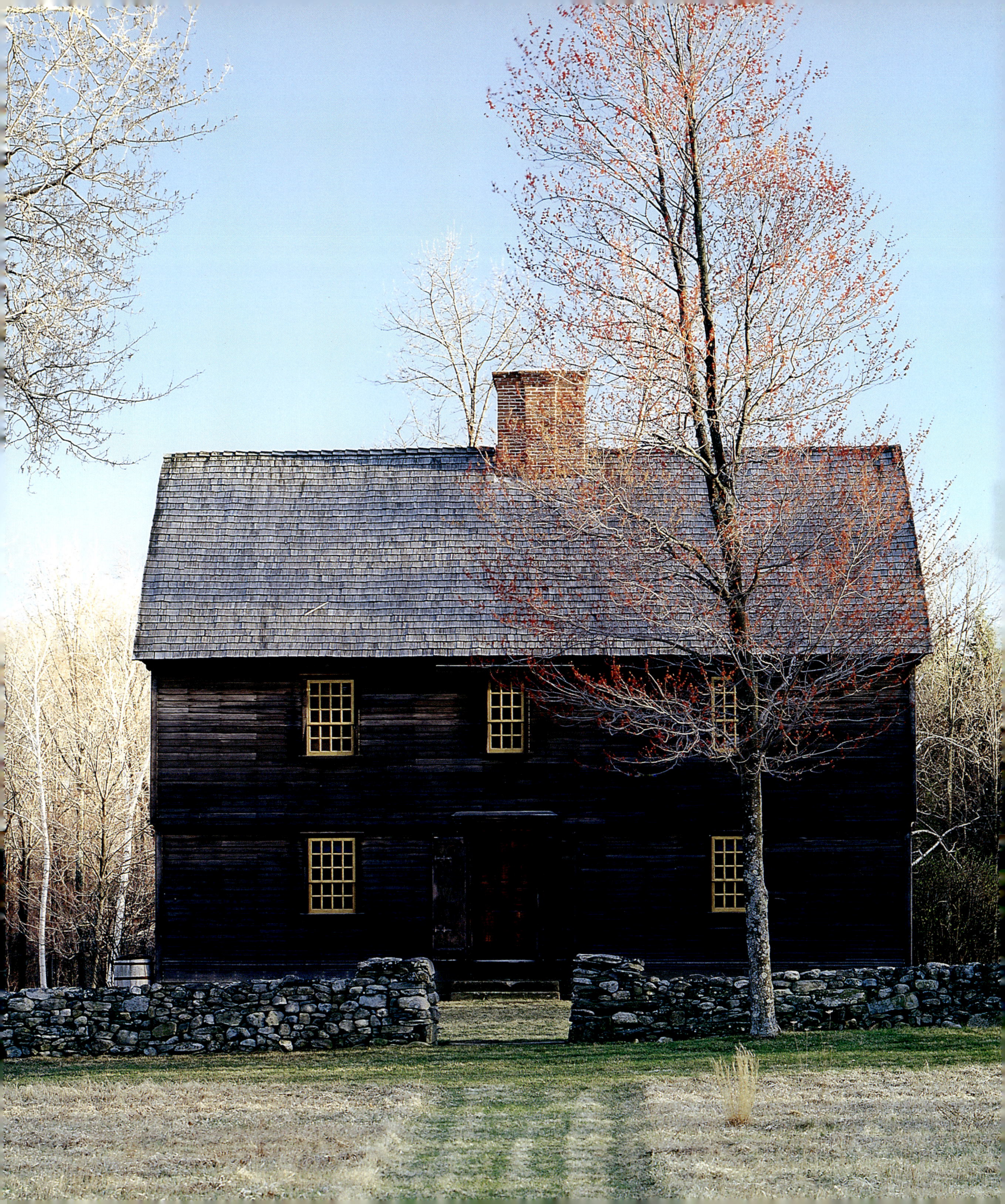

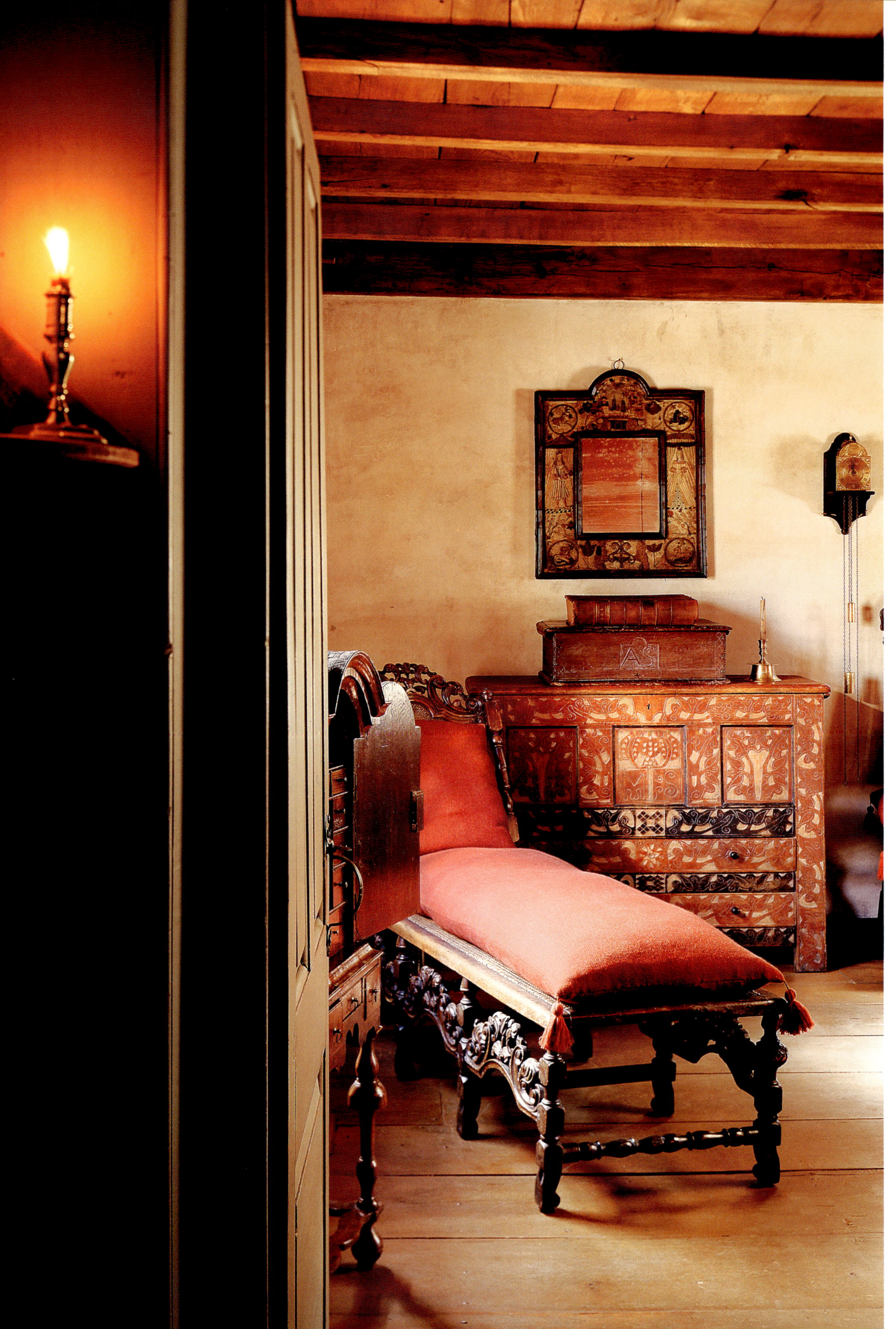

LEFT *From the entryway of the rear el appears the parlor, furnished in the finest style and period of its time.*

FACING PAGE *This Hadley-type chest is inscribed with the initials "MS" for the young lady whose marriage will bring her, the chest, and its textiles—prepared for years by herself—to her new home. A number of these carved and paint-decorated chests, dating between 1680 and 1740, are associated with families in Hampshire County (especially Hadley) in western Massachusetts.*

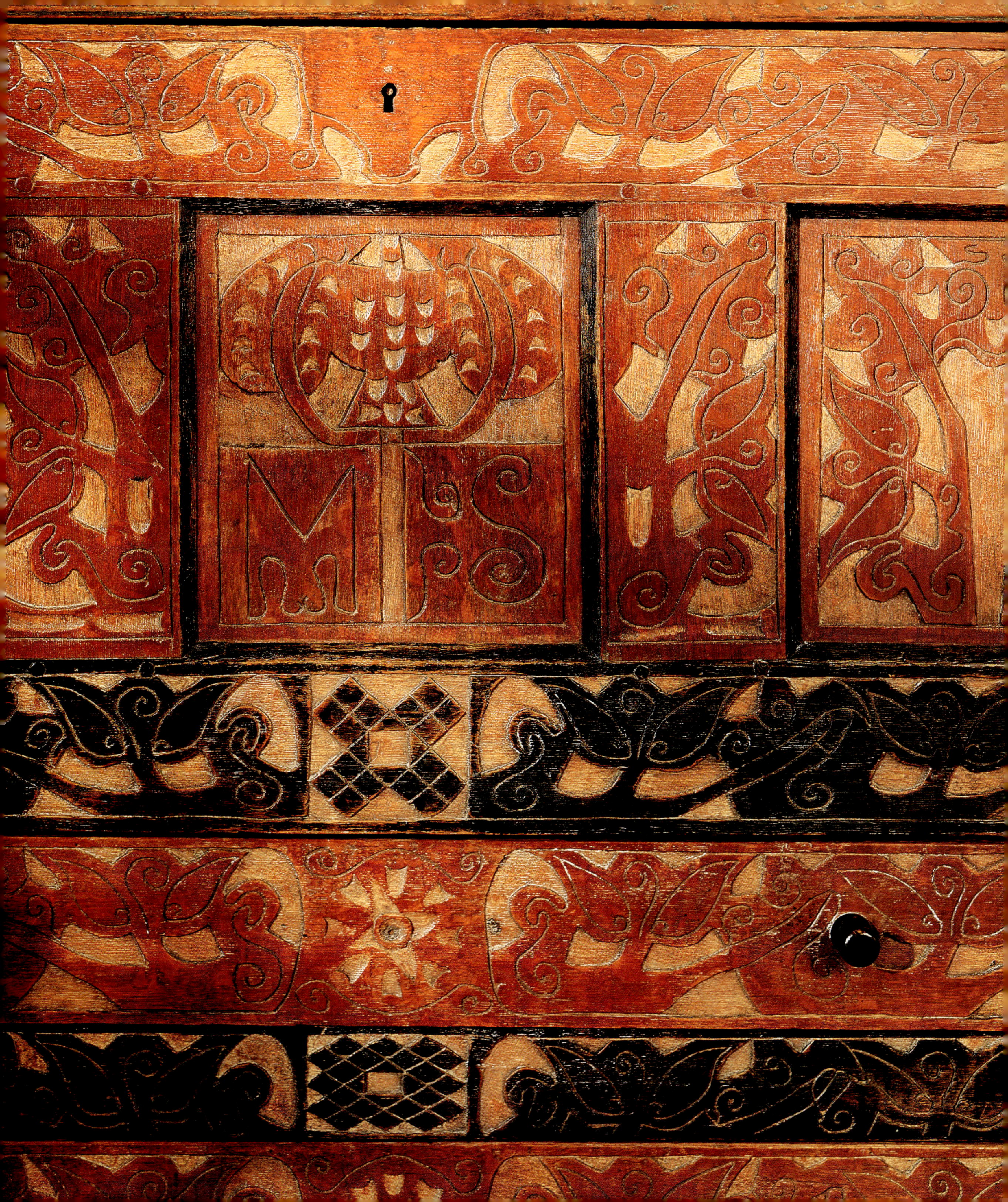
M S

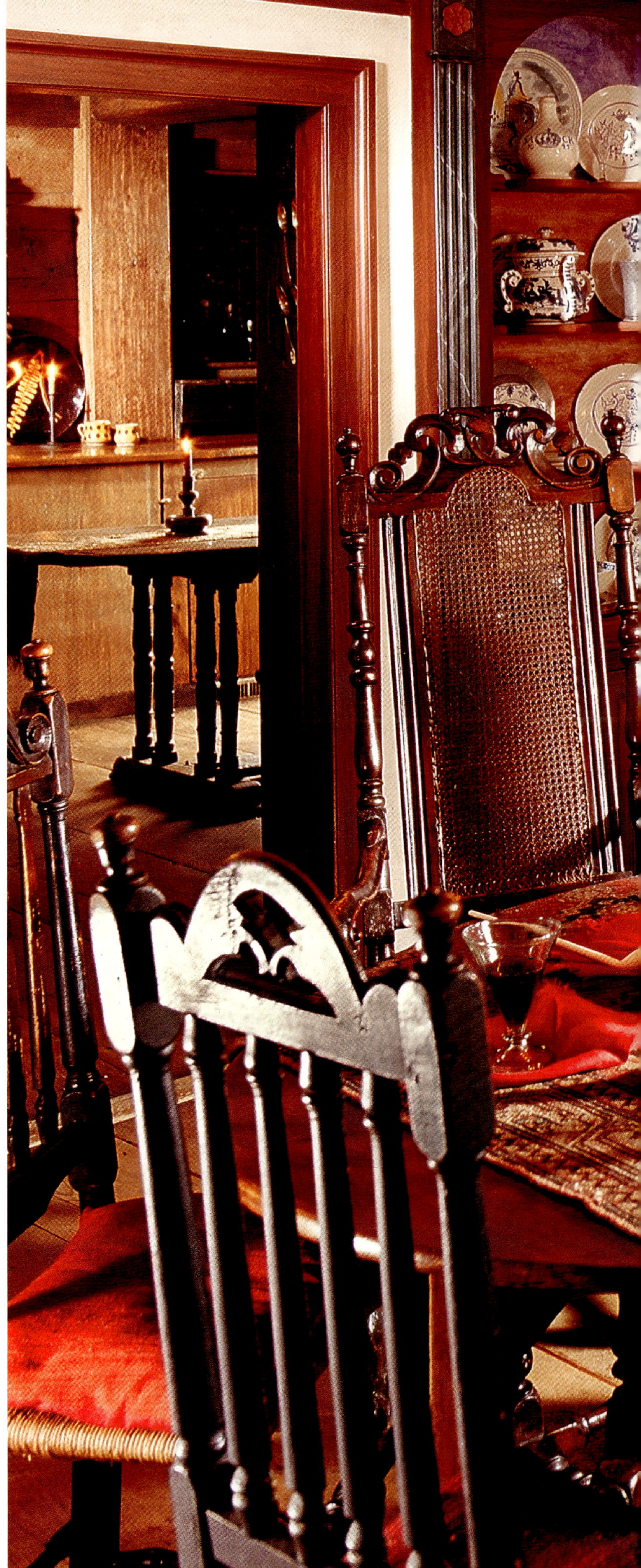

RIGHT *The dining room, adjacent to the kitchen beyond, is furnished in high style with objects of the William and Mary period, which, in New England, carried on for many years after their passing.*

around the date of his marriage to Anna Goodale in 1745, it served as home for their six children. Anna died in 1756, and Samuel married Hannah (Billings) Belding, a recent widow. They remained on the farm until 1781 when, at age sixty-four and his farming days coming to an end, they moved to Conway, where his eldest son Samuel was a physician of note. The old house passed into other hands. A simple two rooms over two rooms, it was smaller than the Crane House—lacking a lean-to extension—and plainer, perfectly in keeping with Ware's yeoman means (he was church deacon).

The two houses were remarkable for their unchanged condition. Both had been inhabited continuously well into the twentieth century yet neither had plumbing or electricity. This originality inspired the current owners' determination to restore the houses with utmost fidelity. It became an extension of their professional work—an art-directed project. Three years went into rediscovering and restoring every detail of the two houses. They developed innovative ways for recreating the feel and appearance of old plaster walls and woodwork. Enthusiasm and fidelity to the past infected the loyalty of their work crew such that they would return years later to show others their accomplishments.

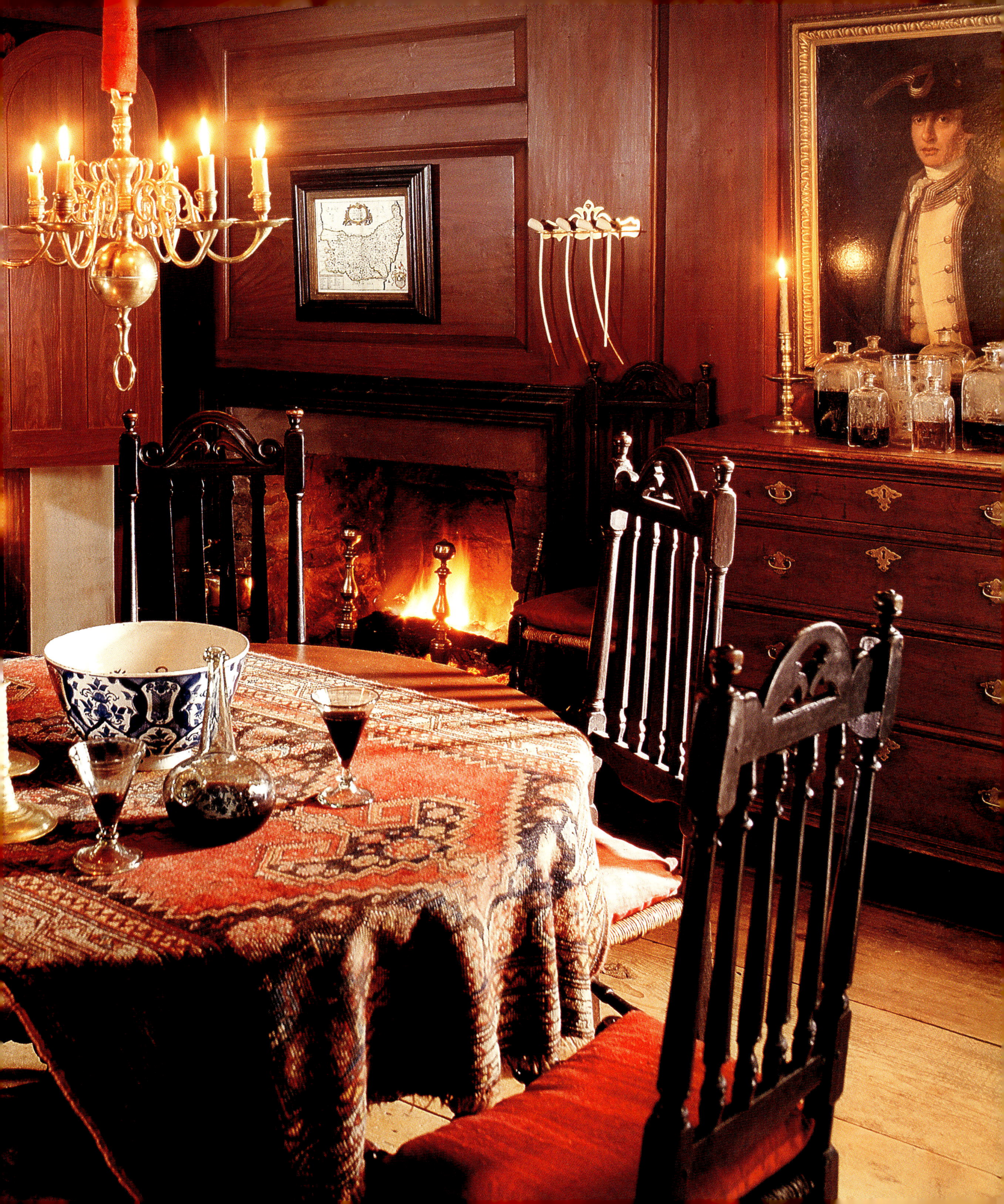

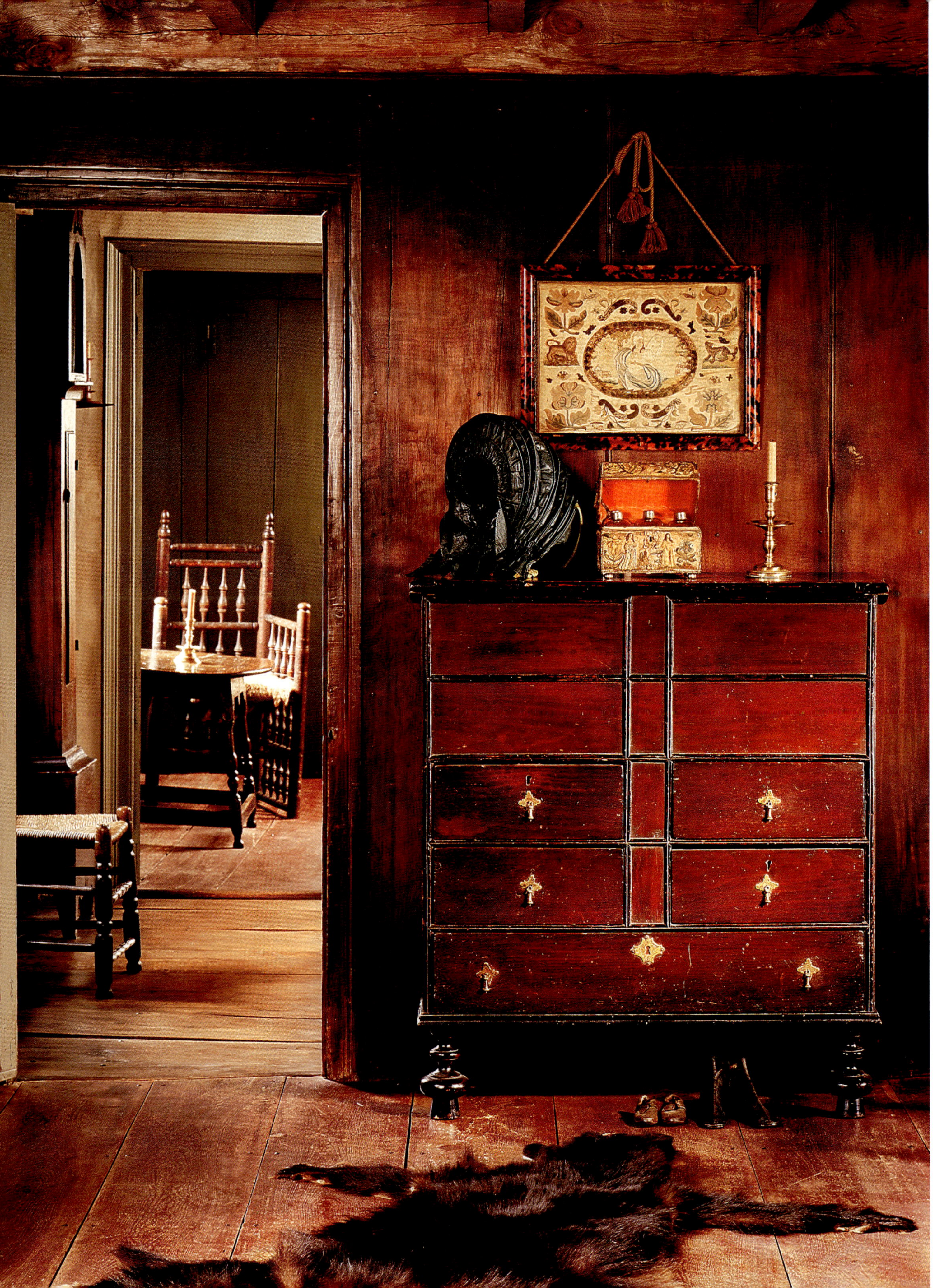

FACING PAGE *In this chamber, a subtle symphony of colors, both natural and manmade, provides visual harmony for both the eye and the mind. This sensibility was a part of early New England culture and, in the right hands, has been brought back again to evoke the same serenity. The chest with the unusual split-drawer configuration is from central Massachusetts, c.1700.*

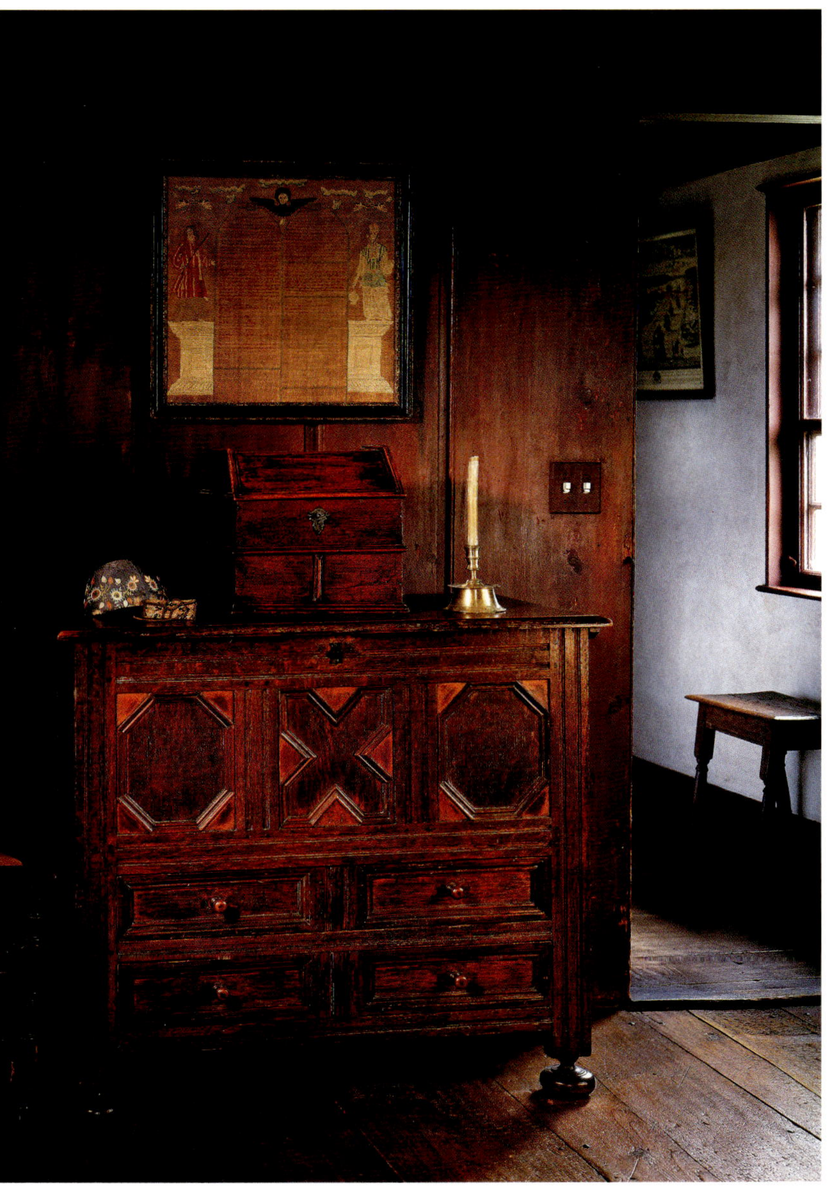

ABOVE *In a bed chamber is a paneled chest from eastern Massachusetts, c.1690, with other objects of the period.*

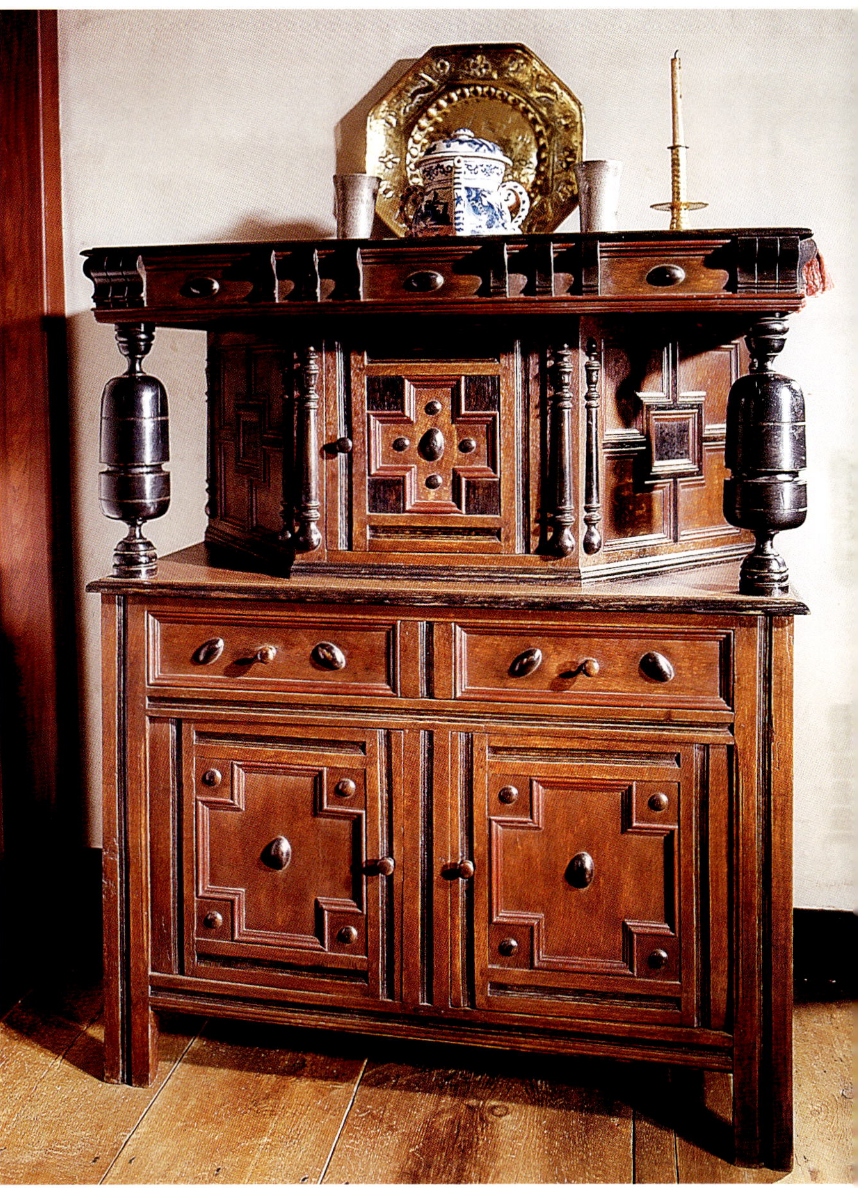

ABOVE *In pride-of-place in the hall (dining room), this eastern Massachusetts court cupboard, c.1680–1700, serves well its intended purpose as a repository of household valuables—textile, silver, liquor, and the like—and as a statement of the wealth and taste of its first owner.*

FOLLOWING PAGES *Like the more elaborate Hadley chest, this simple chest displays "RWS, 1720, 23", the initials, year, and age of the lady for which it was made in Massachusetts or Connecticut. Decorative painting artfully substitutes for unaffordable panels and turnings.*

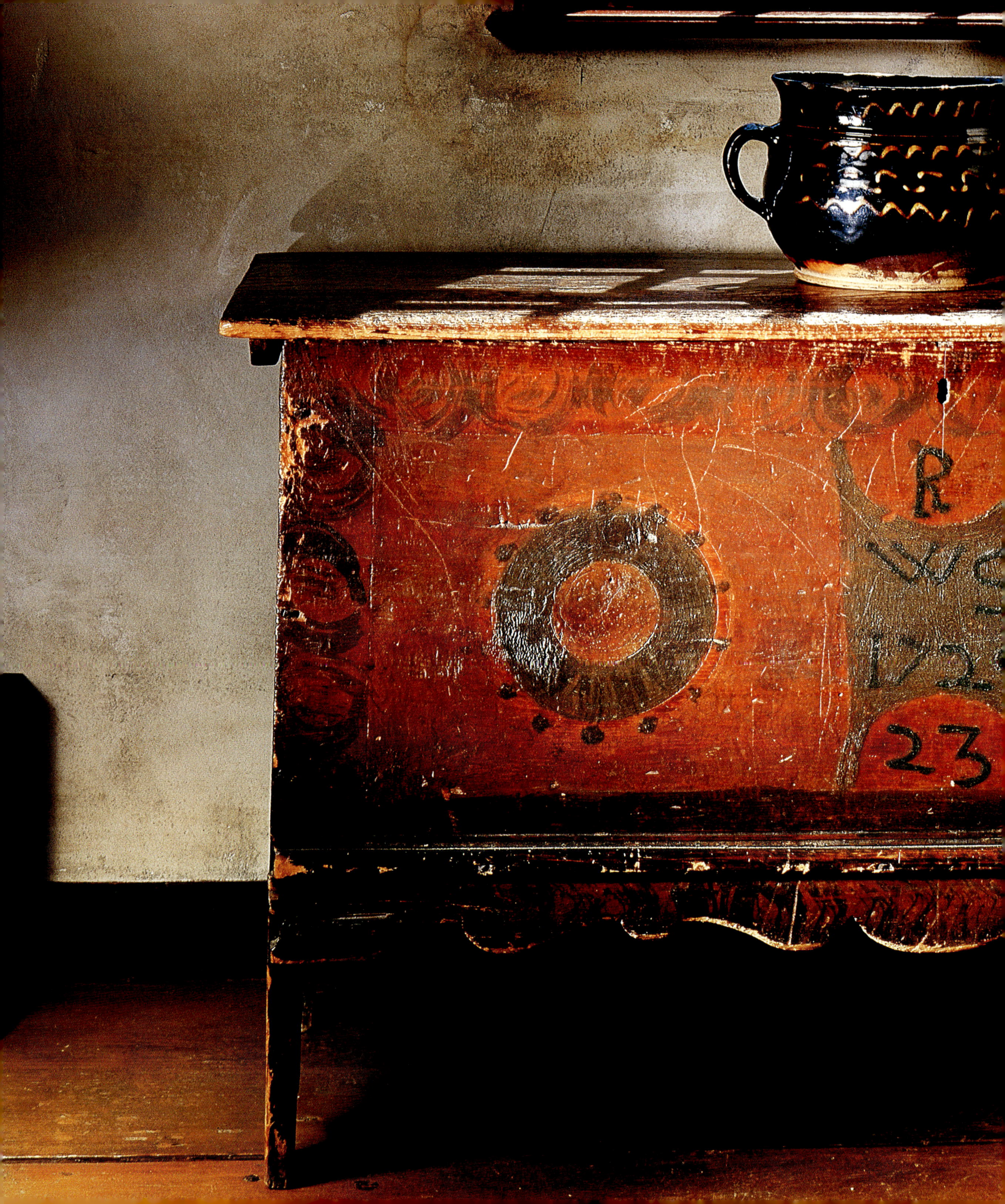
R
23

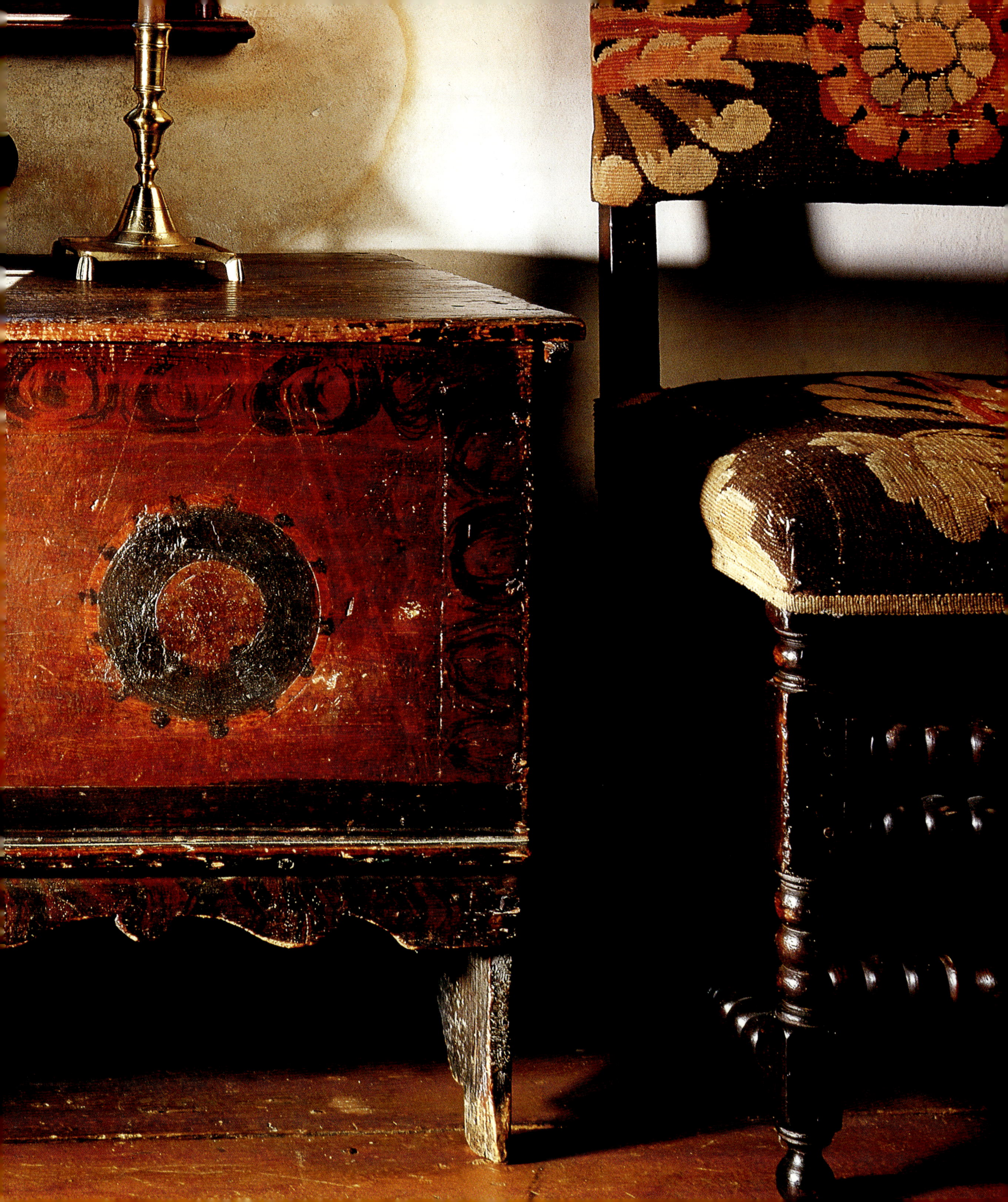

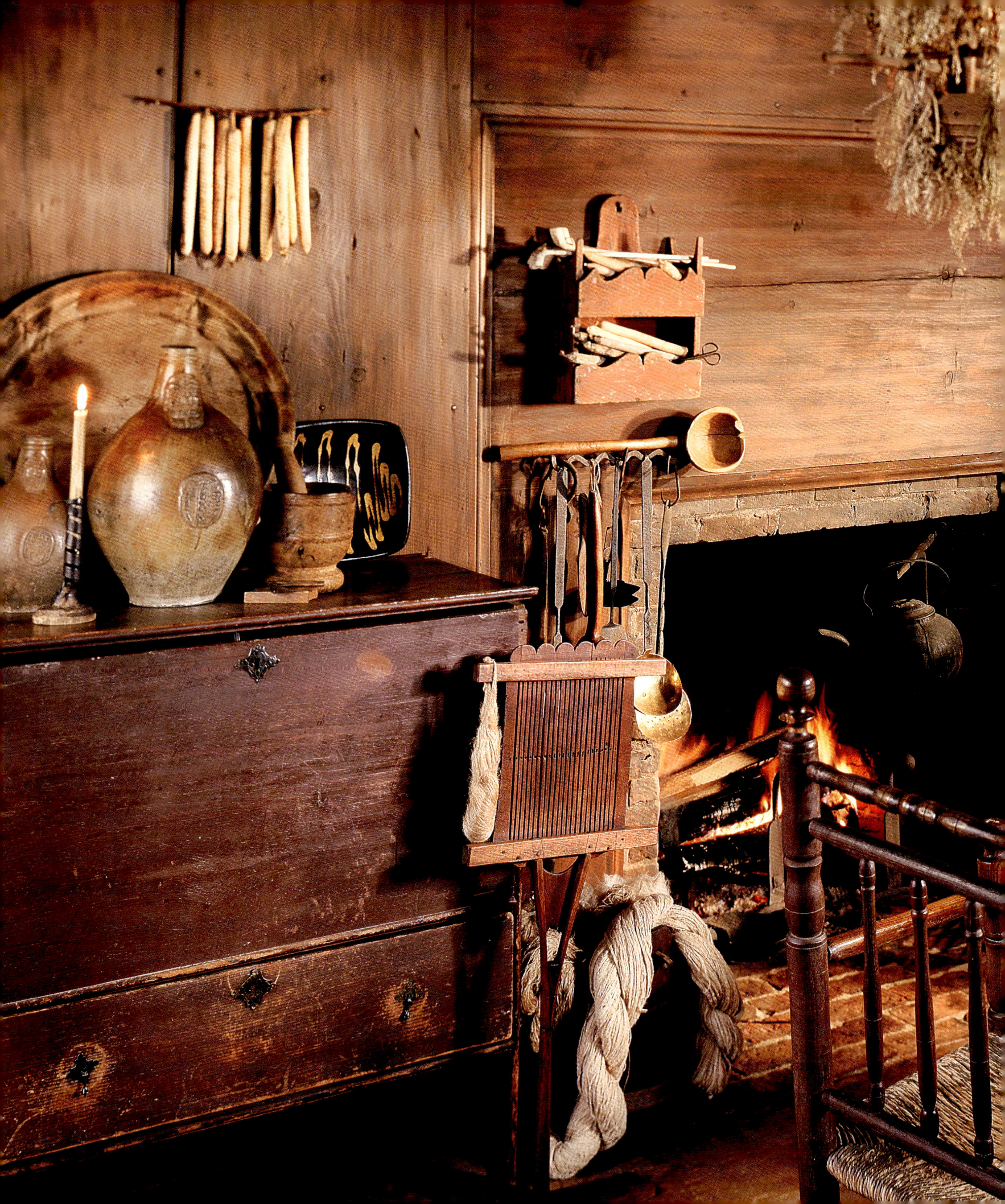

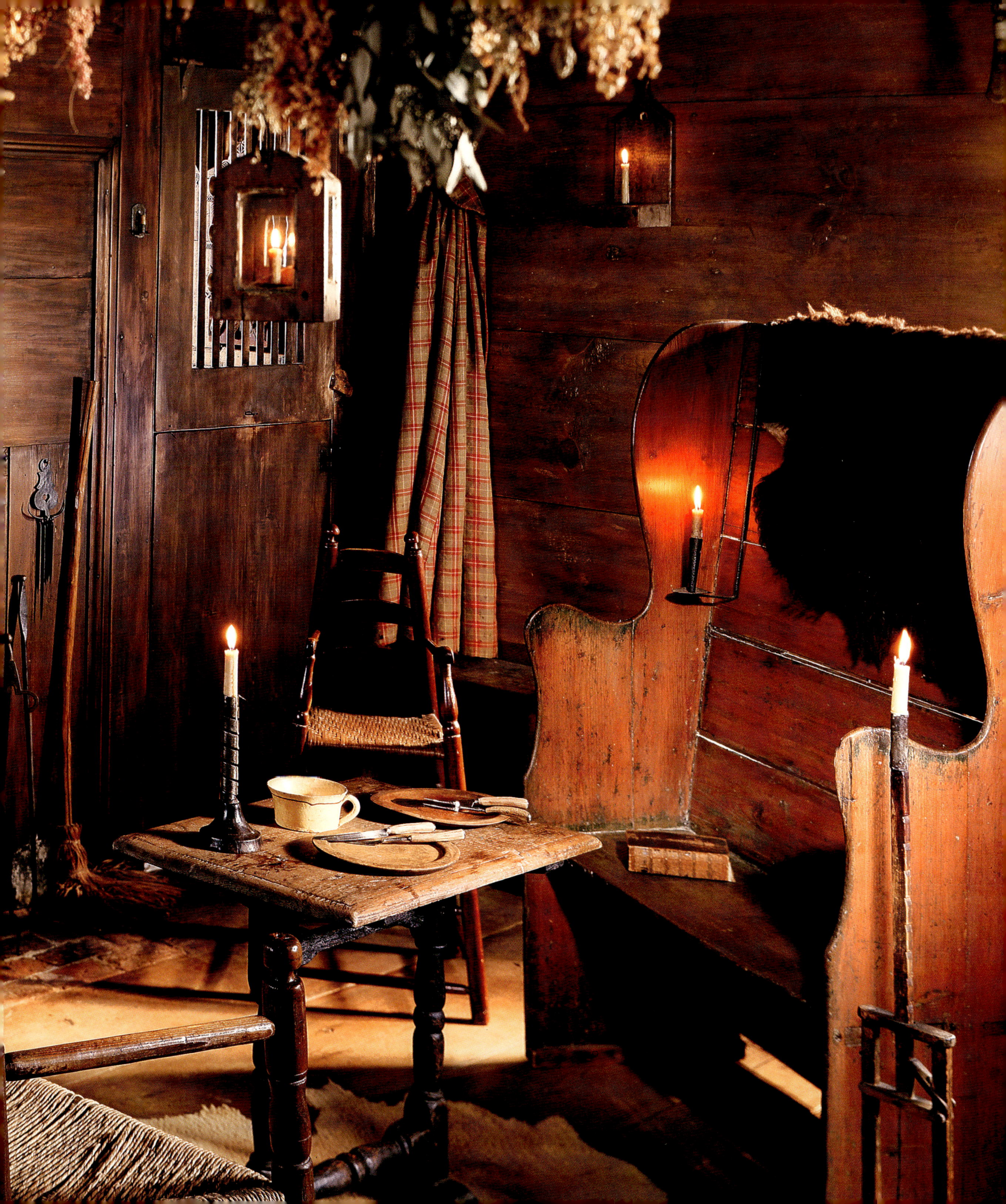

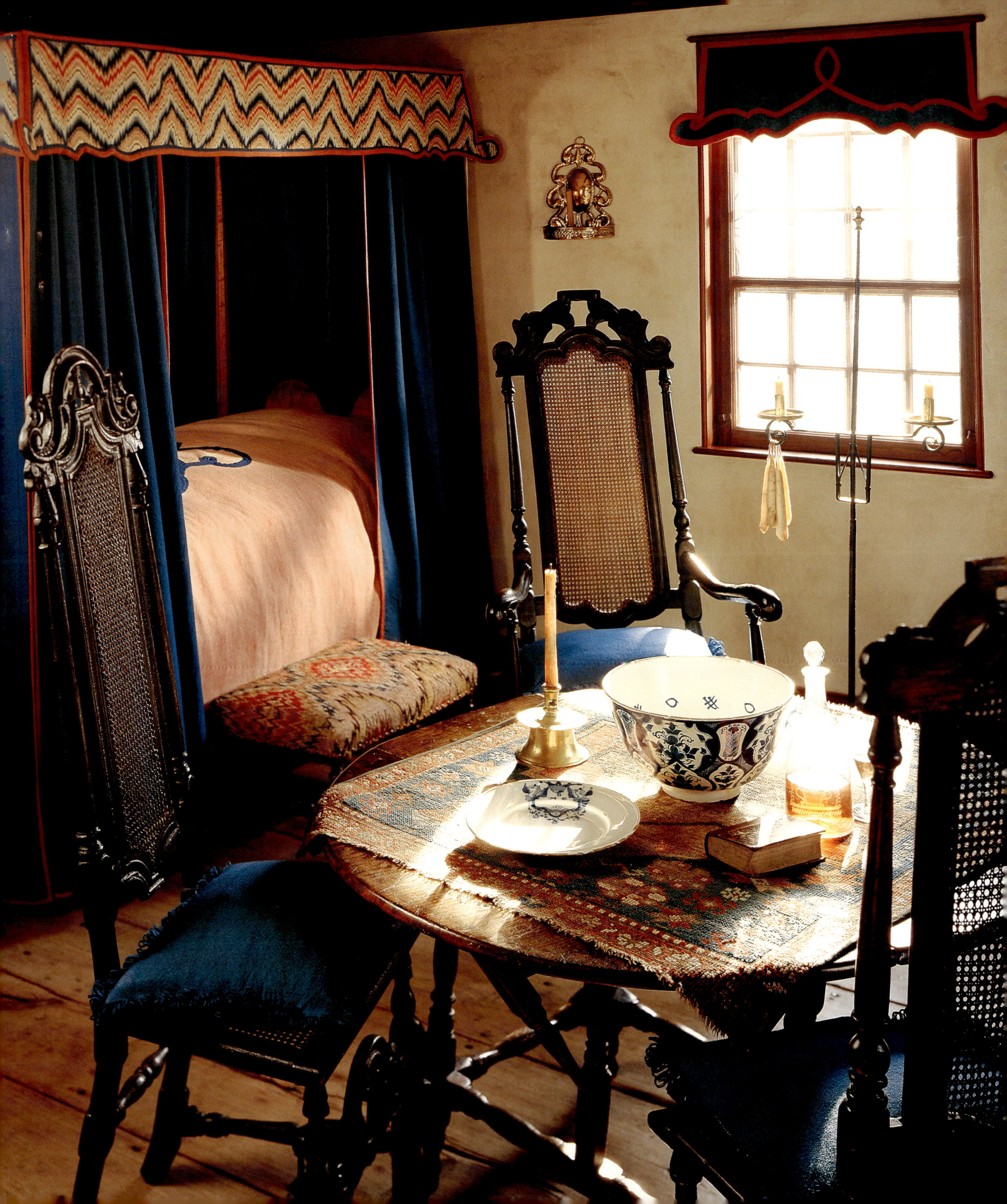

PREVIOUS PAGES *The el of the present house has a center-chimney two-room plan with a small but cozy kitchen with many of the accoutrements of domestic work and pleasure: candle light, draft-blocking tall settle, tea cups, drying herbs, and clay tobacco pipes.*

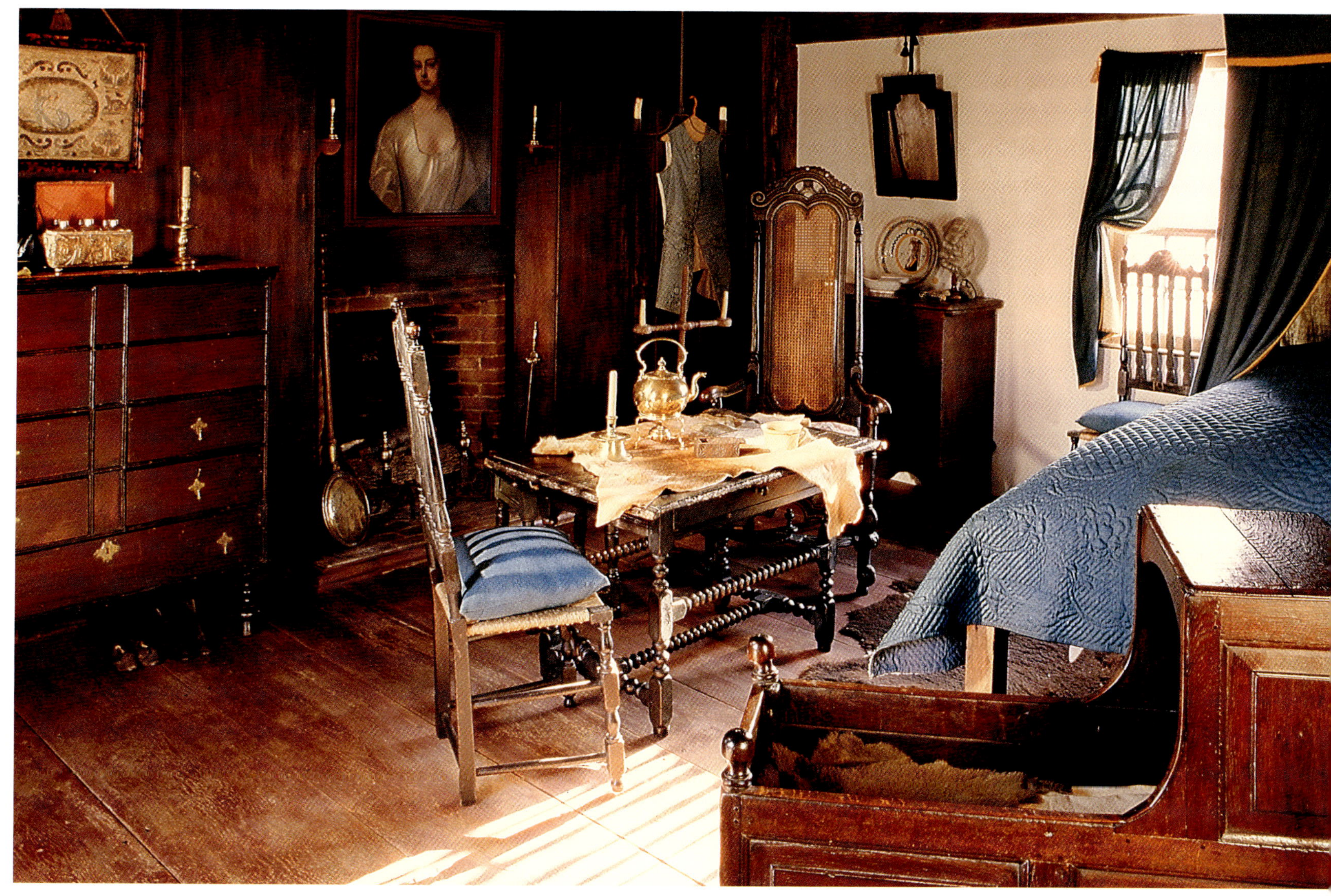

FACING PAGE *The family parlor, to right of the entryway, was the beginning of a long evolving trend toward increasing privacy and formality in New England homes. In the First Period it was reserved as the parents' bedchamber and sitting room, shared only on occasion with special guests, away from the hubbub of the kitchen and family dining room. Many of the finest furnishings were here, especially the tester bedstead, often the most valuable object in inventories because of the high cost of textiles.*

ABOVE *The chamber above the kitchen is now furnished much as a parlor, private yet social. Half tester beds often have a hinged frame to fold it up under the canopy, making way for more daytime space. The analogous cradle canopy is for protective shelter.*

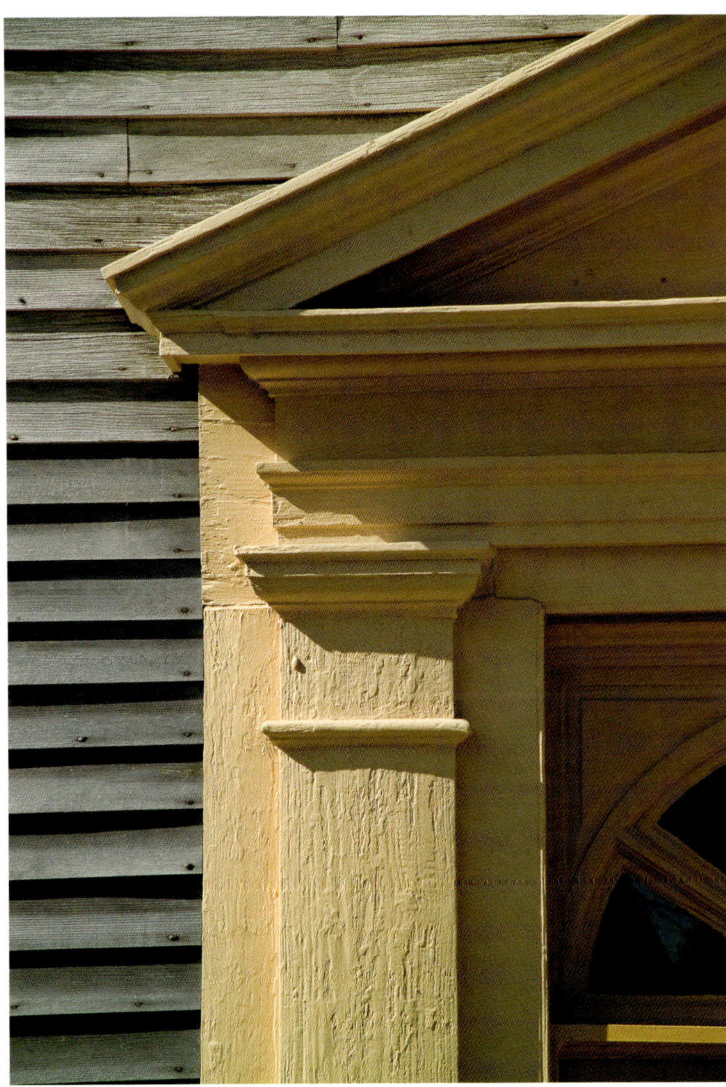

ABOVE AND FACING PAGE *George Tate's 1755 house is a transition, part old style (center chimney, small entryway, and dog-leg stairway) but mostly progressive Georgian (gambrel roof, two rooms deep, large double-hung sash windows, and pedimented doorway with transom lights). He was an established merchant from England when he came to Maine and was well acquainted with the new classically inspired style.*

CAPTAIN GEORGE TATE HOUSE

Portland, Maine, 1755

Maine started off slowly. Claimed by American Indians, French Canada, an English proprietor of the province, and even the Massachusetts Bay Company in the seventeenth century, the threat (and event) of Indian attacks and persistent litigation among land claimants stalled immigration and development until well into the eighteenth century. Maine's great resource was its forest of virgin pines. As New Hampshire's forests were cleared, logging moved to Maine. Around the Casco Peninsula a number of inland rivers converged on a sheltered harbor soon to be called Falmouth (later Portland), where the most lucrative trade was in white pine trees suitable for ship masts for the British navy. Politically connected Massachusetts merchants Colonel Thomas Westbrook and, later, Samuel Waldo had the licenses to supply the London merchants who held a monopoly on contracts with the Navy Board. These and other colonists built the infrastructure at Falmouth and upriver at Stroudwater (later Westbrook) that powered this "giant stick"–based local economy.

Captain George Tate (1700–1794) had been employed by the London monopoly in the Baltic trade in masts. They sent him to Maine to oversee their interests and ensure a reliable supply of masts upon which the largest navy in the world was heavily dependent. Tate arrived in 1751 with his wife and five children. At Stroudwater Landing he bought land, and built a wharf, warehouse, and store to conduct business as well as acting as mast agent. Then in 1755, well established in local business and society, he built a substantial Georgian house on the hill overlooking the landing. In form it is a characteristic mid-century New England home. While retaining the old-fashioned central chimney and short stairway entry hall, the house is otherwise up-to-date in the Classical form with two and a half stories under a gambrel roof,

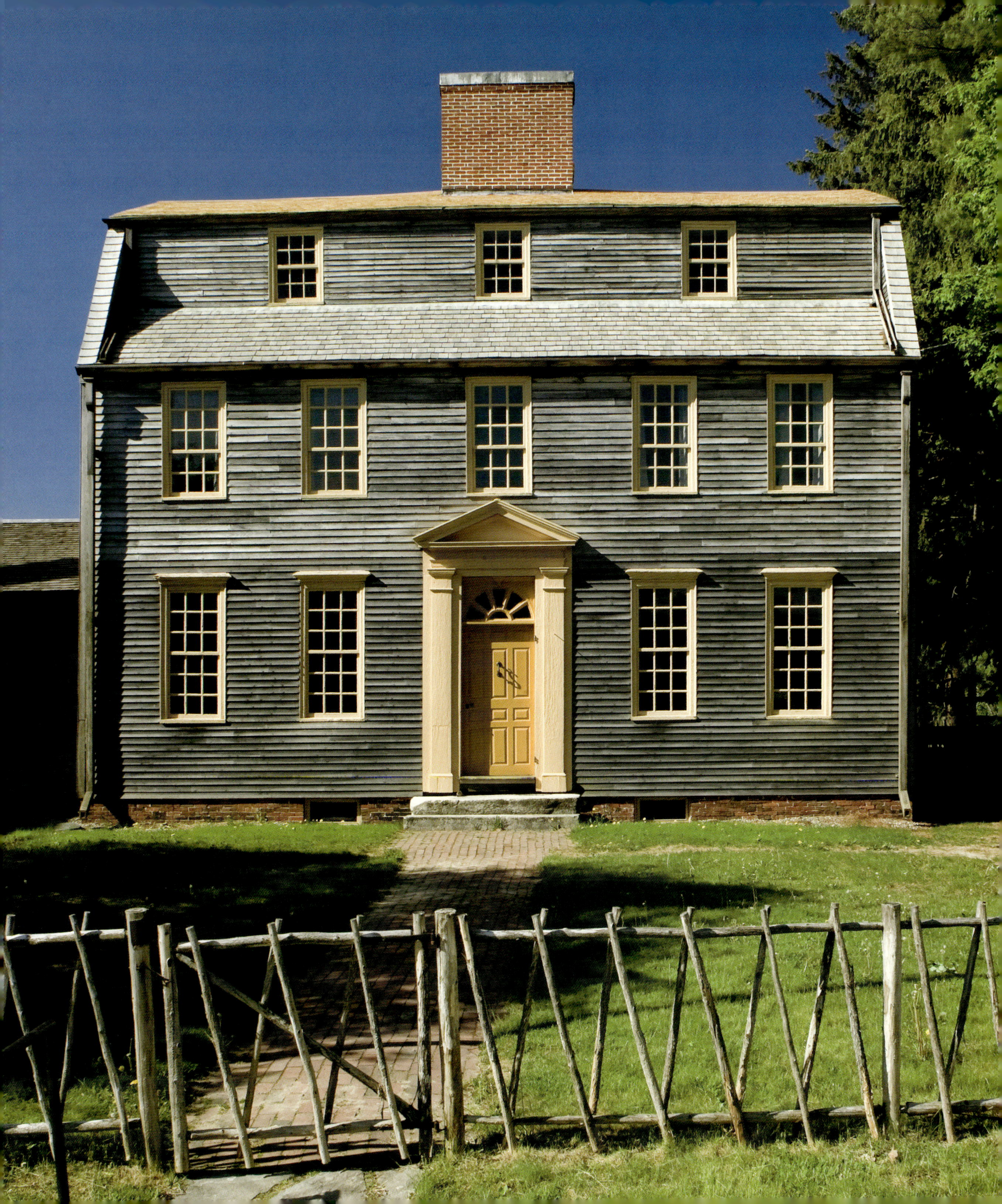

RIGHT *Georgian interiors—here, the parlor inside the entry—are a dramatic break with the past: high ceilings, large windows, trim with classically inspired woodwork, and Georgian-style furniture. The Puritan yeoman has become merchant gentleman. Reserve in manner and decoration has given place to public manners and display.*

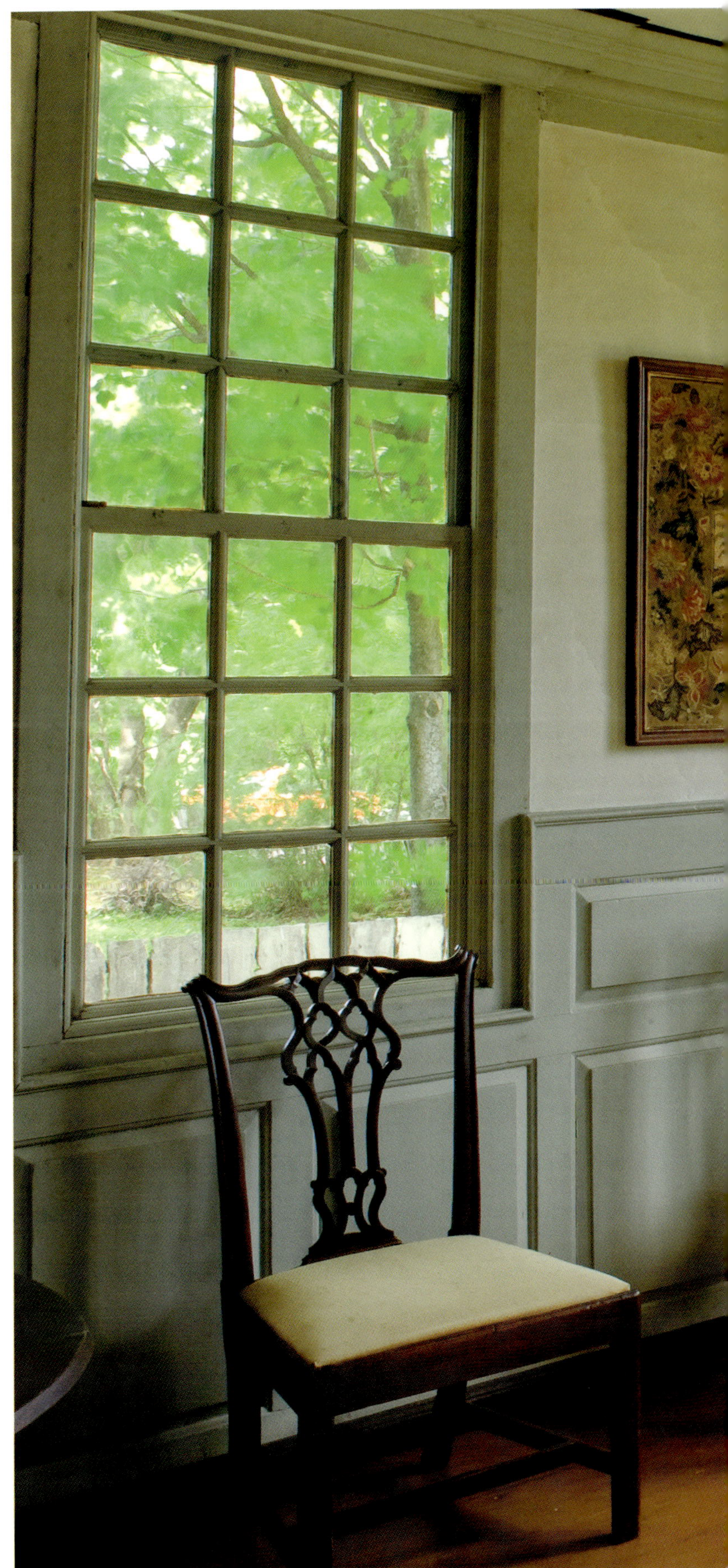

two rooms deep, eight fireplaces, large sash windows, and a pedimented portico front door with fanlight transom window. Though the house overall was not quite unique (another example exists in Maine) or necessarily progressive, Tate had the front side of the gambrel roof altered to accommodate three windows, much like a clerestory. He could have instead installed three dormers, which would have saved more space in the garret.

With the British and colonial defeat of French Canada, by 1763 a tide of reassurance and optimistic expansion swept the northern colonies. It also brought out long-simmering but submerged doubts about the value of being colonies of any power. France had been the greater enemy, and Britain would soon be seen the same way, leading to the Revolution. Issues of loyalty, taxation, and representation affected trade, including the mast business, which, like so many others, deteriorated as the Revolution approached and nearly died during and after the war when the Royal Navy turned again to the Baltic for trees.

As the elder Tate retired, his sons took up the business here and in London. George II, inspired by his father's youthful roll in Tsar Peter's fledgling navy, joined Catherine the Great's navy and became an admiral. His son William's business difficulties, however, caused the home and other properties to be sold in 1803. Years later, Andrew Hawes, whose father had once worked for Captain Tate, acquired the old Tate store, which he operated successfully, and then he acquired the old house in 1888. Somewhat of a historian, he saved the house but never modernized it—no running water, electricity, central heat, just a privy. When he died he left it to the National Society of Colonial Dames in the state of Maine, which has carefully preserved and furnished it.

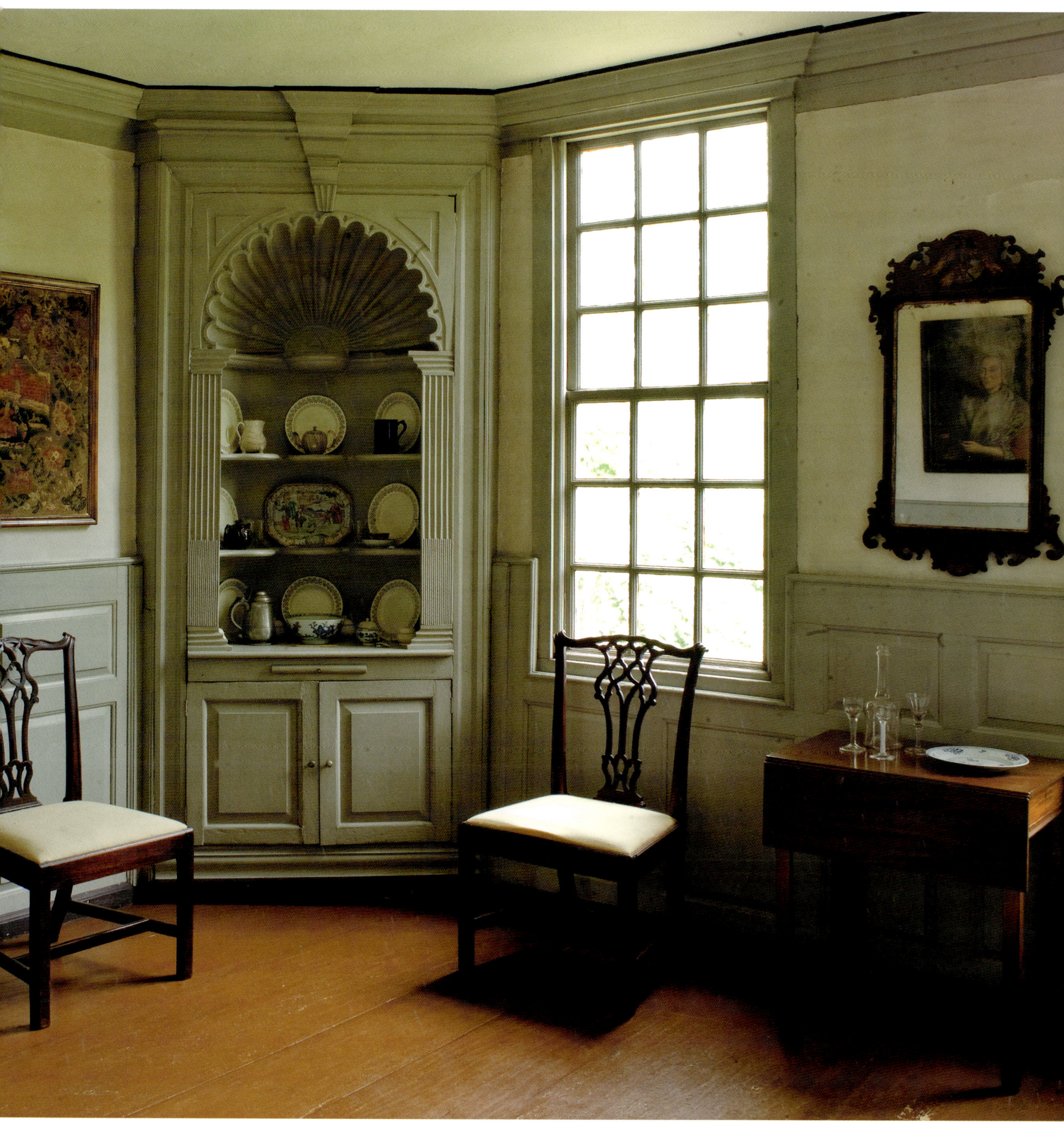

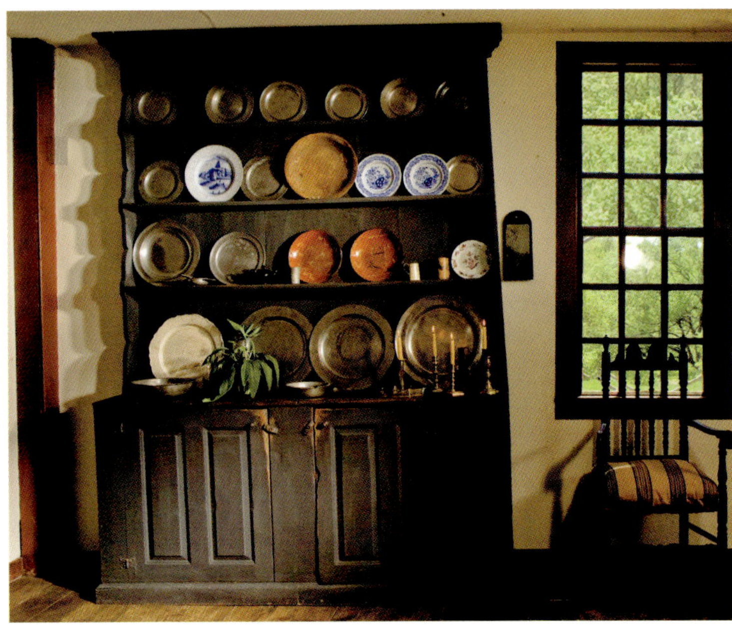

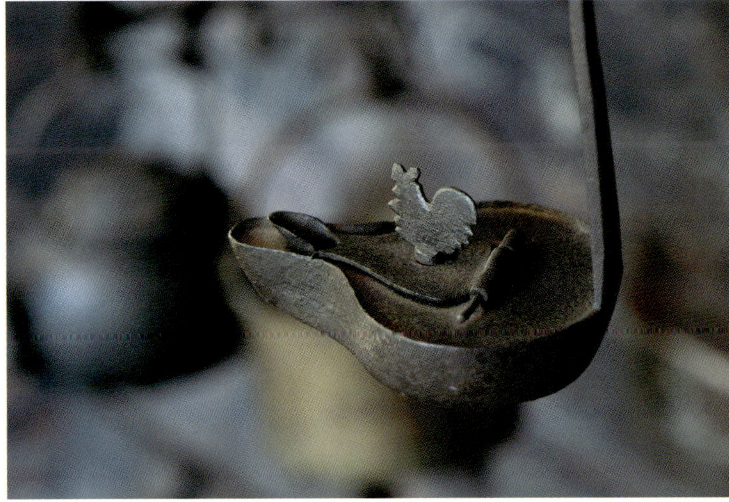

TOP *Increasing separation divides public space (parlor and dining room) from family and work space (bedrooms and kitchen). The kitchen, still served by a large fireplace, continued an old-style look with open dresser cupboards holding containers, though now as much for display as convenience.*

ABOVE *Oil lamps—fed from the chief product of New England's sea-going whaling industry—gave serviceable but dim light. As much as possible, work was done in the daytime since lighting systems had not evolved in centuries. Candles remained an expensive alternative and were time-consuming to make. Photograph by Brandt Bolding.*

RIGHT *The Georgian kitchen in the back part of the house is still old style. It would be decades before the Industrial Revolution would bring in the cast iron stove to revolutionize food cooking. Efficient running water for kitchen and bathroom was still farther away.*

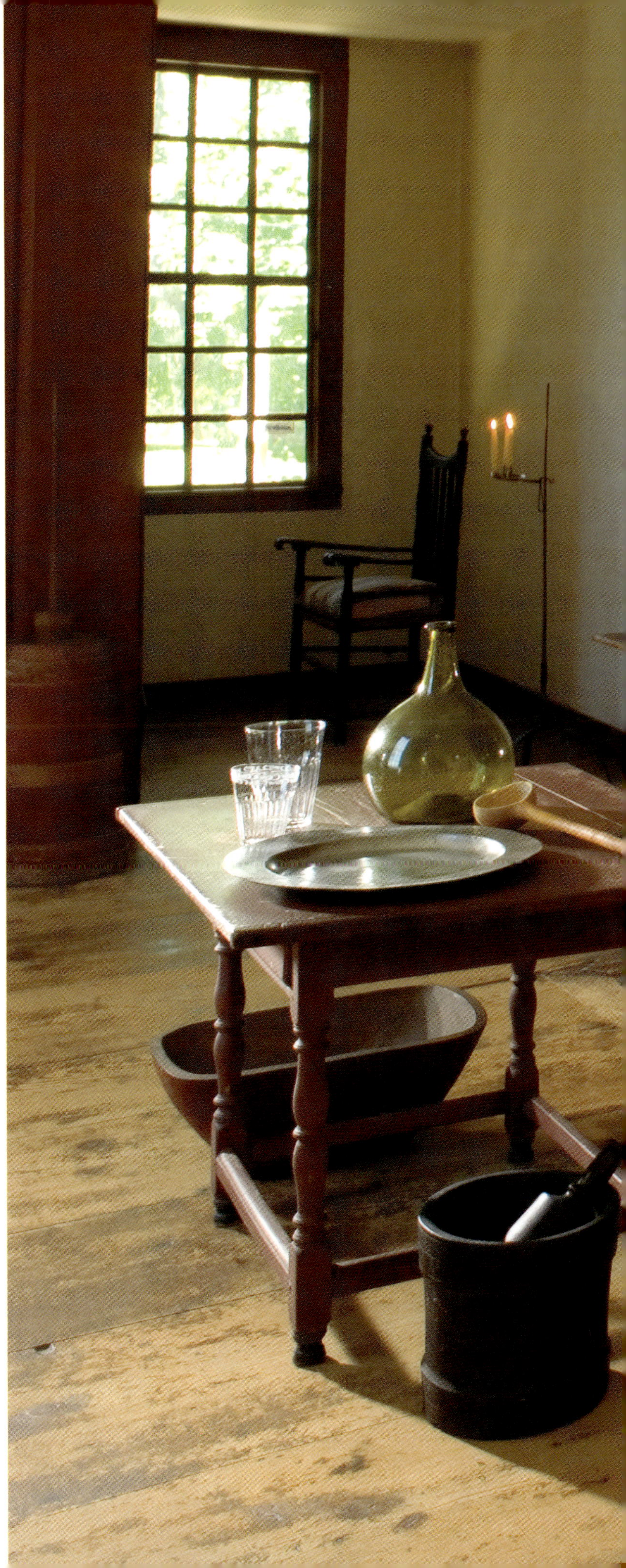

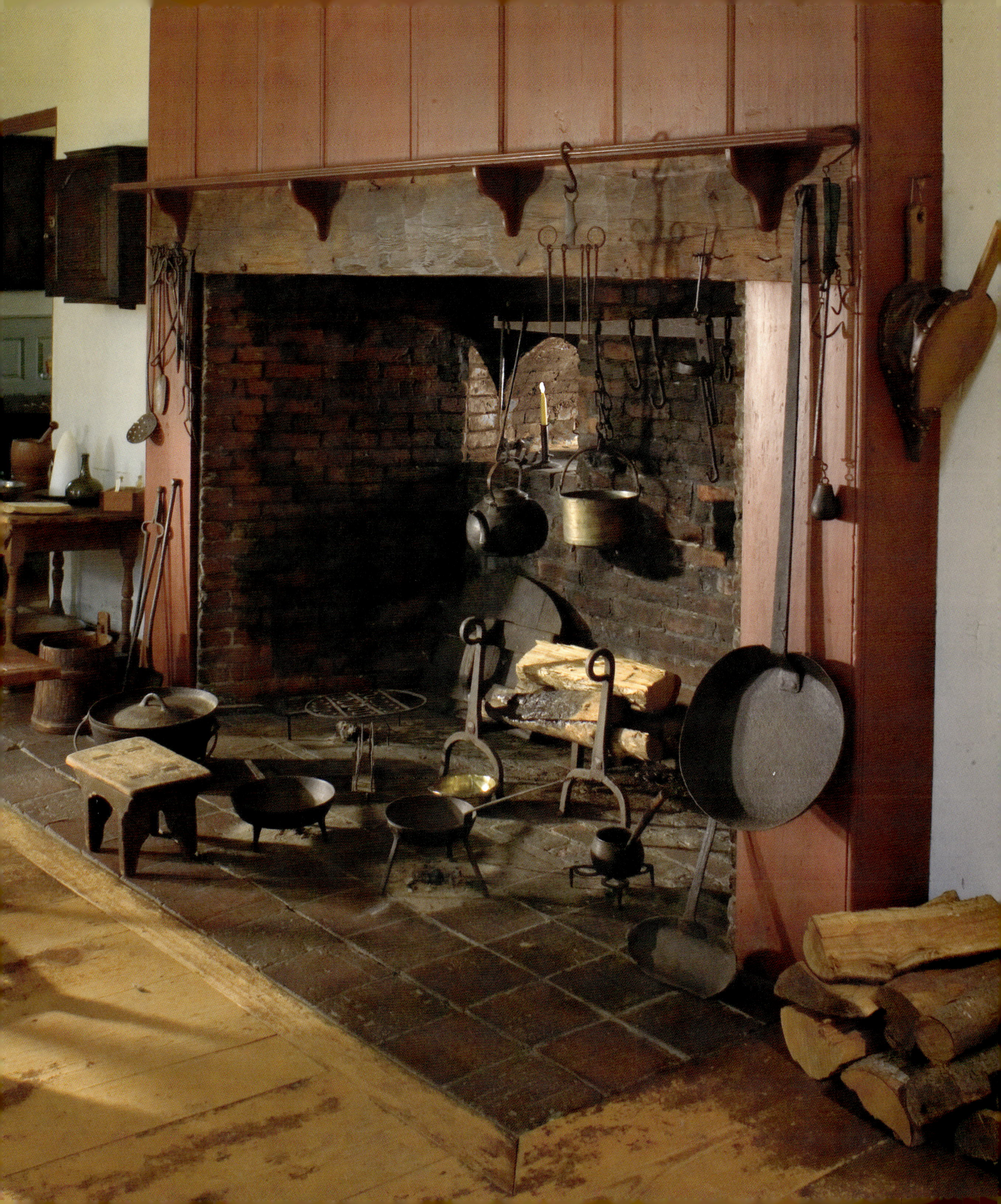

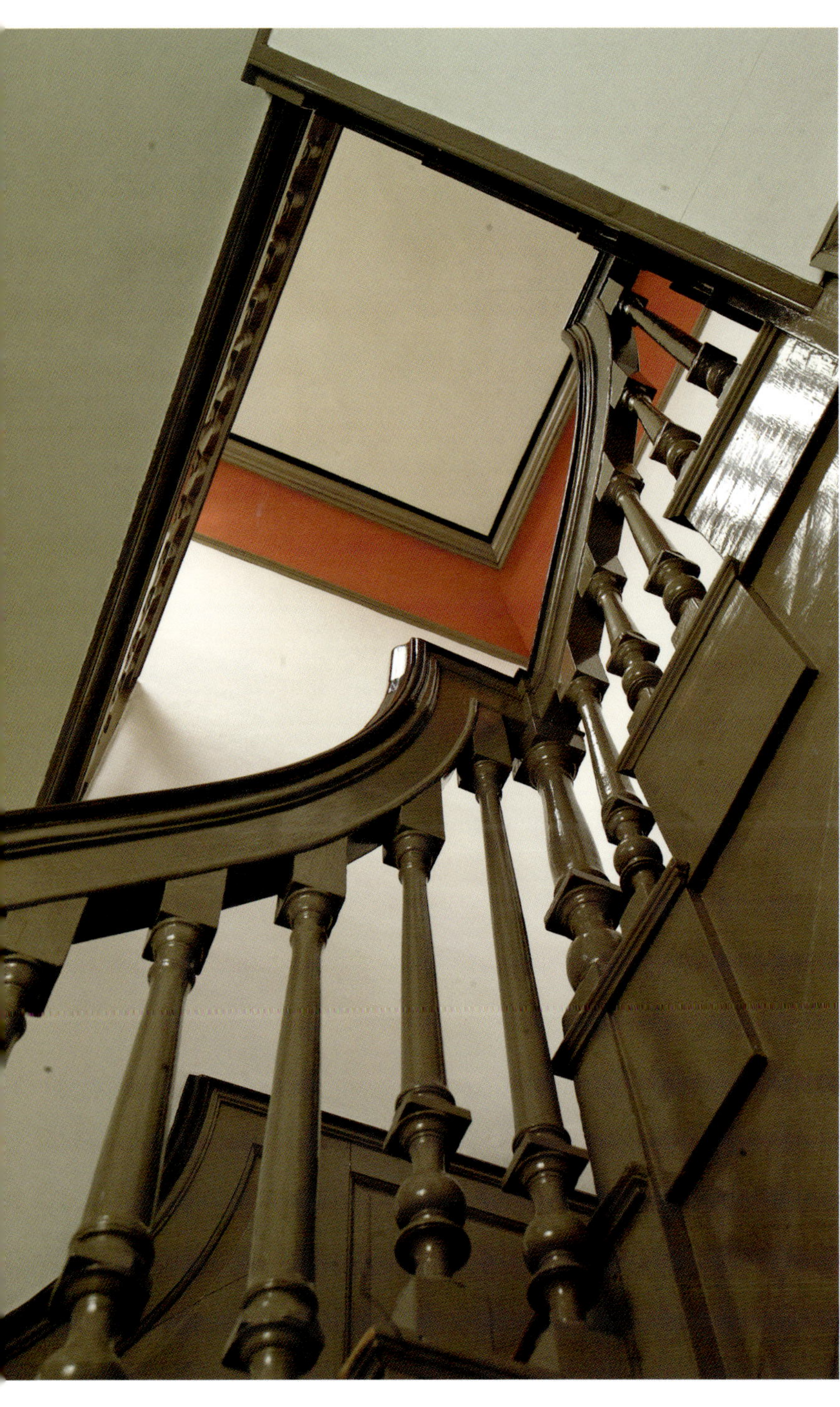

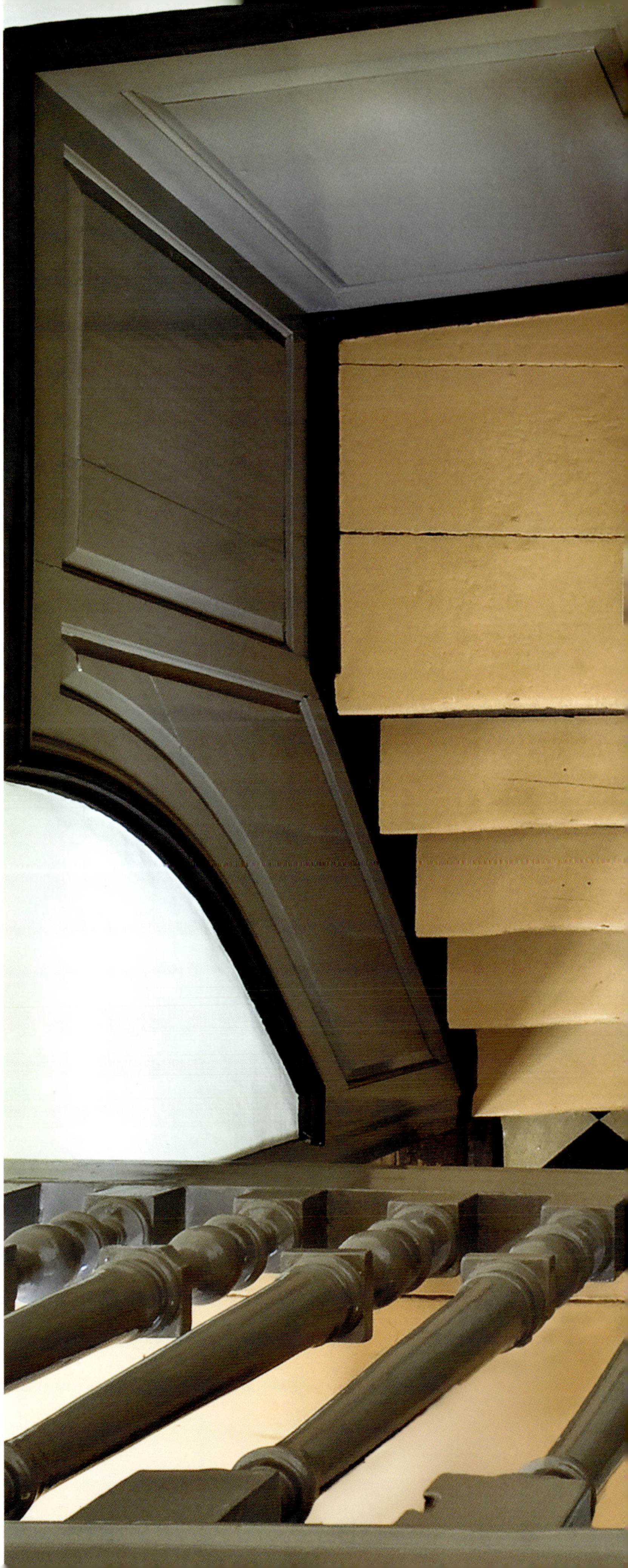

ABOVE *Although the idea of the medieval dog-leg stair structure remained, it is here updated with Georgian balusters and gracefully shaped railing. Carpentry now required sophisticated molding work*

RIGHT *If medieval building emphasized openly expressed structure, Georgian Classical was about dramatic decorative effect, the structure almost completely hidden behind plastered walls and ceiling. Even floors, in the best houses, were being covered—wall-to-wall—with imported machined carpets or painted oil cloths. Although the Tate House features an old style dog-leg stairway, the new style paneled dado, sweeping railing, and contrasting colors are all about visual motion. The legacy of Classical Rome and post-Renaissance English permutations had reached the New World. Photograph by Brandt Bolding.*

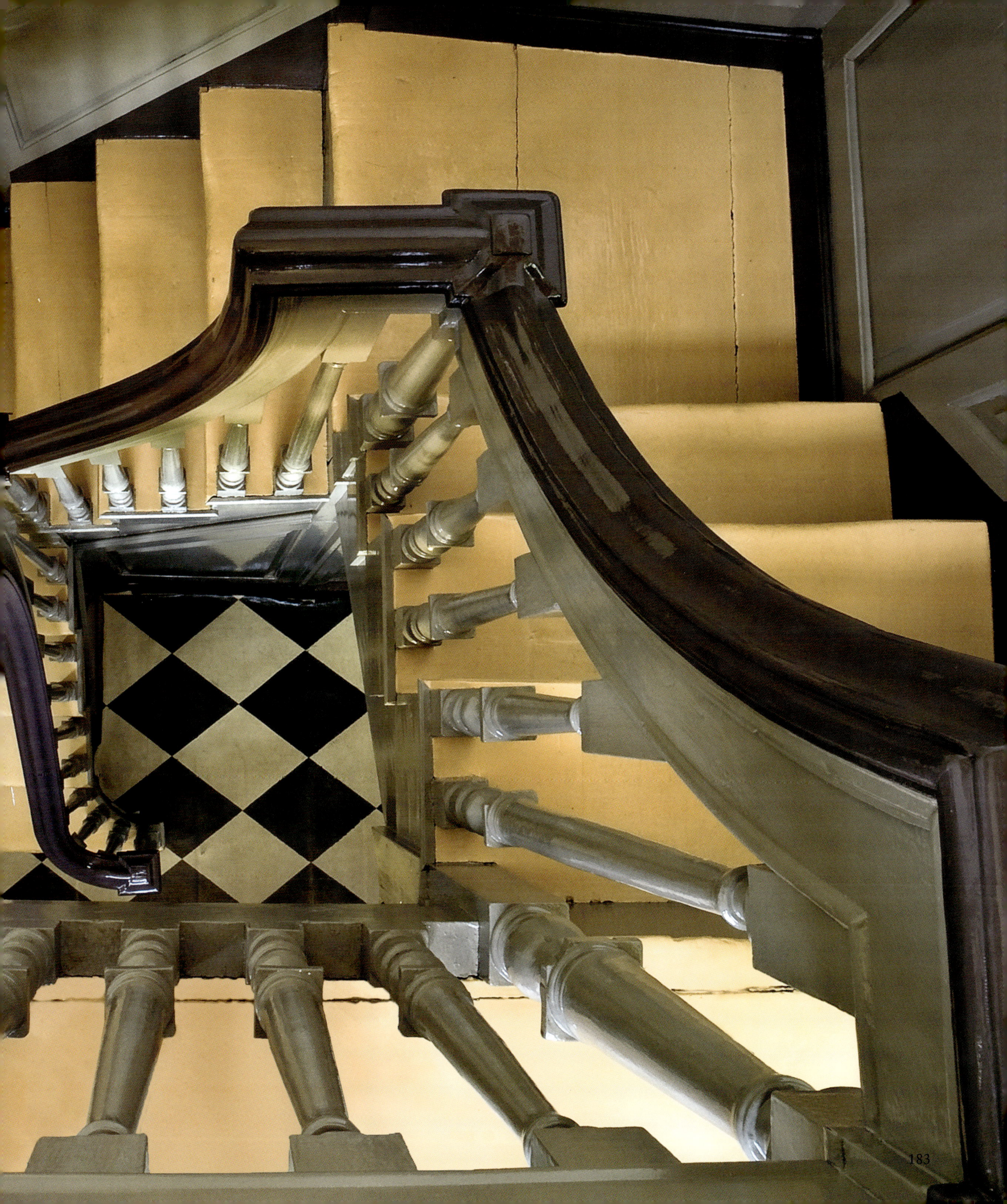

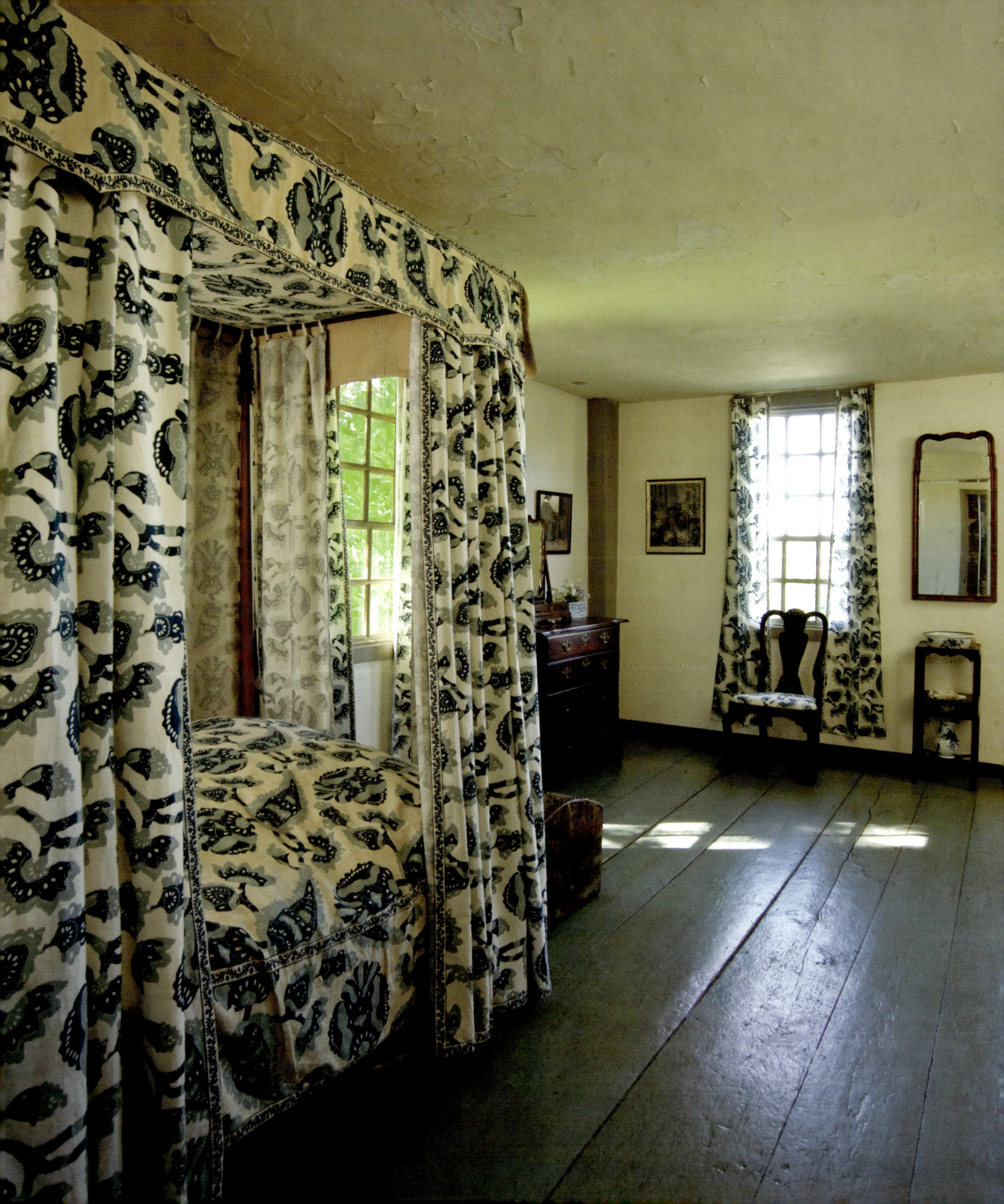

FACING PAGE *In the upstairs chamber, structural beams have nearly disappeared under plaster, which helps reflect light from larger windows. A small fireplace is not only for warmth but for more private socializing than in the parlor. The new style is as much about light and light-heartedness as about new culture.*

RIGHT *The Tate House, in one chimney stack, has eight fireplaces, reflecting the increasing number of bedrooms and privacy in Georgian houses.*

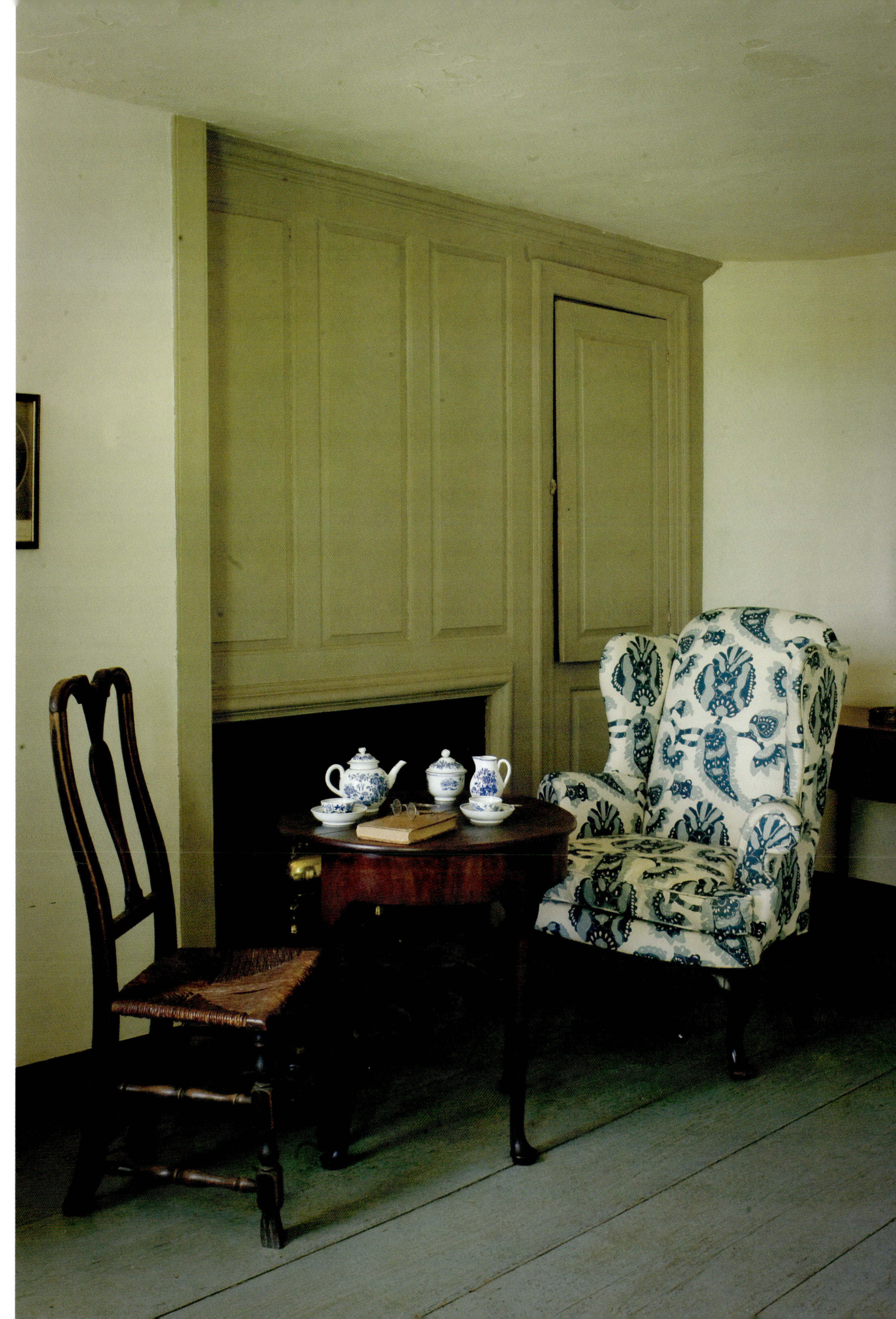

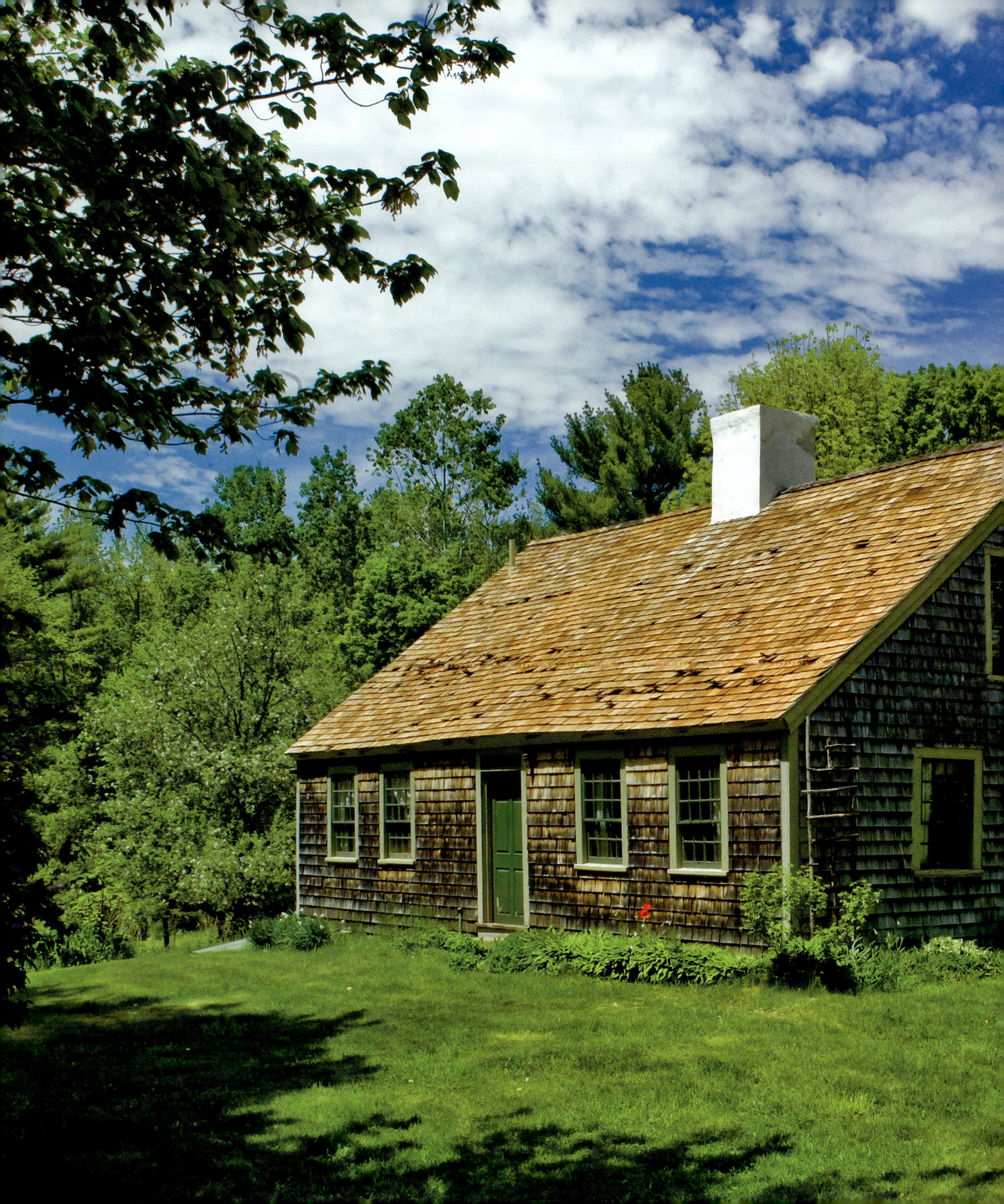

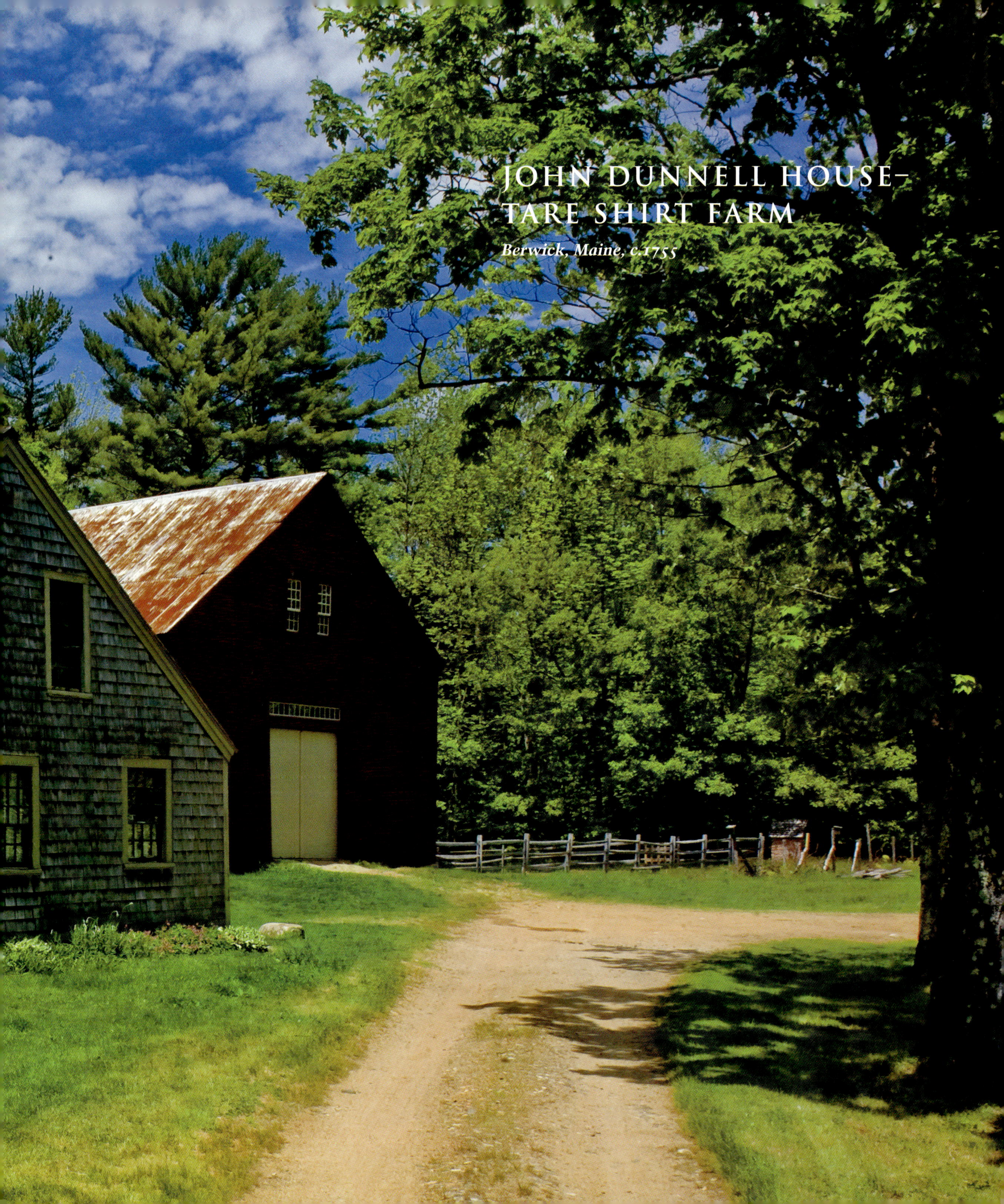

JOHN DUNNELL HOUSE–TARE SHIRT FARM

Berwick, Maine, c.1755

PREVIOUS PAGES *Built at the same time as Tate House, the Dunnell House was far removed from coastal prosperity. Modest in form and features, it is what has become known as a Cape Cod house, not for its origin there—its form comes from England—but for how many were built in that part of Massachusetts.*

RIGHT *The right parlor is an antiquarian's delight. The blue resist-dye fabric was popular in the mid-eighteenth century.*

FOLLOWING PAGES *The principal bedroom on the first floor, to the left of the entry, has one of three fireplaces on the first floor, all of which are contained within a massive twelve-foot square center chimney stack. Emblematic of the scarcity of lime for mortar in early New England, it is entirely laid up with clay, and still intact.*

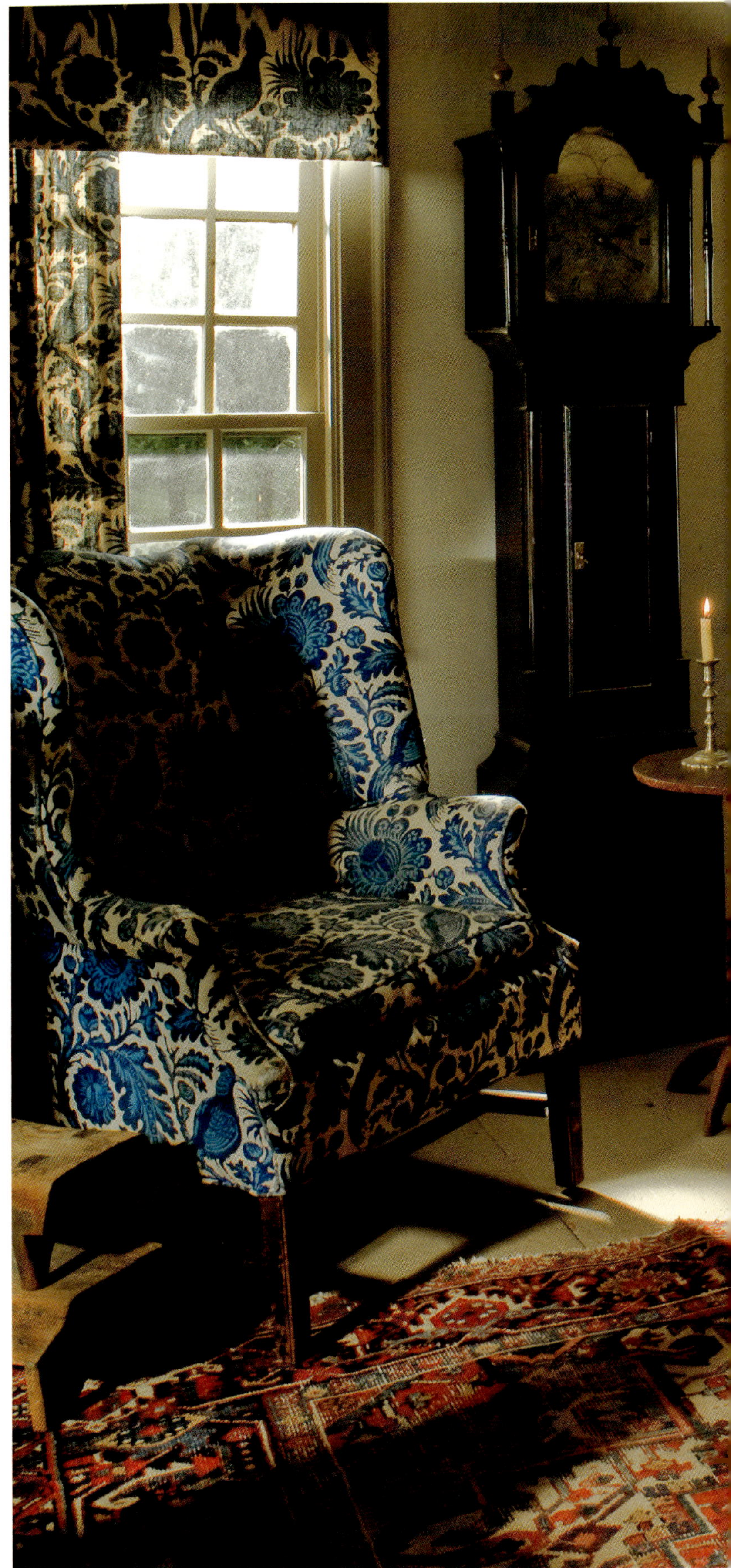

York is the southernmost county of Maine. From Kittery, at the coastal south entrance to the Piscataqua River, settlers pushed north on the river in the 1630s looking for settlement opportunities. They found endless forests and built the first sawmill in America. Known initially as Newichawannock, this settlement on the river was incorporated as Berwick in 1713. As forests were cleared, farms spread through the backcountry, interrupted during four French and Indian wars by destructive raids from Canada. At some time prior to 1755 an as-yet-unidentified family built this house on Tare Shirt Hill Road (now Diamond Hill Road), a few miles northeast of Berwick village.

The next owner of record was John Dunnell, born in 1758 at Buxton, just west of Portland, Maine. In 1777 he enlisted in the Continental Army, serving for a half year as a private. Most likely he moved to Berwick after being discharged and acquired Tare Shirt Farm from its prior, and possibly original, owner. It was known since its origin by the name of the nearby hill and country road. "Tare" meant fine dressed linen yarn, made from flax grown on the local farms well into the twentieth century.

In 1794 he married Molly Farnhum, and they had four children. The family made their living off the farm. He served in the military again, in the War of 1812. A month before his death in 1836, at age seventy-eight, he wrote his will, revealing a little

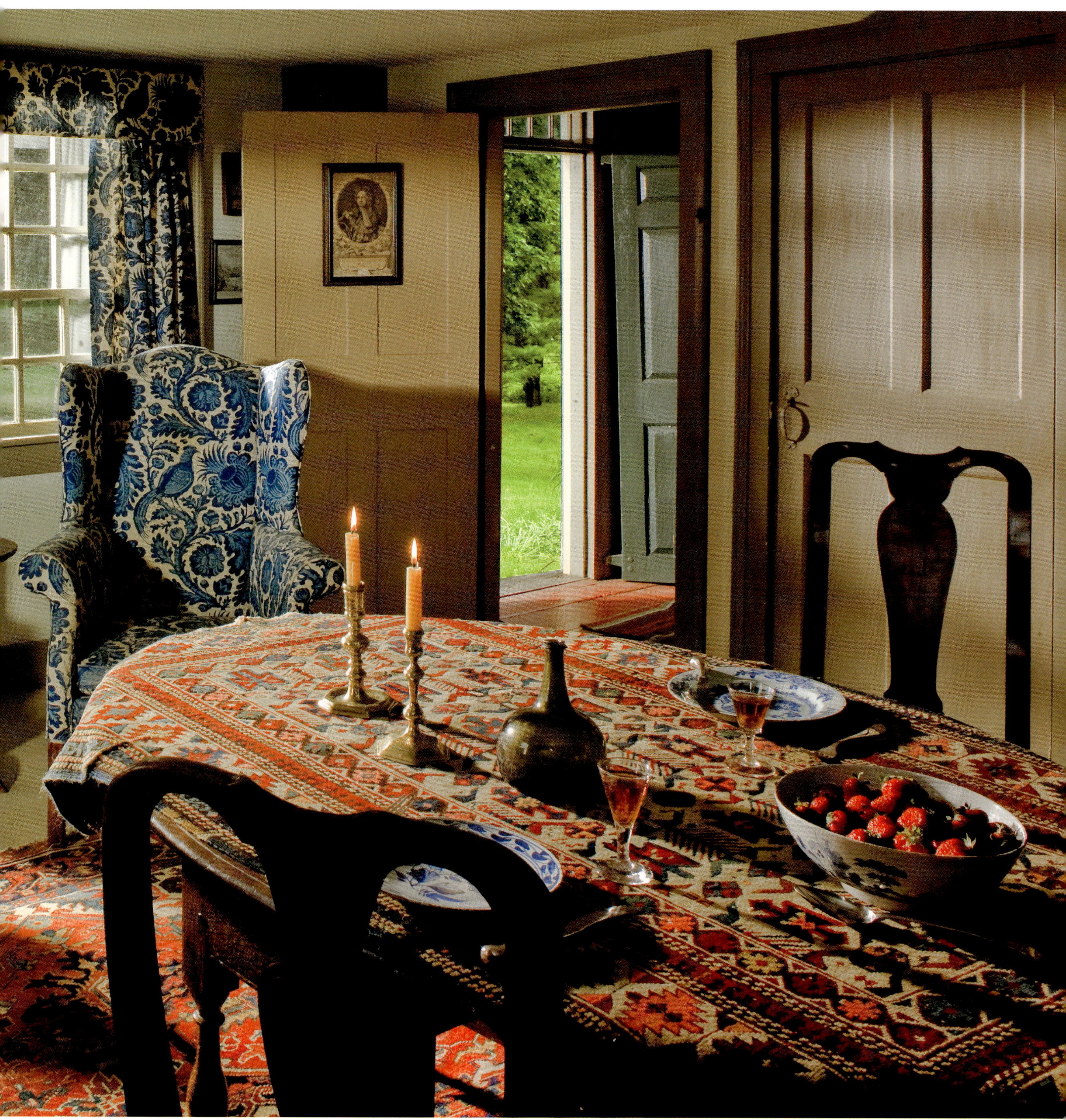

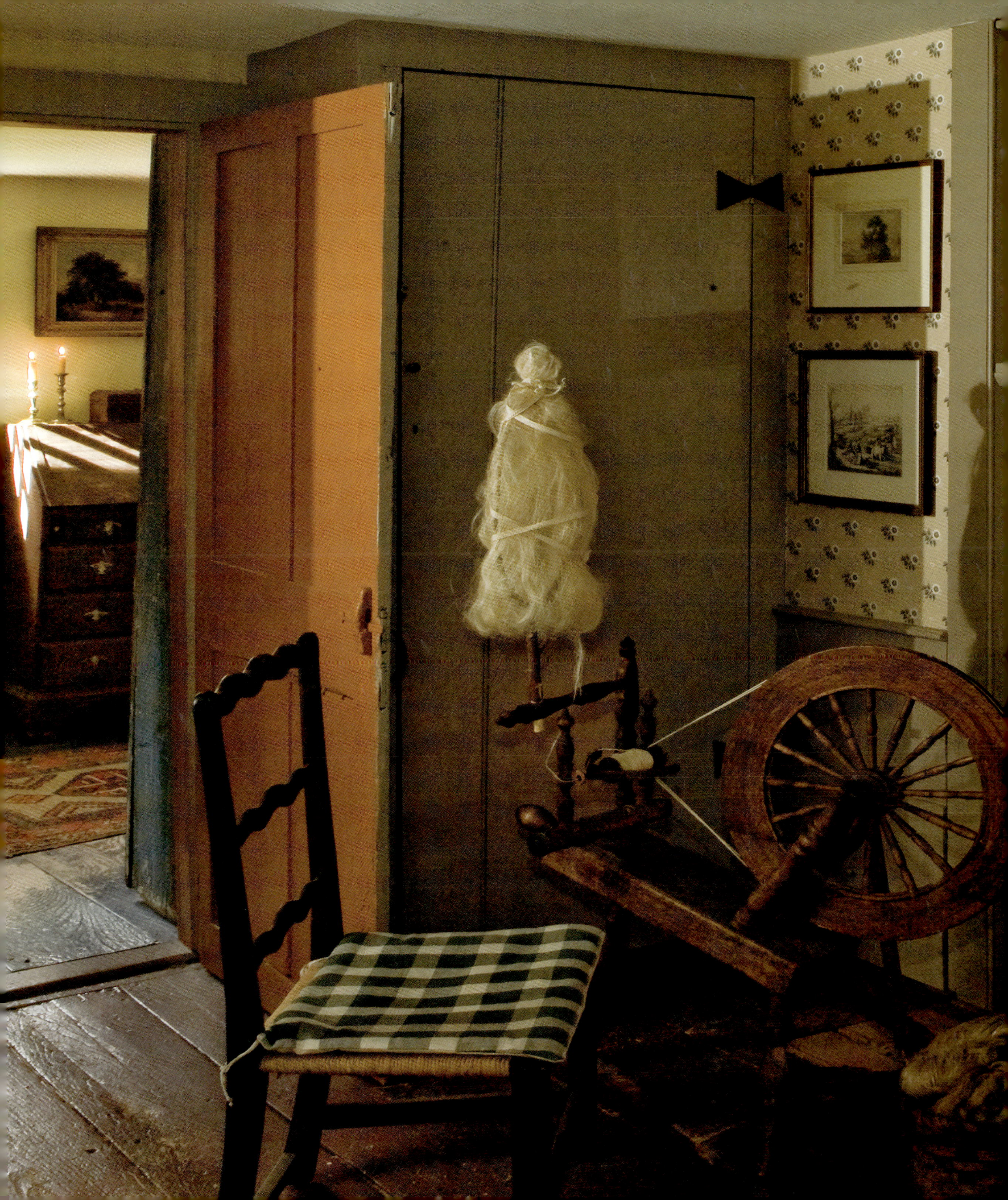

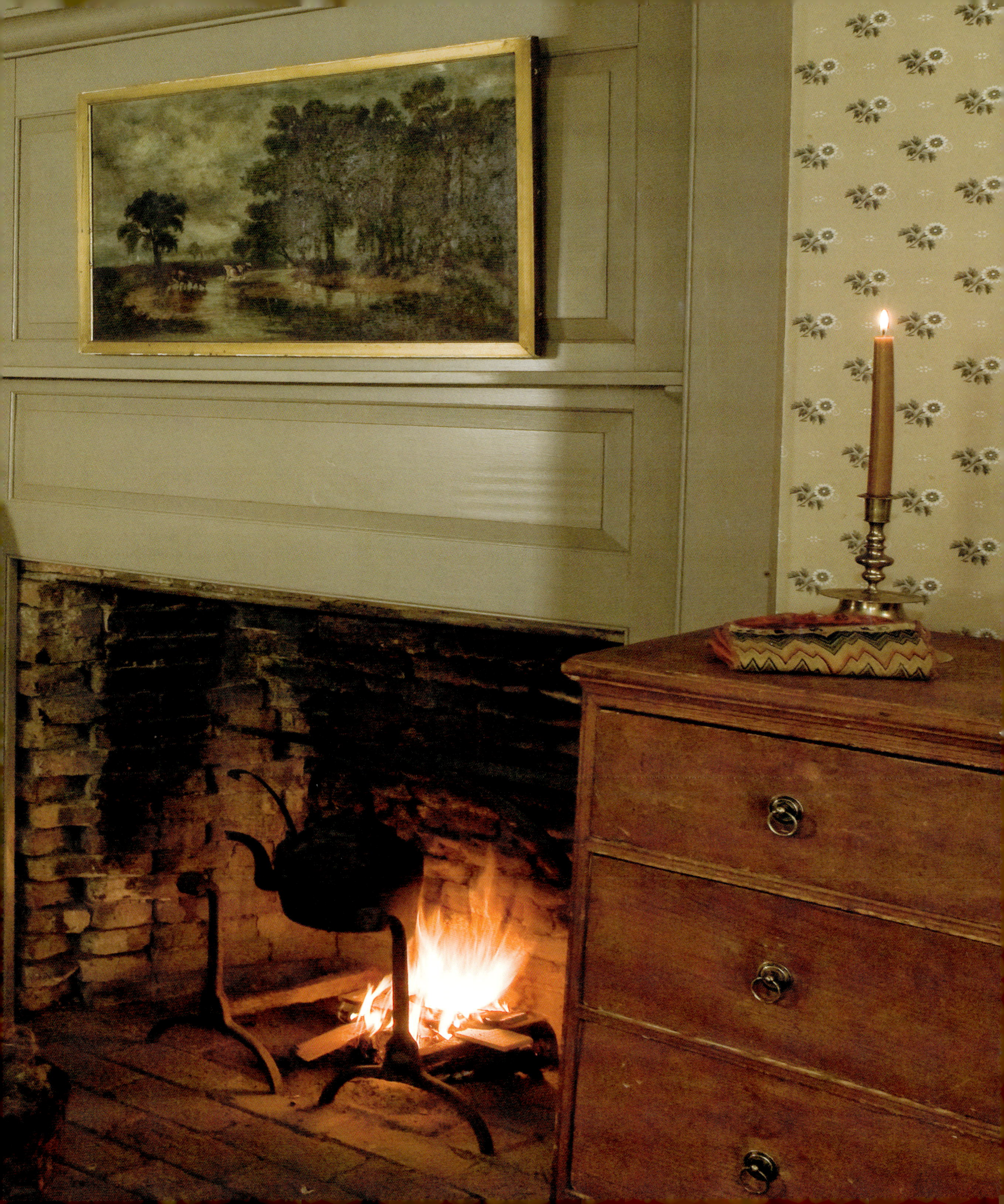

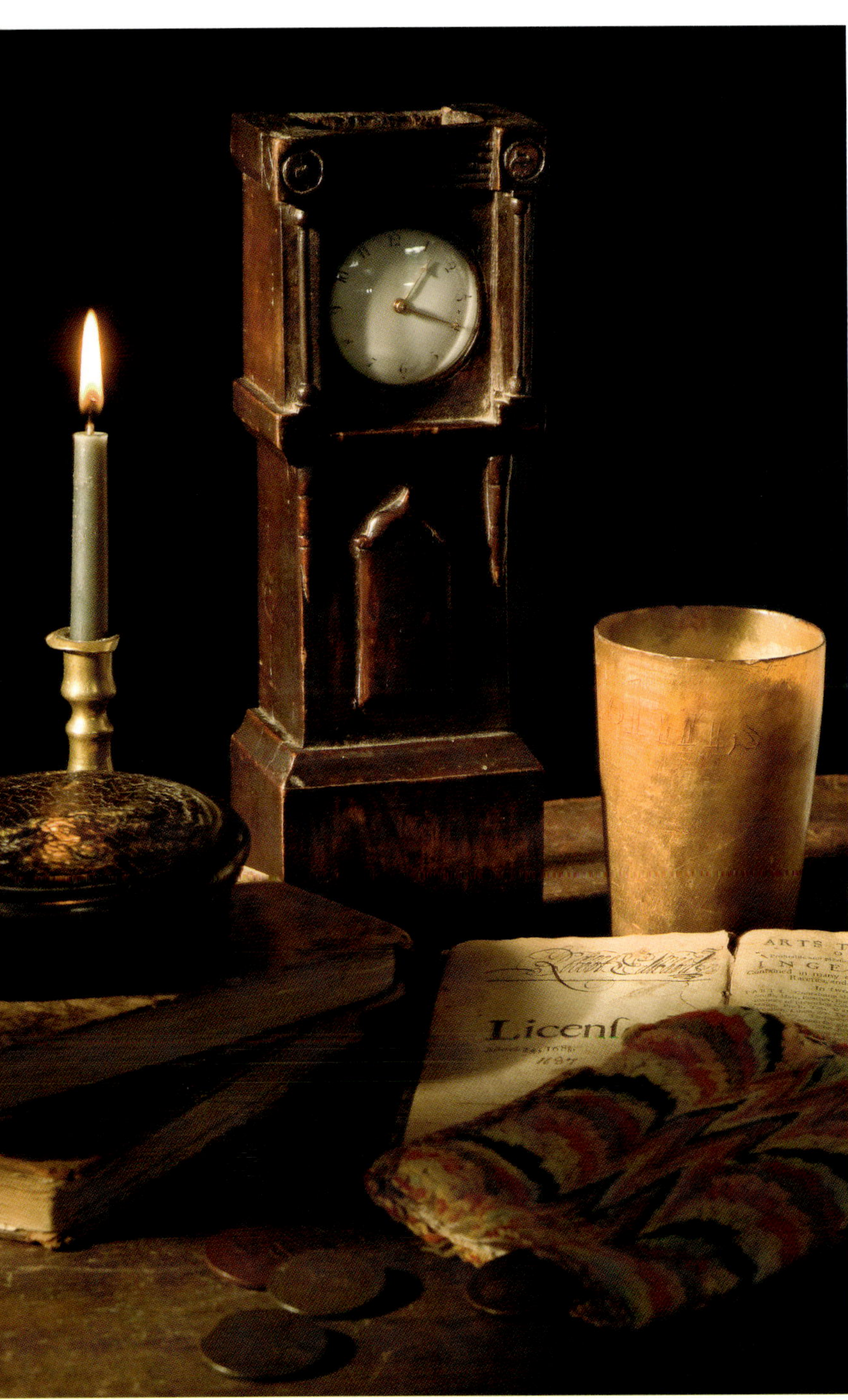

LEFT *Accoutrements of living at home two centuries ago: a horn cup, a pocket watch owner's "tall clock," a few books, a needlepoint pocketbook and change, a snuff box, and a brass candlestick.*

FACING PAGE *The plethora of painted furniture is not just a preference for color per se but a result of the available wood behind the paint. In New England there are many kinds of trees available but only certain species are appropriate for furniture: maple's fine grain turns smoothly on a lathe, and white pine's soft and knot-free wood saws and planes easily. Both woods are initially dead white with no visual character (except tiger maple), making unattractive surfaces demanding to be colored. With the availability of a wide range of powdered pigment in the eighteenth century, those who built and furnished their modest houses with locally made furniture turned to paint for this solution. Wealthier coastal merchants could afford imported mahogany, even for house woodwork.*

about his home and farm. He provided for comfortable support for his wife Molly from rents and profits, gave most of his estate to his son John (who must pay all his debts) and token amounts to son Thomas and daughter Mary, and bequeathed to daughter Sarah, "The use of the back middle bedroom in my dwelling house, the privilege of passing to and from the same through my kitchen to the road, a privilege of the cellar and oven to bake as occasion may require, to hold privileges so long as she will remain a single woman and no longer, but in case of marriage I will her a good cow at that time." He was buried on the farm in what thereafter became Tare Shirt Burying Ground and where several subsequent residents and owners were interred.

The house as built remains essentially the same, a well-preserved survival of a vernacular one-and-a-half-story eighteenth-century Cape Cod–style house with its original fireplaces and room arrangements intact. It is 28 feet deep and 38 feet wide with a massive 12-foot-square stone chimney foundation stack supporting three fireplaces. The bricks laid up in clay, not scarce lime mortar, make up three flues that accommodate each of the fireplaces. The central front door opens into a small vestibule entry with stairway to the garret, which remained unfinished of floor or walls and unused except for storage and occasional sleeping space until the mid-twentieth century.

The grounds immediately adjacent to the house include early features: an 1830s barn on a foundation of an earlier structure, the family cemetery, and a Revolutionary War cemetery for soldiers. A brook passes through the property crossed by two well-used eighteenth-century stone bridges, one for the original road to town, the other to the wood lot. Three stone-lined wells that appear to be early are likely from the period of the house. A well sweep still brings up water from the deepest well.

When the present owners acquired the property in 1985, its post-original features spoke of modest rural survival over generations. The three fireplaces were covered over, the parlor

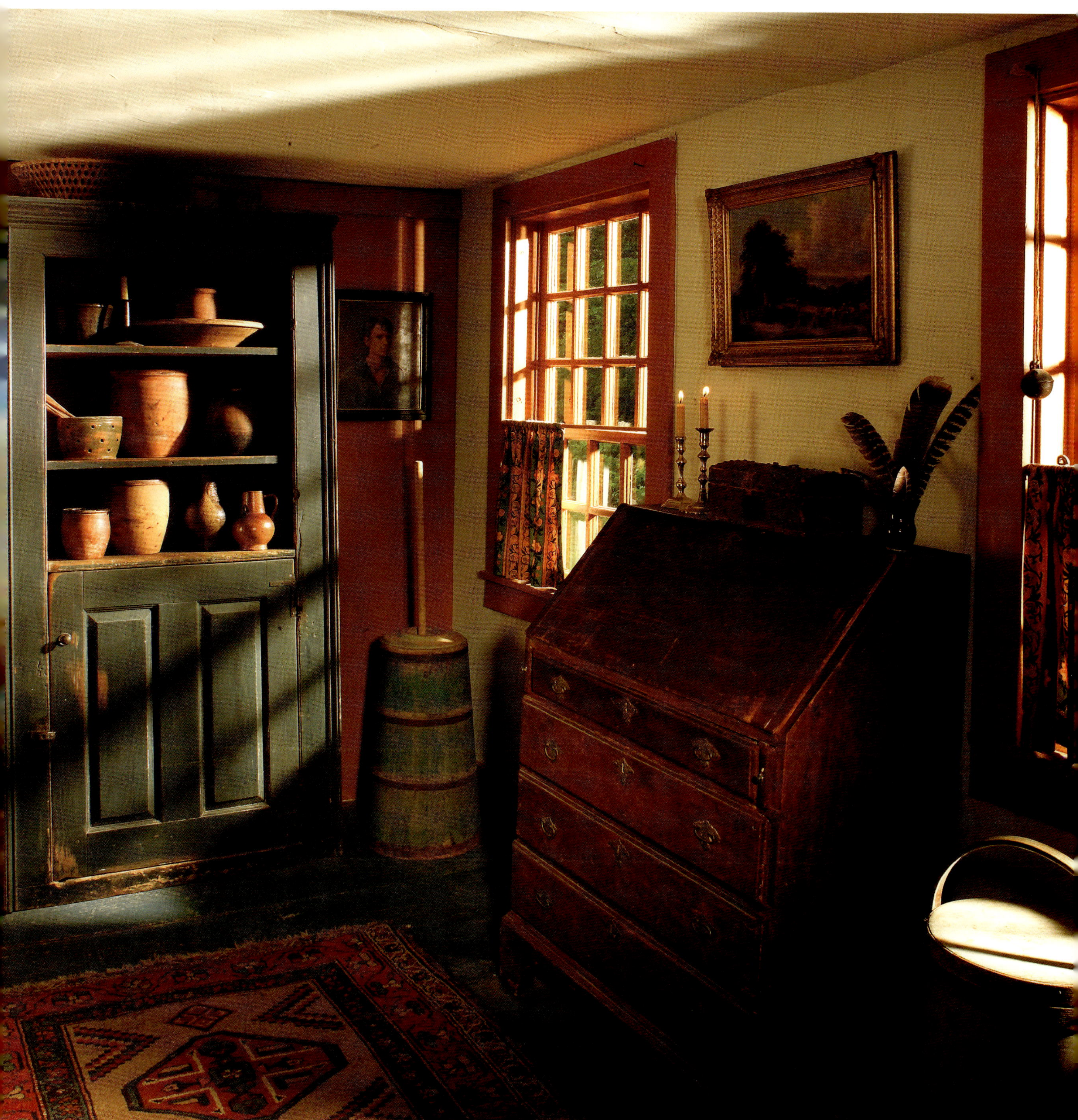

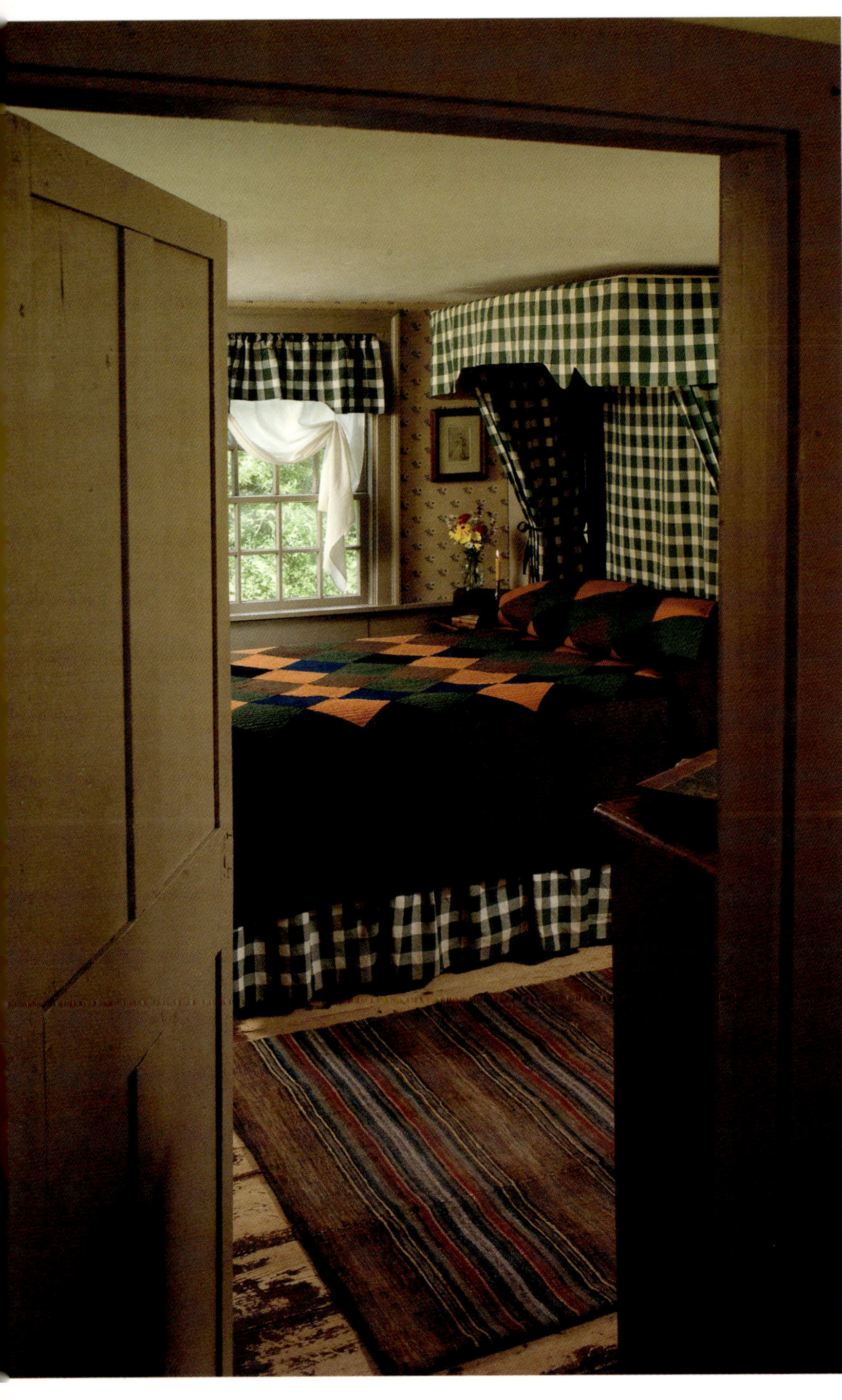

ABOVE *Despite what appears to be a small house, it is actually two rooms deep, dividing the 28-foot depth between the front parlor and kitchen and the rear three bedrooms, one of which enjoyed a fireplace. Until the 1920s the garret remained unfinished, as mere storage for generations.*

RIGHT *In a smaller house functions combine. The shelves found in a larger house pantry are here squeezed up to a kitchen-size fireplace, though the room now serves as a parlor.*

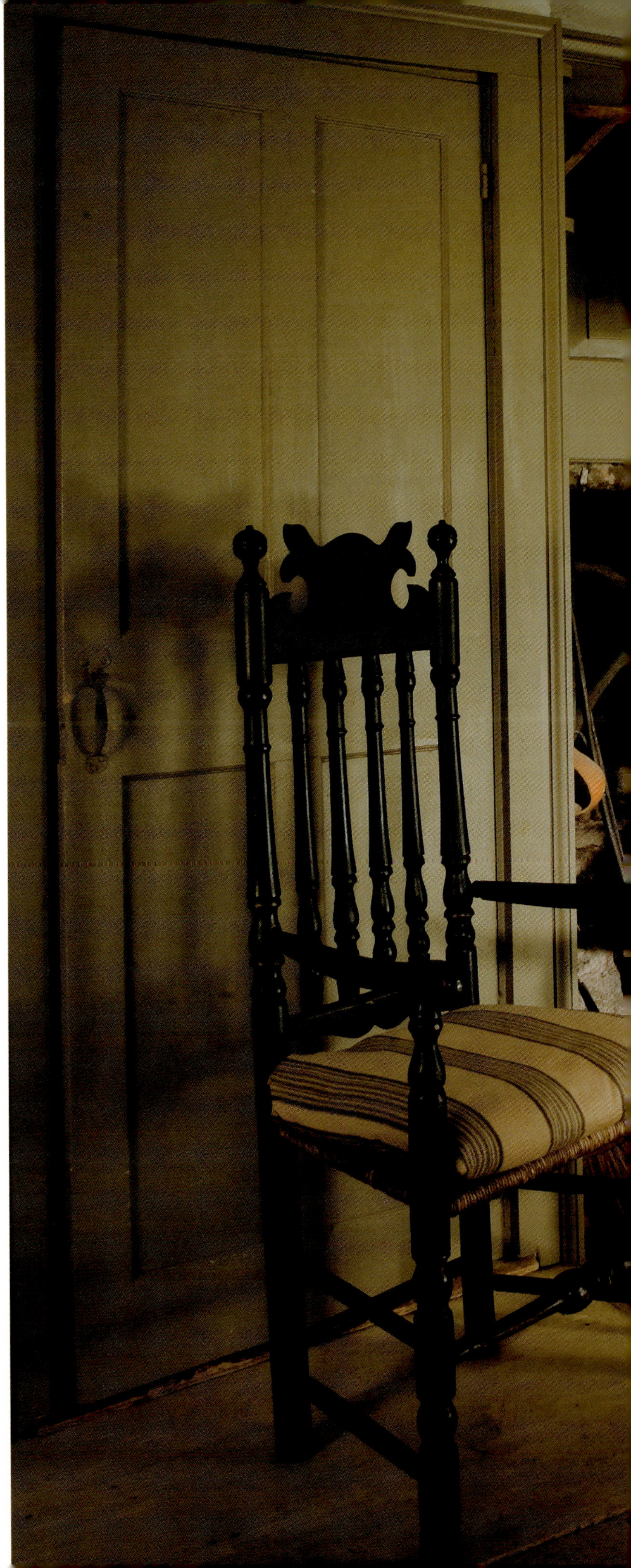

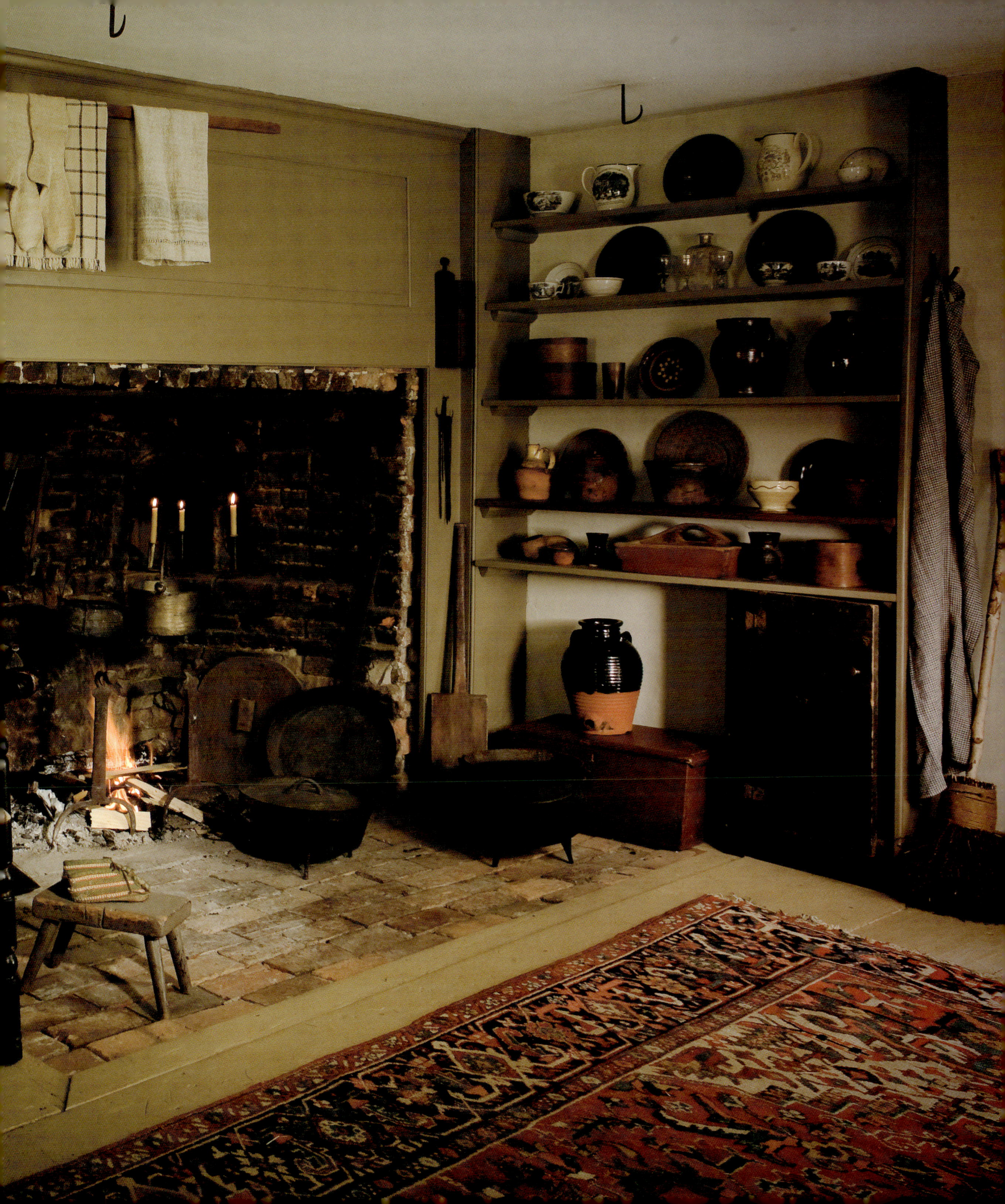

BELOW *The back of the house included three chambers, the center enjoying fireplace warmth, and then another chamber with a doorway.*

FACING PAGE *The 1830s barn, set on an earlier foundation, was for centuries adequate for a farm family. In a modern age of mechanization, vast corporate farms, surpluses, and price deflation, the family farm is slowly vanishing. Unless cherished for storage or a garage, the American barn is following the way of farms.*

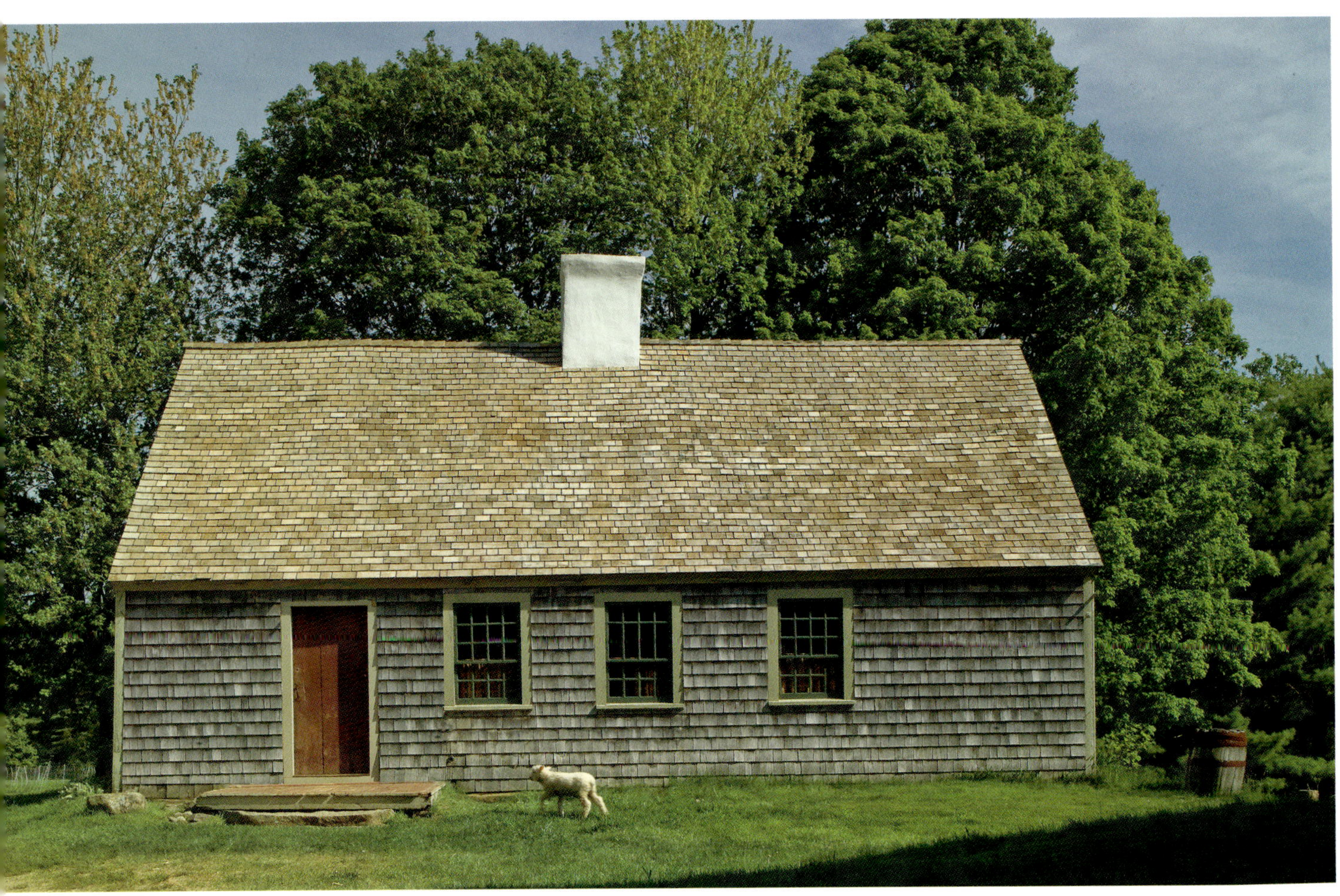

back room was papered with modern gas station road maps, two rooms with three layers each of linoleum floor covering, a single large cast-iron stove used one flue, and the garret was unheated and floored with plywood. Basic electrical service and one very small bathroom had found their way into the house about 1925. Modern prosperity has nearly cleaned out these vestiges of the twentieth-century decline of the family farm.

A new era has since dawned for this and other period farms. The owners have not only restored the house but the entire farm itself, including the reintroduction of early breeds of domestic livestock. The farm consists of American Milking Devon cattle, Dartmoor ponies, Lincoln Longwool sheep, Old English Game fowl, and heritage apples. Today their products supply museums, historic sites, and the film industry. During twenty years of ownership they have expanded the 25-acre farm to nearly its original 60 acres. A smokehouse has been built from early bricks, copying a nearby original. And a 1780s English-style barn has been moved to the adjacent property from Durham, Maine, to serve as a spinning and weaving house. An herb garden of nearly seventy species is cultivated for culinary, dye, and medicinal use. The orchard now includes many strains of ancient apple varieties of English or early New England origin. Even the original stonewalls have been preserved and maintained.

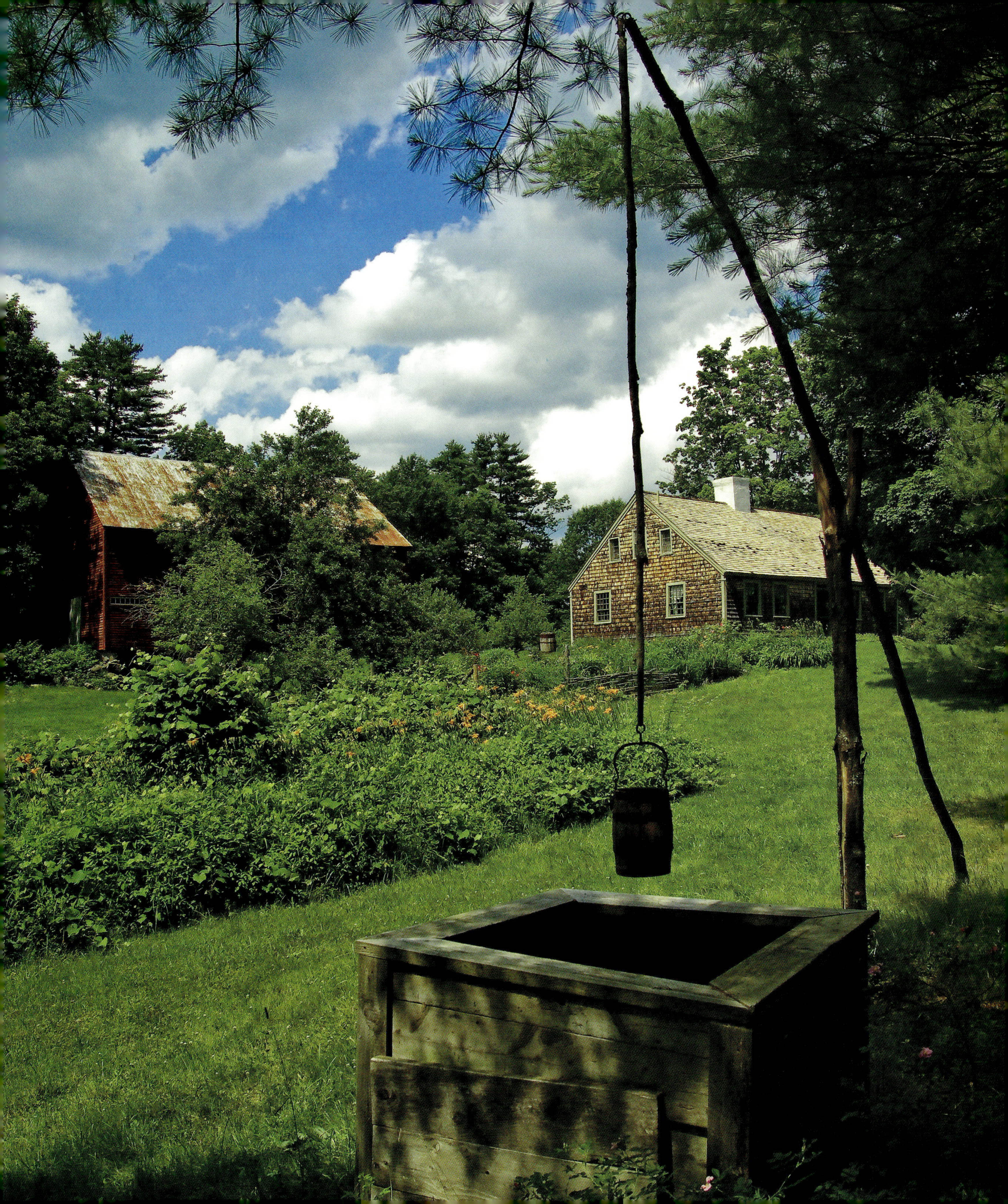

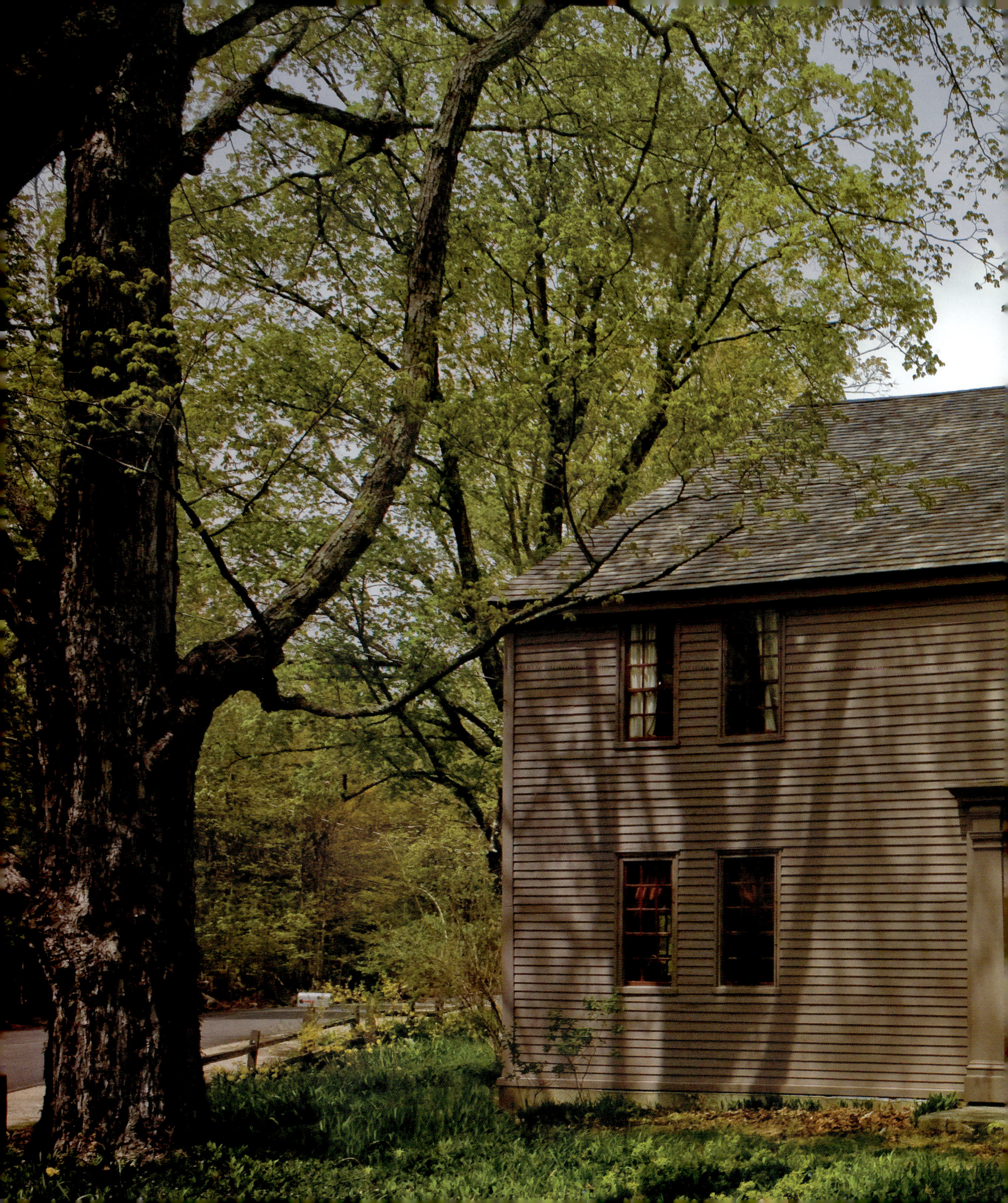

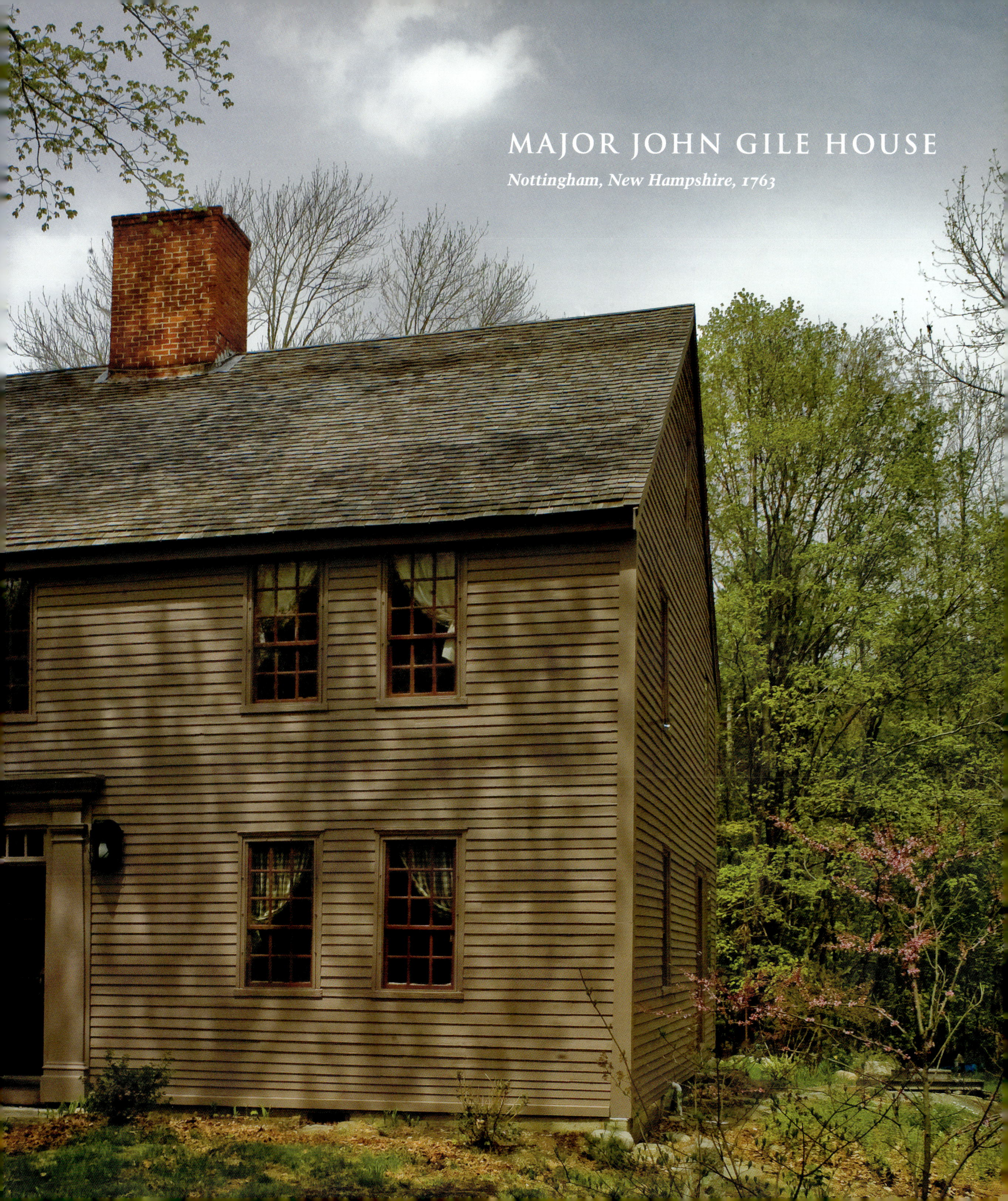

MAJOR JOHN GILE HOUSE

Nottingham, New Hampshire, 1763

PREVIOUS PAGES *With the end of the last French and Indian War, returning veteran Major John Gile built this wholly traditional upcountry home, only its doorway hinting at the new style Georgian.*

RIGHT *This parlor displays the features of what is to come in later houses: plastered ceilings, molded and paneled cupboards, cornice moldings, and double-hung casement windows. Textiles, hardly seen or afforded in First Period houses, now appear as window curtains and, occasionally, floor covering (though the era of the Oriental rug has been reserved for the last hundred years).*

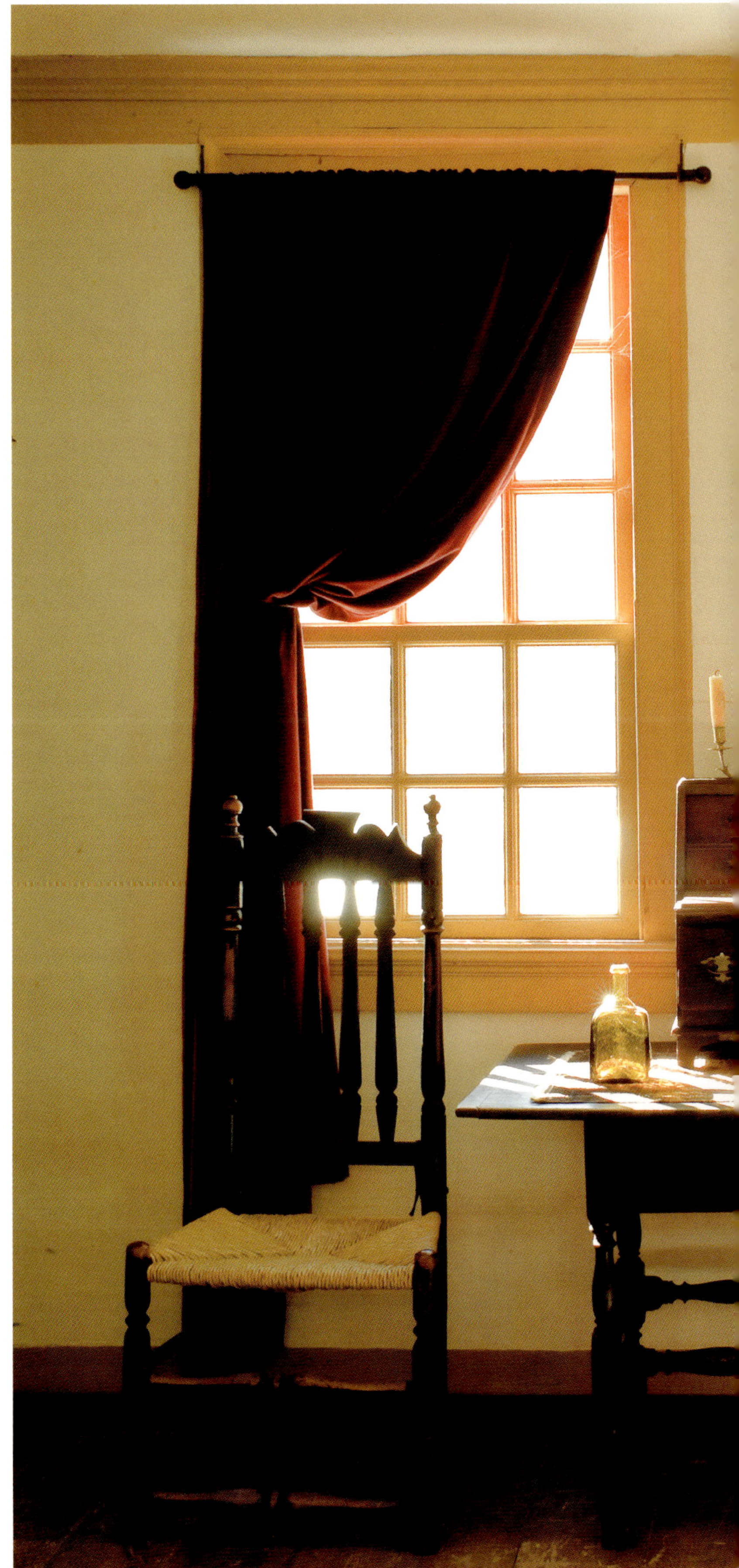

In 1721, 101 residents living along the coast between Boston and Portsmouth petitioned Samuel Shute, governor of the Province of Massachusetts, for property inland from Portsmouth on which to establish a town. The land was heavily forested, the source of most inland prosperity. Rocky soil inhibited agriculture except for family subsistence and sheep raising. Not surprisingly most early proprietors were land speculators (including the governor who received a share), leaving the toil of settlement to others. The region is interlaced with streams suitable for mills—saw, grain, and fulling, the latter a process of cleansing and working up a nap on rough homespun woolen cloth. Later in the century, hardscrabble farmers added income from shoemaking, weaving, and cooperage, the making of barrels.

The Gile family had long been residents of Haverhill on the Massachusetts border with New Hampshire. There, Ephraim Gile was born in 1661, followed by his son Samuel, the father of John (c.1739–1800). John, as a teenager, had joined the militia in 1757, enlisting for the invasion of Canada in the last French and Indian War. He participated in the expedition to Lake George and the taking of forts Ticonderoga and Crown Point. Evidently a man of capability and leadership, at the end of the war in 1763 he returned home with the rank of major, though only twenty-three years old, then quickly moved north from Haverhill to Nottingham in New Hampshire, married Mary Neally, and built this home. Little is known of his life except what we can abstract from his death inventory in 1800: 150 acres of land with buildings, two dwelling houses, a barn, gristmill, cider mill, blacksmith shop, plus domes-

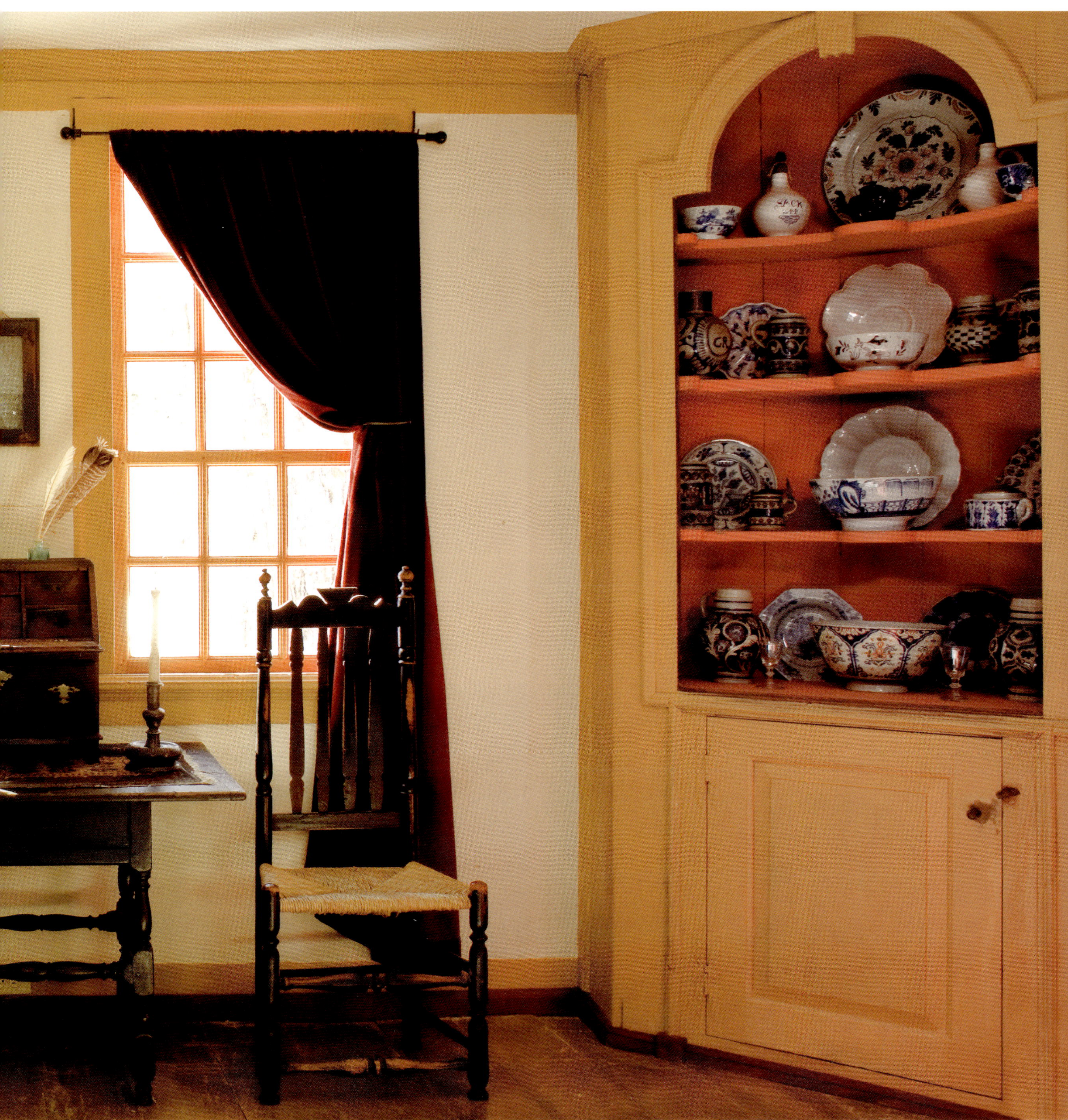
SACK

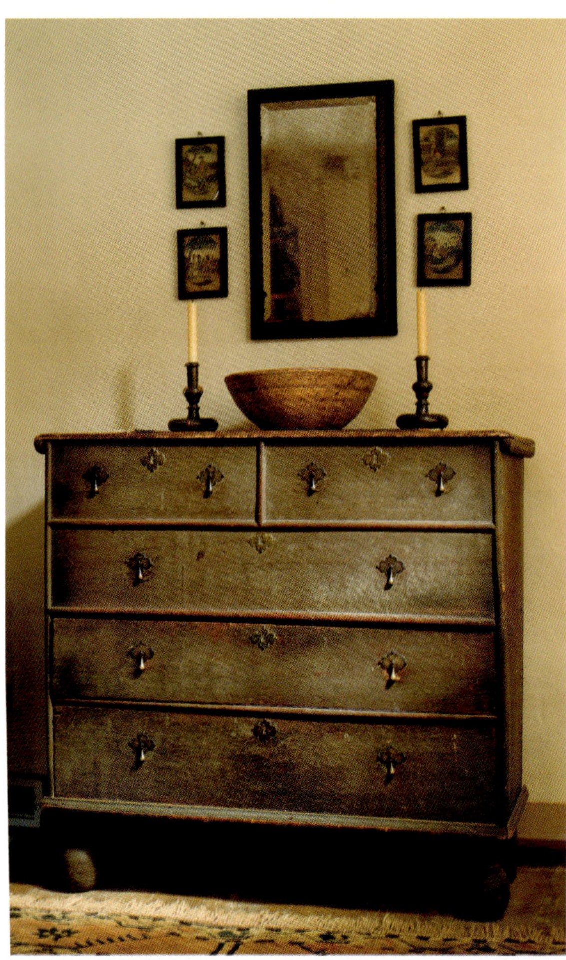

ABOVE *Harking back to an earlier period, the bulbous candlesticks and a ball-foot chest are the survivors of a New England tradition of preservation, which has been fostered by a common culture centered on continuity in community, town governance, and church loyalty.*

RIGHT *Paneled parlors and portraits are a colonial legacy, the visible face of the family tree, hung to be remembered for what they accomplished and as an inspiration to descendants to prosper. Alas, this continuity has broken down except for a dedicated band of restorers who have reassembled the bits and pieces of that legacy for at least their own lifetime.*

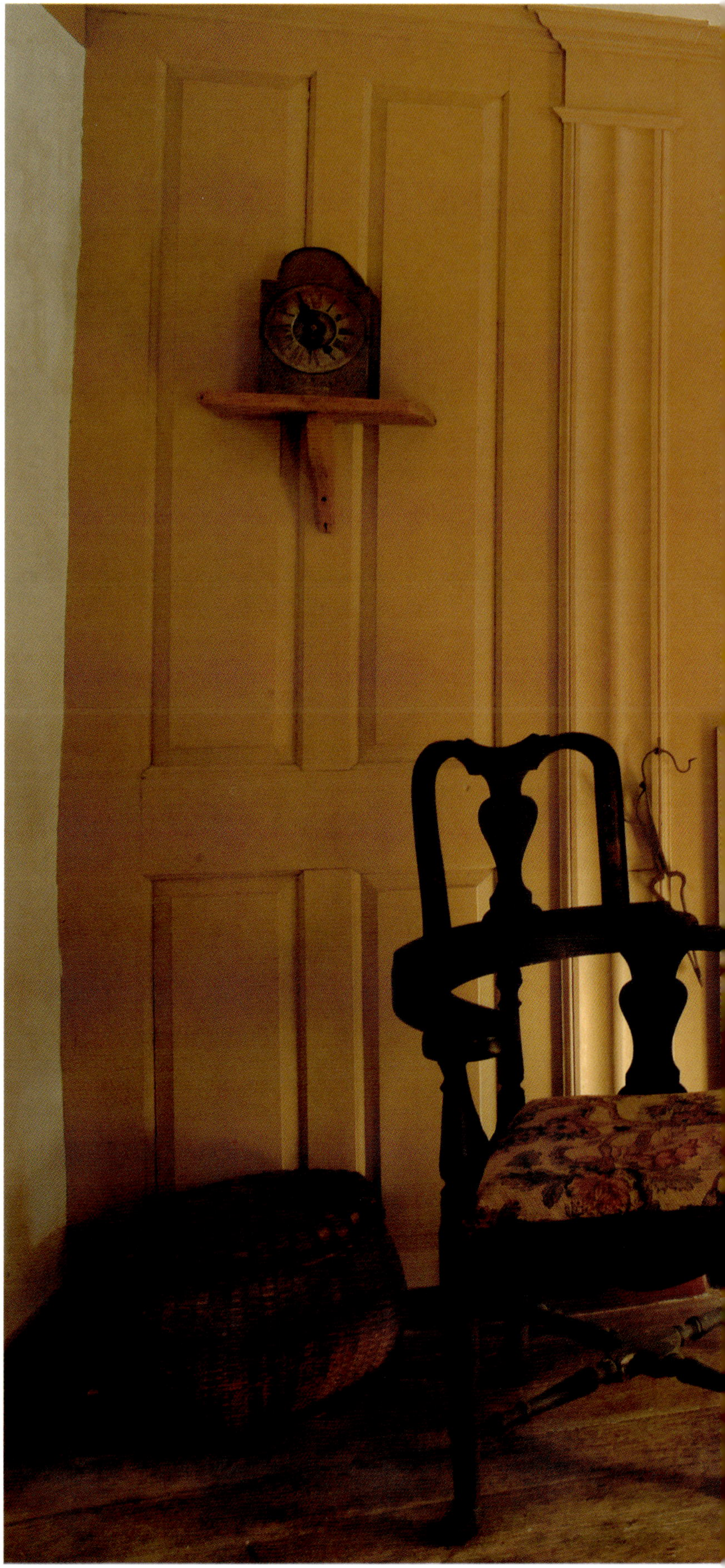

tic animals, household goods, farm tools, and thirty bushels of corn and rye.

Today the house appears much as it did when built, a straightforward two-story house with center chimney and rear kitchen wing, this dating from the 1840s with a built-in iron stove on one side and an oven and set kettle on the other side. The house proportions, features, and colors express John Gile's means, modest but characteristic of upcountry New Englanders. The site has returned to its thickly wooded appearance, similar to when Gile first acquired his acres. The clearing and industry hinted at in his inventory are now gone. Indeed, for much of rural New England the diminution of farming over the last century has left the countryside more woodland than it has been since the Revolution.

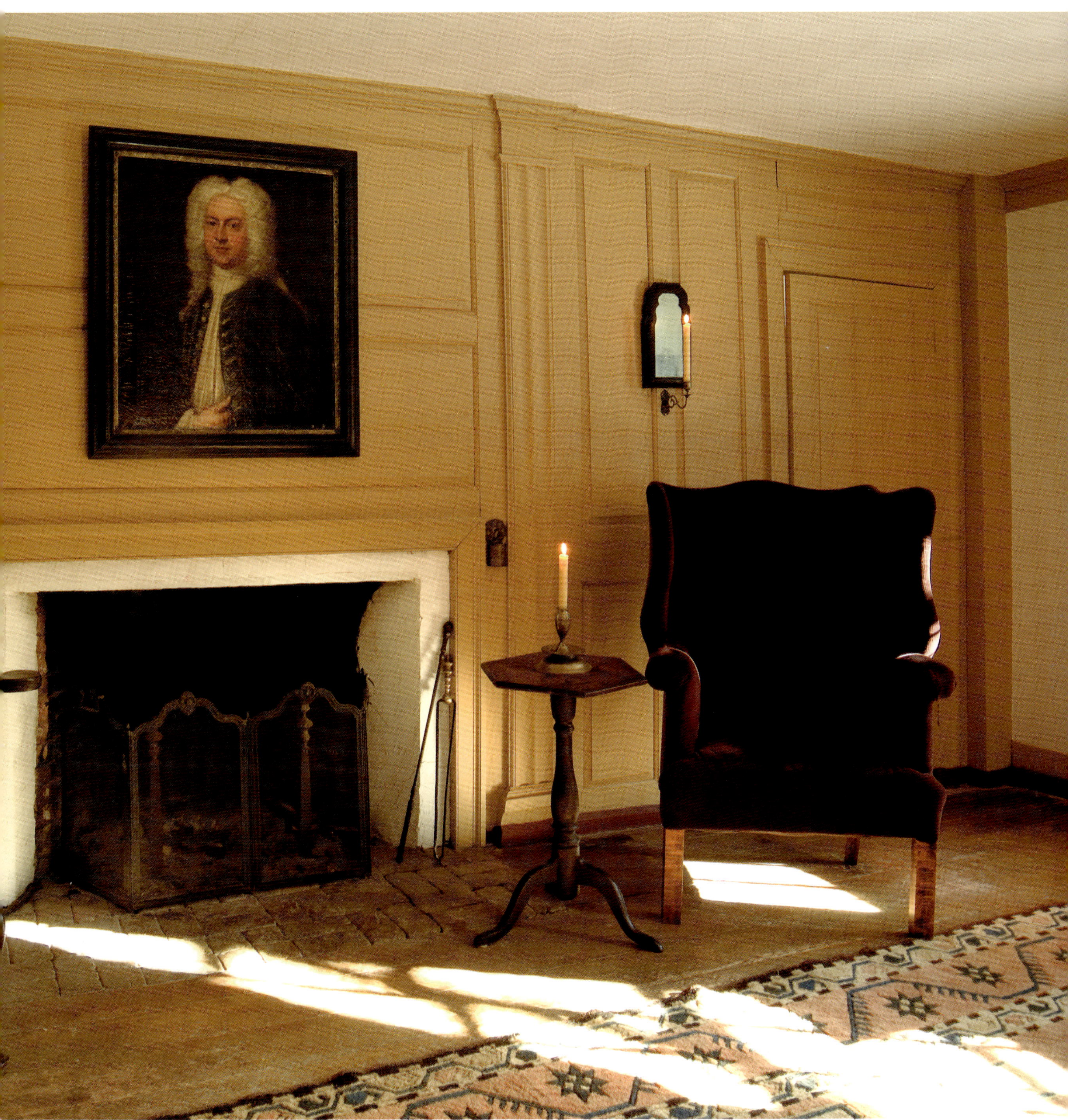

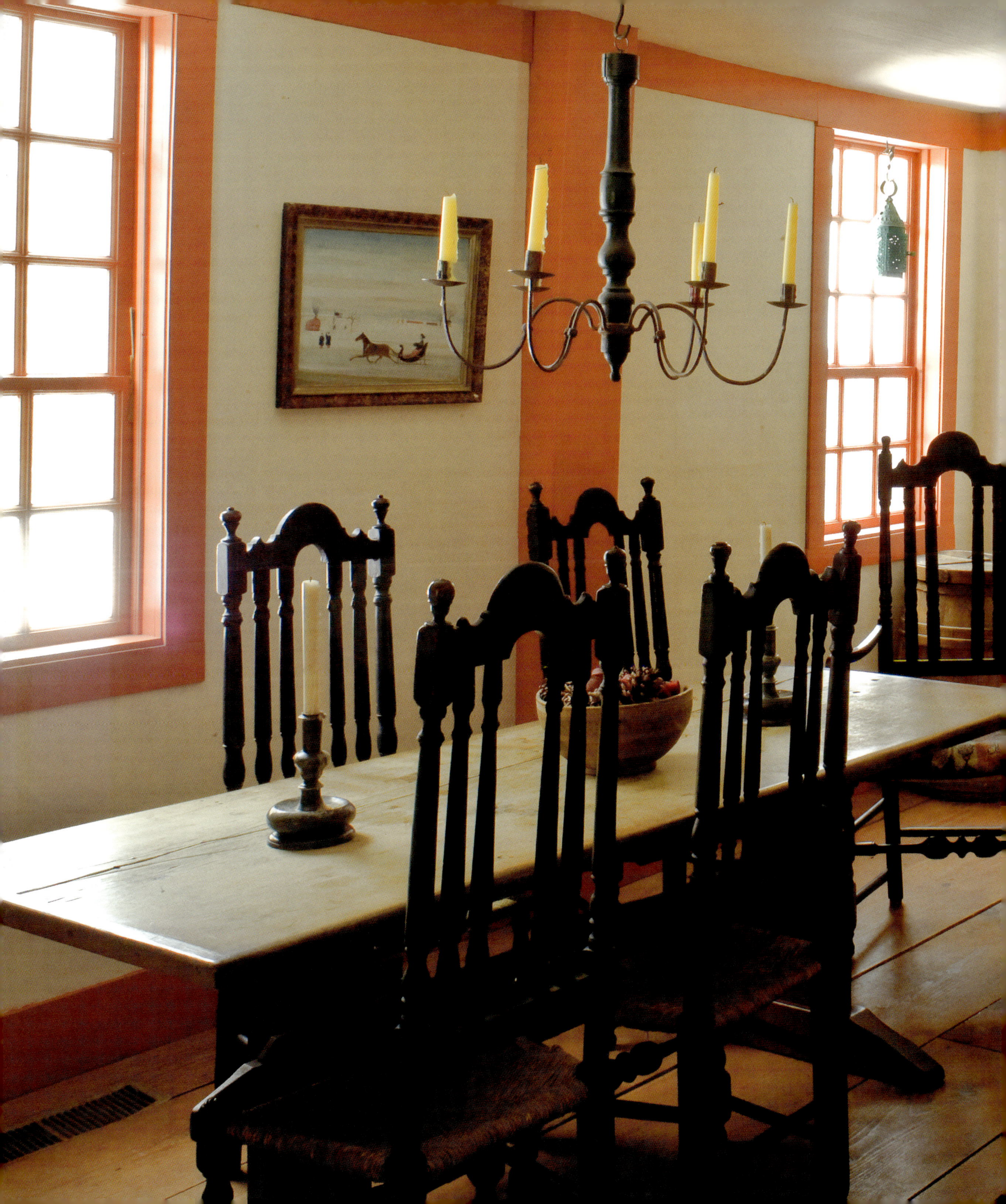

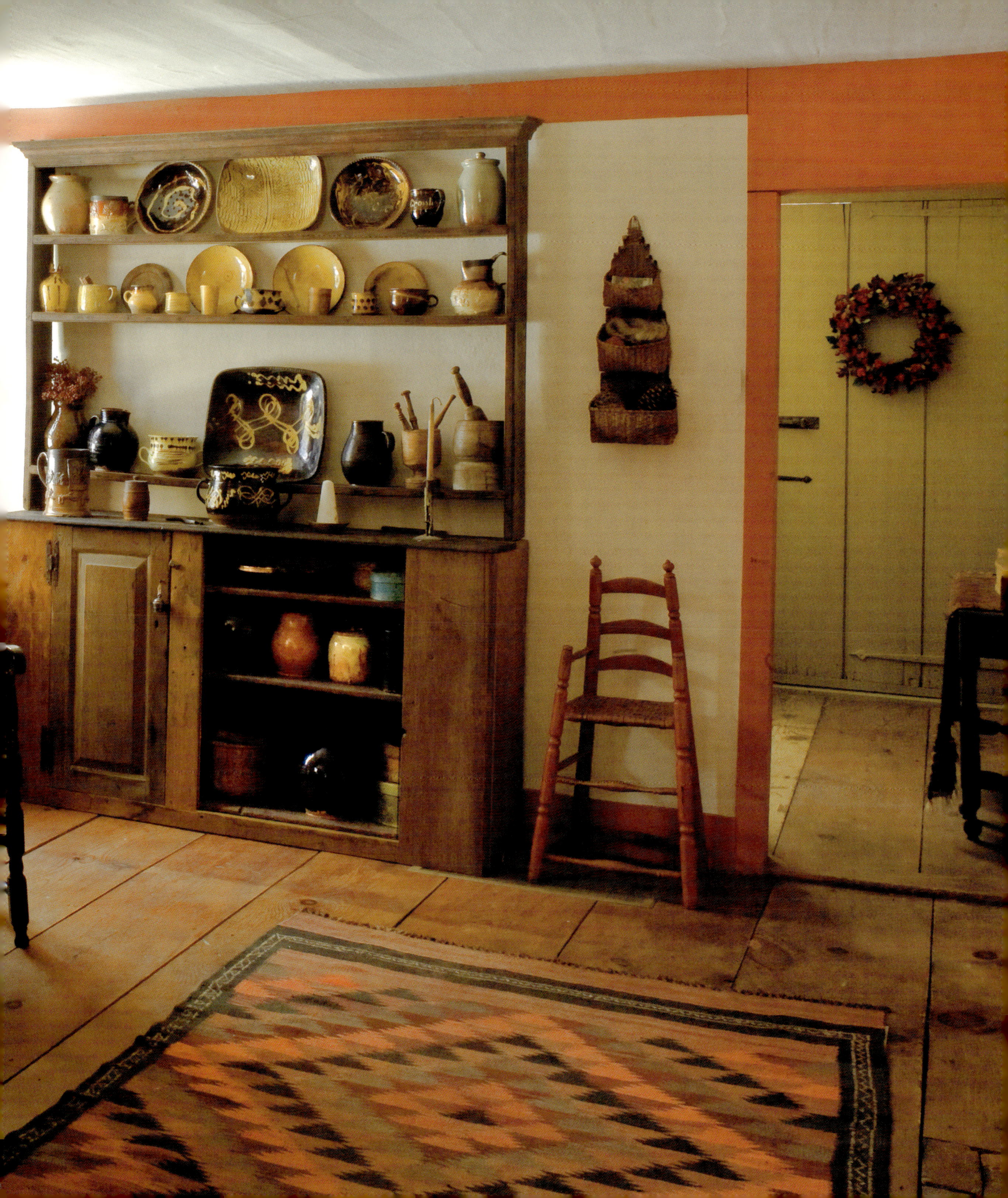

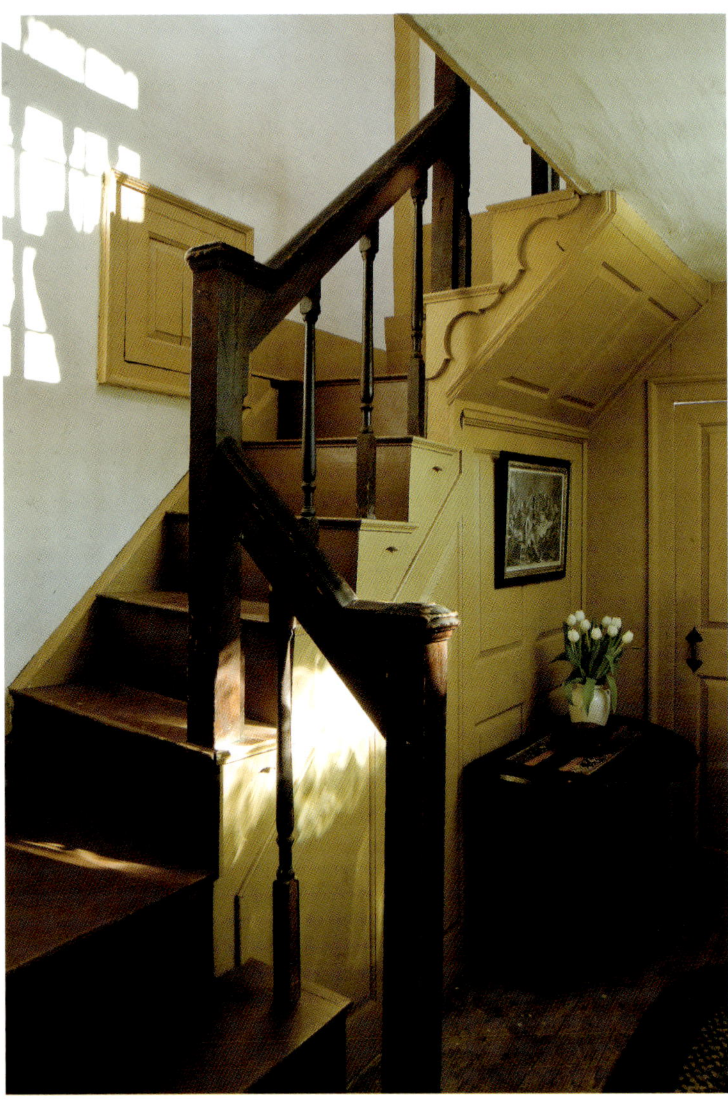

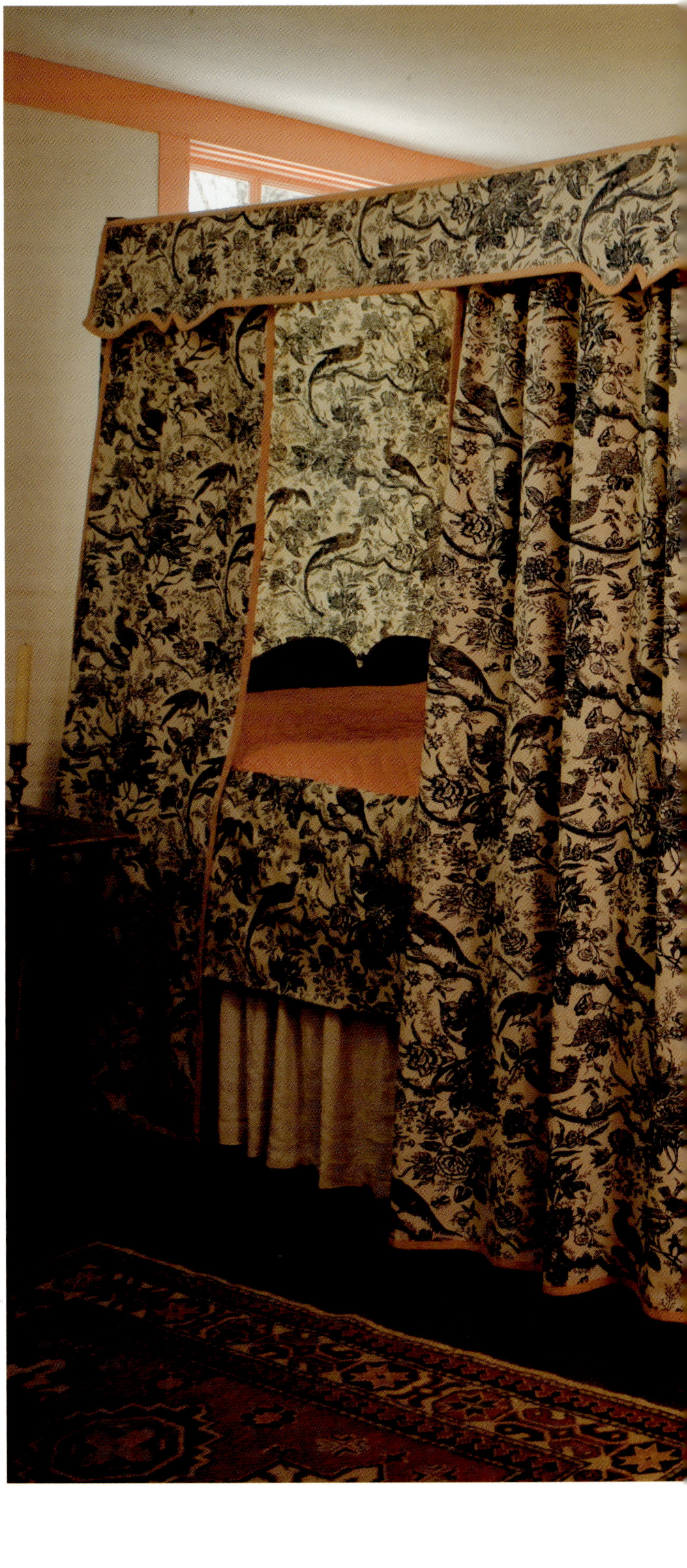

PREVIOUS PAGES *The rear kitchen is large, accommodating dining as well as the preparation for it. In an era when pewter and earthenware vessels were both decorative and functional, they were displayed in open cupboards rather than hidden in kitchen cabinets as in later periods. Straight-back chairs too were purposely built for visual appeal even, as these, at the expense of comfort.*

ABOVE *While seemingly a traditional dog-leg stairway, the curved returns on each tread end and raised panels below declare the owner's cognizance of the new style.*

RIGHT *In a bedchamber the fully draped tester bed was a machine for self heating. As fires cooled down in the night, body warmth and human breath within this tentlike structure helped sustain comfort until the early hours of awakening, when sleepers woke up and left or the fire was rekindled for more comfort.*

FOLLOWING PAGES *Today the house appears much as it did when built, a straightforward two-story house with center chimney and rear kitchen wing. The kitchen wing dates from the 1840s with a built-in iron stove, an oven, and set kettle.*

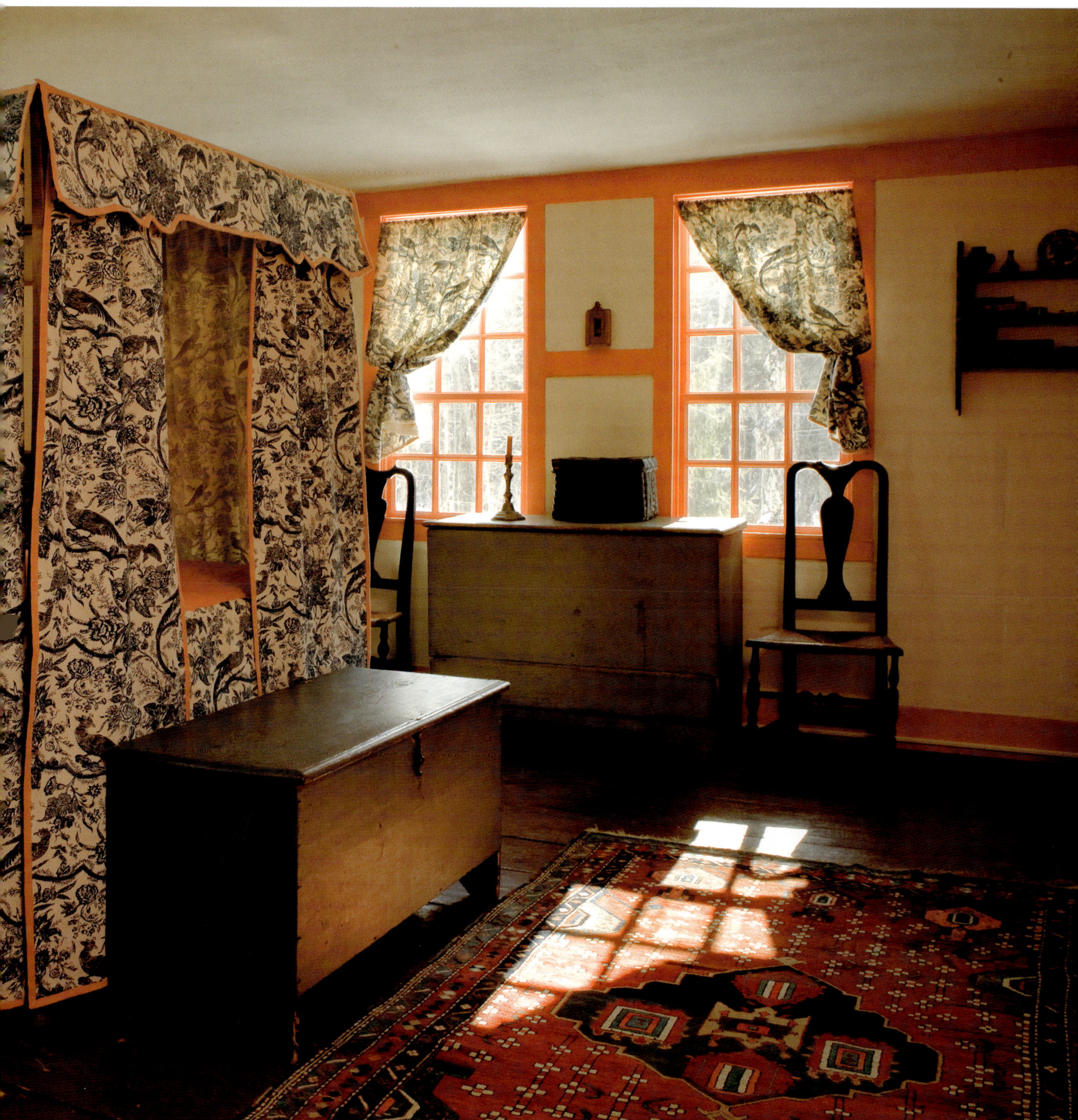

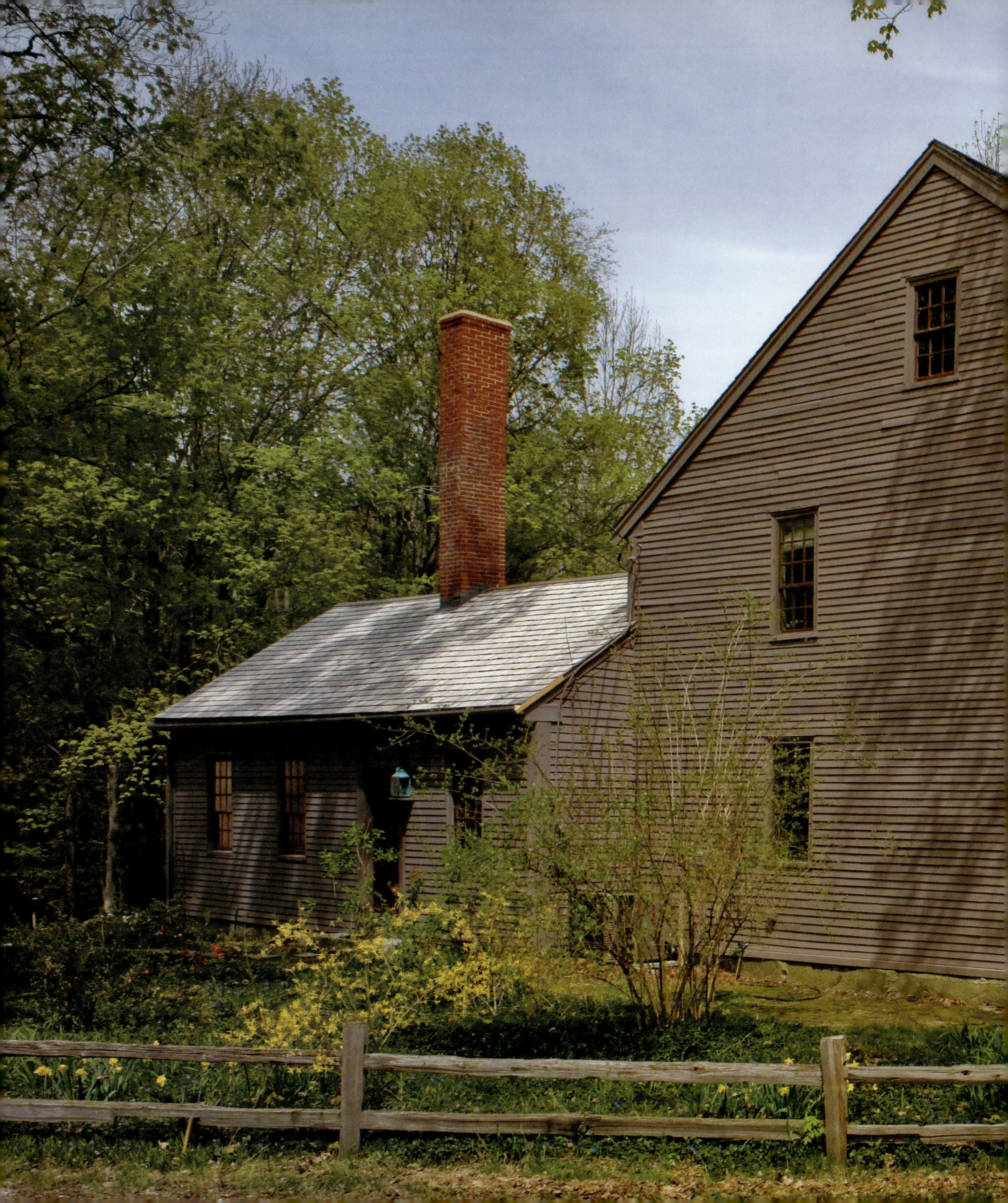

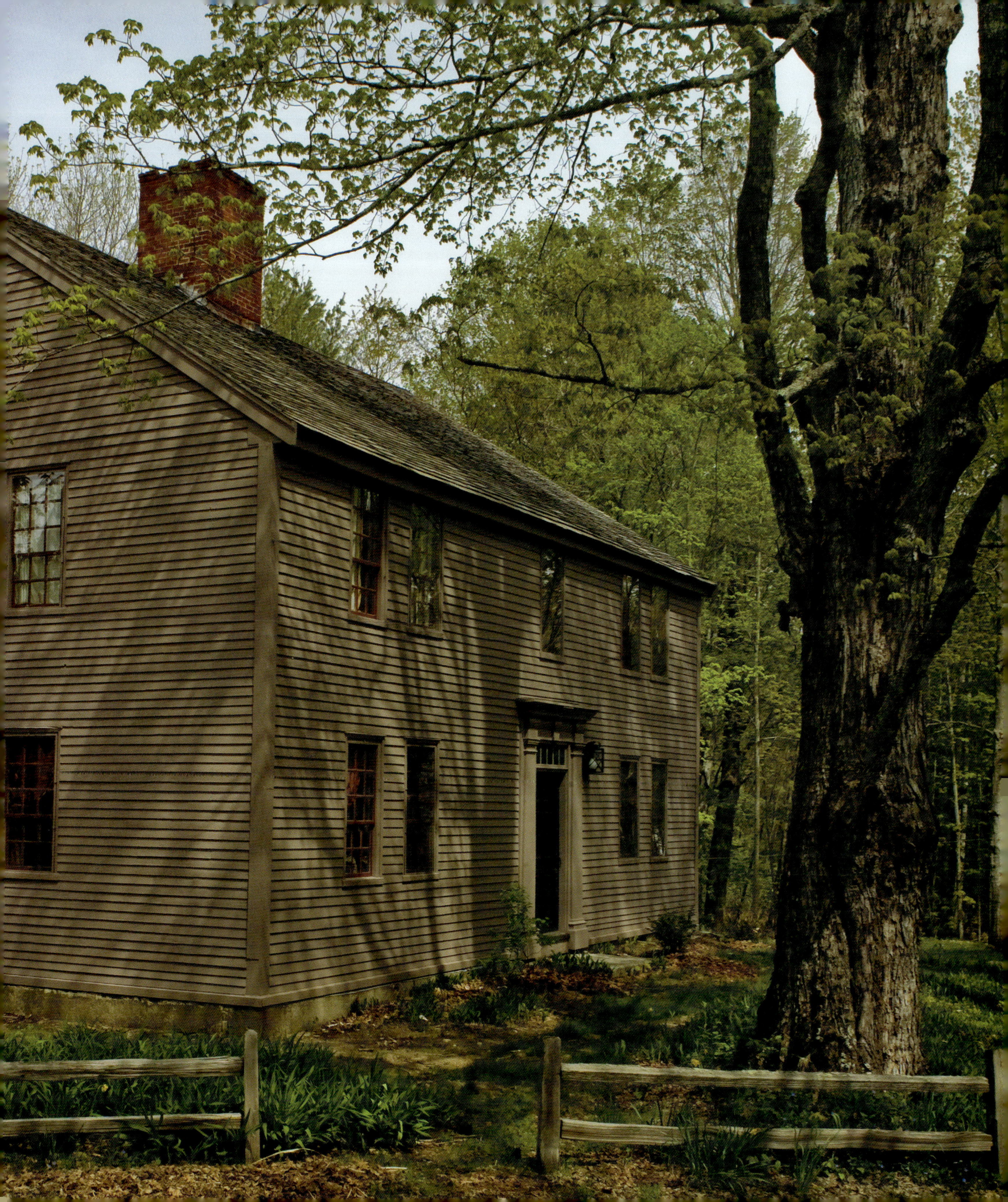

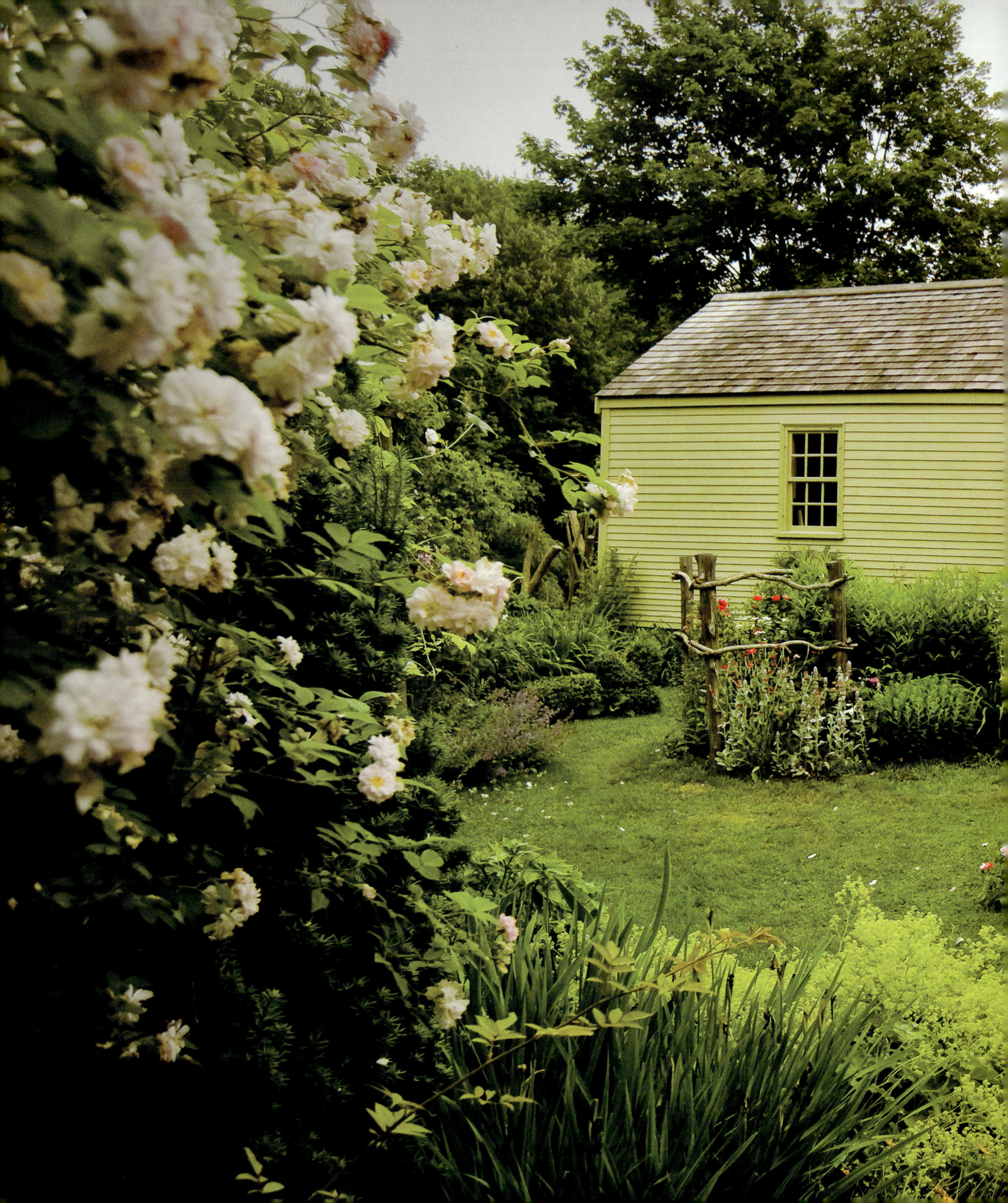

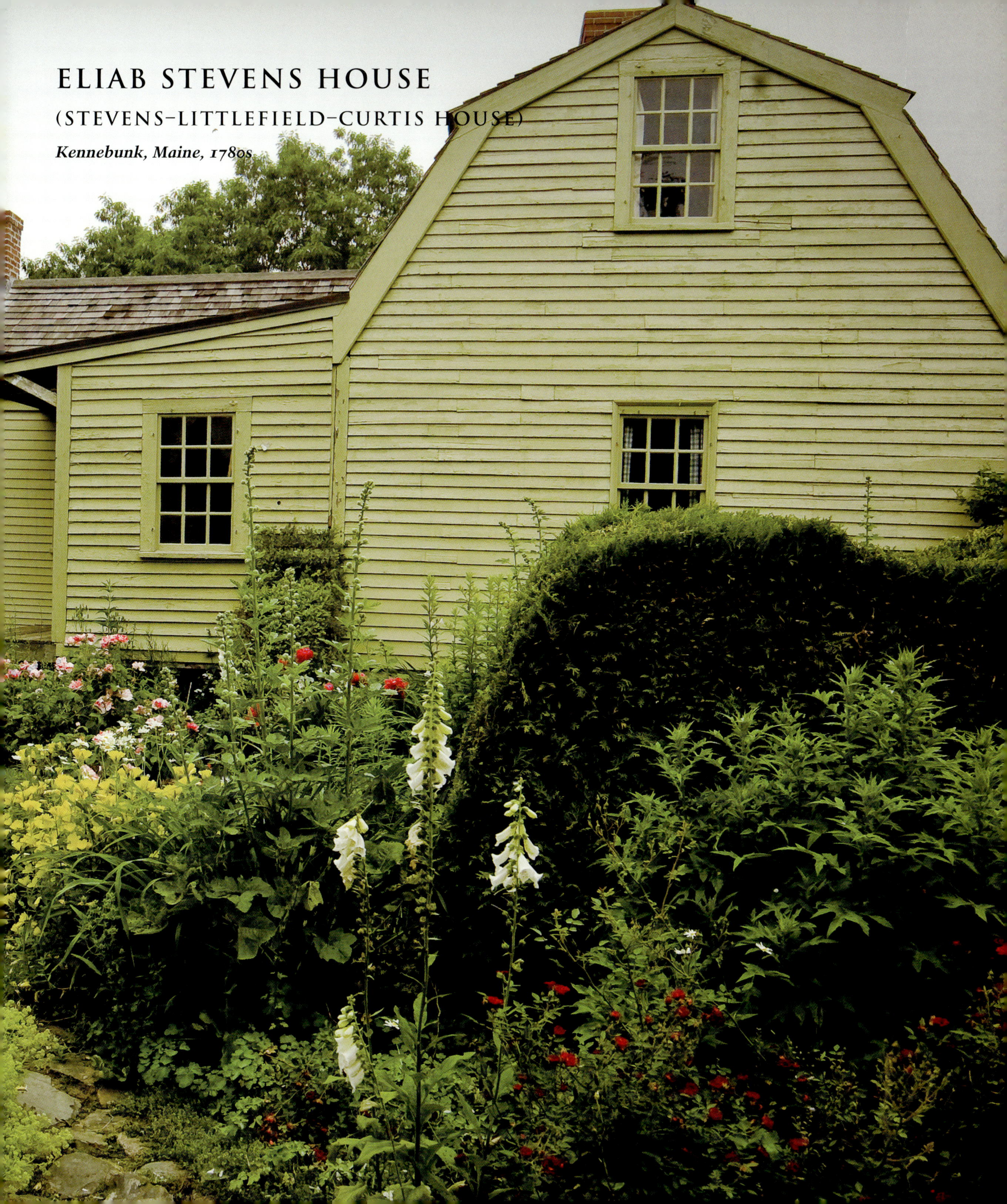

ELIAB STEVENS HOUSE

(STEVENS-LITTLEFIELD-CURTIS HOUSE)

Kennebunk, Maine, 1780s

PREVIOUS PAGES *The gambrel roof—double slant to each side—was in use in New England as early as the seventeenth century and widely adopted in eighteenth-century New York, where its popularity and survival has caused many to assume it was a Dutch invention. The name is standard English and the gambrel roof was known in England before the Puritans brought the idea to America.*

RIGHT *What is today furnished as the parlor retains its early panel-and-board fireplace wall and dado. The variety of plain painted colors used in early periods both enhanced and harmonized the contrast of surfaces and materials. The result was, and still is, emotionally satisfying, like the effect of soothing music.*

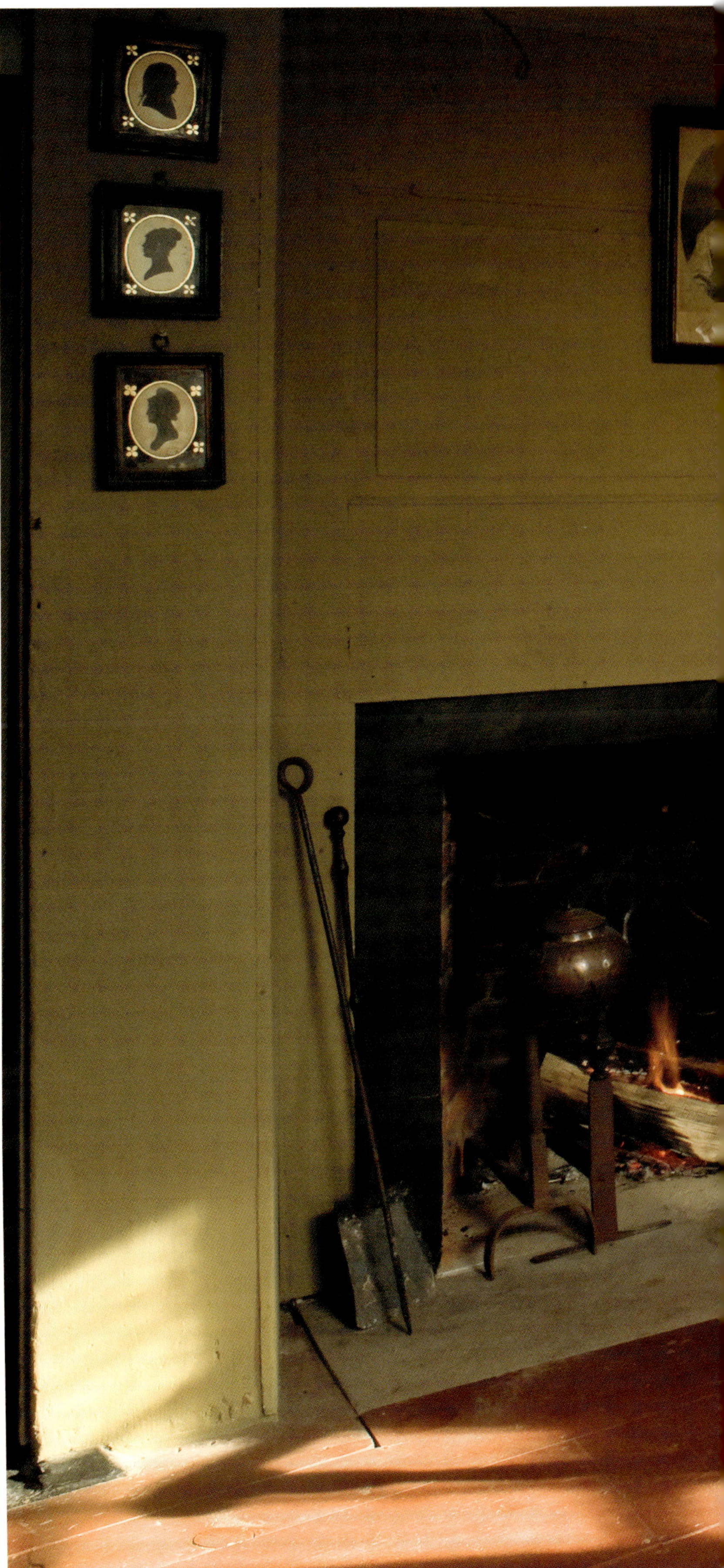

The southern coast of Maine was first visited by Bartholomew Gosnold of Falmouth, England, in 1602 shortly followed by French explorer Samuel de Champlain. Captain John Smith, of later Jamestown fame, came here. Captain Smith's publication *Description of New England* encouraged seasonal fishing parties to visit (forty to fifty ships annually by 1620), before settlers arrived in the 1620s. Besides fishing, they took advantage of the Mousam and Kennebec rivers to gain access to the interior forests of Maine. At the head of navigable waters on the Mousam River, while rapids limited transportation, dams created waterpower for sawmills, the product of which was a shipbuilding industry at what would become Kennebunk town. Slow to grow, in part out of fear of American Indian attacks and later out of competition from better shipyards, Kennebunk turned to other mill industries.

In the heart of this development Eliab Stevens built this house (or possibly acquired it from a prior owner) on the banks of the river in the 1780s. He was a cordwainer (a worker in cordwain, or cordovan leather) and a shoemaker. When he sold the house in 1790, it was to another cordwainer, Moses Littlefield, who then sold the house to tanner Joseph Curtis about 1806. They presaged an active leather and Leatheroid (imitation leather) industry in Kennebunk through the nineteenth century, along with shoe manufacturing, textiles, and iron production.

At 15 by 30 feet, it is a compact one-and-a-half-story house under a gambrel roof. Economy of room size left a front hall, parlor, kitchen, and three rooms and a hall above. The second floor was likely originally an open space for storage and sleeping. In addition to a large center chimney with two fireplaces, there is room for only a small front hall, the stairway being tucked behind the chimney at the rear. To the right, the room is largely intact with original fireplace, overmantel, and board wainscoting. The left room is similar in design but with beaded boards (restored from pieces). The two fireplaces are similar, both smaller than nor-

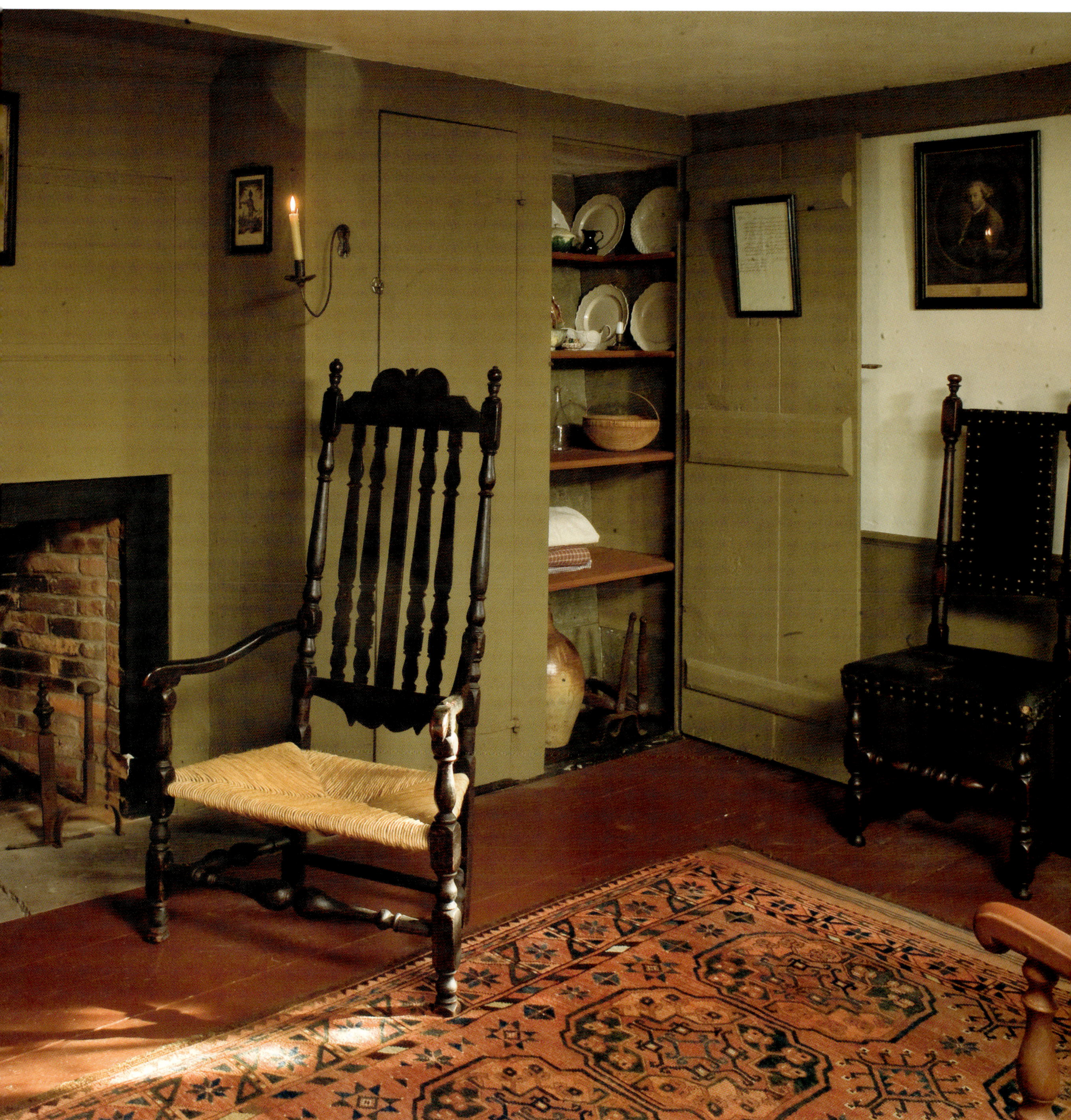

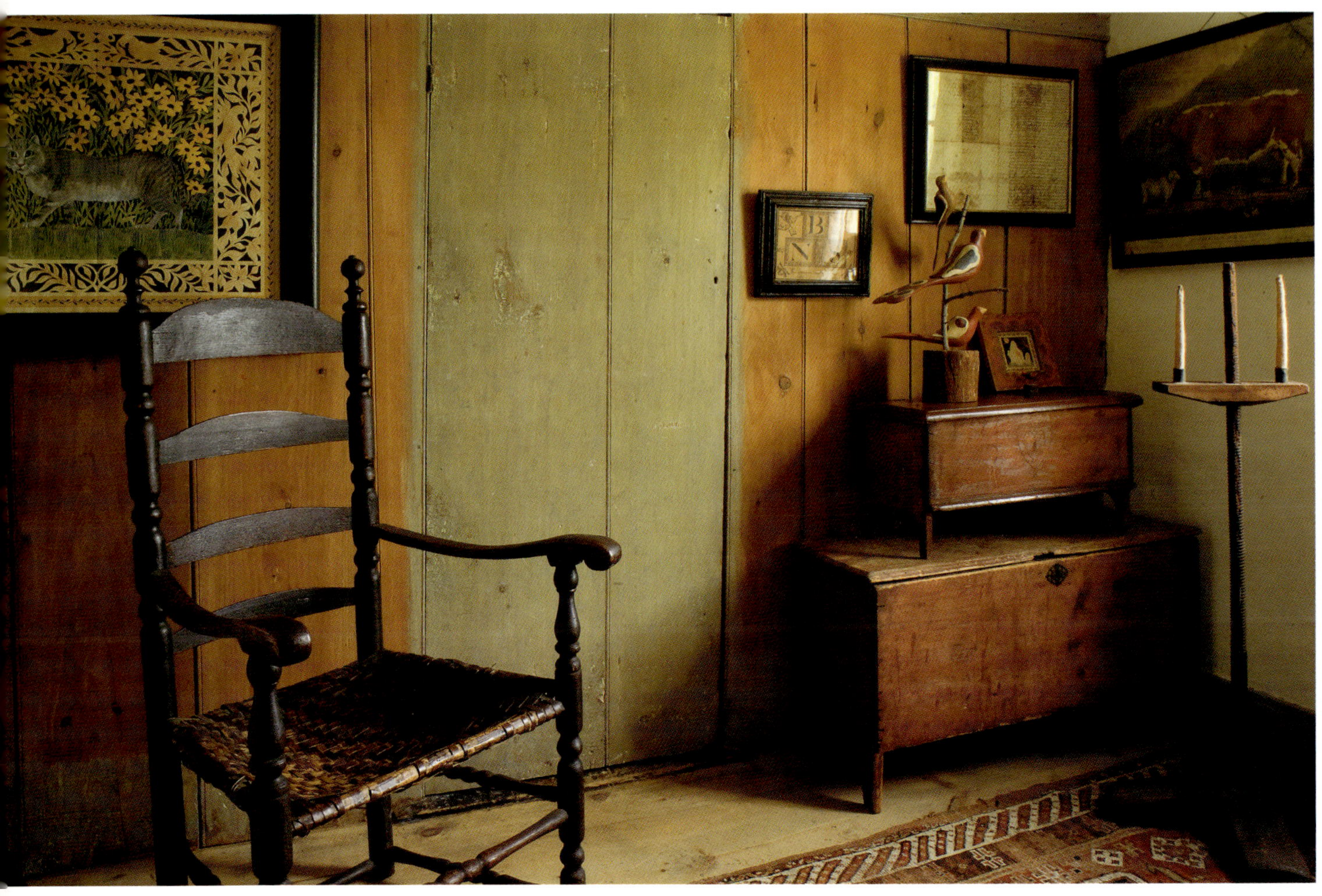

ABOVE *From the right chamber, one can see a door to a closet. This appears unremarkable, but it is a major innovation in house plan and has become increasingly important as affluence spread through the generations ever since.*

FACING PAGE *As both front rooms have similar features, it is not obvious which was originally the kitchen (the kitchen function was moved to a later addition). The entry way (on the right) in this small house (15 by 30 feet) was too small for the conventional dog-leg stairway, and thus the stair was displaced to the left of the fireplace.*

mal kitchen size, and thus it is not possible to say which was parlor and which was kitchen. Perhaps an addition (replaced in the 1870s by another addition) served that purpose. In the attic, half the rafter frames are made of a single piece, hewn from trunks and large branches, unique but strong.

The gambrel roof was more common in Massachusetts where it was an early innovation, providing more headroom in the second floor of two-story houses and, for deep houses, a wider span of roof without the excessive height of the pitch roof.

Through the nineteenth century the house changed hands many times—at one time it served as housing for a leather factory. Being close to the two river dams in town, it witnessed nearby factories erected (and later mostly demolished). In the latter half of that century two rooms were built off the center rear of the house, forming a "T." In the 1870s, the whole structure was reoriented a quarter turn to face the street. It remained in one family most of the twentieth century, until purchased and restored by the present owner in 1992.

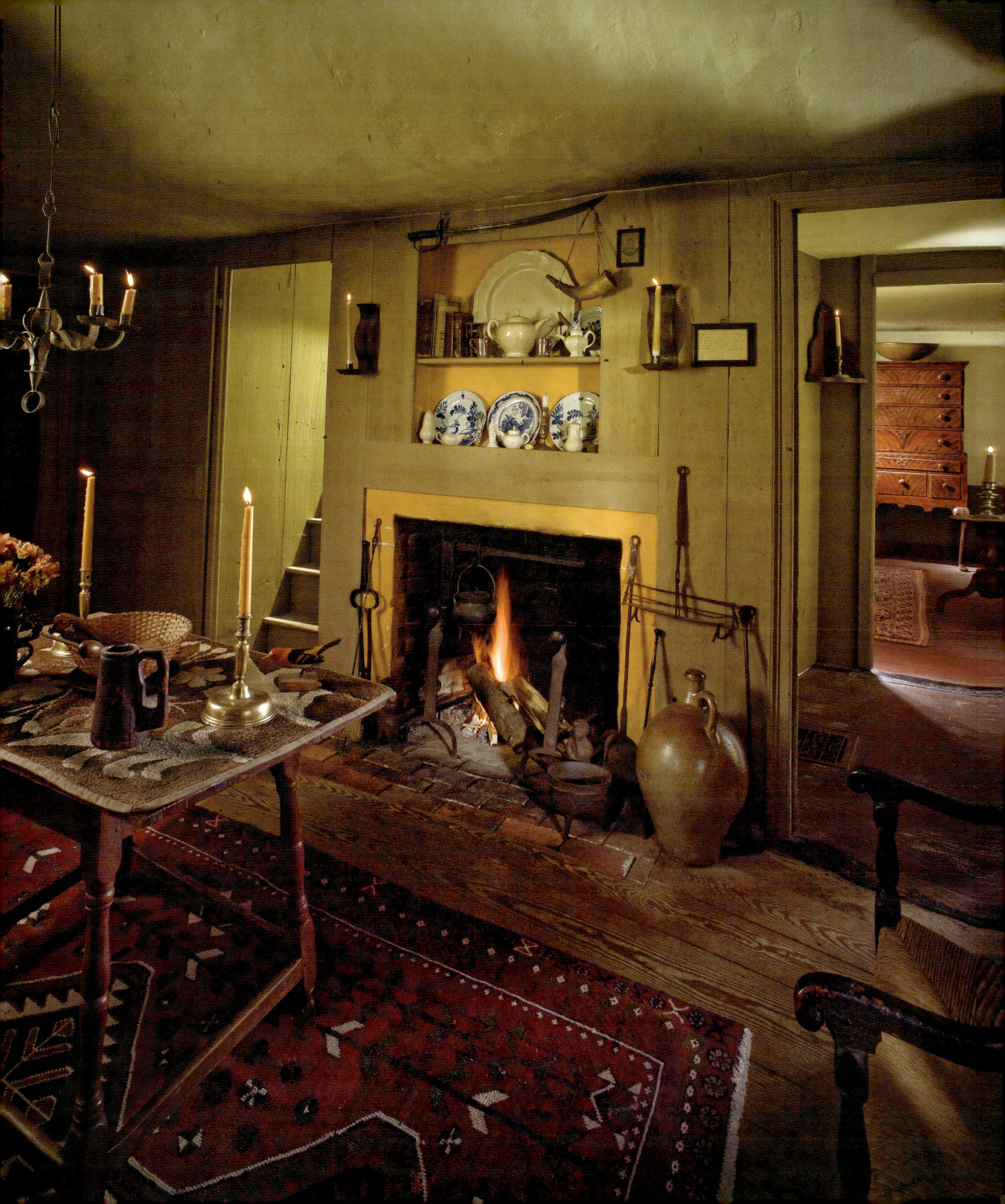

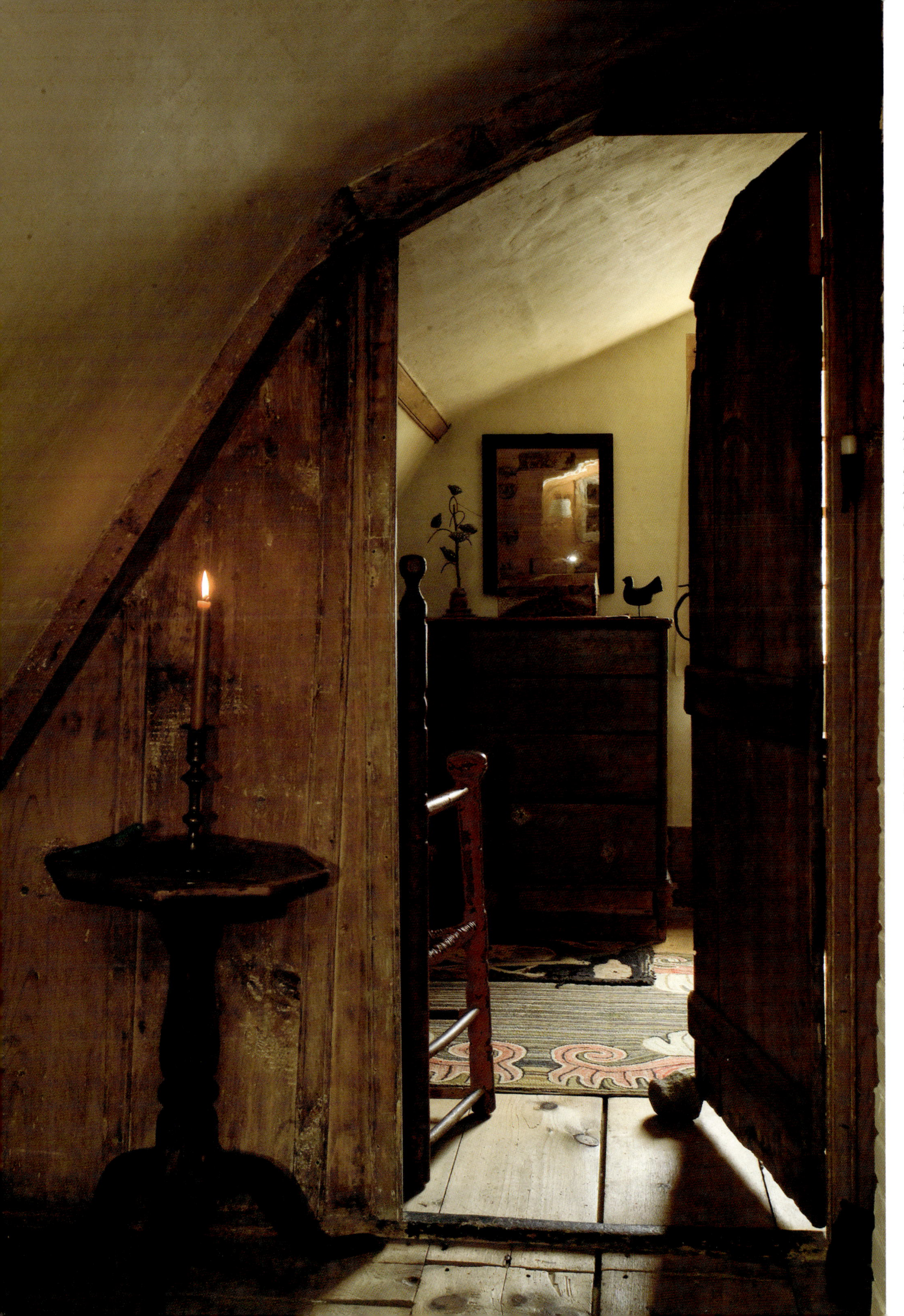

LEFT *A small angle in the gambrel roof rafters was enough to allow more ample headroom in the small upstairs chambers. Bare floors, woodwork, whitewashed plaster, and spare country furniture capture the appearance of the average early home.*

FACING PAGE *Even such a small house could fit four chambers on the second floor. Although Spartan, they were adequate for the purpose of privacy and sleep. Being awake had mostly to do with the hours of sunlight so chambers served little purpose other than sleep at night.*

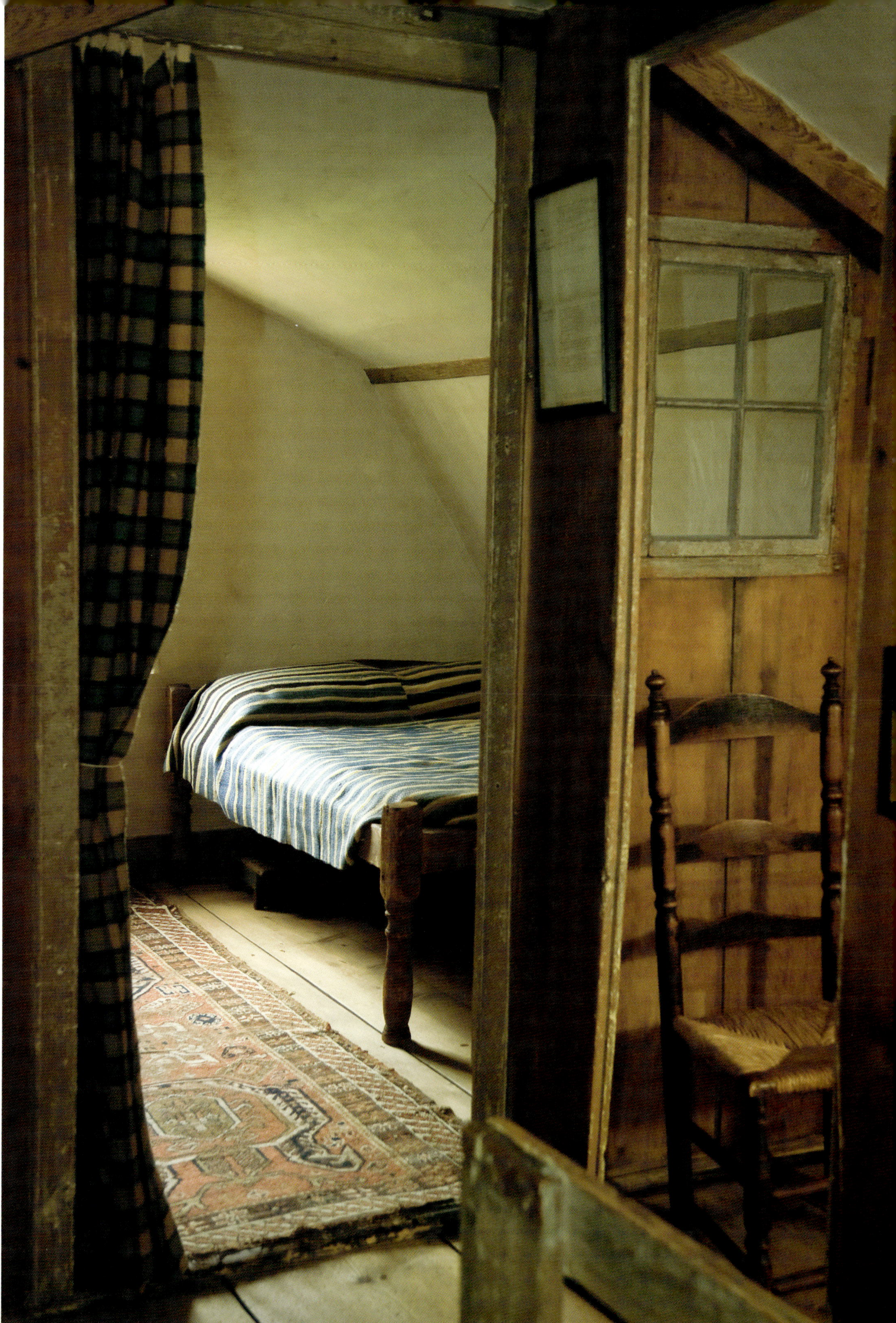

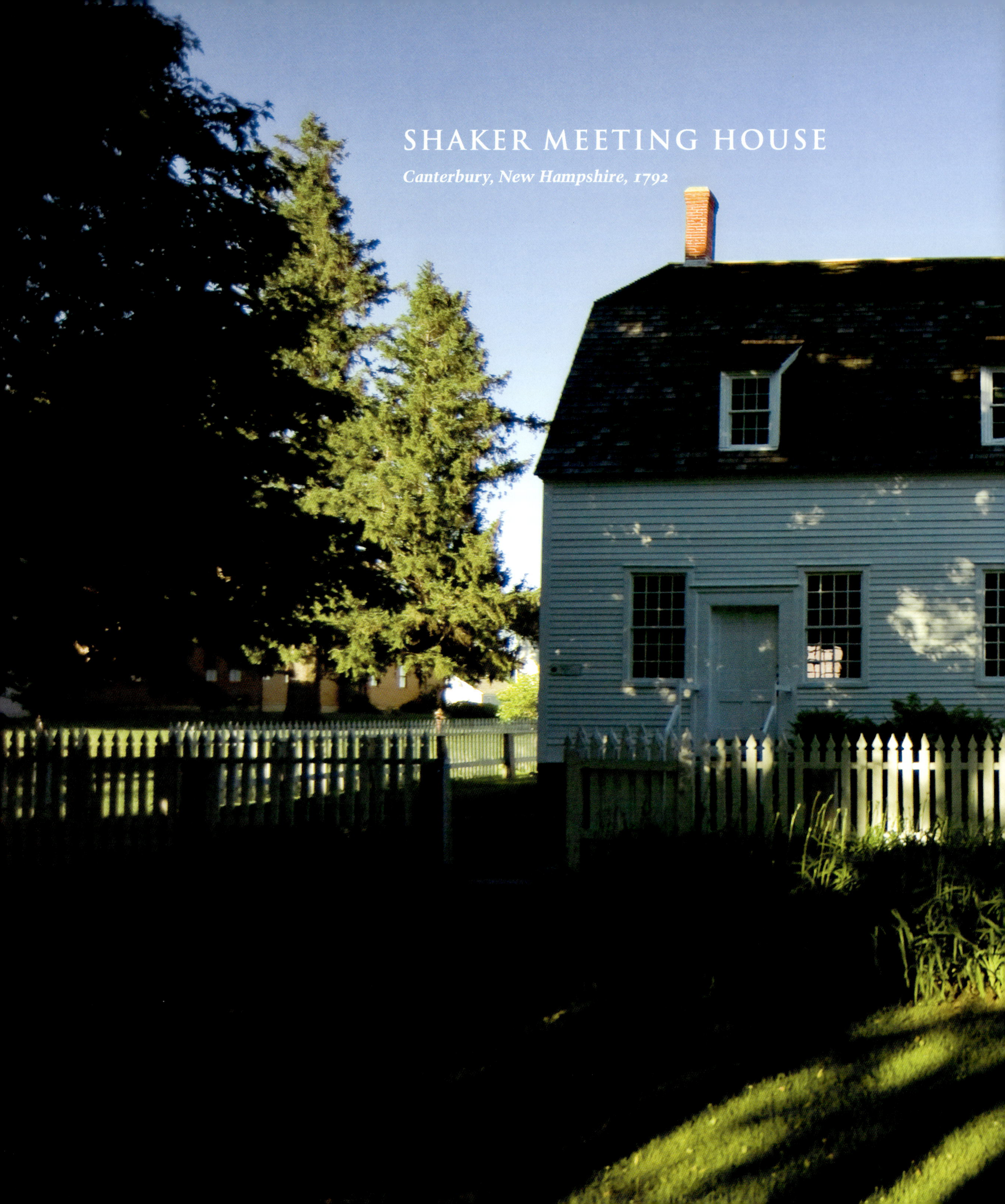

SHAKER MEETING HOUSE

Canterbury, New Hampshire, 1792

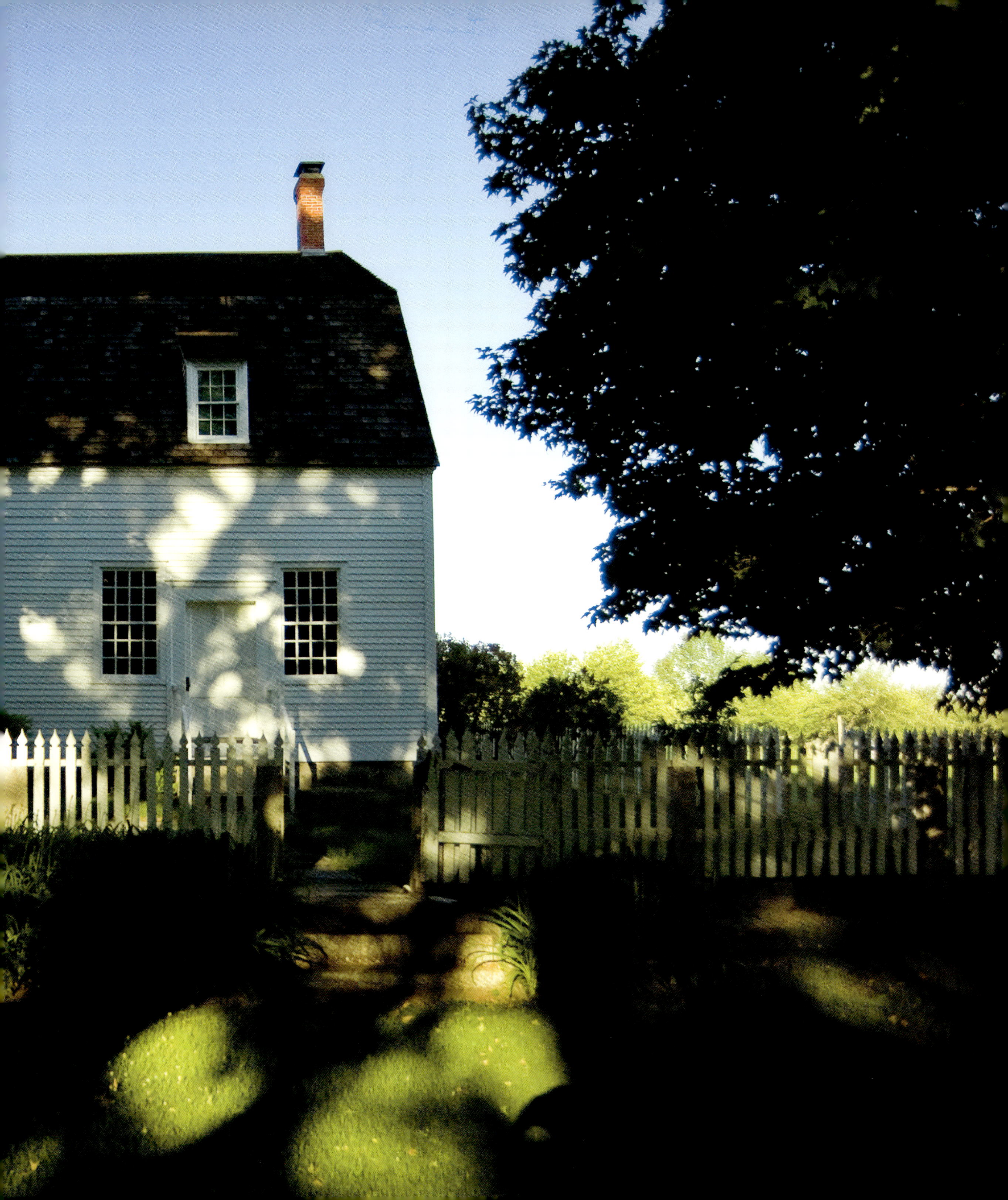

PREVIOUS PAGES *The form of the standard Shaker meeting house began with the 1791 house built by Shaker Moses Johnson at the first Shaker community in Watervliet, New York, near Albany, and was duplicated by him elsewhere. Its structural system is New York Dutch, which allowed for a wide open room where all Shakers could gather on Sunday. The gambrel roof was especially adapted to spanning large spaces, useful for meeting houses and also for two-room-deep dwellings. Two entries for men and women expressed their separate but equal status in this celibate religious society.*

RIGHT *The parallel ceiling beams and braces are characteristic of Dutch framing. A series of "H" frames can be set up for as long a building as desired, a much simpler framing system than the medieval English house. On Sunday mornings, the community gathered for private worship. The afternoon was for a public meeting, which visitors could attend and watch Shaker hymn singing and dancing. Their common name Shaker derived from those who, having seen their vigorous communal dancing, called them the Shaking Quakers.*

The Shakers became the most successful communitarian society in America. Their English origin held little promise of this when dissidents from various religions formed the United Society of Believers based on prophetic doctrine. Just before America exploded in Revolution, a small band of Shakers emigrated, as so many dissidents had before, to the New World, seeking a more hospitable setting to nurture their convictions. Outside of Albany, New York, they obtained land and began their revolutionary experiment based on practices contrary to conventional living. The experiment combined community ownership, monastic-like celibate living (yet with gender equality), pacifism (while surrounded by revolutionaries), devout worship (yet celebrated through ecstatic dancing, whirling, and clapping)—all signifying a communal, not individual, relationship to God. Their popular name, "Shakers" or Shaking Quakers, was derived from their mode of worship to which they invited the outside world to witness. Initially persecuted, they soon grew in numbers by converting individuals and families (who brought all their assets to the Shaker families they joined) and adopting orphans. With "hands to work and hearts to God," they were not a contemplative religion but were organized in families as productive units with multiple manufacturing and agricultural skills, competing successfully in the outside world with their superior quality products, inventions, and practical efficiencies. So successful were they that, within two generations, nineteen communities had been established from Maine to Kentucky.

When New Hampshire was swept by a revivalist revolution in the 1780s, many individuals and families sought a new faith in one of various expressions of the "awakening." Among these was Benjamin Whitcher, a recent Shaker convert who offered shelter to others from local prosecution, donating a large tract of land on which this group decided to form a new community, Canterbury Shaker Village. It was 1792 and within the year the community turned their energy to building dwellings.

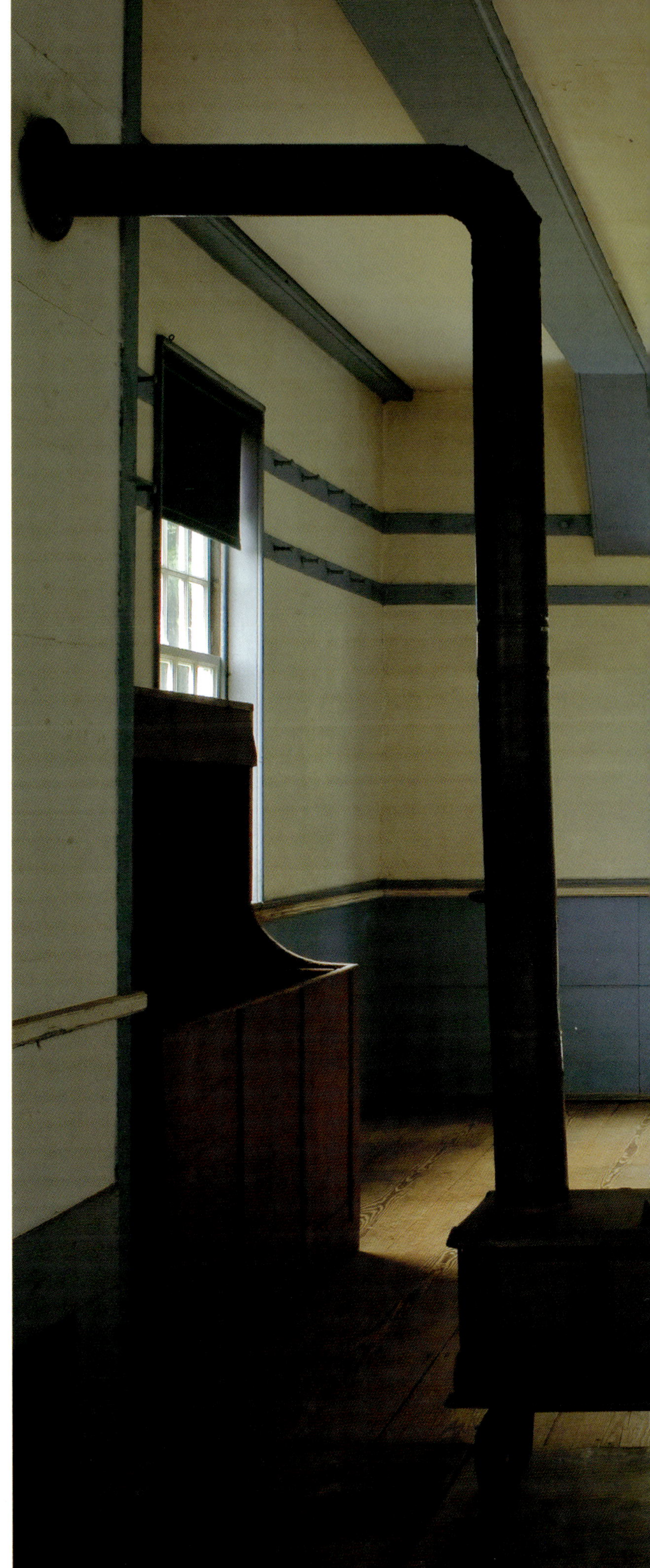

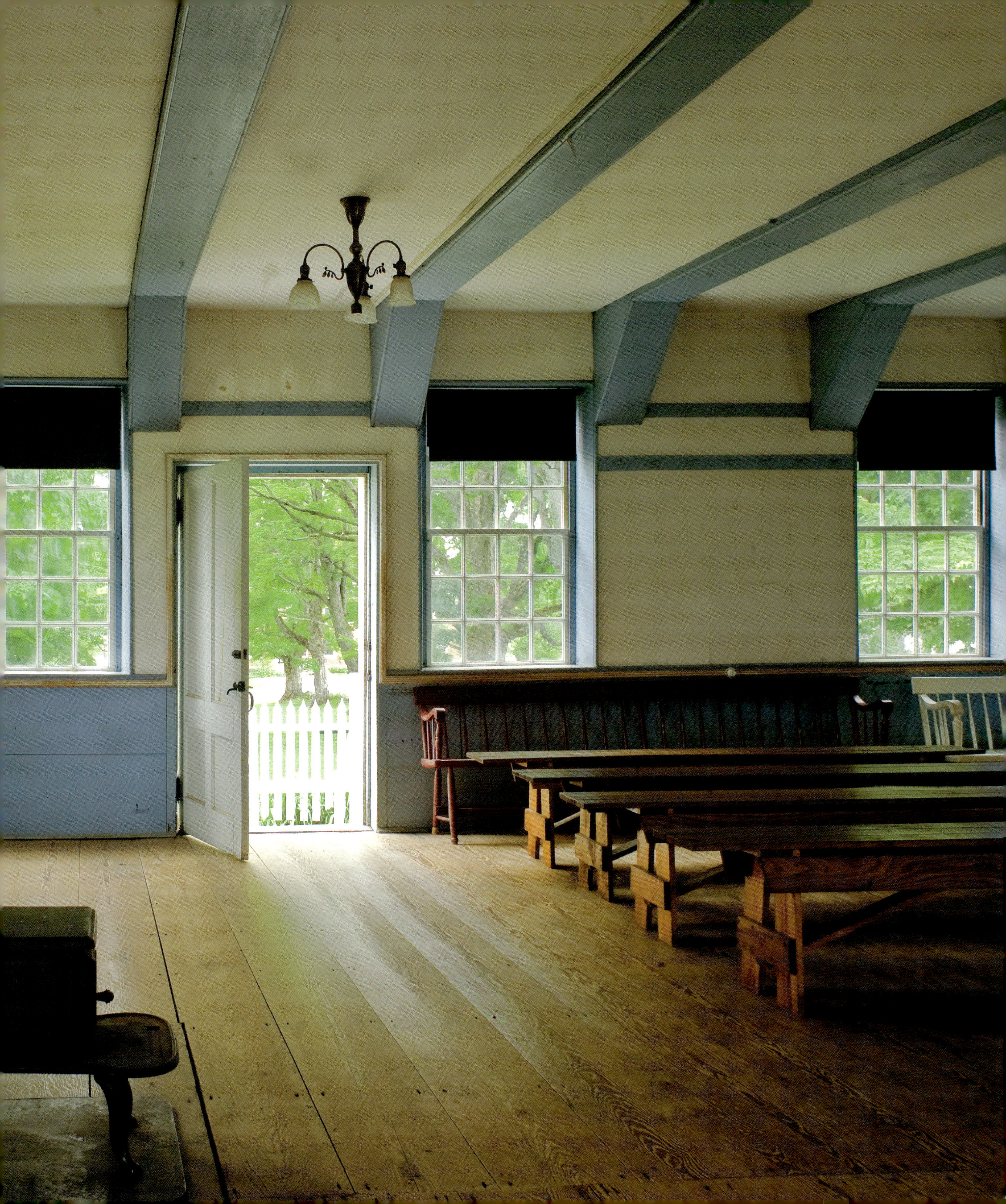

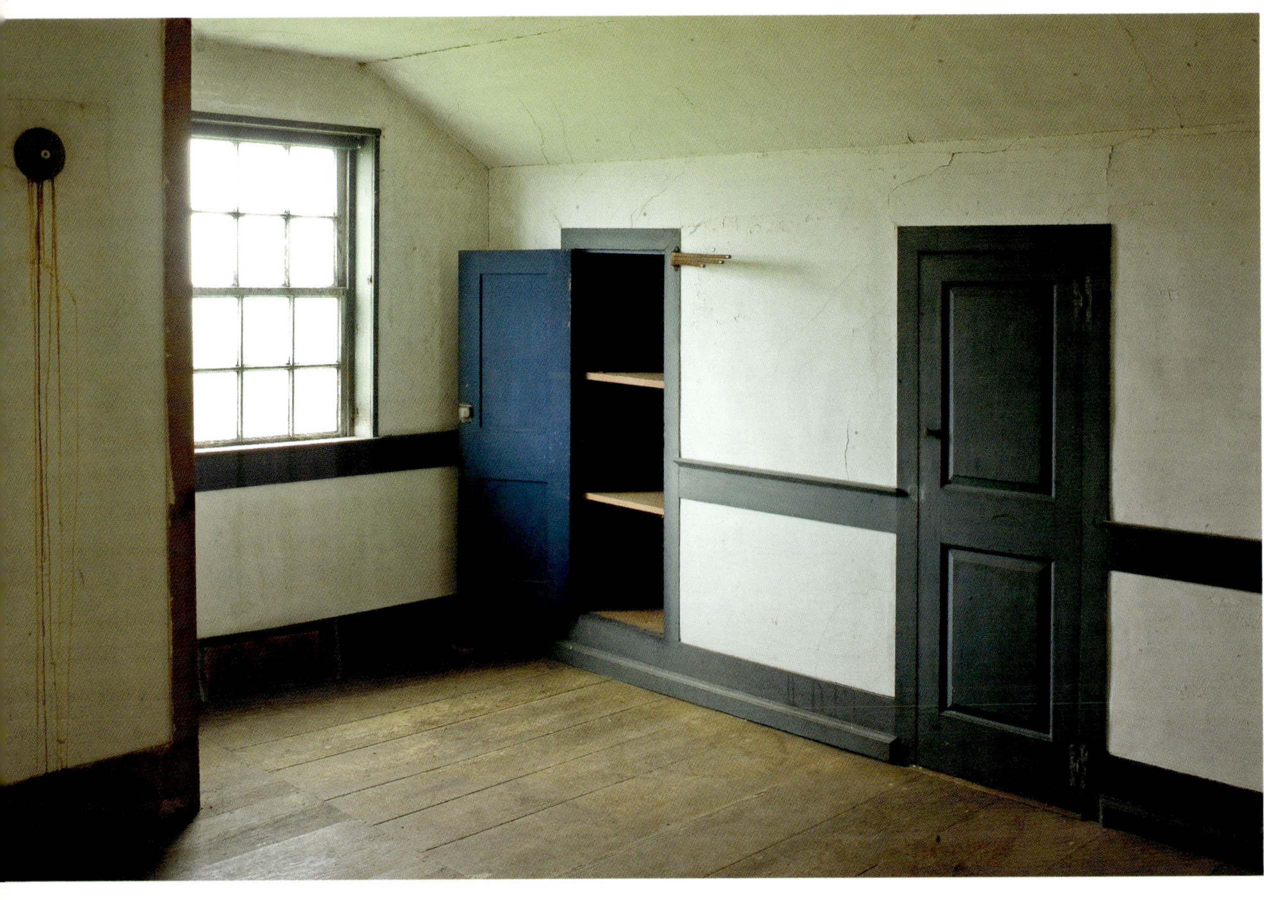

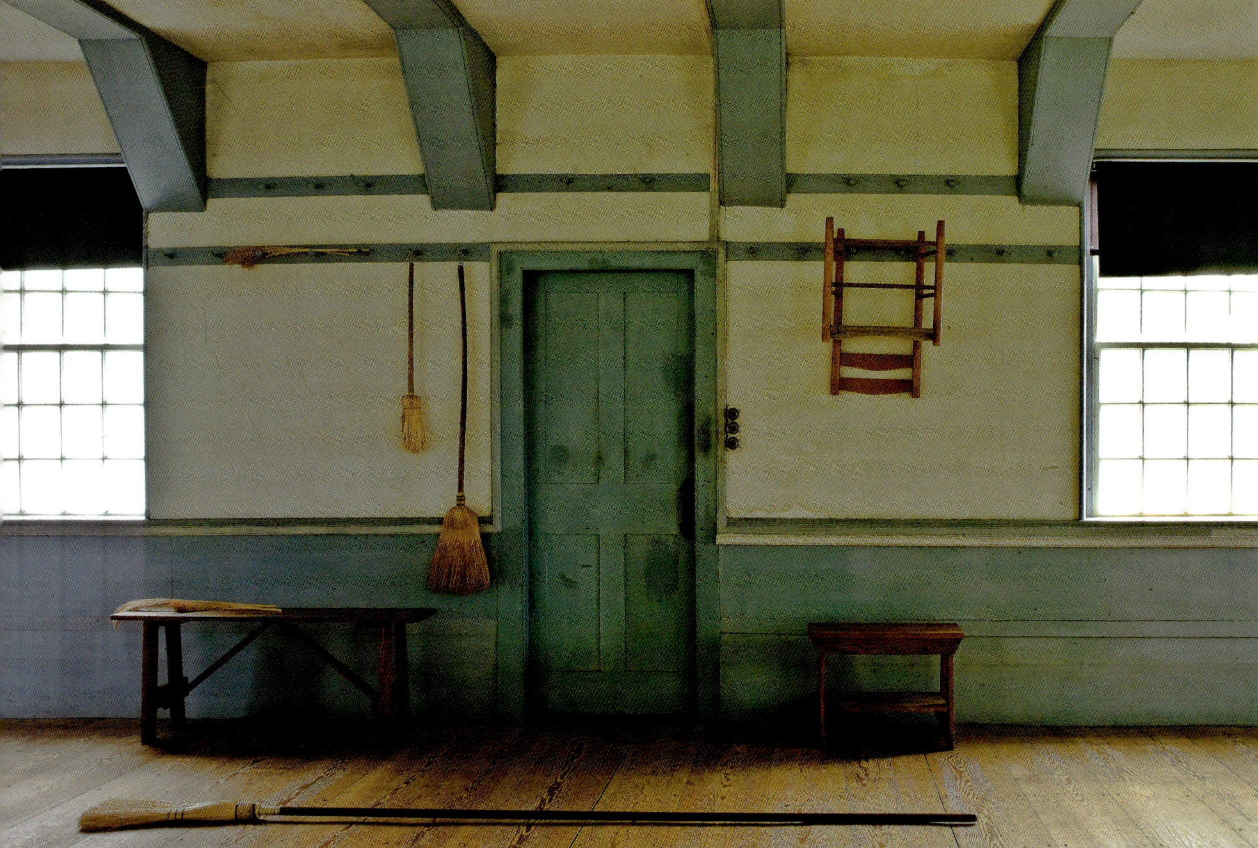

LEFT *While even the Shakers referred to aspects of their life as simple, their buildings were plain, but their construction was undertaken with exquisite attention to fit and finish. Nothing was superfluous or decorative in early Shaker construction. Efficiency and economy is evident in many convenient built-in features, including cupboards and drawers.*

BELOW LEFT *Shaker religious laws required that each meeting house "should be painted white without, and of a bluish shade within." Peg racks served multiple purposes, including clearing chairs from the floor for dancing.*

FACING PAGE *At Sunday meetings men and women faced each other on benches across the open floor. Hymns were sung without accompaniment. More comfortable benches were for worldly people from whom the Shakers hoped to recruit new members.*

FOLLOWING PAGES *The dwelling house (right) was first built in 1793 and enlarged several times until 1837. Here, eighty to a hundred brothers and sisters lived and ate. The belfry was their auditory clock. The creamery (1905), to the left, was for the production of cheese, their famous Golden Guernsey butter, and ice cream using the latest motorized inventions.*

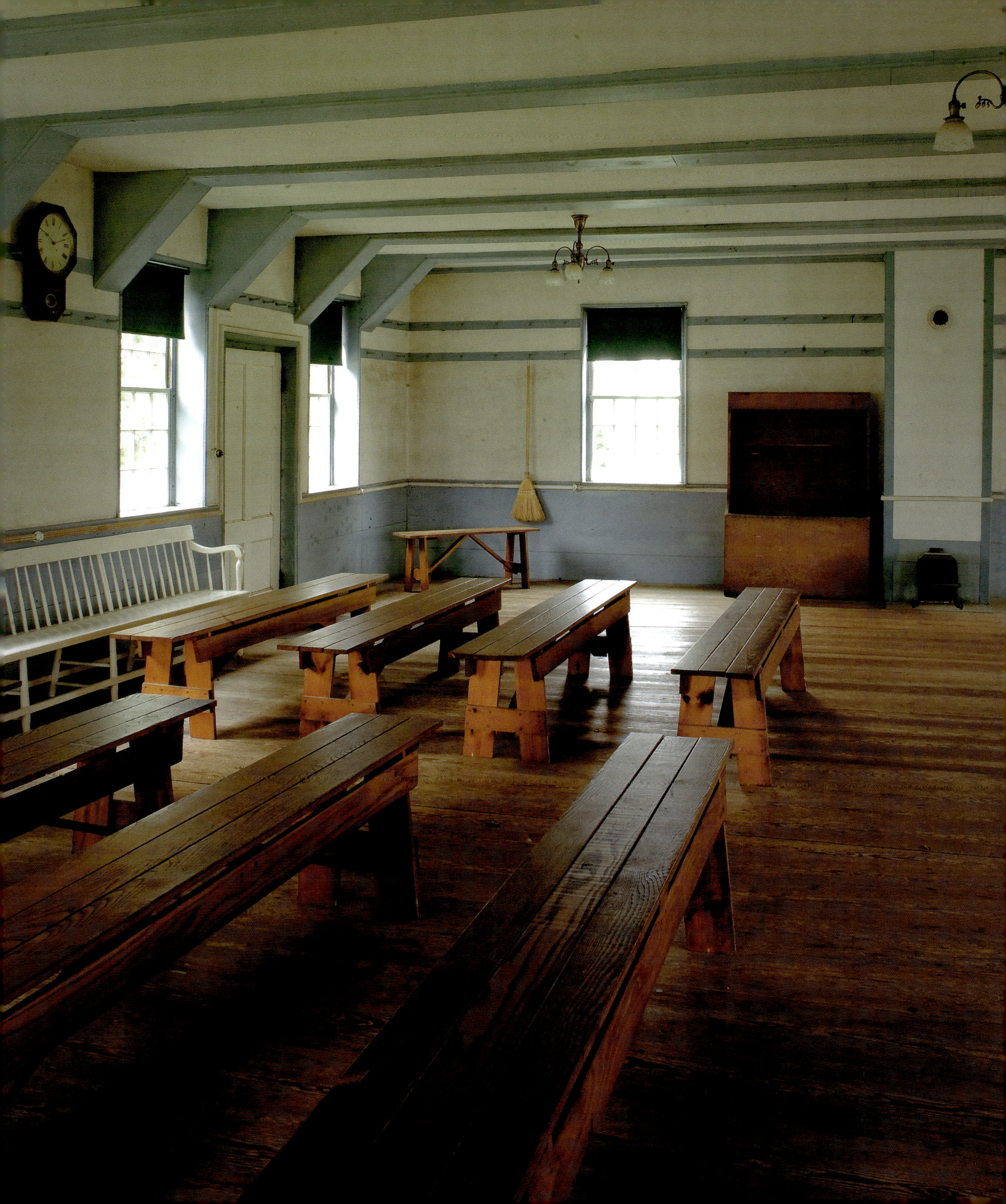

Shaker dedication to perfection extended to buildings, which, though influenced by contemporary worldly architecture, were adapted to multiple uses. Designed without superfluous ornament, each building's refinement of proportions and quality of materials and execution earned worldly admiration then as now. As each new community of families was established, the first structure of importance was the meeting house. Realizing that the unity of the Society among distant communities could be augmented by the unity of architecture, the ministry stipulated that each meeting house be built to a single design. Shaker master builder Moses Johnson erected eleven in as many communities, the one at Canterbury, New Hampshire, was the sixth. This was soon followed by similarly prescribed buildings for multiple purposes: dwelling houses (for three "families"), shops, stables, laundry, school, infirmary, and many more for farming, selling seeds, herbs and herbal medicines, manufacturing textiles, pails, brooms and other products. At its height in the mid-nineteenth century there were four families at Canterbury, three hundred members, more than a hundred buildings, and more than a square mile of productive land.

Moses Johnson's first meeting house, the prototype for others, was built at Watervliet near Albany, New York, in 1791. In form and structure it was similar to some farmhouses built in that area beginning in the 1760s with a gambrel roof and massive parallel ceiling beams. Though the idea of the gambrel roof, so popular in the Dutch area of New York, actually derived from New England, the basic "H" bent framing of the meeting house is Dutch as are the pentice-covered stoops. As a house of communal worship its first-floor interior was a single large space. Two entry doors both symbolized and functioned to express the separation yet equality of the genders as they entered for Sunday services. Two sets of stairways accessed the second and third floors. A pair of granite fireplaces supplied heat. In 1815 the stairways were removed to accommodate for expanded public space. A single stairway in a wing, built on the east side of the structure, would suffice. Heating was now supplied by iron and tin stoves. The second and third floors were for the residence of the ministry, elder men living on the left half, elder women on the right. Following the prototype, this and other meeting houses had white plaster walls, the trim painted blue and cupboards and storage closet interiors painted orange. In 1837 an addition of a winter chapel to the 1794 dwelling house left the meeting house for warm season use. The ministry moved in 1878 to new quarters leaving the upper floors vacant. Electricity for chandeliers was installed in 1910.

Since 1969 the community has been owned by Canterbury Shaker Village Inc., a not-for-profit historical restoration group, which preserved twenty-eight buildings of the original church family settlement and 679 remaining acres. The last active Shaker died in 1992.

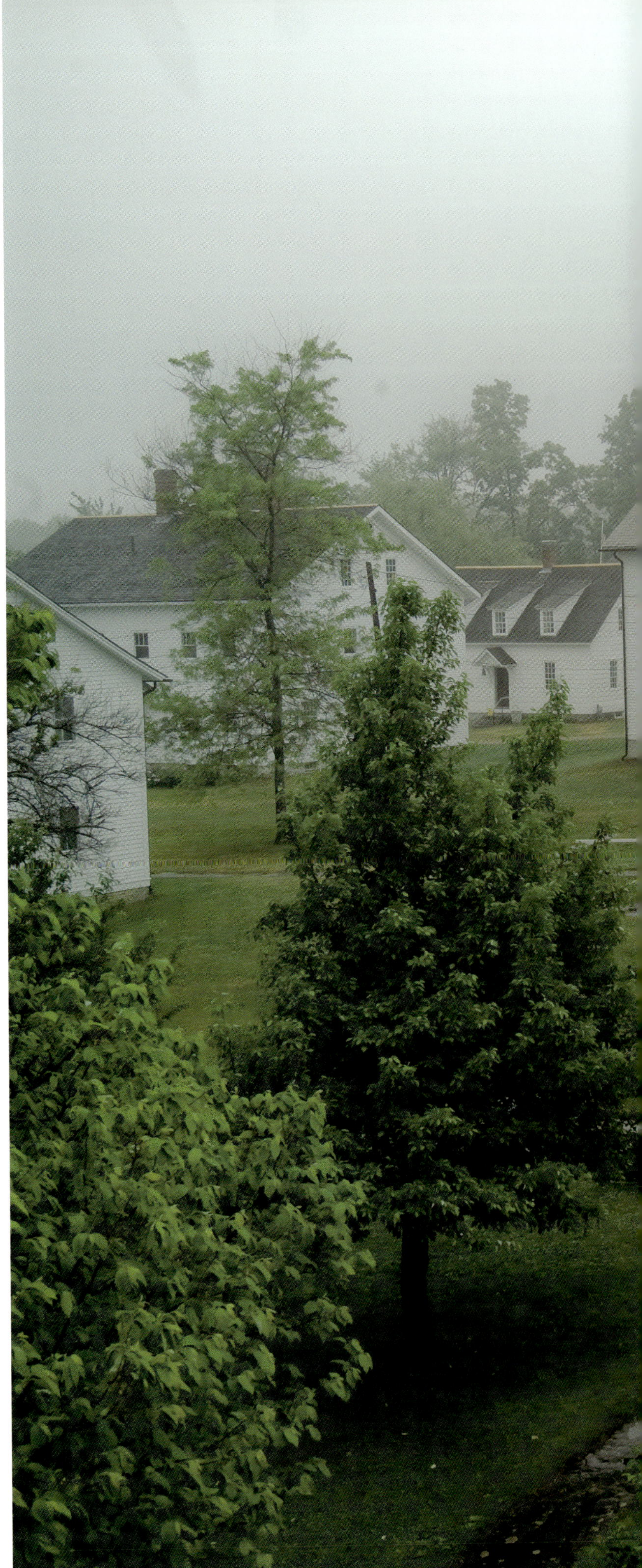

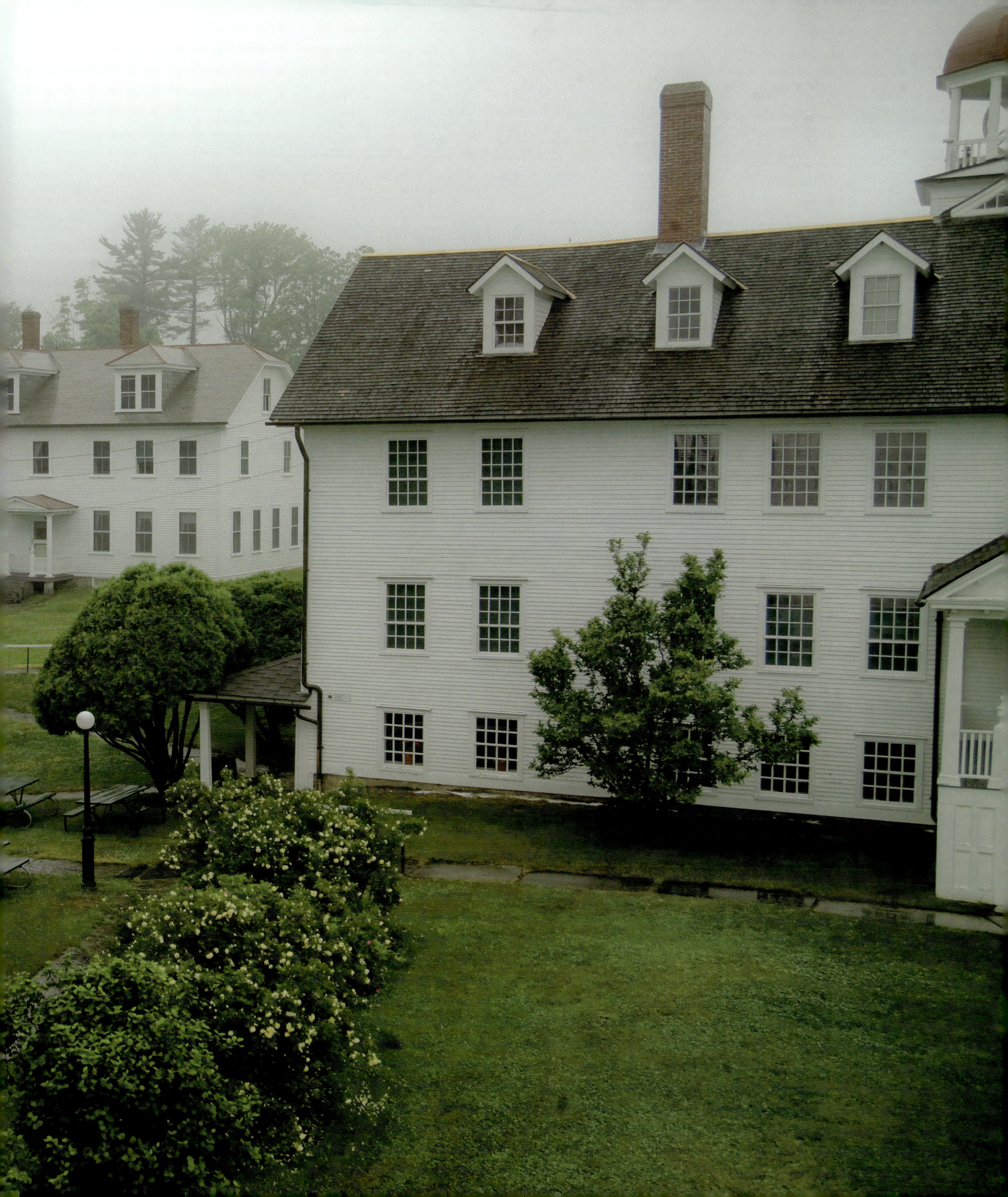

FACING PAGE *Set majestically on a rise overlooking the town common, the Strafford Town House was conceived as both town meeting house and a place of worship for the town's denominations. Its innovative design features a gable end porch tower with entrances, instead of the standard long side entry of prior meeting houses. The idea caught on in New England, and many meeting houses and later churches followed this plan.*

STRAFFORD TOWN HOUSE

Strafford, Vermont, 1799

Vermont, as a result of its remoteness and mountains, was settled later than other colonial regions in New England. The very qualities that caused its neglect, however, have since caused its appeal, especially for visitors from more densely settled states. In the warmer months, Vermont hill-town villages like Strafford draw nostalgic visitors. In many intact villages the sentinel of past and present pride looks serenely down upon the common—the meeting house—reminding all of its purpose to organize faith and governance under one communal roof, suitable for both the sacred and profane as an assembly hall since New England worship and governance both eschewed ornament and ceremony.

Strafford—"the Upper Hollow"—is just such a village. The surrounding town of the same name was chartered in 1761 to sixty-four owners. Initially town meetings and religious services were held in a large house but as the population expanded the need for a sizable meeting house became urgent. Getting agreement on its features to suit both functions took years of discussion and repeated votes. Adherents of the orthodox Congregational Church or "Standing Order" were being challenged by newer evangelical sects, making agreement more difficult. Finally, in 1798, town residents voted for its construction, a location, taxation to pay for it, and a constitution to govern its use. The town would erect and enclose the building, the denominations using it would raise funds to finish the inside. It was initially agreed to build a traditional meeting house with the main entrance in the middle of a long side, a wide aisle of "broad alley" crossing to the pulpit wall opposite. At a December meeting, a new plan was proposed, which called for a space of "fifty feet by sixty feet with a Porch at the South end." "Porch" is an old New England term for an enclosed entryway tower with interior stairway. This time, a second floor with a three-sided gallery was specified. Unusual was the entry in the short (south) gable, not the long side, thus placing the pulpit in the opposite short gable wall. This was apparently too new an idea for the townspeople, who voted it down. Petitioners immediately called for another meeting, marshaled supporters, and when they met in January they had a crowd of 147 men, this time ready to vote for this plan.

The annual town meeting was held in March to elect officers, raise money for town charges, and to discuss some matters concerning school districts and the need to restrict certain animals from running at large. Immediately after a meeting was held on the plan, now modified to 48 feet by 60 feet but not mentioning the porch tower. In fact what got built is more like the prior plan, 50 feet 6 inches by 59 feet 6 inches, the south gable tower 14 feet by 15 feet with all entrances in this tower and gable end. The tower was built with a high steeple and spire and a double set of stairs to the gallery. There is a main entry door in the front of the tower and two side doors. Work must have begun then as the structure was to be erected and enclosed by November 1, 1799.

The master builder is not clearly named, but later remembrances suggest that Leonard Walker with his brother and sons were actively engaged in its building and may have proposed the final design. A talented mechanic, owner of a local sawmill and blacksmith, he also made the 7-foot-tall weathervane for the town house. Granite underpinning rocks had to be excavated and shaped, tree trunks hauled to the site, squared, and joined for wall frames and roof trusses. The latter were massive enough to span fifty feet, each truss with double sets of rafters, purlins, and braces joined by a king post.

At a town meeting on November 13 they voted to sell the right to own pews to pay for interior finish work. Pews to be paid in "Cash or good, What or good Beef Cattle, Rye or Indian Corn at Cash price." The meeting house was to be completed in one year. At the auction one-third of heads of households in the town bought pews. Some cost over $100 near the pulpit, most over $50 on the first floor, and almost all in the gallery went for below $50. Of various denominations, this meant families were thinly scattered around the meeting house during services. As originally built, there were square pews, a high pulpit, and sounding board. The innovative long-axis configuration of entry-to-pulpit proved to be a transitional form. Almost all meeting houses thereafter in New England followed this gable entrance plan. However, the square tower plan quickly evolved into a shallower and wider portico with three entrances facing forward in the classical mode of English churches.

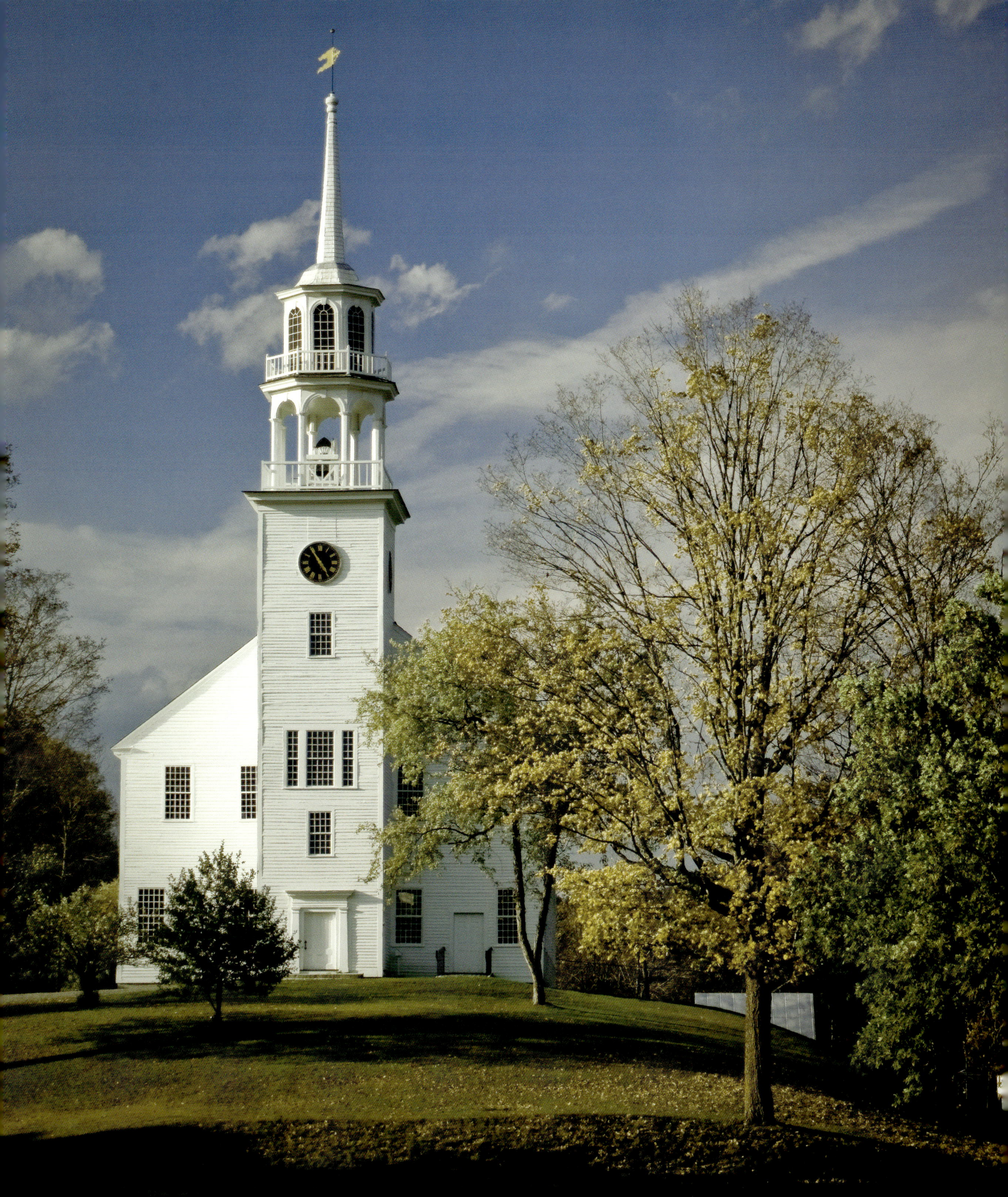

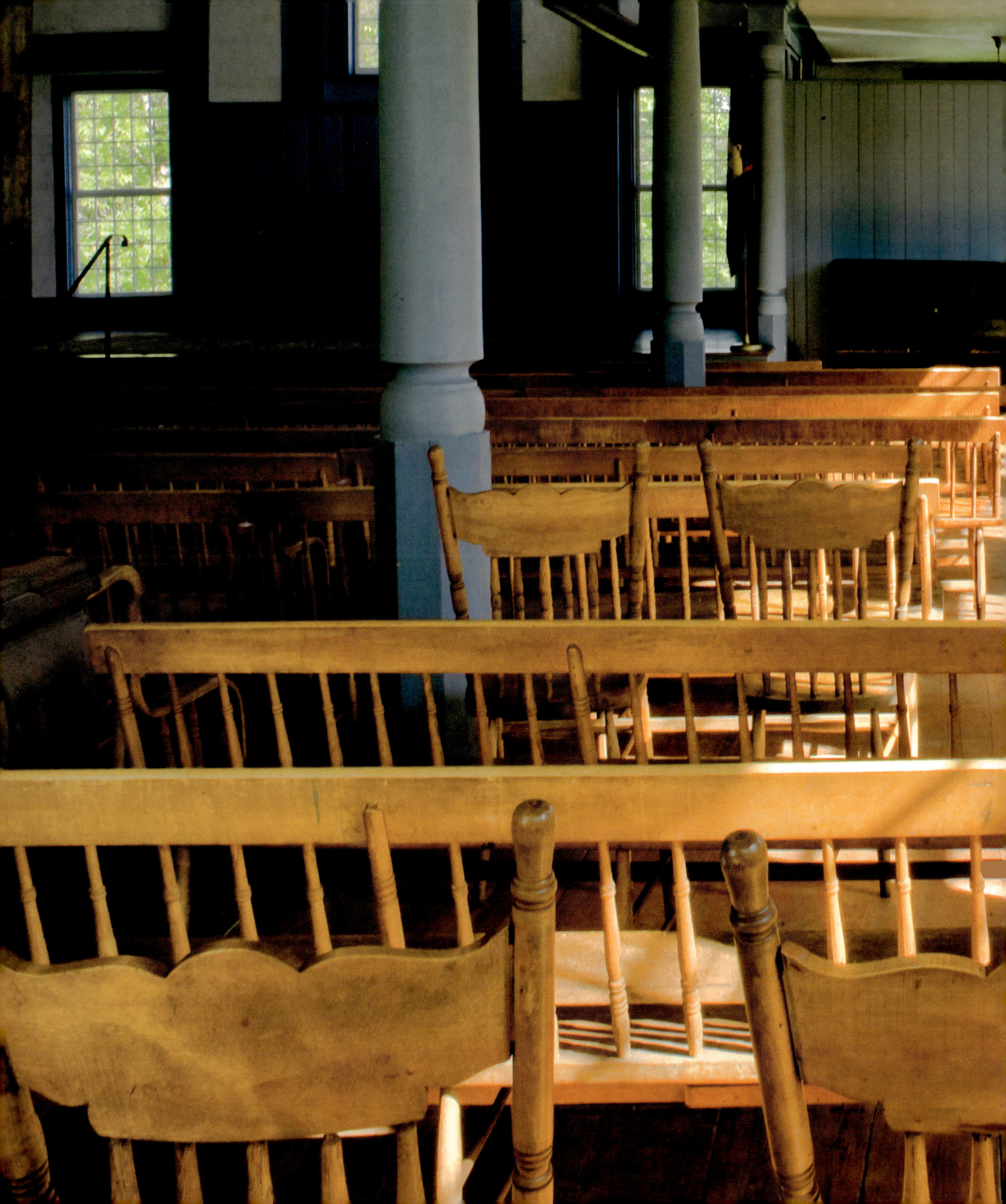

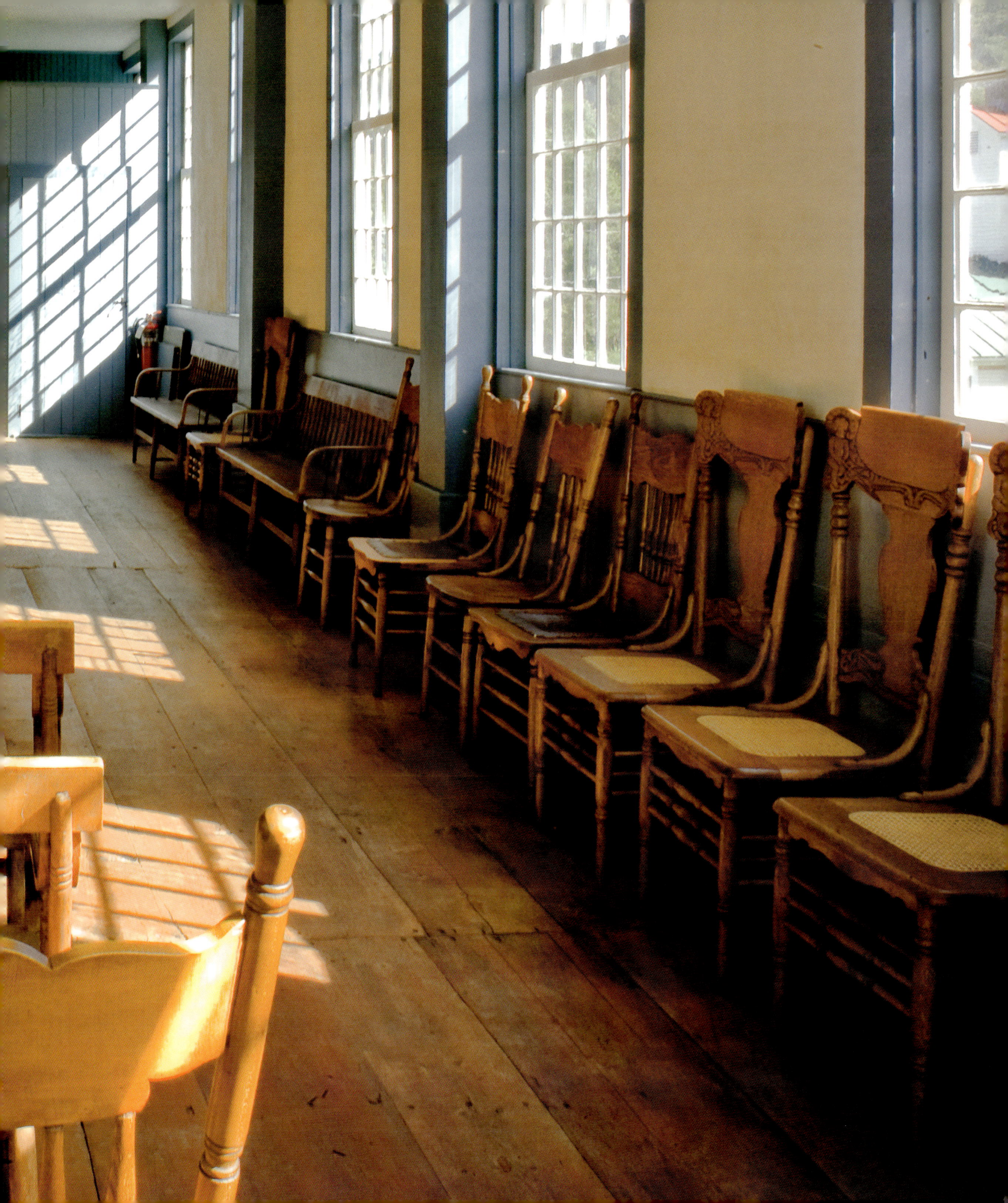

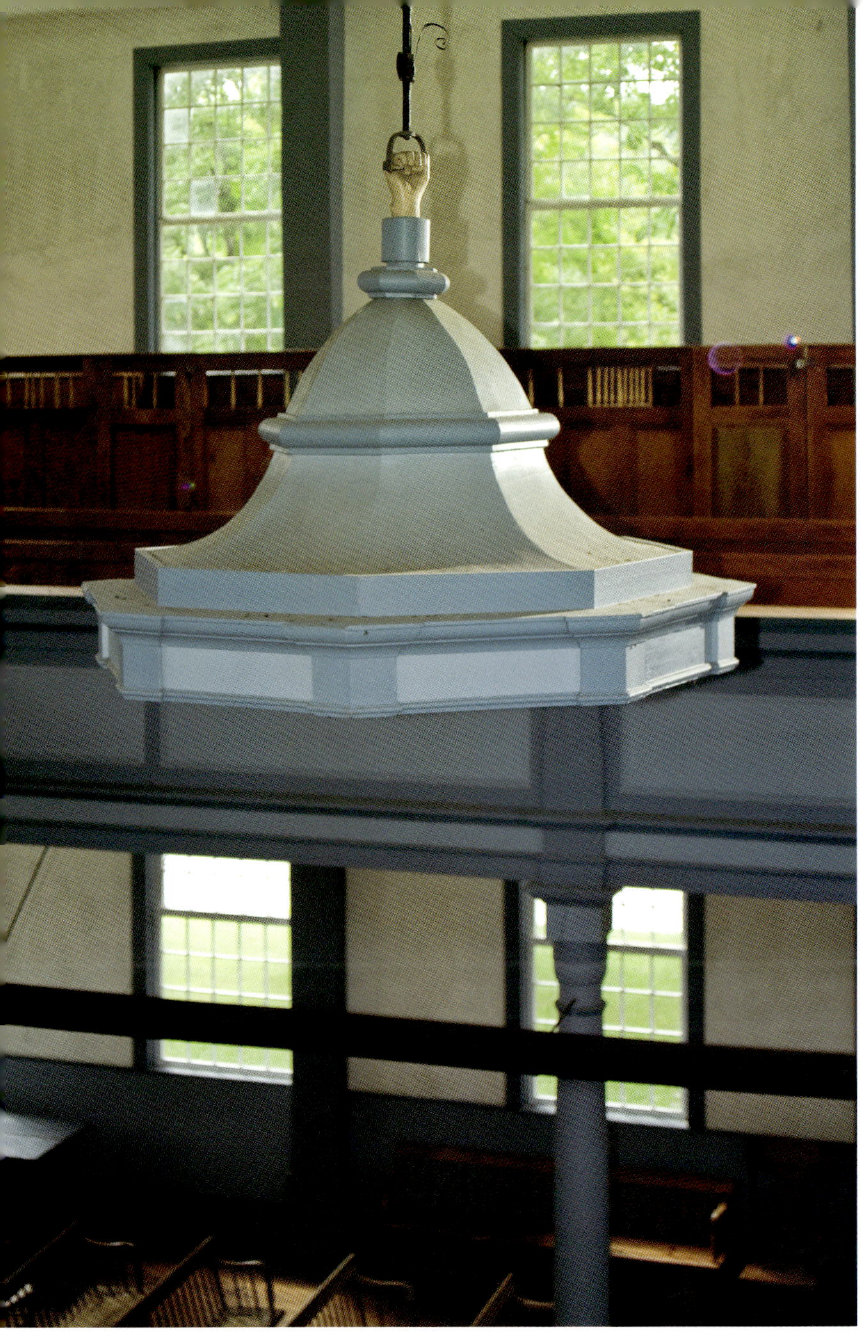

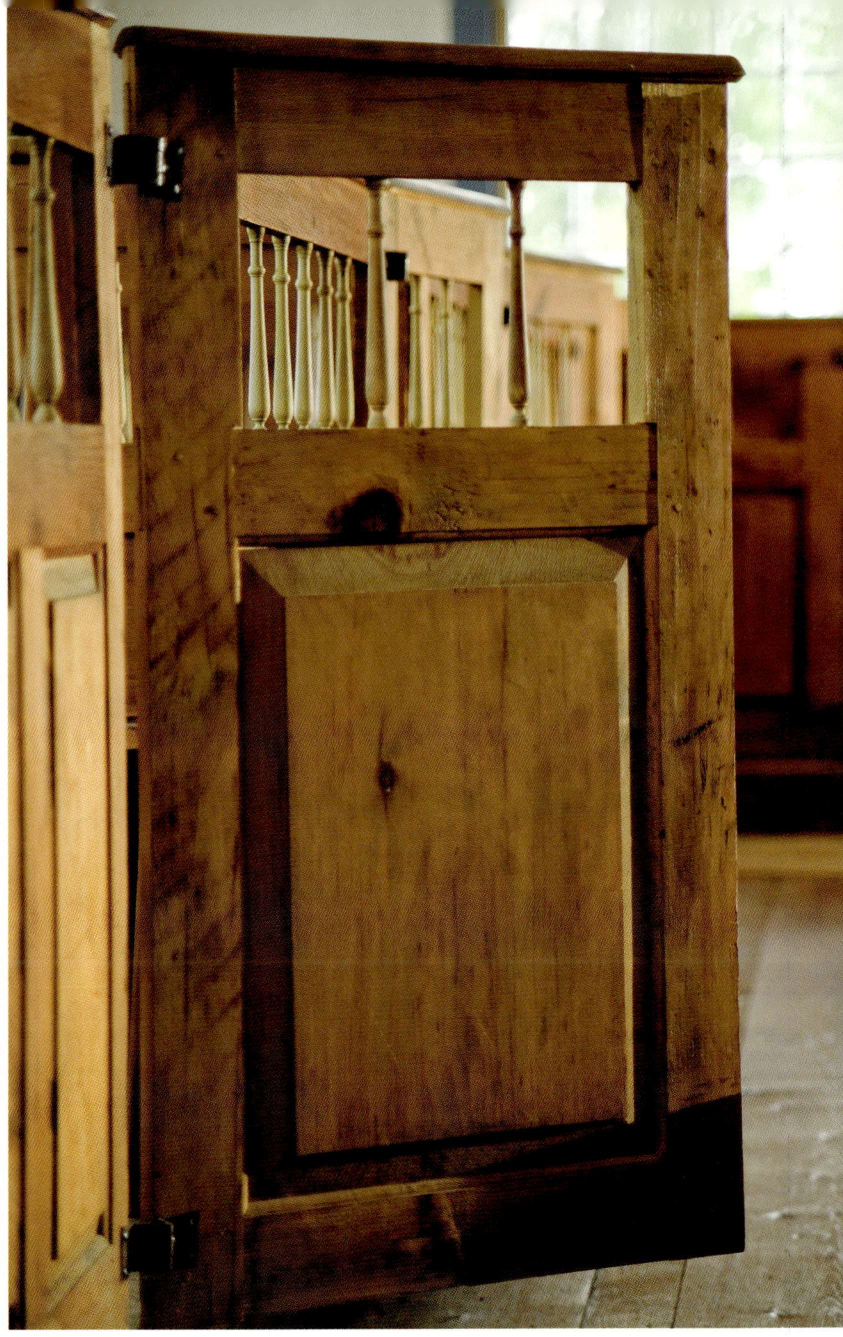

PREVIOUS PAGES *When denominations built their own churches, the building became the town house for meetings resulting in first floor pews being replaced by backed benches, the pulpit removed, and its sounding board retained but in another position.*

ABOVE *Devoid of its purpose but retained out of sentiment, the sounding board literally hangs on by hand.*

ABOVE LEFT *In the balcony early pews survive, which, like the sounding board, are retained for the sake of historic preservation rather than practicality. New England nourishes an admirable affinity for its past.*

All of this coincided with the legal separation of church and state in the early nineteenth century, which led to many church-like meeting houses becoming actual churches, not the property of towns. In Strafford, however, the meeting house retained its dual function until denominations built their own structures and it became what it has been called ever since, the Town House. For this sole purpose the interior was changed to accommodate its public purpose better. The first floor pews were removed but largely remain in the gallery. The pulpit was removed, its sounding board retained in another position out of sentiment. The pulpit wall became a stage (for a while with a proscenium arch) and a large number of spindle settees were placed on the main floor. In recent years the Strafford Historical Society's Town House Preservation Committee has taken responsibility for the care and preservation of this important landmark.

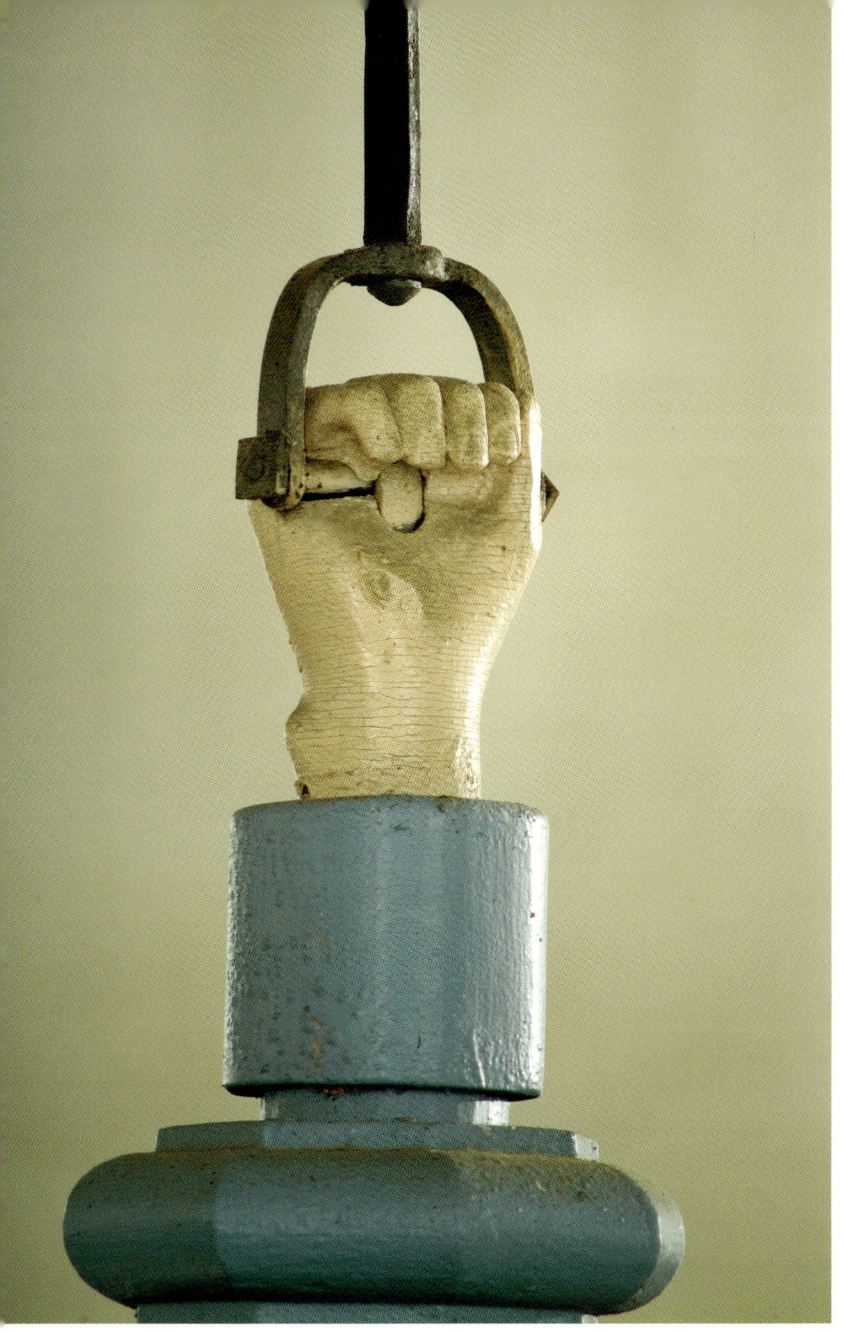

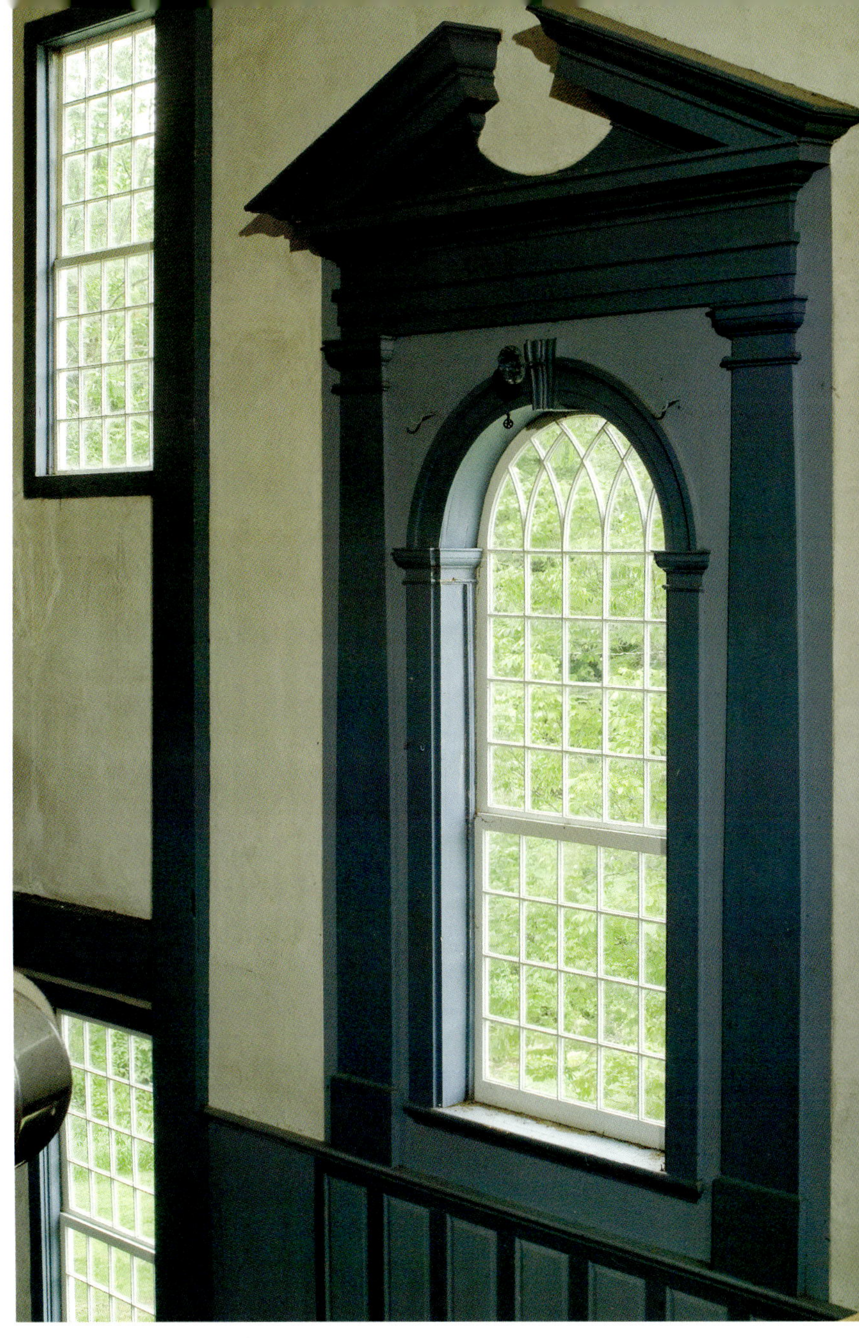

ABOVE LEFT *A hand holds the sounding board.*

ABOVE *The pulpit window marks the place of its earlier purpose room, in which generations of preachers admonished their parishioners.*

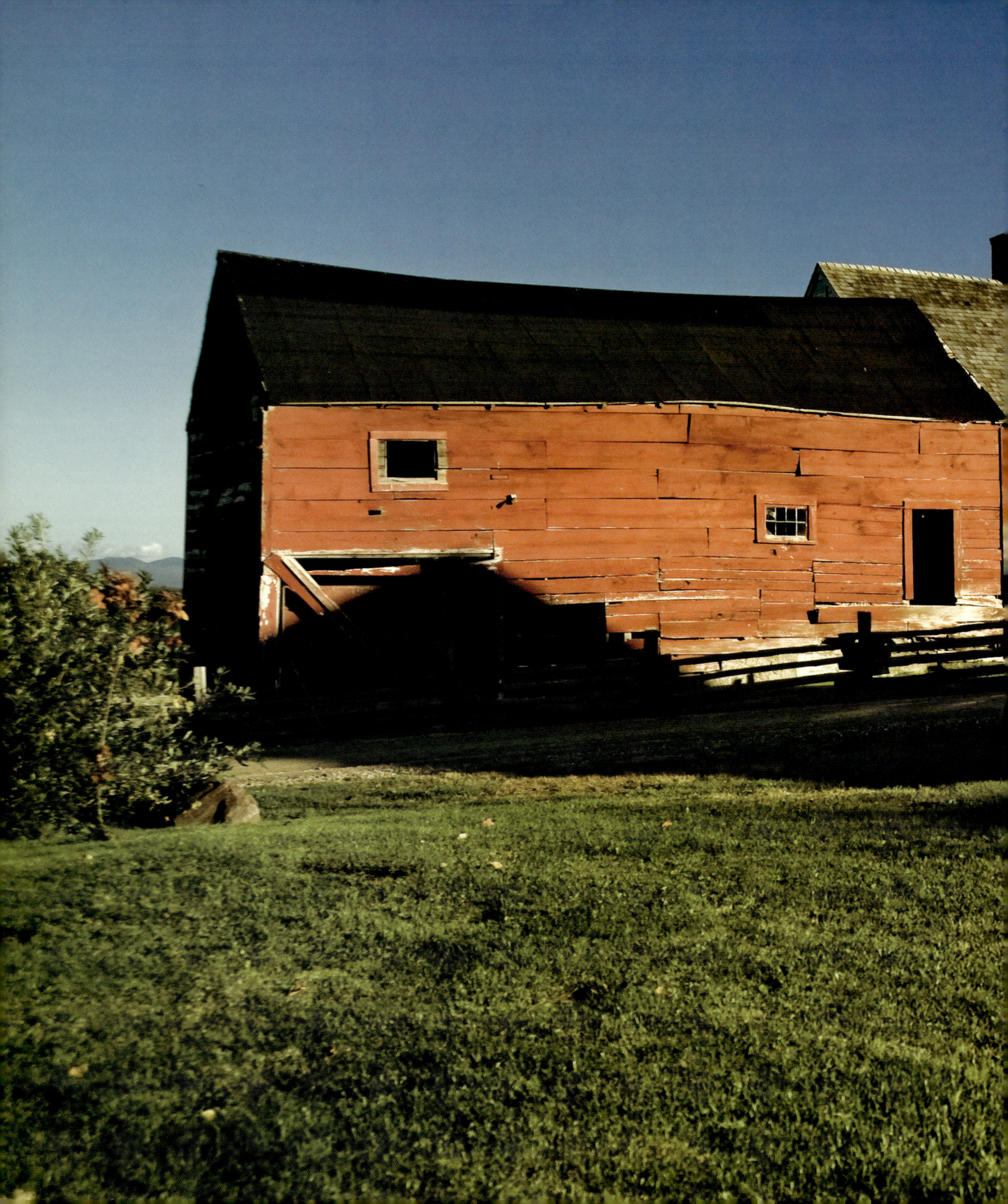

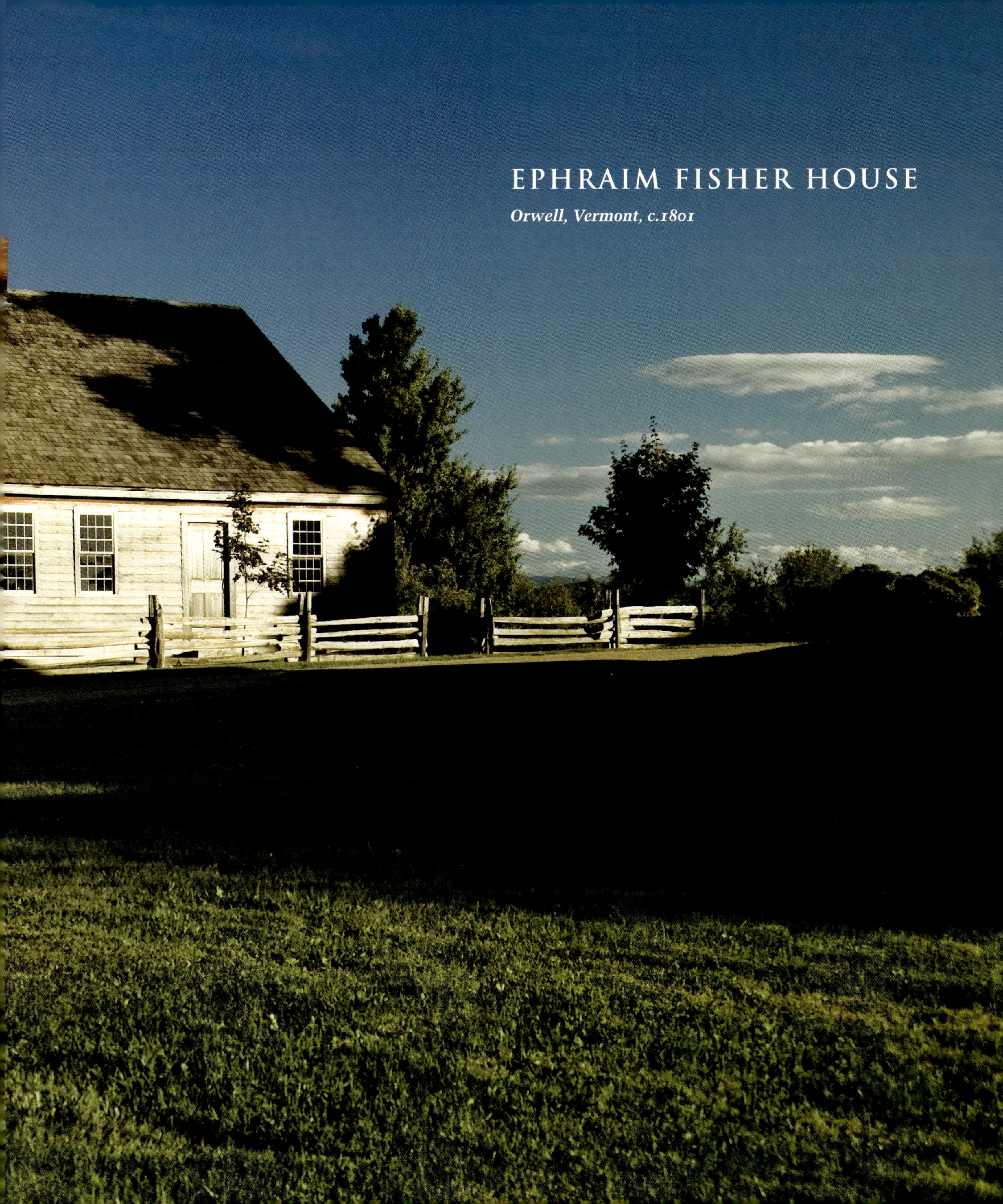

EPHRAIM FISHER HOUSE

Orwell, Vermont, c.1801

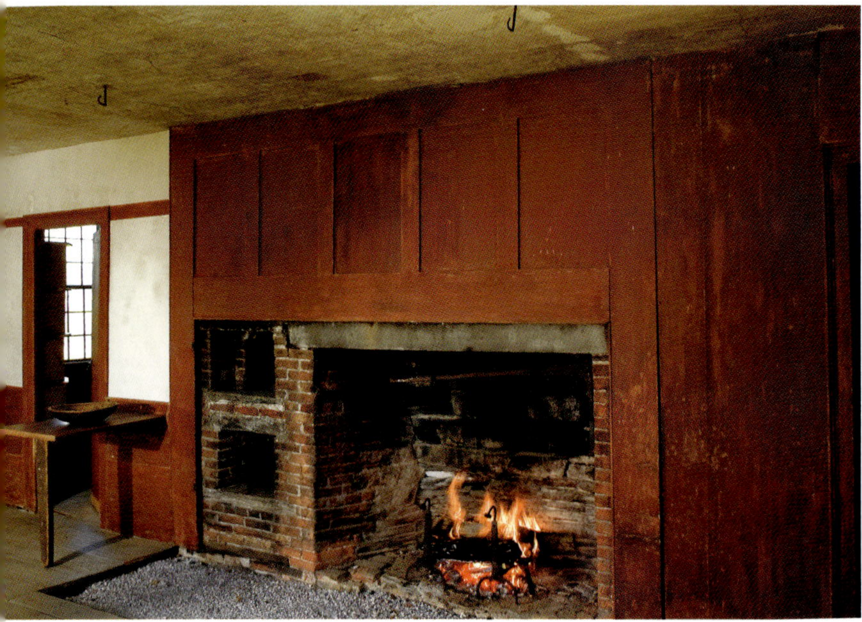

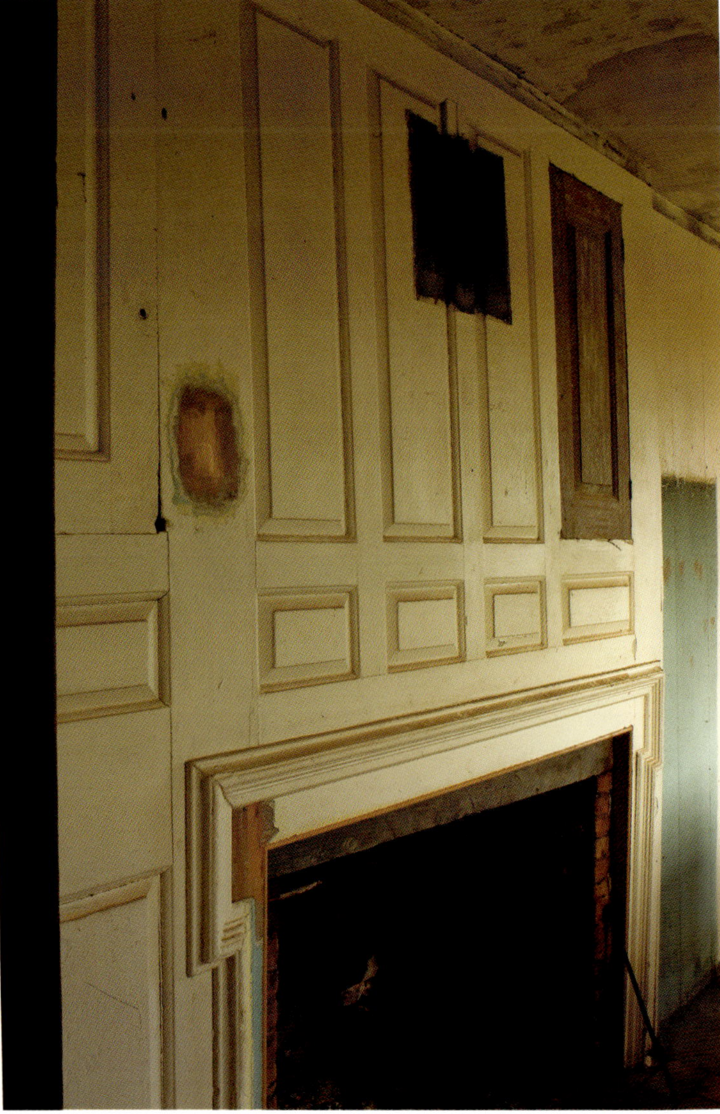

PREVIOUS PAGES *The barn is set prominently near the road, following an old New England farm plan. The house, built in 1801, is basically the same Cape style, dating back a century and more. For those settling distant regions of New England, the familiar and the function was sufficient.*

LEFT *The kitchen is at the front with its fireplace, unusually, facing the front rather than the gable end. Flat recessed paneling retains its original red finish, and the hearth awaits bricks—this is a restoration in progress.*

BELOW LEFT *Unlike the plainer kitchen, the parlor chimney breast is addressed with raised paneling (later pierced by a stove pipe hole for more practical heating). A panel as cupboard door allows one to keep food warm against the brick chimney. A paint scrape reveals it too was originally painted red. The parlor is in the rear room. Unusual to this house is a stairway in the gable end rather than inside the front door.*

FACING PAGE *Throughout the early period regulating indoor temperature was a chore and a problem. In winter the kitchen fireplace's heat was a welcome comfort but in summer it was excessive. A separate summer kitchen, shown here, was the solution, either in the basement (where cool ground temperature moderated the radian heat of the fire), or in a wing.*

The Green Mountains of Vermont remained a relatively isolated northern frontier land, settled by few yet claimed by many. New France claimed it first, Britain later, then Massachusetts, New Hampshire, and New York all laid claim. If its mountains isolated it from south and north, its western boundary, Lake Champlain, was an open corridor of empirical hegemony as French Canada and British America fought several wars through this valley. Peace came in 1765, temporarily, when Britain finally took Canada, but the warring started again with the Revolution and threatened the region still again in the War of 1812. Little wonder Vermont remained underpopulated. New Hampshire, assuming suzerainty, made numerous land grants between 1749 and 1764. New York's attempt to nullify the grants so aroused the independent spirit of Vermont settlers that they declared their land a sovereign republic in 1777, deciding to call it New Connecticut, then, as an afterthought, Vermont. Only in 1791 did Vermont surrender its independence to become the fourteenth state of the Union—peace at last.

Among those land grants was the fertile farmland of Orwell in Addison County, near the southwest corner of the state. Initially the growing of wheat proved the most successful crop. Later, cattle and sheep became the primary farm economy, followed by dairy farming. One of the earlier dairy farmers was Ephraim Fisher (1751–1834) who arrived with family from Freetown, Massachusetts, by 1777, establishing a farm on Crown Point Road, carefully selected for a dependable spring clay soil for grass and loam for grain and pasture. The house oriented to the road (now gone) and a view—though a subsequent survey put it in the corner of his 100 acres which prompted him to buy more land to situate the house handsomely.

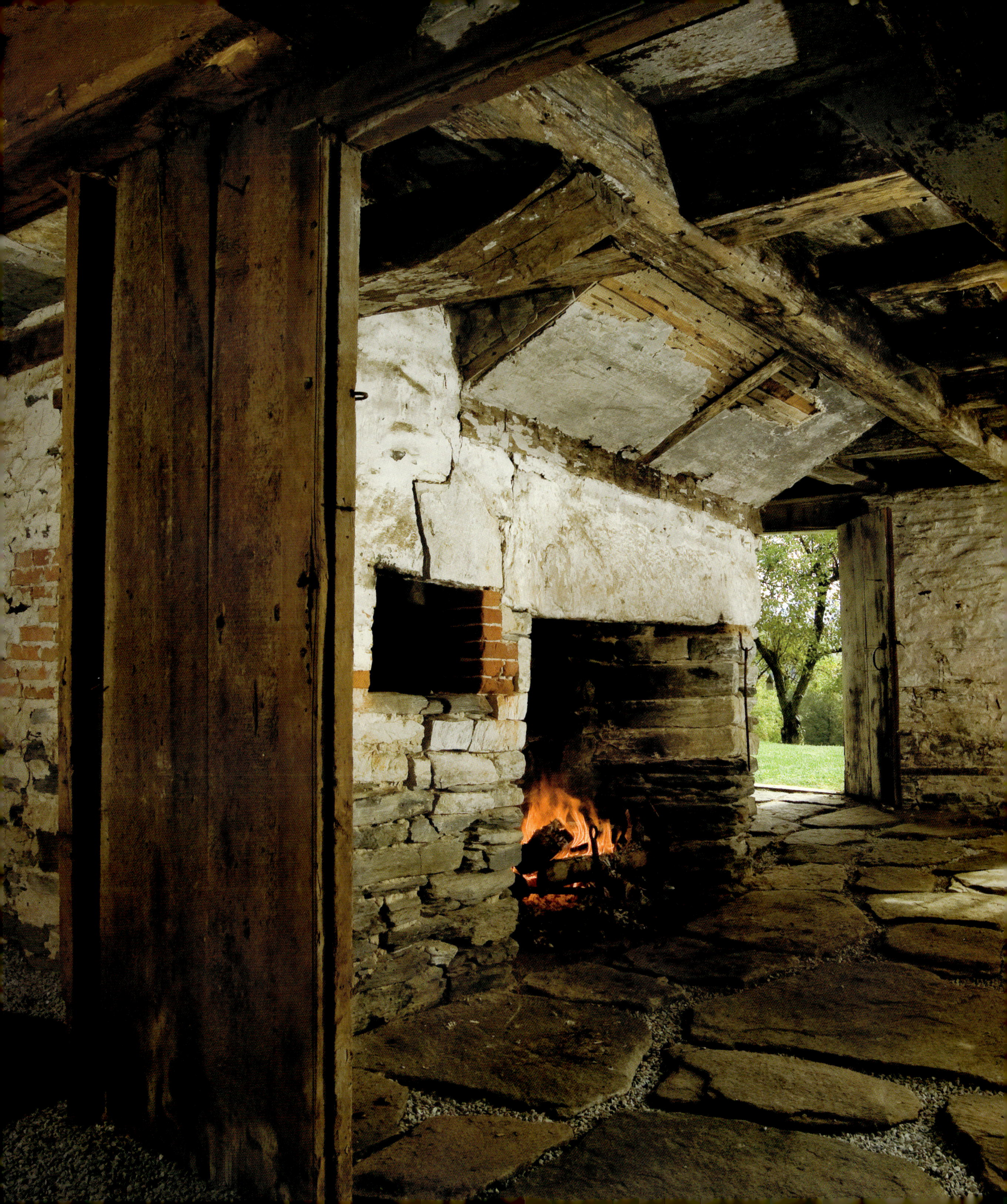

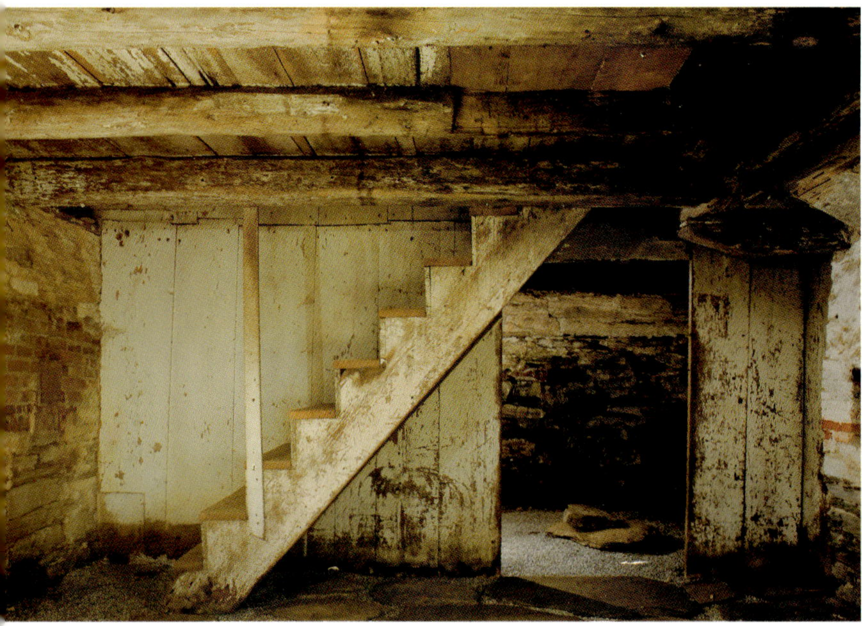

ABOVE *The anchor of traditional New England houses was the chimney stack with several fireplaces. It held up the center of the house while providing a single chimney (multiple flues) for up to seven fireplaces, necessitating a large base. Although this was efficient, it did require a complicated structural system to tie walls to the chimney stack.*

RIGHT *Whitewash is a solution of lime and water, sometimes with additives like salt, brushed onto surfaces in cellars and barns. It is cheap, easily applied, covers over dirty surfaces, reflects light (especially useful in cellars), and has antimicrobial properties, a benefit to food storage and domestic stock. While early New England was deficient in lime, its use in later periods was widespread.*

He built a log cabin, a common first structure for local settlers, in which he lived with his family. Roswell Bottum, Orwell's earliest historian, described Ephraim Fisher: "He was a man who sought little notoriety, but contented himself with the business of his farm and in the company of his family." In the 1800 census we learn that Ephraim and his wife Elizabeth had seven children at home, and three elder daughters married and gone. For such a family he needed a more substantial house, and he began to build the present house when he was about fifty. After his son Isaac (1798–1865) took over the farm in 1820, there were thirty to forty cows producing up to ten thousand pounds of cheese a year, according to the 1825 census (an early cheese press still survives in the barn). It would be decades before the railroad made milk shipment—and a dairy industry—commercially viable. Ephraim died in 1834, likely proud of carving such a farmstead out of the wilderness. His son was proud as well; a photo survives from about 1860 of the family and their prized stock standing before the house and the early cabin, dwarfed by the majesty of the setting.

The Orwell Grant List (for appraisal and taxation) of 1804

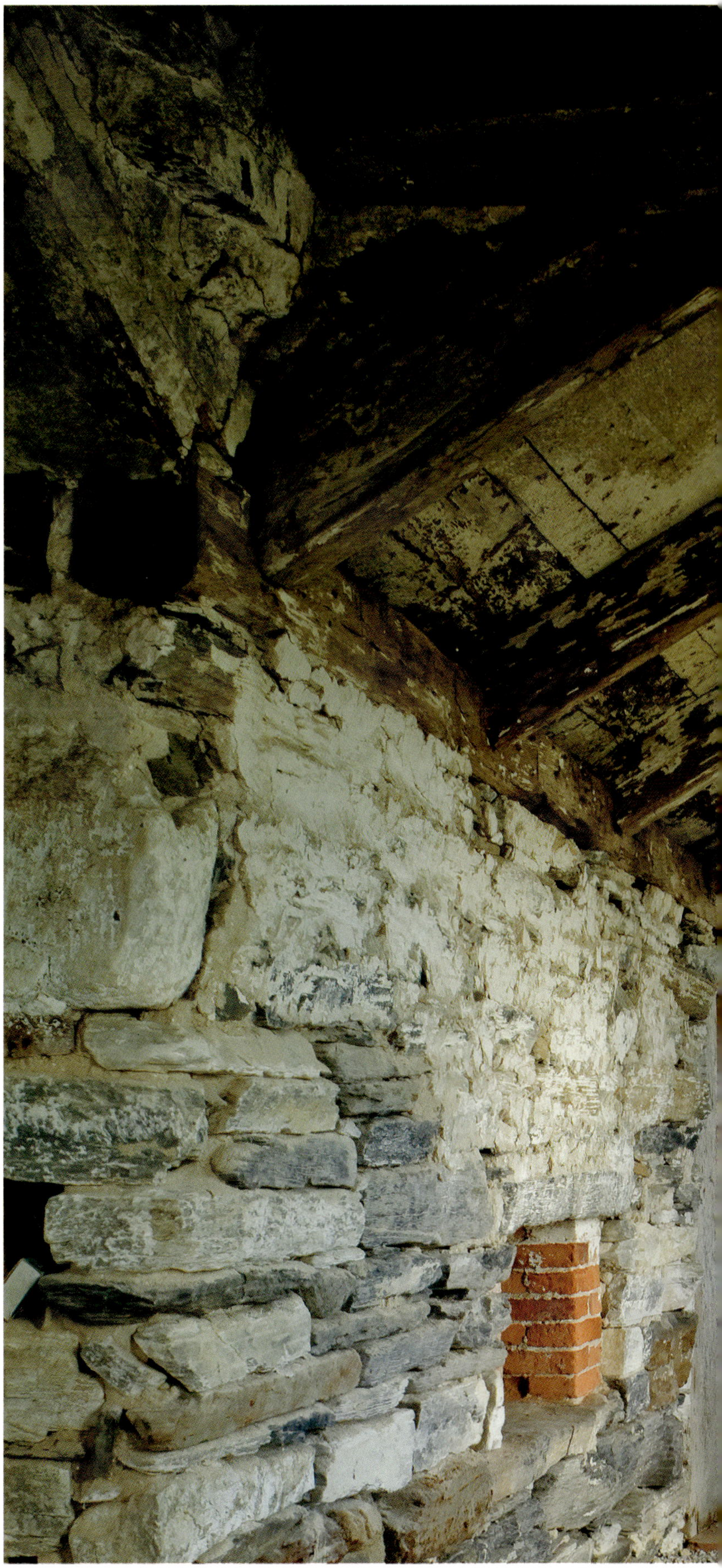

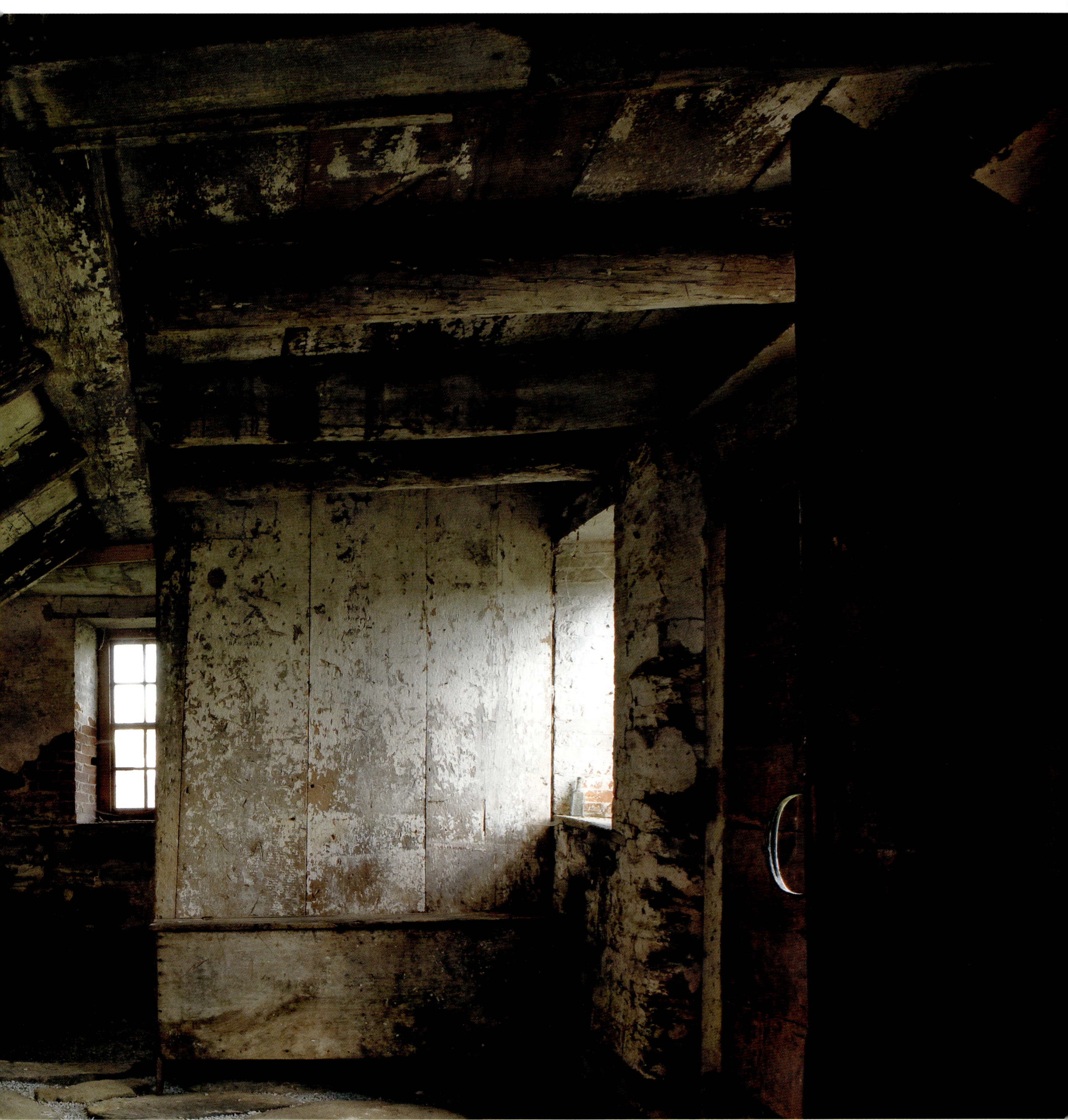

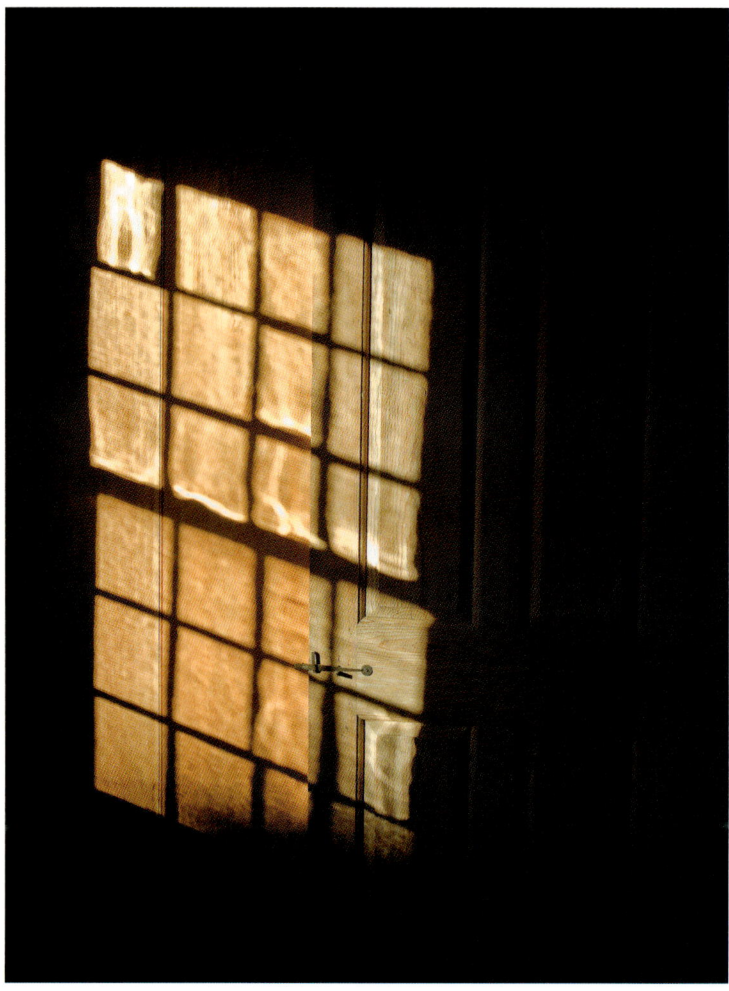

RIGHT *An entry door in a gable end is unusual but relates to the parlor being in the rear of the house rather than near the front door. As a result it was given its own outside entry in the gable end—function trumps tradition.*

FOLLOWING PAGES *Despite his modest means, Ephraim Fisher could afford a grand view. It was free and a joy forever to look out each day across the valley to the Green Mountains.*

lists the present frame house. Despite its Federal Period date, the house harks back to Fisher's past, both in style and location. Its features are akin to houses built in Rhode Island and southeast Massachusetts during the period of 1740–60, the place and time of his youth. It is not a conventional center-chimney Cape Cod–style house. The chimney is not centered, nor is the stairway adjacent to it. With four bays it would be called a three-fourths house. It is a simple, rather small, practical home yet well finished on the inside. Structurally it is a conventional New England house of the post-medieval form—single chimney (five fireplaces, two ovens), post-and-beam timbering with summer beams and joists, and one and a half stories high. It is completely sheathed over the structure with two-inch-thick vertical planking, over which the clapboarding is nailed.

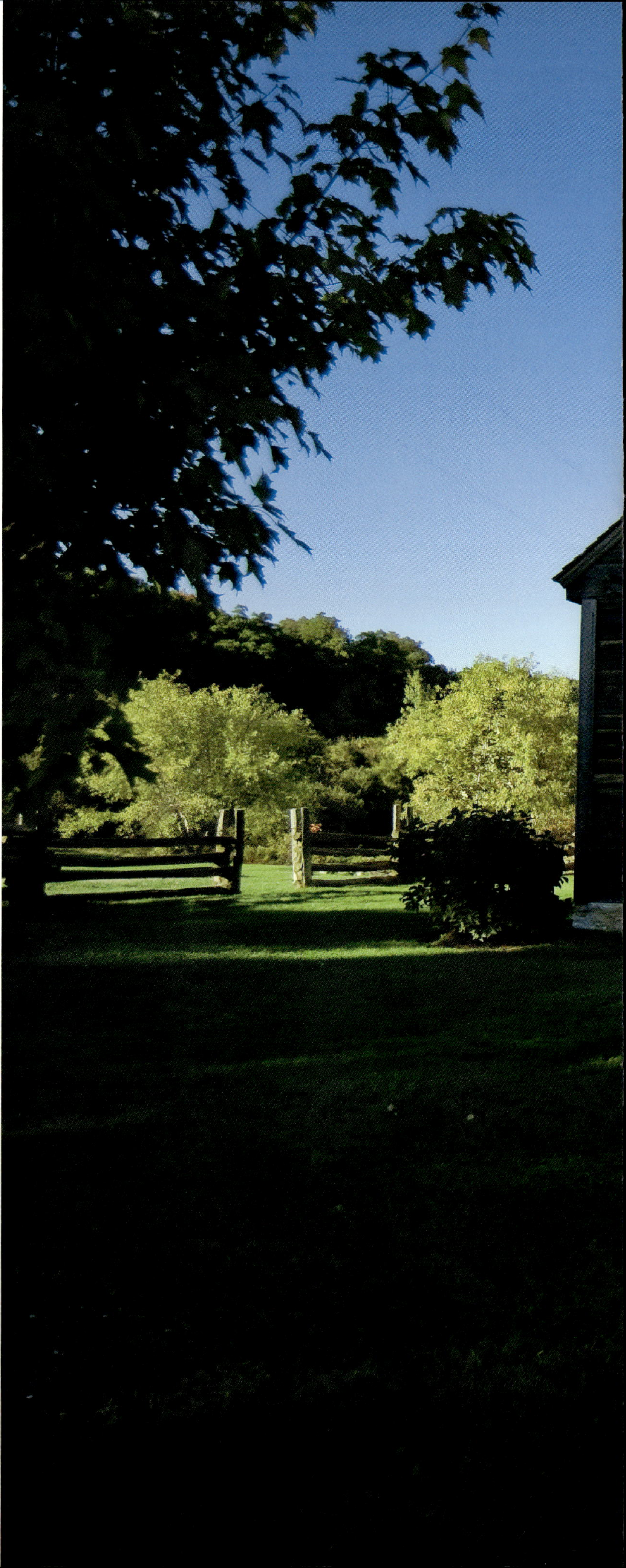

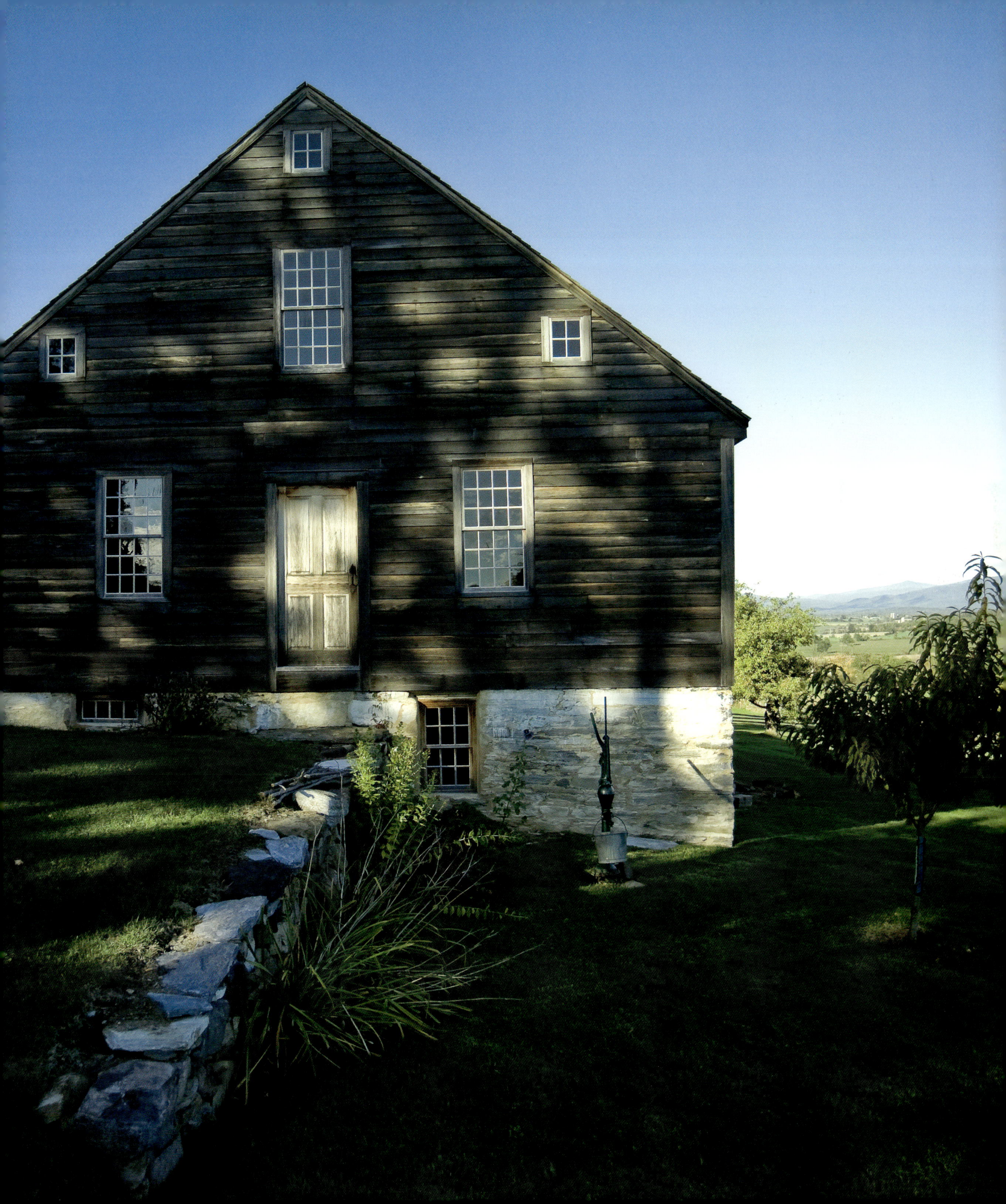

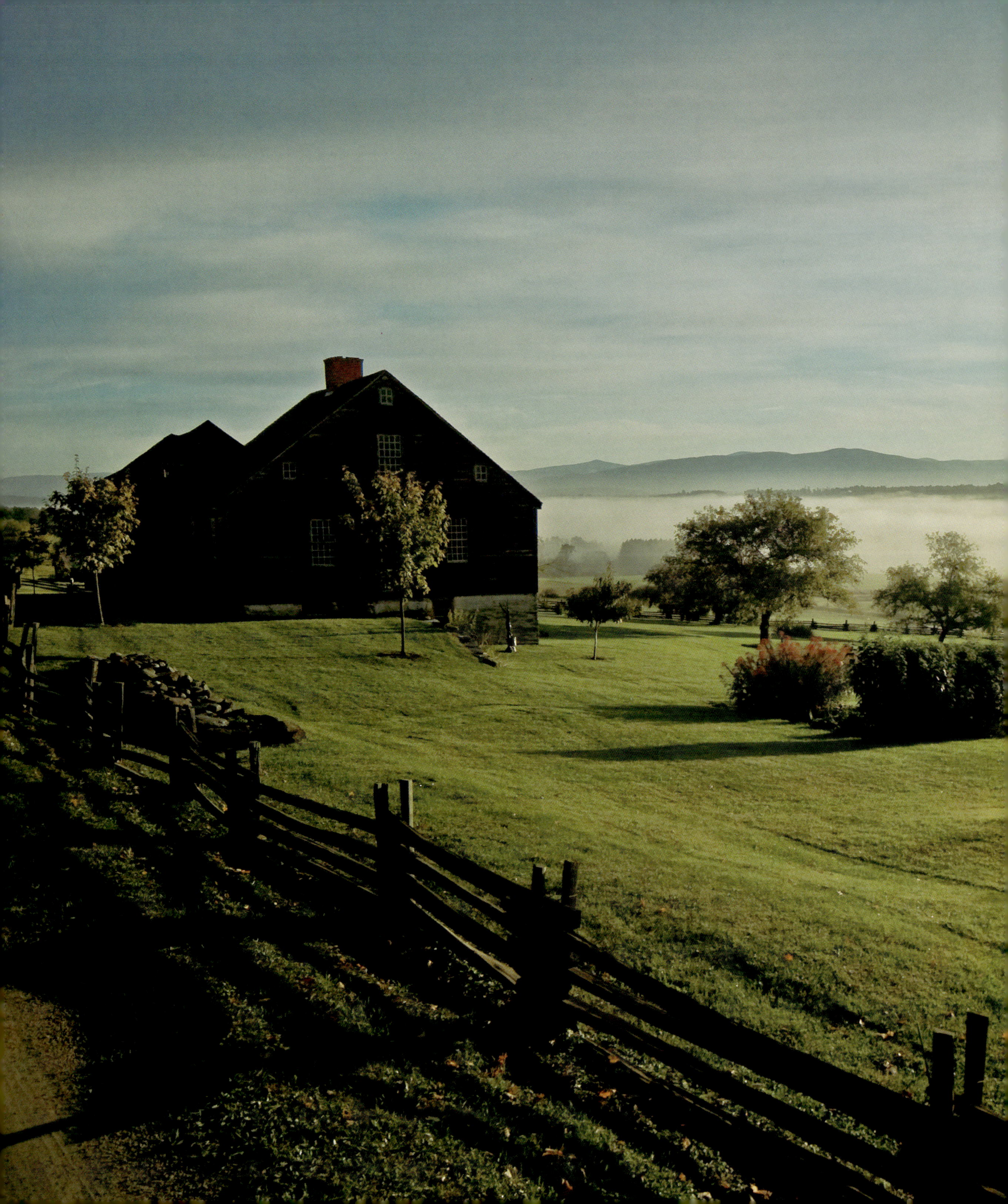

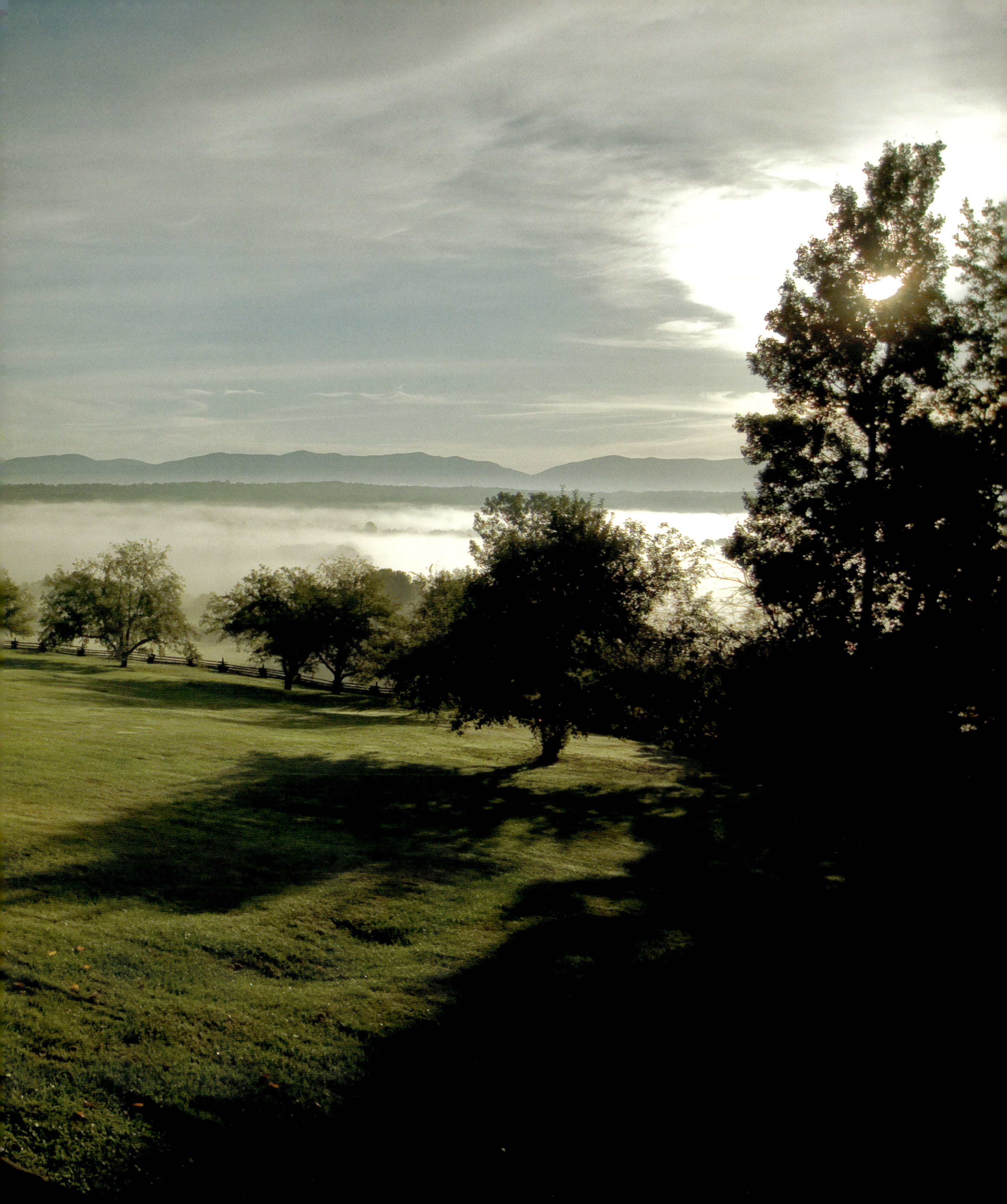

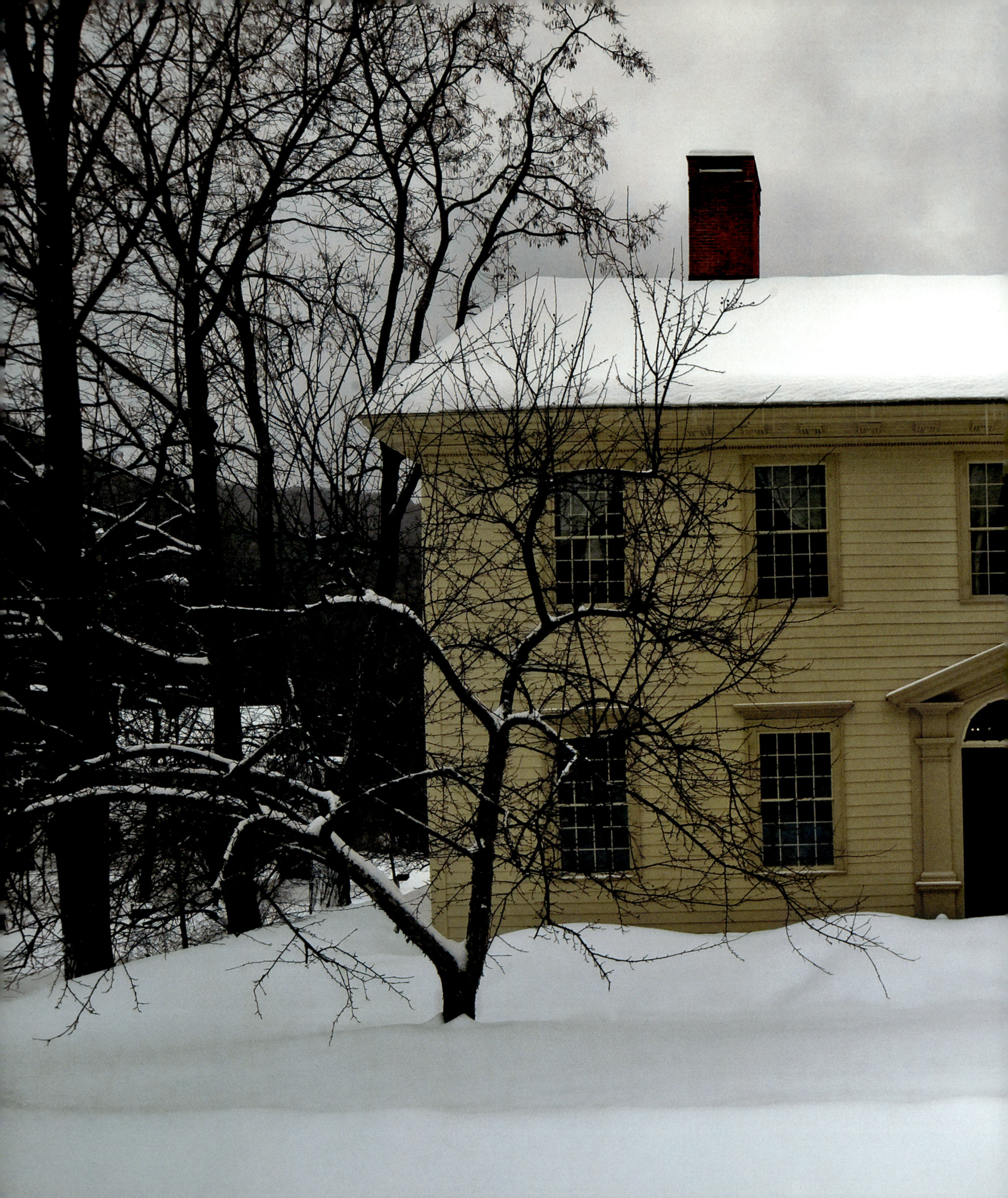

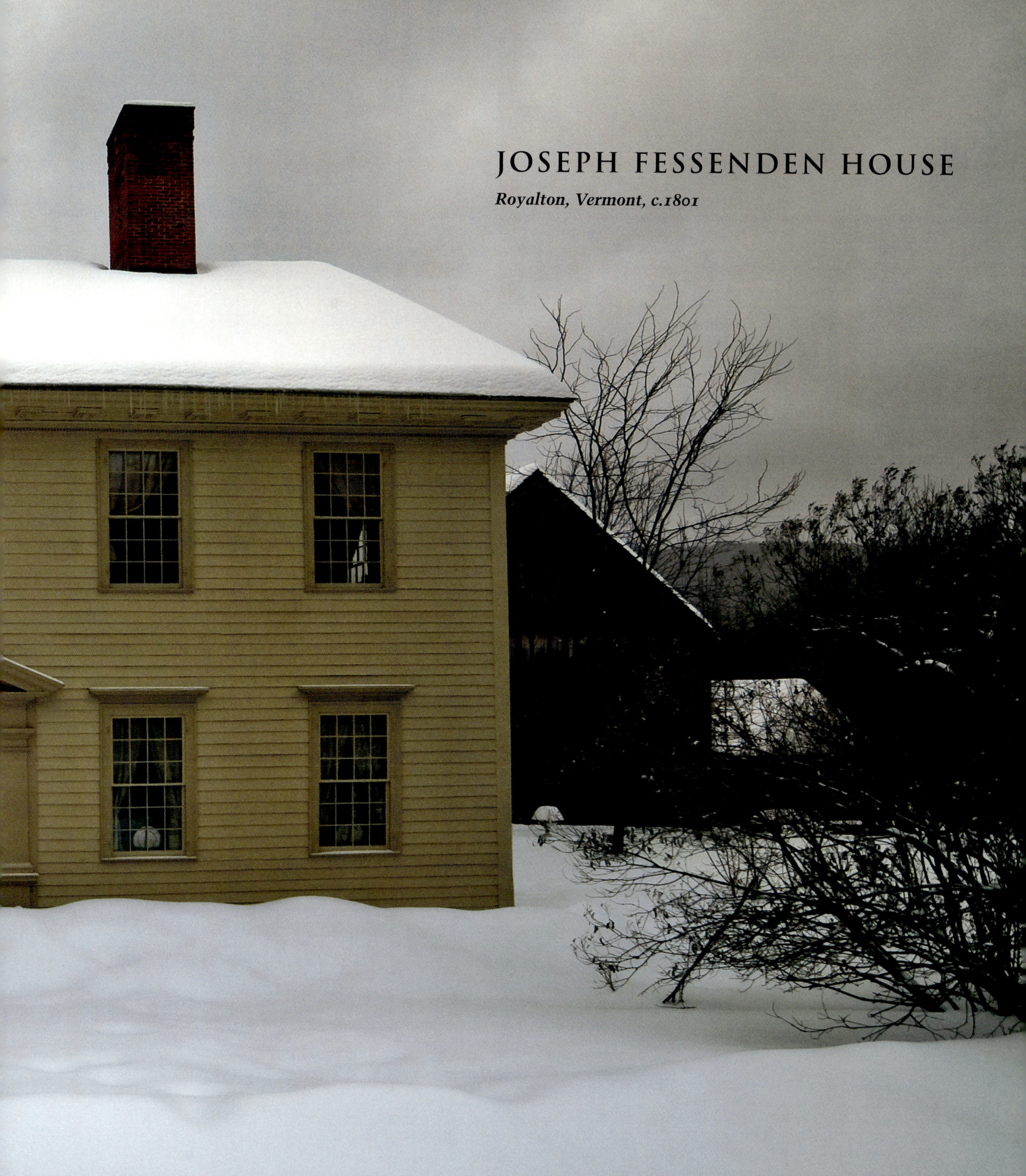

JOSEPH FESSENDEN HOUSE

Royalton, Vermont, c.1801

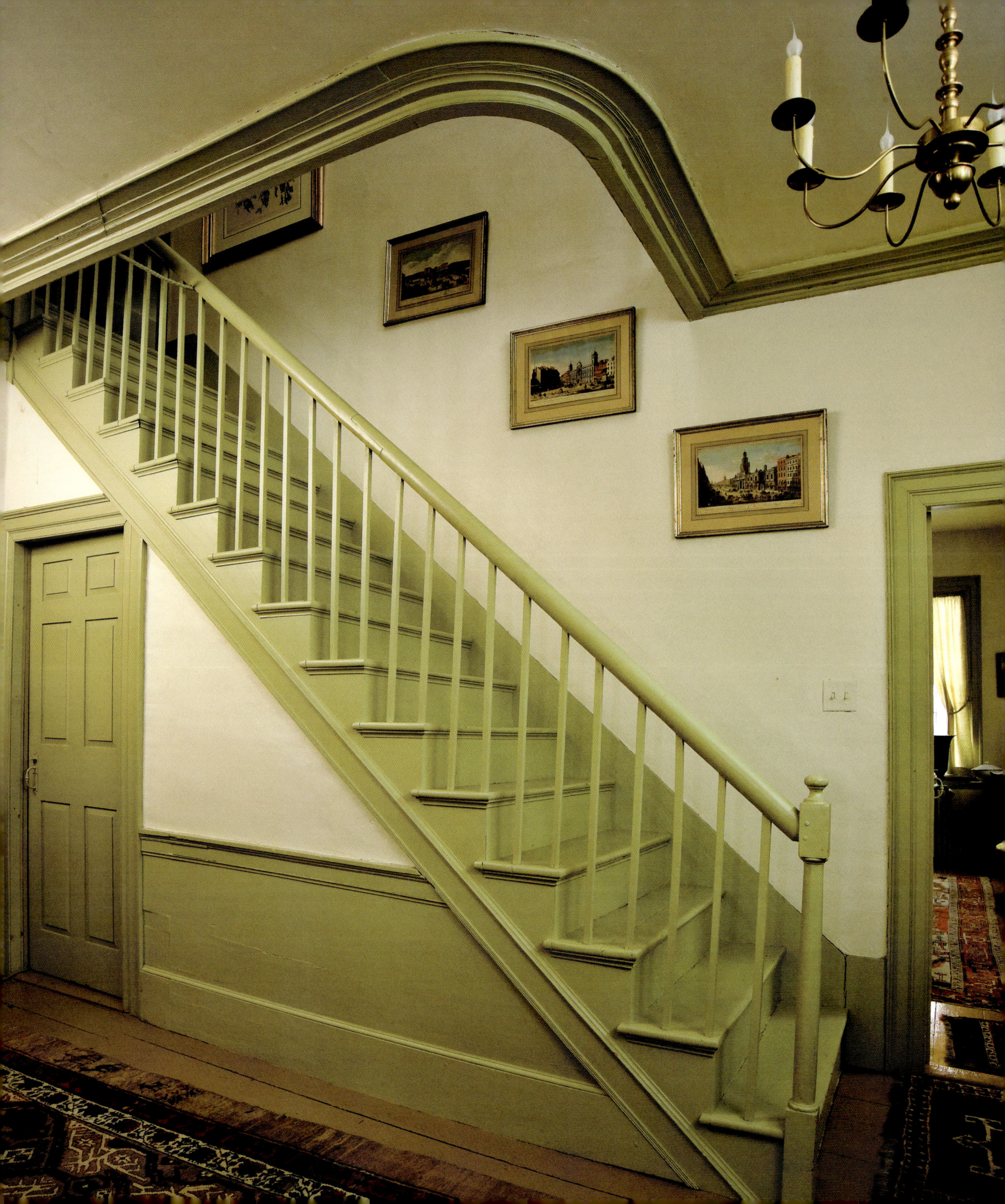

PREVIOUS PAGES *Royalton is geographically fairly remote from the cultural centers of New England, and therefore it is not surprising that its architecture follows suit. Joseph Fessenden's home has a subtle blend of Georgian and Federal features on its exterior: Georgian-sized windows, window panes, pedimented doorway, and large inset chimneys. Yet this 1801 house acknowledges the Federal Period with leaded transom window and imposing but flat dentals under the cornice.*

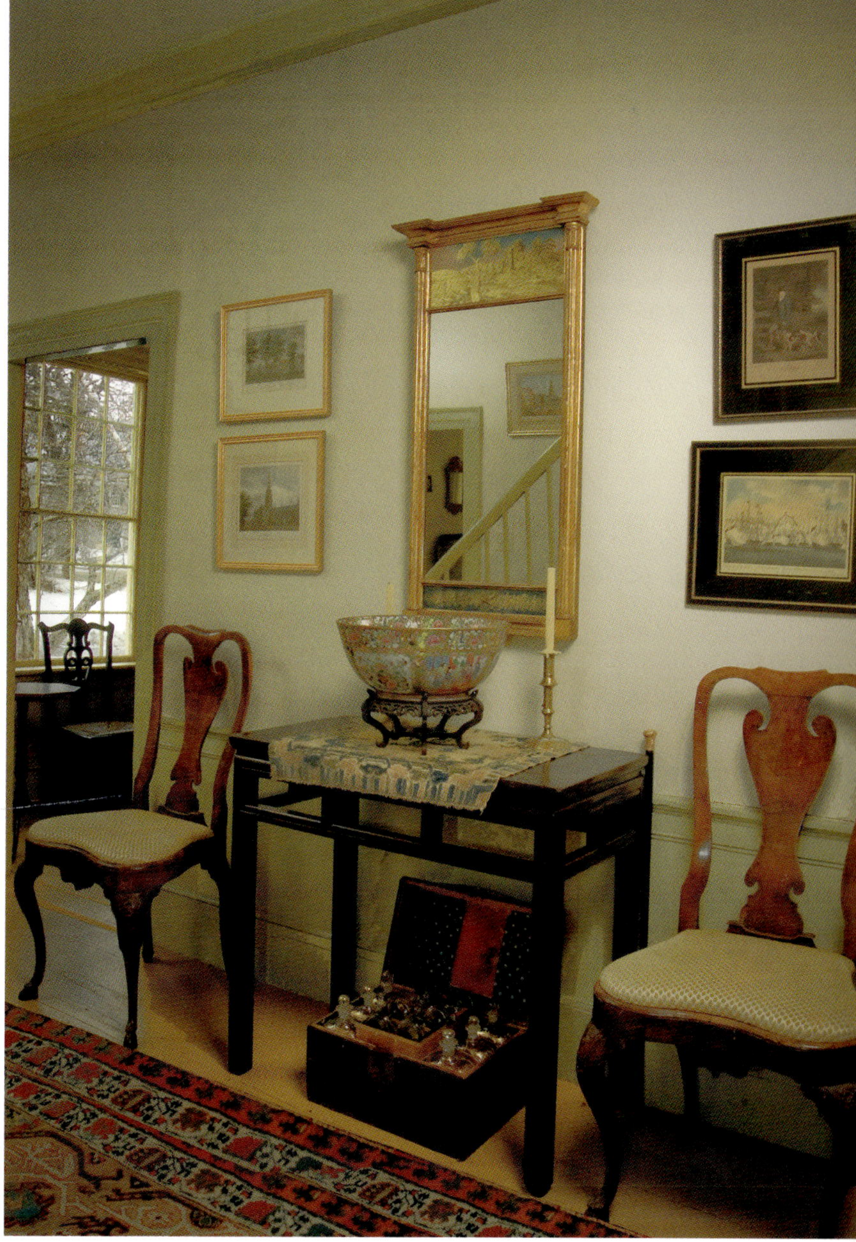

The anomalous position of what later became Vermont—claimed by New York, New Hampshire, and Massachusetts—and being too far away on a dangerous frontier, resulted in late settlement and disputed landholdings. The Town of Royalton received its 1769 charter from New York Province, granted mostly to well-connected New York land speculators. In 1781 the Vermont Legislature, asserting the state's authority, reconfirmed the charter. But before that, Royalton experienced its most spectacular event: late in the Revolution, in 1780, British officers and hundreds of American Indians descended on the disbursed town, attacking every farm and family they found, plundering, burning, killing, and capturing all they desired. Personal accounts by survivors make chilling reading about this last raid of the war in New England, an echo of prior raids throughout the region during a century of wars.

After the raid, when almost all was destroyed, a gift of land for a centralized village resulted in relocating Royalton hamlet to its present position on the White River. Today, the two oldest houses in the village date from this new founding. Representing the next period of houses, the Joseph Fessenden House on the corner of Bridge Street and Royalton Common Road, was built by entrepreneur Joseph Fessenden about 1801. Nearby he had a store where he advertised the sale of an assortment of dry goods: silks, velvets, silk shawls, broadcloths, English, East and West India goods, books, stationery, medicines, saddles, and more.

At first glance this large house has the appearance and proportions of an earlier Georgian house, but some of its details are Federal—notably, the leaded fan-shaped transom window and the shallow-molded cornice dentilation. Although constructed as a single-family house, about 1810 Fessenden converted it to a two-family home, as evidenced by two large chimney stacks with five fireplaces each, two kitchens, double stairways, and a ballroom. Starting in the 1830s it was used as a boardinghouse for the next hundred fifty years, its extra features lending itself to this use. In 1988 the present owners undertook an extensive restoration, and found much of the original features intact.

FACING PAGE *In Fessenden's day, a guest arriving at the front door was expected to read the house for its social message. The hall, parlor, and dining room were the public spaces for entertaining, announced by the elaboration of certain features: a stairway for show as much as function, cornice moldings (without practical function), dado (marginally protecting the plaster wall from bumps and scrapes), and a chandelier.*

ABOVE *Pier tables and mirrors, named for their usual location between windows in public rooms, also serve in the hall. The height of the table denotes its use for display and temporary placement. The height of the mirror indicates that it is for guests to compose themselves on arrival.*

FOLLOWING PAGES *The features of the dining room are less elaborate than those of the parlor or hall, befitting its more functional purpose. However, more shelves and table tops invite the display of silver and porcelain.*

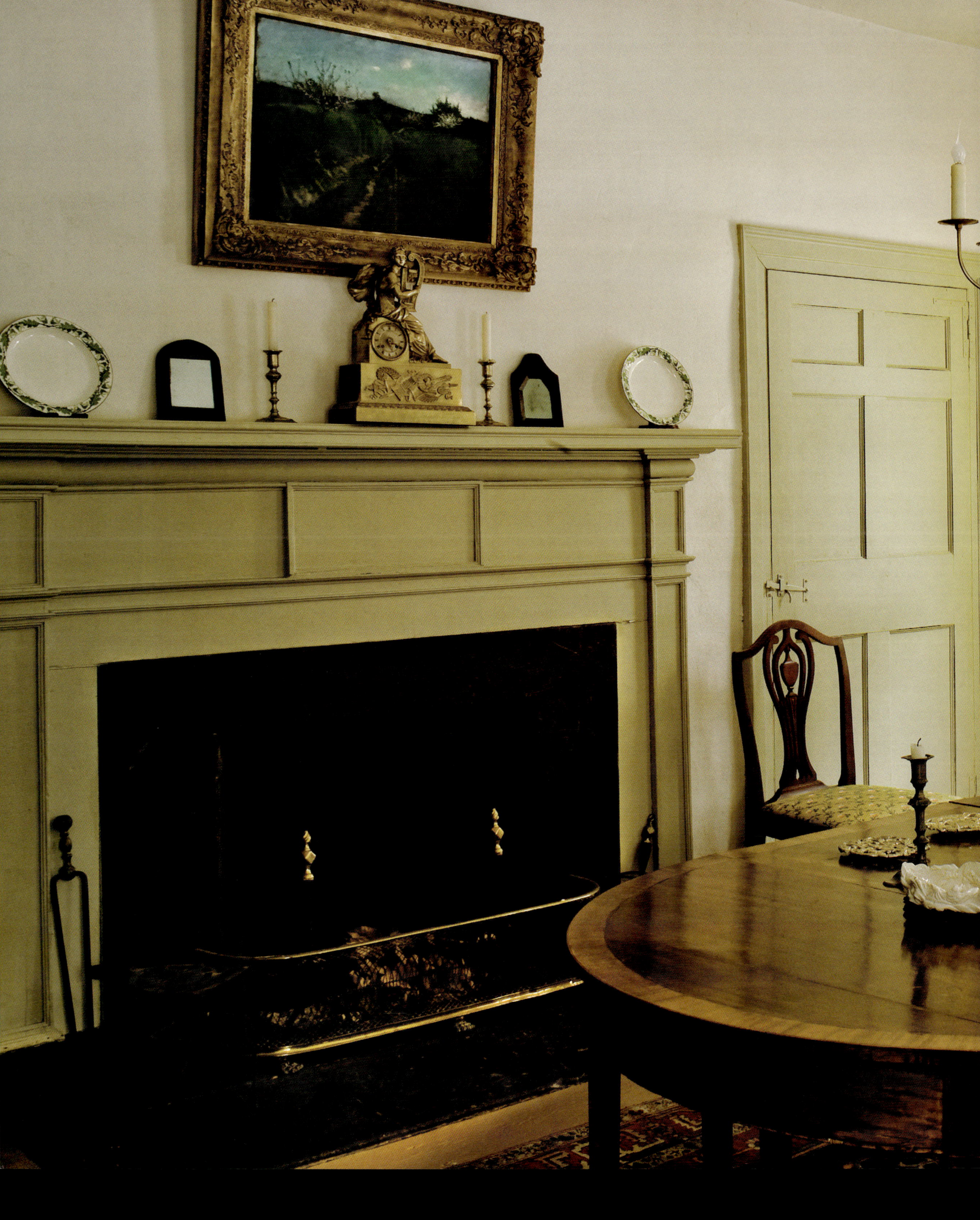

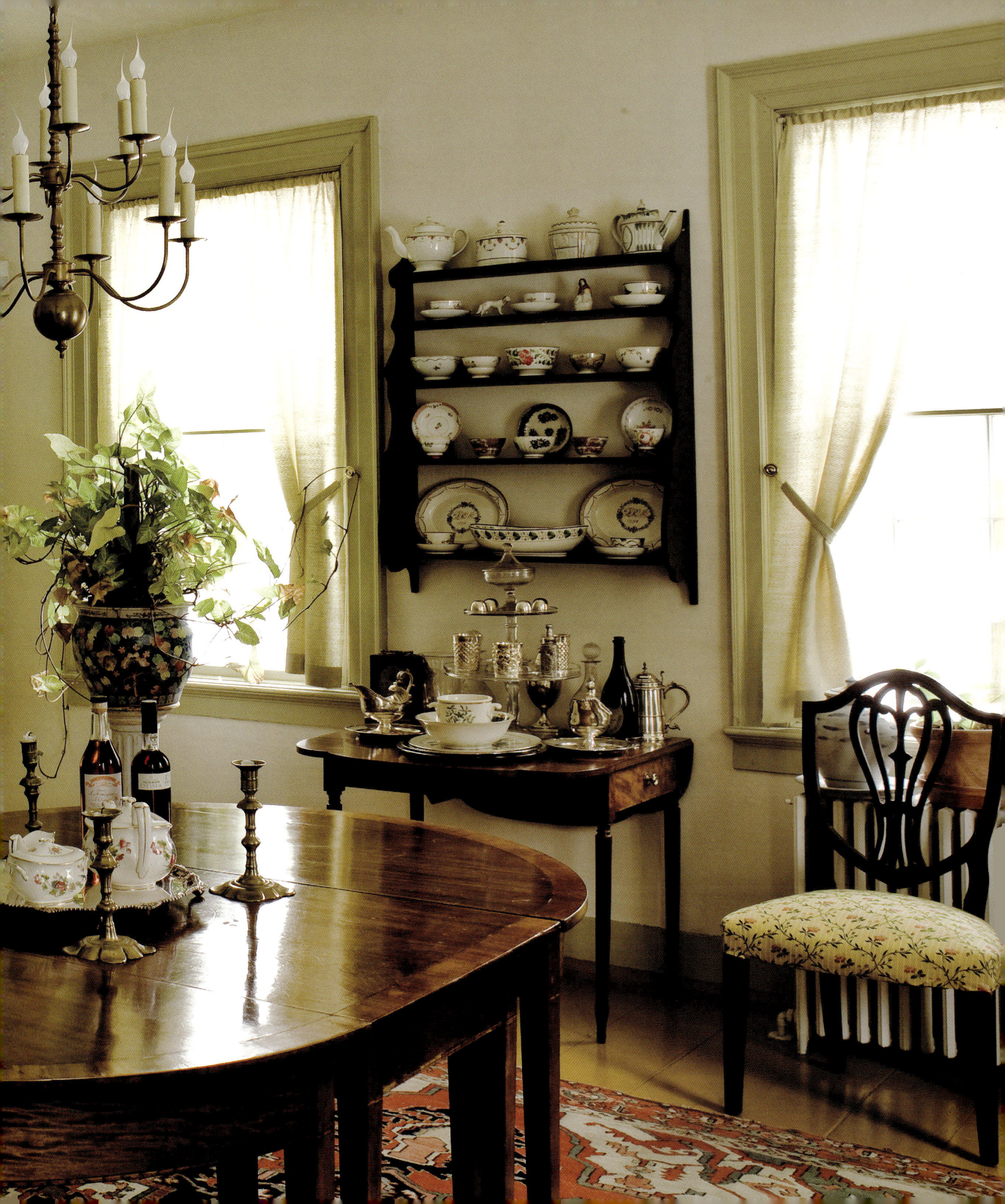

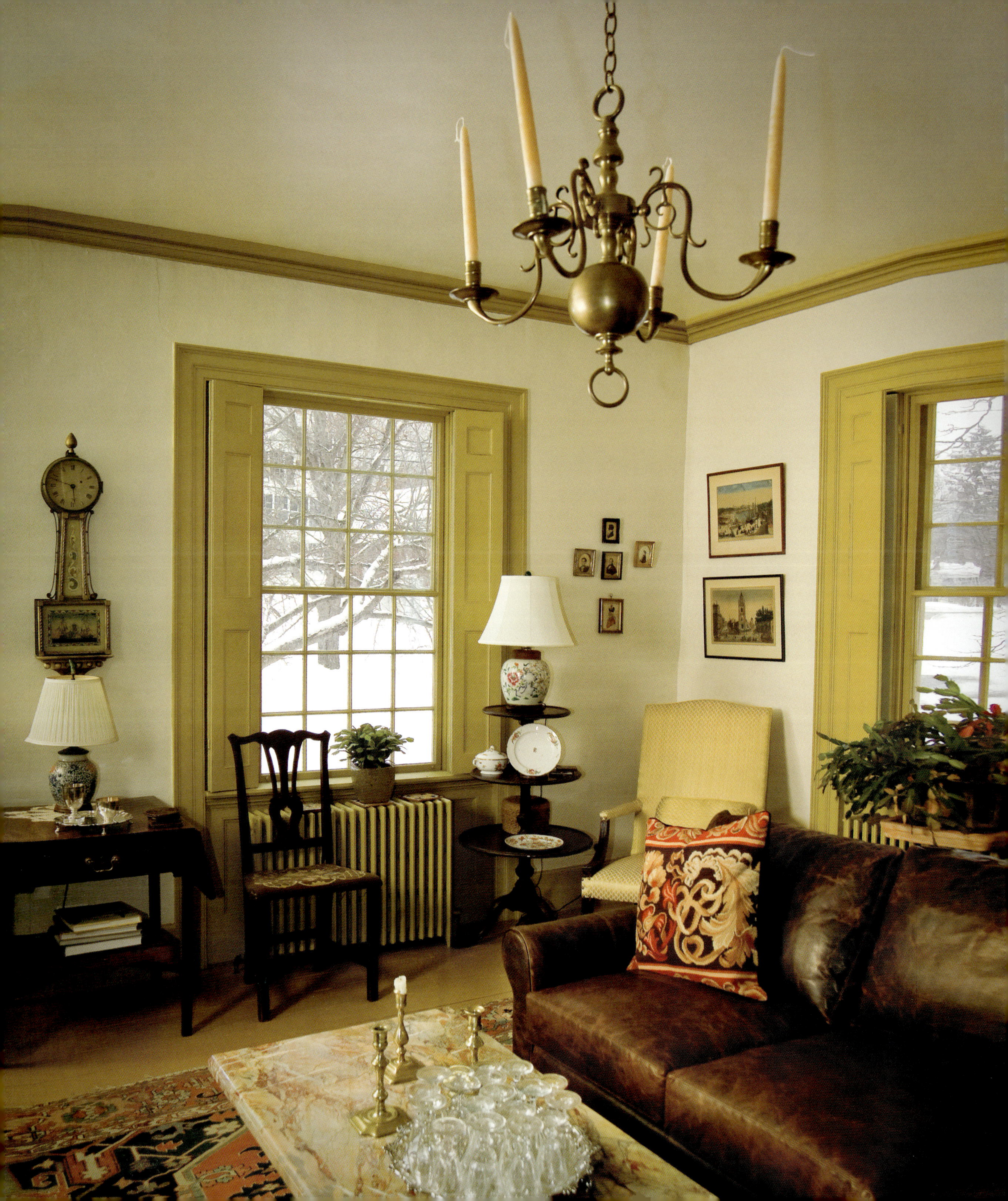

FACING PAGE *Entering the parlor, a guest sees the extra trim continue, a different cornice molding, no dado, and folding interior window shutters. These shutters were more convenient to open and close than exterior shutters but both served similar purposes: closed to deflect the sun's radiant heat in summer and the winter's cold at night. Where valuable fabrics may fade in the sun's light, these shutters were easily adjusted during the day.*

RIGHT *Dining area with paneled fireplace surround.*

FOLLOWING PAGES *A birdhouse garden folly.*

An arbor entry to the barn.

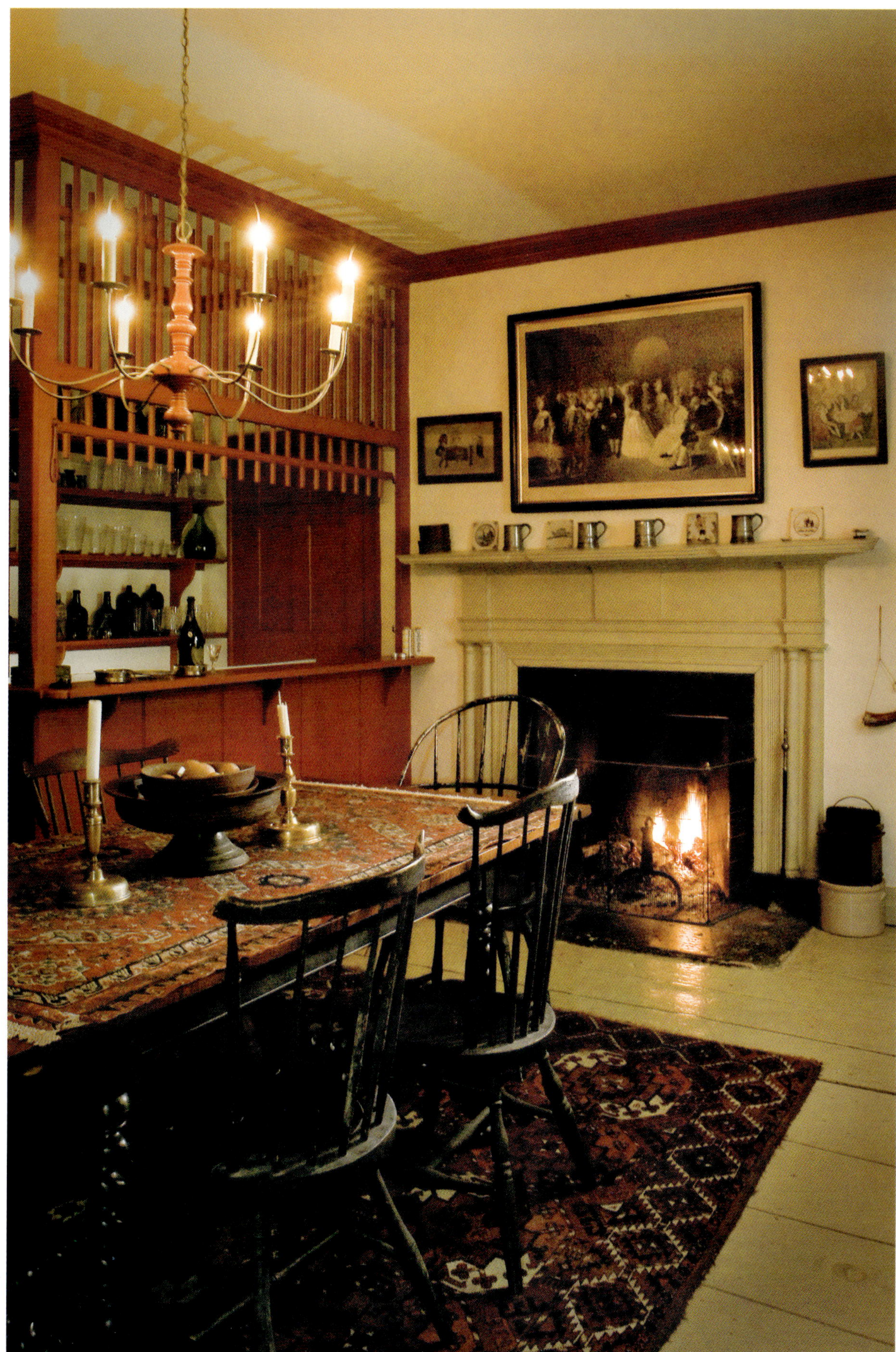

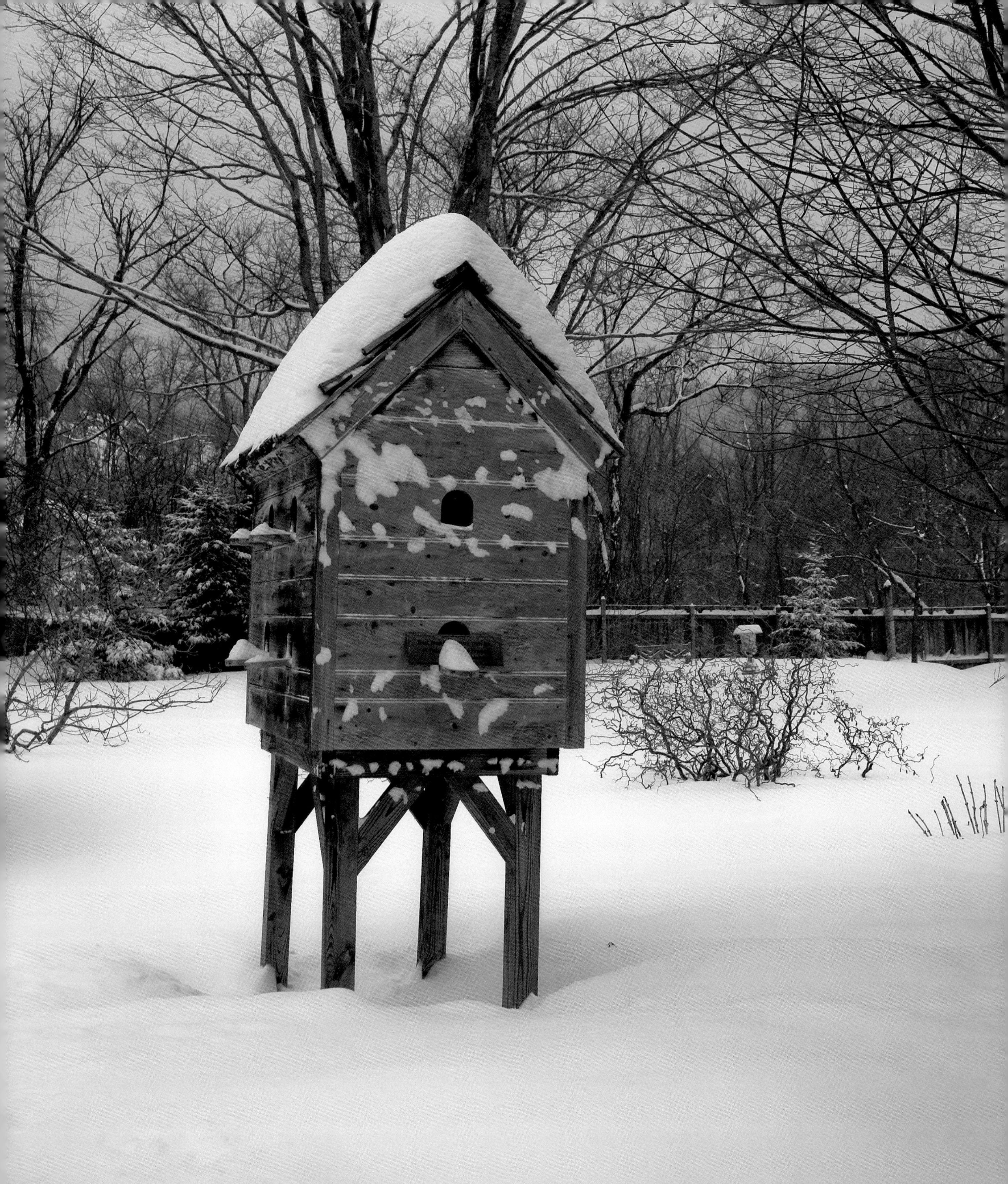

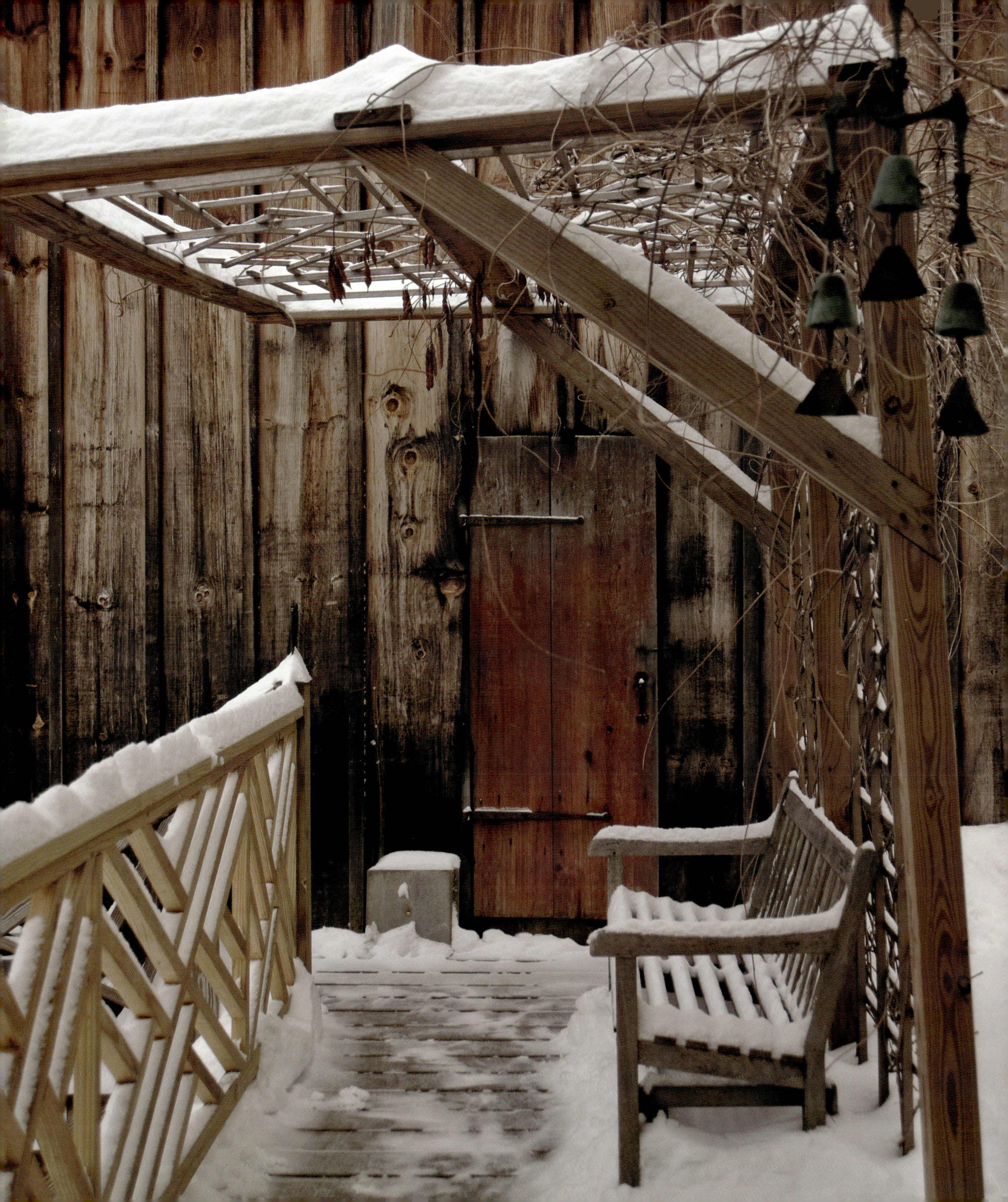

APPENDIX: HOUSES OPEN TO THE PUBLIC

Arranged in order of appearance in the book

THE OLD ROUND CHURCH
The Richmond Historical Society
25 Round Church Road
Richmond, VT 05477
802-828-3226
Open: contact site

PETER TUFTS HOUSE
Medford Historical Society
350 Riverside Avenue, Medford, MA 02155
781-391-8739
www.medford.k12.ma.us/socstud/tuftshouse
www.medfordhistorical.org/contactus.php
Open: variable

HENRY WHITFIELD HOUSE
Henry Whitfield State Museum
248 Old Whitfield Street, Guilford, CT 06437
860-566-3005
karin.peterson@ct.gov
www.whitfieldmuseum.com/history
Open: Apr. 4 to Dec. 14, Wed. to Sun., 10:00 a.m. to 4:30 p.m.
Closed Good Friday, Easter, July 4th, Veterans Day, and Thanksgiving

JONATHAN FAIRBANKS HOUSE
Fairbanks Family Association
511 East Street, Dedham, MA 02026
781-326-1170
fairbankshouse@aol.com
www.fairbankshouse.org
Open: May to Oct., Tues. to Sat. 10:00 a.m. to 5:00pm, and Sun. 1:00 p.m. to 5:00 p.m.

TURNER–INGERSOLL MANSION
(HOUSE OF THE SEVEN GABLES)
Settlement House Association
115 Derby Street, Salem, MA 01970
978-744-0991
info@7gables.org
www.7gables.org
Open: July to Oct. 10 a.m. to 7 p.m., Nov. to June 10 a.m. to 5 p.m.
Closed: Jan. 1 to12, Thanksgiving, Christmas

JUDGE JONATHAN CORWIN HOUSE
(THE WITCH HOUSE)
City of Salem Park and Recreation Department
310 Essex Street, Salem, Massachusetts 01970
978-744-8815
info@corwinhouse.org
www.salemweb.com/witchhouse
Open: Daily, 10 to 5 from early May to mid-Nov. Extended hours in Oct.
Closed: mid-Nov. to early May

JOHN BALCH HOUSE
The Beverly Historical Society & Museum
117 Cabot Street, Beverly, MA 01915
978-922-1186
sgoganian@beverlyhistory.org
www.beverlyhistory.org
Open: May 30 to Oct. 31, Tue. to Sat. 12 noon to 4 p.m.

CAPTAIN JOHN WHIPPLE HOUSE
Ipswich Museum
54 South Main Street, Ipswich, MA 01938
978-356-2811; www.ipswichmuseum.org
Open for tours, May to October, Tue. to Sun. Special hours in winter and fall, please call ahead.

OLD SHIP MEETING HOUSE
First Parish, Old Ship Church
90 Main St, Hingham, MA 02043
781-940-1679; oldship@verizon.net
www.oldshipchurch.org/history
Open: contact site

PARSON JOSEPH CAPEN HOUSE
Topsfield Historical Society
1 Howlett Street, Topsfield, MA 01983
978-887-3998
membership@topsfieldhistory.org
www.topsfieldhistory.org
Open: Sun., Wed., and Fri. afternoons from 1:00 p.m. to 4:30 p.m. from June 15 to Sept. 15

JETHRO COFFIN HOUSE
Nantucket Historical Association
15 Broad Street POB 1016, Nantucket, MA 02554
508-228-1894
www.nha.org
Open: mid-May through mid-Oct., Mon.-Sat. 10 a.m. to 5 p.m., Sun. 12 p.m. to 5 p.m.

ELEAZER ARNOLD HOUSE
Historic New England
487 Great Road, Lincoln, RI 02865
617-227-3956, 617-723-5611
www.spnea.org
Open: Sun. 1 to 4 pm; every second Sunday of the month, June 14 to Oct. 11

THE STEPHEN MUMFORD HOUSE
(WANTON-LYMAN- HAZARD HOUSE)
Newport Historical Society
17 Broadway, Newport, RI 02840
401-846-0813
www.newporthistorical.org/sites_wlhh
Open: contact site

GREAT FRIENDS MEETING HOUSE
Newport Historical Society
29 Farewell Street, Newport, RI 02840
401 846 0813
www.newporthistorical.org/sites_gfmh.htm
Open: contact site

STANLEY-WHITMAN HOUSE
Farmington Village Green and Library Association
37 High Street, Farmington, CT 06032
(860) 677-9222
information@stanleywhitman.org
www.stanleywhitman.org
Open: May to Oct., Wed. to Sun. 12:00 p.m. to 4:00 p.m.; and Nov. to Apr., Sat. and Sun. from 12:00 p.m. to 4:00 p.m.

COGSWELL'S GRANT
Historic New England
Spring Street, Essex, MA 01929
978 768 3632
CogswellsGrant@HistoricNewEngland.org
www.historicnewengland.org/visit/homes/cogswell
Open: June 1 to Oct. 15, Wed. to Sun., Tours at 11 a.m., 12:00 p.m., 1 p.m., 2 p.m., 3 p.m., and 4 p.m.

CAPT. GEORGE TATE HOUSE
The National Society of The Colonial Dames of America in the State of Maine
2 Waldo Street, Portland, ME 04102
(207) 774-6177; info@tatehouse.org;
www.tatehouse.org
Open: Tues. to Sun., June 15 to Sept. 30; and on weekends (Fri., Sat.,and Sun.) to Oct., Tues. to Sat.: 10:00 a.m. to 4:00 p.m. Sun.: 1:00 p.m. to 4:00 p.m.

SHAKER MEETING HOUSE
Canterbury Shaker Village
288 Shaker Road, Canterbury, NH 03224
603 783-9511; tjohnson@shakers.org
www.shakers.org
Open: May 16 to Oct. 31, daily 10:00 a.m. to 5:00 p.m., and on Dec. 5 and 12 for their "Christmas at Canterbury" program

STRAFFORD TOWN HOUSE
Strafford, VT 05072
townofstrafford@wavecomm.com
www.usgennet.org/usa/vt/county/orange/strafford/index.htm
Open: contact site

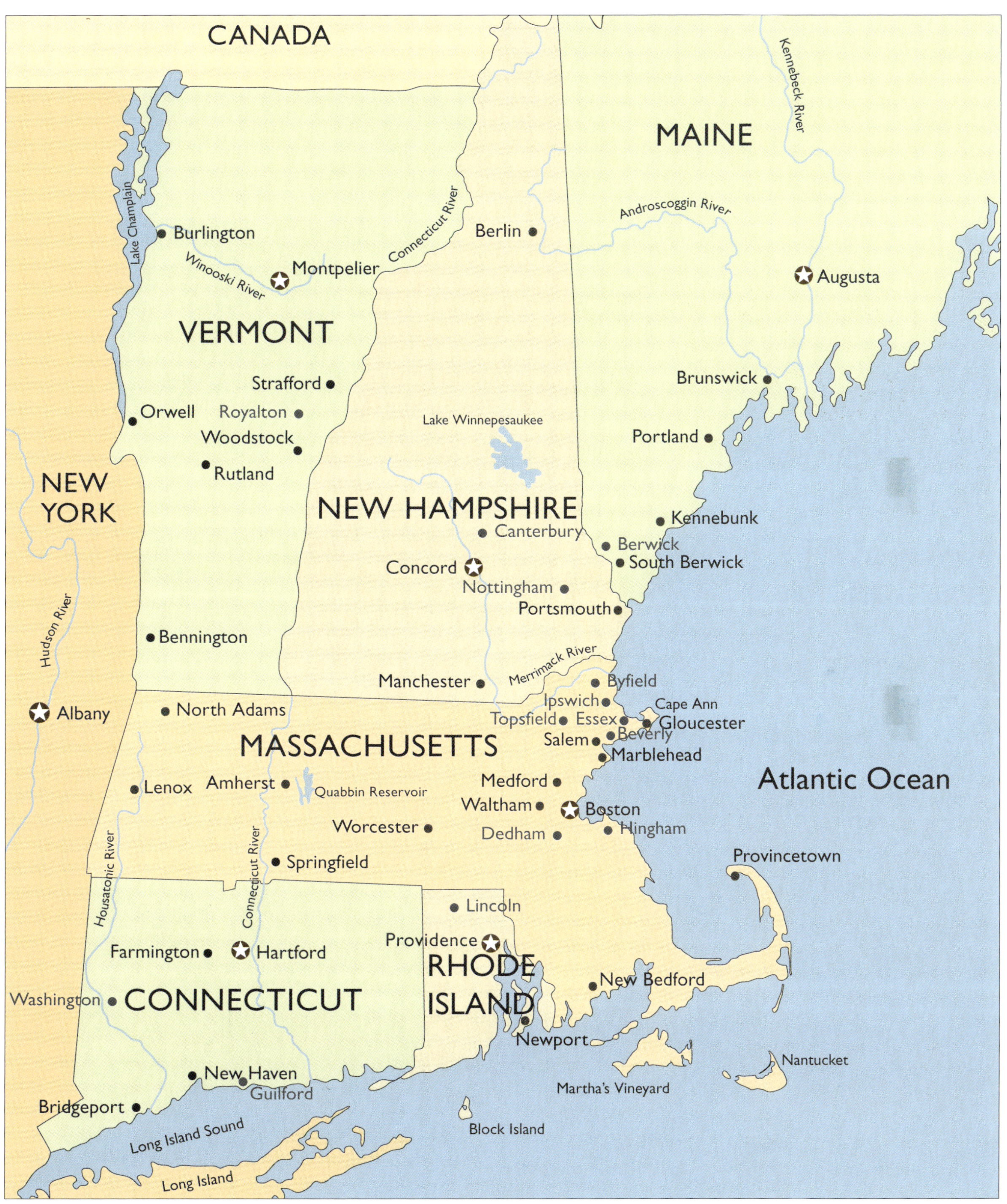
CANADA
MAINE
Kennebeck River
Androscoggin River
Lake Champlain
Burlington
Winooski River
Montpelier
Connecticut River
Berlin
Augusta
VERMONT
Brunswick
Strafford
Orwell
Royalton
Lake Winnepesaukee
Woodstock
Portland
Rutland
NEW YORK
NEW HAMPSHIRE
Kennebunk
Canterbury
Berwick
South Berwick
Concord
Nottingham
Portsmouth
Hudson River
Bennington
Merrimack River
Manchester
Byfield
Albany
North Adams
Ipswich
Cape Ann
Topsfield
Essex
Gloucester
Beverly
Salem
MASSACHUSETTS
Marblehead
Atlantic Ocean
Medford
Lenox
Amherst
Quabbin Reservoir
Waltham
Boston
Worcester
Dedham
Hingham
Housatonic River
Connecticut River
Springfield
Provincetown
Lincoln
Providence
Farmington
Hartford
RHODE ISLAND
New Bedford
Washington
CONNECTICUT
Newport
Nantucket
New Haven
Martha's Vineyard
Guilford
Bridgeport
Block Island
Long Island Sound
Long Island

INDEX

ACKNOWLEDGMENTS

It is a pleasure to look back on the people and places that have made possible this book through the cooperation of organizations and their staff personnel and owners. Providing information on sites to the author and access to the properties for the photographer is gratifying to acknowledge with thanks and real appreciation.

As photographer, Geoffrey wishes to make special mention of those who have sustained his work during the preparation of this book: for his parents, Joan and Mark; for Nancy and Peter Cook; a very special heart felt thanks to Alice Tobin-Gross, for her infinite patience and retouching skills; and much appreciation to Susan Piatt for her support, encouragement and styling; to each of you Geoffrey gives this personal dedication of the book.

Among those others who are not specifically connected to any one site but whose expertise has been especially helpful, we wish to mention Richard Guy Wilson, for his assistance and suggestions and for his wonderful foreword. We have also received helpful advice from Richard Candee, Abbott Lowell Cummings, Randy Brisson of Brisson Restoration, Douglas Barnes, Nora Ostrander (thanks for the chocolates), Lew Sussman, Brandt Bolding, Ken Abramson, Erhard Mahnke, and Sidney Burns. Logan Blackburn was Geoffrey's able assistant, could not have done it all without him.

The staff of Rizzoli we especially thank for their encouragement to undertake this book and the confidence they have placed in our ability to create its content at the level they are accustomed to. These include Charles Miers, David Morton, Douglas Curran, Maria Pia Gramglia, and Colin Hough-Trapp. Abigail Sturges of Sturges Graphic Design has our gratitude for the superior layout she consistently brings to the publications she works on. For all, we wish to convey our appreciation for their kindness, patience, and indulgence.

And our own mutual appreciation:

From Geoffrey: to Rod Blackburn, who has taught me well about old houses.

From Rod: To Geoffrey, who again has taken the lead to make this book a reality, always delighting me with evocative pictures. He has an uncanny ability to bring out the spirit of a house.

We wish to express our appreciation to the site owners, both individuals and associations, who have granted us the liberty to photograph their houses and permission to publish the pictures and text on each in this volume. Likewise we wish to express our appreciation to those individuals at each site who were helpful to us.

The Old Round Church: The Richmond Historical Society; John P. Dumville, Historic Sites Operations Chief, Vermont Division for Historic Preservation.

Peter Tufts House: John Anderson, Medford Historical Society; Daniel Aulenti, Stewardship Manager, Historic New England; Barbara Kerr, Assistant Director, Medford Public Library.

Henry Whitfield House: Karin Peterson, Museum Director; Michael McBride, Curator; Michelle E. Parrish, Assistant Curator; David Block, Museum Volunteer.

Jonathan Fairbanks House: Dr. Alexandra Service, Director/Curator; Jonathan Fairbanks, Trustee.

Turner-Ingersoll Mansion (House of the Seven Gables): Amy Waywell, Curator.

Judge Jonathan Corwin House (The Witch House): Elizabeth Peterson, Director.

Captain John Whipple House: Fred Hale, Executive Director; Pat Tyler, Collections Chair; Judith Hallberg, Secretary, Board of Trustees.

John Balch House: Susan Goganian, Director; Nancy Hood, caretaker and docent.

Old Ship Meeting House: Julianna Dunn, Administrative Assistant; Robert Baynes and other members of the Old Ship community.

Parson Joseph Capen House: Norman Isler, President.

Jethro Coffin House: Ben Simmons; Robyn and John Davis, Chief Curator.

Eleazer Arnold House: Suzanna Crampton, Historic New England.

Micum McIntyre House: Robert M. (Mal) Davis, Daniel B. Davis and James R. Davis, owners.

Dickinson–Pillsbury–Witham House: Barbara Posnansky, owner.

The Stephen Mumford House (Wanton–Lyman–Hazard House) and Great Friends Meeting House: Ruth S. Taylor, Executive Director, Newport Historical Society.

Stanley–Whitman House, Lisa Johnson, Executive Director.

Cogswell's Grant: Kristin Weiss, Site Manager, Historic New England.

The Henry Crane–Samuel Ware House: Linda Dano Attardi, owner.

Captain George Tate House: Dr. Andrea Hawkes, Director; Peter Cook, Trustee.

John Dunnell House–Tare Shirt Farm: Nancy and Peter Cook, owners.

Major John Gile House: Barbara and Robert Betcher, owners.

Eliab Stevens House (Stevens–Littlefield–Curtis House): Perry Hopf, owner.

Shaker Meeting House: Thomas Johnson, Curator; Funi Burdick, Director, Canterbury Shaker Village.

Strafford Town House: Lisa M. Kendall, Town Clerk/Treasurer; Gwenda Smith, Historian.

Ephraim Fisher House: Walter Phelps, owner; Randy Brisson, Brisson Restoration.

Joseph Fessenden House: Richard McGovern and Jacques Tremblay, owners.

Zenus Cowles House: "Oldgate," Ms. Brie Quinby and Mr. Evan Cowles, owners.

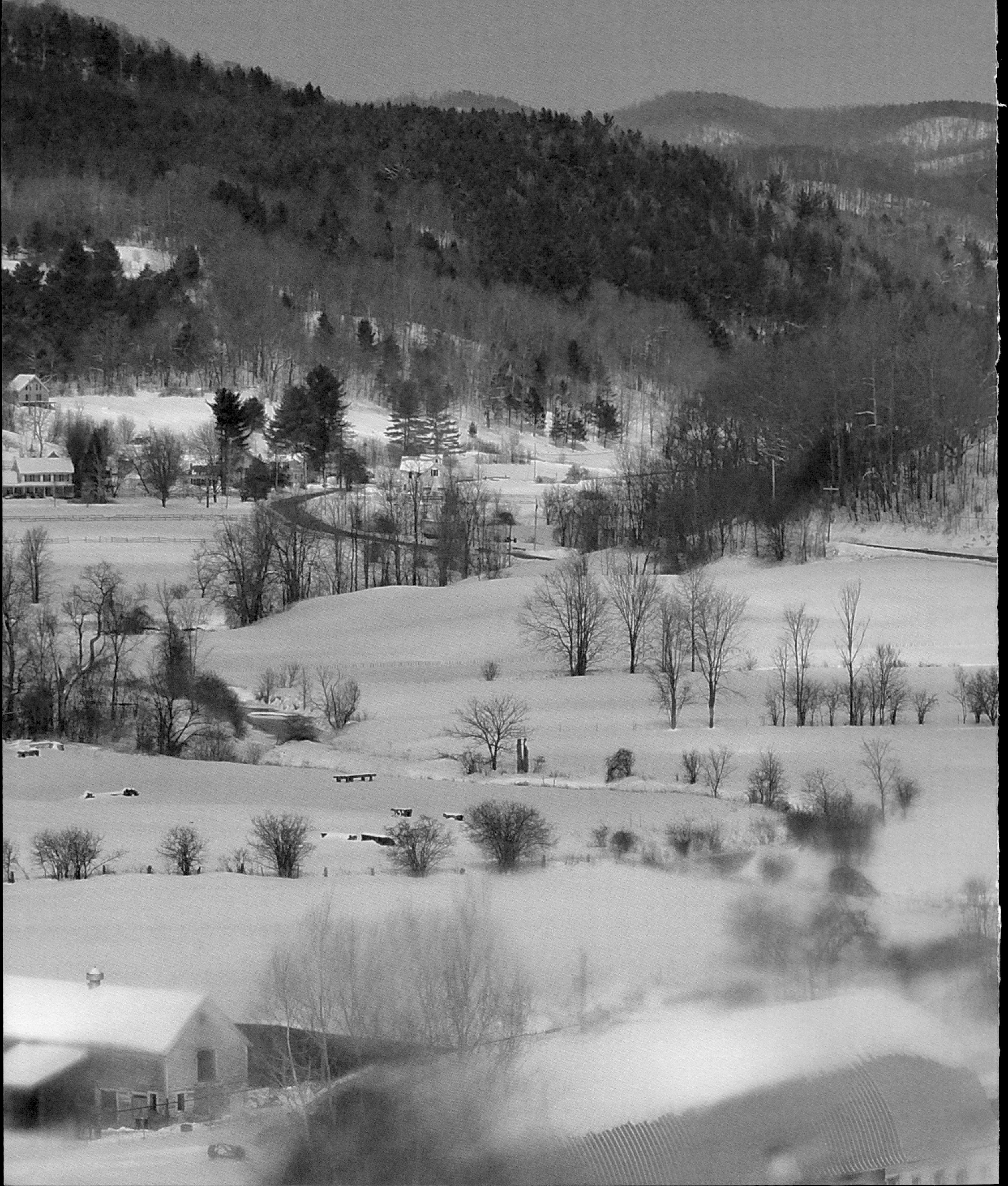